GENDER AND WORK
IN TODAY'S WORLD

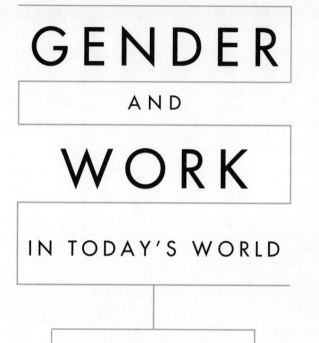

GENDER

AND

WORK

IN TODAY'S WORLD

A READER

edited by NANCY E. SACKS
and CATHERINE MARRONE

Westview
PRESS

A Member of the Perseus Books Group

Copyright © 2004 by Westview Press, A Member of the Perseus Books Group

Westview Press books are available at special discounts for bulk purchases in the United States by corporations, institutions, and other organizations. For more information, please contact the Special Markets Department at the Perseus Books Group, 11 Cambridge Center, Cambridge, MA 02142, or call (800) 255-1514 or (617) 252-5298, or e-mail special.markets@perseusbooks.com.

Published in the United States of America by Westview Press.

Find us on the World Wide Web at www.westviewpress.com

Library of Congress Cataloging-in-Publication Data

Gender and work in today's worlds : a reader / edited by Nancy E. Sacks and Catherine Marrone.
    p. cm.
Includes bibliographical references and index.
ISBN 0-8133-4192-2 (pbk. : alk. paper)
1. Sex role in the work environment. 2. Sex discrimination in employment. 3. Women—
Employment. I. Sacks, Nancy E. II. Marrone, Catherine.
    HD6060.6.G454 2004
    306.3'615—dc22
                                    2004017382
ISBN 0-8133-4192-2 (pbk.)

Interior design by Lisa Kreinbrink
Text set in 10.5-point Adobe Garamond Pro

The paper used in this publication meets the requirements of the American National Standard for Permanence of Paper for Printed Library Materials Z39.48–1984.

10   9   8   7   6   5   4   3   2   1

Contents

Part VIII The Parent Trap, 371

Part IX Work over the Life Course, 419

Part I
WOMEN AT WORK

In this opening section of *Gender and Work in Today's World: A Reader,* we look at some very different work settings and occupational statuses for women. For women and men, the work they do occupies, quite literally, a significant part of their identity formation in the contexts of both paid work and the social response to these jobs. These selections tell of the cumulative experience of being and feeling marginalized on many levels. In the readings to follow, there is the clear sense that uniting, theoretically, notions of work, identity, and status befit the case that work affects women in specific and meaningful ways.

First, in this excerpt from *Nickel and Dimed,* we travel with Barbara Ehrenreich through low-wage work as a Wal-Mart clerk in Middle America. This study is the first, but not the only, research that links work and social class with identity as women struggle to have a real and meaningful life within the low means they earn.

The confining power of work identity reveals itself as obvious social construct in our next reading, from Yuko Ogasawara's *Office Ladies: Power, Gender and Work in Japanese Companies.* Here, the opportunities and potential for power in employment as "office lady" or "business girl," even in a large banking firm, for example, go unexploited by women. Ogasawara argues that the immediate separation carried out through selective recruitment in this Japanese work setting tracks women and men into a two-tiered, and fundamentally stratified, modern workplace.

Perhaps immigrant women, like those in "Domestica," by Pierette Hondagneu-Sotelo, articulate to us even more disturbingly the stark instances whereby some women are clearly reduced to feelings of inadequacy by the work they do. The constant scrutiny of these domestic workers by their household employers of higher social class not only denigrates the tasks these women perform, despite the instrumental function of these tasks to the household, but also further shapes and weakens the workers' individual identities.

Finally, in "Prostitution and Tourism in Southeast Asia," from *Working Women: International Perspectives on Labour and Gender Ideology,* Wendy Lee looks at one of the oldest sources of employment, in which women find that the work is contingent on both their own economic status and the desire of men to set a marketplace. Poor women have always found work like this. Because of the economic circumstances that define what we do for work, and despite the general notion that work defines men's identities more, this section clearly describes how work defines a social experience for women as well. Some of the least exceptional jobs provide the most elucidating windows into women's lives, identities, and their own lack of awareness on the need to connect the two.

1

NICKEL AND DIMED

Selling in Minnesota

Barbara Ehrenreich

For sheer grandeur, scale, and intimidation value, I doubt if any corporate orientation exceeds that of Wal-Mart. I have been told that the process will take eight hours, which will include two fifteen-minute breaks and a half hour for a meal, and will be paid for like a regular shift. When I arrive, dressed neatly in khakis and clean T-shirt, as befits a potential Wal-Mart "associate," I find there are ten new hires besides myself, mostly young and Caucasian, and a team of three, headed by Roberta, to do the "orientating." We sit around a long table in the same windowless room where I was interviewed, each with a thick folder of paperwork in front of us, and hear Roberta tell once again about raising six children, being a "people person," discovering that the three principles of Wal-Mart philosophy were the same as her own, and so on. We begin with a video, about fifteen minutes long, on the history and philosophy of Wal-Mart, or, as an anthropological observer might call it, the Cult of Dam, First young Sam Walton, in uniform, comes back from the war. He starts a store, a sort of five-and-dime; he marries and fathers four attractive children; he receives a Medal of Freedom from President Bush, after which he promptly dies, making way for the eulogies. But the company goes on, yes indeed. Here the arc of the story soars upward unstoppably, pausing only to mark some fresh milestone of corporate expansion. 1992: Wal-Mart becomes the largest retailer in the world. 1997: Sales top $100 billion. 1998: The number of Wal-Mart associates hits 825,000, making Wal-Mart the largest private employer in the nation.

In orientation we learned that the store's success depends entirely on us, the associates; in fact, our bright blue vests bear the statement "At Wal-Mart, our people make the difference." Underneath those vests, though, there are real-life charity cases, maybe even shelter dwellers.[1]

So, anyway, begins my surreal existence at the Comfort Inn.

I live in luxury with AC, a door that bolts, a large window protected by an intact screen—just like a tourist or a business traveler. But from there I go out every day to a life that most business travelers would find shabby and dispiriting—lunch at Wendy's, dinner at Sbarro (the Italian-flavored fast-food place), and work at Wal-Mart, where I would be embarrassed to be discovered in my vest, should some member of the Comfort staff happen to wander in. Of course, I expect to leave any day, when the Hopkins

Park Plaza opens up. For the time being, though, I revel in the splendor of my accommodations, amazed that they cost $5.05 less, on a daily basis, than what I was paying for that rat hole in Clearview. I stop worrying about my computer being stolen or cooked, I sleep through the night, the sick little plucking habit loses its grip. I feel like the man in the commercials for the Holiday Inn Express who's so refreshed by his overnight stay that he can perform surgery the next day or instruct people in how to use a parachute. At Wal-Mart, I get better at what I do, much better than I could ever have imagined at the beginning.

The breakthrough comes on a Saturday, one of your heavier shopping days. There are two carts waiting for me when I arrive at two, and tossed items inches deep on major patches of the floor. The place hasn't been shopped, it's been looted. In this situation, all I can do is everything at once—stoop, reach, bend, lift, run from rack to rack with my cart. And then it happens—a magical flow state in which the clothes start putting *themselves* away. Oh, I play a part in this, but not in any conscious way. Instead of thinking, "White Stag navy twill skort," and doggedly searching out similar skorts, all I have do is form an image of the item in my mind, transpose this image onto the field, and move to wherever the image finds its match in the outer world. I don't know how this works. Maybe my mind just gets so busy processing the incoming visual data that it has to bypass the left brain's verbal centers, with their cumbersome instructions: "Proceed to White Stag area in the northwest corner of ladies', try bottom racks near khaki shorts . . ." Or maybe the trick lies in understanding that each item *wants* to be reunited with its sibs and its clam members and that, within each clan, the item *wants* to occupy its proper place in the color/size hierarchy. Once I let the clothes take charge, once I understand that I am only the means of their reunification, they just fly out of the cart to their natural homes.

On the same day, perhaps because the new speediness frees me to think more clearly, I make my peace with the customers and discover the purpose of life, or at least of my life at Wal-Mart. Management may think that the purpose is to sell things, but this is an overly reductionist, narrowly capitalist view. As a matter of fact, I never see anything sold, since sales take place out of my sight, at the cash registers at the front of the store. All I see is customers unfolding carefully folded T-shirts, taking dresses and pants off their hangers, holding them up for a moment's idle inspection, then dropping them somewhere for us associates to pick up. For me, the way out of the resentment begins with a clue provided by a poster near the break room, in the back of the store where only associates go: "Your mother doesn't work here," it says. "Please pick up after yourself." I've passed it many times, thinking, "Ha, that's all I do—pick up after people." Then it hits me: most of the people I pick up after are mothers themselves, meaning that what I do at work is what *they* do at home—pick up the toys and the clothes and the spills. So the great thing about shopping, for most of these women, is that here *they* get to behave like brats, ignoring the bawling babies in their cars, tossing things around for someone else to pick up. And it wouldn't be any fun—would it?—unless the clothes were all reasonably orderly to begin with, which is where I come in, constantly re-creating orderliness for the customers to maliciously destroy. It's appalling, but it's their nature: only pristine and virginal displays truly excite them.

I test this theory out on Isabelle: that our job is to constantly re-create the stage setting in which women can act out. That without us, rates of child abuse would suddenly
soar. That we function, in a way. as therapists and should probably be paid accordingly,
at $50–$100 an hour. "You just go on thinking that," she says, shaking her head. But
she smiles her canny little smile in a way that makes me think it's not a bad notion.

With competence comes a new impatience: Why *does anybody put up with the wages
we're paid?* True, most of my fellow workers are better cushioned than I am; they live
with their spouses or grown children or they have other jobs in addition to this one. I
sit with Lynne in the break room one and find out this is only a part-time job for
her—six hours a day—with the other eight hours spent at a factory for $9 an hour.
Doesn't she get awfully tired? Nah, it's what she's always done. The cook at the Radio
Grill has two other jobs. You might expect a bit of grumbling, some signs here and
there of unrest—graffiti on the hortatory posters in the break room, muffled guffaws
during our associate meetings—but I can detect none of that. Maybe this is what you
get when you weed out all the rebels with drug tests and personality "surveys"—a uniformly servile and denatured workforce, content to dream of the distant day when
they'll be vested in the company's profit-sharing plan. They even join in the "Wal-
Mart cheer" when required to do so at meetings, so I'm told by the evening fitting
room lady, though I am fortunate enough never to witness this final abasement.[2]

But, if it's hard to think "out of the box," it may be almost impossible to think out
of the Big Box. Wal-Mart, when you're in it, is total—a closed system, a world unto
itself. I get a chill when I'm watching TV in the break room one afternoon and see. . .
a commercial for Wal-Mart. When a Wal-Mart shoes up within a television with a
Wal-Mart, you have to question the existence of an outer world. Sure, you can drive
for five minutes and get somewhere else—Kmart, that is, or Home Depot, or Target,
or Burger King, or Wendy's, or KFC. Wherever you look, there is no alternative to the
megascale corporate order, for which every form of local creativity and initiative has
been abolished by distant home offices. Even the woods and meadows have been
stripped of disorderly life forms and forced into a uniform made of concrete. What
you see—highways, parking lots, stores—is all there is, or all that's left to us here in
the reign of globalized, totalized, paved-over, corporate everything. I like to read the
labels to find out where the clothing we sell is made—Indonesia, Mexico, Turkey, the
Philippines, South Korea, Sri Lanka, Brazil—but the labels serve only to remind me
that none of these places is "exotic" anymore, that they've all been eaten by the great
blind profit-making global machine.

The only thing to do is ask: Why do you—why do *we*—work here? Why do you
stay? So when Isabelle praises my work a second time (!), I take the opportunity to say
I really appreciate her encouragement, but I can't afford to live on $7 an hour, and
how does she do it? The answer is that she lives with her grown daughter, who also
works, plus the fact that she's worked here the last two years, during which her pay has
shot up to $7.75 an hour. She counsels patience: it could happen to me. Melissa, who
has the advantage of a working husband, says, "Well, it's a job." Yes, she made twice as
much when she was a waitress but that place closed down and at her age she's never
going to be hired at a high-tip place. I recognize the inertia, the unwillingness to start

up with the apps and the interviews and the drug tests again. She thinks she should give it a year. *A year?* I tell her I'm wondering whether I should give it another week.

A few days later something happens to make kindly, sweet-natured Melissa mad. She gets banished to bras, which is terra incognita for us—huge banks of shelves bearing barely distinguishable bi-coned objects—for a three-hour stretch. I know how she feels, because I was once sent over to work for a couple of hours in men's wear, where I wandered uselessly through the strange thickets of racks, numbed by the sameness of colors and styles.[3] It's the difference between working and pretending to work. You push your cart a few feet, pause significantly with item in hand, frown at the ambient racks, then push on and repeat the process. "I just don't like wasting their money," Melissa says when she's allowed back. "I mean they're *paying* me and I just wasn't accomplishing anything over there." To me, this anger seems badly mis-aimed. What does she think, that the Walton family is living in some hidden room in the back of the store, in the utmost frugality, and likely to be ruined by $21 worth of wasted labor? I'm starting in on that theme when she suddenly dives behind the rack that separates the place where we're standing, in the Jordache/No Boundaries section, from the Faded Glory region. Worried that I may have offended her somehow, I follow right behind. "*Howard*," she whispers. "Didn't you see him come by? We're not allowed to talk to each other, you know."

"The point is our time is so cheap they don't care if we waste it," I continue, aware even as I speak that this isn't true, otherwise why would they be constantly monitoring us for "time theft"? But I sputter on: "That's what's so insulting." Of course, in this outburst of militance I am completely not noticing the context—two women of mature years, two very hardworking women, as it happens, dodging behind a clothing rack to avoid a twenty-six-year-old management twerp. That's not even worth commenting on.

Alyssa is another target for my crusade. When she returns to check yet again on that $7 polo, she finds a stain on it. What could she get off for that? I think 10 percent, and if you add in the 10 percent employee discount, we'd be down to $5.60. I'm trying to negotiate a 20-percent price reduction with the fitting room lady when—rotten luck!—Howard shows up and announces that there are no reductions and no employee discounts on *clearanced* items. Those are the rules. Alyssa looks crushed, and I tell her, when Howard's out of sight, that there's something wrong when you're not paid enough to buy a Wal-Mart shirt, a *clearanced* Wal-Mart shirt with a stain on it. "I hear you," she says, and admits Wal-Mart isn't working for her either, if the goal is to make a living.

Then I get a little reckless. When an associate meeting is announced over the loudspeaker that afternoon, I decide to go, although most of my coworkers stay put. I don't understand the purpose of these meetings, which occur every three days or so and consist largely of attendance taking, unless it's Howard's way of showing us that there's only one of him compared to so many of us. I'm just happy to have a few minutes to sit down or, in this case, perch on some fertilizer bags since we're meeting in lawn and garden today, and chat with whoever shows up, today a gal from the optical department. She's better coifed and made up than most of us female associates— forced to take the job because of a recent divorce, she tells me, and sorry now that she's found out how crummy the health insurance is. There follows a long story about preexisting conditions and deductibles and her COBRA running out. I listen vacantly because, like most of the other people in my orientation group, I hadn't opted for the health insurance—the employee contribution seemed too high. "You know what we need here?" I finally respond. "We need a union." There it is, the word is out. Maybe if I hadn't been feeling so footsore I wouldn't have said it, and I probably wouldn't have said it either if we were allowed to say "hell" and "damn" now and then or, better yet, "shit." But no one has outright banned the word *union* and right now it's the most potent couple of syllables at hand. "We need *something*," she responds.

After that, there's nothing to stop me. I'm on a mission now: *Raise the questions! Plant the seeds!* Breaks finally have a purpose beyond getting off my feet. There are hundreds of workers here—I never do find out how many—and sooner or later I'll meet them all. I reject the break room for this purpose because the TV inhibits conversation, and for all I know that's what it's supposed to do. Better to go outdoors to the fenced-in smoking area in front of the store. Smokers, in smoke-free America, are more likely to be rebels; at least that was true at The Maids, where the nonsmokers waited silently in the office for work to begin, while the smokers out on the sidewalk would be having a raucous old time. Besides, you can always start the ball rolling by asking for a light, which I have to do anyway when the wind is up. The next question is, "What department are you in?" followed by, "How long have you worked here?"—from which it's an obvious segue to the business at hand. Almost everyone is eager to talk, and I soon become a walking repository of complaints. No one gets paid overtime at Wal-Mart, I'm told, though there's often pressure to work it.[4] Many feel the health insurance isn't worth paying for. There's a lot of frustration over schedules, especially in the case of the evangelical lady who can never get Sunday morning off, no matter how much she pleads. And always there are the gripes about managers: the one who is known for sending new hires home in tears, the one who takes a ruler and knocks everything off what he regards as a messy shelf, so you have to pick it up off the floor and start over.

Sometimes, I discover, my favorite subject, which is the abysmal rate of pay, seems to be a painful one. Stan, for example, a twenty-something fellow with wildly misaligned teeth, is so eager to talk that he fairly pounces on the seat next to mine on a bench in the smoking area. But when the subject arrives at wages, his face falls. The idea, see, was that he would go to school (he names a two-year technical school) while he worked, but the work cut into studying too much, so he had to drop out and now. . . He stares at the butt-strewed ground, perhaps seeing an eternity in appliances unfold before him. I suggest that what we need is a union, but from the look on his face I might as well have said gumballs or Prozac. Yeah, maybe he'll go over and apply at Media One, where a friend works and the wages are higher. . . Try school again, umm. . .

At the other extreme, there are people like Marlene. I am sitting out there talking to a doll-like blonde whom I had taken for a high school student but who, it turns out, has been working full-time since November and is fretting over whether she can afford to buy a car. Marlene comes out for her break, lights a cigarette, and emphatically seconds my opinion of Wal-Mart wages. "They talk about having spirit," she says, referring to management, "but they don't give us any reason to have any spirit." In her view, Wal-Mart would rather just keep hiring new people than treating the ones it has decently. You can see for yourself there's a dozen new people coming in for orientation every day—which is true. Wal-Mart's appetite for human flesh is insatiable; we've even been urged to recruit any Kmart employees we may happen to know. They don't care that they've trained you or anything, Marlene goes on, they can always get someone else if you complain. Emboldened by her vehemence, I risk the red-hot word again. "I know this goes against the whole Wal-Mart philosophy, but we could use a union here." She grins, so I push on: "It's not just about money, it's about dignity." She nods fiercely, lighting a second cigarette from her first. *Put that woman on the organizing committee at once*, I direct my imaginary coconspirators as I leave.

All right, I'm not a union organizer anymore than I'm Wal-Mart "management material," as Isabelle has hinted. In fact, I don't share the belief, held by many union staffers, that unionization would be a panacea. Sure, almost any old union would boost wages and straighten out some backbones here, but I know that even the most energetic and democratic unions bear careful watching by their members. The truth, which I can't avoid acknowledging when I'm in those vast, desert-like stretches between afternoon breaks, is that I'm just amusing myself, and in what seems like a pretty harmless way. Someone has to puncture the prevailing fiction that we're a "family" here, we "associates" and our "servant leaders," held together solely by our commitment to the "guests." After all, you'd need a lot stronger word than *dysfunctional* to describe a family where a few people get to eat at the table while the rest—the "associates" and all the dark-skinned seamstresses and factory workers worldwide who make the things we sell—lick up the drippings from the floor: *psychotic* would be closer to the mark.[5] And someone has to flush out the mysterious "we" lurking in the "our" in the "Our people make the difference" statement we wear on our backs. It might as well be me because I have nothing to lose, less than nothing, in fact. For each day that I fail to find cheaper quarters, which is every day now, I am spending $49.95 for the privilege of putting clothes away at Wal-Mart. At this rate, I'll have burned through the rest of the $1200 allotted for my life in Minneapolis in less than a week.

I could use some amusement. I have been discovering a great truth about low-wage work and probably a lot of medium-wage work, too—that nothing happens, or rather the same thing always happens, which amounts, day after day, to nothing. This law doesn't apply so strictly to the service jobs I've held so far. In waitressing, you always have new customers to study; even housecleaning offers the day's parade of houses to explore. But here—well, you know what I do and how it gets undone and how I just start all over and do it again. How did I think I was going to survive in a factory, where each *minute* is identical to the next one, and not just each day? There will be no crises here, except perhaps in the pre-Christmas rush. There will be no "Code M," meaning "hostage situation," and probably no Code F or T (I'm guessing on these letters, which I didn't write down during my note taking at orientation and which may be a company secret anyway), meaning fire or tornado—no opportunities for courage or extraordinary achievement or sudden evacuations of the store. Those breaking-news moments when a disgruntled former employee shoots up the place or a bunch of people get crushed in an avalanche of piled-up stock are one-in-a-million events. What my life holds is carts-full ones, then empty ones, then full ones again.

You could get old pretty fast here. In fact, time does funny things when there are no little surprises to mark it off into memorable chunks, and I sense that I'm already several years older than I was when I started. In the one full-length mirror in ladies' wear, a medium-tall figure is hunched over a cart, her face pinched in absurd concentration—surely not me. How long before I'm as gray as Ellie, as cranky as Rhoda, as shriveled as Isabelle? When even a high-sodium fast-food diet can't keep me from needing to pee every hour, and my feet are putting some podiatrist's kid through college? Yes, I know that any day now I'm going to return to the variety and drama of my real Barbara Ehrenreich life. But this fact sustains me only in the way that, say, the prospect of heaven cheers a terminally ill person: it's nice to know, but it isn't much help from moment to moment. What you don't necessarily realize when you start selling your time by the hour is that what you're actually selling is your *life*.

Notes

1. In 1988, Arkansas state senator Jay Bradford attacked Wal-Mart for paying its employees so little that they had to turn to the state for welfare. He was, however, unable to prove his point by getting the company to open its payroll records (Bob Ortega, *In Sam We Trust: The Untold Story of Sam Walton and Wal-Mart, the World's Most Powerful Retailer* (Times Books, 2001, p. 193).

2. According to Wal-Mart expert Bob Ortega, Sam Walton got the idea for the cheer on a 1975 trip to Japan, "where he was deeply impressed by factory workers doing group calisthenics and company cheers." Ortega describes Walton conducting a cheer: "Gimme a W!' he'd shout. 'W!' the workers would shout back, and on through the Wal-Mart name. At the hyphen, Walton would shout 'Gimme a squiggly!' and squat and twist his hips at the same time; the workers would squiggle right back" (*In Sam We Trust*, p. 91).

3. "During your career with Wal-Mart, you may be cross-trained in other departments in your facility. This will challenge you in new areas, and help you be a well-rounded Associate" (*Wal-Mart Associate Handbook*, p. 18).

4. Wal-Mart employees have sued the retail chain for unpaid overtime in four states—West Virginia, New Mexico, Oregon, and Colorado. The plaintiffs allege that they were pressured to work overtime and that the company then erased the overtime hours from their time records. Two of the West Virginia plaintiffs, who had been promoted to management positions before leaving Wal-Mart, said they had participated in altering time records to conceal overtime work. Instead of paying time and a half for overtime work, the company would reward workers with "desired schedule changes, promotions and other benefits," while workers who refused the unpaid overtime were "threatened with write-ups, demotions, reduced work schedules or docked pay" (Lawrence Messina, "Former Wal-Mart Workers File Overtime Suit in Harrison County," *Charleston Gazette*, January 24, 1999). In New Mexico, a suit by 110 Wal-Mart employees was settled in 1998 when the company agreed to pay for the overtime ("Wal-Mart Agrees to Resolve Pay Dispute," *Albuquerque Journal*, July 16, 1998). In an e-mail to me, Wal-Mart spokesman William Wertz stated that "it is Wal-Mart's policy to compensate its employees fairly for their work and to comply fully with all federal and state wage and hour requirements."

5. In 1996, the National Labor Committee Education Fund in Support of Worker and Human Rights in Central American revealed that some Kathie Lee clothes were being sewn by children as young as twelve in a sweatshop in Honduras. TV personality Kathie Lee Gifford, the owner of Kathie Lee line, tearfully denied the charges on the air but later promised to give up her dependence on sweatshops.

2

OFFICE LADIES
Power, Gender, and Work
in Japanese Companies

Yuko Ogasawara

At Tōzai Bank, men and women were recruited immediately from colleges and universities for two different positions: *sogoshoku* (integrated track) and *ippanshoku* or *jimushoku* (clerical track). Those in *sogoshoku* were trained to become managers, and *ippanshoku* employees worked as their assistants. The deceptively gender-neutral terms cloaked the fact that integrated-track employees were almost all male and clerical workers were without exception female. In recent years, the bank recruited 50 to 80 university graduates each year for the integrated positions. Among them, only a handful were female. In addition, 100 to 150 women were hired as clerical workers. About half of the women recruited for clerical positions had university diplomas, often from the same institutions as the men in the integrated positions.

The sex-discriminatory policy was reflected in the number of managers in the bank: at the time of the study, there were fewer than ten female managers out of a total of about two thousand (less than one in two hundred). All eleven women on the floor where I worked, as well as four women in the nearby department, were clerical workers.

Recruitment of female university graduates for both *sogoshoku* and *ippanshokus* was virtually unknown before the implementation of the Equal Employment Opportunity (EEO) Law in Japan in 1986. Before implementation of the law, the only women the bank officially employed were junior-college graduates. (Incidentally, the two-year degree program offered in junior college is primarily for female students. There are few junior colleges for male students.) Women graduating from university were penalized for their overqualification. Only those with "personal connections" to the bank, usually through their fathers or relatives, were hired, with the agreement that they would be treated as junior-college graduates.

Even at the time of the study, the hank did not value university education for its clerical staff. A woman who had graduated from university and been with the bank for two years was ranked and compensated the same as a junior-college graduate who had been with the bank four years. This was an improvement over the old policy in effect before the implementation of the EEO Law, which treated the same university graduate as a junior-college graduate who had been with the bank two years. It is clear, however, that the new policy still failed to pay for the price of higher education that the university graduate received. A junior college woman earned money while her university counterpart paid tuition and was nevertheless compensated at the same rate as a university graduate of the same age.[1]

Until shortly after 1982, the bank recruited men and women directly from high school. In the older generation of employees, a number of these people remain. I was told that when the two-track system was introduced, all white-collar male employees, including those with only a high school education, became integrated staff, whereas all female workers were designated as their clerical assistants. At the time of this study, only one such woman had been subsequently promoted to the integrated position. When the bank started recruiting female university graduates for clerical positions, this resulted in the often strained combination of a university graduate assistant and a boss who joined the bank immediately from high school. However, on the floor where I worked, there were no men with only a high school education.

Although people within the bank and the Japanese public in general talked of the two-track system, in reality there was a third category of employees in the bank: *shomu* (miscellaneous jobs). *Shomu* consisted entirely of male employees who worked as company car drivers, messengers, mailmen, bookbinders, building receptionists, and the like. The bank stopped recruiting employees for *shomu* some years ago and began filling these positions with part-time workers in their fifties and sixties who had retired from their primary jobs. Another small group of *shomu* regular employees were physically disabled men.

Shomu workers were present in the everyday life of the bank. For example, one had to pass the receptionist's desk to enter or exit the building, and the mailman came to our room to deliver and pick up mail each day. However, they were curiously absent from the minds of *sarariman* and OLs. People in the office used the words men and women to denote *sōgōshoku* and *ippanshoku* workers, respectively. *Shomu* workers were usually left out in their reference to *men*. OLs had few contacts with *shomu* workers and generally knew little about them. One OL, for instance, stated that they were all part-time workers. I later found out that the man who sat at the nearby receptionist desk was a full-time employee who had been working in the bank for almost thirty years. When I told the OL what I had learned, she was genuinely surprised.

It was not only *shomu* workers but women in the integrated track who were ignored in the dichotomy between men and women, the most salient categorization of people in the company. After the implementation of the EEO Law, the bank adopted the gender-neutral terms *integrated* and *clerical* in its official documents. In everyday life, however, people in the office continued to talk and think in gender dichotomy. A man often asked an OL before picking up a transferred phone call whether the caller was a "man" or a "woman"; what he wished to find out was whether the caller was an integrated staff member whom he must answer with respect, or whether the caller was an ordinary OL. Similarly, OLs frequently replied to a customer's call apologetically, "There's no man on the floor at the moment who can answer your question."

When I called the personnel department of the bank before accepting the job, a woman answered the phone and explained their recruitment policies in a competent manner. When I asked her a further question, however, she said abruptly, "Let me transfer this call to a man." It was apparent from the way she said it that I was to interpret *man* as "someone in a more responsible position to answer your questions." Indeed, because there were still few integrated-track women in the organization (less than twenty among approximately seven thousand employees), people seemed to feel little inconvenience in treating them as an exception to the men–women dichotomy.

In accord with the perception of the overwhelming majority of the people in the office, unless otherwise noted, the words men and women will be used hereafter to denote *sarariman* in the integrated track and OLs in the clerical position, respectively. Despite the fact that the terms reinforce sex discrimination, I use them because to do otherwise would mask the gross unfairness of present conditions.

Office Ladies' Daily Working Lives

Office Ladies as "Girls"

When not referred to as *women*, OLs were often—indeed, more often—referred to as *girls (onnanoko)*. Although they were addressed by the men on the floor by their names, to an outsider both within and out of the hank, OLs were simply "girls." Thus a man speaking to another man on the phone often said, "I'll have one of the girls go get it," or "Our girl made a mistake."[2]

Carole Pateman (1988) compares calling adult women "girls" to calling adult male slaves "boys," and argues that both usages are a graphic illustration of a perpetual nonage that women and slaves cannot cast off. The words suggest "civilly dead beings." By lumping together OLs as "girls," men showed their unwillingness to recognize OLs as individuals. Indeed, respect for OLs' individuality was minimal. For instance, when a woman helped a man prepare a report, her name rarely appeared on it, even if she had done most of the work. The man for whom she worked took all the credit. In the real sense, OLs did not have names in the organization, and hence their names did not appear in the official record.

Working under someone else's name is common in Japan. Young businessmen write many reports on behalf of their bosses, and graduate students in Japanese universities often work for their professors without recognition in print.[3] The difference between the OLs and the businessmen and graduate students is that businessmen and graduate students are serving a form of apprenticeship; it is mutually understood that the boss or professor will eventually help the young person get recognition. However, no such thing can be expected for OLs. Most OLs' work will remain unrecognized forever.

Some women I talked to said that the most humiliating part of being an OL was this "namelessness." Men's individuality was respected. Each man accumulated credit and demerit marks according to his performance. In contrast, differences among individual women were more or less ignored. When a woman made a mistake in her work, the vague "Our girl screwed up" became a legitimate excuse. Seldom did men try to find out which of the women made the error, just as few men were interested in knowing which woman did a splendid job. Being treated as "one of the girls" made many OLs feel that they were mere replaceable cogs in the gigantic machine.

In accordance with the practice of lumping OLs together as "girls" was the fact that OLs in the bank were not seriously evaluated. Men were evaluated according to their performance and were graded on a scale from A to E, which determined the bonus they received. In theory, OLs were supposed to be evaluated as well. In reality, however, I was told that almost every OL received the grade of C, which indicated that she was an average worker.

That evaluation of OLs' performance virtually did not exist was brought home to me one day when two other women and I were discussing the compensation scheme for OLs. Matsumoto-san explained to me that the base payment was the same for all OLs with the same educational background who joined the firm in the same year, but bonuses could, in theory, differ according to their performance evaluations. At this point, Kuze-san gasped in surprise, "Is there such a thing as a performance evaluation?" Apparently, she did not know that OLs, including herself, were being evaluated.

Matsumoto-san informed her bewildered colleague that indeed OLs received grades that ranged from A to E. She then described the way an OL could find out how she had been evaluated by calculating backward from a compensation chart that the union distributed. Kuze-san exclaimed, "Gosh, I didn't know!" Matsumoto-san assured her colleague, "In case of women, it's mostly C anyway. Once Ueda-san [their female colleague on the floor] asked Furukawa-san [one of the board members] about women's grades, and he said that unless there's something gravely wrong, women get Cs." The fact that Kuze-san, who had been with the bank for at least three years, was unaware that there was a performance evaluation attested to its negligible status. Because the performance evaluation did not function properly for OLs, they were oblivious of its existence.

Management's lack of enthusiasm to earnestly evaluate OLs' work was also apparent from the aforementioned organizational arrangement, under which OLs seated at the sales counter reported to a section manager on the second floor of the building who knew little of their actual work. According to this agreement, the men for whom OLs worked were not the people who evaluated their performance. As has been explained, this grouping of OLs under the section manager on the second floor was the result of managers' desire to make it easier to transfer OLs. The arrangement would have caused great inconvenience if OLs' work was to be evaluated seriously. However, since true evaluation for OLs did not exist, the awkwardness of the grouping did not seem to trouble the managers.

Men and women I interviewed confirmed that the situation was similar in other firms. Some managers pointed out that in their company, OLs' performance was reviewed, but most agreed that evaluation of OLs was taken less seriously than evaluation of men. Perhaps more relevant to my discussion is the fact that few OLs considered assessment important. Many women thought that the difference in the appraisal process was of minor significance. OLs working in various companies often used the expressions "unless there's something gravely wrong" or "unless you've done something gravely wrong" (*yohodo no koto ga naikagiri* or *yohodo no koto o shinai kagiri*) to describe to me how little it mattered to them whether they performed well. OLs in general were aware that they had few prospects for promotion. Most did not think of their present job as a lifetime career. Furthermore, references from their current bosses were seldom necessary in obtaining new jobs. There were few incentives for them to worry about the evaluation they received as OLs.

In addition to performance reviews, other customs in the workplace reinforced the notion that OLs commanded less respect than the integrated staff. Some of these practices were supported by the official rules of the company, but most of them functioned as unwritten laws. One example was the custom for a clerical-track woman to leave the company upon marrying a fellow banker. When I asked the OLs whether it was the company rule, they did not know for sure but said that it was expected. A man working in another bank spoke of a similar convention in his workplace, which, according to him, was not laid down in the official company regulation. I suspect that the rule at Tōzai was also unofficial. In practice, however, a woman left the bank if she married a coworker.[4] There was a rumor that once a woman who had married her colleague protested against leaving the company but ultimately conceded when it was hinted that her staying with the bank would "hurt" her husband's career.

Another example was marriage ceremonies. It was customary for a man to invite the general manager of his department as the guest of honor to his wedding party. However, an OL would invite a vice general manager. "A general manager is too important to be asked to come to our parties," explained an OL.

Various day-to-day practices showed that OLs occupied a secondary position to men. For instance, when names were written on a circulation board, OLs' names were indented in the following way.

Ōbayashi (man's name)
Ueda (woman's name)
Kurimoto (woman's name)
Nishida (man's name)

In addition, stamps used by OLs bearing their names were considerably smaller in size than men's. They were called *mame-in* (miniature stamps). More important, OLs did not carry *meishi* (business cards), vital instruments for anyone who wishes to do business in Japan.

Perhaps what most characterized the work life of an OL in contrast to that of a *sararīman* was lack of self-control and independence. First and foremost, a woman was not allowed to manage her own time. Whereas a man might take lunch at any time he found convenient, an OL must dine at the designated time. On the floor where I worked, women alternated taking lunch so that the sales counter would not be deserted. The first group took lunch from 11:30 to 12:30, and the second group from 12:30 to 13:30. The two groups switched times weekly so that the group that took lunch from 11:30 one week would take lunch from 12:30 the next week. What greatly surprised me was the pressure that OLs felt to be punctual. Whenever we were a little late in returning to the office, women ran down the stairs to try to be on time.

It was also customary for an OL to inform fellow OLs seated nearby of every detail of her whereabouts. It was considered necessary to know where to find the person in case she was urgently needed. I could not, however, get used to the way the OL seated next to me

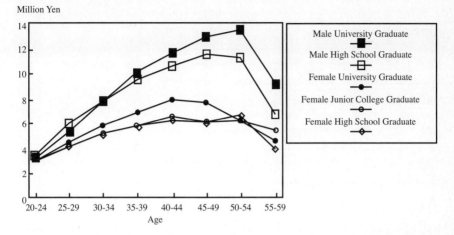

Million Yen

FIGURE 2.1 Average annual gross income in large banks with 1,000 or more full-time employees, 1995. *Source: Rōdōshō, Chingin Kōzō kihon tōkei chōsa* (Basic survey on wage structure), 1996.

told me she was going to the restroom every time she left. I found it hard to do the same myself, feeling that even an OL had at least the freedom to go to the toilet without having to report to someone. Dress was another aspect of OLs' life that was controlled, For they had to wear uniforms. Neither men nor women in the integrated track wore uniforms.

The difference between *sōgōshoku* and *ippanshoku* was perhaps best reflected in their levels of compensation. Because the bank used seniority to determine compensation, wages increased as an employee aged. OLs' compensation curve, however, hit a ceiling (after which there was only a slight increase) much earlier and at a considerably lower level than men's. It was well known among women that an OL who graduated from university must work diligently until she was fifty-one years old to receive the same compensation as a man with the same educational background who had been with the bank for only four years. The women said that if the OL took a maternity leave, her compensation would never reach the level of a man who had been there five years.

Although I was unable to collect precise income data for the employees of the bank, there is a survey conducted by the government on incomes of employees in large banks with one thousand or more employees. Comparison of average annual gross income curves by age for men and women supports the OLs' claim that there was a large difference in the payment received between the two sexes. Incomes for male university and high school graduates rise steeply as they grow older, whereas those for women increase only gradually regardless of education (fig. 2.1). Wage differentials by sex are the largest among people in their late forties, when women, on average, receive less than half as much as men (fig. 2.2).[5]

The bank's policies concerning the treatment of women were typical of many large corporations in Japan (Lam 1992; Lo 1990; McLendon 1983; Rohlen 1974; Saso 1990). The excuse that is often provided by the companies for adopting discriminatory policies is that women's tenure with a company is too short. Because most women quit

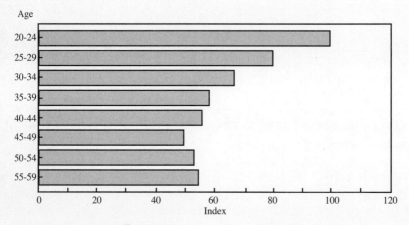

FIGURE 2.2   Wage Differentials by sex (male = 100) in large banks with 1,000 or more full-time employees (annual gross income base), 1995. Source: Rōdōshō, Chingin Kōzō kihon tōkei chōsa (Basic survey on wage structure), 1996.

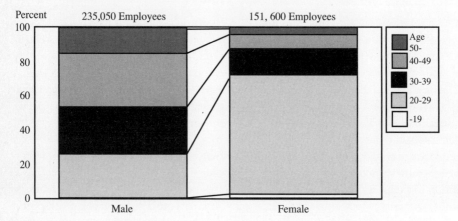

FIGURE 2.3   Employees by age in large banks with 1,000 or more full-time employees, 1995. Source: Rōdōshō, Chingin Kōzō kihon tōkei chōsa (Basic survey on wage structure), 1996.

the firms at marriage, childbirth, or when their husbands are transferred to another part of the country, women do not fit the male pattern of "lifetime" employment and promotion. Figure 2.3 illustrates the skewed breakdown of female employees by age in large banks. Whereas the percentages of male employees in their twenties, thirties, and forties are more or less the same, with a slightly smaller percentage above the age of fifty, as much as 70 percent of female employees are in their twenties. Companies invariably profess that women are an "unreliable" workforce not worth seriously training.[6]

Why is OLs' work evaluated less seriously than men's work? The foremost reasons seem to be that OLs' length of service in a company tends to be short and managers rarely intend to promote them. A director of Itochu, a trading company, who is in charge of personnel management, is reported to have said that because women's tenure was limited, the firm did not feel it necessary to assess their work and thereby distinguish among them. Management hoped that women would get along more harmoniously without appraisal. Apparently, management felt that evaluating women would do more harm than good by encouraging competition and thereby disrupting relationships among them (*Nihon Keizai Shinbun*, 26 September 1994).[7]

In this regard, it is noteworthy that evaluation means different things for (mostly male) white-collar workers in the integrated track in Japan and their counterparts in the United States. Whereas work appraisals are tied to annual discussion of employees' compensation in most American firms, in many Japanese companies a significant portion of employees' salary is negotiated by the corporate union. Japanese *sararīman* usually do not talk about their compensation with supervisors on an individual basis in the way that many American workers do. Appraisals are instead important for *sarariman* to determine who in the long run should be promoted into the next rank of managers and when. In the words of a man working in a bank:

> In our bank, we are always rank ordered unofficially among our *dōki* [those who joined the organization in the same year]. For example, that you rank about xth among 100 *dōki*. Such ordering is not a gross estimation of placing people into high, middle, and low groups. Instead, we are given an exact rank. However, no difference is made in the salary we receive up until we are about thirty-five years old. Managers wait until we are about thirty-five years old. By then consensus is built [concerning each employee's evaluation], and so they begin promoting from among those that are given high evaluation. This way, people will consent to managers' decisions, thinking that it's only proper that those ranked high get promoted first.

As described by this banker, appraisal for white-collar men (and some women) in typical Japanese firms is primarily a means by which to select employees to be promoted into ranks such as *kachō*. It is an instrument to screen workers of high caliber, and its effect becomes apparent only after many years. This, of course, does not imply that men can take appraisal lightly. As the interviewee illustrates, men in his bank are constantly given detailed evaluations. It is just that the result does not become official until the first major promotion. Until then, there is little difference in the amount of pay *dōki* workers receive. The first selection usually does not take place in large Japanese companies until employees have worked for about ten or more years. Given that OLs' length of service is usually short and that management rarely intends to promote them, evaluations of OLs lack major objectives.

In contrast, the majority of blue-collar women in Japan must work under strict surveillance. Scrutiny of their work is usually considered necessary to control factory line productivity. When a worker is slow, her productivity affects the efficiency of the entire line, which may consist of both male and female workers. On the shop floor, the sex of a worker does not normally exempt her from strict evaluation.

In response to the recent slump in the Japanese economy, many companies are attempting to cut costs. Whether corporations can continue to afford the luxury of frivolously evaluating OLs' work remains to be seen. This issue is taken up again in the conclusion of this book.

Office Ladies as "Office Wives"

Rosabeth Kanter writes in her study of women in an American business organization that the marriage metaphor was used to portray the relationships between secretaries and bosses:

> [The marriage metaphor] was. . . implicit in the way many people at Indsco talked about the relationships between secretaries and bosses. Over time, a serious emotional bond could develop. One executive secretary promoted into management described leaving her old boss as a "divorce.". . .
>
> For the first few months after her promotion, she stopped in to see him every morning, hanging her coat in her old office instead of the new one, and finding herself concerned if he had a cold or looked unhappy (1977, 89–90).

Similarly, many OLs at the bank spoke of themselves as "wives," often half in jest. Japanese critics also frequently likened OLs to "office wives."[8] The marriage metaphor was a popular characterization of the relationships between men and women in the office both in the United States and in Japan.

There was, however, a significant difference between American secretaries and Japanese OLs. Whereas many American secretaries worked for specific managers, few OLs did. Among the fifteen OLs at the bank, only one OL held a job that was supervised by one man. Other OLs usually worked in pairs for a group of anywhere from six to fifteen men. Even the two general managers who were members of the board did not have personal secretaries. They had to share the services of two OLs with four other general and vice general managers. This arrangement is typical among Japanese companies. Rodney Clark reports that there were few secretaries in the Western sense of an assistant to a boss at the Japanese box manufacturer where he conducted his research (1979).

Unlike their Japanese counterparts, American bosses were more likely to exercise personal preference in the choice of their female assistants. Whereas some American secretaries were hired by the men they worked for, all OLs, including those working as secretaries for top executives, were hired by the personnel department, which later appointed them to their respective offices.

Because of the working arrangement and hiring procedures, the one-to-one relationship characteristic of American secretaries and bosses that promoted the use of the marriage metaphor in Kanter's case study did not exist in Tōzai Bank. Therefore, what prompted people to refer to OLs as "office wives" could not be the kind of intense bond that existed between American secretaries and bosses. Instead, it seemed to concern the nature of the tasks performed by OLs.

The OLs on the bank floor were assigned all kinds of miscellaneous jobs. They picked up mail from the basement mail room, sorted it, and distributed it to the appropriate addressees. They sorted and distributed various memoranda and notifications. They stored important materials by putting them in order, punching holes in the margins, and filing them in binders. They addressed envelopes. They copied documents and sent them by fax or by air shooter. They printed out deposit balances. They typed letters and documents. They sent telegrams of condolence and congratulation. They bought gifts for customers. They served tea when customers came. They constantly picked up telephones and transferred calls to the appropriate people.

The OLs were also often summoned to fix paper jams and add paper to copiers and fax machines. They were sometimes even asked to paste together papers that had been mistakenly torn apart by men. A woman would, upon being called, jump up from her desk and scurry over to a general manager's desk, only to be asked to fetch him an eraser or refill his stapler. One OL sewed a button back on a general manager's suit.

The term *office wives* compared the OL's role to that of a wife who takes care of her husband at home. The reference emphasized the fact that offices were not all that different from the Japanese home. In each place, woman catered to the needs of men. The metaphor also seemed to comment ironically on men's dependence on women both at home and at the office. It is said that because a wife looks after his daily needs completely, a Japanese man often does not know where to find his socks and handkerchiefs when she is away (Iwao 1993; Lebra 1984). Similarly, in the office, men were often at a loss if OLs were not there to help them.

Without OLs, men on many occasions did not know where to find documents and files, could not fix paper jams or add paper to copiers, and did not know how to operate word processors.[9] Many could not make transportation arrangements for business trips and did not know how to get their expenditures reimbursed. Some men also seemed unsure of the details of paperwork. Men were in the comfortable position of having these nuisances taken care of by OLs, but their comfort was bought at the expense of becoming dependent on women.

The tasks delegated to OLs were simple and mechanical. They were often considered valueless compared with men's jobs. However, no matter how seemingly insignificant, these tasks were essential in that they had to be performed. Even if a man succeeded in negotiating a difficult bargain with an important customer, the contract would not materialize unless an OL completed the necessary forms and saw to it that they went through the required procedure. If a man had not taken time to learn the process himself, he had to rely on OLs to perform a job that was vital for the success of his business.

Several men I interviewed expressed this feeling of dependence on women. For example, a man working in a real estate company, who supervised five salesmen and a woman assistant, said he felt that he must take especially good care of his female assistant. He thought he would be in more trouble if the assistant quit than if one of the salesmen did, for he himself could replace the salesman, but he could not replace the assistant. A man working in a general trading company summarized succinctly, "Women do jobs that you yourself can't do."

Tea Pouring

It is appropriate to consider one aspect of OLs' work—tea pouring (*ochakumi*)—at length because it has attracted attention as a symbol of the drudgery that OLs must endure.[10] Tea pouring helps us understand what it means to be an OL, because it was the task the OLs at the bank detested most.

Customers often visited the departments, and tea had to be served each time. When customers came, the man in charge of their accounts would tell an OL working for his department the number of cups of tea he required and which cubicle to bring them to. The OL had to drop whatever work she had been doing and rush to the kitchen. She would set cups and saucers on a tray, pour Japanese tea, and bring them to the designated cubicle. Some customers, upon being served, murmured "thank you," but more often her service was ignored both by the customers, who were almost always male, and her male colleague. Nevertheless, she would bow politely and retreat with the tray.

When the customers left, the man was supposed to ask the OL to clear up the table for future use. But because he often forgot, the OL had to keep an eye on the cubicle or the man's seat to make sure that the meeting was still going on. When clearing the table, she had to change ashtrays, because many Japanese businessmen smoke. On the floor where I worked, the temporary staff had to clean dirty cups and ashtrays piled in the kitchen sink and were also often asked to serve tea by OLs, who relayed the request made by men.

When an important customer had to be attended by the general or vice general managers, one of the three general managers' rooms located on the second floor was used. OLs did not particularly enjoy serving tea on the second floor, not only because they had to climb stairs but because the group was usually large and many cups of tea had to be balanced on the tray. The serving order was important, and an OL needed to gauge the hierarchical ranking among the guests the moment she entered the room. This was usually done mechanically, taking the cue from the seating arrangement. When I confessed that I had never served tea before, many OLs looked surprised. One of them quickly drew a diagram for me and taught me the rule of thumb in interpreting men's importance from the seating arrangement (fig. 2.4).

Serving tea was a major source of OLs' complaints. They often grumbled that they had to pour tea too many times. During lunch, they soothed their feelings by sharing their annoyance. They were invariably irritated when they had to change ashtrays because a single cigarette had been smoked, or when they had to clear cups of tea that had not been touched. Unfinished cups of tea invited their displeasure by making them feel that their labor was wasted.

To an outsider, typing a letter and serving tea might seem equally tedious and unpleasant tasks, but for an OL, there was a world of difference. Women were far more offended when asked to serve tea than to do other jobs. No matter how many times they had poured tea, OLs said they could not help feeling irritated every time they were asked for the service. I heard many women use the expression *muttosuru* (gets on one's nerves) to describe their annoyance when asked for tea.

One OL working for a food processing company explained the difference between serving tea and other tasks:

> Sure, what we do are all simple things—serving tea, making copies, typing documents. After all, our job is different from men's jobs. But that doesn't mean we feel all right to be ordered to bring tea. I mean, an OL has her own way of doing things. You think of

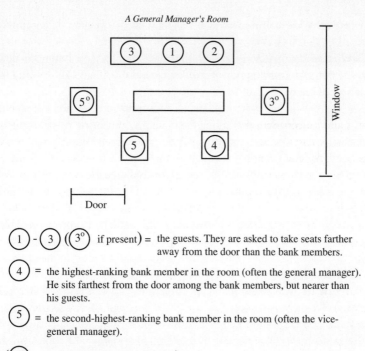

Figure 2.4   Diagram drawn by an office lady indicating the proper tea-serving order.

the procedures, for example, that you'd make copies first, then type this letter, and next that document. In the middle of all that, you're suddenly told to bring tea, and you're supposed to smile cordially and say, "Yes, I'm coming." Every time you serve tea, you interrupt your job and serve for others. It may sound funny to talk about *your* job, when all the jobs are ordered by men. But once you accept them, they become your jobs.

OLs detested serving tea because it emphasized their subordinate position. In typing letters and making copies, women usually had the latitude to decide how and when to do a job. Because OLs were scarce resources, a man could not ordinarily order OLs to type a letter or to make copies immediately, except at a truly pressing moment. It was only in serving tea that women had to put aside whatever they had been doing and follow the orders of men. Tea pouring reminded women that they did not have control over their time.

It was also probable that OLs felt tea pouring was more demeaning than other tasks because it called attention to their subservient role. Susan Pharr (1990) has applied Erving Goffman's definition of "status rituals" to her study of Japanese female civil servants' rebellion against pouring tea. She argues that the asymmetry of the sexes is "ritualized" in women's deferential act of serving tea to male colleagues. She further notes that in order for such status rituals to have meaning for those performing them, the deference behavior must be warmly rewarded by reciprocal conduct. Indeed, OLs at Tōzai had a favorable view of a man who said "thank you" when served tea. An expression of gratitude undoubtedly helped women think well of a certain man. I speculate therefore that the distastefulness of the job would alter somewhat if the emphasis on servile status in pouring tea was weakened by men regularly offering their thanks. The nature of the task, which recalls the domestic, serving role of women, was as much a reason for OLs to dislike the job as the fact that it had to be performed immediately.

OLs frequently mentioned that they would appreciate men's help in serving tea. Many agreed that their burden would be greatly alleviated if men would return dirty cups and ashtrays to the kitchen. Yet it was OLs themselves who made such help unlikely, insofar as they clearly marked the kitchen as women's domain.

The kitchen was called *ochashitsu* (tea room), and OLs took turns tidying up the room. The room was used predominantly to prepare tea for customers, but it was also a place where women touched up their makeup and brushed their teeth after lunch. Despite the fact that they were given a separate space and lockers, women kept their personal belongings in the tea room: the shelves were full of items such as brushes, pins, and cosmetics. In addition, it was a place where women got together to talk privately.

Understandably, men seemed to feel awkward in stepping into the kitchen. Once when I was working in the *ochashitsu*, a man came to the room and asked for a glass of water. My first reaction was to say, "Why don't you open the cupboard, and help yourself to a glass?" But I thought better of it and handed him what he had asked for. By the way he stood uneasily at the doorway, it was apparent that he felt he dare not intrude into the room.

As we have seen, women account for approximately 40 percent of all employees in Japan. One-third of all female employees are clerical workers, and the overwhelming majority of women who work in the office are OLs. Given their numbers, their male colleagues' dependence upon them for essential if simple tasks, and their irritation at chores such as tea pouring, why is it that OLs rarely engage in formal protest against discriminatory company polices such as their exclusion from managerial ranks, the gender-dichotomized two-track employment system, and frivolous evaluations of their performance?

Notes

1. For excellent research on the effects of the EEO Law on the Japanese employment system, see Alice Lam (1992). She finds that although there have been improvements, the law does not fundamentally change Japanese business practices that discriminate against women. Frank Upham has also written a chapter on the passage of the EEO Law (1987). For a more technical aspect of the law, refer to Lorraine Parkinson (1989).

2. Although I feel it inappropriate to refer to adult women as "girls," I use it in translation when it is the word used by the interviewee.

3. I thank Glenda Roberts for calling my attention to this point.

4. Both at Tōzai and in the bank where the interviewee worked, if a woman in the integrated track married a colleague, the custom was that she stayed.

5. For a detailed analysis of the gap between the wages of men and women in Japan, see Kawashima Yoko (1983, 1985), Ōsawa Machiko (1984, 1993), Shinotsuka Eiko (1982), Tomita Yasunobu (1988), and Yashiro Naohiro (1980).

6. Ōsawa Machiko questions the legitimacy of such claims repeatedly made by employers to discriminate against women (1993). She maintains that it is the seniority wage system and the assignment of low-level clerical jobs to women that make women retire early, not women's tendency to retire that make companies assign them low-level jobs. For an analysis of women's rate of leaving jobs, see also Higuchi Yoshio (1991) and Tomita Yasunobu (1988).

7. The cost of evaluating OLs may not be limited to nonpecuniary matters such as damage to human relations in the office. In recent years, women's length of tenure has increased, and a number of companies have reconsidered their policy of not evaluating women. (For further discussion on this issue, see the conclusion of this book.) According to one male interviewee, the reaction of the overwhelming majority of employees in a firm where it was announced that they would start evaluating not only male but female workers was that it was such a nuisance (*mendō*). Everyone who was to assess at least one subordinate's work had to participate in three special training sessions to learn ways to assess another's work. The man felt that it was difficult to justify such training and other expenses accompanying the appraisal of OLs when their work was not taken seriously.

8. On the marriage metaphor, see *Nihon Kcizai Shinbun*, 16 March 1992, "*Tachiagare! Kaishazuma-tachi musume-tachi*" *(Stand Up! Office wives and office daughters), and Nihon Keizai Shinbun,* 1 June 1992, "*Iwaneba naoranu 'shanaizuma atsukai'*" *(Men will not stop treating women as "office wives" unless we speak up).*

9. The OLs at Tōzai had a nickname for men with no sense of using office machines: they, were called *pīchi-chan* (peach-chan). I do not know the origin of the term, but suspect that it has something to do with both words, *copy* and *peach*, sharing the same sound element, *pi*.

10. On the tea pouring, see Nihon Hishokurabu Nōryoko Kōjō Kenyūkai, ed. (1992).

References

Kawashima, Yoko. 1983. "Wage Differentials between Men and Women in Japan." Ph.D. diss., Stanford University.

_____. *Joshi rōdō to rōdō shijō kōzō no bunseki* (An analysis of female labor and labor market structure). Tokyo: Nihon Kezai Hyoronsha.

Nihon Keizai Shinbun. 1992a. "Tachiagare! Kaishazuma-tachi musume-tachi" (Stand up! Office wives and office daughters). March 16.

_____. 1992b. "Kanchigai shiteimasenka OL sōjūjutsu" (Aren't you misunderstanding the way to manage OLs?). June 15.

Osawa, Machiko. 1984. "Women's Skill Formation, Labor Force Participation, and Fertility in Japan." Ph.D. diss., Southern Illinois University.

_____. 1993. *Keizai henka to joski rōdō: Nichibei no hikaku kenkyū* (Economic change and female labor: A comparative study of Japan and the United States). Tokyo: Nihon Keizai Hyoronsha.

Parkinson, Lorraine. 1989. "Japan's Equal Employment Opportunity Law." Columbia Law Review 89, no. 3: 604–661.

Shinotsuka, Eiko. 1982. *Nihon no joshi rōdō* (Female labor in Japan). Tokyo: Toyo Keizai Shinposha.

Tomita, Yasunobu. 1988. "Joshi no koyō kanri to danjokan chingin kakusa" (Management of women employees and the male–female wage gap). In *Shokuba no kyaria uman* (Career women in the workplace). Edited by Kazuo Koiki and Yasunobu Tomita. Tokyo: Toyo Keizai Shinposha.

Yashiro, Naohiro. 1980. "Danjokan chingin sabetsu no yoin ni tsuite" (Factors responsible for wage discrimination between men and women). *Nihon Keizai Kenkyū* 9: 17–31.

3

DOMÉSTICA
Maid in L.A.

Pierette Hondagneu-Sotelo

For Maribel Content, newly arrived from Guatemala City in 1989 at age twenty-two and without supportive family and friends with whom to stay, taking a live-in job made a lot of sense. She knew that she wouldn't have to spend money on room and board, and that she could soon begin saving to pay off her debts. Getting a live-in job through an agency was easy. The *señora*, in her rudimentary Spanish, only asked where she was from, and if she had a husband and children. Chuckling, Maribel recalled her initial misunderstanding when the *señora*, using her index finger, had drawn an imaginary 929 and 939 in the palm of her hand. "I thought to myself, well, she must have two or three bedrooms, so I said, fine. 'No,' she said. 'Really, really big.' She started counting, 'One, two, three, four. . . two-three rooms.' It was twenty-three rooms! I thought, *huy!* On a piece of paper, she wrote '$80 a week,' and she said, 'You, child, and entire house.' So I thought, well, I have to do what I have to do, and I happily said, 'Yes.'"

"I arrived on Monday at dawn," she recalled, "and I went to the job on Wednesday evening." When the *señora* and the child spoke to her, Maribel remembered "just laughing and feeling useless. I couldn't understand anything." On that first evening, the senora put on classical music, which Maribel quickly identified. "I said, 'Beethoven.' She said, 'Yeah,' and began asking me in English, 'You like it?' I said 'Yes,' or perhaps I said, '*Sí*,' and she began playing other cassettes, CDs. They had Richard Clayderman and I recognized it, and when I said that, she stopped in her tracks, her jaw fell open, and she just stared at me. She must have been thinking, 'No schooling, no preparation, no English, how does she know this music?'" But the *señora*, perhaps because of the language difficulty, or perhaps because she felt upstaged by her live-in's knowledge of classical music, never did ask. Maribel desperately wanted the *señora* to respect her, to recognize that she was smart, educated, and cultivated in the arts. In spite of her best status-signaling efforts, "They treated me," she said, "the same as any other girl from the countryside." She never got the verbal recognition that she desired from the *señora*.

Maribel summed up her experiences with her first live-in job this way: "The pay was bad. The treatment was, how shall I say? It was cordial, a little, uh, not racist, but with very little consideration, very little respect." She liked caring for the little seven-year-old boy, but keeping after the cleaning of the twenty-three-room house, filled with marble floors and glass tables, proved physically impossible. She eventually quit not because of the polishing and scrubbing, but because being ignored devastated her socially.

Compared to many other Latina immigrants' first live-in jobs, Maribel Centeno's was relatively good. She was not on call during all her waking hours and throughout the night, the parents were engaged with the child, and she was not required to sleep in a child's bedroom or on a cot tucked away in the laundry room. But having a private room filled with amenities did not mean she had privacy or the ability to do simple things one might take for granted. "I had my own room, with my own television, VCR, my private bath, and closet, and a kind of sitting room, but everything in miniature, Thumbelina style," she said. "I had privacy in that respect. But I couldn't do many things. If I wanted to walk around in a T-shirt, or feel like I was home, I couldn't do that. If I was hungry in the evening, I wouldn't come out to grab a banana because I'd have to walk through the family room, and then everybody's watching and having to smell the banana. I could never feel at home, never. Never, never, never! There's always something invisible that tells you this is not your house, you just work here."

It is the rare California home that offers separate maid's quarters, that doesn't stop families from hiring live-ins; nor does it stop newly arrived Latina migrant workers from taking jobs they urgently need. When live-ins cannot even retreat to their own rooms, work seeps into their sleep and their dreams. There is no time off from the job, and they say they feel confined, trapped, imprisoned.

"I lose a lot of sleep," said Margarita Gutierrez, a twenty-four-year-old Mexicana who worked as a live-in nanny/housekeeper. At her job in a modest-sized condominium in Pasadena, she slept in a corner of a three-year-old child's bedroom. Consequently, she found herself on call day and night with the child, who sometimes went several days without seeing her mother because of the latter's schedule at an insurance company. Margarita was obliged to be on her job twenty-four hours a day; and like other live-in nanny/housekeepers I interviewed, she claimed that she could scarcely find time to shower or brush her teeth. "I go to bed fine," she reported, "and then I wake up at two or three in the morning with the girls asking for water, or food." After the child went back to sleep, Margarita would lie awake, thinking about how to leave her job but finding it hard to even walk out into the kitchen. Live-in employees like Margarita literally have no space and no time they can claim as their own.

Working in a larger home or staying in plush, private quarters is no guarantee of privacy or refuge from the job. Forty-four-year-old Elvia Lucero worked as a live-in at a sprawling, canyon-side residence, where she was in charge of looking after twins, two five-year-old girls. On numerous occasions when I visited her there, I saw that she occupied her own bedroom, a beautifully decorated one outfitted with delicate antiques, plush white carpet, and a stenciled border of pink roses painstakingly painted on the wall by the employer. It looked serene and inviting, but it was only three steps away from the twins' room. Every night one of the twins crawled into bed with Elvia. Elvia disliked this, but said she couldn't break the girl of the habit. And the parents' room lay tucked away at the opposite end of the large (more than 3,000 square feet), L-shaped house.

Regardless of the size of the home and the splendor of the accommodations, the boundaries that we might normally take for granted disappear in live-in jobs. They have, as Evelyn Nakano Glenn has noted, "no clear line between work and non-work time," and the line between job space and private space is similarly blurred. Live-in nanny/housekeepers are at once socially isolated and surrounded by other people's territory; during the hours they remain on the employer's premises, their space, like their time, belongs to another. The sensation of being among others while remaining invisible, unknown and apart, of never being able to leave the margins, makes many live-in employees sad, lonely, and depressed. Melancholy sets in and doesn't necessarily lift on the weekends.

Rules and regulations may extend around the clock. Some employers restrict the ability of their live-in employee to receive telephone calls, entertain friends, attend evening ESL classes, or see boyfriends during the workweek. Other employers do not impose these sorts of restriction, but because their homes are located on remote hillsides, in suburban enclaves, or in gated communities, their live-in nanny/housekeepers are effectively kept away from anything resembling social life or public culture. A Spanish-language radio station, or maybe a *telenovela*, may serve as their only link to the outside world.

Food—the way some employers hoard it, waste it, deny it, or just simply do not even have any of it in their kitchens—is a frequent topic of discussion among Latina live-in nanny/housekeepers. These women are talking not about counting calories but about the social meaning of food on the job. Almost no one works with a written contract, but anyone taking a live-in job that includes "room and board" would assume that adequate meals will be included. But what constitutes an adequate meal? Everyone has a different idea, and using the subject like a secret handshake, Latina domestic workers often greet one another by talking about the problems of managing food and meals on the job. Inevitably, food enters their conversations.

No one feels the indignities of food more deeply than do live-in employees, who may not leave the job for up to six days at a time. For them, the workplace necessarily becomes the place of daily sustenance. In some of the homes where they work, the employers are out all day. When these adults return home, they may only snack, keeping on hand little besides hot dogs, packets of macaroni and cheese, cereal, and peanut butter for the children. Such foods are considered neither nutritious nor appetizing by Latina immigrants, many of whom are accustomed to sitting down to meals prepared with fresh vegetables, rice, beans, and meat. In some employers' homes, the cupboards are literally bare. Gladys Villedas recalled that at one of her live-in jobs, the *señora* had graciously said, "'Go ahead, help yourself to anything in the kitchen.' But at times," she recalled, "there was nothing, nothing in the refrigerator! There was nothing to eat!" Even in lavish kitchens outfitted with Subzero refrigerators and imported cabinetry, food may be scarce. A celebrity photographer of luxury homes that appear in posh magazines described to a reporter what he sees when he opens the doors of some of Beverly Hills' refrigerators: "Rows of cans of Diet Coke, and maybe a few remains of pizza."

Further down the class ladder, some employers go to great lengths to economize of food bills. Margarita Gutiérrez claimed that at her live-in job, the husband did the weekly grocery shopping, but he bought things in small quantities—say, two potatoes that would be served in half portions, or a quarter of a watermelon to last a household of five all week. He rationed out the bottled water and warned her that milk would make her fat. Lately, she said, he was taking both her and the children to an upscale grocery market where they gave free samples of gourmet cheeses, breads, and dips, urging them all to fill up on the freebies. "I never thought," exclaimed Margarita, formerly a secretary in Mexico City, "that I would come to this country to experience hunger!"

Many women who work as live-ins are keenly aware of how food and meals underline the boundaries between them and the families for whom they work. "I never ate with them," recalled Maribel Centeno of her first live-in job. "First of all, she never said, 'Come and join us,' and secondly, I just avoided being around when they were about to eat." Why did she avoid mealtime? "I didn't feel I was part of that family. I knew they liked me, but only because of the good work I did, and because of the affection I showered on the boy; but apart from that, I was just like the gardener, like the pool man, just one more of their staff." Sitting down to share a meal symbolizes membership in a family, and Latina employees, for the most part, know they are just like one of the family.

Food scarcity is not endemic to all of the households where these women work. In some homes, ample quantities of fresh fruits, cheeses, and chicken stock the kitchens. Some employer families readily share all of their food, but in other households, certain higher-quality, expensive food items may remain off-limits to the live-in employees, who are instructed to eat hot dogs with the children. One Latina live-in nanny/housekeeper told me that in her employers' substantial pantry, little "DO NOT TOUCH" signs signaled which food items were not available to her; and another said that her employer was always defrosting freezer-burned leftovers for her to eat, some of it dating back nearly a decade.

Other women felt subtle pressure to remain unobtrusive, humble, and self-effacing, so they held back from eating even when they were hungry. They talked a lot about how these unspoken rules apply to fruit. "Look, if they [the employers] buy fruit, they buy three bananas, two apples, two pears. So if I eat one, who took it? It's me," one woman said, "they'll know it's me." Another nanny/housekeeper recalled: "They would bring home fruit, but without them having to say it, you just knew these were not intended for you. You understand this right away, you get it." Or as another put it, "*Las Americanas* have their apples counted out, one for each day of the week." Even fruits growing in the garden are sometimes contested. In Southern California's agriculture-friendly climate, many a residential home boasts fruit trees that hang heavy with oranges, plums, and peaches, and when the Latina women who work in these homes pick the fruit, they sometimes get in trouble. Eventually, many of the women solve the food problem by buying and bringing in their own food; early on Monday mornings, you see them walking with their plastic grocery bags, carting, say, a sack of apples, some chicken, and maybe some prepared food in plastic containers.

The issue of food captures the essence of how Latina live-in domestic workers feel about their jobs. It symbolizes the extent to which the families they work for draw the boundaries of exclusion or inclusion, and it narks the degree to which those families recognize the live-in nanny/housekeepers as human beings who have basic human needs. When they first take their jobs, most live-in nanny/housekeepers do not anticipate spending any of their meager wages on food to eat while on the job, but in the end, most do—and sometimes the food they buy is eaten by members of the family for whom they work.

Although there is a wide range of pay, many Latina domestic workers in live-in jobs earn less than minimum wage for marathon hours: 93 percent of the live-in workers I surveyed in the mid–1990s were earning less than $5 an hour (79 percent of them below minimum wage, which was then $4.25), and they reported working an average of sixty-four hours a week. Some of the most astoundingly low rates were paid for live-in jobs in the households of other working class Latino immigrants, which provide some women their first job when they arrive in Los Angeles. Carmen Vasquez, for example, had spent several years working as a live-in for two Mexican families, earning only $50 a week. By comparison, her current salary of $170 a week, which she was earning as a live-in nanny/housekeeper in the hillside home of an attorney and a teacher, seemed a princely sum.

Many people assume that the rich pay more than do families of modest means, but working as a live-in in an exclusive, wealthy neighborhood, or in a twenty-three-room house, provides no guarantee of a high salary. I was standing with a group of live-in nanny/housekeepers on a corner across the street from the Beverly Hills Hotel. As they were waiting to be picked up by their employers, a large Mercedes sedan with two women (a daughter and mother or mother-in-law?) approached, rolled down the windows, and asked if anyone was interested in $150-a-week live-in job. A few women jotted down the phone number, and no one was shocked by the offer. Gore Vidal once commented that no one is allowed to fail within a two-mile radius of the Beverly Hills Hotel, but it turns out that plenty of women in that vicinity are failing in the salary department. In some of the most affluent Westside areas of Los Angeles—in Malibu, Pacific Palisades, and Bel Air—there are live-in nanny/housekeepers earning $150 a week. And in 1999, the *Los Angeles Times* Sunday classified ads still listed live-in nanny/housekeeper jobs with pay as low as $100 and $125. Salaries for live-in jobs, however, do go considerably higher. The best-paid live-in employee whom I interviewed was Patricia Paredes, a Mexican who spoke impeccable English and who had legal status, substantial experience, and references. She told me that she currently earned $450 a week at her live-in job. She had been promised a raise to $550, after a room remodel was finished, when she would assume weekend housecleaning in that same home. With such a relatively high weekly salary she felt compelled to stay in a live-in job during the week, away from her husband and three young daughters who remained on the east side of Los Angeles. The salary level required sacrifice.

But once they experience it, most women are repelled by live-in jobs. The lack of privacy mandated separation from family and friends, the round-the-clock hours, the food issues, the low pay, and especially the constant loneliness prompt most Latina immigrants to seek other job arrangements. Some young, single women who learn to speak English fluently try to move up the ranks into higher-paying live-in jobs. As soon as they can, however, the majority attempt to leave live-in work altogether. Most live-in nanny/housekeepers have been in the United States for five years or less; among the live-in nanny/housekeepers I interviewed, only two (Carmen Vasquez and the relatively high-earning Patricia Paredes) had been in the United States for longer than that. Like African American women earlier in the century, who tired of what the historian Elizabeth Clark-Lewis has called "the soul-destroying hollowness of live-in domestic work," most Latina immigrants try to find other options.

Until the early 1900s, live-in jobs were the most common form of paid domestic work in the United States, but through the first half of the twentieth century they were gradually supplanted by domestic "day work." Live-in work never completely disappeared, however, and in the last decades of the twentieth century, it revived with vigor, given new life by needs of American families with working parents and young children—and, as we have seen, by the needs of newly arrived Latina immigrants, many of them unmarried and unattached to families. When these women try to move up from live-in domestic work, they see few job alternatives. Often, the best they can do is switch to another form of paid domestic work, either as a live-out nanny/housekeeper or as a weekly housecleaner. When they do such day work, they are better able to circumscribe their work hours, and they earn more money in less time.

Feeding the children is a big part of the job. Unlike their live-in peers, when live-out nanny/housekeepers talk about food, they're usually concerned with what the children eat or don't eat. Some of them derive tremendous pleasure and satisfaction from bringing the children special treats prepared at their own homes—maybe homemade flan or *pan con crema*, or simply a mango. Some nanny/housekeepers are also in charge, to their dismay, of feeding and cleaning the children's menagerie of pets. Many feel disgusted when they have to bathe and give eyedrops to old, sick dogs, or clean the cages of iguanas, snakes, lizards, and various rodents. But these tasks are trivial in comparison to the difficulties they encounter with hard-to-manage children. Mostly, though, they complain about permissive, neglectful parents.

Not all nanny/housekeepers bond tightly with their employers' children, but most are critical of what they perceive as their employers' careless parenting—or, more accurately, mothering, for their female employers typically receive the blame. They see mothers who may spend, they say, only a few minutes a day with their babies and toddlers, or who return home from work after the children are asleep. Soraya Sanchez said she could understand mothers who work "out of necessity," but all other mothers, she believed, hired nanny/housekeepers because they just didn't like being with their own kids. "*La Americana* is very selfish, she only thinks about herself," she said. "They prefer not to be with their children, as they find it's much easier to pay someone to do that." Her critique was shared by many nanny/housekeepers; and those with children of their own, even if they don't live with them, saw their own mothering as far superior. "I love my kids, they don't. It's just like, excuse the word, 'shitting kids,'" said Patricia Paredes. "What they prefer is to go to the salon, get their nails done, you know, go shopping, things like that. Even if they're home all day, they don't want to spend time with the kids because they're paying somebody to do that for them." For many

Latina nanny/housekeepers, seething class resentments find expression in the rhetoric of comparative mothering.

When Latina immigrant women enter the homes of middle-class and upper-middle-class Americans, they encounter ways of raising children very different from those with which they are familiar. As Julia Wrigley's research has shown, the child-rearing values of many Latina and Caribbean nannies differ from those of their employers, but most are eager to do what middle-class parents want—to adopt "time out" discipline measure instead of swatting, or to impose limits on television viewing and Nintendo. Some of them not only adapt but come to genuinely admire and appreciate such methods of child rearing. Yet they, too, criticize the parenting styles they witness close up in the homes where they work.

Some nanny/housekeepers encounter belligerent young children, who yell at them, call them names, and throw violent temper tantrums; and when they do, they blame the parents. They are aghast when parents, after witnessing a child scratch or bite or spit at them, simply shrug their shoulders and ignore such behavior. Parents' reactions to these incidents were a litmus test of sorts. Gladys Villedas, for example, told me that at her job, a five-year-old "grabbed my hair and pulled it really hard. Ay! It hurt so much I started crying! It really hurt my feelings because never in my own country, when I was raising my children, had this happened to me. Why should this happen to me here?" When she complained to her employer, she said the employer had simply consulted a child-rearing manual and explained that it was "a stage." Not all nanny/housekeepers encounter physically abusive children, but when they do, they prefer parents who allow them the authority to impose discipline, or who back them up by firmly instructing their children that it is not okay to kick or slap the nanny. Nanny/housekeepers spoke glowingly about these sorts of employers.

When nanny/housekeepers see parent-child interactions in the homes where they work, they are often put off and puzzled by what they observe. In these moments, the huge cultural gulf between Latina nanny/housekeepers and their employers seems even wider than they had initially imagined. In the home where Maribel Centeno was working as a live-out nanny/housekeeper, she spent the first few hours of her shift doing laundry and housecleaning, but when a thirteen-year-old boy, of whom she was actually very fond, arrived home from school, her real work began. It was his pranks, which were neither malicious nor directed at her, and parental tolerances of these, that drove her crazy. These adolescent pranks usually involved items like water balloons, firecrackers, and baking soda made to look like cocaine. Recently the boy had tacked up on his parents' bedroom door a condom filled with a small amount of milk and a little sign that read, "Mom and Dad, this could have been my life." Maribel thought this was inappropriate behavior; but more bewildering and disturbing than the boy's prank was his mother's reaction—laughter. Another nanny/housekeeper had reacted with similar astonishment when, after a toddler tore apart a loaf of French bread and threw the pieces, balled like cotton, onto the floor, the father came forward not to reprimand but to record the incident with a camcorder. The regularity with which their employers waste food astounds them, and drug use also raises their eyebrows. Some nanny/housekeepers are instructed to give Ritalin and Prozac to children as young as five or six, and others tell of parents and teens locked in their separate bedrooms, each smoking marijuana.

Nanny/housekeepers blame permissive and neglectful parents, who they feel don't spend enough time with their own children, for the children's unruly behavior and for teen drug use. "The parents, they say 'yes' to everything the child asks," complained one woman. "Naturally," she added, "the children are going to act spoiled." Another nanny/housekeeper analyzed the situation this way: "They [the parents] feel guilty because they don't spend that much time with the kids, and they want to replace that missed time, that love, with toys."

Other nanny/housekeepers prided themselves on taming and teaching the children to act properly. "I really had to battle with these children just to get them to pay attention to me! When I started with them, they had no limits, they didn't pick up their toys, and they couldn't control their tempers. The eldest—oof! He used to kick and hit me, and in public! I was mortified," recalled Ronalda Saavedra. Another woman remarked of children she had looked after, "These kids listened to me. After all, they spent most of the time with me, and not with them [the parents]. They would arrive at night, maybe spend a few moments with the kids, or maybe the kids were already asleep." Elvia Areola highlighted the injustice of rearing children whom one will never see again. Discussing her previous job, she said, "I was the one who taught that boy to talk, to walk, to read, to sit! Everything! She [the child's mother] almost never picked him up! She only picked him up when he was happy." Another nanny/housekeeper concluded, "These parents don't really know their own children. Just playing with them, or taking them to the park, well, that's not raising children. I'm the one who is with them everyday."

Nanny/housekeepers must also maneuver around jealous parents, who may come to feel that their children's affections have been displaced. "The kids fall in love with you and they [the parents] wonder, why? Some parents are jealous of what the kids feel toward you," said Ronalda Saavedra. "I'm not going to be lying, 'I'm your mommy,' but in a way, children go to the person who takes care of them, you know? That's just the way it is." For many nanny/housekeepers, it is these ties of affection that make it possible for them to do their job by making it rewarding. Some of them say they can't properly care for the children without feeling a special fondness for them; others say it just happens naturally. "I fall in love with all of these children. How can I not? That's just the way I am," one nanny/housekeep told me. "I'm with them all day, and when I go home, my husband complains that that's all I talk about, what they did, the funny things they said." The nanny/housekeepers, as much as they felt burdened by disobedient children, sometimes felt that these children were also a gift of sorts, one that parents—again, the mothers—did not fully appreciate. "The babies are so beautiful!" gushed Soraya Sanchez. "How is it that a mother can lose those best years, when their kids are babies. I mean, I remember going down for a nap with these little babies, how we'd cuddle. How is it that a person who has the option of enjoying that would prefer to give that experience to a stranger?" Precisely because such feelings, many Latina immigrants who have children try to find a job that is compatible with their own family lives. Housecleaning is one of those jobs.

Housecleaners

Like many working mothers, every weekday morning, Marisela Ramírez awoke to dress and feed her preschooler, Tomás, and drive him to school (actually, a Head Start program) before she herself ventured out to work, navigating the dizzying array of Los Angeles freeways. Each day she set off in a different direction headed for a different workplace. On Mondays she maneuvered her way to Pasadena, where she cleaned the stately home of an elderly couple; on Tuesdays she alternated between cleaning a home in the Hollywood Hills and a more modest-sized duplex in Glendale; and Wednesdays took her to a split-level condominium in Burbank. You had to keep alert, she said, to remember where to go on which days and how to get there!

By nine o'clock she was usually on the job, and because she zoomed through her work she was able to finish, unless the house was extremely dirty, by one or two in the afternoon. After work, there were still plenty of daylight hours left for Marisela to take Tomás to the park, or at least to take him outside and let him ride down the sidewalk on his kid-sized motorized vehicle before she started dinner. Working as a house-cleaner allowed Marisela to be the kind of wife and mother she wanted to be. Her job was something she did, she said, "because I have to"; but unlike her peers who work in live-in jobs, she enjoyed a fairly regular family life of her own, one that included cooking and eating family meals, playing with her son, bathing him, putting him to bed, and then watching telenovelas in the evenings with her husband and her sister. On the weekends, family socializing took center stage, with carne asadas in the park; informal gatherings with her large Mexican family, which extended throughout Los Angeles; and music from her husband, who worked as a gardener but played guitar in a week-end ranchera band.

Some might see Marisela Ramirez as just another low-wage worker doing dirty work, but by her own account—and gauging by her progress from her starting point—she had made remarkable occupational strides. Marisela had begun working as a live-in nanny/housekeeper in Los Angeles when she was only fifteen years old. Ten years later, the move from live-in work to housecleaning had brought her higher hourly wages, a shorter workweek, control over the pace of work, and flexibility in arranging when she worked. Cleaning different houses was also, she said, less boring than working as a nanny/housekeeper, which entailed passing every single day "*in just one house, all week long with the same routine, over and over.*"

For a while she had tried factory work, packaging costume jewelry in a factory warehouse located in the San Fernando Valley, but Marisela saw housecleaning as preferable on just about every count. "In the factory, one has to work very, very fast!" she exclaimed. "And you can't talk to anybody, you can't stop, and you can't rest until it's break time. When you're working in a house, you can take a break at the moment you wish, finish the house when you want, and leave at the hour you decide. And it's better pay. It's harder work, yes, " she conceded, "but it's better pay."

"How much were you earning at the factory?" I asked.

"Five dollars an hour; and working in houses now, I make about $11, or even more. Look, in a typical house, I enter at about 9:00 A.M., and I leave at 1:00 P.M., and they pay me $60. It's much better [than factory work]." Her income varied, but she could usually count on weekly earnings of about $300. By pooling these together with her husband's and sister's earnings, she was able to rent a one-bedroom bungalow roofed in red tile, with a lawn and a backyard for Tomás's sandbox and plastic swimming pool. In Mexico, Marisela had only studied as far as fifth grade, but she wanted the best for Tomás. Everyone doted on him, and by age four he was already reading simple words.

Of the housecleaners I surveyed, the majority earned, like Marisela, between $50 and $60 per housecleaning, which usually took about six hours. This suggests an average hourly wage of about $9.50, but I suspect the actual figure is higher. Women like Marisela, who drive their own cars and speak some English, are likely to earn more than the women I surveyed, many of whom ride the buses to work. Marisela was typical of the housecleaners whom I surveyed in having been in the United States for a number of years. Unlike nanny/housekeepers, most of the housecleaners who were mothers themselves had all their children with them in the United States. Housecleaning, as Mary Romero has noted, is a job that is quite compatible with having a family life of one's own.

Breaking into housecleaning is tough, often requiring informal tutelage from friends and relatives. Contrary to the image that all women "naturally" know how to do domestic work, many Latina domestic workers discover that their own housekeeping experiences do not automatically transfer to the homes where they work. As she looked back on her early days in the job, Marisela said, "I didn't know how to clean or anything. My sister taught me." Erlinda Castro, a middle-aged women who had already run her own household and raised five children in Guatemala, had also initially worked in live-in jobs when she first came to Los Angeles. Yet despite this substantial domestic experience, she recalled how mystified she was when she began housecleaning. "Learning how to use the chemicals and the liquids" in the different households was confusing, and, as friends and employers instructed her on what to do, she began writing down in a little notebook the names of the products and what they cleaned. Some women learn the job by informally apprenticing with one another, accompanying a friend or perhaps an aunt on her housecleaning jobs.

Establishing a thriving route of *casas* requires more than learning what cleaning products to use or how to clean quickly and efficiently. It also involves acquiring multiple jobs, which housecleaners typically gain by asking their employers if they have friends, neighbors, or acquaintances who need someone to clean their houses; and because some attrition is inevitable, they must constantly be on the lookout for more *casas*. Not everyone who wants to can fill up her entire week.

To make ends meet when they don't have enough houses to clean, Latina housecleaners in Los Angeles find other ways to earn income. They might prepare food—say, tamales and *crema*—which they sell door-to-door or on the street; or they might sell small amounts of clothing that they buy wholesale in the garment district, or products from Avon, Mary Kay cosmetics, and Princess House kitchenware. They take odd jobs, such as handing out flyers advertising dental clinics or working at a swap meet; or perhaps they find something more stable, such as evening janitorial in office buildings. Some housecleaners work swing shift in garment factories, while others work three days a week as a nanny/housekeeper and try to fill the remaining days with housecleaning jobs. Some women supplement their husband's income by cleaning only one or two houses a week, but more often they patch together a number of jobs in addition to housecleaning.

Housecleaning represents, as Romero has written, the "modernization" of paid domestic work. Women who clean different houses on different days sell their labor services, she argues, in much the same way that a vendor sells a product to various customers. The housecleaners themselves see their job as far preferable to that of a live-in or live-out nanny/housekeeper. They typically work alone, during times when their employers are out of the home; and because they are paid "by the job" instead of by the hour, they don't have to remain on the job until 6:00 or 7:00 P.M., an advantage much appreciated by women who have families of their own. Moreover, because they work for different employers on different days, they are not solely dependent for their livelihood on one boss whom they see every single day. Consequently, their relationships with their employers are less likely to become highly charged and conflictual; and if problems do arise, they can leave one job without jeopardizing their entire weekly earnings. Since child care is not one of their tasks, their responsibilities are more straightforward and there are fewer points of contention with employers. Housecleaning is altogether less risky.

Housecleaners also see working independently and informally as more desirable than working for a commercial cleaning company. "The companies pay $5 an hour," said Erlinda Castro, whose neighbor worked for one, "and the women have to work their eight hours, doing up to ten, twenty houses a day! One does the vacuuming, the other does the bathroom and the kitchen, and like that. It's tremendously hard work, and at $5 an hour? Thank God, I don't have to do that." Two of the women I interviewed, one now live-out nanny/housekeeper and the other a private housecleaner, had previously worked for cleaning services, and both of them complained bitterly about their speeded-up work pace, low pay, and tyrannical bosses.

Private housecleaners take enormous pride in their work. When they finish their job, they can see the shiny results, and they are proud of their job autonomy, their houses, their pay, and, most important, what they are able to do with their pay for themselves and for their families. Yet housecleaning brings its own special problems. Intensive cleaning eventually brings physical pain, and sometimes injury. "Even my bones are tired," said fifty-three-year-old Lupe Vélez; and even a relatively young woman like Celestina Vigil at age thirty-three was already reporting back problems that she attributed to her work. While most of them have only fleeting contact with their employers, and many said they work for "good people," just about everyone has suffered, they said, "inconsiderate persons" who exhort them to work faster, humiliate them, fail to give raises, add extra cleaning tasks without paying extra, or unjustly accuse them of stealing or of ruining a rug or upholstery. And the plain old hard work and stigma of cleaning always remain, as suggested by the answer I got when I asked a housecleaner what she liked least about her job. "The least?" she said, with a wry smile. "Well, that you have to clean."

4

PROSTITUTION AND TOURISM IN SOUTHEAST ASIA

Wendy Lee

In the 1960s Franz Fanon warned the poor nations not to become the "brothels of Europe." His warning has taken on new relevance for Southeast Asian countries where an important incentive for tourism is the availability of women, either openly as prostitutes in brothels or performers in sex shows, or less obviously, as bar or hospitality girls, massage and bath attendants, hostesses in hotels, and waitresses in nightclubs and cocktail lounges. It is in Thailand, South Korea, and the Philippines where the most blatant and systemic organization of sex tourism is to be found.

Kate Millet (writing of Western societies) says that "the causes of female prostitution lie in the economic position of women, together with the psychological damage inflicted upon them through the system of sex-role conditioning in patriarchal society" (1975, 50). Prostitution has both a material and ideological basis. The cultural subordination of women takes different forms in different societies, creating a climate where the sexual exploitation of women is not only tolerated, but very often promoted. Some investigators such as Cohen (1962, 406) claim that in the case of Thailand there are specific features that encourage permissiveness and legitimize promiscuity, and that prostitution grows out of traditional cultural practices. However, others, such as Phongpaichit (1982, 47) question this view. While it would be wrong to overemphasize the ideological factors influencing women's recruitment into prostitution, an examination of the historical and cultural background is important in understanding the overall context in which Southeast Asian prostitution takes place. This examination must take account of both the individual level, that is from the standpoint of the women involved, and the collective or institutional basis of prostitution.

In the Philippines, the "Madonna whore" values of Catholicism and its emphasis on virginity have led jilted or raped women to become prostitutes, feeling that they have nothing to lose. In Korean villages, it may not be guilt that drives women into prostitution, yet the traditional Confucian values which demand that women show respect and obedience to their husband and all members of his household are just as oppressive to women. As in the case of Greek women in rural areas, a wife is surrounded by prohibitions that must be observed if she is not to bring discredit to the family:

The Confucian tradition in Korea has a puritanical aspect that emphasizes strict rules of physical modesty and reticence regarding sexual matters. Such values are linked to the subordinate role of women and the emphasis on deference and obligation rather than emotion in personal relations. (Brandt 1971, 133)

Because traditional family systems exert such rigid control over young women, giving them few choices, for example, in marriage, some wish to escape the restrictions of family and the constraints of village life for the bright city lights. Rejection of traditional norms is thought to play a role in female migration to cities. Women who have been drawn into the food and drink business find that the majority of customers are male, a fact that reinforces the pattern of men being served and women serving. Moreover, in the tea rooms and drinking places, the waitresses frequently provide not only nourishment but also sexual services and companionship. "As a consequence, once a woman begins to earn her living by serving food or drink, she finds it very hard to move into another business—both because she thinks of herself as a 'fallen woman' and because other prospective employers regard her in the same way" (Chang-Michell 1985, 23).

Thai women have always taken an active economic role in trading, marketing, and agriculture, while men have traditionally dominated the bureaucracy, the professions, and the religious domain (Thitsa 1980, 15). Despite the fact that there are three times as many women as men in business and trade, women are debarred from real influence by male monopoly of the network of power relations between the Buddhist order, the monarchy, and the military. The Buddhist belief in the transience of worldly things and the dangers of desire has particular implications for women. Karma (the sum of your actions in past lifetimes; a kind of balance sheet of religious merits and demerits) is believed to determine gender. Being born a woman indicates an insufficient store of merit. Women, more worldly beings than men, "may engage in types of activity. . . which might pose threats for men in their merit accumulation, for if women sin, it is only to be expected and the consequences are less" (Kirsch 1975, 185). Prostitution in this context signifies not a rejection of traditional customs nor an attempt to escape family ties, but an alternative means for women to fulfill their obligations as breadwinners. Girls are sometimes pressured by parents to help buy back agricultural land, pay medical expenses and school fees for siblings, or to provide payment for hired labor during the harvest season, and despite customary disapproval of promiscuity, public opinion has shifted somewhat. Since young women are supporting the needs of the family, prostitution is becoming socially validated and accepted as an economic necessity (Phongpaichit 1982, 71).

The new forms that prostitution takes are related to the process of capitalist development and "modernization." When, in 1905, the King of Thailand abolished slavery, the peasantry were freed of service obligations to the king and state, the agricultural economy became oriented to the market rather than to subsistence use, and land grew scarce. Under these conditions poorer landless peasants had few options. Some entered bondage in client relationship with others who were wealthier. "Debts were frequently discharged by selling oneself or, not uncommonly at least, some of one's children into slavery" (Piker 1975, 307). There are still some cases of parents selling a daughter into bondage to pay debts, but this is a measure of their desperation and certainly no longer a socially desired practice. Agents may advance cash to poor peasants and when they are unable to repay the debt, they are forced to sign a promissory note engaging to send a daughter to Bangkok to work as a domestic servant or waitress. On arrival, the girl may be forced to receive clients. It is estimated that about 10 percent of prostitutes in Thailand are deceived or forced into the profession (Hantrakul 1983, 29). But, more commonly, families act as agents of recruitment. Most prostitutes get their jobs through aunts, sisters, or cousins already in the trade. They are socialized into the job by their peers through informal networks.

Phongpaichit does, however, mention a growing band of middlemen and agents developing, and even where prostitution is technically illegal, it is often officially sanctioned; frequently the brokers are government officials (Ong 1985, 5). The 1928 Law on the Traffic in Women and Girls and the 1960 Prostitution Prohibition Act officially banned prostitution in Thailand, but in reality allowed massage parlors and tea houses to be used as fronts for the sale of sex. The 1950s saw some token campaigns against the import of "western permissiveness," but the legislation relating to prostitution was never implemented. This was because the elite still associated power with the amassing of wives and consorts so that their private lives bore little relationship to their public utterances. Former Prime Minister, Field Marshal Sarit Thanarat who had over a hundred wives, was not seen as being in the least inconsistent when he condemned prostitution for corrupting and threatening the family institution (Hantrakul 1983, 28).

In the Philippines, too, women's entry into prostitution is facilitated by an officially endorsed system. Despite an anti-streetwalking ordinance that makes soliciting punishable, prostitution inside clubs is legal, and in cities, employees in the "entertainment" business are issued with a mayor's permit or ID card which licenses them for work. South Korea enacted a Law Prohibiting Decadent Acts in 1962, which provides for penalties on both parties involved, yet prostitutes *(kisaeng)* are still issued special ID cards by the Seoul Tourist Association that permit them to engage in business, and Korean embassies list the telephone numbers of *kisaeng* houses in their official tourist pamphlets.

There are few long-term professionals among Southeast Asian prostitutes; most are amateurs drifting in and out of prostitution depending on need, and their numbers are replenished by a continual stream of girls and women (mostly aged between 15 and 24) migrating from the countryside. The development policies pursued by Thailand, the Philippines, and South Korea have opened a huge gap between the incomes and opportunities available in the city and those in rural areas. In the Philippines the women who come to the military bases or to Manila are fleeing from the economically depressed provinces of Leyte, Samar, and Cebu, areas where the government has done little for agricultural development or land reform (Neumann 1979, 15). In Thailand they come from the north and northeast, areas notorious for their poverty and high rates of out-migration. There, land is poor, there are frequent droughts, the per capita GDP is less than half that of the Central Plain area, and up to one-third of families have no land at all, and depend on tenancy or casual labor to survive (Phongpaichit 1982, 27–30).

Once in the cities, what choices do women have? Finding any kind of job is difficult and for unskilled, poorly educated women, prostitution offers some advantages over petty trading, domestic service, or work in large world market factories, all of which are associated with low wages and poor working conditions. Even if women do opt for factory work, they may eventually be forced to prostitute themselves:

> If a woman loses her job in a world market factory after she has re-shaped her life on the basis of a wage income, the only way she may have of surviving, is by selling her body. There are reports from South Korea, for instance, that many former electronics workers have no alternative but to become prostitutes. (Grossman, quoted in Elson and Pearson 1981, 101)

For some forms of prostitution, there are big financial incentives. Dr. Pawadee Tongudai's 1982 study found that Thai women migrants working in nightclubs and massage parlors earned a monthly average of about £125 (1982 figures), while most female migrants in other occupations earned less than £21 per month (Hantrakul 1983, 28) (although there is a wide disparity between girls working in high-class establishments and those who are bonded to poor owners). Neumann has estimated that prostitutes in the Philippines earn six to ten times as much as sales clerks or factory workers (1979, 15). These figures help to explain the attraction of prostitution for some women, although it should be remembered that while these jobs appear lucrative, prostitutes have a short working life with declining earning power and their health costs may be high. They also retain only a small proportion of their gross income. For example, reports from Thailand found that agents who procure girls aged between 12 and 14 from poor families and take them to Bangkok, receive US $150 from customers paying "to break them in," while the girls themselves receive only US$15 (Barry 1984, 37). Because commercial sex is technically illegal and women working in the street are liable to be arrested, they are forced to use hotels, bars, or other distribution outlets which allows others (bar owners, pimps, and police) to receive a share of their receipts—a kind of market rent (Thanh-Dam 1983, 541). Nevertheless, prostitutes do retain some of the proceeds of their labor, and send home to impoverished parents between one-third and one-half of their earnings (Phongpaichit 1982, 23).

Apart from poverty, there are other reasons that may lead women into prostitution. Some research shows that many prostitutes were abandoned by husbands, have a history of unhappy relationships, or were raped. It is not clear to what extent youthful prostitution is precipitated by sexual abuse, but there is evidence from the child prostitutes in Olongapo that rape (by policemen) was one of the reasons for their recruitment into the profession (Ocampo 1983, 34; Golley 1983, 32). Barry (1984, 29) notes that "trafficking children into prostitution and providing them for pornography is a highly profitable market for pimps and procurers." Although none of the women researchers of this subject appear to concur, Cohen claims that there are additional "positive" recruitment factors. Bangkok bar girls, he says, profess an aversion to Thai men because of past experiences and the women serving tourists are drawn by the excitement of meeting "strange and often attractive foreigners with a respected status and cultural background" (1982, 412).

Some accounts of prostitution do point to other advantages. The flexible working hours are important to single mothers and some prostitutes may enjoy greater autonomy in their personal and sexual lives than middle class women who are repressed by conservative double standards (Hantrakul 1983, 28). A similar case arguing the advantages of not being dependent on any one man is made by they western prostitutes interviewed by Kate Millet (1975, 31): "If one of them gives you trouble, you can just say 'fuck you.' But you can't do that if you're married and you can't do that if you're being kept." In another variation of this argument, some defenders of prostitution justify it as a form of work that, unlike unpaid domestic work, at least gives women some return for their labor and freedom from sexual commitment. According to this view, all women are subject to sexual harassment so prostitution is no more exploitative than other forms of work. Certainly there are reports from the free export zones in South Korea of Japanese supervisors sexually abusing women employees with impunity and many domestic servants suffer the same fate (Elson and Pearson 1981, 100).

If sexual exploitation is possible within marriage and in other jobs, can it be argued that prostitution really offers greater freedom? And are women exercising "free choice" in choosing to become prostitutes? I think not. Avoiding certain personal relations with men and working for oneself may give women the illusion of freedom from economic control, but more probably the prostitutes of Southeast Asia have merely exchanged the domination of fathers, brothers, and husbands for that of male managers, pimps, and police. "The apparent independence of women can be misleading. While women may not be directly subordinate to a particular member of their male kin, they are none the less, subject to an overall culture of male dominance" (Phillips, in Elson and Pearson 1981, 95).

There have been far-reaching changes in female labor patterns in Southeast Asia and with the erosion of kin relations of production, patriarchal control over women's mobility and labor has been somewhat reduced (Thanh-Dam 1983, 536). However, the penetration of capital and extension of capitalist relations of production have tended to reproduce and reinforce the subordination of women as sexual services have become commoditized in a similar fashion to other forms of labor power. New gender divisions are grafted on to, and make use of existing forms of female subordination so that, as Bryceson (1985, 151) points out, women's new "choices" really amount to non-choices: "The working-class woman prostitute represents the epitome of 'freedom' under capitalism. She is 'free' to sell her labor power and her sexuality, but in reality she is forced to do either or both to secure her subsistence."

The issue of sex tourism is related to problems that are fundamental to women's role in the workforce in an international context: women's lack of economic and educational opportunity, their neglect in rural development or land reform schemes, their subjugation within the family, their domestic burdens and family responsibilities, and their exploitation in new forms of factory work. The oppressive character of customary values and much family and employment legislation, together with women's location within the labor process, generally, mean that prostitution becomes a means of survival in a patriarchal world. However, there are forms of resistance, both individual and collective. Individually, many young women retain their self-respect even when working at jobs of which they are ashamed, by emphasizing their self-sufficiency and their ways of contributing to the sustenance of their families. Most use prostitution as a temporary means of livelihood.

References

Barry, K. 1979. *Female Sexual Slavery*. New Jersey: Prentice-Hall.

Barry, K., Bunch, C., and Castley, S. 1984. *International Feminism: Networking Against Female Sexual Slavery*. New York: IWTC.

Brownmiller, S. 1975. *Against Our Will: Men, Women, and Rape*. Toronto: Bantam.

Bryceson, D. F. 1985. "Women's Proleterianization and the Family Wage in Tanzania." In H. Afshar, ed., *Women, Work, and Ideology in the Third World*. London: Tavistock.

Chang-Michell, P. 1985. "Making a Living: South Korean Women in Commerce." *Southeast Asia Chronicle* 96: 17–24.

Cohen, E. 1982. "Thai Girls and Farang Men: The Edge of Ambiguity." *Annals of Tourism Research* 9, no. 3: 403–428.

Elson, D., and Pearson, R. 1981. "Nimble Fingers Make Cheap Workers: An Analysis of Women's Employment in Third World Export Manufacturing." *Feminist Review*, 87–105.

Golley, L. 1983. "For Sale: Girls." *Southeast Asia Chronicle* 89: 32.

Hantrakul, S. 1983. "The Spirit of a Fighter: Women and Prostitution in Thailand." *Manushi* 36: 27–35.

Kirssch, A. T. 1975. "Economy, Polity, and Religion in Thailand." In G. W. Skinner and A. T. Kirsch, eds., *Change and Persistence in Thai Society*. Ithaca: Cornell University Press.

Millet, K. 1975. *The Prostitution Papers: A Candid Dialogue*. St. Albans, U.K.: Paladin.

Neumann, A. L. 1979. "Hospitality Girls in the Philippines." *ISIS International Bulletin* 13: 13–16.

Ocampo, S. 1980. "Philippines Bases and American Guns." *Far Eastern Economic Review*, March, 16.

Ocampo-Kalfors, S. 1983. "The age of innocence lost." *Far Eastern Economic Review*, March, 34.

Ong, A. 1985. "Industrialization and Prostitution in Southeast Asia." *Southeast Asia Chronicle* 96: 2–6.

Phongpaichit, P. 1982. *From Peasant Girls to Bangkok Masseuses*. Women, Work and Development Series, no. 2. Geneva: ILO.

Piker, S. 1975. "The Post-Peasant Village in Central Plain Thai Society." In G. W. Skinner and A. T. Kirsch, eds., *Change in Persistence in Thai Society*. Ithaca: Cornell University Press.

Thanh-Dam, T. 1983. "The Dynamics of Sex Tourism: The Case of Southeast Asia." *Development and Change* 14, no. 4: 533–553.

Thista, K. 1980. *Providence and Prostitution: Image and Reality for Women in Buddhist Thailand*. London: Change International Reports.

Discussion Questions

1. In Ehrenreich's *Nickel and Dimed,* why do Wal-Mart workers "put up with the wages"? Why, according to Ehrenreich and the respondents, do they stay?
2. How do the workers in Ehrenreich's exploration link, or fail to link, their sense of spirit with the high rate of turnover in Wal-Mart?
3. In *Office Ladies,* how does the recruitment process funnel men and women, or "boys and girls," into different occupational and professional tracks?
4. Describe some of the unwritten laws and expectations for behavior that Ogasawara finds at the Tōzai Bank.
5. How is it that the employers in "Domestica" remain so far removed from their employees despite the real physical and emotional proximity in the work setting there?

6. What is the significance of food for domestics employed in *Doméstica*? Do you think it is Hondagneu-Sotelo's intention to tell more about the employer or the maids in this instance?
7. How do economic structures propel women into a life of prostitution?
8. How do the prostitutes in Wendy Lee's selection come to see their place in the work world?

Part II

MEN AT WORK

Work has traditionally been a man's world. Most men work, and their job is a central part of their life and identity. Three key sociological observations about men and work are explored in this section. First, there is a well-embedded notion in U.S. society that men are supposed to work and that men who do not work are failures, losing their identity or developing a poor self-image. Second, research has shown that male personality traits such as rationality and aggression are required and rewarded into the world of work. And finally, gay men have reported that they have not been generally well accepted into the typically straight, "macho" job culture.

Robert Cherry, in "Jobs for Black Men: Missing in Action," explores the economic and emotional trauma of the high rate of joblessness for black men. Cherry presents some compelling evidence that unemployment among black men is embedded in ongoing patterns of discrimination.

Male traits, such as aggressiveness, are correlated with successful careers, particularly for lawyers. Nonetheless, in the second reading, "Rambo Litigators: Emotional Labor in a Male-Dominated Occupation," Jennifer Pierce suggests male litigators need to temper their usual combative, heavy-handed style and integrate female traits, such as empathy, politeness, and friendliness, into their courtroom performances to be effective and to win the support of jurors and judges.

Finally, in the last selection of this section, "The Corporate Closet: Coming Out, Moving On," James D. Woods provides a sensitive portrait of the problems and complexity of "coming out" at work for gay men. Homophobia is reaffirmed as a workplace issue, and several social, economic, and job barriers (e.g., mocking, ostracism, limited promotional opportunities, and job loss) are presented.

In this section, several social problems and identity issues associated with men at work are examined. Although work may be a "man's world," these articles clearly show that it is not an easy world for many men.

5

JOBS FOR BLACK MEN
Missing in Action

Robert Cherry

When civil rights legislation was passed in the 1960s, many advocates hoped that there would be racial equality within a generation. This optimism, however, was dashed during the next decade when it became clear that, among other things, black and white men experience vastly different treatment in the labor market. Over a twenty-four-year period, from 1974 to 1997, the black unemployment rate was never lower than 10 percent, while the white rate was almost never higher than 7 percent. In general, the black rate was at least double the white rate. Interventionists consider these disparities prima facie evidence that strong discriminatory employment practices persist, justifying continued government policies. In contrast, pro-market proponents believe that the racial disparities overwhelmingly reflect skill differences.

The high rate of unemployment over a generation made it difficult for young black men to maintain any confidence that through their efforts they could enter the mainstream of American society. When Federal Reserve chair Paul Volker engineered a deep recession in the early 1980s, raising black unemployment rates to depression levels despair deepened. Not surprisingly, many turned to drug use and crime. Rather than showing compassion and understanding, state and federal governments reacted in a vengeful manner. Civil liberties we reduced, allowing law enforcement more leeway in fighting crime. Stiffer sentencing led to a quadrupling of the prison population so that by the early 1990s, more than one-half of all central-city black men, aged eighteen to thirty years old, were either in jail, on parole, or awaiting trial.

The widespread approval of this get-tough strategy led Republicans to use the image of the black criminal in the 1988 presidential campaign—the infamous Willie Horton ad. Willie Horton killed a woman while on a work release program from a Massachusetts prison. Republicans seized on this tragedy to damage the Democratic candidate, Massachusetts governor Michael Dukakis. Hoping to avoid a similar Republican effort to paint him weak on crime, William Clinton interrupted his presidential campaign in 1992 to fly back to Arkansas to oversee the execution of a mentally retarded black man.

The 1990s economic expansion renewed hopes that racial employment and earnings disparities would be lessened, and indeed, by 1997, official statistics seem to indicate that there has been a modest improvement for adult black men. This assessment was critically dependent, however, on the unemployment measure used. The official unemployment rate of black men had declined not so much because of gained employment but because fewer unemployed black men were eluded in the official count. Moreover, the racial earnings gap among men did not change significantly, even increasing in some parts of the country. Only when the national unemployment rate fell below 5 percent in 1977 did tight labor markets induce a modest decline in racial earnings and employment disparities.

Given the persistence of racial disparities, it becomes important to determine their source: labor market discrimination versus racial skill differences. Assessments are sensitive to the measurement of skills, work experience, educational attainment, and earnings used. In addition, labor market discrimination will vary across educational groups and regions.

Trends in Black–White Earnings Disparities

For most of the last thirty years, the official unemployment rate of black men has been deplorably high. After six years of economic expansion, the 1990 black unemployment rate stood at 10.6 percent. Similarly, after six years of economic expansion, the 1997 rate stood at 10.1 percent. Most troubling, however, was evidence that the unemployment rate was becoming a misleading measure of the labor market difficulties of black men.

During the 1990s expansion, a significant portion of the unemployment decline of black men was due to their withdrawal from the labor market. Between 1994 and 1997, the white male labor force participation rate was unchanged but the black rate declined. Researchers claim that at least one-half of that disparity reflects black workers who had given up using formal job searches because of a lack of employment prospects. Suppose that we assume the "true" participation rate of black men is the same as the white rate. An adjusted black unemployment rate, calculated under this assumption, declined slightly from 19.8 to 19.1 percent between 1994 and 1997, while the official rate dropped from 12 percent to 10.1 percent. This indicates that most of the decline in the official rate reflected the withdrawal of black men from the labor force. In the subsequent two-year period, 1997 to 1999, there was a robust drop in black unemployment rates by both the official and the adjusted measure. However, it is important to note that though the official rate fell to 8.2 percent in 1999, the adjusted rate was still 16.8 percent.[1]

Moreover, even this adjusted rate understates the underemployment of black men. Due to high incarceration rates and undercounting by the census, black men are more likely than white men to be missed in official counts of the noninstitutionalized civilian population. For example, in 1990 among those twenty to sixty-four years old, the female–male ratios for the noninstitutionalized civilian and military populations were 1.189 and 1.017 for blacks and whites, respectively. Only a small fraction of this racial disparity reflects differential death rates. Since the vast majority of black inmates and those missed by the census and employment surveys would be unemployed, their exclusion from the active labor force further understates black unemployment.

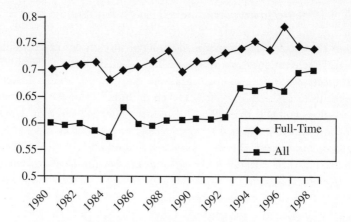

FIGURE 5.1   Black–white earnings ratio, 1980–1998. SOURCE: U.S. Bureau of Labor Statistics, Employment, and Earnings (Washington, D.C.: Government Printing Office, January 2000).

While employment rates are important, there is little progress if employment gains are not matched by earnings gains. In 1980, the black–white earnings ratio, measured by annual income for full-time, year-round workers, stood at 70.4 percent (see Figure 5.1). A decade later it had risen to 71.1 percent and by 1999 to 73.9 percent. One clear reason for the lack of substantial improvement has been the occupational disparities that persist. In January 1999, 29.7 percent of working white men but only 17.8 percent of black men were employed as managers and professionals. Instead, 30 percent of black men but only 19.6 percent of white men were employed as operators, fabricators, and laborers.

Notice that the racial earnings ratio for *full-time* male workers actually declined after 1997 just when tight labor markets were able to help close the racial employment gap. Results are different, however, when all male workers are included. Between 1980 and 1990 this racial earnings ratio was virtually unchanged, rising from 60.1 to 60.7 percent. However, during the next decade, it increased substantially. Indeed, between 1997 and 1999, it rose from 66.1 to 69.9 percent. The rise in the racial earnings ratio for all male workers during these two years suggests the following: An important component of the employment expansion was the ability of low-paid black men to move from part-time and/or part-year employment to full-time, year-round employment.

Data on the employment changes among workers with low educational attainment confirm this shift. In a study conducted in Boston during 1994, economists Barry Bluestone and Mary Stevenson found that black and white men with no more than a high school education were just as likely to have worked sometime in the previous twelve months. However, the expected number of hours worked differed dramatically. Black men averaged 1,327 hours over the previous year, while white men averaged 2,020 hours. National data also show similar disparities. Among non–college educated men, the 1994 probability of full-time employment was 59 percent higher for white men than for black men. As the economic boom tightened labor markets, however, the share of both black and white men with low educational attainment who worked full-time rose. Additionally, this increase was more substantial for black men so that, by the end of 1999, the probability of white men working full-time was only 37 percent higher.[2]

The recent closing of racial disparities in employment and earnings gives us hope for more change. However, our optimism must be tempered by the evidence that during the first six years of the expansion benefits were much more modest. Moreover, even when benefits from tight labor markets kicked in after 1997, racial gaps remain substantial. To understand why these disparities persisted, let us focus more closely on two factors. The severe stigma attached to young black men, especially those with low educational attainment, suggests that we should assess separately how the 1990s economic expansion affected their earnings and employment. And the fact that black men are more heavily concentrated in the non-college labor sector while white men are more heavily concentrated in the college-required labor sector also makes it worthwhile to assess to what degree black men progressed in these two distinct labor markets.

Black Youth Employment Problems

The employment situation of black men under twenty-five years old has been the subject of many studies because of their high rate of joblessness and the social havoc that this can create. The research, however, is complicated by two factors: the inadequacy of the official unemployment measure and distinguishing between those in and those out of school. The inadequacy of the official unemployment rate became apparent during the deep 1980 to 1982 recession. The already high black youth unemployment rate did not rise substantially and, more puzzling, statistics indicated that the vast majority of young black men had very short official spells of unemployment; more than one-half left the unemployment roles within one month.

The ending of spells of official unemployment, however, did not occur because black youths found jobs. Black youth either became discouraged and stopped searching or began to use job search activities that did not meet the government's criterion. Among twenty- to twenty-four-year-old black men, the average duration of joblessness was more than six months for high school graduates and more than ten months for dropouts. During the 1980–1982 recession, 21 percent of all black men between the ages of twenty and twenty-four who were out of school had no work experience in the previous year. This rate was triple the white rate (7.2 percent) and almost double what the black rate had been a decade earlier (12.8 percent). However, this joblessness did not show up in official unemployment statistics because most of these young men did not meet the government criterion for job search so they were not considered part of the active labor force.[3]

Many researchers dismissed any focus on the unavailability of jobs. Instead, they claimed that unemployment problems were caused by the refusal of black youths to accept low-paid employment. Economists Harry Holzer and Kip Viscusi claimed that "outside income generated by illegal activities" was an important reason black youths shun low-paid jobs. Sociologists Christopher Jencks and Elijah Anderson claimed that the civil rights movement had generated a new consciousness that considered these jobs degrading. The political scientist Andrew Hacker believes this explains why black men reject jobs as taxicab drivers that recent immigrants take. Given this viewpoint, it was not surprising that there was broad indifference if not support for increasing the severity of penalties for criminal behavior, which culminated in the explosion of black incarceration rates.[4]

The sociologist William Julius Wilson claimed that the environment faced by low-income black youth also deteriorated as a result of demographic changes. As middle-class blacks moved outside the inner city, black urban ghettos began increasingly to contain only the poor. He suggested that this reduced the presence of role models and middle-class culture available to inner-city black youths, making it less likely that they would develop and maintain the proper behavioral traits necessary for permanent employment. According to William Darity and Samuel Myers, "[The] control and institutionalization of unwanted, superfluous inner-city residents, creat[ed] further marginalization of many young black males, thereby increasing observed pathologies like crime and violence.[5]

Beginning with the 1980–1982 recession, employers were swamped with job applicants. Focusing on the worst jobs advertised, economists Kim Clark and Lawrence Summers found an average of fifteen to twenty responses within two days of an ad's placement. In order to avoid spending substantial personnel resources on interviewing so many applicants, firms increasingly relied upon recommendations from present employees and neighbors. Given segregated housing patterns and little black business ownership, black youths suffered when jobs were filled through informal networks.[6]

The employment difficulties of young black men were particularly severe in older urban areas in the Midwest and mid-Atlantic regions. The interstate highway systems enabled trucking to replace railroads as the principal means of transporting goods. In order to avoid traffic congestion, many manufacturing firms relocated to suburban industrial parks adjacent to interstate highways. Moreover, the growing use of assembly line techniques, which require one-floor operations, made central-city multifloor industrial buildings unsuitable. This further increased the incentive for firms to move to suburban industrial parks.

This relocation of manufacturing production was devastating to black workers. Due to housing market barriers, black workers had difficulty moving close to these new locations, making it more costly to commute and more difficult to obtain information on new job openings.

Between 1975 and 1989 the share of young black men employed in durable manufacturing fell from 40 to 12 percent. By contrast, among young white men, the drop was only ten percentage points. Economists John Bound and Richard Freeman suspected that "an important part of this differential change [was] the closing of older plants in the central cities of the Midwest.[7]

Informal hiring networks continue to dominate the hiring process in low-wage labor markets. They accounted for approximately 35 to 40 percent of new hires in four major metropolitan areas surveyed between 1992 and 1994. In contrast, newspaper advertising accounted for less than 30 percent of new hires. More than one-half of all new hires for low-skilled blue-collar jobs were filled through informal methods.[8] In his more recent work, Wilson found that employers who use these informal networks embrace the notion that black youths tend to have more dysfunctional behavior than white youths.

Wilson found that "roughly two-thirds of the city employers who placed ads in newspapers did so in ethnic, neighborhood, or suburban newspapers instead of or in addition to the metropolitan newspapers." Many of those firms readily admitted that they selectively advertised job openings to avoid having to deal with inner-city black applicants. Not surprisingly, this selective advertising had an impact on hiring practices. Wilson noted: "City employers who placed ads only in local or neighborhood papers, not likely to circulate among inner-city residents, averaged 16 percent black in their entry-level jobs, compared to an average of 32 percent black for those who placed ads in the metropolitan papers.[9] After documenting this racial profiling, Wilson concluded, "Employers make assumptions about the inner-city black workers in general and reach decisions based on those assumptions before they have had a chance to review systematically the qualifications of an individual applicant. The net effect is that many black inner-city applicants are never given the chance to prove their qualifications on an individual level because they are systematically screened out by the selective recruitment process.[10]

Harry Holzer found similar patterns of behavior. He notes that employers preferred Latino workers even though they tended to have less schooling and weaker language skills than black applicants. Holzer suggests that these preferences reflect employer perceptions that Latinos would work for lower wages and have better work ethics. His view builds on the work of Joleen Kirschenman and Kathryn Neckerman, who found that employers perceive blacks to be more troublesome and less compliant than Mexican Americans.[11]

Most striking was the broad black acceptance of these stereotypes. In Chicago, black as well as white employers used racial profiling to exclude young black men living in public housing projects. Even many black workers embraced negative black stereotypes. As one black resident told Wilson:

I say about 65 percent of black males, I say, don't wanna work, and when I say don't wanna work I say don't wanna work hard—they want a real easy job, making big bucks—see? And, and when you start talking about hard labor and earning your money with sweat or just once in a while you gotta put out a little bit—you know, that extra effort, I don't, I don't think the guys really wanna do that. And sometimes it comes from, really, not having a, a steady job or, really, not being out in the work field and just been sittin' back, being comfortable all the time and hanging out.[12]

Similar viewpoints were depicted in Spike Lee's film *Do the Right Thing*. Lee portrays the black pizza worker, Mookie, as an irresponsible employee who takes time off to have sex with the mother of his child whom he is unwilling to support. He also contrasts the lack of industriousness of three black men, who consistently hang out on the street corner with hard-working Asian shopkeepers.

Some data from the early and mid-1990s did suggest that a permanent black underclass has been created. In 1989, the employment rate of young black men equaled only 48.5 percent, well below the white rate of 68.0 percent. By the trough of the cyclical employment downturn in 1992, both employment rates had fallen, but the black rate more dramatically. Whereas the white rate was 94 percent of its peak rate, the black rate was only 85 percent.

It was in this environment that Wilson researched poor black Chicago neighborhoods for his book *When Work Disappears*. "The disappearance of work and its consequences for both social and cultural life," he wrote, "are the central problems in the inner-city ghetto." Wilson was not surprised that ambitious programs like Head Start generally have no lasting impact. He pointed to the inadequate public schools that poor inner-city black children must attend. However, it was the joblessness that is most decisive. When a majority of adults in many inner-city neighborhoods are jobless, social engineering is doomed.[13]

Typical of the men Wilson interviewed was a father of one child from a high-jobless neighborhood who explained why he began to sell drugs to augment his income from part-time work: "Four years I been out here trying to find a steady job. Going back and forth all these temporary jobs and this 'n' that. Then you know you gotta give money at home, you know you gotta buy your clothes which cost especially for a big person. Then you're talking about my daughter, then you talking about food in the house too, you know, things like that.[14]

The economist Chinhui Juhn documented the growing joblessness of black men, especially those with limited education and work experience. She found that on average at any moment during the 1994–1996 time period, about one out of every four black men was not employed. The nonemployment rate among the lowest-paid workers was nearly 50 percent. Juhn found that the nonemployment rate rose primarily because of longer spells of joblessness among a relatively small group.[15]

After an initial spurt upward during the early stages of the expansion, black employment rates fell back again so that in 1997 one could easily begin to view high black youth unemployment as permanent. Clearly, it appeared that the group profiling that Holzer and Wilson documented was taking its toll on black youth as long as employers believed that they had enough white (and Latino) youths available. Indeed, while black rates rose when labor markets tightened, they were no higher in 1999 than they were five years earlier.

These national figures, however, include both the employment situation of those in and those out of school. Over the last decade the proportion of young black men in school has increased. Since those in school tend to work less than those out of school, this shift alone would have caused the overall employment rate of young black men to decline. While the overall black employment rate was unchanged between 1994 and 1999, it increased substantially for those not in school—from 56.6 percent to 61.4 percent. Moreover, there was an even greater increase in full-time employment. The share of young black men, not in school, who held full-time jobs, rose from 43.8 percent to 53.4 percent. Thus, there were two opposing trends among those who were working less than *full-time*, year-round: One group was able to shift to full-time, year-round employment, while Juhn's evidence indicates that another smaller group became more detached from the labor market.

Tight labor markets aided not only employment, but also wage growth. During the first years of the economic expansion, 1992 through 1996, wages after adjusting for inflation declined for young non–college educated black and white men. However, once labor markets tightened, real wages increased dramatically. As a result, for the entire expansion through 1998, real wages increased by 5 and 10 percent for young non–college educated white and black men, respectively. This was above the 4 percent real wage increase for all male workers—the first increase in real wages in over twenty-five years.[16]

The impact of tight labor markets on the real wages of young non–college educated black men was most apparent when comparing different urban areas. Among areas where the unemployment rate was below 4 percent throughout the entire expansion, real wages for young non–college educated black men increased by 11 percent, while in areas where unemployment remained above 7 percent throughout the expansion, real wages declined by 5 percent. In areas where there was a rapid unemployment rate decline, real wages increased by 15 percent.[17]

A typical example of this striking improvement is Brian Bennett. Bennett graduated from an inner-city high school in Raleigh, North Carolina, in June 1997, when the local unemployment rate was 2.2 percent. After working at a series of temporary jobs for a year, he landed a full-time position as a front desk clerk at an Embassy Hotel. Planning to study hotel management part time with tuition help from his employer, Bennett said, "The sky is the limit, no one can hold me back but me."[18]

The manager of the Raleigh Employment Security Commission office said, "Employers are hiring people that two, three, five years ago they weren't hiring." In the early 1990s, four hundred black men between the ages of nineteen and twenty-five from the local area used to take part in a midnight basketball league where networking and interviewing tips were as much on the agenda as foul shots. However, by 1999, there was increasing "difficulty getting enough people to play because they [were] in the job market."[19]

Despite the earnings and employment benefits of tight labor markets, difficulties persist. In 1999, 19 percent of all black men between ages sixteen and twenty-four were neither in school nor at work, higher than during the peak of the previous expansion. Clearly the situations Wilson documented in the early 1990s and Juhn documented for the mid-1990s have not been eliminated. Most disheartening, black teenagers and students continue to have extreme difficulty obtaining employment. Only about one-quarter of black teenagers are employed compared to one-half of white teenagers. Among those sixteen to twenty-four years old, 50.7 percent of white students but only 28.6 percent of black students are employed. The gap is even larger in the cities in which poor blacks are concentrated.[20]

Employment is crucial for teenagers and college students. With the growing expenses of attending even public colleges, they need to accumulate personal funds in order to enter and remain in school. If black youths are unable to work, it is less likely that they will become college graduates. For those black teenagers who do not attend college, employment is crucial if they are to avoid racial profiling.[21]

In localities where the economic boom has not created tight labor markets, the situation of young black workers has remained dismal. This has been particularly true in New York City where more blacks—2.1 million—live than anywhere else in the United States. After seven years of economic expansion, the 1998 New York City unemployment rate stood at 8 percent, almost double the national rate. This contrasted with the peak of the previous expansion when New York City's unemployment rate was below the national rate.

With such a weak general labor market, black workers fared quite poorly. In 1998, black workers had an 18 percent unemployment rate in New York City, well above the 10 percent rate that was typical of other large cities. Indeed, Boston, Dallas, Atlanta, and San Francisco had rates of 6 percent or lower. The New York City employment rate for black men was six percentage points lower than other large cities. Among young black men in school, the New York City employment rate was 12.1 percent, whereas it was 20.7 percent in other large cities.

Most troubling, it does not appear that additional education alone will solve black employment difficulties in New York City. Among college-educated adults, black New Yorkers' 1998 unemployment rate of 9.8 percent was twice the U.S. black average and three times higher than the white rate nationally. Indeed, the poverty rate for New Yorkers with some college stood at 17 percent, up from 7.6 percent a decade earlier; among college graduates, the poverty rate increased from 3.5 to 6 percent. Thus, in the absence of tight labor markets, young black men continue to be at risk.[22]

Regional and Class Differences in Racial Disparities

Discrimination is a particularly important issue in the South Atlantic and Midwest regions since the majority of black workers live in these two regions. Furthermore, the historical importance of these regions cannot be underestimated: The history of slavery and Jim Crow in the South and the Midwest's importance as the primary destination of the black exodus indicate that the trajectory of discrimination in these regions is essential for understanding racial inequality in America. This section will present results from a study that analyzed changes in the racial earnings ratio in these two regions over the first five years of the 1990s economic expansion.[23]

The share of black and white workers can be placed into three occupational groupings: (1) fourteen college-required occupations in which at least 70 percent of those employed have some college education; (2) ten manual noncollege occupations that require physical labor and are low paid; and (3) twenty-one noncollege skilled occupations (see Table 5.1). In order to have a sufficient sample size, data were combined for three-year time periods, 1992 to 1994 and 1995 to 1997.

As noted earlier, nationally black men are overrepresented in blue-collar employment and underrepresented in managerial and professional occupations. The degree of over- and underrepresentation seems to vary substantially among regions. In the Midwest, at the beginning of the expansion 21.54 percent of black men but 25.42 percent of white men were employed in the college-required sector so that black men were 85 percent as likely to be employed there as white men. However, South Atlantic black men were only 54 percent as likely as white men to be employed in the college-required sector in that region. In the manual occupations, South Atlantic blacks were twice as likely to be employed as whites but only 57 percent more likely in the Midwest.

This more favorable black Midwest occupational distribution, however, was at least partially due to a selectivity bias. Our data included only those who are working. At the beginning of the economic expansion in 1992, employment rates among black

TABLE 5.1 Male Occupational Employment Shares by Race

	BLACK (%)		WHITE (%)		BLACK-TO-WHITE RATIO	
	1992–1994	1995–1997	1992–1994	1995–1997	1992–1994	1995–1997
South Atlantic						
College	15.81	18.19	29.47	30.79	0.54	0.59
Skilled	55.54	55.65	56.77	55.81	0.98	1.00
Manual	28.65	26.16	13.76	13.40	2.08	1.95
Midwest						
College	21.54	22.28	25.42	26.68	0.85	0.84
Skilled	55.58	56.26	60.05	59.92	0.93	0.94
Manual	22.88	21.46	14.53	13.40	1.57	1.60

SOURCE: Author's caluclations from the U.S. Bureau of the Census, Current Population Survey Outgoing Rotation Group Files (Washington, D.C.: Government Printing Office, 1992–1997).

men in these regions differed dramatically—63.9 percent in the South Atlantic but only 53.5 percent in the Midwest region, a 10.4-percentage point gap. In contrast, the white male employment rate was higher in the Midwest than in the South Atlantic region. Virtually the entire regional differential reflected Midwest black men who, if working, would have been employed in low-paid noncollege occupations. Thus, their exclusion artificially enhanced the Midwest occupational distribution for black men.

Over the expansion, many of these missing Midwest black men became employed so that the 1996 regional employment rate gap was only 8.7 percentage points. As a result of the disproportionate entry of low-paid black workers, however, there was an "unfavorable" shift in the Midwest black occupational distribution. The relative share of black employment in the college-required sector declined, while in the manual sector it increased. In contrast, in the South Atlantic region, the relative share of black employment in the college-required sector increased, while in the manual sector it declined. These shifts reduce regional occupational differences and, indeed, most of the remaining difference is due to the persistence of regional employment rate disparities.

Wage data are also influenced by the increased employment of low-paid Midwest black workers. At the beginning of the economic expansion, among Midwest black men, the average wage in the combined noncollege labor sector was 61.2 percent as much as the average wage in the college-required sector. The "class" ratio among white men was only 60.6 percent. Over the economic expansion, the class ratio remained the same among Midwest white workers but declined to 58.7 percent among black workers. By contrast, the class ratio among South Atlantic black men actually increased, indicating growing equality among black workers there.

During the economic expansion, the racial earnings ratio among men declined in the Midwest but improved in the South Atlantic region. As with the racial earnings ratio among women in the previous chapter, the overall change can be decomposed into

TABLE 5.2 Decomposition of Changes in the Black-to-White Male Earnings Ratio by Region, 1992–1994 and 1995–1997

| | RACIAL EARNINGS RATIO | | DECOMPOSITION INTO: | | | |
REGION	*1992–1994*	*1995–1997*	*Total change*	*Sector shares*	*College wage*	*Noncollege wage*
South Atlantic	72.07	73.24	1.17	0.68	-1.01	1.48
Midwest	81.49	80.51	-0.98	-0.25	0.11	-0.84

SOURCE: Author's calculations from the U.S. Bureau of the Census, Current Population Survey Outgoing Rotation Group Files (Washington, D.C.: Government Printing Office, 1992–1997).

three distinctive components into the sector-shares, college-wage, and non–college wage effects (see Table 5.2).

In the South Atlantic region, the racial earnings ratio among men increased by 1.17 percentage points. Black men in this region shifted more rapidly into the college-required sector than white men and, in the noncollege sector, the wages of black men increased by more than the wages of white men. These favorable changes were par-tially offset by an adverse college-wage effect; the wages of black workers increased by less than the wages of white men in the college-required sector.

As a result of the entry of low-earning, less-skilled black men, the Midwest racial earnings ratio among men decreased by 0.98 percentage points. Midwestern black men shifted less rapidly into the college-required sector than white men and, in the noncollege sector, the wages of black men increased less than the wages of white men. These adverse effects were marginally offset by a small favorable college-wage effect, as the wages of black workers increased by slightly more than the wages of white workers in the college-required sector.

In the Midwest, the major source of racial earnings ratio decline was the adverse noncollege wage effect. This was anticipated, given the large entry of low-paid black workers there. However, these entrants did not depress black wages in the manual oc-cupations. Instead, the major source of the adverse effect was the more rapid rise of white than black wages in the skilled occupations. The wages of black workers did not lag because white workers were able to increase their share of employment in the better-paying skilled occupations. Instead, the wages of black men lagged because they were less able to obtain the higher-paid positions within occupations in which they were employed. Thus, black men experienced a glass ceiling effect where they can enter occupations but not advance at as high a rate as white men.

There are discriminatory barriers to advancement in the skilled labor sector. Indeed, economists Joyce Jacobsen and Laurence Levin estimate that almost one-half of the racial wage differential among non–college educated men is the result of differential returns to tenure and experience.[24] There are additional reasons for the growing racial wage gap within skilled occupations. Over the economic expansion black and white Midwest men experienced different sources of labor mobility. For black men, the expansion enabled them to move into full-time employment so that they would be disproportionately at the bottom rung of the ladder in each skilled occupation. At the same time, having secure employment at the beginning of the expansion, white men were able to advance within skilled occupations.

The dynamics in the skilled labor sector were different in the South Atlantic region. Because black men had more secure employment at the beginning of the expansion, they experienced the same rise up the occupational ladder as white workers. In addition, black men were able to shift into the higher-paying skilled occupations. Both of these factors enabled black wages to rise faster than white wages in the skilled occupations.

In the college-required labor sector, at the beginning of the expansion, black men in both regions were somewhat underrepresented in the highest-paying occupations and overrepresented in the lowest-paying ones. The expansion eliminated this racial disparity completely. This improvement contrasted with the experience of black women who lagged behind white women in the ability to gain access to the higher-paying professional and managerial occupations.

In the Midwest, black and white men shifted to the college-required sector in relatively the same proportions, so that black men did not have a disproportionate share of the lowest-rung positions. However, glass ceiling effects did not lessen, so that there was virtually no change in the relative wages within occupations. In the South Atlantic region, the positive sector-shares effect indicates that black workers increased their share of employment in college-required occupations. Most likely, this reflected a growing number of new black college graduates entering the job market. These new entrants would have disproportionately concentrated at the bottom rung in each occupation. Since this dampened the average growth of black wages within occupations, there was an adverse college-wage effect in the South Atlantic region.

Measuring Labor Market Discrimination

Racial disparities do not necessarily demonstrate labor market discrimination. They could primarily reflect skill and behavioral differences. The data, however, seem to reject this viewpoint, instead indicating that wage gaps among equally educated black and white workers twenty-five to thirty-four years old grew in the 1980s and persisted through the 1990s (see Table 5.3). Using similar findings, Andrew Brimmer estimated that if black men earned the same wages as comparably educated white men, total gross domestic product (GDP) would increase by 2.15 percent.[25]

The pro-market economist June O'Neill—appointed by President Clinton in 1995 to direct the Congressional Budget Office—also found that there were substantial and growing racial earnings gaps among men during the 1980s. Indeed, her reported ratios are lower than those of Mishel, Bernstein, and Schmitt for that time period. However, O'Neill firmly rejected claims that this demonstrated persistent labor market discrimination against black men.[26]

Pro-market economists claim that these estimates are incomplete since they do not fully adjust for skill differences between black and white men. In particular, comparisons must take into account the following additional factors: the region of residency,

TABLE 5.3   Black-to-White Earnings Ratio (Percentage) Among Men Twenty-Five to Thirty-Four Years Old, 1979–1995

	YEARS OF SCHOOLING			
	8-10	*12*	*13-15*	*16 and more*
	Mishel, Bernstein, and Schmitt*			
1979	81.6	85.8	90.1	92.8
1989	81.1	81.1	81.6	77.6
1995	82.9	80.9	82.4	87.1
	O'Neill**			
1979/80	75.2	80.4	84.6	90.6
1987	81.6	75.5	82.1	74.4

*Hourly wage rate comparisons among all workers who had positive income during that year.
**Usual weekly wage, averaged over a three-year period, including only individuals who worked at least twelve weeks and full-time for at least one-half of the weeks worked.

actual work experience, and the measure of basic skills. With these adjustments, O'Neill estimated that young black men in 1987 would have earned 99.1 percent of comparably skilled young white men.

O'Neill's estimate was based on a comparison of the usual weekly wage of men who worked at least twelve weeks during the previous year and were full-time for at least half of the time they worked. Interventionists contend that the choice of income measure and restrictions on which workers are included understates racial earnings disparities. They argue that direct controlled studies of hiring practices are the most effective method of measuring labor market discrimination.

Conclusion

Evidence presented indicates that severe employment problems persist for black men even after the longest uninterrupted economic expansion in U.S. history. This is particularly the case once nonemployment, incarceration, and census undercounting of black men is accounted for. Indeed, only when labor markets tightened after 1997 did racial earnings and employment disparities lessen. Just as with black women, these tight labor markets forced many employers to hire job applicants for whom they held negative stereotypes. This enabled those black men who had some work experience to gain full-time, year-round employment. However, it did not reverse the continued detachment of a significant share of young black men from the labor market.

Black employment problems were most severe in areas that had an excess supply of workers. This was the case in the Midwest at the beginning of the economic expansion and in New York City throughout the expansion. In the Midwest, these employment difficulties were reflected in the particularly high nonemployment rate of black men that artificially made employment and earnings disparities seem smaller. In New York City, these employment difficulties were severe enough to substantially adversely affect college-educated black men.

Racial earnings disparities among college graduates does not appear to be significant, especially if adjustments are made for skills, either through class rank or standardized test scores. Racial earnings disparities in the noncollege labor sector, however, were larger and more persistent. These disparities primarily reflect the inability of black men to advance within skilled occupations. In addition, because of racial profiling, young black men have difficulty gaining employment, limiting their work experience as they age.

Instead of discriminatory practices, liberal economists tend to emphasize structural factors to explain racial disparities within the noncollege labor sector: the increasing use of informal hiring practices and the changing location of manufacturing firms. Since blacks have a weak set of business contacts, they are unlikely to be in the personal network of suburban employers. Since blacks are trapped in central cities, many are unable to commute to suburban jobs. Thus, they argue that the lack of black employment occurs even if employers hold neither racial preferences nor stereotypes.

These economists tend to minimize the extent to which racial preferences and stereotypes influence the decisions of firms about where to locate and what hiring procedures to use. As Wilson and Holzer documented, however, hiring practices were consciously developed so that black workers would have difficulty finding out about job openings. For example, when the Japanese automobile manufacturers expanded production facilities in the United States, their location decisions seemed to be at least partially based on a desire to avoid hiring black workers. They built almost all of their plants in semi-rural locations distant from cities in which black workers were concentrated. One particular example was a decision to locate an auto plant two miles outside the census definition of the Columbus, Ohio, metropolitan area. If it had located within the official metropolitan area, the firm would have been subject to equal employment opportunity (EEO) guidelines that require firms to hire in proportion to available labor supplies in the metropolitan area. Since about 20 percent of the Columbus metropolitan area is black, the firm would have been under pressure to hire a work force that was 20 percent black. However, by locating just outside the metropolitan area, the firm could still tap the Columbus labor market but would not be subject to the 20-percent goal since few blacks lived in the particular locality in which it located.

Many conservative policy analysts focus on the personal decisions of non–college educated black men to explain their employment problems. These analysts often claim that much of the problem stems from the unwillingness of black men, especially in the Northeast and Midwest, to take service jobs that they perceive as demeaning. Indeed, this argument surfaced when it was found that black men had a disproportionately low representation among the waiting work force in New York City. Though 26 percent of the city's population in 1996, they represented only 10.5 percent of those employed as waiters. When surveyed, many black waiters "acknowledge that black Americans may be rejecting what they perceive as a servile profession." This reflected not a particular political perspective but the attitudes of white customers. Typical was the experience of one black waiter at an exclusive restaurant who was told, "For a colored boy, you're not too bad.[27]

Black waiters were quick to point out that discriminatory practices are a more important explanation of the low numbers of black waiters. When he was trying to gain a toehold in the industry, George Thomas remembered, "I faxed my qualifications to restaurants and they expressed excitement. Then they saw me in person, and the whole conversation changed." Given this experience, Harlem political leader David Paterson suggests that black men don't seek employment as waiters because "they think those jobs are closed off to them." Fortunately, Mr. Thomas did not give up and worked his way up to becoming waiter captain at a three-star restaurant.[28]

While racial equality is in reach in the college-required labor sector, the continuation of EEO policies is still necessary if the remnants of discriminatory practices are to be rooted out and the advances already made are to be sustained. In noncollege labor markets, black men continue to be victimized by glass ceiling effects that limit their ability to advance. Black men also continue to be last in the hiring queue. For these reasons, EEO policies must be expanded and strengthened in the noncollege sector.

In addition, government can be more sympathetic to the employment difficulties faced by black men. Despite poor labor markets, New York City treats black men as if they were responsible for their joblessness. Rather than hiring them as fully paid workers, they are hired on workfare programs that pay them minimum wage or lower. The *New York Times* reporter Steven Greenhouse documented how, between 1994 and 1998, New York City was able to reduce its government work force by 10 percent through the hiring of 34,000 workfare recipients. This was most striking in the parks department where government employees declined from 1,925 to 1,156.[29]

That the government has the ability to absorb young workers with low education is most apparent in Germany. Economists Francine Blau and Lawrence Kahn documented that in 1991, among all men aged eighteen to twenty-nine years old without a high school diploma, 17 percent had government employment in Germany but less than 2 percent had government employment in the United States. Moreover, unlike workfare programs that pay minimum wages, government employment in Germany narrowed the wage gap between these workers and private sector workers. If the government in the United States followed the German example, the situation of young black men could be improved dramatically.[30]

Notes

1. Robert Cherry, "Impact of Tight Labor Markets on Black Employment," *Review of Black Political Economy*, Summer 2000, 27–41; Chinhui John, "Decline of Male Labor Market Participation," *Quarterly Journal of Economics*, February 1992, 79–121.

2. Barry Bluestone and Mary Stevenson, "Racial and Ethnic Gaps in Male Earnings in a Booming Urban Economy," *Eastern Economic Journal*, Spring 1999, 209–238.

3. Kim Clark and Lawrence Summers, "The Dynamics of Youth Unemployment," in *The Youth Labor Market Problem*, ed. Richard Freeman and David Wise (Chicago: University of Chicago Press, 1982), 199–230; Richard Freeman and James Medoff, "Why Does the Rate of Youth Labor Force Activity Differ across Surveys?" in *Youth Labor Market Problem*, 75–114.

4. Elijah Anderson, "Some Observations on Black Youth Unemployment," in *Youth Employment and Public Policy*, ed. Bernard Anderson and Isabel Sawhill (Englewood Cliffs, N.J.: Prentice-Hall, 1980), 37–46; Harry Holzer, "Black Youth Nonemployment: Duration and Job Search," in *Black Youth Employment Crisis*, ed. Freeman and Holzer, 23–74; Christopher Jencks, "Genes and Crime," *New York Review of Books* 12 (February 1987): 3341; Kip Viscusi, "Market Incentives for Criminal

Behavior," in *Black Youth Employment Crisis*, ed. Freeman and Holzer, 301-346; Andrew Hacker, *Two Nations: Black and White, Separate, Hostile, Unequal* (New York: Random House, 1995).

5. Wilson, *The Truly Disadvantaged*; Darity and Myers, *The Underclass*, 150.

6. Clark and Summers, "Dynamics of Youth Unemployment."

7. John Bound and Richard Freeman, "What Went Wrong? The Erosion of the Relative Earnings of Young Black Men during the 1980s," *Quarterly Journal of Economics*, February 1992, 215 n.; Marc Breslow, "The Racial Divide Widens," *Dollars and Sense*, January–February 1995, 10–11.

8. Harry Holzer, *What Employers Want: Job Prospects for Less-Educated Workers* (New York: Sage, 1996).

9. William J. Wilson, *When Work Disappears* (New York: Vintage, 1996), 134.

10. Wilson, *When Work Disappears*, 136–137.

11. Holzer, *What Employers Want*; Joleen Kirshenman and Kathryn Nickerman, "'We'd Love to Hire them But. . .': The Meaning of Race for Employers," in *The Urban Underclass*, ed. Christopher Jencks and Paul Peterson (Washington, D.C.: Brookings Institution, 1991), 203–234.

12. Wilson, *When Work Disappears*, 139.

13. Wilson, *When Work Disappears*, 139.

14. Wilson, *When Work Disappears*, 58–59.

15. Chinhui Juhn, "Black-White Employment Differential in a Tight Labor Market," in *Prosperity for All? The Economic Boom and African Americans*, ed. Cherry and Rodgers, 88–109.

16. Richard Freeman and William Rodgers, "Area Economic Conditions and the Labor Market Outcomes of Young Men in the 1990s Expansion," in *Prosperity for All? The Economic Boom and African Americans*, ed. Cherry and Rodgers, 50–87.

17. Freeman and Rodgers, "Area Economic Conditions," 50–87.

18. Sylvia Nasar and Kirsten Mitchell, "Booming Job Market Draws Young Black Men into Fold," *New York Times*, May 23, 1999, A1.

19. Nasar and Kirsten Mitchell, "Booming Job Market," A1.

20. Greg DeFreitas, "Urban Racial Employment Differentials: The New York Case," in *Prosperity for All? The Economic Boom and African Americans*, ed. Cherry and Rodgers, 11–126.

21. John Ballen and Richard Freeman, "Transitions between Employment and Unemployment," in *Black Youth Employment Crisis*, ed. Freeman and Holzer, 223–274; Bruce Elmslie and Stanley Sedo, "Persistent Consequences of Initial Discrimination: Young Black Workers in the 1960s," *Review of Black Political Economy*, Spring 1996, 97–110.

22. Greg DeFreitas, *More Work, More School, More Poverty?* (New York: Community Service Society of New York, 2000).

23. Boushey and Cherry, "Exclusionary Practices and Glass-Ceiling Effects across Regions," 160–187.

24. Joyce Jacobsen and Laurence Levin, "Looking at the Glass Ceiling: Do White Men Receive Higher Returns to Tenure and Experience?" in *Prosperity for All? The Economic Boom and African Americans*, ed. Cherry and Rodgers, 211–238.

25. Andrew Brimmer, "The Economic Cost of Discrimination Against Black Americans," in *Economic Perspectives on Affirmative Action*, ed. Margaret Simms (Washington, D.C.: Joint Center for Political and Economic Studies, 1995), 11–29.

26. June O'Neill, "The Role of Hurnau Capital in Earnings Differences Between Black and White Men," *Journal of Economic Perspectives*, Fall 1990, 2546; Mishei et al., *The State of Working America*, table 3.56.

6

RAMBO LITIGATORS
Emotional Labor in a
Male-Dominated Occupation

Jennifer Pierce

Litigation is war. The lawyer is a gladiator and the object is to wipe out the other side.
—Cleveland lawyer quoted in the *New York Times*

A recent spate of articles in the *New York Times* and a number of legal dailies characterized some of America's more flamboyant and aggressive trial lawyers as "Rambo litigators."[1] This hypermasculine, aggressive image is certainly not a new one. In popular culture and everyday life, jokes and stories abound that characterize lawyers as overly aggressive, manipulative, unreliable, and unethical individuals.[2] What jokes, as well as the popular press, fail to consider is that such behavior is not simply the result of individual failings but is actually required and reinforced by the legal profession itself.

Legal scholar Carrie Menkel-Meadow (1985) suggests that the adversarial model with its emphasis on "zealous advocacy" and "winning" encourages a "macho ethic" in the courtroom (51–54). Lawyers and teachers of trial lawyers argue that the success of litigators depends on their ability to manipulate people's emotions (Brazil 1978; Turow 1987). Trial lawyers must persuade judges and juries, as well as intimidate witnesses and opposing counsel in the courtroom, in deposition, and in negotiations. The National Institute of Trial Advocacy, for example, devotes a three-week training seminar to teaching lawyers to hone such emotional skills, thereby improving their success in the courtroom (Rice 1989). This chapter makes this aspect of lawyering explicit by examining the emotional dimension of legal work in a particular specialty of law litigation. Sociological studies of the legal profession have yet to seriously examine the emotional dimension of lawyering.[3] Although a few studies make reference to the emotional dimension of work, it is not the central focus of their research.[4] For example, Nelson (1988) reduces lawyering to three roles, "finders, minders and grinders," meaning "lawyers who seem to bring in substantial clients. . . lawyers who take care of the clients who are already here and there are the grinders who do the work" (senior partner quoted in Nelson 1988, p. 69). Nelson's reduction of these roles to their instrumental and intellectual dimensions neglects the extent to which instrumental tasks may also contain emotional elements.

The sparse attention other sociological studies have given to this dimension of lawyering is contradicted by my 15 months of field research (from 1988 to 1989) at two large law firms in San Francisco 6 months at a private firm (Lyman, Lyman, and Portia) and 9 months in the legal department of a large corporation (Bonhomie Corporation).[5] Litigators make use of their emotions to persuade juries, judges, and witnesses in the courtroom and in depositions, in communications with opposing counsel, and with clients. However, in contrast to the popular image, intimidation and aggression constitute only one component of the emotional labor required by this profession. Lawyers also make use of strategic friendliness, that is, the use of charm or flattery to manipulate others. Despite the apparent differences in these two types of emotional labor, both use the manipulation of others for a specific end—winning a case. Although other jobs require the use of manipulation to achieve specific ends, such labor may serve different purposes and be embedded in a different set of relationships. Flight attendants, for example, are friendly and reassuring to passengers so as to alleviate their anxiety about flying (Hochschild 1983). However, flight attendants' friendliness takes the form of deference: Their relationship to passengers is supportive and subordinate. By contrast, in litigation, the goal of strategic friendliness is to win over or dominate another. As professionals who have a monopoly over specialized knowledge, attorneys hold a superordinate position with respect to clients, witnesses, and jurors and a competitive one with other lawyers. If trial lawyers want to win their cases, they must be able to successfully manipulate and ultimately dominate others for their professional ends.

By doing whatever it takes within the letter of the law to win a case, lawyers effectively fulfill the goal of zealous advocacy: persuading a third party that the client's interests should prevail. In this way, intimidation and strategic friendliness serve to reproduce and maintain the adversarial model. At the same time, by exercising dominance and control over others, trial lawyers also reproduce gender relations. The majority of litigators who do dominance are men (88 percent of litigators are male) and those who defer are either female secretaries and paralegals, other women, or men who become feminized in the process of losing.[6] In addition to creating and maintaining a gendered hierarchy, the form such emotional labor takes is gendered. It is a masculinized form of emotional labor, not only because men do it but because dominance is associated with masculinity in our culture. West and Zimmerman (1987) argue, for example, that displays of dominance are ways for men to "do gender."[7] Similarly, psychoanalytic feminists equate masculinity with men's need to dominate women (Benjamin 1988; Chodorow 1978). In the case of trial lawyers, the requirements of the profession deem it appropriate to dominate women as well as other men. Such conquests or achievements at once serve the goals of effective advocacy and become the means for the trial lawyer to demonstrate a class-specific form of masculinity.

Gamesmanship and
the Adversarial Model

Popular wisdom and lawyer folklore portray lawyering as a game, and the ability to play as gamesmanship (Spence 1988). As one of the trial attorneys I interviewed said,

> The logic of gamesmanship is very interesting to me. I like how you make someone appear to be a liar. You know, you take them down the merry path and before they know it, they've said something pretty stupid. The challenge is getting them to say it without violating the letter of the law.

Lawyering is based on gamesmanship—legal strategy, skill, and expertise. But trial lawyers are much more than chess players. Their strategies are not simply cerebral, rational, and calculating moves but highly emotional, dramatic, flamboyant, and shocking presentations that invoke sympathy, distrust, or outrage. In my redefinition of the term, gamesmanship involves the utilization of legal strategy through a presentation of an emotional self designed specifically to influence the feelings and judgment of a particular legal audience—the judge, the jury, the witness, or opposing counsel. Furthermore, in my definition, the choices litigators make about selecting a particular strategy are not simply individual, they are institutionally constrained by the structure of the legal profession, formal and informal professional norms such as the American Bar Association's (1982) *Model Code of Professional Responsibility* and training in trial advocacy through programs sponsored by the National Institute of Trial Advocacy.

The rules governing gamesmanship derive from the adversarial model that underlies the basic structure of our legal system. This model is a method of adjudication that involves two advocates (e.g., the attorneys) presenting their case to an impartial third party (i.e., the judge and the jury) who listens to evidence and argument and declares one party the winner (Luban 1988; Menkel-Meadow 1985). As Menkel-Meadow (1985) observes, the basic assumptions that underlie this set of arrangements are "advocacy, persuasion, hierarchy, competition and binary results (win or lose)." She writes, "The conduct of litigation is relatively similar. . . to a sporting event—there are rules, a referee, an object to the game, and a winner is declared after play is over" (51).

Within this system, the attorney's main objective is to persuade the impartial third party that his client's interests should prevail (American Bar Association 1982, 34). However, clients do not always have airtight, defensible cases. How, then, does the zealous advocate protect his clients interests and achieve the desired result? When persuasion by appeal to reason breaks down, an appeal to emotions becomes tantamount (Cheatham 1955, 282–283). As legal scholar John Buchan (1939) writes, "The root of the talent is simply the *power to persuade*" [italics added] (211–213). By appealing to emotions, the lawyer becomes a "con man."[8] He acts "as if" he has a defensible case, he puffs himself up, he bolsters his case. Thus, the successful advocate must not only be smart, but as famous turn-of-the-century trial lawyer Francis Wellman (1903/1986, 13) observes, he must also be a "good actor." In his book, *The Art of Cross-Examination,* first published in 1903 and reprinted to the present, Wellman describes how carefully the litigator must present himself to the judge and jury.

> The most cautious cross-examiner will often elicit a damaging answer. Now is the time for the greatest self-control. If you show by your face how the answer hurt, you may lose by that one point alone. How often one sees a cross-examiner fairly staggered by such an answer. He pauses, blushes. . . [but seldom regains] control of the witness. With the really experienced trial lawyer, such answers, instead of appearing to surprise or disconcert him, will seem to come as a matter of course, and will fall perfectly flat. He will proceed with the next question as if nothing happened, or else perhaps give the witness an incredulous smile, as if to say, "Who do you suppose would believe that for a minute?" (13–14).

More recently, teacher and lawyer David Berg (1987) advises lawyers to think of themselves as actors, and the jury, an audience. He writes,

> Decorum can make a difference, too. . . . Stride to the podium and exude confidence, even if there is a chance that the high school dropout on the stand is going to snake you look like an idiot. Take command of the courtroom. Once you begin, do not grope for questions, snuffle through papers, or take breaks to confer with co-counsel. Let the jury know that you are prepared, that you do not need anyone's advice, and that you care about the case. . . because if *you don't care, the jurors won't care.* (1987, 28, italics added)

Wellman (1903/1986) and Berg (1987) make a similar point: Trials are the enactment of a drama in the courtroom, and attorneys are the leading actors. Appearance and demeanor are of utmost importance. The lawyer's manner, his tone of voice, his facial expressions, are all means to persuade the jury that his client is right. Outrageous behavior is acceptable, as long as it remains within the letter of the law. Not only are trial lawyers expected to act but with a specific purpose in mind: to favorably influence feelings of the juror. As Berg points out, "If you don't show you care, the jurors won't care."

This emphasis on acting is also evident in the courses taught by the National Institute for Trial Advocacy (NITA) where neophyte litigators learn the basics in presenting a case for trial. NITA's emphasis is on "leaning by doing" (Kilpatrick, quoted in Rice 1989). Attorneys do not simply read about cases but practice presenting them in a simulated courtroom with a judge, a jury, and witnesses. In this case, doing means acting. As one of the teacher-lawyers said on the first day of class, "Being a good trial lawyer means being a good actor. . . . Trial attorneys love to perform." Acting, in sociological terms, translates into emotional labor, that is, inducing or suppressing feelings in order to produce an outward countenance that influences the emotions of others. Teacher-lawyers discuss style, delivery, presentation of self, attitude, and professionalism. Participants, in turn, compare notes about the best way to "handle" judges, jurors, witnesses, clients, and opposing counsel. The efforts of these two groups constitute the teaching and observance of "feeling rules" or professional norms that govern appropriate lawyerlike conduct in the courtroom.

The three-week course I attended took students through various phases of a hypothetical trial jury selection, opening and closing statements, and direct and cross-examination.[9] Each stage of the trial has a slightly different purpose. For example, the objective of jury selection is to uncover the biases and prejudices of the jurors and to develop rapport with them. On the other hand, an opening statement sets the theme for the case, whereas a direct examination lays the foundation of evidence for the case. Cross-examination is intended to undermine the credibility of the witness, whereas closing represents the final argument. Despite the differing goals that each of these phases has, the means to achieve them is similar in each case, that is, the attempt to persuade a legal audience favorably to one's client through a particular emotional presentation of self.

In their sessions on direct and cross-examination, students were given primarily stylistic, as opposed to substantive, responses on their presentations. They were given finer legal points on the technicalities of their objections—the strength or weakness of their arguments. But in the content analysis of my field notes, I found that 50 percent to 80 percent of comments were directed toward the attorney's particular style. These comments fell into five categories: (a) personal appearance, (b) presentation of self (nice, aggressive, or sincere manner), (c) tone and level of voice, (d) eye contact, and (e) rapport with others in the courtroom.

For example, in one of the sessions, Tom, a young student-lawyer in the class, did a direct examination of a witness to a liquor store robbery. He solemnly questioned the witness about his work, his special training in enforcing liquor laws, and how he determined whether someone was intoxicated. At one point when the witness provided a detail that Tom had not expected, rather than expressing surprise, Tom appeared nonchalant and continued with his line of questions. At the end of his direct, the teacher-lawyer provided the following feedback:

> Good background development of a witness. Your voice level was appropriate but try modulating it a bit more for emphasis. You also use too many thank-you's to the judge. You should ingratiate yourself with the judge but not overly so. You also made a good recovery when the witness said something unexpected.

When Patricia, a young woman attorney, proceeded nervously through the same direct examination, opposing counsel objected repeatedly to some of her questions, which flustered her. The teacher-lawyer told her,

> You talk too fast. And you didn't make enough eye contact with the judge. Plus, you got bogged down in the objections and harassment from opposing counsel. Your recovery was too slow. You've got to be more forceful.

In both these examples, as in most of the sessions that I observed, the focus of the comments was not on the questions asked but on how the questions were asked. Tom was told to modulate his voice; Patricia was told not to talk so fast. In addition, the teacher-lawyer directed their attention to rapport with others in the courtroom. Tom was encouraged not to be overly ingratiating with the judge, whereas Patricia was told to pay more attention to the judge. Moreover, the teacher commended Tom for his "recovery," that is, regaining self-composure and control of the witness. He criticized

Patricia, on the other hand, for not recovering well from an aggressive objection made by opposing counsel.[10]

In my fieldwork at NITA and in the two law offices, I found two main types of emotional labor: intimidation and strategic friendliness. Intimidation entails the use of anger and aggression, whereas strategic friendliness uses politeness, friendliness, or playing dumb. Both forms are related to gamesmanship. Each involves an emotional presentation of self that is intended to favorably influence the feelings of a particular legal audience toward one's client. Many jobs appear to require strategic friendliness and intimidation. Domestic workers, for example, sometimes "play dumb" so as not to alienate their white female employers (Rollins 1985). For domestic workers, however, this strategy is a means for someone in a subordinate position to survive a degrading job. By contrast, for litigators, strategic friendliness, like intimidation, is a means for an individual with professional status to control and dominate others in an effort to win one's case. Although both the litigator and the domestic worker may play dumb, in each job, the behavior serves different goals that are indicative of their divergent positions in relationship to others.

Intimidation and strategic friendliness not only serve the goals of the adversarial model, but they exemplify a masculine style of emotional labor. They become construed as masculine for several reasons. First, emotional labor in the male-dominated professional strata of the gendered law firm is interpreted as masculine, simply because men do it. Ruth Milkman (1987), for example, suggests that "idioms of sex-typing can be applied to whatever women and men happen to be doing" (50). Male trial attorneys participate in shaping this idiom by describing their battles in the courtroom and with opposing counsel as "macho," "something men get into," and "a male thing." In addition, by treating women lawyers as outsiders and excluding them from professional networks, they further define their job as exclusively male.

In addition, the underlying purpose of gamesmanship itself, that is, the control and domination of others through manipulation, reflects a particular cultural conception of masculinity. Connell (1987), for example, describes a hegemonic form of masculinity that emphasizes the domination of a certain class of men (middle- to upper-middle class) over other men and women. Connell's cultural conception of masculinity dovetails neatly with feminist psychoanalytic accounts that interpret domination as a means of asserting one's masculinity (Benjamin 1988; Chodorow 1978). The lawyers I studied also employed a ritual of degradation and humiliation against other men and women who were witnesses or opposing counsel. The remainder of this chapter describes the two main components of emotional labor intimidation and strategic friendliness—the purpose of each, and shows how these forms become construed as masculine. These forms of emotional labor are explored in practices, such as cross-examination, depositions, jury selection, and in opening and closing statements.

Intimidation

The first and most common form of emotional labor associated with lawyers is intimidation. In popular culture, the tough, hard-hitting, and aggressive trial lawyer is portrayed in television shows, such as *L.A. Law* and *Perry Mason* and in movies, such as *The Finn, A Few Good Men,* and *Presumed Innocent.* The news media's focus on famous trial attorneys such as Arthur Liman, the prosecutor of Oliver North in the Iran-Contra trial, also reinforces this image. Law professor Wayne Brazil (1978) refers to this style of lawyering as the *professional combatant.* Others have used terms such as *Rambo litigator, legal terrorists,* and *barbarians of the bar* (Margolick 1988; Miner 1988; Sayler 1988). Trial attorneys themselves call litigators from large law firms "hired guns" (Spangler 1986). The central figure that appears again in these images is not only intimidating but strongly masculine. In the old West, hired guns were sharpshooters, men who were hired to kill other men. The strong, silent movie character Rambo is emblematic of a highly stylized, super masculinity. Finally, most of the actors who play tough, hard-hitting lawyers in the television shows and movies mentioned above are men. Thus, intimidation is not simply a form of emotional labor associated with trial lawyers, it is a masculinized form of labor.

Intimidation is tied to cultural conceptions of masculinity in yet another way. In a review of the literature on occupations, Connell (1987) observes that the cult of masculinity in working class jobs centers on physical prowess and sexual contempt for men in managerial or office positions (180). Like the men on the shop floor in Michael Burawoy's (1979) study who brag about how much they can lift or produce, lawyers in this study boast about "destroying witnesses," "playing hardball," "taking no prisoners," and about the size and amount of their "win." In a middle-class job such as the legal profession, however, intimidation depends not on physical ability but on mental quickness and a highly developed set of social skills. Thus, masculinizing practices, such as aggression and humiliation, take on an emotional and intellectual tone specific to middle-class occupations and professions.

This stance is tied to the adversarial model's conception of the "zealous advocate" (American Bar Association 1982). The underlying purpose of this strategy is to intimidate, scare, or emotionally bully the witness of opposing counsel into submission. A destructive cross-examination is the best example.[11] Trial attorneys are taught to intimidate the witness in cross-examination, "to control the witness by never asking a question to which he does not already know the answer and to regard the impeachment of the witness as a highly confrontational act" (Menkel-Meadow 1985, 54). Wellman (1903/1986) describes cross-examination in this way:

> It requires the greatest ingenuity; a habit of logical thought; clearness of perception; infinite patience and self-control; the power to read men's minds intuitively, to judge of their characters by their faces, to appreciate their motives; ability to act with force and precision; a masterful knowledge of the subject matter itself; an extreme caution; and, above all *the instinct to discover the weak point in the witness under examination. . . .* It is a *mental duel* between counsel and witness. (8, italics added)

Berg (1987) echoes Wellman's words when he begins his lecture on cross-examination by saying, "The common denominator for effective cross-examination is not genius, however. It's a combination of preparation and an instinct for the jugular" (27).

Again, cross-examination involves not only acting mean but creating a specific impression on the witness.

In the sections on cross-examination at NITA, teachers trained lawyers how to act mean. The demonstration by the teachers on cross-examination best exemplified this point. Two male instructors reenacted an aggressive cross-examination in a burglary case. The prosecutor relentlessly hammered away, until the witness couldn't remember any specific details about what the burglar looked like. At its conclusion, the audience clapped vigorously. Three male students who had been asked to comment on the section responded unanimously and enthusiastically that the prosecutor's approach had been excellent. One student commentator said, "He kept complete control of the witness." Another remarked, "He blasted the witness's testimony." And the third added, "He destroyed the witness's credibility." The fact that a destructive cross-examination served as the demonstration for the entire class underlines the desirability of aggressive behavior as a model for appropriate lawyerlike conduct in this situation. Furthermore, the students' praise for the attorney's tactics collectively reinforce the norm for such behavior.

Teachers emphasized the importance of using aggression on an individual level as well. Before a presentation on cross-examination, Tom, one of the students, stood in the hallway with one of the instructors trying to "psyche himself up to get mad." He repeated over and over to himself, "I hate it when witnesses lie to me, it makes me so mad!" The teacher coached him to concentrate on that thought, until Tom could actually evoke the feeling of anger. He said to me later in an interview, "I really felt mad at the witness when I walked into the courtroom." In the actual cross-examination, each time the witness made an inconsistent statement, Tom became more and more angry: "First, you told us you could see the burglar, now you say your vision was obstructed! So, which is it, Mr. Jones?" The more irate he became, the more intimidated and confused the witness became, until he completely backed down and said, "I don't know," in response to every question. The teacher characterized Tom's performance as "the best in the class," because it was the "the most forceful" and "the most intimidating." Students remarked that he deserved to "win the case."

NITA's teachers also used mistakes to train students in the rigors of cross-examination. For example, when Laura cross-examined the same witness in the liquor store case, a teacher commented on her performance:

> Too many words. You're asking the witness for information. Don't do that in cross-examination. You tell them what the information is. You want to be destructive in cross-examination. When the other side objects to an answer, you were too nice. *Don't be so nice* [italics added]. Next time, ask to talk to the judge, tell him, "This is crucial to my case." You also asked for information when you didn't know the answer. Bad news. You lost control of the witness.

By being nice and losing control of the witness, Laura violated two norms underlying the classic confrontational cross-examination. A destructive cross-examination is meant to impeach the witness's credibility, thereby demonstrating to the jury the weakness in opposing counsel's case.

In situations that call for such an aggressive cross-examination, being nice implies that the lawyer likes the witness and agrees with his or her testimony. By not being aggressive, Laura created the wrong impression for the jury. Second, Laura lost control of the witness. Rather than guiding the witness through the cross with leading questions that were damaging to opposing counsel's case, she allowed the witness to make his own points.[12] As we will see in the next section of the chapter, being nice can also be used as a strategy for controlling a witness; however, such a strategy is not effective in a destructive cross-examination.

Laura's violation of these norms also serves to highlight the implicitly masculine practices used in cross-examination. The repeated phrase, "keeping complete control of the witness," clearly signals the importance of dominating other women and men.[13] Furthermore, the language used to describe obtaining submission ("blasting the witness," "destroying his credibility," or pushing him to "back down") is quite violent. In addition, the successful control of the witness often takes on the character of a sexual conquest. One brutal phrase used repeatedly in this way is "raping the witness." Within this discursive field, men who "control," "destroy," or "rape" the witness are seen as "manly," whereas those who lose control are feminized as "sissies" and "wimps" or, in Laura's case, as "too nice."

The combative aspect of emotional labor carries over from the courtroom to other lawyering tasks, such as depositions. Attorneys not only "shred" witnesses in the courtroom but in depositions as well. When I worked at this private firm, Daniel, one of the partners, employed what he called his "cat and mouse game" with one of the key witnesses, Jim, in a deposition that I attended. During the deposition, Daniel aggressively cross-examined Jim. "When did you do this?" "You were lying, weren't you?" Jim lost his temper in response to Daniel's hostile form of interrogation—"You hassle me, man! You make me mad!" Daniel smiled and said, "I'm only trying to get to the truth of the situation." Then, he became aggressive again and said, "You lied to the IRS about how much profit you made, didn't you, Jim!" Jim lost his temper again and started calling Daniel a liar. A heated interchange between Daniel and opposing counsel followed, in which opposing counsel objected to Daniel's "badgering the witness." The attorneys decided to take a brief recess.

When the deposition resumed, Daniel began by accusing John, the other attorney, of withholding crucial documents to the case, while pointing his index finger at him. Opposing counsel stood up and started yelling in a high-pitched voice, "Don't you ever point your finger at me! Don't you ever do that to me! This deposition is over. . . I'm leaving." With that he stood up and began to cram papers into his briefcase in preparation to leave. Daniel immediately backed down, apologized, and said, "Sit down, John, I promise I won't point my finger again." He went on to smooth the situation over and proceeded to tell John in a very calm and controlled voice what his objections were. John made some protesting noises, but he didn't leave. The deposition continued.

In this instance, the deposition, rather than the courtroom, became the stage and Daniel took the leading role. His cross-examination was confrontational and his behavior with the witness and opposing counsel was meant to intimidate. After the deposition, Daniel boasted to me and several associates about how mad he had made the witness and how he had "destroyed his credibility." He then proceeded to reenact the final confrontation by imitating John standing up and yelling at him in a falsetto voice. In the discussion that followed, Daniel and his associates gave the effects of his behavior on the "audience" utmost consideration. Hadn't Daniel done a good job forcing the witness to lose control? Hadn't he controlled the situation well? Didn't he make opposing counsel look like a "simpering fool"?

The reenactment and ensuing discussion reveal several underlying purposes of the deposition. First, it suggests that the deposition was not only a fact-finding mission for the attorney but a show designed to influence a particular audience—the witness. Daniel effectively flustered and intimidated the witness. Second, Daniel's imitation of John with a falsetto voice, "as if" he were a woman, serves as a sort of "degradation ceremony" (Garfinkel 1956). By reenacting the drama, he ridicules the man on the other side before an audience of peers, further denigrating him by inviting collective criticism and laughter from colleagues. Third, the discussion of the strategy builds up and elevates Daniel's status as an attorney for his aggressive, yet rational control of the witness and the situation. Thus, the discussion creates a space for collectively reinforcing Daniel's intimidation strategy.

In addition to highlighting the use of intimidation in depositions, this example also illustrates the way aggression as legal strategy or rule-governed aggression (Benjamin 1988; Lyman 1987) and masculinity become conflated, whereas aggression, which is not rule governed, is ridiculed as feminine. John shows his anger, but it is deemed inappropriate, because he loses control of the situation. Such a display of hostility does not serve the interests of the legal profession, because it does not achieve the desired result—a win for the case. As a result, Daniel and his associate regard John's behavior —his lack of control, his seeming hysteria and high voice—with contempt. This contempt takes on a specific sexual character. Just as the working class "lads" in Paul Willis's (1977) book, *Learning to Labor*, denigrate the "earholes" or sissies for their feminine attributes, Daniel and his colleagues ridicule John for his female-like behavior. Aggression as legal strategy or maleness is celebrated; contempt is reserved for aggression (or behavior) that is not rule governed and behavior that is also associated with the opposite sex.

Attorneys also used the confrontational approach in depositions at Bonhomie Corporation. In a deposition I sat in on, Mack, a litigator, used an aggressive cross-examination of the key witness.

Q: What were the names of the people that have migrated from one of the violators, as you call it, to Bonhomie Corporation?
A: I don't remember as of now.
Q: Do you have their names written down?
A: No.
Q: Well, if you don't remember their names and they're not written down, how can you follow their migration from one company to another?
A: You can consider it in the process of discovery that I will make some inquiring phone calls.

Q: Did you call anyone to follow their migration?
A: Well, I was unsuccessful as of yet to reach other people.
Q: Who have you attempted to call?
A: I can't tell you at this time. I have a list of processes in my mind to follow.
Q: Do you recall who you called and were not able to reach?
A: No.
Q: What's the list of processes in your mind to follow?
A: It's hard to describe.
Q: In other words, you don't have a list?
A: [quietly] Not really.
Q: Mr. Jensen, instead of wasting everyone's time and money, answer the question yes or no!
Opposing Counsel: Don't badger the witness.
Q: Answer the question, Mr. Jensen, yes or no!
Opposing Counsel: I said, don't badger the witness.
Q: Mr. Jensen, you are still required to answer the question!
A: [quietly] No.

In this case, Mack persisted in badgering the witness, who provided incoherent and vague answers. In response to the question, "Well, if you don't remember their names and they're not written down, how can you follow their migration from one company to another?" the witness gave the vague reply: "You can consider it in the process of discovery that I will make some inquiring phone calls." As the witness became more evasive, the attorney became more confrontational, "Answer the question, Mr. Jensen, yes or no!" By using this approach, the lawyer succeeded in making the witness appear even more uncooperative than he actually was and eventually pushed him to admit that he didn't have a list.

Later, in the same deposition, the attorney's confrontational tactics extended to opposing counsel.

Q: Let's change the subject. Mr. Jensen, can you tell me what representations were made to you about the reliability of the Bonhomie Corporation's spider system?
A: Nancy, the saleslady, said they use it widely in the United States, and could not be but very reliable. And, as we allege, fraudulent, and as somebody referred to it, was the, they wanted to give us the embrace of death to provide us more dependency, and then to go on and control our operation totally [sic].
Q: Who said that?
A: My attorney.
Q: When was that?
Opposing Counsel: Well, I . . .
Mack: I think he's already waived it. All I want to know is when it was supposedly said.
A: Well . . .
Opposing Counsel: I do use some great metaphors.

Mack: Yes, I know, I have read your complaint.
Opposing Counsel: Sorry?
Mack: I have read your complaint. That will be all for today, Mr. Jensen.

Here, the attorney did not stop with badgering the witness. When the witness made the statement about the "embrace of death," Mack was quick to find out who said it. And when opposing counsel bragged about his "great metaphors," Mack parried back with a sarcastic retort, "Yes, I know, I have read your complaint." Having had the final word, he abruptly ended the deposition. Like the other deposition, this one was not only an arena for intimidating the witness but for ridiculing the attorney on the other side. In this way, intimidation was used to control the witness and sarcasm to dominate opposing counsel. In doing so, Mack had achieved the desired result—the witness's submission to his line of questioning and a victory over the other side. Furthermore, in his replay of the deposition to his colleagues, he characterized his victory as a "macho blast against the other side," thereby underscoring the masculine character of his intimidation tactics.

Strategic Friendliness

Mr. Choate's appeal to the jury began long before final argument. His manner to the jury was that of a *friend* [italics added], a friend solicitous to help them through their tedious investigation never an "pen combatant, intent on victory, and looking upon them as only instruments for its attainment. (Wellman 1903/1986, 16–17)

The lesson implicit in Wellman's anecdote about famous nineteenth-century lawyer Rufus Choate's trial tactics is that friendliness is another important strategy the litigator must learn and use to be successful in the courtroom. Like the use of aggression, the strategic use of friendliness is another feature of gamesmanship and, hence, another component of emotional labor. As Richard, one of the attorney-teachers at NITA stated, "Lawyers have to be able to vary their styles, they have to be able to have multiple speeds, personalities and style." In his view, intimidation did not always work and he proposed an alternative strategy, what he called "the toe-in-the-sand, aw shucks routine." Rather than adopting an intimidating stance vis-à-vis the witness, he advocated "playing dumb and innocent." "Say to the witness, 'Gee, I don't know what you mean. Can you explain it again?' until you catch the witness in a mistake or an inconsistent statement." Other litigators, such as Leonard Right (1987), call this the "low-key approach." As an illustration of this style, Ring describes how opposing counsel delicately handled the cross-examination of a child witness.

The lawyer for the defendant. . . stood to cross-examine. Did he attack the details of her story to show inconsistencies? Did he set her up for impeachment by attempting to reveal mistakes, uncertainties and confusion? I sat there praying that he would. But no, he did none of the things a competent defense lawyer is supposed to do. He was old enough to be the girl's grandfather. . . the image came through. He asked her very softly and politely: "Honey, could you tell us again what you saw?" She told it exactly as she had on my direct. I felt relieved. He still wasn't satisfied. "Honey, would you mind telling us again what you saw?" She did again exactly as she had before. He still wasn't satisfied. "Would you do it once more?" She did. She repeated, again, the same story—the same way, in the same words. By that time I got the message. The child had been rehearsed by her mother the same way she had been taught "Mary Had a Little Lamb." I won the case, but it was a very small verdict. (35–36)

Ring concludes that a low-key approach is necessary in some situations and advises against adhering rigidly to the prototypical combative style.

Similarly, Scott Turow (1987), lawyer and novelist, advises trying a variety of approaches when cross-examining the star witness, lie cautions against adopting a "guerrilla warfare mentality" in cross-examination and suggests that the attorney may want to create another impression with the jury:

Behaving courteously can keep you from generating hurt, and, in the process, smooth the path for a win. [In one case I worked on] the cross examination was conducted with a politesse appropriate to a drawing room. I smiled to show that I was not mean-spirited. The chief executive officer smiled to show that he was not beaten. The commissioners smiled to show their gratitude that everybody was being so nice. And my client won big. (40–42)

Being nice, polite, welcoming, playing dumb, or behaving courteously are all ways that a trial lawyer can manipulate the witness to create a particular impression for the jury. I term this form of gamesmanship strategic friendliness. Rather than bully or scare the witness into submission, this tactic employs the opposite—friendliness, politeness, and tact. Despite this seeming difference, it shares with the former an emphasis on the emotional manipulation of another person for a strategic end—winning one's case. For instance, the attorney in Ring's account is gentle and considerate of the child witness for two strategic reasons. First, by making the child feel comfortable, he brings to light the fact that her testimony has been rehearsed. Second, by playing the polite, gentle grandfatherly role, he has created a favorable impression of himself with the jury. Thus, he simultaneously demonstrates to the jury that the witness has been rehearsed and that he, as opposing counsel, is a nice guy. In this way, he improves his chances for winning. And, in fact, he did. Although he didn't win the case, the verdict for the other side was "small."

Although strategic friendliness may appear to be a softer approach than intimidation, it carries with it a strongly instrumental element. Consider the reasoning behind this particular approach. Ring's attorney is nice to the child witness not because he's altruistically concerned for her welfare. He utilizes gentility as a strategy to achieve the desired result—a big win in the courtroom. It is simply a means to an end. Although this approach may be less aggressive than intimidation, it is no less manipulative. Like the goal of intimidation, the central goal of this component of gamesmanship is to dominate and control others for a specific end. This end is best summed up by litigator Mark Dombroff (1989) who writes, "So long as you don't violate the law, including the rules of procedure and evidence or do violence to the canons of ethics, winning is the only thing that matters" (13).

This emphasis on winning is tied to hegemonic conceptions of masculinity and competition. Sociologist Mike Messner (1989) argues that achievement in sporting competitions, such as football, baseball, and basketball, serve as a measure of men's self-worth and their masculinity. This can also be carried over into the workplace. For example, in her research on men in sales, Leidner (1993) finds that defining the jobs as competition becomes a means for construing the work as masculine.

For litigators, comparing the number of wins to the courtroom and the dollar amount of damages or settlement awards allows them to interpret their work as manly. At Bonhomie Corporation and at Lyman, Lyman, and Portta, the first question lawyers often asked others after a trial or settlement conference was "Who won the case?" or "How big were the damages?" Note that both Ring and Turow also conclude their pieces with descriptions of their wits "I won the case, but the verdict was small" and "I won big." Trial attorneys who did not "win big" were described as "having no balls," "geeks," or "wimps." The fact that losing is associated with being less than a man suggests that the constant focus on competition and winning is an arena for proving one's masculinity.

One important area that calls for strategic friendliness and focuses on winning is jury selection or *voir dire*. The main purpose of *voir dire* is to obtain personal information about prospective jurors, to determine whether they will be fair, "favorably disposed to you, your client, and your case, and will ultimately return a favorable verdict" (Mauet 1980, 31). Once an attorney has made that assessment, biased jurors can be eliminated through challenges for cause and peremptory challenges. In an article on jury selection, attorney Peter Perlman (1988) maintains that the best way to uncover the prejudices of the jury "is to conduct *voir dire* in an atmosphere that makes prospective jurors comfortable about disclosing their true feelings" (5). He provides a checklist of strategies for lawyers to use that enable jurors to feel more comfortable. Some of these include the following:

> Given the initial intimidation that jurors feel, try to make them feel as comfortable as possible; approach them in a *natural, unpretentious, and clear manner*.
> Because jurors don't relate to "litigants" or "litigation," humanize the client and the dispute.
> *Demonstrate the sincere desire* to learn of the jurors's feelings. (5–9, italics added)

Perlman's account reveals that the underlying goal of jury selection is to encourage the jury to open up so that the lawyer can eliminate the jurors he doesn't want and develop a positive rapport with the ones who appear favorable to his case. This goal is supported not only by other writings on jury selection (Blinder 1978; Cartwright 1977; Mauet 1980; Ring 1983) but also through the training offered by NITA. As a teacher-judge said after the class demonstration on jury selection, "Sell your personality to the jury. Try to get liked by the jury. You're not working for a fair jury but one favorable to your side."

At NITA, teachers emphasized this point on the individual level. In their sessions on *voir dire*, students had to select a jury for a case that involved an employee who fell down the steps at work and severely injured herself. (Jurors in the class were other students, in addition to myself.) Mike, one of the students, proceeded with his presentation. He explained that he was representing the wife's employer. He then went on to tell the jury a little bit about himself "I grew up in a small town in Indiana." Then, he began to ask each of the jurors where they were from, whether they knew the witness or the experts, whether they played sports, had back problems, suffered any physical injuries, and ever had physical therapy. The instructor gave him the following comments:

The personal comments about yourself seem forced. Good folksy approach, but you went overboard with it. You threw stuff out and let the jury nibble and you got a lot of information. But the main problem is that you didn't find out how people feel about the case or about their relatives and friends.

Another set of comments:

Nice folksy approach but a bit overdone. Listen to what jurors say, don't draw conclusions. Don't get so close to them, it makes them feel uncomfortable. Use body language to give people a good feeling about you. Good personality, but don't cross certain lines. Never ask someone about their ancestry. It's too loaded a question to ask. Good sense of humor, but don't call one of your prospective jurors a "money man." And don't tell the jury jokes! You don't *win them over* [italics added] that way.

The sporting element to *voir dire* becomes "winning over the jury." This theme also became evident in discussions student lawyers had before and after jury selection. They discussed at length how best "to handle the jurors," "how to get personal information out of them," "how to please them," "how to make them like you," and "how to seduce them to your side." The element of sexual seduction is no more apparent than in the often used phrase, "getting in bed with the jury." The direct reference to sexual seduction and conquest suggests, as it did with the intimidation strategy used in cross-examination, that "winning over the jury" is also a way to prove one's masculinity. Moreover, the desired result in both strategic friendliness and intimidation is similar: obtaining the juror's submission and winning.

Strategic friendliness is used not only in jury selection but in the cross-examination of sympathetic witnesses. In one of NITA's hypothetical cases, a husband's spouse dies of an illness related to her employment. He sues his deceased wife's former employer for her medical bills, her lost wages, and "lost companionship." One of the damaging facts in the case that could hurt his claim for lost companionship was the fact that he had a girlfriend long before his wife died. In typical combative adversarial style, some of the student lawyers tried to bring this fact out in cross-examination to discredit his relationship with his wife. The teacher-judge told one lawyer who presented such an aggressive cross-examination,

It's too risky to go after him. Don't be so confrontational. And don't ask the judge to reprimand him for not answering the question. This witness is too sensitive. Go easy on him.

The same teacher gave the following comment to another student who had "come on too strong":

Too stern. Hasn't this guy been through enough already! Handle him with kid gloves. And don't cut him off. It generates sympathy for him from the jury when you do that. It's difficult to control a sympathetic witness. It's best to use another witness's testimony to impeach him.

And to yet another student:

Slow down! This is a dramatic witness. Don't lead so much. He's a sympathetic witness—the widower—let him do the talking. Otherwise you look like an insensitive jerk to the jury.

In the cross-examination of a sympathetic witness, teachers advised students not to be aggressive but to adopt a gentler approach. Their concern, however, is not for the witness's feelings but how their treatment of the witness appears to the jury. The jury already thinks the witness is sympathetic, because he is a widower. As a result, the lawyers were advised not to do anything that would make the witness appear more sympathetic and them less so. The one student who did well on this presentation demonstrated great concern for the witness. She gently asked him about his job, his marriage, his wife's job, and her illness. Continuing with this gentle approach, she softly asked him whether anyone had been able to provide him comfort during this difficult time. By doing so, she was able to elicit the testimony about the girlfriend in a sensitive manner. By extracting the testimony about the girlfriend, she decreased the jury's level of sympathy for the bereaved widower. How much companionship did he lose, if he was having an affair? At the same time, because she did so in a gentle manner, she increased the jury's regard for her. She presented herself as a nice person. Her approach is similar to Laura's in using "niceness" as a strategy. However, in Laura's case, being nice was not appropriate to a destructive cross-examination. In the case of cross-examining a sympathetic witness, such an approach is necessary.

Opening statements also provide an opportunity for using the nonconfrontational approach. NITA provided a hypothetical case called *BMI v. Minicom,* involving a large corporation that sues a small business for its failure to pay a contract. Minicom signed a contract for a $20,000 order of computer parts from BMI. BMI shipped the computer parts through UPS to Minicom, but they never arrived. According to the law in the case, the buyer bears the loss, typically through insurance, when the equipment is lost in mail. Mark gave an opening statement that portrayed Minicom as a small business started by ambitious, hard-working college friends "on their way to the big league in business." He played up the difficulties that small businesses face in trying to compete with giant corporations. And at a dramatic moment in the opening, he asked the jury to "imagine a world where cruel giants didn't squeeze out small companies like Minicom." The teacher provided the following comments:

> Good use of evocative imagery. BMI as cruel giant. Minicom squeezing in between the cracks. Great highlighting of the injustice of the situation.

The lawyer for Minicom attempted to gain sympathy from the jury by playing up the underdog role of his client—the small company that gets squeezed between the cracks of the cruel, dominating giant.

In his attempt to counter this image, Robert, the lawyer for BMI, used a courteous opening statement. He attempted to present himself as a nice guy. He took off his jacket, loosened his tie, smiled at the jury, and said, in a friendly conversational tone, "This case is about a broken contract. BMI fulfilled their side of the contract, Mr. Blakey, my client, worked round the clock to get the shipment ready for Minicom. He made phone call after phone call to inventory to make sure the parts got out on time. He checked and rechecked the package before he sent it to Minicom." He paused for dramatic emphasis and, looking sincere and concerned, said, "It's too bad UPS lost the shipment, but that's not BMI's fault. And now, HMI is out $20,000." He received the following comments from the teacher:

> Great use of gestures and eye contact. Good use of voice. You made the case sound simple but important. You humanized yourself and the people at BMI. Good building of sequence.

Here, the attorney for BMI tried to play down his client's impersonal, corporate image by presenting himself as a nice guy. Before he began his opening statement, he took off his jacket and loosened his tie to suggest a more casual and ostensibly less corporate image. He smiled at the jury to let them know that he was friendly—not the cruel giant depicted by opposing counsel. He used a friendly conversational tone to begin his opening statement. And he even admitted that it was not fair that the other side didn't get their computer parts. As the teacher's comments suggest, this strategy was most effective for this particular kind of case.

This approach can also be used in closing statements. In a hypothetical case, during which an insurance company alleged that the claimant set fire to his own business, the lawyer for the store owner tried to defuse the insurance company's strategy with a highly dramatic closing statement:

> Visualize Elmwood Street in 1952. The day Tony Rubino came home from the Navy. His father took him outside to show him a new sign he had made for the family business. It read "Rubino & Son." Standing under the sign "Rubino & Son" with his father was the happiest day of his life. [Pause] The insurance company wants you to believe, ladies and gentlemen of the jury, that Tony set fire to this family jewel. "I'll carry on," he told his father, and he did. . . . [With tears in her eyes, the lawyer concludes] You don't set fire to your father's dream.

The teacher's comments for Janine's closing statement were effusive:

Great! Well thought out, sounded natural. Good use of details and organization. I especially liked "I don't know what it's like to have a son, but I know what it's like to have a father." And you had tears in your eyes! Gave me the closing-argument goose bumps. Pitched emotion felt real, not phony.

Janine's use of sentimental and nostalgic imagery, the son returning home from the navy, the beginning of a father and son business, the business as the "family jewel" is reminiscent of a Norman Rockwell painting. It also serves to counter the insurance company's allegation that Tony Rubino set fire to his own store. With the portrait the lawyer paints and the concluding line, "You don't set fire to your father's dream," she rallies the jury's sympathy for Tony Rubino and their antipathy for the insurance company's malicious claim against them. Moreover, her emotional presentation of the story is so effective that the instructor thought it "sounded natural" and "felt real, not phony." The great irony here is that this is not a real case—it is a hypothetical case with hypothetical characters. There is no Tony Rubino, no family store, and no fire. Yet Janine's "deep acting" was so convincing that the teachers believed it was true—it gave him "the closing-argument goose bumps."

Strategic friendliness carries over from the courtroom to depositions. Before deposing a particularly sensitive or sympathetic witness, Joe, one of the attorneys in the private firm, asked me whether "there is anything personal to start the interview with—a sort of warm-up question to start things off on a personal note?" I had previously interviewed the woman over the phone, so I knew something about her background. I told him that she was a young mother who had recently had a very difficult delivery of her first child. I added that she was worried about the baby's health, because he had been born prematurely. At the beginning of the deposition later that afternoon, Joe said in a concerned voice that he understood the witness had recently had a baby and was concerned about its health. She appeared slightly embarrassed by the question, but with a slow smile and lots of encouragement from him, she began to tell him all about the baby and its health problems. By the time Joe began the formal part of the deposition, the witness had warmed up and gave her complete cooperation. Later, the attorney bragged to me and one of the associates that he had the witness "eating out of his hand."

After recording these events in my field notes, I wrote the following impressions:

> On the surface, it looks like social etiquette to ask the witness these questions, because it puts her at ease. It lets her know he takes her seriously. But the "personal touch" is completely artificial. He doesn't give a shit about the witness as a person. Or, I should say, only insofar as she's useful to him.

Thus, something as innocuous as a personal remark becomes another way to create the desired impression with a witness and thereby manipulate him or her. Perhaps what is most ironic about strategic friendliness is that it requires a peculiar combination of sensitivity to other people and, at the same time, ruthlessness. The lawyer wants to appear kind and understanding, but that is merely a cover for the ulterior motive—winning. Although the outward presentation of self for this form of emotional labor differs from intimidation, the underlying goal is the same: the emotional manipulation of the witness for a favorable result.

Conclusion

In this chapter, I have redefined gamesmanship as the utilization of legal strategy through a presentation of emotional self designed specifically to influence the feelings and judgments of a particular legal audience, such as the judge, the jury, opposing counsel, or the witness. Gamesmanship as emotional labor constitutes two main components—intimidation and strategic friendliness. Despite their apparent differences, both share an emphasis on the manipulation of others toward a strategic end, that is, winning a case. Whereas, the object of intimidation is to "wipe out the other side," playing dumb and being polite represent strategically friendly methods for controlling legal audiences and bringing about the desired "win." Furthermore, 1 have shown that the attempt to dominate and control judges, juries, and opposing counsel not only serves the goals of the adversarial model but also becomes a means for trial lawyers to assert a hegemonic form of masculinity. Lawyers who gain the other side's submission characterize their efforts as a "macho blast," "a male thing," or "something men get into," whereas those who do not are regarded as "sissies" and "wimps." Thus, it is through their very efforts to be successful litigators that emotional labor in this male-dominated profession is masculinized.

This chapter also suggests many questions for future research on the role of masculinity and emotions in organizations. Masculinity is often a taken-for-granted feature of organizational life. Yet the masculinization of occupations and professions has profound consequences for workers located within them. Not only do male litigators find themselves compelled to act in ways they may find morally reprehensible, but women working in these jobs "are increasingly marginalized facing sex discrimination and sexual harassment (Rhode 1988; Rosenberg, Perlstadt, and Phillips 1993). At the same time, because of its informal and seemingly invisible nature, emotional labor too is often unexamined and unquestioned (Fineman 1993). Given that organizations often intrude on emotional life means that the line between the individual and the job becomes a murky one. The litigator who refuses to play Rambo may not only be unsuccessful, he may find himself without a job. Thus, many questions still require our attention. Is emotional labor-gendered in other jobs? Under what conditions? When does emotional labor take on racialized or classed dimensions? When is it exploitative and when is it not? And finally, what role, if any, should emotions play in the workplace?

Notes

This chapter first appeared as Jennifer Pierce, "Rambo Litigators: Emotional Labor in a Male-Dominated Occupation," in Cliff Cheng, ed., *f*, 1–27, Sage Publications, 1993.

1. For examples, see Goldberg (1987), Margolick (1988), Miner (1988), and Sayler (1988).

2. For example, see the *National Law Journal's* (1986) article, "What America Really Thinks About Lawyers."

3. Classic studies on the legal profession have typically focused on the tension between professionalism and bureaucracy. For examples, see Smigel (1969), Carlin (1962), Spangler (1986), and Nelson (1988).

4. For example, in their classic book, *Lawyers and Their Work*, Johnstone and Hopson (1967) describe nineteen tasks associated with the lawyering role. In only two of these nineteen tasks do Johnstone and Hopson allude to the emotional dimension of lawyering—"emotional support to client" and "acting as a scapegoat," 119–120.

5. In addition to my field research, I also conducted sixty interviews with lawyers, paralegals, and secretaries, as well as eight interviews with personnel directors from some of San Francisco's largest law firms. Field work and interviews were also conducted at the National Institute of Trial Advocacy where I spent three weeks with litigators during a special training course on trial preparation. These methodological decisions are fully discussed in the introductory chapter to my book, *Gender Trials* (Pierce 1995). Please note, names of organizations and individuals have been changed throughout to protect confidentiality.

6. See Chapter 4, "Mothering Paralegals: Emotional Labor in a Feminized Occupation," in *Gender Trials*.

7. West and Zintmerman (1987) conceptualize gender as "a routine accomplishment embedded in everyday interaction," 1.

8. Blumberg (1967) describes lawyers as practicing a "confidence game." In his account, it is the client who is the "mark" and the attorney and other people in the court who collude in "taking him out." In my usage, litigators "con" not only their clients but juries, judges, and opposing counsel as well.

9. Special thanks to Laurence Rose, Lou Natali, and the National Institute of Trial Advocacy for allowing me to attend and observe NITA's special three-week training seminar on trial advocacy. All interpretations of NITA and its practices are my own and are not intended to reflect the goals or objectives of that organization.

10. Women were much more likely to be criticized for being "too nice." The significance of women being singled out for these kinds of "mistakes" is examined in Chapter 5, "Women and Men as Litigators," in *Gender Trials*.

11. Mauet (1980) describes two approaches to cross examination. In the first, the purpose is to elicit favorable testimony by getting the witness to agree with the facts that support one's case. On the other hand, a destructive cross-examination "involves asking questions which will discredit the witness or his testimony," 240.

12. The proper form of leading questions is allowed in cross-examination but not in direct examination. Mauet (1980) defines a leading question as "one which suggests the answer" and provides examples, such as "Mr. Doe, on December 13, 1977, you owned a car, didn't you?" 247. In his view, control comes by asking "precisely phrased leading questions that never give the witness an opening to hurt you," 243.

13. Women trial lawyers negotiate the masculinized norms of the legal profession in a variety of ways. See Chapter 5, "Women and Men as Litigators," in *Gender Trials*.

References

American Bar Association 1982. *Model Code of Professional Responsibility and Code of Judicial Conduct*. Chicago. National Center for Professional Responsibility and ABA.

Benjamin, J. 1988. *The Bonds of Love: Psychoanalysis, Feminism, and the Problem of Domination*. New York: Pantheon.

Berg, D. 1987. "Cross-examination." *Litigation: Journal of the Section of Litigation, American Bar Association* 141: 25–30.

Blinder, M. 1978. "Picking Juries." *Trial Diplomacy* 11: 8–13.

Blumberg, A. 1967. "The Practice of Law As Confidence Game: Organizational Co-Optation of a Profession." *Law and Society Review* 12: 15–39.

Brazil, W. 1978. "The Attorney As Victim: Toward More Candor About the Psychological Price Tag of Litigation Practice." *Journal of the Legal Profession* 3: 107–117.

Buchan, J. 1939. "The Judicial Temperament." In J. Buchan, *Homilies and Recreations.* 3rd ed. London: Hodder & Stoughton.

Burawoy, M. 1979. *Manufacturing Consent.* Chicago: University of Chicago Press.

Carlin, J. 1962. *Lawyers on Their Own.* New Brunswick, N.J.: Rutgers University Press,

Cartwright, R. 1977. "Jury Selection." *Trial* 28: 13.

Cheatham, E. 1955. *Cases and Materials on the Legal Profession.* 2nd ed. Brooklyn, N.Y.: Foundation.

Chodorow, N. 1978. *The Reproduction of Mothering: Psychoanalysis and the Sociology of Gender.* Berkeley: University of California Press.

Connell, R. W. 1987. *Gender and Power: Society, the Person, and Sexual Politics.* Stanford, Calif.: Stanford University Press,

Dombroff, M. 1989. "Winning Is everything!" *National Law Journal,* September 25, p. 13.

Fineman, S., ed. 1993. *Emotions in Organizations.* Newbury Park, Calif.: Sage.

Garfinkel, H. 1956. "Conditions of Successful Degradation Ceremonies." *American Journal of Sociology* 61, no. 11: 420–424.

Goldberg, D. 1987. "Playing Hardball." *American Bar Association Journal,* July 1, 48.

Hochschild, A. 1983. *The Managed Heart: Commercialization of Human Feeling.* Berkeley: University of California Press.

Johnstone, Q., and Hopson, D., Jr. 1967. *Lawyers and Their Work.* Indianapolis: Bobbs-Merrill.

Leidner, R. 1993. *Fast Food, Fast Talk: Service Work and the Routinization of Everyday Life.* Berkeley: University of California Press.

Luban, D. 1988. *Lawyers and Justice: An Ethical Study.* Princeton, N.J.: Princeton University Press.

Lyman, P. 1987. "The Fraternal Bond as a Joking Relationship: A Case Study of Sexist Jokes in Male Group Bonding." In M. Kimmel, ed., *Changing Men: New Directions in Research on Men and Masculinity,* pp. 148–163. Newbury Park, Calif.: Sage.

Margolick, D. 1988. "At the Bar: Rambos Invade the Courtroom." *New York Times,* August 5, p. B5.

Mauer, T. 1980. *Fundamentals of Trial Techniques.* Boston: Little, Brown.

Menkel-Meadow, C. 1985. "Portia in a Different Voice: Speculations on a Women's Lawyering Process." *Berkeley Women's Law Review,* Fall, pp. 39–63.

Messner, M. 1989. "Masculinities and Athletic Careers." *Gender and Society* 31: 71–88.

Milkman, R. 1987. *Gender at Work.* Bloomington: University of Indiana Press.

Miner, R. 1988. "Lawyers Owe One Another." *National Law Journal,* December 19, pp. 13–14.

Nelson, R. 1988. *Partners with Power.* Berkeley: University of California Press.

Perlman, P. 1988. "Jury Selection." *The Docket: Newsletter of the National Institute for Trial Advocacy* 122, 1.

Pierce, J. L. 1995. *Gender Trials: Emotional Lives in Contemporary Law Firms.* Berkeley: University of California Press.

Rhode, D. 1988. "Perspectives on Professional Women." *Stanford Law Review* 40: 1163–1207.

Rice, S. 1989. "Two Organizations Provide Training, In-House or Out." *San Francisco Banner,* May 24, p. 6.

Ring, L. 1983, July. "*Voir Dire*: Some Thoughtful Notes on the Selection Process." *Trial,* July, 72–75.

Ring, L. 1987. "Cross-Examining the Sympathetic Witness." *Litigation: Journal of the Section of Litigation, American Bar Association* 41, 35–39.

Rollins, J. 1985. *Between Women: Domestics and Their Employers.* Philadelphia: Temple University Press.

Rosenberg, J., Perlstadt, H., and Phillips, W. 1993. "Now That We Are Here: Discrimination, Disparagement and Harassment at Work and the Experience of Women Lawyers." *Gender and Society* 73, 415–433.

Sayler, R. 1988. "Rambo Litigation: Why Hardball Tactics Don't Work." *American Bar Association Journal,* March 1, p. 79.

Smigel, E. 1969. *The Wall Street Lawyer: Professional or Organizational Man?* 2nd ed. New York: Free Press.

Spangler, E. 1986. *Lawyers for Hire: Salaried Professionals At Work.* New Haven: Yale University Press.

Spence, G. 1988. *With Justice for None.* New York: Times Books.

Turow, S. 1987. "Crossing the Star." *Litigation: Journal of the Section of Litigation, American Bar Association* 141: 40–42.

Wellman, F. [1903] 1986. *The Art of Cross-Examination: With the Cross-Examinations of Important Witnesses in Some Celebrated Cases* 4th ed. New York: Collier.

West, C., and Zimmennan, D. 1987. "Doing Gender." *Gender and Society* 12: 125–151.

"What America Really Thinks About Lawyers." 1986. *National Law Journal,* October, p. 1.

Willis, P. 1977. *Learning to Labor.* Farnborough, U.K.: Saxon House.

7

THE CORPORATE CLOSET
Coming Out, Moving On

James D. Woods

L ong before Stuart learned that he would not make partner, he has begun to contemplate a change in strategy. "Everything seemed to hinge on my coming out," he recalls. "I was feeling more and more pressure to be social at work, and was increasingly convinced that that would be impossible until I came out. Being in the closet seemed to be the primary barrier." As the pressure mounted, Stuart considered his various options. "I was terrified, and I told myself that if I could get through the conversation itself, I would be fine. Everything else would fall into place if I could get my big, terrible secret out in the open."

These concerns were foremost in Stuart's mind as he sat through his performance review. "When the partners told me that I needed to be more social at work, I just let them talk. My assumption was that if we could identify the particular problem I faced in making partner, then I could do something about it. So when they said I should make more of an effort to socialize and chitchat with the other attorneys, I decided to address the issue head on." Stuart paused and uttered the words he thought would be so hard to say. "I explained that there was a good reason I wasn't hanging out with the other attorneys. I said that I was glad we were being clear about the problem—that the criticisms were of my social performance, not my work. If that's the case, I told them, I can identify the reason for it: I'm gay."

As Stuart made his announcement, the partners shifted in their seats. One of them took a quick puff on his cigar. "I realized that I had made both of them extremely nervous," Stuart says. "First there was this stunned silence. Then they both jumped in to assure me that they didn't care one way or another if I was gay. They said that their criticisms had nothing to do with my being gay or straight, and they insisted that it had never been a problem at the firm. To illustrate the point, one of them told a peculiar story. He said that homosexuality had never even been mentioned in the partnership meetings, except when they were discussing another associate who was 'openly gay,' by which I assume he meant flamboyant or effeminate. One of the senior partners had made a negative comment about the associate, but that partner had since left the firm."

Leaving the room, Stuart realized that he had just confronted one of his most longstanding fears. "It was as if the floor dropped out from beneath me," he says. "I knew that for the next several months—perhaps for the rest of my career—everything would be different. I had opened Pandora's box. What I didn't realize, before I came out, was just how different it would be. My intention at the time was just to get through that conversation. I didn't think much beyond that."

•　•　•

Like Stuart, gay men often speak of coming out as if it were the final frontier, the destination of a long and arduous journey. Yet in many ways coming out is less an arrival than a change in direction, the first step down a different but no less arduous road. There are at least as many ways of shaping a gay identity as there are of trying to evade one, and while the man who reveals his homosexuality no longer finds it necessary to hide, his change in strategy brings with it a new set of obligations. Where he was previously concerned with the maintenance of secrecy, he now faces decisions about where, when, and how often his sexuality is to be displayed. His responsibilities shift from the suppression of information to the mechanics of its disclosure: How should others be informed? How much should they know? And what will be the consequences of these choices? By coming out, a man trades one set of managerial tasks for another.

Integration strategies, which are characterized by the authentic expression of a man's sexuality, are increasingly common among gay professionals. Of the men we interviewed almost half had revealed themselves to one or more of their coworkers. Likewise, a 1992 survey of *Out/Look* readers found that 93 percent of lesbians and gay men had revealed themselves to one or more coworkers. Sixty-eight percent had discussed a same-sex lover with someone at work; 30 percent had displayed a photograph, ring, or some other symbol of the relationship; and 74 percent had been vocal about their beliefs on lesbian and gay political issues. In the gay press as well as in many mainstream publications stories now abound about lesbian and gay professionals who are openly gay at work.

The first step in using such a strategy is to come out. Except in those rare organizations that do not take heterosexuality for granted, a man must usually say or do something explicit to let others know that he is homosexual; silence on the subject constitutes an implicit claim to be heterosexual. A man's coming out is thus a crucial turning point in any relationship, marking a transition from the use of one strategy to another. It is also one of the quintessential gay experiences, a rite of passage familiar to all within the community. Dozens of books have been written on the proper ways to come out to parents and friends. Gay support groups, public meetings, and cocktail parties are often sites at which tips on coming out are freely sought and provided. Before the arrival of AIDS no subject was burdened with greater significance or prompted more advice, nervous laughter, or abject terror within gay circles.

The net effect has been a tendency, especially among those who remain in the closet, to focus their attention on the transition itself. In retrospect a man can usually pinpoint the precise encounter, telephone call, or letter in which he came out to a boss or coworker. He remembers laying the groundwork for his disclosure, giving his listener some kind of explanatory context. Sometimes he can recall the exact words that were used—and he rarely forgets the response. "You spend so much time worrying about the best way to come out," says Stuart, "that your attention is really focused on the coming out itself, not on what follows it."

The particular form of the disclosure is crucial, given that the initial revelation serves to "frame" a man's sexual identity for a specific audience. It supplies a context for it, establishing the terms of the discourse. The information itself may be conveyed in a gesture of friendship, "I'm telling you this because I want us to be closer"; a political demand, "This policy discriminates against lesbians and gay men, myself included"; even an expression of sexual interest "Can I buy you a drink?" Some men introduce their disclosures with talk about honesty, framing them as a matter of integrity, "I can't lie to you." Still others, sadly, must reveal themselves during conversations about HIV illness, as part of an appeal for compassion or financial assistance.

Whichever frame is used, it has consequences for the way a man's sexuality will be interpreted by others. Indeed, without such a frame, his coming out will strike them as puzzling. It will seem unmotivated, irrelevant; they will see no reason for it. As Kath Weston observed in *Families We Choose*, "The idea of going up to someone and bluntly stating, 'Hi, I'm gay,' without further elaboration elicits laughter from a lesbian or gay audience." As Milton explains, "You can't just *say* it. There has to be a reason for it, or it will seem ridiculous. People will think, 'Why is he telling me this?'"

Gay men often struggle to establish the appropriate frame, the right context for their disclosures. Indeed, they often complain that their inability to find the proper frame prevents them from coming out altogether. "Having everyone know is one thing," says Glen. "But *how* they find out adds another whole dimension." Glen worries that a formal announcement would seem too "political" or "aggressive." He doesn't want people to view his disclosure as "a conversation about sex. . . If they just learned that I was gay because their brother-in-law told them or something, I don't think there would be any problem. They'd say, 'Oh yeah, we knew that already,' or 'He's kind of an aloof jerk anyway, so it doesn't make any difference.' But if I *told* them, I think the emphasis would be more on my reason for coming out than on the essence of the message." Finding no such reason, Glen has never formally come out at work.

When Carter comes out to clients, he wants them to view his disclosure as a sign of their growing rapport, a token of trust between business partners. He tries to frame it accordingly. Only after a successful deal or two, after he's fully established his credentials with a client, does he mention the fact that he is gay. Until then he avoids sexual small talk altogether. Because he considers the particular form of the disclosure crucial, Carter was upset recently when a coworker preempted his handling of it. A new client let it be known that she was attracted to Carter but was told by one of his associates "not to waste [her] time. Carter's gay." Carter wasn't upset that his secret had been revealed but was furious that he had not been permitted to handle the matter himself. "I get mad about that sometimes," he says. "I mean, I should be the one to tell them. Other people in the office know I'm real open about it, so they don't think there's a problem with saying something. It's hard for me to make them understand that I'd like to be in control." Rather than learn about Carter's sexuality in a professional context—a company party, a business lunch—his client made the discovery when a third party discouraged her from making a romantic overture.

As he chooses the particular way in which to reveal his sexuality—and then manages its ongoing visibility—a man may be guided by one of several aims. Sometimes his goal is to accommodate, to put others at ease as they grapple with new and potentially discomforting information. Like Carter, a man may have no interest in creating a stir. Others hope to educate and enlighten, to create change, even to provoke. As with other strategies, there are a number of tactics at one's disposal.

Minimizing Visibility

Some men want others to be aware of their sexuality, but take steps to ensure that it will be as unobtrusive as possible. They strike a low profile, expressing their sexuality only in limited ways. They favor tacit acknowledgment of it to direct references or discussions. While their sexuality is no longer a secret, neither is it especially visible.

The minimizing approach is often used by stigmatized individuals who try to lessen their vulnerability by limiting their visibility. They fear that if they become too conspicuous or appear too numerous, they will invite retaliation. At Yale in the 1940s and 1950s, Jews tried to downplay their significant presence on campus, wary of provoking a backlash. Likewise, Rosabeth Kanter has observed that professional women sometimes try to become "socially invisible" when working in male-dominated environments. In order to blend into the predominant male culture, they try "to minimize their sexual attributes." Some adopt "mannish dress" or speech patterns. Others avoid public events and occasions for performance, staying away from meetings, working at home rather than in the office, keeping silent at meetings. Unlike male peers who seize every opportunity to make themselves noticed, these women try to blend. Like gay men who use a minimizing strategy, they are not trying to disguise their gender per se. Rather, they are trying to play down its visibility and the conspicuous status it bestows on them in male-dominated environments.

By coming out in indirect or unobtrusive ways, gay men hope to downplay the significance of their revelation. Some invite speculation by making suggestive remarks, encouraging their peers to read between the lines. Others allow coworkers to stumble across evidence—a photograph of a lover, a gay magazine—or to decode some subtlety in a conversation—the mention of what "we" plan to do for Christmas while denying them more explicit verbal cues. "I assume my secretary knows 'my deal' because of the demography of my phone calls," says Arthur. "So overwhelmingly male, so overwhelmingly cute and perky and *that age*, all with weird names, as she puts it, like Trevor and Thad and Biff. She says, 'Don't you have any friends with real names?'" Al seems to have reached a similar understanding with his secretary. "She knows I'm gay, because she takes phone calls from all my male friends. She chats to them and actually knows some of them because they have business relationships with the company. We talk about restaurants—I'm her 'cultural coordinator.' We also talk about the occurrence of AIDS among professional men." Some men say that their sexual identity is conveyed by their mere status as middle-aged bachelors. "Anyone who's a forty-one-year-old man, who's never been married, and who's never talked about a social life with women, has got to be an anomaly," says Burt. "The only explanation is that he's gay. Or that he has an old war wound."

Allusions and oblique signs of acknowledgment thus take the place of explicit conversation. Mitch feels that he has this sort of relationship with Neil, one of the other associates in his firm. The two men travel together and have worked closely on a number of important cases. Mitch feels certain that Neil "has me figured out." But until last summer he didn't give it much thought. "Neil wanted to rent a place in the Hamptons for his wife and daughter," Mitch recalls, "and I said, 'Well, if you want to rent my house for a week and a half, I'll rent it to you.' The only problem was that the house was full of photos of me and Jay [his lover]—there was no way you could stay in this house and not understand that this person was gay and lived here with his lover. Neil went out the next day and spent ten days in the house, and when he came back, he couldn't have been more cordial." Still, the men's shared understanding was never formally acknowledged until Jay and Mitch broke up. At this point it became obvious that Mitch was upset due to "relationship problems." When he finally confided in Neil that this relationship with Jay had ended, Neil tried to be supportive, asked questions, expressed sympathy.

Quite often, the men's reticence is encouraged by the fear that to go further, to be more explicit, would be to overstep the limits of their coworkers' tolerance. For seven years Les has worked in the same office, and feels certain that the other staff members perceive Brad, the man with whom he lives, to be his lover. "I'm sure the boss knows where I'm at with Brad. The first time you go on a vacation with your roommate, fine. But I go someplace with my roommate every year. And I talk too much. If my roommate were sixty there might not be much thought about it. But when your roommate's thirty-six—I'm sure that my boss knows." Les says that he'd like to be more up-front about his relationship with Brad. "I'd love to shout it from the treetops. It's really irritating that I have to be careful," he says. "But in a way I suppose I already have. If I didn't have Brad, I'd probably be more frustrated than I already am because no one would know where I'm at. By having a lover and doing things with him, I've already stated where I'm at."

Chuck confronted these same boundaries several years ago when his boss asked him to dinner, encouraging him to "bring a date." Although his coworkers know he is gay, Chuck was reluctant to invite his lover, John. "I guess if I felt completely comfortable that everybody knew and didn't have a problem with it, then it would be easier," he explains. "I just didn't know how well that would mix and go over." Craig, a VP of finance at American Express, says that while coworkers know about his sexuality, they may not be ready for an explicit display of it. "I've never spoken to anyone about sexuality, but I assume they all know," he says. "Craig's lover, Roland, frequently calls at work, and everyone knows that they live together. "There are people who've called me on the weekends or at seven in the morning and gotten Roland. I assume they at least suspect." When asked to imagine a hypothetical situation in which he and Roland were publicly identified as a couple, Craig shrugs. "I think many people are accepting as long as they're not confronted with it. It's easier for them that way."

There is a big difference, these men point out, between knowing about and actually facing a gay man's sexuality. Even men who are clearly identified with gay causes or activities are often reluctant to participate in personal conversations on the subject. Don cofounded the lesbian and gay employee association at Levi Strauss in San Francisco, and is known for his work on its behalf. His name and photograph have appeared in magazines and company newsletters. Yet despite his public role as an advocate, he is wary of drawing attention to his own personal life. "One thing about the company is that while I feel everybody is pretty accepting overall of working with a gay or lesbian person, they don't want to hear anything more about it. It's a more subtle form of discrimination is okay to be gay, but don't bring your partner to me and introduce him to my wife and have me confront that in my personal life." Although the company has an explicit nondiscrimination policy and is subject to city ordinances that protect lesbian and gay workers, the social barriers remain. "Nobody's going to come up and point to the photograph of a man on my bulletin board, and ask, 'Who's that?' They'll only ask the people who have children and families and a conventional relationship."

Even when coworkers seem interested and supportive, even when there is no immediate threat of discrimination, gay men are often wary of making explicit, unambiguous mention of their sexuality. Most feel safer behind veiled comments and insinuations. George has a flamboyant personal manner and recognizes that "my voice and walk give me away." He has even learned, through his boss, that his sexuality was discussed long ago by the committee that hired him. Nor are his romantic activities much of a secret in the office. Yet George remains reserved when speaking about his personal life. "Somebody I had a crush on called the office the other day," he recalls. "The secretary walked up with a message while I was talking to Rose and Jean, and they were both teasing me. It was a male name, obviously. Those two know I'm gay, though we've never actually used the word."

These signs of acceptance notwithstanding, George is afraid to push the envelope. "The acknowledgment issue is a big step for me," he says. "It's one thing for it to be understood, but it's another to go into open dialogue." In particular George decided not to invite a guest to the company's Christmas party and doesn't plan to take anyone next year. "I'm not real comfortable having people experience that interaction. It's probably a little bit of self-consciousness when it comes to the work environment." When asked how he would respond if someone else used "the word," explicitly asking him about his sexuality, George shudders. "It would be difficult to answer a direct question," he says. "I would never say no, because I think it's obvious that I'm gay." Yet George doesn't think he will hear a direct question until his coworkers are ready to take the next step. "I'd love to feel so comfortable that I could say it to anybody, but I don't think that will ever happen. I'm really responding to my coworkers' fears. Until that changes I'll have to position it a certain way to be socially acceptable."

Whether the boundary is the product of internalized fears or the discomfort of a man's peers, it limits expression of his sexuality. At thirty-eight, Roy has begun to find these boundaries restrictive. "I think virtually everyone has me figured out by now," he says. "My approach has been to gently send out signals over time. I wasn't terribly outgoing on this issue at first, but as I've felt more comfortable and safe, professionally, I've sent out more and more signals that I'm gay. My colleagues know that I went to Key West a couple of Christmases in a row. I have a share in Fire Island. I vacation in Provincetown. We're all in a small group of offices together, and if you hear my phone calls you know that there are a lot of men calling. Some of them call quite regularly. Last week I probably did my most 'outish' thing yet. I was invited to a screening of the new Quincy Jones movie, and I brought a guy that I've been seeing. It wasn't a major social function, but a lot of my business colleagues were there, and they saw me there with a guy whose name they may have recognized from my phone messages."

Roy hopes that these signals will facilitate his transition to full disclosure. "I'm looking for an opportunity to make a comment that explicitly puts on record the fact that I'm gay, so that everyone will understand that it's perfectly okay to talk about it. There have been a few occasions, not many, where we would be in a meeting and someone from outside would make some comment, and I would notice one of my colleagues artfully trying to move the conversation, trying to avoid an embarrassing train of thought. I would prefer that everyone be comfortable."

As his own comfort level grows, Roy wants to be more open, to dispense with caution and restraint. At the moment he fears that his sexuality is a "sensitive" issue at work, and he wants to desensitize it, to make it more of an everyday matter. He wants, in other words, to normalize his identity.

Normalizing the Abnormal

It's hard to be inconspicuous when others consider you extraordinary in some way. Men and women who are "abnormal"—whether the norm relates to sexuality, national origin, race, or job performance—receive special attention and scrutiny. They become the *gay* engineer, the *foreign* boss, the *black* accountant, the *top-ranked* salesman. Their difference, whether valued or devalued, sets them apart. "Everyone gets hung up about the fact that you're gay," says Barry. "It's hard to be just one of the gang."

To normalize his sexual identity, a gay man must make it seem mundane and familiar; he must assimilate it to the norm. He does this by downplaying differences between gay and straight lives, highlighting instead their many commonalities. He presents information about an unfamiliar sexuality in familiar, heterosexual terms. With his initial disclosure, in particular, he tries to establish common ground.

"Lovers" and "boyfriends" are the categories most often invoked by men who wish to normalize their identities in this way. Kirk has lived with his lover, Bruce, for a number of years. He was initially secretive at work about his life with Bruce but soon grew dissatisfied with the resulting sense of detachment. He wanted to share more of his personal life with the staff, and needed a way to broach the subject. An opportunity finally came in the form of the hospital Christmas party. "I spoke to the divisional chairman, and told him that I was going to bring someone," Kirk recalls. "He said, 'That's fine. I'd be more worried if you didn't bring someone.'"

The groundwork laid, Kirk invited Bruce to the party. He then spoke to the department chairman's wife and told her that he would be bringing Bruce. "It was the first time I'd actually mentioned Bruce to anybody," he recalls. "I asked if she thought her husband was going to be too nervous about it. She said, 'Don't worry, he lived in San Francisco. He can deal with it.'" As it turned out, Bruce was warmly received. He was introduced as Kirk's "spouse" and was accepted as such by the other doctors and nurses. "Although I hate myself for saying it," Kirk adds, "it helped that Bruce doesn't fit any of the stereotypes about gay people. If it came to that, it wouldn't have made any difference, but it just wasn't an issue." Several years later Kirk and Bruce are known as an established couple, an identity that supplies a "normal" interpretation of Kirk's sexuality. As plans were made for last year's Christmas party, the chairman asked if Kirk would be bringing Bruce again.

"Bruce couldn't come because he was on call at the hospital, but the chairman said, 'Well, tell him we're sorry he couldn't make it.'"

Rob, a music instructor at a private school in the Philadelphia suburbs, reveals his sexuality in a similar fashion. For forty years Rob has lived with his lover, Albert, and frequently brings him to performances and recitals. "They've all known Albert for so many years," Rob says. "They always knew him, because I always brought him to everything." For Rob revealing his sexuality amounts to revealing his "marital" status. "Everyone knows, without me having a badge on my chest, that I'm gay. They know that I live with another man and have for forty years."

As friendships develop at work, Rob eventually mentions his relationship with Albert. "Last year, there was a young woman, Sarah, who taught violin. We wanted to do a performance of the Ravel Trio. It was obvious to me that she was a lesbian. I mean, good Lord. We started to work on the piece, and Sarah said to me, 'You'll have to come out to my house. Kathy and I would love to have you.' And I said, 'Well, you'll have to come out to our house. Albert and I would love to have you.' So it was that kind of mutual thing." Rob and Sarah both divulged their sexuality in the familiar and expected context of a conversation about their respective domestic relationships. "If a teacher came up to me and asked if I was gay, I'd say, 'Yes, of course,'" Rob says. "But it has never come up that way."

Domestic events can also be arranged to demonstrate normalcy, to make gay households seem ordinary to coworkers. Russ recalls a dinner party he threw, in part because he wanted to put his home life on display. He invited four of his coworkers to the apartment he shares with his lover, Ed. He gave them a tour of the house, the shared bedroom, and the shared automobile. "Ed and I bought a Jeep, and I used to talk about the fact that it was his idea, that it was too expensive and we can't afford it, and that kind of stuff." His peers apparently got the message and are now comfortable talking about Ed. Sometimes they even joke about it. "Ed's a plumber, and maybe they'll say, 'Well, you gonna get your pipes cleaned out tonight?' Something like that."

For others the end of a romance supplies common ground, an opportunity for gay men to share a familiar experience with nongay peers. "Jay was a major part of my life," says Sean of his former lover. "Whenever I talked about weekend plans, Jay's name automatically cropped up. If I hadn't been dating someone, they probably wouldn't have known that I'm gay." When Sean and Jay ultimately broke up, Sean's coworkers were supportive. They expressed concern and told him of their own disappointments. It was a bonding experience, Sean recalls, and it gave him a chance to talk about things that usually went unsaid. Peers who might otherwise have avoided the subject were comfortable using the language and gestures of sympathy.

Gay men also emphasize the normalcy of their lives by stressing beliefs or interests they share with straight colleagues despite the differences in their sexual orientation.

Indeed, some find it easiest to come out in the course of a discussion about political beliefs and civil rights. By raising the subject of homosexuality in these contexts they depersonalize it, even as they reveal their own particular relationship to the subject at hand. Al unintentionally revealed himself when his boss spied him mailing a letter to a gay organization. "I put an envelope with a dues check in my out bin, to Philadelphia Attorneys for Human Rights. PAHR is the gay attorneys group, and my boss noticed it. He's liberal, and was involved in other human rights organizations. He said, 'Tell me about this organization. What do they do?' I wasn't going to lie and tell him it was something else. So we talked about it." The ensuing conversation was framed as a dialogue about civil rights and the role attorneys play in their defense.

In recent years AIDS activism has become another route through which many gay men reveal their sexuality. "Everyone knows that I work for Action AIDS," according to Rob, "and while that's not really a gay organization, in the eyes of most people it is. Like it or not, AIDS is a gay men's disease for many, many people. You work with a gay organization, you're a gay man." Jerry's activism became public news when he cosponsored the first AIDS Walk in New York. "My name ends up getting plastered all over the city," he says, "because the posters for the AIDS Walk have the names of the major sponsors. A lot of the other traders came up to me and said, 'I saw your name in the press.'" Glen expressed his concern in more personal terms. "I identified myself as being part of a vulnerable minority," he says, recalling a conversation with the CEO of his company. "We were talking about AIDS in another context. I admitted that it was a personal concern because I considered myself more susceptible than the average person, because I belong to an affected minority." In doing so Glen emphasized the civil rights and public health implications of his sexuality, concerns he knew his boss, as an attorney, would feel comfortable discussing.

In their efforts to make the unusual seem usual, gay men often find that they have assumed the role of instructor, educating or enlightening their peers on the subject of homosexuality. To normalize their own identities, they set themselves up as authorities. They encourage others to use them as a resource. They also try to debunk some of the more absurd myths they encounter about gay people. Patrick recalls a question he got from a coworker. "My administrative assistant, Diane, asked me, 'Who's the girl?' She didn't ask the question directly. She said, 'Patrick, I've been meaning to ask you'. . . . We were talking about my ex-boyfriend, and I said, 'You want to know who's the girl, John or me, right?' And she said, 'Yeah, how'd you know?' And I said, 'I get asked that occasionally.'" The question led to a conversation in which Patrick tried to fill a few gaps in Diane's understanding. "She had decided, at first, that I was the girl. Then she decided he was the girl because he's much more nurturing. I tried to explain that things don't work that way."

Barry is especially fond of enlightening his coworkers with carefully placed comments and rebukes. Shortly after joining a large Manhattan firm, Barry began dating a man named Leonard. When talking about Len at work, he routinely found that his associates assumed he was dating a woman named Lynn. One time, he recalls, "one of the summer associates said, 'Well, what's she like?' I replied, 'You mean, what's he like?'" After a quick "Oops," the associate recovered and the conversation moved on. On other occasions, when coworkers ask about his marital status, Barry offers a quick rectification. "I'd say, 'We've got to get some things straight here.' And they'd say, 'What?' And I'd say, 'Well, I'm not married, but if you know a nice guy, I'd like to be.' Something like that."

With these pointed "corrections," Barry hopes to make his sexuality seem mundane, un-extraordinary. During recruiting lunches, for example, he raises the issue in a casual way. "I take the summer associates out to lunch, and we go to Lutece. It's a big deal, a three-hour lunch, and they always get smashola drunk. And they always ask me about being gay, with maybe three exceptions out of a hundred candidates that I took there. They say, 'You know, you're the first gay person I've ever known.' And I say, 'No, I'm not, I'm just the first one you know about.'" Even when these lessons get out of hand, Barry tries to normalize the situation. "Some guys try to be smart," he says. "They try to say things that will make me say, 'That's none of your business.' And I would never do that. So they ask, 'Well, how many people have you slept with?' And I just tell them. Anything they ask, I answer straight out, in a totally matter-of-fact way. That shuts them up after a while."

Other men joke with their peers as a way of desensitizing the subject. Keith uses this tactic with one of his coworkers. "She found out that I'm gay, and I knew that she was having trouble with it. So I told her a joke. I said, 'Do you know what's worse than a guy with a switchblade?' And she said, 'I don't know.' So I said, 'A fag with a chipped tooth.' She kind of stood there for a second; she didn't know what to say. Then she started to laugh. Later she told me, 'Keith, you just took me aback; I didn't know what to think then.' Then after we started talking and stuff, she told me, 'I used to think that all gays were sick, that they were perverts. I'm really glad I got to meet you, because you've helped change my opinion of that. I realize now that when I was growing up and started liking little boys, that you did, too.'"

Especially when this sort of sexual banter is part of the daily routine, it can be an effective way of making others comfortable with a potentially troubling issue. "Sometimes we just sit around the lunch table and dish," says Peter, a Philadelphia realtor. "A lot of rude jokes go back and forth, which is par for the course." Some of these jokes are about gay people, which Peter hopes will make the subject "less of a big deal." Sean is also fond of jokes and says they help make his sexuality "more run of the mill. When they see that it's not an issue with me, that I don't have a problem with it, hopefully they won't have a problem with it, and it becomes more of an everyday situation for them. They can joke about it and make little asides, jests. I like that because it means that I'm getting somewhere with them, and they're able to see things in a different way than before. Hopefully when they have children, that will be passed on."

Carter, likewise, finds that his sense of humor is often the best way of putting coworkers at ease. His office is populated largely by women, and they often meet after work for a meal or cocktail together. "We just have a blast," says Carter, describing a typical lunch hour. "I show them pictures from a trip, with all guys, and they critique the different guys. Whoever I'm seeing will come to the office, and I'll introduce him around, stuff like that. We go cruise at the mall, and they'll go, 'Do you think he is?' and I'll go 'yeah' or 'no.' Then they'll say, 'Do you think he likes me or you?' Stuff like that. It's just a real open thing." By making his sexuality a casual subject—a matter of flirtations, vacations, and fleeting attractions—Carter has tried to normalize it for his coworkers.

Quite often other gay people are the subject of Carter's jokes. "I make fun of being gay sometimes," he says. "I'll say, 'Look at those faggots' or something like that, to get it out in the open." In June the office staff watched part of Houston's gay pride parade on television. "Some of our people, some office people, were on TV dressed up like girls, and the other people in the office thought that was kind of revolting. Laura was saying, 'Did you see them dressed up like girls? Wasn't that disgusting?'" Carter played along. "I can't get too nellie around them," he says, "and I think 90 percent of the negative comments involve somebody acting like a girl or being effeminate." Rather than question these stereotypes about gender-appropriate behavior, Carter joins the chorus of criticism. By playing to his coworkers' stereotypes about homosexuality he hopes to put them at ease. He makes fun of "effeminate" men and "dykey" women. He is careful not to seem "faggy" at work. At one point he got rid of a bathing suit that a woman at work told him was "really queer."

Whatever one thinks of Carter's tactics, his goal is to normalize his identity, to make homosexuality the functional equivalent of heterosexuality. Indeed, the chief aim of all normalizing strategies is the attainment of equality. Men who use them often say that they want only what their straight coworkers already have. They want the same privileges when it comes to talking about their sexuality. To achieve this, they become attentive, in their interactions with peers, to matters of balance and fairness. Jack explains, "After putting up with the frustration, for years, of having my male drinking buddies talk so openly about what was going on sexually—by God, now that I'm open, I'm going to discuss my life as openly as they discuss theirs." When the conversation turns to personal topics, Jack tries to balance his own revelations against those made by others. "Sometimes drawing that line is very hazy, and I have to be careful to stop short of deliberately rubbing people's noses in my sexuality when I don't have to. It's not an easy line to walk."

To draw this line some men look for analogues in the behavior of their peers. When a coworker reveals something about his sexual life, the remark is often taken as an invitation. "Once I know people fairly well, I'll say, 'So-and-so and I spent the weekend together' or something like that," says Chris. "They know I have a house in Virginia, and I take friends there. It becomes a part of conversation just like they talk about their own husbands or wives." Patrick simply monitors the ebb and flow of information between his coworkers, matching his own disclosures to those made by peers. "People talk about their families and their kids constantly," he says, "so I chime in with, 'We did this' and 'That's my family.' Or I'll mention gay friends who want to adopt, if we're talking about kids."

The result, for Patrick, is the sense that he is treated much like everyone else. "I think my relationship with people at work is probably much the same as a straight person's. Where I'm reserved, a lot of people are reserved. I don't really care that much who Diane's date was with, so I don't go into details about mine and say, 'He's really cute and his name is Mark, and he's five foot eleven inches.' I don't do that. But if Diane says something about her dates, I counter with something about mine. Sometimes when people are telling me a lot about their lives, I think, 'Well, it's my turn to talk now.'"

By educating their peers, and by highlighting the familiar aspects of an unfamiliar identity, gay men attempt to transform the unusual into the commonplace and acceptable. They situate self-disclosure in everyday narrative contexts—family, romance, civil rights—showing the connections between gay and straight lives. They remind straight peers that they share many of the same concerns—finding a date, making house payments, dealing with in-laws—thus supplying them a framework for thinking about gay relationships. With the parallels made evident, they encourage others to treat them as equals.

Dignifying Difference

An exclusive normalization strategy strikes some men as absurd. "Of course I'm different," says Sean. "My life has been shaped, in a profound way, by my sexuality." The real issue, he says, isn't the mere fact of his difference, but the particular use he has made of it. "My sexuality is more positive than negative, because that's how I've used it. I can see how it would easily be a negative, if you let it be. I personally don't let anything become a negative. Give me lemons, and I'll make lemonade."

Dignifying strategies assert control over the terms in which homosexuality is understood at work. Rather than emphasize how normal homosexuality is, assimilating it to the mainstream, these tactics preserve its marginality. Differences are transformed into assets. Instead of highlighting the many things gay men have in common with their heterosexual peers, these men draw favorable attention to the differences that do in fact exist.

Some men find themselves in work situations that require knowledge of the lesbian and gay community, and this becomes the basis for their choice of strategy. A man's employer may have a product it wants to market to gay consumers; others recognize that a large segment of their clientele is gay and thus has particular needs or concerns. In these situations, gay men have special access or insight that can be of use to their employers. While working on a marketing project involving a new AIDS medication, for example, Sean encouraged coworkers to take advantage of his familiarity with the community. "I was always deferred to in those situations," he recalls. "My opinion was always sought, and they pretty well took what I said as gospel." As far as Sean's boss was concerned, "My being gay was a boon for the company, because I knew how to deal with situations that came up on the AIDS drug we were working on, and was able to explain a lot of things they didn't understand. I thought of problems that there was absolutely no way a person who wasn't gay could possibly conceive of, like the ways we might be slighting certain subgroups."

Peter identified his connections to the gay community in his first interview with his current employer, a Philadelphia real estate firm. "When I interviewed with my boss, I told her that I wanted to advertise in the *Philadelphia Gay News*. She was completely open to it. I'd sold to several gay men before, and I suggested that I do an ad just for me, promoting myself as a realtor. There's a market out there for me, I told her. I just have to tap into it." Since that time she has encouraged Peter to handle the firm's advertising and public relations to the gay community. The other realtors, most of whom are heterosexual, seek his advice: What special living needs do gay clients have? How can I best reach gay customers?

Peter thinks that being gay can also be an asset in more indirect ways. As a marginal person, he has cultivated other, transferable talents that he now brings to the workplace. He says that he is a highly individualistic, creative person, traits that are useful in his line of work. "There are a lot of gay people in real estate, especially in residential real estate," he says. "I guess it's because in homosexuality there tends to be a lot of individuality, and this is a very individualized business." Michael says that gay people also have an edge in his line of work, a branch of consulting best known by the euphemism "competitive intelligence." Michael's job often requires him to work under cover, posing as a college student or researcher, to dig up information on companies that compete with his clients. "I think that for what we do, being gay is an advantage," he says. "I genuinely believe that in corporate spying—whether it's called competitive intelligence or whatever—being sensitive to context, to what is said and how it's being said, is a really important part of the business. Being gay, in this culture, means being sensitive to context." When hiring junior associates, Michael favors other gay people.

John says that his sexuality is crucial to the work he does. Although he does not consider himself "corporate" in the usual sense, he faces the same pressures from his boss the bishop and his peers in other congregations. John began his career as the associate pastor at a large, fashionable congregation in the Philadelphia suburbs. Most of his parishioners were married, and John felt that this limited his effectiveness. Upon his retirement, the head pastor told John that the church needed a replacement who would understand these people's lives. 'I can't give you the job because we really need a married man in that job,' he told me. That's as close as he came to saying that he would have been embarrassed to have a gay man. He used the word single. He wouldn't use the word gay."

Several years later John was invited to interview for a position with a congregation in downtown Philadelphia. He met with the vestry, who told him that the congregation was a diverse group of single, elderly, and gay people. They were worried that the church had not managed to attract many married couples, and wanted to know how John would tackle that problem. John encouraged them to see that "the common theme in the congregation is 'singleness.'" He urged them not to worry about courting married people, to take pride in the fact that they made single people feel at home.

As a single gay man, he told them that he could "model singleness" for the congregation. His marital status, which had been a handicap in the suburbs, became an asset in his new congregation; rather than hide or downplay his experiences as a marginal person, John made them a selling point. "In the interview, I said that in many ways, being gay saved my life. I've always been very positive about being gay once I came out, because I really think it's the best thing that ever could have happened to me. I'm looking at all these faces in the interview, and I said, 'I'm like you. I'm an upper-middle-class white kid from the suburbs. I'm male, and there's nothing in my background that would have enabled me to make a connection with the oppression of other people if I weren't gay.' Being gay helped me make sense of the world, to some degree—the way the world really is."

Unfortunately no more than a handful of gay professionals manage to turn their sexuality into an asset in the eyes of their peers. They often point out that their sexuality is an asset in one way or another. They recount experiences and insights that would have eluded them had they lived more conventional lives. They describe risks taken and opportunities pursued, and explain these as a function of an avant-garde sensibility, freedom from marital responsibilities, or a deep-seated insecurity that drives them to work—traits that are tapped in subtle, often unrecognized ways. Yet rarely do they feel that coworkers recognize the role their sexuality has played in the kind of professionals they have become. While employers are only too happy to exploit a gay man's unique or special qualifications, they usually do not want to know about the personal struggles in which he acquired them.

Discussion Questions

1. How has men's work changed in the past ten years?
2. What ten jobs would you say most people in U.S. society would consider primarily men's jobs? What characteristics make certain jobs men's jobs?
3. What special barriers do black men and gay men face in the world of work?
4. How could a young black male job applicant overcome the perception of many employers, as reported by Cherry, that young black men are troublesome and often noncompliant employees? How can the negative perception of employers about young black males be changed?
5. Do you believe that the most aggressive litigators are the most successful? Using the ideas in Pierce's article, discuss the role of aggression versus empathy and friendly politeness as strategies to win cases.
6. In your chosen field, if one of your co-workers were a gay man, how do you think Woods would predict that your personal and professional interactions would be affected?

Part III

WOMEN AND MEN IN NONTRADITIONAL JOBS

Women and men who work apart from most others in their own gender find that the work setting provides a unique opportunity to experience, and at times suffer with, the same larger gender issues that confront them away from work. For the groundbreaking women and men who cross female- and male-dominated occupational lines, employment becomes more than paid labor. It provides an opportunity to test the role reversal of genders in work. However, for women who enter male fields, the road to promotion and acceptance is quite unlike a man's experience there, and often much less positive.

In the first piece for this section, "The Glass Escalator: Men Who Do Women's Work," Christine Williams looks at men who enter the feminized fields of nursing, primary teaching, library science, and social work. She finds, in addition to myriad other positive outcomes, that men fare quite well when they cross the road. This positive outcome arises because the men who work in "women's jobs" increase the status of that work, and along with status enhancement often come salary increases and promotions.

In this selection from *Ladies on the Lot: Women, Car Sales, and the Pursuit of the American Dream*, Helen Lawson writes of the interesting and traditionally masculine field of car sales. She explains that, unlike Williams's environment, which provides entitlement in a unique turn of token status for men in typically feminine work, car dealerships are replete with regular instances of gender-related harassment. The case of car sales is a good example of how men's and women's early socialization (in which, for example, boys are encouraged to learn about cars long before their jobs in dealerships) will leave the genders differentially qualified.

Finally, Susan Martin's "Outsiders Within the Station House: The Impact of Race and Gender on Black Women Police," presents a terrific case of how race and sex combine to create a distinct social consciousness for the women who work in the very masculine field of police work. In her work, discrimination with a "one-two" punch, otherwise known as double jeopardy, is tested. Although the opportunities for minority men and women to work in police departments has increased, both subtle and overt barriers remain.

These three authors describe atypical work settings and the unanticipated consequences of moving across gender in them—consequences often related to the original gender orientation of the work.

8

THE GLASS ESCALATOR
Men Who Do Women's Work

Christine Williams

*This chapter addresses men's underrepresentation in four predomi-
nantly female professions: elementary school teaching, librarianship,
and social work. Specifically, it examines the degree to which discrimination disadvantages men in hiring and promotion decisions,
the work place culture, and in interactions with clients. In-depth interviews were conducted with ninety-nine men and women in these
professions in four major U.S. cities. The interview data suggest that
men do not face discrimination in these occupations; however, they
do encounter prejudice from individuals outside their professions. In
contrast to the experience of women who enter male-dominated professions, men generally encounter structural advantages in these occupations that tend to enhance their careers. Because men face
different barriers to integrating nontraditional occupations than
women face, the need for different remedies to dismantle segregation
in predominantly female jobs is emphasized.*

The sex segregation of the U.S. labor force is one of the most perplexing and tenacious
problems in our society. Even though the proportion of men and women in the labor
force is approaching parity (particularly for younger cohorts of workers) (U.S. Department of Labor 1991, 18), men and women are still generally confined to predominantly
single sex occupations. Forty percent of men or women would have to change major occupational categories to achieve equal representation of men and women in all jobs
(Reskin and Roos 1990, 6), but even this figure underestimates the true degree of sex segregation. It is extremely rare to find specific jobs where equal numbers of men and women
are engaged in the same activities in the same industries (Bielby and Baron 1984).

Most studies of sex segregation in the work force have focused on women's experiences in male-dominated occupations. Both researchers and advocates for social

change have focused on the barriers faced by women who try to integrate predominantly male fields. Few have looked at the flip side of occupational sex segregation: the exclusion of men from predominantly female occupations (exceptions include Schreiber 1979; Williams 1989; Zimmer 1988). But the fact is that men are less likely to enter female sex-typed occupations than women are to enter male-dominated jobs (Jacobs 1989). Reskin and Roos, for example, were able to identify thirty-three occupations in which female representation increased by more than nine percentage points between 1970 and 1980, but only three occupations in which the proportion of men increased as radically (1990, 20–21).

In this chapter, I examine men's underrepresentation in four predominantly female occupations—nursing, librarianship, elementary school teaching, and social work. Throughout the twentieth century, these occupations have been identified with "women's work," even though prior to the Civil War, men were more likely to be employed in these areas. These four occupations, often called the female "semiprofessions" (Hodson and Sullivan 1990), today range from 5.5 percent male (in nursing) to 32 percent male (in social work) (See Table 8.1). These percentages have not changed substantially in decades. In fact, as Table 8.1 indicates, two of these professions—librarianship and social work—have experienced declines in the proportions of men since 1975. Nursing is the only one of the four experiencing noticeable changes in sex composition, with the proportion of men increasing 80 percent between 1975 and 1990. Even so, men continue to be a tiny minority of all nurses.

Although there are many possible reasons for the continuing preponderance of women in these fields, the focus of this paper is discrimination. Researchers examining the integration of women into "male fields" have identified discrimination as a major barrier to women (Jacobs 1989; Reskin 1988; Reskin and Hartmann 1986). This discrimination has taken the form of laws or institutionalized rules prohibiting the hiring or promotion of women into certain job specialties. Discrimination can also be "informal," as when women encounter sexual harassment, sabotage, or other forms of hostility from their male coworkers resulting in a poisoned work environment (Reskin and Hartmann 1986). Women in nontraditional occupations also report feeling stigmatized by clients when their work puts them in contact with the public. In particular, women in engineering and blue-collar occupations encounter gender-based stereotypes about their competence that undermine their work performance (Epstein 1988; Martin 1980). Each of these forms of discrimination—legal, informal, and cultural—contributes to women's underrepresentation in predominantly male occupations.

The assumption in much of this literature is that any member of a token group in a work setting will probably experience similar discriminatory treatment. Kanter (1977), who is best known for articulating this perspective in her theory of tokenism, argues that when any group represents less than 15 percent of an organization, its members will be subject to predictable forms of discrimination. Likewise, Jacobs argues that "in some ways, men in female-dominated occupations experience the same difficulties that women in male-dominated occupations face" (1989, 167), and Reskin contends that any dominant group in an occupation will use their power to maintain a privileged position (1988, 62).

TABLE 8.1   Percentage of Men in Selected Occupations, Selected Years

Profession	1990	1980	1975
Nurses	5.5	3.5	3.0
Elementary teachers	14.8	16.3	14.6
Librarians	16.7	14.8	18.9
Social workers	31.8	35.0	39.2

SOURCE: U.S. Department of Labor. Bureau of Labor Statistics. *Employement and Earnings* 38:1 (January 1991), Table 22 (Employed civilians by detailed occupation), 185; 28:1 (January 1981), Table 23 (Employed persons by detailed occupation), 180; 22:7 (January 1976), Table 2 (Employed persons by detailed occupation), 11.

However, the few studies that have considered men's experience in gender atypical occupations suggest that men may not face discrimination or prejudice when they integrate predominantly female occupations. Zimmer (1988) and Martin (1988) both contend that the effects of sexism can outweigh the effects of tokenism when men enter nontraditional occupations. This study is the first to systematically explore this question using data from four occupations. I examine the barriers to men's entry into these professions; the support men receive from their supervisors, colleagues and clients; and the reactions they encounter from the public (those outside their professions).

Methods

I conducted in-depth interviews with seventy-six men and twenty-three women in four occupations from 1985 to 1991. Interviews were conducted in four metropolitan areas: San Francisco/Oakland, California; Austin, Texas; Boston, Massachusetts; and Phoenix, Arizona. These four areas were selected because they show considerable variation in the proportions of men in the four professions. For example, Austin has one of the highest percentages of men in nursing (7.7 percent), whereas Phoenix's percentage is one of the lowest (2.7 percent) (U.S. Bureau of the Census 1980). The sample was generated using "snowballing" techniques. Women were included in the sample to gauge their feelings and responses to men who enter "their" professions.

Like the people employed in these professions generally, those in my sample were predominantly white (90 percent).[1] Their ages ranged from 20 to 66 and the average age was 38. The interview questionnaire consisted of several open-ended questions on four broad topics: motivation to enter the profession; experiences in training; career progression; and general views about men's status and prospects within these occupations. I conducted all the interviews, which generally lasted between one and two hours. Interviews took place in restaurants, my home or office, or the respondent's home or office. Interviews were tape-recorded and transcribed for the analysis.

Data analysis followed the coding techniques described by Strauss (1987). Each transcript was read several times and analyzed into emergent conceptual categories. Likewise, Strauss's principle of theoretical sampling was used. Individual respondents were purposively selected to capture the array of men's experiences in these occupations.

Thus, I interviewed practitioners in every specialty, oversampling those employed in the most gender atypical areas (e.g., male kindergarten teachers). I also selected respondents from throughout their occupational hierarchies from students to administrators to retirees. Although the data do not permit within group comparisons, I am reasonably certain that the sample does capture a wide range of experiences common to men in these female-dominated professions. However, like all findings based on qualitative data, it is uncertain whether the findings generalize to the larger population of men in nontraditional occupations.

In this paper, I review individuals' responses to questions about discrimination in hiring practices, on-the-job rapport with supervisors and coworkers, and prejudice from clients and others outside their profession.

Discrimination in Hiring

Contrary to the experience of many women in the male-dominated professions, many of the men and women I spoke to indicated that there is a preference for hiring men in these four occupations. A Texas librarian at a junior high school said that his school district "would hire a male over a female."

> I: Why do you think that is?
> R: Because there are so few, and the. . . ones that they do have, the library directors seem to really. . . think they're doing great jobs. I don't know, maybe they just feel they're being progressive or something, [but] I have had a real sense that they really appreciate having a male, particularly at the junior high. . . . As I said, when seven of us lost our jobs from the high schools and were redistributed, there were only four positions at junior high, and I got one of them. Three of the librarians, some who had been here longer than I had with the school district, were put down in elementary school as librarians. And I definitely think that being male made a difference in my being moved to the junior high rather than an elementary school.

Many of the men perceived their token status as males in predominantly female occupations as an advantage in hiring and promotions. I asked an Arizona teacher whether his specialty (elementary special education) was an unusual area for men compared to other areas within education. He said,

> Much more so. I am extremely marketable in special education. That's not why I got into the field. But I am extremely marketable because I am a man.

In several cases, the more female-dominated the specialty, the greater the apparent preference for men. For example, when asked if he encountered any problem getting a job in pediatrics, a Massachusetts nurse said,

> No, no, none. . . I've heard this from managers and supervisory-type people with men in pediatrics: "It's nice to have a man because it's such a female-dominated profession."

However, there were some exceptions to this preference for men in the most female-dominated specialties. In some cases, formal policies actually barred men from certain jobs. This was the case in some rural Texas school districts, which refused to hire men in the youngest grades (K-3). Some nurses also reported being excluded from positions in obstetrics and gynecology wards, a policy encountered more frequently in private Catholic hospitals.

But often the pressures keeping men out of certain specialties were more subtle than this. Some men described being "tracked" into practice areas within their professions which were considered more legitimate for men. For example, one Texas man described how he was pushed into administration and planning in social work, even though "I'm not interested in writing policy; I'm much more interested in research and clinical stuff." A nurse who is interested in pursuing graduate study in family and child health in Boston said he was dissuaded from entering the program specialty in favor of a concentration in "adult nursing." A kindergarten teacher described the difficulty of finding a job in his specialty after graduation: "I was recruited immediately to start getting into a track to become an administrator. And it was men who recruited me. It was men that ran the system at that time, especially in Los Angeles."

This tracking may bar men from the most female-identified specialties within these professions. But men are effectively being kicked upstairs in the process. Those specialties considered more legitimate practice areas for men also tend to be the most prestigious, better paying ones. A distinguished kindergarten teacher, who had been voted citywide Teacher of the Year, told me that even though people were pleased to see him in the classroom, "there's been some encouragement to think about administration, and there's been some encouragement to think about teaching at the university level or something like that, or supervisory-type position." That is, despite his aptitude and interest in staying in the classroom, he felt pushed in the direction of administration.

The effect of this "tracking" is the opposite of that experienced by women in male-dominated occupations. Researchers have reported that many women encounter a "glass ceiling" in their efforts to scale organizational and professional hierarchies. That is, they are constrained by invisible barriers to promotion in their careers, caused mainly by the sexist attitudes of men in the highest positions (Freeman 1990).[2] In contrast to the "glass ceiling," many of the men I interviewed seem to encounter a "glass escalator." Often, despite their intentions, they face invisible pressures to move up in their professions. As if on a moving escalator, they must work to stay in place.

A public librarian specializing in children's collections (a heavily female-dominated concentration) described an encounter with this "escalator" in his very first job out of library school. In his first six-months' evaluation, his supervisors commended him for his good work in storytelling and related activities, but they criticized him for "not shooting high enough."

> Seriously. That's literally what they were telling me. They assumed that because I was a male—and they told me this—and that I was being hired right out of graduate school, that somehow I wasn't doing the kind of management-oriented work that they thought

I should be doing. And as a result, really they had a lot of bad marks, as it were, against me on my evaluation. And I said I couldn't believe this!

Throughout his ten-year career, he has had to struggle to remain in children's collections. The glass escalator does not operate at all levels. In particular, men in academia reported some gender-based discrimination in the highest positions due to their universities' commitment to affirmative action. Two nursing professors reported that they felt their own chances of promotion to deanships were nil because their universities viewed the position of nursing dean as a guaranteed female appointment in an otherwise heavily male-dominated administration. One California social work professor reported his university canceled its search for a dean because no minority male or female candidates had been placed on their short list. It was rumored that other schools on campus were permitted to go forward with their searches (even though they also failed to put forward names of minority candidates) because the higher administration perceived it to be easier to fulfill affirmative action goals in the social work school. The interviews provide greater evidence of the "glass escalator" at work in the lower levels of these professions.

Of course, men's motivations also play a role in their advancement to higher professional positions. I do not mean to suggest that the men I talked to all resented the informal tracking they experienced. For many men, leaving the most female-identified areas of their professions helped them resolve internal conflicts involving their masculinity. One man left his job as a school social worker to work in a methadone drug treatment program not because he was encouraged to leave by his colleagues, but because "I think there was some macho shit there, to tell you the truth, because I remember feeling a little uncomfortable there. . . ; it didn't feel right to me." Another social worker, employed in the mental health services department of a large urban area in California, reflected on his move into administration:

> The more I think about it, through our discussion, I'm sure that's a large part of why I wound up in administration. It's okay for a man to do the administration. In fact, I don't know if I fully answered a question that you asked a little while ago about how did being male contribute to my advancing in the field. I was saying it wasn't because I got any special favoritism as a man, but. . . I think. . . because I'm a man, I felt a need to get into this kind of position. I may have worked harder toward it, may have competed harder for it, than most women would do, even women who think about doing administrative work.

Elsewhere I have speculated on the origins of men's tendency to define masculinity through single-sex work environments (Williams 1989). Clearly, personal ambition does play a role in accounting for men's movement into more "male-defined" arenas within these professions. But these occupations also structure opportunities for males independent of their individual desires or motives.

The interviews suggest that men's underrepresentation in these professions cannot be attributed to discrimination in hiring or promotions. Many of the men indicated that they received preferential treatment because they were men. Although men mentioned gender discrimination in the hiring process, for the most part they were channeled into more "masculine" specialties within these professions, which ironically meant being "tracked" into better paying and more prestigious specialties.

Supervisors and Colleagues: The Working Environment

Researchers claim that subtle forms of work place discrimination push women out of male-dominated occupations (Jacobs 1989; Reskin and Hartmann 1986). In particular, women report feeling excluded from informal leadership and decisionmaking networks, and they sense hostility from their male coworkers, which makes them feel uncomfortable and unwanted (Carothers and Crull 1984). Respondents in this study were asked about their relationships with supervisors and female colleagues to ascertain whether men also experienced "poisoned" work environments when entering gender atypical occupations.

A major difference in the experience of men and women in nontraditional occupations is that men in these situations are far more likely to be supervised by a member of their own sex. In each of the four professions I studied, men are overrepresented in administrative and managerial capacities, or, as is the case of nursing, their positions in the organizational hierarchy are governed by men (Grimm and Stern 1974; Phenix 1987; Schmuck 1987; Williams 1989; York, Henley and Gamble 1987). Thus, unlike women who enter "male fields," the men in these professions often work under the direct supervision of other men.

Many of the men interviewed reported that they had good rapport with their male supervisors. Even in professional school, some men reported extremely close relationships with their male professors. For example, a Texas librarian described an unusually intimate association with two male professors in graduate school:

> I can remember a lot of times in the classroom there would be discussions about a particular topic or issue, and the conversation would spill over into their office hours, after the class was over. And even though there were. . . a couple of the other women that had been in on the discussion, they weren't there. And I don't know if that was preferential or not. . . It certainly carried over into personal life as well. Not just at the school and that sort of thing. I mean, we would get together for dinner. . .

These professors explicitly encouraged him because he was male:

> I: Did they ever offer you explicit words of encouragement about being in the profession by virtue of the fact that you were male?. . .
> R: Definitely. On several occasions. Yeah. Both of these guys, for sure, including the Dean who was male also. And it's an interesting point that you bring up because it was, oftentimes, kind of in a sign, you know. It wasn't in the classroom, and it wasn't in front of the group, or if we were in the student lounge or something like that. It was. . . if it was just myself or maybe another one of the guys, you know, and just talking in the office. It's like. . . you know, kind of an opening up and saying, "You know, you are really lucky that you're in the profession because you'll really go to the top real quick, and

you'll be able to make real definite improvements and changes. And you'll have a real in-fluence," and all this sort of thing. I mean, really, I can remember several times.

Other men reported similar closeness with their professors. A Texas psychotherapist recalled his relationships with his male professors in social work school:

> I made it a point to make a golfing buddy with one of the guys that was in administra-tion. He and I played golf a lot. He was the guy who kind of ran the research training, the research part of the master's program. Then there was a sociologist who ran the other part of the research program. He and I developed a good friendship.

This close mentoring by male professors contrasts with the reported experience of women in nontraditional occupations. Others have noted a lack of solidarity among women in nontraditional occupations. Writing about military academies, for example, Yoder describes the failure of token women to mentor succeeding generations of fe-male cadets. She argues that women attempt to play down their gender difference from men because it is the source of scorn and derision.

> Because women felt unaccepted by their male colleagues, one of the last things they wanted to do was to emphasize their gender. Some women thought that, if they kept company with other women, this would highlight their gender and would further iso-late them from male cadets. These women desperately wanted to be accepted as cadets, not as women cadets. Therefore, they did everything from not wearing skirts as an op-tion with their uniforms to avoiding being a part of a group of women. (Yoder 1989, 532)

Men in nontraditional occupations face a different scenario—their gender is construed as a positive difference. Therefore, they have an incentive to bond together and em-phasize their distinctiveness from the female majority.

Close personal ties with male supervisors were also described by men once they were established in their professional careers. It was not uncommon in education, for exam-ple, for the male principal to informally socialize with the male staff, as a Texas special education teacher describes:

> Occasionally I've had a principal who would regard me as "the other man on the cam-pus" and "it's us against them," you know? I mean, nothing really that extreme, except that some male principals feel like there's nobody there to talk to except the other man. So I've been in that position.

These personal ties can have important consequences for men's careers. For exam-ple, one California nurse, whose performance was judged marginal by his nursing su-pervisors, was transferred to the emergency room staff (a prestigious promotion) due to his personal friendship with the physician in charge. A Massachusetts teacher ac-knowledged that his principal's personal interest in him landed him his current job

I: You had mentioned that your principal had sort of spotted you at your previous job and had wanted to bring you here [to this school]. Do you think that has anything to do with the fact that you're a man, aside from your skills as a teacher?
R: Yes, I would say in that particular case, that was part of it. . . . We have certain things in common, certain interests that really lined up.
I: Vis-à-vis teaching?
R: Well, more extraneous things—running specifically, and music. And we just seemed to get along real well right off the bat. It is just kind of a guy thing; we just liked each other. . .

Interviewees did not report many instances of male supervisors discriminating against them, or refusing to accept them because they were male. Indeed, these men were much more likely to report that their male bosses discriminated against the females in their professions. When asked if he thought physicians treated male and female nurses differently, a Texas nurse said:

I think yeah, some of them do. I think the women seem like they have a lot more trouble with the physicians treating them in a derogatory manner. Or, if not derogatory, then in a very paternalistic way than the men [are treated]. Usually if a physician is mad at a male nurse, he just kind of yells at him. Kind of like an employee. And if they're mad at a female nurse, rather than treat them on an equal basis, in terms of just letting their anger out at them as an employee, they're more paternalistic or there's some sexual harassment component to it.

A Texas teacher perceived a similar situation where he worked:

I've never felt unjustly treated by a principal because I'm a male. The principals that I've seen that I felt are doing things that are kind of arbitrary or not well thought out are doing it to everybody. In fact, they're probably doing it to the females worse than they are to me.

Openly gay men may encounter less favorable treatment at the hands of their supervisors. For example, a nurse in Texas stated that one of the physicians he worked with preferred to staff the operating room with male nurses exclusively—as long as they weren't gay. Stigma associated with homosexuality leads some men to enhance, or even exaggerate their "masculine" qualities, and may be another factor pushing men into more acceptable specialties for men.

Not all the men who work in these occupations are supervised by men. Many of the men interviewed who had female bosses also reported high levels of acceptance, although levels of intimacy with women seemed lower than with other men. In some cases, however, men reported feeling shut out from decision making when the higher administration was constituted entirely by women. I asked an Arizona librarian whether men in the library profession were discriminated against in hiring because of their sex:

Professionally speaking, people go to considerable lengths to keep that kind of thing out of their [hiring] deliberations. Personally, is another matter. It's pretty common around here to talk about the "old girl network." This is one of the few libraries that I've had any intimate knowledge of which is actually controlled by women. . . . Most of the department heads and upper level administrators are women. And there's an "old-girl network" that works just like the "old-boy network," except that the important conferences take place in the women's room rather than on the golf course. But the political mechanism is the same, the exclusion of the other sex from decision making is the same. The reasons are the same. It's somewhat discouraging. . .

Although I did not interview many supervisors, I did include twenty-three women in my sample to ascertain their perspectives about the presence of men in their professions. All of the women I interviewed claimed to be supportive of their male colleagues, but some conveyed ambivalence. For example, a social work professor said she would like to see more men enter the social work profession, particularly in the clinical specialty (where they are underrepresented). Indeed, she favored affirmative action hiring guidelines for men in the profession. Yet, she resented the fact that her department hired "another white male" during a recent search. I questioned her about this ambivalence:

I: I find it very interesting that, on the one hand, you sort of perceive this preference and perhaps even sexism with regard to how men are evaluated and how they achieve higher positions within the profession, yet, on the other hand, you would be encouraging of more men to enter the field. Is that contradictory to you, or. . . ?
R: Yeah, it's contradictory.

It appears that women are generally eager to see men enter "their" occupations. Indeed, several men noted that their female colleagues had facilitated their careers in various ways (including mentorship in college). However, at the same time, women often resent the apparent ease with which men advance within these professions, sensing that men at the higher levels receive preferential treatment that closes off advancement opportunities for women.

But this ambivalence does not seem to translate into the "poisoned" work environment described by many women who work in male-dominated occupations. Among the male interviewees, there were no accounts of sexual harassment. However, women do treat their male colleagues differently on occasion. It is not uncommon in nursing, for example, for men to be called upon to help catheterize male patients, or to lift especially heavy patients. Some librarians also said that women asked them to lift and move heavy boxes of books because they were men. Teachers sometimes confront differential treatment as well, as described by this Texas teacher:

As a man, you're teaching with all women, and that can be hard sometimes. Just because of the stereotypes, you know. I'm real into computers. . . and all the time people are calling me to fix their computer. Or if somebody gets a flat tire, they come and get me. I mean, there are just a lot of stereotypes. Not that I mind doing any of those things, but it's. . . you know, it just kind of bugs me that it is a stereotype, "A man should do that." Or if their kids have a lot of discipline problems, that kiddo's in your room. Or if there are kids that don't have a father in their home, that kid's in your room. Hell, nowadays that'd be half the school in my room (laughs). But you know, all the time I hear from the principal or from other teachers, "Well, this child really needs a man. . . a male role model" (laughs). So there are a lot of stereotypes that. . . men kind of get stuck with.

This special treatment bothered some respondents. Getting assigned all the "discipline problems" can make for difficult working conditions, for example. But many men claimed this differential treatment did not cause distress. In fact, several said they liked being appreciated for the special traits and abilities (such as strength) they could contribute to their professions.

Furthermore, women's special treatment sometimes enhanced, rather than poisoned the men's work environments. One Texas librarian said he felt "more comfortable working with women than men" because "I think it has something to do with control. Maybe it's that women will let me take control more than men will." Several men reported that their female colleagues often cast them into leadership roles. Although not all savored this distinction, it did enhance their authority and control in the work place. In subtle (and not too subtle) ways, then, differential treatment contributes to the "glass escalator" men experience in nontraditional professions.

Even outside work, most of the men interviewed said they felt fully accepted by their female colleagues. They were usually included in informal socializing occasions with the women, even though this frequently meant attending baby showers or Tupperware parties. Many said that they declined offers to attend these events because they were not interested in "women's things," although several others claimed to attend everything. The minority men I interviewed seemed to feel the least comfortable in these informal contexts. One social worker in Arizona was asked about socializing with his female colleagues:

I: So in general, for example, if all the employees were going to get together to have a party, or celebrate a bridal shower or whatever, would you be invited along with the rest of the group?
R: They would invite me, I would say, somewhat reluctantly. Being a black male, working with all white females, it did cause some outside problems. So I didn't go to a lot of functions with them. . .
I: You felt that there was some tension there on the level of your acceptance. . . ?
R: Yeah. It was OK working, but on the outside, personally, there was some tension there. It never came out, that they said, "Because of who you are we can't invite you" (laughs), and I wouldn't have done anything anyway. I would have probably respected them more for saying what was on their minds. But I never felt completely in with the group.

Some single men also said they felt uncomfortable socializing with married female colleagues because it gave the "wrong impression." But in general, the men said that they felt very comfortable around their colleagues and described their work places as very congenial for men. It appears unlikely, therefore, that men's underrepresentation in these professions is due to hostility towards men on the part of supervisors or women workers.

Discrimination from "Outsiders"

The most compelling evidence of discrimination against men in these professions is related to their dealings with the public. Men often encounter negative stereotypes when they come into contact with clients or "outsiders"—people they meet outside of work. For instance, it is popularly assumed that male nurses are gay. Librarians encounter images of themselves as "wimpy" and asexual. Male social workers describe being typecast as "feminine" and "passive." Elementary school teachers are often confronted by suspicions that they are pedophiles. One kindergarten teacher described an experience that occurred early in his career which was related to him years afterwards by his principal:

> He indicated to me that parents had come to him and indicated to him that they had a problem with the fact that I was a male. . . I recall almost exactly what he said. There were three specific concerns that the parents had: One parent said, "How can he love my child; he's a man." The second thing that I recall, he said the parent said, "He has a beard." And the third thing was, "Aren't you concerned about homosexuality?"

Such suspicions often cause men in all four professions to alter their work behavior to guard against sexual abuse charges, particularly in those specialties requiring intimate contact with women and children.

Men are very distressed by these negative stereotypes, which tend to undermine their self-esteem and to cause them to second-guess their motivations for entering these fields. A California teacher said,

> If I tell men that I don't know, that I'm meeting for the first time, that that's what I do. . . sometimes there's a look on their faces that, you know, "Oh, couldn't get a real job?"

When asked if his wife, who is also an elementary school teacher, encounters the same kind of prejudice, he said,

> No, it's accepted because she's a woman. . . I think people would see that as a. . . step up, you know. "Oh, you're not a housewife, you've got a career. That's great. . . that you're out there working. And you have a daughter, but you're still out there working. You decided not to stay home, and you went out there and got a job." Whereas for me, it's more like I'm supposed to be out working anyway, even though I'd rather be home with [my daughter].

Unlike women who enter traditionally male professions, men's movement into these jobs is perceived by the "outside world" as a step down in status. This particular form of discrimination may be most significant in explaining why men are underrepresented in these professions. Men who otherwise might show interest in and aptitude for such careers are probably discouraged from pursuing them because of the negative popular stereotypes associated with the men who work in them. This is a crucial difference from the experience of women in nontraditional professions: "My daughter, the physician," resonates far more favorably in most peoples' ears than "My son, the nurse."

Many of the men in my sample identified the stigma of working in a female-identified occupation as the major barrier to more men entering their professions. However, for the most part, they claimed that these negative stereotypes were not a factor in their own decisions to join these occupations. Most respondents didn't consider entering these fields until well into adulthood, after working in some related occupation. Several social workers and librarians even claimed they were not aware that men were a minority in their chosen professions. Either they had no well-defined image or stereotype, or their contacts and mentors were predominantly men. For example, prior to entering library school, many librarians held part-time jobs in university libraries, where there are proportionally more men than in the profession generally. Nurses and elementary school teachers were more aware that mostly women worked in these jobs, and this was often a matter of some concern to them. However, their choices were ultimately legitimized by mentors, or by encouraging friends or family members who implicitly reassured them that entering these occupations would not typecast them as feminine. In some cases, men were told by recruiters there were special advancement opportunities for men in these fields, and they entered them expecting rapid promotion to administrative positions.

> I: Did it ever concern you when you were making the decision to enter nursing school, the fact that it is a female-dominated profession?
> R: Not really. I never saw myself working on the floor. I saw myself pretty much going into administration, just getting the background and then getting a job someplace as a supervisor, and then working, getting up into administration.

Because of the unique circumstances of their recruitment, many of the respondents did not view their occupational choices as inconsistent with a male gender role, and they generally avoided the negative stereotypes directed against men in these fields.

Indeed, many of the men I interviewed claimed that they did not encounter negative professional stereotypes until they had worked in these fields for several years. Popular prejudices can be damaging to self-esteem and probably push some men out of these professions altogether. Yet, ironically, they sometimes contribute to the "glass escalator" effect I have been describing. Men seem to encounter the most vituperative criticism from the public when they are in the most female-identified specialties. Public concerns sometimes result in their being shunted into more "legitimate" positions for men. A librarian formerly in charge of a branch library's children's collection, who now works in the reference department of the city's main library, describes his experience:

> R: Some of the people [who frequented the branch library] complained that they didn't want to have a man doing the storytelling scenario. And I got transferred here to the

central library in an equivalent job. . . . I thought that I did a good job. And I had been told by my supervisor that I was doing a good job.

I: Have you ever considered filing some sort of lawsuit to get that other job back?

R: Well, actually, the job I've gotten now. . . well, it's a reference librarian; it's what I wanted in the first place. I've got a whole lot more authority here. I'm also in charge of the circulation desk. And I've recently been promoted because of my new stature, so. . . no, I'm not considering trying to get that other job back.

The negative stereotypes about men who do "women's work" can push men out of specific jobs. However, to the extent that they channel men into more "legitimate" practice areas, their effects can actually be positive. Instead of being a source of discrimination, these prejudices can add to the "glass escalator effect" by pressuring men to move out of the most female-identified areas, and *up* to those regarded more legitimate and prestigious for men.

Conclusion: Discrimination Against Men

Both men and women who work in nontraditional occupations encounter discrimination, but the forms and consequences of this discrimination are very different. The interviews suggest that unlike "nontraditional" women workers, most of the discrimination and prejudice facing men in the "female professions" emanates from outside those professions. The men and women interviewed for the most part believed that men are given fair—if not preferential—treatment in hiring and promotion decisions, are accepted by supervisors and colleagues, and are well integrated into the work place subculture. Indeed, subtle mechanisms seem to enhance men's position in these professions, a phenomenon I refer to as the glass escalator effect.

The data lend strong support for Zimmer's (1988) critique of "gender neutral theory" (such as Kanter's [1977] theory of tokenism) in the study of occupational segregation. Zimmer argues that women's occupational inequality is more a consequence of sexist beliefs and practices embedded in the labor force than the effect of numerical underrepresentation per se. This study suggests that token status itself does not diminish men's occupational success. Men take their gender privilege with them when they enter predominantly female occupations; this translates into an advantage in spite of their numerical rarity.

This study indicates that the experience of tokenism is very different for men and women. Future research should examine how the experience of tokenism varies for members of different races and classes as well. For example, it is likely that informal work place mechanisms similar to the ones identified here promote the careers of token whites in predominantly black occupations. The crucial factor is the social status of the token's group—not their numerical rarity—that determines whether the token encounters a "glass ceiling" or a "glass escalator."

However, this study also found that many men encounter negative stereotypes from persons not directly involved in their professions. Men who enter these professions are often considered "failures," or sexual deviants. These stereotypes may be a major impediment to men who otherwise might consider careers in these occupations. Indeed, they are likely to be important factors whenever a member of a relatively high status group crosses over into a lower status occupation. However, to the extent that these stereotypes contribute to the "glass escalator effect" by channeling men into more "legitimate" (and higher paying) occupations, they are not discriminatory.

Women entering traditionally "male" professions also face negative stereotypes suggesting they are not "real women" (Epstein 1981; Lorber 1984; Spencer and Podmore 1987). However, these stereotypes do not seem to deter women to the same degree that they deter men from pursuing nontraditional professions. There is ample historical evidence that women flock to male-identified occupations once opportunities are available (Cohn 1985; Epstein 1988). Not so with men. Examples of occupations changing from predominantly female to predominantly male are very rare in our history. The few existing cases—such as medicine—suggest that redefinition of the occupations as appropriately "masculine" is necessary before men will consider joining them (Ehrenreich and English 1978).

Because different mechanisms maintain segregation in male- and female-dominated occupations, different approaches are needed to promote their integration. Policies intended to alter the sex composition of male-dominated occupations—such as affirmative action—make little sense when applied to the "female professions." For men, the major barriers to integration have little to do with their treatment once they decide to enter these fields. Rather, we need to address the social and cultural sanctions applied to men who do "women's work," which keep men from even considering these occupations.

One area where these cultural barriers are clearly evident is in the media's representation of men's occupations. Women working in traditionally male professions have achieved an unprecedented acceptance on popular television shows. Women are portrayed as doctors *(St. Elsewhere),* lawyers *(The Cosby Show, L.A. Law),* architects *(Family Ties),* and police officers *(Cagney and Lacey).* But where are the male nurses, teachers, and secretaries? Television rarely portrays men in nontraditional work roles, and when it does, that anomaly is made the central focus—and joke—of the program. A comedy series (1991–1992) about a male elementary school teacher *(Drexell's Class)* stars a lead character who *hates children!* Yet even this negative portrayal is exceptional. When a prime time hospital drama series *(St. Elsewhere)* depicted a male orderly striving for upward mobility, the show's writers made him a physician's assistant, not a nurse or nurse practitioner—the likely real-life possibilities.

Presenting positive images of men in nontraditional careers can produce limited effects. A few social workers, for example, were first inspired to pursue their careers by George C. Scott, who played a social worker in the television drama series, *Eastside/Westside.* But as a policy strategy to break down occupational segregation, changing media images of men is no panacea. The stereotypes that differentiate masculinity and femininity, and degrade that which is defined as feminine, are deeply entrenched in culture, social structure, and personality (Williams 1989). Nothing short of a revolution in cultural definitions of masculinity will effect the broad scale social transformation needed to achieve the complete occupational integration of men and women.

Of course, there are additional factors besides societal prejudice contributing to men's underrepresentation in female-dominated professions. Most notably, those men I interviewed mentioned as a deterrent the fact that these professions are all underpaid relative to comparable "male" occupations, and several suggested that instituting a "comparable worth" policy might attract more men. However, I am not convinced that improved salaries will substantially alter the sex composition of these professions unless the cultural stigma faced by men in these occupations diminishes. Occupational sex segregation is remarkably resilient, even in the face of devastating economic hardship. During the Great Depression of the 1930s, for example, "women's jobs" failed to attract sizable numbers of men (Blum 1991, 154). In her study of American Telephone and Telegraph (AT&T) workers, Epstein (1989) found that some men would rather suffer unemployment than accept relatively high paying "women's jobs" because of the damage to their identities this would cause. She quotes one unemployed man who refused to apply for a female-identified telephone operator job:

> I think if they offered me $1,000 a week tax free, I wouldn't take that job. When I. . . see those guys sitting in there [in the telephone operating room], I wonder what's wrong with them. Are they pansies or what? (Epstein 1989, 577)

This is not to say that raising salaries would not affect the sex composition of these jobs. Rather, I am suggesting that wages are not the only, or perhaps even the major impediment to men's entry into these jobs. Further research is needed to explore the ideological significance of the "woman's wage" for maintaining occupational stratification.[3]

At any rate, integrating men and women in the labor force requires more than dismantling barriers to women in male-dominated fields. Sex segregation is a two-way street. We must also confront and dismantle the barriers men face in predominantly female occupations. Men's experiences in these nontraditional occupations reveal just how culturally embedded the barriers are, and how far we have to travel before men and women attain true occupational and economic equality.

Notes

This research was funded in part by a faculty grant from the University of Texas at Austin. I also acknowledge the support of the Sociology Departments of the University of California–Berkeley, Harvard University, and Arizona State University. I would like to thank Judy Auerbach, Martin Button, Robert Nye, Teresa Sullivan, Debra Umberson, Mary Waters, and the reviewers at *Social Problems* for their comments on earlier versions of this chapter.

1. According to the U.S. Census, black men and women compose 7 percent of all nurses and librarians, 11 percent of all elementary school teachers, and 19 percent of all social workers (calculated from U.S. Census 1980: Table 278, 1197). The proportion of blacks in social work may be exaggerated by these statistics. The occupational definition of "social worker" used by the Census Bureau includes welfare workers and pardon and parole officers, who are not considered "professional" social workers by the National Association of Social Workers. A study of degreed professionals found that 89 percent of practitioners were white (Hardcastle 1987).

2. In April 1991, the Labor Department created a Glass Ceiling Commission to "conduct a thorough study of the underrepresentation of women and minorities in executive, management, and senior decision-making positions in business" (U.S. House of Representatives 1991, 20).

3. Alice Kessler-Harris argues that the lower pay of traditionally female occupations is symbolic of a patriarchal order that assumes female dependence on a male breadwinner. She writes that pay equity is fundamentally threatening to the "male workers sense of self, pride, and masculinity" because it upsets his individual standing in the hierarchical ordering of the sexes (1990, 125). Thus men's reluctance to enter these occupations may have less to do with the actual dollar amount recorded in their paychecks, and more to do with the damage that earning "a woman's wage" would wreak on their self-esteem in a society that privileges men. This conclusion is supported by the interview data.

References

Bielby, William T., and James N. Baron. 1984. "A Woman's Place Is with Other Women: Sex Segregation Within Organizations." In *Sex Segregation in the Workplace: Trends, Explanations, Remedies,* ed. Barbara Reskin, 27–55. Washington, D.C.: National Academy Press.

Blum, Linda M. 1991. *Between Feminism and Labor: The Significance of the Comparable Worth Movement.* Berkeley: University of California Press.

Carothers, Suzanne C., and Peggy Crull. 1984. "Contrasting Sexual Harassment in Female-Dominated and Male-Dominated Occupations." In *My Troubles are Going to Have Trouble with Me: Everyday Trials and Triumphs of Women Workers,* ed. Karen B. Sacks and Dorothy Remy, 220–227. New Brunswick, N.J.: Rutgers University Press.

Cohn, Samuel. 1985. *The Process of Occupational Sex-Typing.* Philadelphia: Temple University Press.

Ehrenreich, Barbara, and Deirdre English. *For Her Own Good: 100 Years of Expert Advice to Women.* Garden City, N.Y.: Anchor.

Epstein, Cynthia Fuchs. 1981. *Women in Law.* New York: Basic Books.

_____. 1988. *Deceptive Distinctions: Sex, Gender, and the Social Order.* New Haven: Yale University Press.

_____. 1989. "Workplace Boundaries: Conceptions and Creations." *Social Research* 56: 571–590.

Freeman, Sue J.M. 1990. *Managing Lives: Corporate Women and Social Change.* Amherst, Mass.: University of Massachusetts Press.

Grimm, James W., and Robert N. Stern. 1974. "Sex Roles and Internal Labor Market Structures: The Female Semi-Professions." *Social Problems* 21: 690–705.

Hardcastle, D. A. 1987. "The social work labor force." Austin, Tex.: School of Social Work, University of Texas.

Hodson, Randy, and Teresa Sullivan. 1990. *The Social Organization of Work.* Belmont, Calif.: Wadsworth.

Jacobs, Jerry. 1989. *Revolving Doors: Sex Segregation and Women's Careers.* Stanford, Calif.: Stanford University Press.

Kanter, Rosabeth Moss. 1977. *Men and Women of the Corporation.* New York: Basic Books.

Kessler-Harris, Alice. 1990. *A Woman's Wage: Historical Meanings and Social Consequences.* Lexington: Kentucky University Press.

Lorber, Judith. 1984. *Women Physicians: Careers, Status, and Power.* New York: Tavistock.

Martin, Susan E. 1980. *Breaking and Entering: Police Women on Patrol.* Berkeley: University of California Press.

_____. 1988. "Think Like a Man, Work Like a Dog, and Act Like a Lady: Occupational Dilemmas of Policewomen." In *The Worth of Women's Work: A Qualitative Synthesis,* ed. Anne Statham

Miller, Eleanor M., and Hans O. Mauksch, 205–223. Albany: State University of New York Press.

Phenix, Katharine. 1987. "The Status of Women Librarians." *Frontiers* 9: 36–40.

Reskin, Barbara. 1988. "Bringing the Men Back In: Sex Differentiation and the Devaluation of Women's Work." *Gender and Society* 2:58–81.

Reskin, Barbara, and Heidi Hartmann. 1986. *Women's Work, Men's Work: Sex Segregation on the Job.* Washington, D.C.: National Academy Press.

Reskin, Barbara, and Patricia Roos. 1990. *Job Queues, Gender Queues: Explaining Women's Inroads into Male Occupations.* Philadelphia: Temple University Press.

Schmuck, Patricia A. 1987. "Women School Employees in the United States." In *Women Educators: Employees of Schools in Western Countries,* ed. Patricia A. Schmuck, 75–97. Albany: State University of New York Press.

Schreiber, Carol. 1979. *Men and Women in Transitional Occupations.* Cambridge.: MIT Press.

Spencer, Anne, and David Podmore. 1987. *In a Man's World: Essays on Women in Male-Dominated Professions.* London: Tavistock.

Strauss, Anselm L. 1987. *Qualitative Analysis for Social Scientists.* Cambridge: Cambridge University Press.

U.S. Bureau of the Census. 1980. Detailed Population Characteristics, 1:D. Washington, D.C.: Government Printing Office.

U.S. Department of Labor. Bureau of Labor Statistics. 1991. *Employment and Earnings: January.* Washington, D.C.: Government Printing Office.

U.S. Congress. House. 1991. *Civil Rights and Women's Equity in Employment Act of 1991.* Report 102-40, pt. 1. Washington, D.C.: Government Printing Office.

Williams, Christine L. 1989. *Gender Differences at Work: Women and Men in Nontraditional Occupations.* Berkeley: University of California Press.

Yoder, Janice D. 1989. "Women at West Point: Lessons for Token Women in Male-Dominated Occupations." In *Women: A Feminist Perspective,* ed. Jo Freeman, 523–537. Mountain View, Calif.: Mayfield.

York, Reginald O., H. Carl Henley, and Dorothy N. Gamble. 1987. "Sexual Discrimination in Social Work: Is It Salary or Advancement?" *Social Work* 32: 336–340.

Zimmer, Lynn. 1988. "Tokenism and Women in the Workplace." *Social Problems* 35: 64–77.

9

LADIES ON THE LOT
Women, Car Sales, and the Pursuit of the American Dream

Helene Lawson

One time I was on the phone with somebody and the owner walks by and he goes, "Why are you being so nice? I want to make sure that it is clear that if somebody needs prodding you are there to give it to them. You need more backbone."

—Martha, six-month sales agent novice

There are tough women who work in the city. They sell more cars and make more money, go in for the close right away and they get it most of the time. All the sweetness they show when they meet customers disappears. They have long red claws and are very menacing. The control they have would not make it in a small suburban store. That is something for a big store with a large clientele. It is hard, because, like the used car salesman with the white shoes, plaid jacket, and stripped tie, women get a bad reputation from them. But they are very successful. They have learned how to make a lot of money.

—June, ex-preschool teacher

Work socializes people. Formal and informal on-the-job training and experience combine to produce the technical and cognitive abilities, as well as values, attitudes, and social skills, necessary to function within the subculture of a job.[1] This socialization causes people to behave in ways they may not have before in order for them to adapt and conform to the common needs of the work group. Our society seldom questions this type of socialization because it equates learning to work with becoming a mature adult.[2] However, not all work changes people for the better, and selling cars—especially used ones—suggests dishonesty and deviance to the public. Sales training literature says salesworkers are "made." And theorists believe they are "made" to behave in a callous, aggressive, and untrustworthy manner because the "kind of thinking required to master the sales process is pragmatic and instrumental, not reflexive" (Oakes 1990:96). Successful sales agents cannot concern themselves with the morals and ethics of their behavior. They are concerned only with the results of their behavior, that is, how much it profits them. Simmel (1978) felt this fixed focus caused trading agents to lack character, objectivity, and commitment to the welfare of others.

When workers are trained to be concerned only with their own success, it is difficult to build trust.[3] Each person in the transaction is in a situation in which he or she must have defensive strategies in order to negotiate his or her way in the system. Trust in a community involves openness. There is a boundary around the group, not around the person.[4] In the community of car sales, everyone knows everyone else is "out to get you," so workers are warned to get others first.

Learning the Trade

Informal Training

There are two types of informal training. (1) Socialization is a type of informal training that occurs before one is actively involved in the work. It refers to imagining or anticipating what it would be like to be a member of a group of which an individual is not presently a me on the basis of information given by people acquainted with the occupation.[5] (2) Once on the job, Informal training in occupations is usually gained through peer networking that occurs once the individual is accepted into the work group or community. People learn what to expect from the job and how to handle themselves by getting insider information from those already experienced in the role.[6]

Mentors, Friends, and Relatives

Women in car sales discussed receiving advice from individual mentors and friends who were familiar with the car sales. These women developed assumptions abort work from these informants. They were given insider tips and advice on how to avoid problems with management and coworkers before they began to work. Fran said her ex-husband prepared her for what to expect in the business by cautioning her not to trust alone:

> My ex and I are friendly, so I got a lot of knowledge from him as far as what happens in a car dealership. I was coached as far as "watch this and watch that" because this is typically what happens to newcomers at dealerships—other salesmen steal your customers, management does not credit you for the actual number of cars you sell, and buyers lie to you about their credit ratings and what prices other dealerships gave them. So I had somebody watching over my shoulder and warning me to look for certain types of things.

Ann's brother similarly cautioned her to distrust everyone in the business:

> He said, "I know many people in the business, but I don't trust any of them. You've got to understand their motivation. They're in it for the money. If they are making money, if they are successful, they feel whatever they do, they must be right."

Barbara's steady date sold cars at one time. He warned her not to trust customers:

> Watch out for customers. You spend time with them and they won't give you their trust. They won't give you their real telephone numbers, and some of them won't even give you their real names, because they're just shopping or their credit is bad and they aren't really going to buy.

Denise's mother, Marsha, warned her to distrust sales agents at other dealerships:

> Salesmen at other dealerships will say anything to take a deal away. They "low ball." They take customers out of the market that way and try and talk them into buying another car when the car they promised doesn't come in. Don't cut your commission just because a customer was lied to.

And Nora dated a car sales agent who told her to distrust management, because managers lied about the prices cars were taken in for so they could cut commissions:

> Owners doctor the books. They register the car at a much higher price than it was really bought for, so their profit is probably double what their books show. Try to find out what the car was really taken in for and keep your own books.

Thus these women were taught to distrust coworkers, customers, and management before they began to work. And, once the women began to sell, they found that bosses, coworkers, and customers also distrusted them.

Bosses and Coworkers

Women new to car sales wanted support and help from bosses and coworkers. They were moving into a new situation and, as yet, did not have a good perspective on themselves. Women devalue themselves and think something must be wrong with them when they understand the world differently from men.[7]

Women respondents entered the field with different backgrounds from men and were not quite sure how to apply their experiences or even if their experiences were valuable. Their self-concept was low and their fears were validated, because what newcomer women saw in the men they worked with was distrust and a lack of faith in women as agents. Edith and Joan, two newcomers to car sales, summed up the inferiority newcomer women felt when they were hired and the ways in which their bosses and coworkers reinforced their feelings of inadequacy. Edith said:

I can't say that I was overly confident about taking the job, and when I started, the manager said, "I don't know what is going to happen. I don't know how the customers are going to accept you. I don't know how the salesmen are going to accept you."

Joan, a newcomer of two weeks, was also concerned about being able to do the work:

I didn't know anything. I said to my boss, "Give me a month. You don't even have to pay me. I have never done this before. I'm coming in fresh. I don't know how good I'll be." And he said he was as worried about hiring me as I was about doing the job.

Men's lack of trust in women as colleagues concerns their cultural role as wives and mothers. Women are expected to put their work before their children's welfare or domestic needs and are expected to drop out if family responsibilities require it.[8] Women's initial self-concepts based on fear of incompetence are usually enhanced by harassment related to these assumptions regarding their primary loyalty. Three sales managers—Pete, Marvin, and Larry exemplified this negative point of view. They wanted women workers because other women liked buying from them, but they thought most women could not be good car salespersons. They based their judgment on two major stereotypes of competency in woman workers in male fields: a lack of technical knowledge and presupposed dropout due to family responsibilities and breadwinner husbands. John, the general manager at Wendy's dealership, said women in general did not do well, but a token woman on the lot was okay as long as she sold to other women, because most men customers did not like dealing with her:

As far as women in the business, I think they are finding they really don't like the business. You don't find very many women that are real, real good, that are real outstanding in the business as far as sales. A lot of people don't even like talking to a woman when it comes to a car. A lot of men are offended. I can give you a perfect example of this woman we hired.

She had a customer about a week ago, and she was explaining the car to him. He just jumped all over her. He said her information was inadequate. He started telling her the thickness of the metal. He started getting into real detail things and she didn't know how to respond to it because she doesn't really know the technical background of the car. I think dealerships try not to have too many women because they're weaker than men. Yet, on the other hand, I like the idea of having a woman because a lot of women that come in the store like to deal with a woman. They feel they can trust her more.

Frank, a sales manager at a dealership next door to Ida's and under the same ownership, brought up old stereotypes, asserting that women would not advance in the business because they were too concerned with marriage and family problems or were supported by husbands:

I've had women working for me, but as for becoming managers or owners, I think it would be very difficult as far as the way the hours are set up. The latest I have left the store is 4:00 in the morning. For a woman because, quote unquote, a lot of women are married, and' therefore it is additional income, not sole income—or they have kids to take care of.

Mike, an ex-manager brought up similar stereotypes. He felt that divorced women with children would always be concerned about what was going on at home with the children. And single women would be looking for husbands, getting married, and quitting:

> I have had a couple women working for me over the years. The problem I have had is that many women try to sell cars with their own personal life in disarray. You get into these divorcees where they have an unstable personal situation. I had a woman coming to me looking for a job one day and she had a baby less than a year old. I looked her right in the eye and I said, "Go home and raise your baby. You don't need the job." Her husband had a job and she wanted to get out of the house and sell cars. Now I can't believe any woman in her right mind would take a job from 9:00 [in the morning] till 10:00 at night with young children at home. One of the problems we run into with divorced women is they've got the children. Something happens in school or after school and they have to run home. The other problem is with younger women you don't know how soon they are going to get married and have children and then their family life will control their activities so they don't want a job anymore. They don't go into it as permanently as men.

At most dealerships, themes of gender-related harassment and overall distrust were evident and vividly illustrated. These themes were replicated in differing forms and woven throughout the varied paths of women workers as they continued on in their careers. This added to the framework of the distressful nature of the business and its resulting lack of support for workers.

Formal Training Methods

In sales occupations, the content and substance of formal knowledge transmitted by administration is mainly concerned with meeting a payroll and turning a profit for the agency.[9] In car sales, that means how to sell enough cars at a high enough price to make money for the dealer. The reprimands sales agents get from their bosses come because they are not paying attention to those things the sales philosophy says they should. For example, perhaps they have not been aggressive enough, have not created a great enough need or desire for the product in the customer, or have let the customer go before the manager got a chance to close the deal. Formal training, according to informants, ranged from structured one- to two-week programs conducted outside or on the site of the agency, to one- to three-day seminars and workshops, to less structured offerings, where management trained newcomers on a one-on-one basis, to various types of quasi-apprenticeships. However, training did not always begin when newcomers started work. A majority of women said they got little to no training before they were expected to sell.[10]

In-House Management Training

What training newcomers did get centered on issues of customer manipulation. From the very first in-house training session, agents are told to convince customers they (agents) have a genuine interest in them and their needs, rather than just in making a sale. This is especially stressed at one-price dealerships. Sales agents must convince customers that they are on their side, getting them the best possible deal, when agents actually have no real control over the final price. This is an exaggeration of a problem that we all confront in many ways in everyday life: convincing people of who we are and that we are genuine, especially when we have an interest in their behavior.[11] By understanding the in-house training sessions, we learn about dealers' perspectives on customers, employees, and work. First, the sales agent must learn to be aggressive in order to create a need and desire in the customer. Sales agents do not just sell a car; they must also sell themselves, the service department, and add-ons. In addition, the manager makes sure the new sales agent, anxious to get a sale, does not sell the car for less than what the dealership wants, because management controls the closing.

There are a variety of ways in which new sales agents understand this training situation and learn to manage it. Through training, they begin to reconstruct their understandings of the sales encounter and how to pursue a customer. Jean, a ten-year veteran, said:

> That's how people cut their teeth in the business. The more inexperienced people tend to go to track or one-price stores. They get hired there because that way management has more control over them and the customers and makes sure the dealership gets a high price for the car. At my dealership I do my own thing. I've been in the business for a while so I know how to sit down with the customer. I don't need their crap.

Betsy, a two-year veteran who left a track store, agreed. She said that she was forced to use a sales spiel that she thought inappropriate in many cases, and that the manager interfered with her completion of sales as well as sexually harassed her:

> They had a ten-step process that they wanted people to follow. They wanted new people, everyone that had never been in the business before, for the purpose of training them the way they wanted them trained. They wanted to have complete control over you which they did beautifully. You role play. I always started out, "Welcome to Jones Chevrolet. My name's Betsy. May I assist you?" Then you ask the customer questions like where they live, how long they've been on the job, what they did for a living, if they bought the car they were driving new or used, then you show them the car. You open the hood. You tell them about the extras. You drive the car with them. You drive their trade-ins. If you didn't get the answers to the questions, you were sent right back out to ask the customer. You had to do all the steps their way. This is basically what they did in the training session. They just taught you the steps. They didn't teach you anything mechanical or technical about cars.

Some novices liked the track method because they were not sure they could close on their own. Edith, in sales for ten months, learned by watching her manager. She said, "I am new. I don't care if a manager does it if I can't close it. I'll come right in and stand while they are closing. I learn that way." The uncertainty of the newcomer is an issue here. New sales agents are uncertain about learning the ropes; they know their salary and their job depends on how successful they are. The track method adds some control in the situation. Even if control is given to the manager, the newcomer feels more secure about closing the sale:

> I was not allowed to close a deal by myself. I had to present all the information to a manager and say, "Where do I go from here?" He'd say, "Want me to close this deal for you? Well, what are you gonna do for me if I close this deal for you?" And, oh, my God, while he was harassing me, I would see my customers leaving! And then he would turn and run out the door after them and talk to them in the parking lot. Sometimes he would sell them, so he would help me, but torture me first.

At one-price dealerships, sales agents may not need to go to a manager to get a price. But they still have a routine to follow, according to Roger, a sales consultant:

> The customer usually sees a greeter first. Then I explain the one-price concept to prove to the customer that they are getting the best deal possible. I interview them and find out what their needs are. Then I help them find the right car with the right features and we go for a test drive. If we agree on the car, I bring them to the finance specialist.

Other new sales agents did not agree with the philosophy behind routines or track methods. Leah said she knew how to sell by instinct and not by following a prescribed sales program that called for cornering every walk-in and going through a long sales talk and asking a series of prescribed questions. But she was unable to identify what her skill or innate quality was:

> I am a human being. I possess certain innate qualities that allow me to know when to strike and when to be still. If I thought it was more advantageous to let this guy go at this particular time, having given him what he came in for, brochure information, whatever, I'm going to believe that when it is time to seriously shop, he will come back and spend the necessary time involved for the amount of money he is spending.

Because management at some dealerships checked up on every walk-in, sales agents had to justify why walk-ins did not buy a car. Leah, who had too many customers leave, excused herself by saying, "He only wanted a brochure." She was reprimanded by her manager, who expected her to keep customers long enough to turn over to him. Sales agents such as Leah were punished if people left without getting a sales pitch or seeing a manager. She said, "I have been threatened to be suspended for a day, no pay." My general manager said, "Listen, nobody can exit people until I see them. I have not let anybody else let people go. You're not going to start."

As previously mentioned, autonomy was a prime motivator for many women to pursue a career in car sales. Loss of autonomy in this area was upsetting to women, who described autonomy as the freedom they wanted in deciding how they were going to sell and the excitement they felt in creating a successful sales style. They spoke of the enjoyment and satisfaction they received from creative interactions with customers. Most men defined autonomy differently. Regardless of where they worked, men sales agents agreed they had to learn to follow a designated script to produce desired outcomes early in their careers. They did not feel they had freedom or autonomy in how they sold. Instead, men found freedom in their ability to easily find another job if things were slow at their dealership, or if they got fired.

Seminars

Sometimes dealerships contracted out for short seminars to be held on their premises or sent people to seminars or workshops of varying lengths. This training covered attributes of new car models being added to a line. Carol, who had been in business over two years, described this training as helpful:

> I went through a week of in-house training. I watched films and read pamphlets to get product knowledge. You have to know your automobiles. You have to know the product that you are selling. You have to know each individual car, car line, colors, options, add-ons.

Other seminars relied heavily on managers. Managers gave sales agents product brochures and showed them in-house videos on the cars. Timing was an important issue in this training. Even the best of programs were held at times that did not necessarily coincide with the hiring of newcomers and the sporadic and uncoordinated manner in which most training was presented meant that some agents did not attend training sessions until long after they had started selling cars. Most agents got little to no training before they started selling cars. Isabel was put on the floor on the busiest day of the week, after only two days of training, and felt this was too much pressure for a novice:

> The general manager said, "I will teach you." Thursday I watched videos on a closed circuit TV about the product. The next day he said, "Now say this and do that and bring the deal into my office." Saturday he said, "You're going on the floor." He worked me twelve hours that day, no lunch, no breaks, no nothing. I think he really wanted to see how far he could push me before I cracked.

Martha started selling without formal training. Then she got fired and went to a new dealer. There she got more information than she needed on product knowledge:

> I didn't really get to go to any classes until I had been in sales for about six months because they offer them at weird times, and I got fired after three months on my first job because sales were slow. At my new place, my training has been all on product knowledge basically about the car. I went to a workshop, where I learned physically about the car, getting in and out of the vans, campers. Then they sent me to a class, like when the [Audi] Fox first came out we all had to get certified about the Fox. They told me things—like colors they came in and stuff—I already knew about from experience and reading the brochures. The owner says he wants to make sure his employees are taught so they can make money because he would rather they stay here than have a turnover. But, in the short period of time that I've been selling [six months], the training has not

helped me. I know I have to use my own personality to sell, because that's what it's about. But I'm not sure how to do it.

This is an interesting comment on socialization and the career. Martha was having difficulty becoming a car sales agent. As a group, newcomers differed in their reactions to training and were uncertain about what they needed or wanted. Most women had no prior sales experience. All these women wanted to know more about cars, including the women who had prior sales experience with other products. All were dissatisfied with the initial training they got and talked about using natural ability to sell their first cars. The novice woman was confused, saying, "There is something I need to know but I can't tell you what it is." To add to this confusion, many managers sent new women out on the floor during the first week with no training, giving them advice such as: "Follow someone around. Here you go, sell cars! Go ahead kid, sell!" Sales agents called this the "sink or swim" method.

Apprenticeships

In situations in which management did not train newcomers and seminars were unavailable, newcomers tried to attach themselves to a more experienced sales agent. Despite the fact that management often suggested this approach, men were resistant to accept a newcomer, especially a woman, as an apprentice. More experienced car sales agents did not generally bother with newcomers until they had proven themselves. Men sales agents did not want to be followed around by women trying to learn their jobs. Distrust was especially high because women were seen as a foreign presence in the work culture of car lots. To follow an experienced sales agent around was therefore a difficult, if not an impossible, task for a woman entering the field.[12] When newcomers like Isabel went to men for help, they were ignored or refused. Isabel said both new and experienced men ignored her:

I missed the training program, so they told me to follow someone around. Actually I had to be on my own because hardly any salesmen would talk to me because I was infringing on their territory. Guys that were here for a long time didn't care about me, they cared about themselves. And new salesmen wouldn't talk to me either.

Jean recalled her early days as a sales agent and the cliques from which she was excluded:

Every sales floor has little cliques. They use each other as sounding boards and support systems. If you have a sales floor that has twenty people, you can have six in one clique, six in another clique and six in a third clique. Then you have a couple loners—usually a woman or a minority. I am not on the sales floor anymore. When I was, it was hard to get in with any male clique. If I would walk over, they would walk away or ignore me.

By contrast, Bill, a newcomer who worked at Ida's store, explained his experience:

We are a team. We help each other. We are in it together and trying to make our store the best in the business. If there is something I don't know, one of the guys is always ready to help me. We spend weekends and evenings together talking things over and watching ball games.

Yet this is not always the experience of male newcomers in sales. Christopher, a beginning chemical sales agent whose progress I followed for a year, was allowed to join the group but was kept on the fringes and got little help:

> Sometimes a bunch of us would meet for breakfast, but the more experienced guys wouldn't discuss sales with me. When I asked other men about what chemicals were best for certain cleaning jobs, they gave me the wrong information. I knew they talked to each other about which chemicals to push because they paid higher commissions. I knew they stold customers from new sales agents who dropped out after a few months, even if they weren't in their territory. But they wouldn't tell me those things.

Therefore incoming men sales agents are also excluded from the work group. However, while men are excluded from insider information, women face a very different experience. They are also subjected to physical and verbal sexual harassment as a means forcing them to keep their distance. Yolanda talked about what she learned from her attempts at apprenticeship:

> When I first started, I wanted to learn from the guys, but that led to stuff like "Jesus Christ, why don't you go out with me? I've really got something to offer you. When are we going on a date? C'mon. Sex between us would be really great." If that didn't get me to leave, somebody would say, "Leave the room so I can tell this joke." This one guy finally said, "What are you doing here? You're taking up space where a male could be supporting—his family." Now I keep my distance.

Thus, right at the start, most women learned that the sales floor was male territory on which they should tread carefully. Through sexist jokes, exclusion, and other forms of harassment, they began to understand that they were infringing on male territory and were seen as potential competitors.[13] If they succeeded in making a connection, they would learn how to do their job and they might steal a sale from a coworker. The problem with informal training and following people around is that you must rely on your potential competitors to teach you what you need to know. Most inexperienced women therefore went out on the selling floor with little training and no support system.

Selling the First Car: Luck and Magic

In occupations such as car sales where there is a very short training period that provides only minimal skills and a rudimentary sense of what membership in the occupation means, most of what makes the person a member of the occupation is learned on the job. "In many cases, learning a job and doing it are one and the same" (Pavalko 1988, 105). With minimal training, some women sold their first day out. When asked how they did it, they were not aware of what skills they used and gave themselves little credit for their success. They said it was luck or that it came "naturally." All women sales agents told me they began selling before they were certain of cars and sales techniques. They thought they did not know enough and needed to know more, but when they made a big sale they said they discovered they did not have to know very much in order to do it. They spoke in fatalistic ways. When they made a sale, they did not understand what they were doing or how they were doing it. They knew they had something in them that came out, but they did not know what it was. They thought they had not taken an active role in the sale. This passive voice was part of their self-concept. They said their sales were a "matter of luck" rather than ability. They said, "I had nothing to do with it," a very passive way of understanding their success. They saw chance, luck, and then mimic as the cause of success. Dorene was unexpectedly hired at a dealership that sold expensive foreign cars. She talked about an "easy" first sale where she did not even know what she was doing:

I'll tell you the first sale because that one I remember very well. That's when they hired me to sell Alfa Romeos and I never saw one and I never heard of them. They didn't even have one in stock. They just said, "You're gonna sell Alfa Romeos." And my first thing was, "What is an Alfa Romeo?" Well, I was there for about a couple weeks and it was right after the auto show and a young dentist came in with his wife and he had his hands in his pockets, jiggling his money, and he goes, "I want to buy a car." And I go, "Well, what kind of car do you want to buy?" And he says, "I want to buy a Spider." And I said, "Well, we don't have any." And he goes, "Well, I want to buy one." And I didn't know a thing. It was my first car. I never wrote up a deal or anything. I was like, "Well, okay, what would you like in it?" So we sat down and we started writing this deal and I didn't even know the price of the car. I wrote down everything he wanted. I found out what the list price was and I wrote it down. I sold him an alarm, which I was good at, because I sold alarms before. I sold him a radio and I knew about those. I sold him everything there was. I wrote it all down. I got a $5,000 deposit from him and he took his credit out and I knew nothing. I went into the boss and he almost died. So he goes, "Don't lose this one!" It was an order car and we called New Jersey immediately and ordered the car for him. It was the most exciting thing I ever did. After that we laughed and the guy even laughed when he came in to pick up the car. He goes, "You were new at selling and I was new at buying. I bet you really screwed me." And I did. I made more money on that car than I made on a Mercedes. I didn't even know I was doing it. It was really fun, and I said, "This is so easy."

For many women, this is how it worked. They started out selling without knowing how or why they made the sale. Roberta told me the skills she brought from her previous sales work with Tupperware helped her with her first sales, but she did not recognize what her specific skills were. Even Renita, who worked at a top-of-the-line dealer, could not say how she made her first sale. "My first month I sold a new and a used Rolls Royce. I got lucky." Betsy, who had been selling for over two years, still described her ability in vague terms:

It comes natural. At first the manager told me what to do. Now say this or do this and bring the deal into my office and I ended up selling a convertible. You know what was good? First of all, I was lucky. If it was a bad experience, it would have been a real trauma. Once you get one success in anything, it will breed another and another.

Bev was the only sales agent at her suburban store during the first two weeks it was opened. So although the manager told her to watch the other sales agents, there were none and she sold by "magic":

They said, "Don't worry about selling for a couple months. We'll put you on salary. Just watch all the other salesmen and see what you can learn." It turned out I was the only sales agent for about two and a half weeks. I sold a convertible my very first night. And I'm like, "What am I going to do now?" I went to our manager and I said, "They said, 'Yes'." And he said, "Well go write it up." And I said, "How?" It was funny. It was magic.

Women attributed sales to qualities that were out of control, such as natural ability. Yet often, they were using skills learned from experiences in service jobs or in family situations which taught communication and interaction skills that they carried into car sales. However, they negated and minimized their experiences because much of what they did was invisible to them. It is these finely honed skills that novice sales-women called upon to sell cars. Because they are unnamed, they were not treated as learned skills but as natural attributes.[14]

Though women newcomers did not know why they had early successes, those that did agreed that selling their first car was a turning point in their careers. They had new positions as car sales agents and new self-concepts and identities. It gave them an incredible high that led to the confidence needed to sell more cars. They were hooked into staying in the field. Carol talked about the turning point where she decided there was nothing she would rather do than sell cars:

I love this business. I really do. It's great. It's crazy, but it gets under your skin and there's nothing else for you to do. You really wouldn't want to do anything else. I can't explain it. I feel good about myself. Every time I have a customer come in, it's a challenge all over again, and the sky's the limit.

Cathy also talked about expanded horizons. Whereas before she was a struggling waitress with a limited income, now she was a successful career woman with limitless options:

Before I was unhappy and depressed. But this is different. It's very challenging. You go from high to low and there's really no middle. You're either on top or you're on the bottom. But I'm successful and there's no limit to what I can do.

Thus filled with hope, inexperienced women began to learn the ropes and negotiate the hostile environment of the dealership, eventually understanding what skills they needed to use to sell cars.

Notes

1. Symbolic interactionists theorize that socialization is an ongoing interactional process and that we can only see ourselves in relation to our community. Furthermore our selves are continually being constructed and reconstructed in interaction and negotiation in this community (Mills 1959; Denzin 1978). Work is such a community. For literature on socialization through work, see Howard S. Becker and James Carper, "The Development of Identification With an Occupation," *American Journal of Sociology* 6 (1956): 289–298; Everett C. Hughes, *The Sociological Eye* (Chicago: Aldine 1971); and Robert A. Rothman, *Working: Sociological Perspectives* (Englewood Cliffs, N.J.: Prentice-Hall, 1987).

2. Erik Erikson, *Identity: Youth and Crisis* (New York: Norton, 1968).

3. If workers are to behave in a responsible and ethical manner toward each other as well as those they service, they must have values that encompass more than their own perceived needs in the immediate situation. Furthermore in order to recognize their own ethical involvement, workers must experience "an element of self-determination, freedom and the demand for responsible life enhancing interpretations" (Quigley 1994, 54). For literature (both theoretical and in applied work settings) on trust and what conditions are necessary for its development, see T. R. Quigley, "The Ethical and the Narrative Self," *Philosophy Today* 38, no. 1 (1994): 43. Lawrence A. Blum, *Friendship, Altruism, and Morality* (Boston: Routledge & Kegan Paul, 1980); Morton Deutsch, "Trust and Suspicion," *Journal of Conflict Resolution* 4 (1958): 165–179; Fred Davis, "The Cabdriver and His Fare: Facets of a Fleeting Relationship," *American Journal of Sociology* 65 (1959): 158–165; Jack Haas, "Learning Real Feelings: A Study of High Steel Ironworker's Reactions to Fear and Danger," *Sociology of Work and Occupations* 4 (1977): 147–170; and Robert Jackall, *Mora Mazes: The World of Corporate Managers* (New York: Oxford University Press, 1988).

4. Erving Goffman, *The Presentation of Self in Everyday Life* (Garden City: N.Y.: Doubleday, 1959).

5. Ronald M. Pavalko, *Sociology of Occupations and Professions* (Itasca, Ill.: Peacock, 1988).

6. George Ritzer, *Man and His Work: Conflict and Change* (New York: Appleton-Century-Crofts, 1977).

7. Carol Gilligan, *In a Different Voice* (Cambridge: Harvard University Press, 1982).

8. Judith Lorber, "*Trust, Loyalty and the Place of Women in the External Organization of Work*," in Jo Freeman, ed., *Women: A Feminist Perspective* (Palo Alto, Calif.: Mayfield, 1984), 370–378.

9. C. Wright Mills, *White Collar* (New York: Oxford University Press, 1951).

10. Employers utilize extremely simple methods of formal training with low-status employees because there is little danger that a single employee can cause damage to the operation as a whole. If an employee does not produce the desired results, he or she can easily be fired and replaced. See Ritzer, *Man and His Work*.

11. Goffman, *Presentation of Self in Everyday Life*.

12. This situation is similar to those of blue-collar women in studies by Mary Walshok (1981) and women medical interns studied by Cynthia Fuchs Epstein (1988) who had difficulty finding men to mentor them. Rosabeth Kanter (1977) finds women in corporate management having similar difficulties because they are token women in territory belonging to men. They eat in separate lunchrooms and are not included in informal gatherings where insider information is passed along. Jessie Bernard (1964) finds academic women are also excluded in this way.

13. This is found to be the case in other occupations dominated by men, such as coal mining, police work, and the military. See Rustad 1984; Schroedel 1985; Walshok 1981; Yount 1991; Zimmer 1987. It is also true for newcomers in other high-commission jobs such as insurance and commercial real estate. See Leidner 1991 and B. Thomas 1990. And it is true for professionals such as women lawyers. See Rosenberg, Perlstadt, and Phillips 1993. For a current anthology, see Dana Dunn, *Workplace/Women's Place* (Los Angeles: Roxbury, 1997).

14. See Arlie Russell Hochschild, *The Managed Heart: Commercialization of Human Feelings* (Berkeley: University of California Press, 1983), for a discussion of emotional labor in service work.

10

OUTSIDERS WITHIN THE STATION HOUSE
The Impact of Race and Gender on Black Women Police

Susan Martin

Most of the research on the effects of discrimination on occupational behavior has focused either on race or gender, ignoring the unique social location of black females. Recent feminist scholarship has identified the need for an interactive model articulating the interlocking nature of racial and sexual systems of subordination. This chapter examines the interactive effects of race and gender in one male-dominated occupation—police work. Based on in-depth interviews with 106 black and white officers and supervisors from five large municipal agencies, it explores the perspectives, experiences, and structural barriers black women officers face in dealing with white female and black and white male coworkers. This study finds that the combination of their race and gender statures leads to both unique problems and perspectives for black women. The interaction of racism and sexism results in each form of expression modifying the nature and impact of the other.

In the past thirty years more women and persons of color have entered occupations previously limited to white men. Although some studies have examined the factors that have aided or hindered women's advancement into nontraditional occupations and others have focused on changes in the occupational status of blacks and other ethnic minorities, few have systematically focused on the interactive effects of race and gender on black women's occupational perspectives and behavior.

This chapter examines how race and gender interact and affect the workplace status and perspectives of black women by closely examining one occupation long dominated by white males—police work. It explores how racism enlarges cleavages among women and how sexism divides black women and men, while police work itself, in controlling "the dangerous classes," contributes to these divisions. By focusing on these interlocking systems of oppression in one particular setting, this chapter seeks to expand understanding of the interconnections among these elements of an overarching structure of domination and resistance to it.

The Intersection of Race and Gender

Most studies of occupational attainment and the effects of discrimination focus separately on the effects of gender or race, ignoring the fact that black women must deal with the joint effect of multiple disadvantaged statuses.[1] Several early studies of the effects of race and gender adopted an additive approach, suggesting that the combination of their gender and race statures expose black women to "double jeopardy" (Beale 1970) or multiple disadvantages in the labor market or, alternatively, provide extra benefits arising from "the positive effects of the double negative" of their minority statuses, particularly for affirmative action decisions (Epstein 1973).

Two recent studies testing the competing "double jeopardy" and "double advantage" hypotheses, however, find little support for either in their examinations of black female managers (Nkomo and Cox 1989) and chemists (Koelewijn-Strattner et al. 1991). Both suggest the need for a more qualitative approach to explore how black women perceive themselves vis-à-vis white women and black and white men.

Feminist critics of the additive approach note that much of the literature has generalized about women on the basis of data on white women and about blacks on the basis of the experience of black men (Dugger 1988; Hooks 1981) or has treated black women as invisible or as deviant cases (Gilkes 1981). Additional studies have compared the dynamics and effects of racism and sexism, ignoring qualitative differences in the scope and intensity of the physical and psychological impact of racism compared to sexism (King 1988).

Other analysts have proposed an interactive model, noting that black women's unique social location at the intersection of different hierarchies has produced a distinct feminist consciousness different from that of white women (Collins 1986, 1990; Dill 1983; King 1988; Smith and Stewart 1983). White women have ample contact with white men and the potential for increased power by association with one of them. But they have limited their influence by internalizing an image of helplessness and allowing themselves to be "put on a pedestal." In contrast, due to racism, black women have experienced far less protection and a far greater element of fear based on white hostility, physical separation, and intimidation. Thus Hurtado (1989, 845) suggests that white women experience "subordination through seduction" while black women face "subordination through rejection." For the latter, the result is "a unique angle of vision" that "merges thought and action. . . and espouses a both/and orientation that views them as part of the same processes" (Collins 1990, 26).

Differences in class and occupational status intersect with those of race and gender in separating black and white women. Historically white middle-class women accepted and contributed to the domestic code that enabled them to slough off burdensome domestic work onto more oppressed groups of women. As service work moved from the home to institutionalized urban labor markets segmented by race and gender, the race and gender hierarchy also moved into public settings. This divergence in the experiences of black and white women with respect to access to power, their workplace activities, and their roles in their respective communities has contributed to black women's "acute consciousness of the interlocking nature of race and gender oppression" (Glenn 1992, 34–35).

Kanter's (1977) structural approach identifies power, opportunity, and group representation as key determinants of occupational behavior and work-related contingencies in work organizations. Inequalities in opportunities for mobility and the distribution of power within an organization lead some members toward success and consign others to failure. In addition, "tokens," whose type is underrepresented in majority-dominated groups, face barriers to occupational achievement including performance pressure, exclusion as "outsiders," and treatment according to familiar stereotypes.

Kanter's theory of tokenism was conceived as gender neutral and as broadly applicable to racial and other minorities. However, it ignores both the specific effects of sexism that male tokens do not suffer (Zimmer 1988; Williams 1992) and the effects of other dimensions of domination including race, class, sexual orientation, and age. As Acker (1990:146) observes, neither mobility opportunities nor the organizations in which they are found are "gender neutral." Rather,

> advantage and disadvantage, exploitation and control, action and emotion, meaning and identity are patterned through and in terms of a distinction between male and female, masculine and feminine. Gender is not an addition to ongoing processes, conceived as gender neutral. Rather, it is an integral part of those processes.

Organizations are gendered in terms of physical and social divisions (e.g., job titles and physical space); symbols and images (e.g., language and dress) that explain and reinforce those divisions; interaction processes and patterns that enact dominance and submission (e.g., nonverbal door ceremonies); and the production of organizational identities that are gendered.

Furthermore, organizations are structured by racial divisions, stereotypes, and patterns of dominance and deference that intersect with gender distinctions. In one of the few studies examining these patterns of interaction that focused explicitly on black women, Collins (1990) identifies four stereotypes or "controlling images." In contrast to the key virtues of piety, purity, submissiveness, and domesticity to which white women have been encouraged to aspire, black women have been portrayed as mammies, matriarchs, welfare recipients, and "hot mommas." These images have maintained the political economy of domination by making racism, sexism, and poverty appear to be normal and inevitable. They have kept black women as "others," at the margins of society, while their labor market opportunities have been severely restricted to low paying service jobs (Collins 1990).

To provide a clearer picture of the interlocking effects of gender and race, this paper explores their impact on one occupation that traditionally has been monopolized by white men. While a fully interactive model would compare the experiences and perspectives of incumbents from all groups, this paper focuses on black women as the pivotal group in defining the commonalities and differences between: (1) black and white women in their experiences of sexism; and (2) black men and women in the face of racism, in police organizations, which have long been dominated by and served the interests of dominant white men.

The Police and Discrimination

Police work has a long tradition of discriminatory selection criteria and assignment practices. Until recently, most black men were rejected by racially discriminatory selection procedures that excluded persons that did not "fit" (Gray 1976); those that became officers walked foot beats in ethnic neighborhoods and were prohibited from arresting white offenders (Leinen 1984).[2] Regardless of race, women were employed as "policewomen," got lower pay, and worked with "women, children, and typewriters" (Milton 1972).

In 1972, the Equal Employment Opportunity Act outlawed discrimination by public employers on the basis of race, color, religion, sex, or national origin. Since that time, most police agencies have altered discriminatory selection criteria related to education, age, height, and weight, as well as their use of arrest records, agility tests, and veterans' preference (Sulton and Townsey 1981). They have modified the agility tests and personal interview procedures that disproportionately eliminated women and the written examinations that disproportionately eliminated minority candidates; many departments now are guided by affirmative action plans.[3]

As a result, the representation of women and black men in policing has grown. By the end of 1986, in municipal departments serving populations of more than 50,000 people, white men comprised 72.2 percent of the sworn personnel, nonwhite men made up 19 percent, white women constituted 5.3 percent, and nonwhite women 3.5 percent. Although black women made up only 2.5 percent of all sworn officers, they constituted 31 percent of the female officers, whereas black men composed only 12 percent of male personnel (Martin 1990). Above the entry officer rank, the proportion of women police was 3.3 percent and that of black women a mere 1 percent.

While the door to the station house has opened to minority men and all women, both racist (Leinen 1984; Christopher et al. 1991) and sexist attitudes and behaviors remain widespread within police departments (Home 1980; Hunt 1990; Martin 1980, 1990; Pike 1991). Nevertheless, in comparing the discrimination experienced by female and minority male officers, Pike (1991, 275) suggests that minority men do not challenge the quintessential police officer role in the same way women do. Stereotypes of black men fit into the traditional police model since they are seen as physically strong, street-wise, and masculine; their integration did not require organizational changes. In contrast, the integration of women required changes in facilities, uniforms, and physical training programs. In addition, the organizational stereotype of "what women are like" means that women are much less likely to match the ideal type of the officer and those that do risk being labeled "butch" or "bitch." None of these studies, however, has addressed the issue of the unique situation of black women officers and the interactive effects of racism and sexism.

Data Sources and Research Design

The data reported here come from case studies in five large municipal agencies that were part of a larger study designed to assess the current status of women in policing (Martini 1990). The case studies explored departmental policies and procedures for integrating women into policing and officers' perspectives on changes in the status of women over the past two decades. As shown in Table 10.1, the agencies were diverse with respect to size, region, representation of minorities and women, and the nature of their affirmative action policies.

The data were collected in two phases. First, approximately ten command staff and other administrators in each department were interviewed regarding historical and current departmental policies and procedures related to women. Interviews were conducted with persons in charge of recruitment, psychological services, the training academy, promotion process, EEO and legal officials, field operations, a precinct or district, the union or bargaining agent for the officers, and with other individuals regarded as knowledgeable about department policies affecting the status of women. This included a total of about fifteen high-ranking women (some in top civilian positions), nearly half of whom were black. In addition, statistical data, policy documents, and personnel rosters from which to select an interview sample were obtained.

In the second phase, approximately thirty female and twenty male officers and midlevel supervisors were randomly selected and invited to participate in an interview conducted during on-duty time. Approximately half of these persons were interviewed in each agency (see Table 10.1), depending on the contingencies of scheduling and their willingness to participate. Because the case studies were designed to identify changes in the status of women officers during the past decade and to explore the problems of women supervisors, midlevel supervisors were oversampled and compose 54 percent of the females and 60 percent of the males that were interviewed. Most were in their thirties and had about ten years of police experience at the time of the interviews.

The interviews were semistructured, lasted about two hours, and explored a wide range of work issues. In four of the five sites, half of the interviews were conducted by the author (who is white) and half by a black female research associate.[4] When the interview schedule permitted a choice, we each interviewed persons of our own race in order to increase rapport and disclosure of potentially embarrassing information.

Officers' Perceptions of Discrimination

The interviews indicated that across the five case study departments the experience of discrimination is widespread but that officers differ in their perceptions of it both on the basis of gender and race.[5] These differences help explain why female officers rarely have acted in concerted political fashion, despite their common experience of sex discrimination, including sexual harassment.

Most of the female but only a minority of the male respondents believe that they had been victims of discrimination as police officers. As shown in Table 10.2, 68 percent of the black women and 80 percent of the white women reported encountering

TABLE 10.1   Characteristics of the Case Study Departments, End 1986

	Washington, D.C.	*Birmingham*	*Detroit*	*Phoenix*	*Chicago*
Department Size-end 1986	3,869	644	5,049	1,757	12,448
Region	Mid-Atlantic	South	N. Central	West	N. Central
% female	13	15	18	7	10
% non-white	56	25	48	15	25
% female supervisors	7	10	12	2	2
Affirmative Action	*voluntary court ordered*		*court ordered and voluntary*	*voluntary court ordered*	
# women interviewed	16	17	15	12	12
# men interviewed	9	6	12	6	7
# sergeant and above	19	11	15	10	9

discrimination based on either race or sex, in contrast to 43 and 32 percent of the white and black men, respectively (X^2 = 58.5; df = 9; p **is less than** .001). Yet white and black women differed in their experiences of discrimination. The majority of white women reported facing sex discrimination (77 percent) but were unlikely to believe they had been victims of racial discrimination (20 percent). Black women reported racial discrimination as the more frequent experience (61 percent) than sex discrimination (55 percent), although a substantial minority (48 percent) of the black women reported experiencing both. Black women also were much more likely than black men to report racial discrimination (24 percent compared with 61 percent).

Among the men, whites claimed to be victims of racial discrimination more frequently than blacks (43 percent versus 24 percent) and most of their complaints were related to racial discrimination (made by 33 percent). Complaints of sex discrimination came only from white men.[6]

Respondents also were asked whether they had benefited or been favored because of their race or sex. Black women were as likely as white women (36 percent versus 38 percent) to report being favored, but the former were more likely to believe they had benefited from both statuses while the white women felt favored only on the basis of their sex. A third of the black men but none of the white males believe they had been favored.

The meaning of discrimination varied among the four groups. Some whites, particularly, the men, regard themselves as having been victimized by affirmative action programs which resulted in promotion of black men and women who scored lower than they did on the promotion exam. Male respondents never mentioned and women infrequently commented on the inequities that arise from assignments attributable to informal sponsorship by powerful mentors or from membership in old-boy networks. Thus the measure of discrimination is the decisionmaking process related to a specific opportunity or position, particularly when there are formalized rules that confer advantage to a class rather than individuals. In contrast, there is little recognition of

TABLE 10.2   Percentage of Case Study Police Officers Who Experienced Discrimination by Gender and Race

Type of Discrimination	White Female (N=35)	Black Female (N=31)	White Male (N=21)	Black Male (N=17)
Sex only	60	7	10	—
Race only	3	13	19	24
Both race and sex	17	48	14	—
Neither	20	32	57	76
Total	100%	100%	100%	100%

inequities built into the organizational logic (Acker 1990) or the ways that decision rules related to policies, procedures, and systems of evaluations structure advantages or disabilities in ways that are both gendered and racially biased. If everyone competes according to the same formal criteria (whether or not these are appropriate, job related, or biased in some fashion), then there is no perception of discrimination. Conversely, when the playing field is not level, persons are promoted out of turn or from a race or sex-based list, or an assignment is earmarked for a person of a particular race and/or gender, the decision is viewed as discriminatory.

Men, both black and white, also expressed indignation at the discrimination arising from women's taking advantage of their sexuality to gain sponsorship, protection, and coveted assignments. That as males, some men took advantage of informal buddy relationships and insider status and were involved in exchanges of other types of favors was ignored by the men and infrequently articulated by the women. Many women also were critical of those (other) women who exchanged sexual favors for job-related benefits. Although they recognized that this had a negative impact on women as a group (and some observed that individually they had had to work harder because they did not "play"), few labeled it discrimination.

Affirmative Action Policies, Counting Rules, and the Intersection of Race and Sex

Given the presence of discrimination on the basis of both race and gender, how to "count" black females has an important effect on the implementation of affirmative action efforts. Clearly some individual black women have benefited, but in three of the case study departments the rules applied to counting in court orders and affirmative action plans have worked to black women's disadvantage.

This disadvantage was most strikingly illustrated by the legal battle over promotion procedures in the Chicago police department, as black men and white women protected their own interests at the expense of the black women. The department's hiring and promotion process came under supervision of the federal courts as a result of *U.S. vs. City of Chicago*. In 1973, after a finding that the sergeant's promotional exam was discriminatory, the judge imposed quotas for promotions. The black women, as black plaintiffs, were represented by the Afro-American Police League and initially were drawn from the promotion list as blacks, regardless of gender. When the white women realized some black women were being promoted to sergeant ahead of them, however, they filed a claim asserting that all females should be treated as a single minority group. The judge ruled that black women could not be given double benefits. He asked the Afro-American League's legal representative whether it was acceptable to count the black women as women, not as blacks, for the purpose of the quota. Without consulting the women, the lawyer agreed.

Perhaps in accepting the change the lawyer recognized that he would increase the number of positions for which blacks were eligible. Alternatively, one might interpret his actions as knowingly undercutting the black women. While the change increased promotion opportunities for black men by removing the women from competition with them, it forced the black women to compete with the white women whose test scores were better than theirs (whereas those of black men were not). When the black women legally protested the decision several years later, the judge agreed that they had a valid complaint but ruled that it was "not timely." As one black woman observed, "Nobody was looking out for our interests."[7]

In another department, although black females now outnumber white females three to one, the affirmative action practice remains the promotion of one white woman for every black woman. In a third department, black women have been double counted, but the result in counting them twice is to shrink rather than expand either the quota for women or for minorities.

Despite these generally disadvantageous counting rules, the black women often have incurred the hostility of both white women and black men who feel that the black women have taken "their" places. Furthermore, when black females act in concerted fashion with black men, as the Chicago lawsuit illustrates, they have less power to share, lower status as women, and face being betrayed or undermined by their allies in the latter's quest for advantage.

Race and Gender Effects on Street Patrol Activities

The initial resistance to both racial integration and the assignment of women to police patrol was strong, organized, and sometimes life threatening (Bloch and Anderson 1974; Martin 1980; Leinen 1984; Hunt 1984). Such systematic harassment has largely ended. Nevertheless, both racism and sexism continue, although they are expressed in different ways. Many men—both white and black—still openly voice negative views of women as officers prefer not to work with them, and alter their behavior when they have a female partner. In contrast, black men are accepted as capable officers, although racial politics abounds and seating at roll calls and most off-duty socializing remain racially separate. Overt expression of racism, however, are taken seriously by command staff and have led to disciplinary action in the departments in this study.

How do these patterns of racism and sexism affect black women officers' perceptual world, street patrol behavior, and opportunities for mobility? All rookie officers face a "reality shock" when they begin street patrol. This initial training period is important in developing skills and self-confidence and establishing a reputation. An officer who does not have or take opportunities to develop patrol skills due to limiting assignments, inadequate instruction. Lion, or overprotection is likely to be hesitant or fail to act in a confrontation. Such incompetent officers are regarded by others as potential dangers they are anxious to avoid, thus perpetuating the cycle of incompetence on patrol. Gender-based patterns of occupations socialization and expectations of patrol performance influence the way rookies respond, creating self-fulfilling prophecies for many women officers (Martin 1980).

These patterns are most visible for the first generation of women officers who faced organized resistance designed to drive them out of police work. They faced insufficient instruction, coworker hostility, and the "silent treatment" that "made eight hours seem like eight days," close and punitive supervision, exposure to danger and lack of backup, and paternalistic overprotection. As one black woman recounted:

> Males didn't want to work with females, and at times, I was the only female or black on the shift. I had to do a lot to prove myself. I was at the precinct 10 days before I knew I had a partner 'cause. . . [the men] called in sick and I was put in the station. The other white guys called the man who was assigned to work with me the 11th day and told him to call in sick. . . . He came in anyway.

Another noted:

> My first day on the North side, the assignment officer looked up and said, "Oh shit, another fucking female." That's the way you were treated by a lot of the men. The sergeant called me in and said the training officer doesn't want to ride with you but I've given him a direct order to work with you.

Although both white and black women were targets of the men's hostility, several black women observed differences in their treatment that reflect differences in the cultural image and employment experiences of black and white women. Historically, white women have been put on a pedestal—idealized as frail and spared from physical labor. In contrast, black women have assumed the beast of burden role (Dill 1979), performing heavy physical labor in fields, factories, and the homes of white women, as well as coming "to symbolic sexuality, prowess," and. . . embody the "myth of the superwoman" (Palmer 1983, 158). Faced with these dual images of womanhood, white women formed their identities around "good" womanhood, accepted their difference from black women, and adopted a sense superiority, although, in reality, they were powerless, having accepted economic and psychological dependence on white men who control their sexuality.

On patrol, women tend to be treated according to those traditional patterns. In all five departments the initial cohorts of white women assigned to patrol, particularly those who were physically attractive or attached to influential white men, were more likely than black women to be protected from street patrol assignments by being given station house duty and rapid transfers to administrative units. As one woman noted,

White women were put on a pedestal, treated like wives. . . [Many] got jobs doing typing for commanders and downtown assignments. They're high priced secretaries.

On street patrol, too, there were and continue to be differences in expectations and treatment of black and white women. Patrol officers rely heavily on fellow officers for backup in dangerous situations; providing backup when another officer calls for help is a central norm policing (Westley 1970). Police also may support, control, or sanction others by their willingness to "slide in" on calls to provide added police presence and by the speed with which they provide assistance.

Both the lack of reliable backup and overprotectiveness are likely to reduce an officer's willingness to take risks or display initiative. But the officer who fails to act appropriately is shunned as a coward. And when such behavior is displayed by a woman, rather than being an individual failure, the stigmatizing label is generalized to all women.

Many of the white patrolmen are protective of white women, and the latter acquiesce by enacting the stereotyped roles of pet, mother, or seductress (Kanter 1977) to gain personal acceptance and backup. Black women also are told to remain "back covers" by male partners who do not expect them to perform as equals. When they defer to white men and accept a passive role, however, they cannot count on being protected as females and may instead be viewed as lazy (thereby fitting the welfare mother stereotype). A black woman explained:

> Black women don't expect to be nice to them (white men) because white males won't protect us on the street.

Another noted that when she had a white female partner, the white men backed them up; when she worked with a black partner the white men would not do so. Several stated they had faced outright racial harassment, illustrated by the following incident that occurred in 1977:

> My training officer and I went to a call. . . When we got back, our car door was open and there was a cut out arrow from a sheet of paper taped to the window. The word "nigger" was written on the arrow which was pointing to my seat. My training officer told me not to pay attention to it, but it bothered me. I didn't report it; it wouldn't have done any good. . . but the incident let me know where I stood.

Black women face uncertainties related both to coworker backup and to unpredictable responses of citizens to a black woman exercising authority. They also are aware of the historical role of the police as oppressors in the black community. These factors contribute to their reluctance to adopt the policing style characteristic of white men who are enthusiastic about "aggressive patrol" and seeking out crime and criminals. This difference in occupational perspective and role performance style was illustrated in interviews with two rookie officers for whom similar assignments to the projects posed starkly contrasting problems. The black female was troubled by responding to conflicts involving people she had grown up with and was embarrassed to learn intimate information about their lives. The white male fumed out after acting as the macho enforcer zealously arresting for drug offenses persons he views as "animals" that he had to fight "tooth and claw."

Nonpatrol Assignments and Station House Interaction

Inside the station, women face a hostile working environment filled with sexual propositions, pornographic material, and cursing (Martin 1980; Swerdlow 1989). Several black woven asserted that they faced additional displays of deliberate disrespect shown to them as women by the men's use of language.[8] One black woman observed:

> White males generally have very little respect for black females, especially if they don't know you. . . . If a white female is around and they start their cueing, they'll say "excuse me." If a black female is around they don't stop. Their attitude is, "Oh it is only a black female, who cares."

Black men also tend to be protective of women but black women cannot count as heavily on them for backup. First, they are fewer in number and, therefore, less available when needed. In addition, they face pressures from the white men (or shared their resistance to women on patrol), not to back the women up.

Interacting with these gender-based stereotypes, black women face widespread racial stereotypes as well as outright racial harassment. Stereotypically, blacks are assumed to be less knowledgeable, reliable, and able to manage power as supervisors. For example, a black female burglary detective observed that white men are reluctant to recognize her expertise. Precinct supervisors often call her unit for information. However, when she answers calls from white males they tend to argue with what she says. Another black woman asserted:

> A white male can goof off all day and nobody'd say a thing. But a woman, especially a black woman. . . has to work twice as hard.

Another woman did just that when she took over the administrative work of two sergeants who retired at the same time in her detective unit. Although, she explained, "I had an advantage; I knew how to type." The difference was also one of attitude. The men would wait for a typist; she did the work herself, to assure that the records were current. While she observed, "now everything runs smoothly," her performance may also contribute to the subsequent downgrading of such administrative support positions and to their resegregation (Reskin and Roos 1990).

As part of the gendering of organizations, job tasks come to be "loaded with gender meanings" (Hall 1993, 454). Even before integration, not only was policing done by men and thus viewed as men's work, police attached gendered meanings to various tasks and aspects of the job. Hunt (1984) observed that police symbolically construct their occupational world in terms of oppositional categories with masculine and feminine significance. "Real police work" is associated with the outside domain of the street where men engage in high-status, dirty, dangerous crime-fighting activities. In contrast, inside administrative work, formal rules, and cleanliness are associated with femininity. As women officers have moved into symbolically feminine inside positions, those jobs have become more strongly gender labeled and devalued in the eyes of male officers.

It probably was no accident that men in administrative support jobs emphasized their masculine policy and administrative responsibilities, letting the typing pile up rather than perform the task regarded as women's work. As women gain these assignments, by using their feminine typing and office management skills to make the unit operate more efficiently, they also risk transforming the gender and racial meanings of the work so that it confers less prestige and authority.[9]

In some instances, the black women's combination of race and gender has made the nature of their problems ambiguous. One explained:

> Sometimes I couldn't tell if what I faced was racial or sexual or both. The black female is the last one on the totem pole in the department, so if things are okay, you thank God for that.

A black female supervisor reported having problems with a white male subordinate who deliberately violated procedures. After he transferred, she learned that his new male supervisor also had problems with him,

> so it wasn't a female thing. . . but at the time I couldn't be sure. . . I felt he was rebelling against me because I was a female lieutenant and a black lieutenant. I had a double whammy on me as female and black.

Facing the double whammy, however, emboldened some black female supervisors to stand up to harassment and challenge the systemic racial and gender discrimination they perceived, perhaps because of their detachment from the informal work culture. Like Simmel's "marginal man" [sic], the black female has been the "outsider within" (Collins 1986). Nowhere is this truer than in the "macho" world of police work, where black women are separated both from many black male officers who have enthusiastically embraced its crime-fighting activities and from white women by the latter's expectations of protection as stereotypic women. Having survived isolation and performance pressures as officers and as sergeants, they relished their access to power and sought to use it in broadly political ways.[10] Several told of challenging evaluation and assignment practices they regarded as racist, not simply for individual career advancement but on behalf of black officers. One black woman in a command position related the following:

> I took a beating for changing things (regarding race). Whites are tribal in this community 'cause they see all blacks as the enemy and as criminals. I understand their ethnocentrism. . . . but cannot tolerate some of the stuff that was going on. When I insisted on doing things by the book there was rebellion. . . . Now they're on the right path but they call me "that woman" because I caused them problems.

A female sergeant related the following experience. When she observed that blacks were receiving lower service ratings, regardless of their productivity, she began recording all activities for the unit. The next rating period, when the lieutenant called all sergeants in to justify their ratings, the whites and the black male sergeant had rated blacks lower than the whites; she rated females and blacks higher. The lieutenant refused to approve her ratings and demanded an explanation. She stated that her ratings were based on her six-month log on all officers' activities and threatened to file a grievance and let the records speak for themselves if the ratings were not changed. She added:

> The lieutenant sat back in his chair and said that in his 15 years as a lieutenant he'd never had a black officer challenge him. He wondered how long it would take for a black to speak up. He added it took guts, but that the service ratings would be changed.

A third black woman supervisor stated that she challenged the disproportionate number of detective positions held by white men after feeling empowered by the model provided by Jesse Jackson when he ran for president.

Dealing with Black Men

Although black women often have worked closely with black men to reduce the effects of racial discrimination, their relations with them also are strained by tensions and dilemmas associated with sexuality and competition for desirable assignments and promotions. Like white women, in the struggle for power and acceptance in policing, black males have sometimes allied with white men. The bases for their alliance, however, rest largely on their shared resistance to the integration of women into the policemen's world. Yet the open hostility of black men to white women—particularly those with close personal bonds to white male police—always poses the threat of reprisals. Consequently, the black men appear to display less hostility to white than black women with whom they compete for positions and promotions earmarked "black" by affirmative action programs.

Illustrating such competition, a black woman observed that when she was promoted her black male peers suggested that she had taken "their" slot. Another noted, "If you speak up or show you can think for yourself. . . you have problems from black men." For example, a black female lieutenant told of being verbally abused by a white lieutenant. When she hung up on him, he called her commander to complain. When her black commander asked why she could not be nicer to the lieutenant, her response was, "The only thing that I hate more than a white man trying to run over me is a black man clearing the way."

Others recounted instances of sexual harassment and the dilemmas it posed in choosing between fighting for one's personal interests as a woman and recognition of a larger concern arising from racism and the need to preserve racial solidarity. One black woman observed, "The black men have assumed they could make sexual approaches to black women they would hesitate making to whites." Another reported:

> The worst harassment I got came from a black male lieutenant. . . . The only reason I didn't (file a sexual harassment suit) is because the lieutenant's black. I guess that makes

me a racist but I looked at the overall problem it would have caused and how it would be played up in the press and didn't do it.

Elaborating on the competition theme, one woman mused:

For some reason the black men tend to hurt us more [than white men]. . . Maybe they're afraid of us, although they won't admit it.

Several recounted instances of competition for scarce resources, from being denied lockers in the station house to jealousy regarding assignments. For example, a black woman asserted:

The white commanders put white women on desk jobs for years. As soon as black females got desk assignments, however, the black guys complained.

Other black women, however, observed that they have had support from black men but poor treatment from whites. One stated, for example:

Black males are generally good to work with, but white males generally have very little respect for black females, especially if they don't know you.

In departments with a large proportion of black personnel or a black chief the effects off racism seem to diminish, but this tends to heighten black women's awareness of sex discrimination, particularly in the selection of members of the command staff:

No woman in the department is considered capable of operating in the inner circle. . . . It's an exclusive club. . . . and having a woman as the right hand man, the Chief would suffer ridicule from ranking men. They'd say "what can she offer," implying what is done by a woman can't be of value.

Ironically, she did not comment on the implied sexual innuendo.

Relations Among Women Officers

All respondents agreed that there is little unity among the women. They are divided by divergent perspectives on occupational performance, gender enactment, racism, and by white men's success using a divide-and-conquer strategy, playing on the racism of white females and the sexism of black males. Consequently, most women do not see it in their best interest to organize.

All police must find a personal style that solves certain work-related problems: dealing with fear and danger; gaining citizen compliance; and relating to peers and supervisors. In addition, women officers must cope with discrimination, sexual harassment, gender stereotypes, and the interactional scripts that incorporate race and gender in what is considered appropriate behavior for a policeman. They must negotiate an occupational identity and respond to the gender role stereotypes into which they are cast.

Martin (1980) observes that women officers are pressured to enact the police role either as *police*women or police*women*. The former behave in a manner that conforms to existing male behavioral norms and emphasizes being professional, dedicated, aggressive, and controlling even though this means acting "unladylike" and being labeled dyke or bitch. The latter, in contrast, emphasize their femininity, adopt a less assertive policing style, and consequently fail to meet work-related expectations.

Most female respondents stated that they seek to negotiate an identity that allows them to maintain their femininity, succeed as officers, and gain individual acceptance as "just me." Nevertheless, most were critical of other women, including those who "behave like clinging vines" or "act mannish" on the job and those who "act like sluts" or "try to make their way around the department on knee pads" because each of these behaviors contributes to negative stereotyping that "rubs off on us."

Although some women—both white and black—have succeeded in creating a new "woman cop" identity by combining valued masculine and feminine attributes and self-definitions (Hunt 1984), the opportunities, options, and the way they arrived at their identities also are affected by racial scripts for policing styles and prevailing stereotypes of and structural constraints on black and white women.[11]

A few of the women belong to state or national women's law enforcement organizations, but efforts to organize the women in their own agencies have been short-lived or sporadic. Chicago is the only case study site with an active (but still fledgling) departmental women officers' organization, the Coalition of Law Enforcement Officers (CLEO). Formally open to all officers, CLEO is designed to address the concerns of black women officers through educational growth and support activities.[12] Commenting on a recent meeting held by CLEO, one white Chicago officer admiringly observed:

> White women won't be organized. (At the CLEO meeting) they were talking about day care! . . . White women have the housewife syndrome; many black women are single, used to running a family, and are more assertive. . . . Black women have much more consciousness of abuse; white women are less aware of abuse as women.

Another white woman added:

> Black females are more militant and don't think white females are suffering. I wish they could see how white males treat white females.

Of course, the black women do see that white women who do not conform to stereotypes are punished for their independence, but that others have been willing to remain on the pedestal, and that both types have actively used their personal ties to white men to gain occupational advantages less frequently available to black women.

Several white women complained that they were isolated politically and personally. Most appear to share the view that:

Had we organized as a group, it would have hampered our acceptance. We went out as individuals and fitted in as individuals and that was the best thing we did for acceptance. If we'd set ourselves apart, it would have turned people off.

Clearly the people to whom she is referring are white men who become the reference group and persons in power to be appeased rather than turned off. Unity threatens her with guilt by association with the women whose occupational performance and personal behavior the respondent and others like her find objectionable, namely women who do not adopt a "kick-ass" aggressive patrol style.

Black women less frequently articulated such an individualistic strategy for gaining acceptance. Despite widely differing gender performance styles and approaches, they rarely were openly critical of other black women. Their barbs and expressions of anger were reserved for the frequent racism and sexism they encountered. They also consistently expressed both pride and frustration in their identity as a black woman officer or a black female in management rather than as simply a black or a female.

Racism compounds the divisions among women. Several blacks noted that white women are as racist as white men. For example, one woman stated:

White females seem to think that minorities are totally incompetent, dirty, don't know what we are doing, and need to be led by the hand and told what exactly has to be done, so that we won't screw up anything. That's insulting to me.

Others recounted incidents of racism involving women. Some incidents were individual; others involved organized actions such as that illustrated by the white women's legal action that blocked black women from accessing both their identities in *U.S. vs. Chicago*.

Joining a women's group, the men assert and white women perceive, means implicitly joining "them" (the other racial group) which makes you not part of "us." For women of both races acceptance by the men (of the same race) is more important than the support of other women, for both work-related and social reasons. Since women usually work with men and depend on them for backup, their support is often a matter of life and death. Men have more experience, "muscle," and are available in greater numbers than women officers. They also are the supervisors who have the power to reward and punish. In addition, social activities including dating and marriages occur along racial lines. Men of each race control women's duty behavior by threatening them with social isolation.

Both white and black men have used racism to control the women of their race and prevent women from unifying to address sex discrimination. A white female, for example, said that when she rejected the sexual advances of a white male, he started the rumor that she only slept with blacks. This attempt to assert white male control used both racism and sexism: doubly impugning the woman's behavior as promiscuous and disloyal.

In departments where blacks have gained political and numerical power, overt racism has diminished. However, the salience of their oppression as women is heightened. As one black female supervisor observed:

They keep us competing, fat versus thin, old versus young, and women seem to fall for it. Getting unity is like pulling teeth. The women say (of a female supervisor who tries to counsel them), "she doesn't want to help us" and while the women are feuding, the men are moving up.

Conclusion

This chapter goes beyond dichotomous approaches to understanding race and gender that have characterized much of the study of racism and sexism. Instead of the prevailing either/or approach, it has sought to treat them as interlocking systems of oppression and has employed a both/and approach to focus on black women as a unique class or group. It has done so using a narrowly targeted in-depth strategy of examining workplace experiences and perceptions in an occupation long dominated by white men—policing. Such a strategy has both strengths and weaknesses.

On the positive side, police work provides rich opportunities for exploring interlocking dimensions of discrimination and black women's "unique angle of vision" (Collins 1990, 26). Gender is deeply embedded in the police culture, while historically police departments have excluded black officers and have served as enforcers of a system of racial injustice in the black community. Despite changes in the past two decades, the idealized image of the representative of the forces of law and order and protector who maintains the "thin blue line" between "them" and "us" remains white and male. As "outsiders within," black women have a perspective on policing that challenges the prevailing notions, including the naturalness of the police role as it currently is enacted, and hints at an alternative vision of policing. Moreover, their experiences suggest the complexity of the interconnections of racism and sexism, which themselves are parts of the larger "matrix of domination" (Collins 1990, 225). They also illustrate some of the ambiguities in distinguishing among the bases for differential treatment.

Domination occurs not only with respect to race and gender but class, age, sexual orientation, and ethnicity, and operates on three levels at which people experience and resist it: the individual; the group or community; and social system. Thus this examination has focused on only one cell of the matrix and explored it for only one particular occupation. Even in this narrowly focused effort, however, the reception of black and white women, and nature of the "discrimination" they experienced appears to have varied across specific work settings, depending on whether or not they were introduced as a result of legal action against the department as well as the racial and social climate in the study sites.

The in-depth strategy has the advantage of reducing the likelihood of either overgeneralization or oversimplification that have characterized studies of both racism and sexism. It suggests that experiences and perspectives are situated not only historically but within organizational and occupational contexts that vary. And, in studying an occupational or organizational setting in which both black and white men are present, it has expanded the "three-way relationship involving white men, white women, and women of color" in which "race and gender dynamics are played out" (Glenn 1992, 34) to give black men a role.

At the same time, it has excluded several important issues and elements of that matrix that should be noted. It "controlled" for several variables by ignoring or excluding them. The class backgrounds of the officers were presumed to be the same for black and white officers; this clearly is questionable and merits further study. Most of the persons that were interviewed were experienced officers who had been promoted. The perspectives expressed by these black women may point to useful strategies for survival but understate the problems of average women officers, particularly those who left police work. The experiences of a wider segment of the occupational or organizational group also merit future exploration.

The data rest entirely on intensive interviews without observing actual behavior or gathering intensive personality measures. Since discrimination often is subtle, the findings illustrate the ways in which one may easily confuse whether discrimination is based on race, gender, age, experience, or personality style. Thus the "by the book" behavior of the female supervisor cited in this paper illustrates how a personality or interactional style that is offensive to others may elicit punishment or be perceived in race or gender terms.

The both/and conceptual perspective allows one to view all groups as having varying amounts of penalty and privilege in a single system that changes over time. White women are penalized by gender but privileged by their race. Depending on the context, an individual may be oppressor and member of an oppressed group or both simultaneously. For example, the interactions of white women officers with other police and with citizens most likely were affected by their age, rank, and by the authority of their office. Similarly, black men alternately were shown to act as mediators and oppressors of black women in divide and conquer politics characteristic of many organizational settings.

Assuming the perspective of persons who are multiple minorities illuminates the unique uncertainties and heightened consciousness that result, as well as the advancement strategies likely to be different from those of other groups. As outsiders within who have limited expectations of climbing onto the pedestal or becoming one of the boys, black women have been able to distance themselves from the occupational culture and adopt a more critical view of it as well as their place in it.

It is hoped that these findings stimulate a variety of further studies. In exploring the matrix of domination, not only the intersection of race and gender but consideration of class, ethnicity, and sexual orientation are important factors for further examination in a variety of occupational settings as well as across occupations and work contexts which vary widely from each other. Studies too are needed that go beyond resistance of the oppressed to examine structural reversals, as persons who are not white males move into positions of authority. Finally, these findings suggest the value of exploring sources of strength and resilience as well as the nature of the barriers that limit achievement.

Notes

The author thanks especially Hattie Carrington without whose assistance this study would not have been possible, as well as Lynn Zimmer and other anonymous reviewers for their helpful comments and criticisms. This research was completed when the author was a project director at the Police Foundation and was supported in part with funding from the Ford Foundation. This chapter is a revised version of a paper presented at the American Sociological Association Meetings in San Francisco in August 1989.

1. Although Hispanic, Native American, and Asian American women share many of the disadvantages of black women, this chapter focuses only on black women, given the limitations of my data and the history of police integration.

2. The term "police officer" has replaced "policeman" and "policewoman" as the generic term referring to sworn police personnel of all ranks. While the word "officer" sometimes is used to mean police at the lowest rank in a semimilitary organization, I will use it in the generic sense unless otherwise specified.

3. By the end of 1986, 15 percent of the departments in cities serving populations of more than 50,000 were operating under court orders or consent decrees (most of these were in jurisdictions with populations over 250,000) and 42 percent had adopted voluntary affirmative action plans (Martin 1990). Only 4 percent of municipal agencies still had minimum height and weight standards as entry criteria (Fyfe 1987).

4. Personal contingencies prevented the research associate from leaving Washington, D.C., to conduct the interviews in Phoenix. The proportion of blacks in that city and police department, however, is very small.

5. After relating their history of assignments and experiences during initial training, respondents were asked directly, "Have you experienced discrimination on the basis of race or sex as members of the police department?" No definition of discrimination was provided but all positive responses were probed. Even before getting to this question, however, many of the women described treatment by training officers, supervisors, and fellow officers that was subsequently described as discrimination or as sexual harassment. A separate question regarding both their definition and experience of sexual harassment was included late in the interview schedule (if the subject had not already been explored).

6. The low proportion of black men reporting discrimination is puzzling. Although it is possible that women's "radar" for detecting discrimination was more sensitive, the fact that the interviews focused largely on women in policing led the black men to minimize discussion of their own experiences of racial discrimination. Furthermore, the higher proportion of white than black males claiming to have been a victim of discrimination suggests both a reluctance of some of the latter to discuss their experiences and the strength of the white backlash and resentment of affirmative action. The perception of being a victim of "reverse discrimination" was only expressed by respondents in the agencies with court ordered affirmative action policies including racial quotas for promotions. The acrimony over integration was particularly intense in Detroit where a powerful police union dominated by white men had initiated a number of lawsuits challenging several court ordered affirmative action policies.

7. This case clearly illustrates the problem of judicial treatment of black women's employment discrimination claims. If courts shifted from looking one at a time at "protected categories" to conceptualizing black women as a distinct class protected by Title VII of the Civil Rights Act, it would have a substantial impact on current antidiscrimination efforts (Scarborough 1989).

8. White men sometimes combined expressions of racism and sexism by yoking stereotypes of black women to their sexuality. The mechanism was strikingly displayed by a white male respondent in his interaction with the black female interviewer. In discussing the racial integration of the police work he strayed from the question to gratuitously assert: "I can't accept it that it is acceptable for black women to have babies out of wedlock and give them over to grandparents. These women prefer to date married men. They don't care how men treat them. He responded to a question about how white females are accepted in policing saying: on a par with black females. I don't want to offend you but if I was reincarnated, I wouldn't want to come ball as a black female. But of course he was deliberately offending, by making clear his stereotypic view of black women as both sexually promiscuous and willing victims of black men."

9. This energetic black woman also stated: "Initially they (the men) couldn't stand the thought of you being around them: now all administrative units are run by females. Few men type so they seek out good females." Similarly, an internal audit by the Chicago police determined that women held 53 percent of the "inside" permanent station assignments in violation of the seniority rules.

10. In addition to bringing structural changes, a high proportion of the black women related at least one instance of resisting oppression, bias, or discrimination at a personal level. For example, one woman stated: "When I was (assigned to work) at the jail I had a lieutenant who didn't like blacks period. . . . He wouldn't speak to me. One day I was the only one in the office and if he wanted to get out, I'd have to let him out (by opening the electronically controlled door). I deliberately turned my back to him so he'd have to ask me to let him out. He stood five minutes before saying anything." Nevertheless, ultimately she "won" by forcing him to recognize and address her as a fellow officer.

11. Examining the structural constraints on correctional officer role enactment, Zimmer (1986) found that they affected black and white in different ways. A woman who wanted to enact the "modified" (or policewoman-like) style of work performance required protection from male coworkers and noncontact assignments from male supervisors. Since most coworkers and virtually all supervisors in the prisons were white men, they forced black women into direct contact assignment. The latter perceived this distribution of assignments as racial prejudice although it was due primarily to the lack of "connections" also faced by white women from urban areas who lacked ties to male supervisors. Harlan and O'Farrell (1982) also note that black women who entered traditionally male blue-collar jobs in large industrial firms felt similarly disadvantaged vis-à-vis white women.

12. At the time the data were collected, CLEO was only eighteen months old, had been inactive in its first year, and included only fifty-five members (out of approximately 1,000 women in the department, 455 of whom are black). Its continuation and success under a new leader are uncertain. Its focus on concerns of black women, however, may have removed one source of tension that has hampered organizing efforts in other departments.

References

Acker, Joan. 1990. "Hierarchies, Jobs and Bodies: A Theory of Gendered Organizations." *Gender and Society* 4: 139–158.

Beale, Francis. 1970. "Double Jeopardy: To Be Black and Female." In *The Black Woman: An Anthology,* ed. Toni Cade. New York: New American Library.

Bloch, Peter D., and Deborah Anderson. 1974. *Policewomen on Patrol: Final Report.* Washington, D.C.: Urban Institute.

Christopher, Warren, J. A. Arguelles, R. Anderson, W. R. Barnes, L. F. Estrada, Mickey Kantor, R. M. Mosk, A. S. Ordin, J. B. Slaughter, and R. E. Tranquada. 1991. *Report of the Independent Commission on the Los Angeles Police Department.*

Collins, Patricia H. 1986. "Learning from the Outsider Within: The Sociological Significance of Black Feminist Thought." *Social Problems* 33: 14–32.

_____. 1990. *Black Feminist Thought: Knowledge, Consciousness, and the Politics of Empowerment.* New York: Routledge.

Dill, Bonnie T. 1979. "The Dialectics of Black Womanhood." *Signs* 4: 543–555.

_____. 1983. "Race, class, and gender: Prospects for an all-inclusive sisterhood." *Feminist Studies* 9: 131–150.

Dugger, Karen. 1988. "Social Location and Gender-Role Attitudes: A Comparison of Black and White Women." *Gender and Society* 2: 425–448.

Epstein, Cynthia F. 1973. "The Positive Effects of the Multiple Negative: Explaining the Success of Black Professional Women." *American Journal of Sociology* 78: 912–935.

Fyfe, James. 1986. *Police Personnel Practices, 1986.* Baseline Data Report 18, no. 6. Washington, D.C.: International City Management Association.

Gilkes, Cheryl T. 1981. "From Slavery to Social Welfare: Racism and the Control of Black Women." In *Class, Race, and Sex: The Dynamics of Control,* ed. Ann Swerdlow and H. Lessing, 288–300. Boston: G. K. Hall.

Glenn, Evelyn N. 1992. "From Servitude to Service Work: Historical Continuities in the Racial Division of Paid Reproductive Labor." *Signs* 18: 1–43.

Hall, Elaine J. 1993 "Waitering/Waitressing: Engendering the Work of Table Servers." *Gender and Society* 7: 329–346.

Harlan, Sharon L., and Brigid O'Farrell. 1982. "After the Pioneers: Prospects for Women in Non-Traditional Blue Collar Jobs." *Work and Occupations* 9: 363–386.

hooks, belle. 1981. *Ain't I a Woman: Black Women and Feminism.* Boston: South End.

Home, Peter. 1980. *Women in Law Enforcement.* 2nd ed. Springfield, Ill.: Thomas.

Hunt, Jennifer. 1984. "The Development of Rapport Through Negotiation of Gender in Field Work Among Police." *Human Organization* 43: 283–296.

―――― 1990. "The Logic of Sexism Among Police." *Women and Criminal Justice* 1: 3–30.

Hurtado, Aileen. 1999. "Relating to Privilege: Seduction and Rejection in the Subordination of White Women and Women of Color." *Signs* 14: 833–855.

Kanter, Rosabeth M. 1977. *Men and Women of the Organization.* New York: Basic Books.

King, Deborah. 1988. "Multiple Jeopardy, Multiple Consciousness: The Context of a Black Feminist Ideology." *Signs* 14: 42–72.

Koelewijn-Strattner, Gijsberta J., Joseph L. Lengermann, and Marina A. Adler. 1991. "Race and Gender in the Chemistry Profession: Double Jeopardy or Double Negative." Paper presented at the annual meeting of the American Sociological Association, Cincinnati, Ohio.

Leinen, Stephen. 1984. *Black Police, White Society.* New York: New York University Press.

Martin, Susan E. 1980. *"Breaking and Entering": Policewomen on Patrol.* Berkeley: University of California Press.

――――. 1990. *On the Move: The Status of Women in Policing.* Washington, D.C.: Police Foundation.

Milton, Catherine. 1972. *Women in Policing.* Washington, D.C.: Police Foundation.

Nkomo, Stella M., and Taylor Cox Jr. 1989. "Gender Differences in the Upward Mobility of Black Managers: Double Whammy or Double Advantage." *Sex Roles* 21: 825–839.

Palmer, Phyllis. 1983. "White Women/Black Women: The Dualism of Female Identity and Experience in the United States." *Feminist Studies* 9: 151–171.

Pike, Diane L. 1991. "Women in Police Academy Training: Some Aspects of Organizational Response." In *The Changing Roles of Women in the Criminal Justice System: Offenders, Victims, and Professionals,* ed. Imogene Moyer, 261–280. 2d ed. Prospect Heights, Ill.: Waveland.

Reskin, Barbara, and Patricia Roos. 1990. *Job Queues, Gender Queues: Explaining Women's Inroads into Male Occupations.* Philadelphia: Temple University Press.

Scarborough, Cathy. 1989. "Conceptualizing Black Women's Employment Experiences." *Yale Law Journal* 98: 1457–1478.

Smith, Althea, and Abigail J. Stewart. 1983. "Approaches to Studying Racism and Sexism in Black Women's Lives." *Journal of Social Issues* 39: 1–13.

Sulton, Cindy, and Roi Townsey. 1981. *A Progress Report on Women in Policing.* Washington, D.C.: Police Foundation.

Swerdlow, Marion. 1989. "Men's Accommodations to Women Entering a Nontraditional Occupation: A Case of Rapid Transit Operatives." *Gender and Society* 3: 373–387.

Westley, William. 1970. *Violence and the Police.* Cambridge: MIT Press.

Williams, Christine. 1991. "The Glass Escalator: Hidden Advantages for Men in the 'Female' Professions." *Social Problems* 39: 253–266.

Zimmer, Lynn. 1986. *Women Guarding Men.* Chicago: University of Chicago Press.

――――. 1988. "Tokenism and Women in the Workplace: The Limits of Gender Neutral Theory." *Social Problems* 35: 64–77.

Discussion Questions

1. Why is there an apparent preference to hire men to work in female-dominated occupations like nursing and social work?
2. According to Williams's research, supervisors play an important role in the socialization that goes on at work. How does their influence change the work experience for men and women in a female-dominated work setting?
3. For the "ladies on the lot," the apprenticeship-type training in car sales becomes supplanted by the "sell or else" kind of choruses typical of commission work. How are women disadvantaged compared to men who work in this environment?
4. According to Lawson, how does the existence of cliques at work on the sales floor affect experience for men and women there?
5. How do men and women working in police stations perceive discrimination differently, according to Martin?
6. What effect has affirmative action had on the hiring and retention of minority police officers in the station houses Martin researches?

Part IV

NONTRADITIONAL
WORK STRUCTURES

n today's world of work, there appears to be a dramatic growth in nontraditional work structures and schedules. Led mainly, but not exclusively, by women, this trend has more workers situated in a variety of work settings that deviate from traditional full-time, Monday-through-Friday, nine-to-five jobs. There are many forms of the new work structure, such as job sharing, flex time, and telecommuting, as well as a growth in part-time, temporary, and self-employment positions. Days and times of work also have become more disparate and include variable days and hours, late shifts, early shifts, and concentrated weeks (such as four-day schedules consisting of four ten-hour shifts). In this section, part-time and temporary positions and self-employment will be featured as examples of three growing trends in employment, which each have gendered implications.

This section begins with the most frequently mentioned nontraditional job structure option for working mothers: part-time work. Cynthia Epstein and her colleagues, in "Part-Time Work as Deviance: Stigmatization and Its Consequences," show that part-time lawyers are stigmatized and that this stigmatization is gendered, since most part-time lawyers are women. Among the stigma effects endured by part-time lawyers are snide comments, sarcasm, and slights, as well as the loss of desirable assignments and clients.

In the next reading, "Temps: De-skilled and Devalued," Jackie Kraas Rogers explores the world of temporary workers. She concludes with a negative assessment of this job option. Primarily, Rogers says that most temporary work is tedious and consists of "de-skilled" tasks. Another critique of this work structure is that temporary work agencies often recruit aspiring full-time workers with the false claim of the likelihood of a low-skilled, temporary job's leading to a full-time, higher-skilled job.

A historically less typical work structure for women has been self-employment. In "Self-Employment as a Response to the Double Day for Women and Men in Canada," A. Bruce Arai suggests that the flexibility of self-employment is a good job option as a way for women (and men) to balance the time conflicts between job and home. In this study of Canadians, Arai finds that among many categories of respondents to their national survey, women with children are most likely to choose self-employment.

In conclusion, experimentation with alternative work structures has apparently had mixed results so far. The authors in this section indicate there are some potential job penalties and lack of advancement opportunities associated with part-time and temporary work, but that self-employment may be a growing, positive option for women with children.

11

PART-TIME
WORK AS DEVIANCE
Stigmatization and Its Consequences

Cynthia Fuchs Epstein, Carroll Seron,
Bonnie Oglensky, and Robert Saute

The image of the totally dedicated professional creates a sharp contrast with the image of the part-timer. In the invidious comparison with full-time lawyers, the part-timer is often seen as less dedicated and less professional—a "time deviant."

Our research found clear evidence that part-time lawyers are stigmatized. It also noted the function this stigma serves in reinforcing time ideals for the majority of lawyers. It led us to seek and ponder the conditions under which part-time attorneys are insulated from stigmatization.

Lawyers who take on part-time status learn they are stigmatized directly (e.g., when they are taken off the track to partnership) or indirectly (e.g., when they become the butt of jokes about their schedules). Some just feel "it's in the air." Arthur Kant, one of the few male lawyers we encountered who worked a reduced schedule, anticipated that he would be stigmatized for his part-time status later in his career even though he had not thus far drawn negative comments; he was well aware that the legal profession honors workaholism, and he expected to be punished for doing less.

We use the term "stigma" here in its sociological sense to convey the way in which "otherness" is determined by social definition—by labeling. This is played out in interaction, through understandings commonly shared and communicated by comments that carry messages regarding socially appropriate behavior. Stigma, as Erving Goffman (1963) pointed out, has to do with relationships, not attributes.[1]

Stigma serves to place a boundary around the "normal." What is at issue is deviation from the norm.

Facing Stigma

The definition and enunciation of the stigma on part-time work as a deviation from the normal is captured by the comment of Georgia Lamm, a tenth-year associate in a large firm who felt she had to remove herself from a partnership track when her son was born but who nonetheless felt professionally committed:

> There are both explicit and implicit beliefs in law firsts that the best lawyers don't have lives. . . [A colleague] was told gratuitously in an elevator by a partner that she couldn't be serious about her work because she worked part-time. I am serious about my work. But not in the way he meant, which is totally single-minded with nothing else mattering.

And, as Leslie Reiff, a former part-time partner who recently had switched back to full-time work, reported, "The institutional perception of part-time as bad can't be battled via policy—it's a mind-set among lawyers." August Covington White hoped to circumvent this mind-set by getting approval for a title as consulting tax counsel in a part-time job. As he jokingly commented: "Call it anything, but don't call it part-time!"

The mind-set seemed fairly clear to one of the authors of this book during a dinner party conversation with a noted professor at a major law school who also was a consultant for a major New York law firm. Describing this study, the author asked his opinion of the feasibility of part-time work in the New York firm. "Impossible," he asserted without hesitation. "But don't you work part-time for the firm?" she asked. "That's different," he said, "I provide expertise they need." "But couldn't a woman who wanted to limit her hours also provide expertise on a part-time basis as you do?" the questioner continued. "I don't think we are getting anywhere with this conversation," the professor snapped as he turned away, obviously irritated at being categorized as a "part-timer" rather than a "consultant."

Part-time lawyers are well aware of the different evaluations they are apt to confront both inside and outside the legal workplace. There are consequences for them personally, with regard to their self-images and their reputations.

The intensity of the stigma experienced by attorneys working part-time varies with the sector of the law in which they work (large law firms, corporations, or government): with whether their part-time status is regarded as temporary or whether they have a formal designation as part-time or temporary workers; and with whether they have negotiated their part-time status from a permanent full-time position or have become contract lawyers hired through an agency that handles temporary employment.[2] (This study was almost entirely limited to part-time lawyers who are not temporary contract lawyers.) The attitudes of coworkers and supervisors also help to create an environment in which part-time lawyers find themselves either valued or belittled.

Mechanisms That Stigmatize Part-Time Status

While a number of lawyers who work part-time schedules find it to be a positive personal experience at work and at home, a substantial number find they must confront reactions that range from nonspecific and unarticulated resentment and anger to almost hostile behavior.

Verbal and Nonverbal Communication

Because part-time positions are officially legitimate in any work environment in which they have developed, it is rare for coworkers or supervisors to openly state their opposition to them. Disapproval is communicated nonetheless through snide comments, sarcasm, slights, and nonverbal behavior.

It was good fortune, according to Stephanie Laughton, when a merger between her old firm and a new firm created the opportunity to negotiate a part-time partnership. Still, as she settled into her new job and tried to manage the stress of stretching her part-time schedule to cover a full-time workload, she found herself the target of colleagues' comments such as "Where are you when we need you?" Two years later, Laughton returned to a full-time schedule because she couldn't any longer face the stigma of part-time status.

An older associate in a midsize firm who entered law school and began a second career in her late 30s, Donna Carter, said she knew exactly why colleagues forget which days she works. "It's just a little whack, getting the dig in," she said. This carried a particular sting because Carter worked part-time out of necessity; one of her children had a grave illness. Similarly, Nancy Drager, a part-time litigator at a small firm, reported a continual trickle of snide remarks.

Sometimes lawyers who have worked part-time fail to support their part-time colleagues. Laurel Anderson, a corporate finance lawyer at a large firm, took offense when a former part-time attorney who returned to a full-time schedule made obnoxious comments about part-time people.

Others said they heard "playful" wisecracks from colleagues when they first started part-time work. Charlotte Wise, one of two attorneys in a large corporation who were granted part-time schedules, has heard her share of these wisecracks. Though Wise feels many were meant to belittle her, she also thinks they revealed a bit of envy among colleagues and clients:

> Gee, I'd love to have a day off. . . ha ha ha. I'd say, "Look, they're not. If you knew what I did on my days 'off,' I think you'd rather be at work."

Clarissa Hoskins reported she was the target of "slighting by forgetting" in the legal department of the large corporation where she works:

> They use. . . [voice-mail messages] to joke: "It's Wednesday—are you here?" or, "It's Thursday—are you home?". . . I think to some extent they are really jealous that I don't have the grind every single day. I think in some ways they are being kind of ribbing in a nice and friendly way. I think it is just a topic of conversation like, "Oh, hi, are you here today?" But it annoys us—it really annoys us.

Clients' Objection to Part-Time Work

Clients' reactions to working with a part-time lawyer run a range from cooperative to feeling inadequately served. Ruth Tucker, a specialist in real estate law, made the request to go part-time at a large firm three years ago so she could spend part of her time doing volunteer tenant/landlord work at a legal services agency. Her colleagues supported her, but a major client complained "six times over the course of this year that he lost a lawyer by getting her because she wasn't there the entire time."

As an ultimate sign of rejection, clients stigmatize part-time lawyers by avoiding or refusing to work with them. Some attorneys reported that clients wanted to know why they have to work with someone who "could be gone tomorrow," falsely equating reduced hours with a lack of long-term job commitment. Yet we found that the part-time lawyers we interviewed rarely leave jobs they enjoy unless they are laid off.

Symbolic Treatment That Highlights Differential Status

In addition to slights and digs, a few part-time attorneys reported dismissive treatment in law offices that highlighted their second-class citizenship in other ways. These included not being given offices, business cards, or other tangible indicators of professional status.

A lawyer at a large insurance company, Jean Graber, described the status consciousness of the culture and how it undermined her rank within the organization. She was made to feel like a second-class citizen by not being given a name plate on her office door. She also was not permitted to have business cards or letterhead with her name on them. Further indignities included not being invited to the departmental retreat and exclusion from the company's organizational chart.

Examples of second-class treatment were offered by Katherine Marx, a civil litigator in a small firm before she was laid off. The full-time partners rented her office on the days she was not at work, highlighting her contingent status, and as a further insult, held the firm's cocktail hour on the days she was not in the office. Miriam Greer was assigned work space in a paralegal's office by the managing partner in the firm. She mounted a successful campaign to get a lawyer's office, well aware of the symbolic message the assignment carried:

> The lawyer who brought me in said "Don't worry. . . [a lawyer's office] was promised to you.". . . He fought for me. But if I hadn't gotten involved. . . I might have gotten stuck in a paralegal's office.

Second-class status was reinforced by pension inequities for part-time work, according to part-timers and their colleagues in a government agency we studied. There, pensions accrued not according to the calendar but according to the proportion of a year worked. A lawyer working on a half-time schedule had to work twenty years for her pension to vest rather than the ten years required of full-time lawyers. Attorneys regard this rule as punitive rather than economically based. Ellen Russell, a part-time attorney in the office, explained:

> The way the [pension] law is written it's supposed to include part-time lawyers who are permanent. . . . We weren't temporary folks who came on for six months and. . . [were expected] to disappear. . . The pension really ought to vest in the same ten years, because it's ten years of real time.

Stigma also was implicit in the ways in which time was calculated for seniority and advancement of part-time lawyers. Arthur Kant, the attorney who earlier was quoted as anticipating stigmatization, had a telecommuting arrangement in a government agency. Although he found support as "a test case" in his agency, he was concerned that he would have to hide his work arrangement when applying for a better job elsewhere because of the sentiment that work performed outside the office didn't count as "real work."

Collateral Damage: The "Halo Effect" of Part-Time Stigmatization

Holding a stigmatized status may prompt others to unfairly attribute failures to the person in question. For example, the lawyer in the job-sharing situation described earlier told us that when work is not completed efficiently it's blamed on the job-sharing arrangement, whereas if one works full-time, failure is blamed on a heavy workload:

> If you're in a job share, they'll blame it on the fact you're not there every day—that you're not getting your work done. Instead of if you're full-time, you're just overburdened because you're busy.

Gender and Stigma

Stigma attached to part-time work cannot be separated from attitudes and general norms toward gender roles in the larger society.

As the sociologist Arlie Hochschild (1979) has noted, these extend to the "emotion norms" that attach to the nurturing aspect of the mother's role, which involves not only feeding and educating children, for example, but deeply felt mother love. Although elsewhere in this book we argue for the legitimacy of motherhood as a justification for part-time schedules, it is important to point out that men may be stigmatized if they request or engage in part-time work in order to spend more time with their children (Goffman 1963).

The reasons one gives for requesting a part-time schedule are taken into account by those who grant the option in many circumstances. In the past, it would have been unimaginable for men to request a part-time schedule to take care of children (unless they had been widowed). Firms accepted as legitimate, however, men's requests for time off to participate in public domain activities, such as a political campaign or business venture. In rare cases, an attorney might take a sabbatical to write a book, or an extended leave to hold elective political office.

In these cases, the reduced schedule (in terms of yearly output) was not called part-time and was regarded as temporary. Thus the less-than-full-time schedules that men have had recourse to have not been called part-time. Labeling, according to the sociologist Howard Becker (1963), places the actor in circumstances where it is hard to continue the routines of everyday life. Thus part-time professionals develop repertoires for avoiding the label that stigmatizes them if they can.

Stigmatizing the Performance
of Multiple Roles

Antipathy to women's assumption of multiple roles contributes to the stigmatization of part-time work. Some writers attribute the hostility reported by a number of part-time lawyers to a backlash against women's progress in high-level occupations (Epstein 1987; Faludi 1991).

Lawyers reported comments expressing disapproval of their attempts to play roles historically regarded as incompatible: those of attorney and mother. Song reported that colleagues and acquaintances seemed to think that anyone performing these roles part-time showed a lack of commitment to both roles. Thus we find an underlying disapproval for attempts to perform multiple roles. For example, when Melissa Fiske asked for a reduced schedule in the large financial institution for which she worked, her supervisor commented: "If you ant to be a lawyer, be a lawyer. If you want to be a mother, be a mother." Ellen Barnes, who worked for more than ten years in a government legal office, said:

> It's a very tricky thing to work part-time. . . You're really neither fish nor fowl. . . For full-time committed attorneys, you've copped out or. . . fallen off the track, or you've made much too big a compromise. . . [they] can't take you that seriously. And conversely, you have the same sort of stuff from stay-at-home mothers who, of course, view their role as very important. . . . It is. . . but they think you're some other creature because. . . part of the day you're someplace else.

A double stigma was experienced by George Marks, the part-time lawyer-husband of a part-time attorney. He suffers an even greater onus than his wife, because he violates both time and manhood norms by attempting to combine his professional role with an active role as an involved father. As his wife reported, feedback from colleagues and friends communicated their view that "real men do not work at home."

Techniques for Reducing
the Stigma of Part-Time Status

Erving Goffman (1963) wrote in his book *Stigma* that Some people try to anticipate and evade the negative consequence of a stigmatized status. One way is "passing"—that is, acting as if one were "normal"—in this case, as if one were a full-time professional; another is information control.[3]

Passing

The ability to pass by making the stigmatized status invisible reflects the relational aspect of stigmatization. One can bluff opposing litigators by seeming to work full-time or by keeping clients unaware of one's schedule so that opponents and clients feel they are interacting with and relying on a fulltime professional. In these cases, the relationship with the part-time lawyer is based on the client's perception that she or he is diligently at work and available at all times.

Information Control

Passing rests partly on the ability and opportunity to manage information about one-self (Goffman 1963: 91). As we shall describe later, technology is helpful for this, and so is the use of gatekeepers such as secretaries. Part-time lawyers consider these factors all the time in making decisions about whether to reveal their status or hide it.

A part-time associate pointed out that unless she has ongoing work with clients or co-counsel, she is not inclined to reveal she works part-time. She feels it is important to acknowledge the fact to continuing clients, not only for scheduling purposes but also as a way to explain why she does not have a supervisory title.

Sandra Karp felt no need to hide or play down her part-time arrangement. Her boss, a woman Karp described as extremely supportive, worked well with her. But she took the advice of a colleague working in her department on a contract basis that she shouldn't let her arrangement be widely known and should maintain a low profile. Thus, while others talked about the career advantages of high visibility, she noted wryly that she "was striving for invisibility." The same kind of invisibility was sought by Deborah Finkelstein, a lawyer who had left a large firm that had several part-timers, but, she said, "You couldn't tell who they were; or they wouldn't tell you what their deal was. These were always secret things."

The passing strategy, called "covering" by Goffman (1963: 102), was cultivated by Deborah Pinkerton, a part-time associate. Pinkerton found ways to remain physically invisible even when she was working in the office, keeping the door closed and ordering lunch to be sent in, so that she would not be missed when not in the office. She hoped to give the impression that she was always there even if unseen.

John Logan, a supervisor in the legal department of a government agency who has worked part-time in the past, told us that he had felt he had to hide his part-time status from adversaries. As he reported: "Litigation is a game of bluff, and you want your adversaries to think you're working hard all the time against them." Karen Scott, a recently laid-off part-time government staff attorney, told of her subterfuge:

> Part-timers also have to accommodate court schedules, but it was an unwritten rule that we developed, we never *ever* advised the court that we were working less than 100 percent. . . . We would never say that we were unavailable because we had a part-time schedule. . . . We decided that it was [a bad idea] to be asking for more time [to accommodate our limited work-time schedule]. . . . We didn't think that the court would buy it, we didn't think that it was any of their business.

And another part-time government attorney commented:

> I don't like to bring it up. . . because I think it connotes an unserious[ness] to an awful lot of people. . . It's amazing how most people don't notice. . . It's not like they expect a phone call to be returned within three hours. If it's returned the next day, that's perfectly legitimate.

Orders from her firm to pass as a full-time attorney were reported by Serena Woodward, a part-time associate in a major firm. Her secretary transferred calls to her home on her day off. Other respondents reported that some lawyers gave their home phone numbers to clients without telling them it was a home number.

The lack of face-to-face interaction (or "face time") was not a problem to clients, according to one lawyer:

[My part-time schedule] wasn't really advertised, because lots of the people that I dealt with were not in the same location. They would just call. And I would either be there or not. And I would always call back within a day or two. And I found that most people. . . weren't confronting me as full-time or part-time; all they cared about was, "Was my work done?" And "Were my calls returned within a reasonable amount of time?" And since I always returned my phone calls—which was something that a lot of other people didn't do—that [gained me] a lot of good will. People didn't care.

A part-time in-house counsel who rose to become a vice president of her corporation did not tell clients she was part-time because "it didn't come up."

"Passing" was a game for some attorneys, but a number of them played the game out of shame they felt front perceived negative evaluations. As the sociologist Thomas Scheff (1988) has described, even in the absence of obvious sanctions, the part-time lawyer may anticipate rejection (criticism, passive-aggressive jokes, withdrawal by colleagues)—and consequently may behave in ways that minimize the visibility of his or her deviance. A continual process of self-monitoring—in which one takes cues from the situation and from the self-imagined disgrace—serves as a mechanism of social control.

Although part-time work is often stigmatized, its definition as a deviant professional work style varies depending on the institution, attitudes of coworkers and supervisors, and the acceptance or rejection of the lawyer who has chosen to work that way. The stigmatizing process is compounded because most part-time lawyers are women, who still are confronting the consequences of stereotypes that question their professional roles.

We have seen that lawyers are sensitive to the ways in which part-time status is depreciated by unnecessary and unwarranted behavior by colleagues whose intent, conscious or not, is to undermine its legitimacy.

In the next chapter we identify the structural, cultural, and psychological factors that act to make part-time work possible without social stigma.

Conclusion

Part-time work arrangements in the legal profession are seen as a solution to the work/family time dilemmas faced by many lawyers in their child rearing years. Most lawyers who work on these alternative schedules are women, because women are normatively more free to choose to do so and because child care, considered to be women's responsibility, is the most commonly accepted justification for granting part-time schedules. Despite the fact that women attorneys are a significant and growing proportion of the profession, part-time work is neither typical nor common.

This study shows the benefits and pitfalls of part-time status for lawyers and the institutions they work for. Reluctance to ask for part-time schedules, and the resistance of employers to grant it, have to do not only with the practical problems of co-ordination and economics but go to the heart of what it means to be a true professional. In law, as in other professions, commitment and excellence are often measured by the seemingly unlimited number of hours practitioners work, indicating that their first priority is their vocation. Practitioners who work circumscribed hours are considered to be "time deviants." Although the "greediness" of different spheres of law varies, the norms demanding constant availability of the individual lawyer persist, especially in private sector law firms, where they have become even more pronounced in today's competitive environment. Thus, even as part-time work is becoming institutionalized because of the profession's growing awareness of the problems lawyers have in integrating family and work lives, and of their discontent with escalating time demands, part-time work is often stigmatized for its violation of the profession's norm.

Technology is part of the problem because it speeds the pace of practice with rapid turnaround times that are created and enforced by the use of computers, fax machines, cell telephones, and other devices. However, it is also part the solution because it permits part-timers to work effectively at sites outside the office. Here, too, new problems arise as the boundary between work and home life becomes blurred.

While much of the focus of this research has been on the experiences of individuals, alternative work arrangements pose both advantages and disadvantages for the organizations permitting them. Part-time work options are a way attract or keep legal talent, and in a procession in which women make up an increasingly large proportion of practitioners, it has become less possible to ignore their desires to be responsive to contending commitments at home and work. Indeed, the government sector uses defined part-time policies to tract a level of legal talent and experience that would not be otherwise available. Because it is usually lawyers with a number of years of experience who desire part-time work, these arrangements save organizations from losing substantial investments in attorneys they have trained.

Part-time status has career consequences. Most part-timers appear to be locked from promotion into supervisory or partnership positions. Indeed, lost of the attorneys in this study agreed this is a quid pro quo for their withdrawal from a full-time commitment and, while disappointed, they felt it is reasonable and understandable from the standpoint of the organization. With such understandings in place, all sectors of the legal workplace may employ the talents of experienced lawyers without having to commit to the career progression of part-time attorneys or acquire obligations to them. Of course, there are consequences for the organizations in terms of lower commitment. For the part-timers who return to full-time work, however, it is possible to go back, although they may lose years of seniority.

Part-time arrangements may also pose difficulties for the internal life of organizations. Norms of professionalism require a commitment to contribute to the quality of work life of the organization; and attorneys, like all professionals, are expected to be good colleagues. Without time to socialize and communicate informally, part-time arrangements compromise an intangible but essential part of collegial life—the camaraderie and social bonds that create high morale and a sociable place to work.

A firm's reputation is in part contingent on its contribution to the collegial life of the profession at large. Because they place limits on their hours of work, part-timers are rarely able to contribute to this aspect of the professional calling. For example, part-timers are less available to share in responsibilities for bar association activities, in training and mentoring of younger colleagues, or in expanding the knowledge base of the profession by studying and writing on professional matters.

While many part-timers bring sophisticated legal expertise to their work they rarely have the time to develop the social ties necessary for effective client development, although some have acquired client loyalty in past full-time work. In an increasingly competitive market for legal services, this may be a serious shortcoming.

Finally, because the number of part-timers in any one organization remains small, there is little pressure for change in administrative or personnel rules to address their needs. Should part-time arrangements become more common, however, the profession will have to answer the growing number of questions about part-time seniority, remuneration, pensions, benefits, and promotion.

Lawyers who make policy in their organizations have differing views about the feasibility of alternative work arrangements. The federal government has worked out formal guidelines to provide solutions to some of the problems of part-time employment for their lawyers, and the more defined government work schedules make it possible to implement them when they are supported by the positive attitudes of supervising attorneys. The private sector faces different kinds of challenges, and the mind-sets of the top people are also crucial. Although management committees of large law firms are concerned about losing young lawyers who resist the workaholic demands that intrude on their family lives, there does not seem to be great interest in strengthening arrangements for part-time work. Some firms see such changes as inevitable given the attrition rates of associates. Some believe no changes will take place until men begin to pressure firms for more flexible schedules, a "solution" that others hold to be unlikely because of the costs of breaking with tradition and the competitive pressures facing the legal world today. Some others believe change may come when women partners commonly participate in the management of large firms. Yet because there are still so few women partners, and because they have less power than male partners, most did not believe they could accomplish serious change. Further, as we have seen, not all women partners agree on the feasibility of part-time work. Yet, sympathies of women clients—women are now a rising number of directors of corporate legal departments—could encourage firms to accept more flexibility, according to some other attorneys.

Now that part-time work schedules are a growing option, the profession at large should address its traditional stereotypes about what is required to be a successful practitioner. Senior attorneys in large firms, who came of professional age in a different era, need to accept a new model of the excellent attorney, one that includes the many younger attorneys who are deeply committed to their work and to their families and the part-time attorneys who have decided not to leave their profession. While old stereotypes tend to linger on the screen of social life, it is time for the profession to acknowledge that one may be both a dedicated professional and a dedicated family member.

We may expect that changes in the law profession's existing power structures and the willingness of men to join with their women colleagues in challenging the prevailing order will result in legitimation of greater workplace flexibility. Resolutions of conflicting pressures will be difficult, however, since the issue of work hours goes far beyond its immediate importance to lawyers seeking change and those who manage the legal workplace. Long hours of work and visibility of effort have symbolic meaning, and serve as proxies for commitment and excellence. Long hours of work also bond professionals socially as well as professionally, placing those who are not always "there" in a marginal position. Furthermore, the gendered nature of part-time work is a reflection of strong cultural values about the proper roles of the two sexes and the division of labor in society. These are values and conditions that are not easy to disrupt, and they make the question of part-time work contested terrain and a proxy for many issues beyond lawyers' work schedules.

Notes

1. The stigma attached to contract lawyers is widely acknowledged. A contract lawyer quoted in the *New York Times* remarked, "There is sometimes a stigma attached to being a contract attorney" (Kirk 1995, 13). However, there is a growing use of temporary lawyers, about 30 percent a year (Pristin 1998), with New York the largest market. Some firms use them for special projects (e.g., White and Case, a large New York firm hired 100 to work on an antitrust case), but lawyers from other firms interviewed for the article voiced concern about the quality of temporary contract lawyers.

2. As Goffman (1963) writes, "Because of the great rewards in being considered normal, almost all persons who are in a position to pass will do so on some occasion" p. 74).

3. Rogers (n.d.) reports that contract lawyers are paid for below the hourly rates of regular lawyers. In California the pay rates are between $35 or as high as $100. But clients are billed between $100 and $300 an hour for their services (p. 10).

References

Becker, Howard. 1963. *Outsiders: Studies in the Sociology of Deviance.* London: Free Press.
Epstein, Cunthia Fuchs. 1987. "Multiple Demands and Multiple Roles." In *Spouse, Parent Worker: On Gender and Multiple Roles,* ed. Faye Crosby. New Haven: Yale University Press.
Faludi, Susan. 1991. *Backlash.* New York: Crown.
Goffman, Erving. 1963. *Stigma: Notes on the Management of Spoiled Identity.* Englewood Cliffs, N.J.: Prentice Hall.
Hochschild, Arlie Russell. 1979. "Emotion Work, Feeling Rules and Social Structure." *American Journal of Sociology,* November, 551–595.
Scheff, Thomas. 1988. "Shame and Conformity: The Deference-Emotion System." *American Sociological Review,* June, 395–406.

12

TEMPS
De-skilled and Devalued

Jackie Krasas Rogers

Doug Larson is a thirty-nine-year-old white man who occasionally gets work as an extra on a popular soap opera. After losing a secure managerial job with a trucking company, he took six months off to find direction in his life. Three years earlier, he came to Los Angeles to pursue an acting career. Divorced, with no children, he feels he can accommodate the instability of both his lines of work, temping and acting. He described one of the aspects that is most troubling to him:

> Usually they think of temps as being morons for some reason. And they give you very little work to start out. I'd be done in a matter of minutes and they look at you like, "Why did you do that so quickly?" I didn't find any of the work difficult. It was quite numbing on the brain. It wasn't creative. It wasn't challenging. It was just mundane work.

I asked him what made him think people thought of temporary workers as morons:

> The type of work they give you and how they present it to you. They present it to you like you're a third grader. You have to do this and make sure you don't fold the corner of the envelope to the left. And if you lick that stamp, be careful you don't cut your tongue!

Although Doug's sense of humor shows through in this exchange, he was greatly troubled by what he described as the monotony of the work and his sense that others looked down on him. Many temporaries in this study as well as those in other studies complain about the lack of interesting and challenging work. Without invalidating these findings, I found that unskilled work is only part of the story. Not all workers felt that the work was unskilled at all times. In fact, some felt they had the opportunity to really "show their stuff" while on an assignment. These workers felt, however, that they were not being paid an appropriate wage for the highly skilled work they were performing. Temporary clerical work contains within it two kinds of work: unskilled/low-paid and highly skilled/low-paid. In this sense, temporary work can be seen as a lose-lose situation—an abundance of monotonous work that requires little or no skill or the use of high-priced skills in a setting that pays only a low-price wage.

In this chapter, I sketch out two different dynamics in the organization of temporary jobs. One is de-skilling. By that I mean the shifting of monotonous and low-skill tasks to temporary clerical workers. The second dynamic, devaluing, refers to the circumstance of temporary clerical workers who perform highly skilled work with little recognition. Both de-skilled and devalued work are low paid; however, devalued work more closely resembles high-end clerical work or work that could easily be argued to fall outside clerical work altogether, such as human resource management, advertising, or supervision. Outside the context of temporary employment, these tasks are typically higher paid than what these workers made. In the context of temporary employment, the performance of special tasks draws no more pay for the temporary, nor is it cause for changing the worker's title or job classification.

Understanding the simultaneous existence of these two dynamics can help us reconcile opposing reports regarding the effects of temporary employment, the temporary industry's efforts at defining the situation, and the salience of gender, class, and race in disentangling the range of experience. Let us explore in depth the first claim, that temporary work is unskilled.

Changes in the
Technical Work Process: De-skilling

The jury is still out with regard to whether clerical work has become de-skilled since the change from a male dominated to a female-dominated workforce. Clerical work has always been an amalgam. As a male-dominated field at the turn of the century, clerical work offered good pay, autonomy, and a chance for advancement for many men (Crompton and Jones 1984). Many women were able to use clerical work as an entry point to a managerial career; however, many clerical jobs even at this time could be considered low-skill and even monotonous for the men who performed them. As women entered the occupation in large numbers, they were typically found in the lower strata without paths into management. Today, most types of clerical work are female-dominated, and since the 1970s people of color have increased their representation in clerical work (Hartmann et al. 1986).

Much ado has been made about the degradation or "proletarianization" of the clerical workforce. The growth of clerical work after World War II and the introduction of new technologies spurred criticism that clerical work was being "degraded" to become more like assembly line factory work. At the same time, others have argued that the advent of technology such as computers has increased the skill level in certain kinds of clerical work. Both points of view seem to have some validity. Much of clerical work *is* routinized, however, significant packets of skill do exist. The use of word processors has removed some skill from letter composition, yet a new set of skills is required to use the software package (Machung 1984). The diversity of jobs within the occupation is such that generalizations about de-skilling or upgrading become nearly meaningless. Two more fitting questions to ask may be "Who is doing which jobs?" and "To what extent are those jobs skilled?"

We know that many clerical jobs are truly monotonous, and that these types of jobs, along with "back office" clerical jobs, are disproportionately reserved for women of color.

Then there are those clerical jobs that are highly skilled, requiring not only technical ability and organizationally specific knowledge, but also deftness at handling interpersonal communications. Regardless of the work, however, the skills of clerical workers often are not acknowledged. Because skills are at least partly socially constructed, any "skill" can be passed off as a talent, a knack, a personality trait, or as an ability inherent in a particular social group, such as women, thus diminishing the value of that skill. Cultural beliefs enter into even our most "scientific" evaluations of job skill, such as the Hay System. When a job is primarily performed by women, several cultural assumptions enter into its valuation. First, women's jobs historically have been seen as providing supplemental income to a family with a male breadwinner, allowing for the payment of lower wages that can in part be justified by constructing the job as low-skill.

Second, the skills of women are considered to be merely reflections of natural, "feminine" abilities. Typing sixty words per minute is not seen so much as a valuable skill that has been honed as it is simply something that women tend to do well. Therefore one can look at a female-dominated job and easily surmise that the competencies are but a reflection of women's natural abilities. Why else would so many women be crowded into the same job? Women are said to be "good with people," thus the secretary's savvy with clients can be accounted for as a gender trait rather than a skill to be valued and thus rewarded.

Men and male-dominated jobs historically have been associated with skill, while women and female-dominated jobs have not. Men have contributed to the naturalization of women's skills because they have had the power to define their jobs as skilled, sometimes at the expense of women's jobs." The ideologically based process through which work (usually women's work) comes to be labeled as unskilled or semi-skilled is called devaluing. What could arguably be seen as a skill is labeled in a way that makes the competency seem less of an achievement and more of a natural talent. The failure to acknowledge skill devalues competencies by casting them as trivialities—something an entire gender tends to do well—and they don't see the need to pay for that. They pay for skill.

Investigating the concept of skill in clerical temporary work is an onerous task because the diversity of jobs within clerical temporary work nearly mirrors the diversity in the larger occupation. Temporary clerical work encompasses such diverse assignments as data entry and filing to receptionist and executive secretary; therefore the skill involved in temporary work cannot he characterized in singular terms. Neither are temporary jobs immune from the ideological processes that are often involved in skill definition. There is no reason to assume that temporary clerical jobs use the same skills even when labeled as their traditional counterparts. Nor can we assume that the ideological defining of "skill" in temporary clerical work is identical to that of traditional clerical work. What may be assumed as skill in a full-time receptionist job is often different from the definition of skill in a temporary receptionist job. It therefore makes sense to compare the skill content of "permanent" jobs with their temporary counterparts. In other words, to what extent is the skill content of a job related to the fact that it is a temporary rather than a "permanent" job? Does temporary employment upgrade or de-skill clerical work?

All of the temporary clerical workers I interviewed reported at least some assignments in which they felt they were given the worst work in the office. They referred to this type of work with a variety of terms, including (but not limited to) "shit work" "dreg work" or "scat work." Regardless of the specific moniker, one is able to infer the quality of this type of work and the way the temporaries who often performed it felt about being assigned such work. Many of the workers I spoke with identified a consistent pattern of dreg work while only occasionally being called in for the use of their "special skills."

A lot of times you'll be called to do, you'll have to know this program and it's supposed to be a lot of word processing but it ends up being like opening the mail and answering phones all day. (Harold Koenig, twenty-nine-year-old white man)

And at this assignment now I'm processing declination and reply letters for insurance. And it's basically all I do. And when it's done, I don't have anything to do. And when I was at the other assignment I was keeping a log of various telephone accounts because I was working in the telecommunications department. And keying logs of the telephone bills and sending out the telephone bills to the customers. Very simple phones, nothing difficult. No real brains involved. Or at least the bare minimum. (Albert Baxter, thirty-one-year-old white man)

I worked in a bank and stuffed envelopes for five days straight. It was terrible; it was sooo monotonous. [My supervisor] delegated me these huge boxes of stuff, so like I would only have to go to him two days later. I'd just go to him when I ran out of stuff to stuff. (Sarah Tilton, twenty-five-year-old white woman)

The probability of being assigned to such tedious tasks and the abundance of dreg work did not seem to vary based on one's human capital. Despite the range of educational and work backgrounds of my interviewees, they seemed to share frequent feelings of overqualification for the work that they were performing. Most jobs, it seemed to them, did not require even a high school diploma much less a college degree. Yet temporary agencies routinely test for a host of skills, including math, spelling, and computer software skills. A quick check of publicly available temporary agency materials found on the Internet demonstrates the emphasis that agencies place on their skills evaluation systems. One agency boasts their applicant testing procedures were developed by a highly prestigious consulting firm. Another claims the best skills-testing software in the business. But is this all just hype to lure potential temporaries to work for agencies, only to assign them later to the surplus of low-skill jobs available? Many temporary workers were unable to see any point to the screening process when they are routinely placed into jobs below their capability levels.

They give you spelling tests, math tests, yeah, they do that, too. The ten-key test [data entry of numbers]. And most of the time when you go to a job, you never basically do those things. I mean, it's like the ten-key. Unless you're really doing an accounting job and you have to add up, I can see that. But the jobs I mostly got weren't like that. I was always overqualified for the job). (Linda Mejia, thirty-one-year-old Latina)

So while temporary workers are tested to determine their individual skill level (that is, the maximum skill of the person), like Linda, many of my informants were seldom given assignments that required the use of their maximum skills. In this sense, temporary work can be understood to be a form of underemployment for many (Parker 1994). Indeed, temporary workers can experience temporary work exclusively in this fashion. Take Ellen Lanford for example. Her agency told her that she was one of their most "placeable" temporaries because of her extensive educational background. While she was given many assignments from the agency, Ellen expected the work to be different.

Yes, there were some days when I thought, this is ludicrous. I am so miserable. I can't believe that I'm however many years old, thirty-six, thirty-seven, and I'm making nine thousand copies of this script or something. I have two master's degrees. (Ellen Lanford, thirty-eight-year-old white woman)

Again, to the degree that the temporary industry focuses on the human capital that temporaries hang to the job rather than the job itself, the industry can misrepresent temporary workers' experiences by equating the skill of the worker with the job). The worker and the job are treated as virtually the same, when in fact the worker may possess (and often is required to possess) a bundle of skills ranging from computer to social knowledge. Having extensive qualifications is no guarantee of receiving work that will match the temporary worker's needs.

From the client company's perspective, Ellen may appear to be the perfect match for the job. Based on her extensive educational background, the company may assume that she's capable of doing the work, she needs minimal supervision, and she shows up on time. That the particular assignment might not utilize her skills to the fullest is of little concern. Overqualification poses less of a problem for the client than for the temporary worker, unless it results in undesirable behavior on the part of the temporary worker. From the temporary's point of view, there is a disjuncture of their skills and the job tasks they are required to perform. They see the matching process as oriented toward meeting the client's needs. Because overqualification is not typically framed as problematic by the agency, finding a challenging assignment is seen by temporary workers as a lucky happenstance rather than an outcome of a managed matching process.

If temporary clerical workers believe the work they are asked to perform is lacking in skill, then to what end is this occurring? Is it simply a byproduct of a general tendency toward de-skilling? Or is there a trend toward some workers maintaining or increasing the skill content of their jobs at the expense of temporary workers? Either implicitly or explicitly, temporaries acknowledge that their performance of dreg work insulates permanent employees from having to perform those low-skill tasks that they find unsavory.

Yeah, the temp is the one who gets the shit work. And the temp is the one who is last considered for anything. (Michael Glenn, twenty-five-year-old Asian American)

When you're a temp, you get all the shitty work. . . You usually got stuck in the back to do the work that either someone put off or was on maternity leave or sick. Work that no one else wanted to do. (Doug Larson, thirty-nine-year-old white man)

This idea that the work assigned to temporaries is work that has been sitting untouched because no one else in the office would do it is a commonly held belief among temporary workers. My fieldwork supports what many of my informants described. I found myself doing this kind of work in several assignments. On one assignment, I was asked to replace pages in reference manuals. The manuals held information on various pension and legal codes. There were several sets of manuals on many topics. Each month, the companies that printed the reference manuals would send replacement pages (anywhere from thirty to one hundred pages per set) that required someone to go to the correct binder, pull out the old page, and insert the new page. Complicating matters was the fact that the pages were tissue-thin and separating them was quite tedious. When I was hired, the replacement pages had backed up for over fourteen months because none of the permanent workers would do this work. It had been assigned in turn to two or three permanent workers who told me (with a knowing smile) that they could just never get to it. That is why I was "the lucky one" (field notes, June 1994).

These research findings also suggest that the de-skilling process in temporary clerical work is not conducted by management alone. De-skilling of temporary clerical work takes place not simply as part of a management strategy but as part of the social relations of the workplace, which may include management prerogatives as well. Therefore we see that "permanent" workers also participate in the assignment of less desirable, simple tasks to temporary workers.

In fact, my supervisor was really gung-ho about giving me all this grant work to do, and I spent the entire time typing in there while she was pigging out on Doritos and whatnot. So it seemed as though she had taken the opportunity to give me all her crap work. (Irene Pedersen, twenty-four-year-old white woman)

Temporaries with similar experiences report that their entrance into an office is seen as a signal for the permanent clerical workers to transfer the work they do not want to do and have been putting off onto the temporary workers. Ironically, literature from the temporary industry demonstrates a similar understanding of this role being one of the functions of temporary work.

Companies often call on temporary help for supplemental stalling during peak production periods, special projects, transitions, the introduction of new products or technology, and to relieve *"core" employees of excess overtime and tedious work.* (pamphlet from a temporary help firm, my italics)

This is a notable contradiction to the scenario portrayed by temporary agencies in which temporary workers are hired as short-term experts. Thus it seems that the "expert" notion of the temporary worker is not always applicable beyond the role of pumping up the agency's reputation in its literature, at least in the case of clerical work.

While temporary work does not necessarily change the overall technical labor process of clerical work, it can result in two categories of jobs, and differential experiences of work for permanent and temporary workers. Temporary employment can therefore serve as a type of occupational segregation that "pushes up" the skill level in the core of workers (who delegate low-skill dreg work) while "pushing down" the skill level in the periphery of temporary workers. Permanent workers are relieved from monotonous work, and (happily for the employer) these higher-paid core workers do not spend their time doing routine tasks.

Using temporary workers in this way provides a further realization of the Babbage principle. Under the Babbage principle, work is divided so that highly skilled, high-priced workers spend their time exclusively on high-priced tasks, while unskilled, low-priced workers spend their time on low-priced tasks. Thus, implementing the Babbage principle is said to reduce overall labor costs. If the work was not divided, one would have to find and employ higher-skilled workers and pay the higher rate to ensure the capability of the worker for performing the high-end tasks. For example, if I am proficient at desktop publishing, having me make photocopies is not an economical use of my time. According to the Babbage principle, my time doing desktop publishing should be maximized, and someone else should be hired and paid less to do the photocopying. If the work is not divided and I must also do the photocopying, unfortunately for my employers, it will cost them the higher rate to have me perform this low-price task.

Temporary employment can then be seen as a means for bringing in low-priced workers to do low-priced work. The permanent core is where high-skilled, high-priced work is done. Therefore, it seems that the de-skilling and the upgrading of clerical jobs are occurring simultaneously with the introduction of temporary workers. The overall content of clerical work may be unchanged, but the distribution of tasks now takes place with regard to the temporary/permanent division. While this is good news for core individuals who are buffered by the temporary ring, every silver lining does have its cloud. That core of skilled workers seems to be shrinking, for even in times of economic recovery the use of temporary help is rising (Parker 1994).

Changes in the
Technical Work Process: Devaluing

The image of temporary work as widening the division between higher-skilled jobs and lower-skilled jobs is only partially correct. Not all temporary work is unskilled. In some cases, clerical temporaries perform complex, skilled work that is either equivalent or superior to the work of "permanent" employees. In these instances, the only distinguishing factors between permanent and temporary work often seems to be that temporary work is lower-paid and brief or uncertain in duration. Moreover, the skilled work of temporaries is not recognized as such—it is devalued or ideologically stripped of skill. This ideological de-skilling can result in temporary workers receiving lower compensation than permanent workers for similarly skilled work. The following description, although seemingly extreme, is reflective of the type of skilled labor that temporary workers may be called on to perform. Michael was hired for a long-term assignment as a word processor:

Nine dollars an hour. I am publication coordinator. I do all the billing for the magazine. I do all the billing for the advertisers, which means I'm sort of accounts receivable. I answer phones. I'm front office for phones. I do the filing, of course, for certain things. I place the ads. I cut and paste and place all the ads. I proof the entire magazine before it goes to the printer. (Michael Glenn, twenty-six-year-old Asian American)

For those temporaries who come to the labor market highly skilled, their skills do not necessarily provide them with "market power" that translates into job security, high pay, and promotional opportunities when they enter temporary employment. While his duties required in-depth knowledge and tremendous responsibility in addition to his clerical skills, Michael was unable to increase his hourly pay rate or to become permanent in the position. If the need arises, companies can get highly skilled individuals like Michael at "bargain basement" rates by paying for a clerical temporary worker and using the hill range of that worker's abilities.

Ludy describes a situation in which she wrote speeches for her temporary boss. While he showed gratitude for help, he did not offer to increase her pay.

He was just used to having a girl who would answer his phone and take messages and type the letters. That's cool. But you don't get any more money for that, you don't get any more money for being smart. (Ludy Martinez, thirty-six-year-old Filipina)

In my own temping experience. I was a human resources clerical worker. One day I was asked to bring coffee for the company's insurance representative, and to keep him occupied while the director of human resources finished up some other work. I was supposed to keep him occupied until she was ready. Not long after we started talking, he asked why I was temping. I gave my standard answer. Then he asked what I did before graduate school and I told him I worked in insurance. The next thing you know, we were discussing self-insured plans and preferred provider organizations, and it seemed like he was quizzing me. He told me about some changes he thought the company should implement when the director walked in.

Later that week, I was asked to help with the insurance plan changes because apparently the insurance rep thought I was quite knowledgeable.

He told the director that she better use my talents while I was there. She was really enthusiastic about my "newly discovered" background. I thought it was nice to work with her like this. Of course, I still had to do the filing and mailing, but I could easily fit those things in (field notes, July 1994).

In addition to finding highly skilled individuals they can hire out at low hourly rates, temporary agency representatives prefer temporaries with a willingness to do a wide variety of work, either above or below the skill level for which they were hired.

An applicant who if we tell her you're gonna be doing some word processing and the client asked if she can do some backup on the switchboard and says, "I wouldn't do that. I'm above that. I may have a degree or I'm working on a degree, and I have good skills, why should I do that?" Well you know, in the meantime, you're out of work. *We're paying you the same rate if you're gonna be answering phones or doing a proposal*, so that would be someone we would consider a prima donna. (Manny Avila, temporary agency representative, twenty-eight-year-old Latino)

Many times in my experience and the experiences of my interviewees, the temporary was hired to perform simple clerical work only to wind up doing highly skilled clerical work or even something altogether different. Instances of temporary workers being hired to write proposals and ending up answering phones are much less common, but they do exist. For those who were hired as clerical workers, many resented being brought into the workplace under the guise (and pay) of a clerical worker while being asked to perform complex tasks that often required extensive training or experience.

And I went to some agencies right away, and they're like, "Well, OK, so do you speak Sanskrit, do you ride a bicycle?" It's like. "Well, no, I uh, I know this program fairly well and type and. . . " Oh well, so does everyone so that's not good enough. You need to know Lotus and Windows and desktop publishing, and you need to have had a master's in finance. . . Sometimes they get you in there and they want you to like be their junior CEO and still pay you nine bucks an hour. (Harold Koenig, twenty-nine-year-old white man)

Certain businesses find it useful to hire overqualified temps if they can find them. Because they will get those extra skills out of them even though they're just paying an hourly wage. I mean, it's like when certain businesses found out that I could at least spell and write and compose and that's how I ended up writing speeches and stuff like that. They're getting wise to the fact that not all the temps have the same skills, and that they will try to bilk you. I mean, it's like when people found out I could translate French and Spanish, and they were like "Whoa!" (Ludy Martinez, thirty-six-year-old Filipina)

Although agencies seem willing to put to use the many skills of temporary workers, many temporaries report feeling that their education and work experience are not recognized by the agency as having been instrumental in the development of the skills they use while on assignment.

I have worked as a secretary in a law firm for twenty, over twenty years now. But that didn't matter to the agency, didn't seem to make a difference. They wanted specific programs, and I hadn't used them. Sure, I could learn them. I worked twenty years! Doesn't that count for something? (Ramona Geary, forty-eight-year-old white woman)

It was kind of depressing for me, but I needed money. I remember being given like spelling tests and very simplified math tests to make sure I had a brain even though I had a résumé that said I graduated from college. . . I think they should say, "I recognize that this may be a bit condescending, but its just a way to screen. We know you're smart and you have a degree." Some sort of acknowledgment about that. (Carol Ketchum, twenty-nine-year-old white woman)

Thus, many temporary workers bring substantial skills and "human capital" with them to jobs that are defined and remunerated as unskilled. While employers may find themselves in the fortunate position of paying for a receptionist who ends up doing accounting, computer-aided design, or translating documents from French and Spanish, the job remains defined as clerical. Temporary agencies and their clients benefit from temporary workers' education and work experience, but the temporary workers themselves do not. Therefore, in addition to de-skilling, we find either no change in the technical labor process or an upgrading that goes unrewarded by money or recognition. Agencies often fail to recognize (verbally or monetarily) the types of skills developed through education or work experience, while at the same tune they are happy to market those same skills to their clients.

De-skilling and devaluing might at first appear to be contradictory tendencies because one involves highly monotonous work while the other involves highly skilled work. They are better understood as complements, however: One constitutes material de-skilling, and the other constitutes ideological de-skilling. Together, de-skilling and devaluing help construct temporary work as the most monotonous work in an office. If we attend only to the de-skilling tendency, we miss an important facet of the experience of temporary workers. In effect, we buy into the devaluing of temporary workers' skills.

Although the discussion to this point has proceeded as though material and ideological de-skilling are easily demarcated categories, real-life experience reflects a more complicated relationship. Some temporary workers mainly experienced de-skilled work, while others mainly experienced devalued work. Many temporary workers, however, experienced a combination of the two, and even an oscillation between de-skilled and devalued work.

For example, Ludy, the woman who was translating French and Spanish as well as writing speeches, also had to spend hours transcribing audiotapes of depositions. And Cheryl Hansen (a twenty-five-year-old white woman) reported filing in a bank as well as running computer-aided design software while working as a temporary clerical worker. In my own temping experience, I worked as a receptionist and at cleaning out old files as well as rewriting personnel policies. In the receptionist and filing jobs, I was hired as a clerk. In the situation where I rewrote personnel policies, I was also hired as a clerk. For all three assignments I received an identical pay rate.

Ideologies Concerning Skill

Let's take a look at the temporary help services (THS) industry rhetoric about the skills required of its workers. The understanding of skill and the messages regarding this understanding are complex and vary according to the industry's projected audience. The industry uses notions of skill to their advantage in both marketing and eliciting consent front temporary workers. On occasions when the industry's intended audience is potential clients, temporary workers are characterized as being highly skilled. In these situations, the temporary industry claims to be filling a niche left by a dearth of skilled labor in the United States. In this excerpt from a temporary agency's promotional kit aimed at generating clients, temporary workers are cast as possessing high-level yet scarce skills:

> There is a chronic shortage of skilled clerical and technical help in this country. The Occupational Outlook Handbook, published annually by the Department of Labor, has outlined this fact since at least 1974. The forecasted growth in demand for skilled clerical and technical help is significantly faster than the growth for the workforce as a whole. At the same time, supply side factors, such as the *women's movement*, and aging workforce, the decline of the classic secretarial school, and increased labor force nobility and opportunity have created a supply imbalance/shortfall. This fact is reflected in the newspaper classified ad sections every week. . . . Rapidly changing technology in both the clerical and technical fields have created new skill requirements to which the workforce in this country responds slowly. (Temporary agency promotional kit 1994; my italics)

Business and the temporary industry are cast as responding to a shortage and a rigidity in the U.S. workforce, for which the educational system and even the women's movement are to blame. This ideological sleight of hand acts to shift the impetus for temporary work from the temporary industry itself and employers to workers, when in fact Golden and Appelbaum (1992) have found it to be just the opposite. The large increases in temporary work are employer- rather than employee-driven, but by focusing on the "human capital" of workers, the temporary industry dodges questions regarding their role (and employers' roles) in creating a large contingent workforce. The THS industry is the skill-matcher, the void filler, and the workforce educator. Temporary employment agencies are seen as the savior, as entrepreneurs supplying the solution to a desperate demand rather than as a co-creator of that demand.

The industry also often likes to make use of a military analogy by portraying temporary workers as office commandos who swoop in to solve an office crisis, after which they ride off into the sunset and their next mission. One item in a public relations kit from National Association of Temporary and Staffing Services provides an example of the heroism attributed to temporary workers and, of course, the industry that supplies these courageous men and women:

> A good secretary is an executive's right arm. So what does the boss do if that right arm is home with the flu? A competent temporary employee eases executive tensions by handling a secretary's chores. And temps, as they are called, can do much more.

Temporary workers save the day by being able to pick up a job, any job, on a moment's notice or by providing scarce skills for an urgent but limited time period. For office work, knowledge of certain software packages is one of the primary office-saving devices. One company suggests that they can provide "someone who can fill in when the resident desktop publishing expert is out, or someone who can pull together a presentation using all of the latest software."

This portrayal of temporary workers does not always mesh with reports from temporaries, who often feel overqualified for assignments while they perform unskilled work despite their "human capital" or capabilities. An experience I shared with many temporaries was being called in on what had been described to me as an "urgent" assignment, only to find little actual work to perform. One particular assignment left me wondering whether the client company would have been better off renting an answering machine for the day. I think I answered the phone a grand total of five times during the course of nine hours (field notes 1994).

Ideologies Concerning Upward Mobility

Yet another powerful ideology operating on temporary workers regards temporary employment as a means to upward mobility. Temporary agencies prominently advertise skill development as a benefit of temporary employment that will surely bring upward mobility for the hard-working temporary.

> The temporary help industry acts to increase the skills and real wages of the workforce through its training and upgrading programs, and through the productive experience it provides. (Press release, National Association of Temporary Services 1994)

> As workers compete in an ever-changing and complex workplace, temporary help offers numerous benefits that give temporary employees an inside tract to more advanced skills and better jobs. (Press kit, National Association of temporary Services 1994)

In cases where temporary workers continually perform de-skilled work, they obviously are inhibited from acquiring or using skills on the job. And white temporary industry representatives sing the praises of the in-house computer training they offer to temporary workers, my interviewees' reports seldom matched what was advertised. Not all temporary agencies have computer training available. The hardware, software, and space required represent a substantial investment for a smatter agency. In those agencies that do have computer training available, the "training" most often consists of the worker following an on-screen, computer-led tutorial. Temporary workers who have used these tutorials have found them to be inadequate because they offer little opportunity for the student to practice in a meaningful way.

> They advertise that they have the tutorial. And it's not really a tutorial that anyone teaches you. It's something that you, you hit the button on the computer and it says [speaking slowly with emphasis], "Welcome to tutorial. We will now learn about a computer. This is your keyboard. This is the screen." And it takes you step by step by step. And the software is geared specifically for that, and you type up the little thing

they give you to type up or whatever. You don't have the option to write your own letter or whatever. (Bernice Katz, thirty-four-year-old white woman)

At the temporary agency where I worked (a large regional agency), computer training consisted mainly of tutorials in WordPerfect, Microsoft Word, WordStar, Dis-
playWrite, MultiMate, Wang, and Samna Word. Also offered were Lotus 1-2-3
(version 2.2) and dBASE III Plus. Many of the tutorials were for outdated versions of
the software, and tutorials for Lotus and dBASE are not adequate to produce profi-
ciency in those who use them. Exceptions do exist to this training scenario, and they
are well-publicized. The experiences of temporary workers, however, reflect the rarity
of the high-quality training opportunities.

In addition to the lack of quality training programs, not all temporary workers are eligible for the computer training that does exist. Agencies sometimes require a certain
number of hours to be worked before a temporary may access these tutorials—an ironic
fact considering how agency literature emphasizes qualified individuals and promises to
help temporaries develop marketable skills. At the agency where I worked, temporaries
are required to have a staggering 500 hours of work (almost three months full-time) before they are eligible for computer training. Because most temporaries must work
through more than one agency in order to secure enough hours of work, eligibility for
such programs becomes more remote the more agencies a temporary worker uses.

Many temporary workers who do qualify and would like to acquire additional computer training are inhibited from doing so because of the very nature of temporary
work. Temporary workers are constrained by the uncertainty of their situation and do
not have the free time or flexibility that many believe they do (Martella 1991; Negrey
1993). Temporary workers who are working full-time find it difficult if not impossible
to take advantage of computer training because temporary agencies typically have the
same hours as the businesses they service and offer training only during those hours.

I say I like to go once a week. That would be ideal. Truth is, maybe I'm lucky if I can
do it one time a month for an hour or so. But I like to go to keep up my skills and to be
seen as a presence—that I'm doing something to improve my skills. (Jean Masters,
thirty-four-year-old African American)

Jean found it difficult to practice her computer skills because her agency closed at 5:30
P.M. and was not open on the weekends. Most of the time, Jean's assignments ended between 5 and 5:30 P.M. With commuting time, she could not even get to the agency before it closed, much less find time to practice new skills or develop new competencies.

When temporary workers are not working full-time, many are involved in looking for
work or running their time cards to the different agencies they use. These activities can
take a substantial amount of time. In addition, temporaries must be available immediately
to the agencies should an assignment arise. For many, this means waiting by the phone or
calling all "your" agencies to find work, rather than isolating yourself at just one agency
and making use of the computer training program. As most temporary workers will tell
you, if an agency calls with an assignment, you had better be accessible or you will lose the

assignment. Some temporary workers I interviewed even carry beepers. Overall, I found very little use of agency-provided training owing to the constraints placed on temporary workers by their status as temporary. Thus the picture of temporaries gaining upward mobility from skills development is not always accurate for these workers.

Another way in which agencies use the ideology of upward mobility is through portraying temporary work as a good way for workers to get into a desirable organization or occupation. Temporary work is represented as a vehicle for workers to demonstrate their skills so that their talents can be discovered. The industry portrays itself as providing good jobs that could lead to something better (permanent) in tough economic times.

> Working as a temporary can be a meaningful and useful bridge to full-time employment by providing. . . an opportunity for workers to showcase their talents to a wide variety of potential employers. (Press kit from the National Association of Temporary Services 1994)

> The temporary help/staffing services industry can act as a "jobs bridge" to full-time employment. Temporary work offers workers, who may have been displaced during current workforce restructuring, a critical safety net of income, benefits, and skills training which often provides access back to full-time employment. (Pamphlet from a temporary help company 1993)

Indeed, the most common reason that temporaries consent to perform de-skilled or devalued work is that they believe they may gain a "permanent" job through temporary employment.

> After working three months there I'd probably have the references from the people I work with to get a permanent job there. And I guess that's kind of a starting gate. That's pretty much what I looked for. It's just too bad because the company is moving to Sacramento or something like that. (Mark Cranford, twenty-year-old white man)

> I'm temping. . . because eventually somewhere I will get an offer. And I won't have to go through the interview process in the same way everyone else does. They go, "We love you, this is a formality." And you know you've got the job basically. (Michael Glenn, twenty-six-year-old Asian American)

> It's temporary, and there's a possibility. The key is here, something maybe I haven't touched on, too. There's that possibility that someone might see me and say, "Hey, he would be able to do this job." Maybe not the one I'm doing, but another job. And [there's] the possibility of acting, too. (Doug Larson, thirty-nine-year-old white man)

Thus the ideology that skills gained through temporary employment are a means to upward mobility and permanency pushes temporary workers to work hard (at de-skilled or devalued work) and stay with temporary employment. They come to believe that developing and using such skills on temporary assignments will lead them out of temporary employment to their dream job, whether inside or outside the corporate world. Temporary workers become workers-in-waiting, waiting for their reward, which is a "good," full-time job. Some workers take this view to the extreme, as did one man who told me that by working in the kitchen at an entertainment company, he might be discovered for his talents as a sound engineer:

> If you do well, I mean, if you're doing something in the kitchen and they really like you, and you say, "Well I work on audio" they may pull you over and say, "Here, we've got this," or something like that. . . . It's easier to find out about jobs at a particular place if you're already in the place than it is to submit unsolicited resumes. (Arnold Finch, twenty-three-year-old white man)

Unfortunately, Arnold never was hired as a sound engineer by the entertainment company. Still other workers feel that their writing skills or management skills will be recognized and they will be offered a permanent job that differs significantly from their temporary assignment." In fact, among those temporary workers I interviewed who were offered permanent jobs, the jobs offered were almost exclusively the same as their temporary assignments. Thus temporary workers often turned down permanent offers because they did not represent upward mobility through temping. Rather than take a permanent position that resembled a temporary position and its attendant de-skilled or devalued work, temporary workers waited in hopes that the next offer would be more in line with their expectations. They felt that they could perform de-skilled or devalued work if it was a means to an end (upward mobility) but not as a permanent job.

> During the time I temped I must have been offered at least eight or nine permanent jobs at places, and like I didn't know how to tell them I would never consider working for them, not full-time, not at the same job. They'd have to give more than that. (Ludy Martinez, thirty-six-year-old Filipina)

> And I was offered a lot of full-time positions from the temp jobs. But I. . . was fortunate that I didn't have to take a job right away just to make ends meet. I could wait for the job I really wanted, one that I could use my degrees and talents for. (Ellen Lanford, thirty-eight-year-old white woman)

Thus the characterization of work as "temporary" represents an effective strategy for eliciting workers to do work they would otherwise not perform because they felt it was "beneath them." This scenario is reminiscent of women college graduates feeling they could get into the management of an organization through the secretarial pool. Temporary work alters internal labor markets in such a way, however, as to significantly separate temporary workers from permanent workers and access to internal labor markets. To the extent that the secretarial pool was ever a successful route into managerial positions, it is even less so in temporary clerical employment, particularly when temporary employees are used as a buffer around permanent employees to secure their jobs and cushion them against monotonous work. As such, temporary workers find a considerable distance between temporary employment and access to the internal labor market of a company unless they specifically were hired into a position for a trial run.

When temporary workers perform work that lacks skill content, they are unable to demonstrate their capability for performing a more skilled, permanent job. Temporary industry figures reflect that 35 percent of temporary workers eventually are offered permanent jobs. Of course, this leaves 65 percent, the overwhelming majority, who are not offered jobs. Obviously, the industry's claims about temporary work being the road to a permanent position should be tempered. When assessing the success of temporary employment for job placement, keep in mind that the industry does not provide data regarding the type of jobs offered, or whether these offers are ultimately accepted by the temporary worker. In my research, those workers who were offered permanent jobs recounted that they did not take the jobs because of low pay or low skill requirements. In other words, temporary workers who did filing for eight hours a day were not typically offered a position in the management training program. More often than not, they were offered permanent jobs that entailed filing for eight hours a day. Jobs offered to temporaries more often resembled temporary work in skill and pay level. To make a definitive statement about work transitions, additional research is needed to examine these transitions from temporary to permanent work. Such research must be carefully designed to discern which temporaries are offered permanent employment and how often this occurs, which temporaries accept permanent employment offers, and which reject such offers and why.

An interesting phenomenon that indicated the effectiveness of the industry's marketing claims about temporary work as the means to a desirable permanent job was that many of my informants remained hopeful for their shot at upward mobility despite having been offered de-skilled or devalued jobs they did not accept.

> I didn't want to go into an agency, you know, with a lot more, with being really overqualified and going to do clerical work. I felt that would be too devastating to me. Now I just don't care. I'll take ten bucks and keep my mouth shut and go home. And you never know who you're gonna meet [while temping]. (Cindy Carson, thirty-eight-year-old white woman)

This is not to say that temporaries never find their perfect job through temping. Indeed, this must happen often enough to perpetuate and legitimize the myth of the full-time job, which aids in securing a docile temporary workforce. Cases of "temp finds wonder job" are paraded out by temporary agencies to the media and their own workers.

> In 1993, George Williams accepted a temp assignment with Ethereal Gas Company, where his cheerful smile, reliability, and willingness to work made a good impression. Within a few months, he was offered a full-time position with the gas company and has since received a promotion and an opportunity for additional training. (temporary agency newsletter)

One agency even ran a contest soliciting "temp stories" from temporary workers in Los Angeles. The ad gave examples of the kinds of temp stories they were looking for.

Prominently featured are the examples of temporary workers finding great jobs through temporary employment.

> The client falls in love with you and you get offered a regular, full-time position with a company you've come to know and like. . . . IT REALLY HAPPENS. Just listen to [April's] story. She started off as a temporary receptionist at a literary agency in Century City, and now she heads up the entire TV literary department! (full page back-cover color advertisement placed by a temporary agency)

Thus ideologies concerning skill and upward mobility help to secure temporary workers' consent and labor in an environment of economic and structural constraints owing to changes in the organization of work. Much has been said about the declining loyalty of workers to companies that ate regularly shedding employees. Despite the limits on consent produced through direct, contradictory experiences, temporary workers often embraced these ideologies, at least initially in the interviews, perhaps partially as a way to justify their position to me. Continued discussion, however, revealed a measure of control that was far from complete. Indeed, the extent to which workers embraced a particular ideology seemed to be intertwined with the extent to which they perceived themselves as having other options. In this way, structural constraints and ideologies act as mutually reinforcing means for producing consent in temporary workers.

In the case where temporary workers are performing de-skilled work, the lack of skill acts as a mechanism of control over the temporary employee. The worker is unable to gain any organizationally specific skills that would increase individual bargaining power with the client. Furthermore, in this context, temporary workers are unable to increase their bundle of skills. Frederick Taylor, the "father" of scientific management, understood that removing knowledge from workers was a means to better control them. While Taylor undertook this through scientific management, the same process can occur when skilled work is allocated by permanent and temporary status.

• • •

The picture of skill in temporary work is a complex one. Employers, in conjunction with permanent employees, can divide clerical tasks in order to insulate "core" workers from routine jobs, which results in the material de-skilling of jobs for temporary workers. The overall technical work process remains unchanged, while material skill is reallocated based on one's status as a periphery or core employee. Alternatively, companies can hire temporaries into clerical jobs that are clerical in name only (upgrading the content of the job while leaving the pay unchanged), which results in the devaluing of temporary jobs. We have seen that temporary work is both de-skilled and devalued, with some temporary workers experiencing both material and ideological de-skilling tendencies.

A significant alteration has evolved in the operation of internal labor markets. Although represented by the temporary industry as "a foot in the door," temporary jobs do not provide the route to upward mobility as promised. Relatively unskilled temporaries can be structurally inhibited from developing the very skills that may help them to acquire less marginal work, while highly skilled temporaries can be constrained from demonstrating their capabilities on the job because they are required to do relatively de-skilled work. Yet even those who are able to demonstrate their skills on the job feel that potential employers have little motivation to hire them permanently because of added benefit costs and the hiring fees charged by temporary agencies, and because they are already doing the job at a relatively low rate of pay. In these cases, temporary jobs can truly be described as a lose-lose situation—dead-end jobs regardless of the human capital that temporary workers bring with them.

Consider the high-wage, high-skill workforce touted by the Clinton administration (see also Reich 1992). The temporary industry holds that it can be central to the upgrading of U.S. workers' skills.

> The U.S. Department of Labor estimates that 75% of the people who lose their jobs today will have to be retrained before going back into the workforce because their skills will have become obsolete. Currently businesses are hard-pressed to fill jobs requiring specific expertise (computer operators, word processing operators, etc.). Temporary help companies have the unique ability to provide workers with distinctive or hard to find skills. By using such workers, businesses maintain their operations even as workforce skill shortages intensify. (Sample letter to the editor, National Association of Temporary Services promotional material for National Temporary Help Week 1994)

As made evident by the stories of the workers I spoke with, some of the more grandiose claims made by the industry need to be viewed with a skeptic's eye. The temporary industry's relationship to workers' skill development is more complex than portrayed here. Even when agencies make training available, the unstable nature of much temporary employment has the unintended consequence of prohibiting skill acquisition. One possible consequence of increased temporary usage explored and supported to a degree herein might be a further bifurcation of the workforce into higher-wage, higher-skill "winners" and lower-wage, lower-skill "losers."

In addition, considering the overrepresentation of women and people of color in contingent forms of employment, we should take warning that continuing increases in temporary employment may exacerbate existing gender and racial inequalities in employment, regardless of the skills one obtains through increased educational efforts. The "winners" and "losers" are as likely to be divided by race, class, and gender as they are in many other aspects of social life. Indeed, rewards in the world of the temporary worker often are dispersed with regard to these social categories.

References

Crompton, R., and G. Jones. 1984. *White-Collar Proletariat: De-skilling and Gender in Clerical Work.* Philadelphia: Temple University Press.

Hartmann, H., R. E. Kraut, and L. A. Tilly, eds. 1986. *Computer Chips and Paper Clips: Technology and Women's Employment.* Washington, D.C.: National Academy Press.

Machung, A. 1984. "Word Processing: Forward for Business, Backward for Women." In *My Troubles Are Going to Have Trouble with Me: Everyday Trials and Triumphs of Women Workers*, edited by K.B. Sacks and D. Remy. New Brunswick, N.J.: Rutgers University Press.

Martella, M. 1991. *"Just a Temp": Expectations and Experiences of Women Clerical Temporary Workers*. Washington, D.C.: U.S. Department of Labor, Women's Bureau.

National Association of Temporary Services. 1992. *Report on the Temporary Help Services Industry*. Alexandria, Va.: DRI/McGraw Hill.

Negrey, C. 1993. *Gender, Time, and Reduced Work*. Albany: State University of New York Press.

Parker, R. E. 1993. "The Labor Force in Transition: The Growth of the Contingent Workforce in the United States." In *The Labor Process and Control of Labor*, edited by B. Berberoglu. Westport, Conn.: Praeger.

Reich, R. 1992. *The Work of Nations*. New York: Vintage.

13

SELF-EMPLOYMENT AS A RESPONSE TO THE DOUBLE DAY FOR WOMEN AND MEN IN CANADA

A. Bruce Arai

Malgré une augmentation récente de la participation masculine aux tâches de la maison, les femmes assurent encore la plus grande partie de ce travail, que ce soit les soins apportes aux enfants, le nettoyage, la cuisine, les courses, la gestion financière, l'education ou les conseils personnels. Toutefois, de nombreuses femmes mènent une activité professionnelle rémunérée, qui viert s'ajouter à leurs responsabilités au sein du foyer. Cet article pose la question de savoir si les femmes choisissent le travail autonome comme un moyen d'alléger quelque peu les pressions rigides que leur impose leur "double travail." Alors que les femmes semblent effectivement se tourner vers le travail autonome pour cause de conflits entre travail et vie de famille, les hommes ne semblent pas guidés par les mêmes raisons.

• • •

Despite recent increases in the amount of work done in the home by men, most of this work is still performed by women. These duties range from child care, cleaning, and cooking to shopping, financial management and domestic discipline and counselling. Yet many women also hold down paid jobs in addition to their domestic responsibilities. This paper investigates whether women turn to self-employment as a way of introducing some flexibility into the rigid pressures from both sides of this "double day." While women do appear to turn to self-employment as one way of coping with conflicting family and work pressures, the same is not true for men.

There is wide agreement that women still have responsibility for much of the work that is done in the home (Kalleberg and Rosenfeld 1992; Blain 1993). For example, on average, women do 78 percent more unpaid housework than do men (Jackson 1996). This discrepancy persists even when women also work outside the home, which they have been doing in record numbers recently. The gap is also unaffected by type of household (e.g., married partners versus cohabiters). South and Spitze (1994) found that men in all household situations except for divorced and widowed men, do about the same amount of housework and in all cases it is significantly less than the amount women perform.

Balancing the demands of this "double day" (Luxton 1980, 179) or "second shift" (Hochschild 1989, 3) is not always easy for women. Ginn and Sandall (1997) speculate on some of the reasons that meshing home and work demands may be even more problematic now than in the past. They suggest that women's earnings are now a more significant component of family finances, and that it may now be more important for women to earn their own income because of higher divorce rates, higher chances of male unemployment and shrinking pension benefits for widows. Additionally, the proportion of working women with responsibilities for small children or the elderly has increased dramatically.

Ginn and Sandall further claim that the conflicting demands of work and home lead to greater stress levels for both men and women, and they test three specific hypotheses about this connection on a sample of British social work professionals. The first hypothesis is that stress levels will be higher for people with young children, responsibilities for the elderly and longer work hours than for people without young children, elderly care duties and long work hours because these responsibilities are less flexible than other elements of home and work. Second, the effect of young kids on stress levels will be greater for women than for men because young children tend to make more demands on their mothers than on their fathers. Finally, stress levels should be higher for full-time than for part-time workers. Their analyses reveal support for all three postulates. In explaining their results, they conclude that

> because of gender ideology which allocates family caring work primarily to women, employed women with dependent children are under more pressure than similar men to work reduced hours and in relatively undemanding jobs which may be beneath their capabilities. (Ginn and Sandall 1997, 429)

In other words, when women are faced with a conflict between rigid demands in the home and rigid demands at work, they are under more pressure than men to find a way to accommodate those demands. Some of the ways in which women in their sample responded to these pressures were to move into part-time work, or into lower-level positions.

Similar patterns may operate in Canada where the stress of managing the work—family interface is also prevalent. Beaujot (1997) reports on a Conference Board of Canada survey that found that one-third of all respondents experienced "severe tension" in balancing home and work demands while a further quarter of the respondents experienced "moderate tension."

Dealing with Stress

While these findings are instructive, there are other issues that must be considered when we move from documenting stress levels to ways in which women attempt to diffuse this stress. First, when faced with competing demands from home and work, women may use many techniques to introduce some flexibility into the demands from one or both sides. For example, they may take steps to make their domestic responsibilities more flexible by transferring some of the demands to another household member, hiring outside help, or relaxing some of the less pressing needs such as household cleanliness (Kalleberg and Rosenfeld 1992; Presser 1994). They may also make changes in their work situation, such as moving into part-time employment or leaving the labor force altogether.

A second issue concerns the composition of the second shift. That is, household tasks are not completely interchangeable, and transferring some of these tasks to others can be difficult. For example, children, especially young children, may make emotional demands for care that cannot always be scheduled or transferred to others. As Blain (1993) shows, virtually all of the medical care of children—from scheduling appointments and deciding on care routines to staying home from work to look after sick children—falls on their mothers, even when fathers are present in the household.

The inflexibility of domestic demands may also depend on the age and number of children in the home. The demands of younger children may be more inflexible than those of older offspring. Additionally, the more children in the household, the more people there are making demands on the mother. South and Spitze (1994) show that having kids, especially younger kids, increases the average number of housework hours for women, but not for men. Waldfogel (1997) shows that the earnings penalty for women with one child is 4 percent and 12 percent for two or more kids compared to women without children. Estes and Glass (1996) found that women often make job changes following childbirth in an attempt to minimize both income and time with family, but that they often fail to achieve this because of their relative lack of power in the labor market. Clearly then, the presence of children significantly affects both the nature of household demands for women, and the different ways of managing the work–family nexus.

Aside from adjustments in the home, Kalleberg and Rosenfeld (1992) show that we cannot assume that the way women adjust their work patterns in response to the pressures of the double day will be the same across all countries. Specifically, women in Canada and the United States have more difficulty balancing home and work schedules while Scandinavian women are more likely to continue in full-time work or to drop out of the labor force altogether. This difference is partly due to better welfare state provisions for child care and parental leaves in Scandinavia compared to North America. But Kalleberg and Rosenfeld found no national differences in how men balance home and work responsibilities. They speculate that men may face different pressures than women, with women being pressured to manage the conflicts of the double day and men being pressured to continue in full-time work, even when other options are available.

There are also other reasons that might affect how people respond to the double day, especially when there are young children in the home. Munch, McPherson, and Smith Lovin (1997) show that women with children under age five have fewer and less intense job-related network contacts, but this pattern does not hold for men. We know that much valuable information passes through these networks (Granovetter 1984). To the extent that women are at least temporarily deprived of this information resource, this may limit their chances of reacquiring work after a maternity leave. In other words, the particular ways in which women respond to the stress of the double day likely depends upon both individual and state level processes.

Crompton and Harris (1998) have further argued that some occupations allow women to plan their careers around family aspirations while others do not. They show that in professional occupations such as medicine, women can "satisfice" or reach some level of accomplishment in both their domestic and work spheres. By "satisficing," women attain a level of satisfaction in their home and work lives, but also realize that to do so they must sacrifice some initial goals or hopes in each sphere. In other occupations such as banking, this type of planning is not possible and women end up relinquishing or scaling back either their familial or work aspirations.

The reason that occupation is important, Crompton and Harris contend, is that certain occupations are structured such that preplanning of families and careers is possible. In some professions like medicine, long training periods outside the place of employment, the portability of skills, and the flexibility in hours once employed allow women to plan their careers around family aspirations. In other "managerial" occupations like banking, the quick, organization-specific training and constant flux of managerial tasks and situations do not allow women in these jobs the ability to plan either careers or families.

While their argument is interesting, there is another way to explain Crompton and Harris's difference between professional and managerial women. The differences they find could also be due to the distinction between employment and self-employment. Although self-employment does not usually involve a long training period, the portability of skills, flexibility of hours and ability to choose one's work could produce the "satisficing" pattern found among Crompton and Harris's doctors. This is even more plausible given that self-employment among medical professionals is much higher than average in many countries.

In contrast, the organization-specific and other-directed nature of employed work is similar to that found in "managerial" occupations, and may prevent planning careers around families for all employees and not just managers. Indeed, it may be the case that managers often have more ability to satisfice than other employees, given their generally superior benefit plans and employment prospects.

The Self-Employment Option

So part-time employment, moving into lower level positions and choosing family-friendly occupations may not be the only work-based responses of Canadian women to balancing employment and family. It may also be the case that women turn to self-employment in these situations. In an analysis of earlier American data, Carr (1996) found that women, but not men, did turn to self-employment in these situations (see also Jurik 1998). There are at least three reasons why the odds that a woman will become self-employed should increase when faced with inflexible schedules.

First, one of the primary reasons that many entrepreneurs (both male and female) give when asked why they are self-employed is the flexibility that this form of work offers (Bechhofer and Elliott 1978; Nisbet 1997). Among the Canadian self-employed, 6 percent said that the major reason they chose to start their own business was because of its flexibility. A further 42 percent said their primary rationale was because of the independence it afforded them and a further 13 percent chose self-employment because it allowed them to work at home (Statistics Canada 1997).

Second, as job-related networks deteriorate, women often replace them with other networks, usually based around family and community contacts (Munch et al. 1997). These networks may lead to increased chances of self-employment. We know that family and community networks are a vital source of capital and information for male entrepreneurs, especially in immigrant and ethnic enclave economies (Waldinger et al. 1990; Light and Rosenstein 1995; Portes 1905). It may be the case that these networks could play a similar role for women with children.

Finally, self-employment for women is more of an option now than in the past. Several studies have documented the resurgence of self-employment in Canada since the 1970s, and particularly the number of women entrepreneurs. Moreover, this rise in self-employment is not simply the product of cyclical fluctuations in unemployment (Arai 1997; Statistics Canada 1997). As more and more women become self-employed, its appeal to other women is enhanced, which produces further growth. Many women have become quite successful entrepreneurs and average earnings in self-employment can be comparable to those in paid work (Belcourt et al. 1991; Arai 1995; Statistics Canada 1997). This, along with its potentially greater flexibility may attract women as a way to alleviate some of the pressure of the double day.

These factors would not be expected to push men into self-employment to the same degree as women. Kalleberg and Rosenfeld (1992) argue that men do not seem to experience the same pressures to balance the double day as women. Carr (1996) also found if—at having a child under six, plus one between six and seventeen only increased a man's odds of self-employment by 18 percent but it increased a woman's odds by 66 percent. Further, men also enjoy the flexibility and independence of self-employment, but it is more likely that these features are important to men for work-related reasons (Light and Rosenstein 1995). Also, men do not experience the deterioration of job networks that women do when they have children.

However, there are also good reasons for believing that women will not turn to self-employment as a way of balancing home and work responsibilities. There are factors that may cancel out the above benefits of self-employment, lead to greater exploitation (Jurik 1998) or may even make it less likely that women will choose self-employment over some form of paid employment as a way of dealing with the double day.

First, the supposed flexibility of being an independent business operator, able to set your own hours and conditions of work may be largely illusory. Clearly, self-employment in some industries such as retail sales, hospitality and tourism, and day-care provision do not have flexible hours and are probably more rigid and involve longer hours than most forms of paid employment. So the flexible character of self-employment may only be true in some industries, or it may be the case that flexibility and independence is simply part of the ideology rather than the reality of self-employment (Linder 1992).

Second, the appeal of decent earnings in self-employment is also problematic, especially in relation to the flexibility of running a business. Specifically, self-employment earnings, although on average they are similar to earnings from paid employment, are significantly more polarized. Achieving high earnings in self-employment is usually only possible by working longer hours (Statistics Canada 1997), which would probably exacerbate rather than alleviate the problems of the double day. Also, higher earnings are more common among male than female entrepreneurs, so its attractiveness to women may be reduced.

Given what is known about the general characteristics of the self-employed population, it is not clear whether women turn to it to balance work and family. For instance, most of the self-employed are still male, although the number of women is rising rapidly (Statistics Canada 1997). And while the rate of self-employment among immigrants is generally high (Waldinger et al. 1990), they remain a small segment of Canadian entrepreneurs (Arai 1995). Average earnings in self-employment are slightly below those found in wage work, although the average number of hours worked is slightly higher. Only a small proportion of entrepreneurs work primarily from home, although the percentage of women who do so is much higher than that of men. Also the self-employed and employee populations are relatively distinct, with few entrepreneurs also holding down a paid job and vice versa. Finally, the occupational distribution of the self-employed shows that most women and men start their own businesses in the service sector (Arai 1995; Statistics Canada 1997).

The major question to be addressed in this paper then is whether Canadian women with children turn to self-employment as a way of easing the demands of the double day. Four specific hypotheses will be tested:

1. Women with children have greater odds of being self-employed than women without children.
2. The more children a woman has, the greater her odds of being self-employed.
3. Women with young children have greater odds of self-employment than women with older children.
4. Having children will increase the odds of self-employment for women more than for men.

Each of these hypotheses investigates a different dimension of the potential flexibility of self-employment for women, and in all cases the hypotheses apply only to people who are employed. Data for this paper comes from statistics in Canada's 1995 Survey of Work Arrangements (SWA).

Results

As can be seen in Table 13.1, flexible working arrangements for employees are the exception rather than the rule in Canada. Only 10 percent of employees have a job sharing arrangement, and less than one-quarter of employees can choose the start and end times of their jobs. Similarly of those employees who regularly do some of their work

TABLE 13.1   Percentage of Employees Enjoying Selected "Flexibility" Benefits

Benefit	*Percent of Workers*
Job sharing arrangement	10.1
Choose start/end times for work	23.8
For working at home, employer provides:	
Computer	20.5
Modem	12.2
Fax machine	9.8
Other Equipment	18.6
Reimbursement for costs	6.7

SOURCE: Survey of Work Arrangements, 1995.

TABLE 13.2   Main Reason for Choosing Self-Employment, Women and Men

Reason	*Women*	*Men*
Make more money	7.8	9.3
Enjoy independence	29.0	46.0
Flexible schedule	9.6	4.2
Work from home	15.5	2.1
Family business	21.1	21.5
Other	16.4	17.0

SOURCE: Survey of Work Arrangements, 1995.

at home (11.3 percent of all employees) employers provide equipment and/or reimbursement to 20.5 percent or less of these people. In other words, despite the fact that many companies promote "family friendly" employment practices, only a small minority of employees are actually able to take advantage of them. In many cases, employees must look elsewhere for flexibility.

Turning to the self-employed, Table 13.2 presents some of the different reasons that women and men choose to start a business. And while none of the reasons can be directly equaled with a desire to balance work and family, some of them do provide an indirect indication. Choosing self-employment because of a desire for flexible schedules, or to work from home, are consistent with choosing it to ease the conflicts of home and work. If this is the case, then up to 25.1 percent of women but only 6.3 percent of men may be opening businesses to ease the pressures of the double day. This indicates that women may use self-employment as a source of flexibility four times as often as men.

A more sustained examination of the hypotheses outlined above is presented in Tables 13.3 and 13.4. Table 13.3 shows that hypotheses 1 and 2 are supported by these data. The effect of the number of children a woman has on her odds of self-employment is both positive and significant, meaning that women with children do have greater odds of being self-employed than women without children. In addition, for each additional child that a woman has, her odds of self-employment increase by between 5 and 22 percent. Although this effect is relatively small, it is consistent with the idea that women are turning to self-employment to escape the rigid pressures from

TABLE 13.3 Logistic Regression of the Odds of Self-employment for Women on Selected Variables

Variable	B	S.E. B	Exp B	95 % C.I. for Exp B Low	High
Number of children	.125***	.033	1.130	1.050	1.220
Child(ren) present by age group (ref: none)					
Children aged 0-2 yr.	.561***	.169	1.750	1.260	2.440
Children aged 3-5 yr.	-.134	.249	.875	.538	1.42
Children aged 6-15 yr.	.215*	.101	1.240	1.020	1.51
0-2 and 3-5 only	.221	.223	1.250	.805	1.93
0-2 and 6-15 only	.817***	.237	2.270	1.420	3.610
3-5 and 6-15 only	.518***	.162	1.680	1.220	2.300
Education (ref.: university degree)					
0 to 8 years	-.921***	.183	.398	.278	.570
Some high school	-.608***	.132	.544	.420	.705
High school graduate	-.680***	.123	.506	.398	.644
Some post-secondary	-.264	.145	.767	.578	1.020
Post-secondary diploma	-.381***	.111	.683	.550	.850
Age group (ref.: 55-69 yr.)					
15-24	-1.64***	.164	.194	.441	.268
25-34	-1.34***	.135	.261	.201	.340
35-44	-.960***	.127	.383	.299	.491
45-54	-.615***	.120	.541	.428	.684
Number of hours worked	.032***	.004	1.030	1.020	1.040
Part-time	.958***	.124	2.610	2.050	3.320
Not married	-.266	.178	.766	.540	1.090
Spouse's labour force status (ref.: full-time)					
Part-time	.011	.110	1.010	.815	1.250
Unemployed	-.190	.195	.827	.565	1.210
No spouse	.192	.162	1.210	.882	1.660
Spouse's class worker (ref.: employee)					
Self-employed	1.390***	.084	4.010	3.400	4.720
No spouse	.158	.137	1.170	.895	1.530
Constant	-3.400***	.228	-		
Initial -2 log likelihood			8965.27		
Model -2 log likelihood			6646.39		
Model chi-square			2318.88***		
DF			44		
R^2			.26		
N			11828		

* p < .05   ** p < .01   *** p < .001

TABLE 13.4 Logistic Regression of the Odds of Self-Employment for Men on Selected Variables (occupational categories not shown)

Variable	B	S.E. B	Exp B	95 % C.I. for Exp B Low	High
Number of children	-.014	.032	.986	.926	1.050
Child(ren) present by age group (ref: none)					
Children aged 0-2 yr.	.004	.132	1.000	.776	1.300
Children aged 3-5 yr.	-.046	.178	.956	.674	1.360
Children aged 6-15 yr.	-.059	.083	.943	.801	1.110
0-2 and 3-5 only	.168	.158	1.180	.869	1.610
0-2 and 6-15 only	-.125	.217	.882	.576	1.350
3-5 and 6-15 only	-.046	.138	.955	.729	1.250
Education (ref.: university degree)					
0 to 8 years	-.555***	.127	.574	.447	.737
Some high school	-.342***	.103	.711	.581	.869
High school graduate	-.358***	.096	.699	.579	.844
Some post-secondary	-.425***	.121	.654	.516	.830
Post-secondary diploma	-.376***	.086	.686	.580	.813
Age group (ref.: 55-69 yr.)					
15-24	-2.530***	.163	.080	.058	.110
25-34	-1.400***	.100	.246	.202	.299
35-44	-.868***	.095	.420	.349	.505
45-54	-.533***	.089	.587	.494	.698
Number of hours worked	.055***	.003	1.060	1.050	1.060
Part-time	2.300***	.119	9.930	7.860	12.540
Not married	-.327	.139	.721	.549	.947
Spouse's labour force status (ref.: full-time)					
Part-time	.222***	.077	1.250	1.070	1.450
Unemployed	-.080	.089	.923	.776	1.100
No spouse	.315*	.137	1.370	1.050	1.790
Spouse's class worker (ref.: employee)					
Self-employed	1.160***	.085	3.190	2.700	3.760
No spouse	.004	.096	1.000	.832	1.210
Constant	-5.870***	.218			
Initial -2 log likelihood			14060.03		
Model -2 log likelihood			9880.09		
Model chi-square			4179.94***		
DF			44		
R^2			.30		
N^L			13766		

* p < .05   ** p < .01   *** p < .001

home and work. It is also consistent with the idea that the more children a woman has, the more pressure she may be under from both family and career, which increases her odds of self-employment.

In contrast, the results in Table 13.3 are not completely consistent with hypothesis 3. The data reveal that the effect of children's ages on a woman's odds of self-employment are considerably more complex than available theory would suggest. In order to be consistent with hypothesis 3, the effect and significance of children on a woman's odds of self-employment should diminish with the presence of older kids. However, women with very young children and with school-age children have higher odds of self-employment, but the odds of self-employment for women with preschoolers are no different than for women without children.

Interestingly, the effect of having preschoolers cancels out the increase in the odds of self-employment for women who also have very young children, but it does not do so for women with school-age children. As is shown in the table, the odds of self-employment for women with both preschoolers and very young children are not significantly different than women without children, but these odds are higher for women with preschoolers and school-age children. Also, having very young and school-age children has a greater positive effect on the odds of self-employment than having preschoolers and school-age children.

One plausible explanation for this result is the frequency and duration of long-term work interruptions for women. Fast and Da Pont (1997) show that over 60 percent of working women have experienced a work interruption of six months or more, usually in their twenties and thirties when the likelihood of having small children in the household is greatest. The average duration of these interruptions is 4.6 years. In addition, over 700 percent of women returned to paid employment, and over half of these women went back to a job with the same or similar duties, although many of them returned to part-time rather than full-time employment. Further, 62 percent of women experienced a work interruption for child and family reasons, although that percentage appears to be decreasing in recent years. If these women began the interruption when their child was born and returned to paid work about five years later, this would be consistent with the results in Table 13.3. In other words, this could explain, but does not show conclusively, why women with preschoolers do not have increased odds of self-employment, as was predicted.

These results paint a different picture of the effect of children on self-employment in Canada than what Carr found for the United States. There, preschool-age children increased a woman's odds of self-employment significantly, as did having preschoolers and school-age children, but there was no effect for women with only school-age children. Carr (1996) explained this result by arguing that it is consistent with the idea that preschoolers require more care than children in school.

One reason for these differences between Canada and the United States could be simply that a difference in the time period of the surveys is showing up as a national difference. With the steady growth of female self-employment since 1980 (the year of Carr's data) it may be the case that women are more committed to self-employment now in both countries, and once they start a business when their children are young, they may continue running the business when their kids head off to school. It is also possible that, with school days getting shorter and shorter, and the number of professional development days increasing, even school children require more care now than in the past. Finally, it may be that self-employment is currently more popular among women, and even women with school-age children are turning to it to juggle family and career.

In general, the control variables have the anticipated effects on the dependent variable. Women who have higher levels of education tend to have greater odds of self-employment, suggesting that opportunities for self-employment are generally greater for women with more education. However, the fact that women with only some post-secondary education have equally high odds of self-employment as those with university degrees suggests that graduation from university is not necessary to maximize a woman's odds of self-employment.

The age categories reveal that the odds of self-employment are greater for older women than for younger women. This is consistent with Ginn and Sandall's suggestion that women's earnings may be more important now than in the past, and self-employment, particularly for those older women who do remain in the labor force, may be one of the few options available.

The result that working more hours increases a woman's odds of self-employment shows that regardless of whether they work full-time or part-time, self-employment usually requires a greater time commitment than paid work. However, the results suggest that this commitment can be met in a more flexible manner because women with children still have greater odds of self-employment. Women who work part-time have higher odds of self-employment, although there is no difference in the odds of self-employment for married and unmarried women. This is somewhat surprising given the importance of marriage for the success of family businesses (Bertaux and Bertaux-Wiame 1981; Light and Rosenstein 1995). However, much of this research has focused on male entrepreneurs, and the present results indicate that this importance may not apply to women.

The labor force characteristics of a woman's spouse seem to have little effect on her odds of self-employment. The only spousal attribute that has any positive effect on a woman's odds of self-employment is having a partner who is also self-employed. This is consistent with the idea that self-employment runs within a family.

Hypothesis 4 about the effects of children on a person's odds of self-employment being greater for women than for men is strongly confirmed in Table 13.4. Neither the number of children that a woman has, nor the ages of his children have any positive effect on his odds of self-employment. Indeed, if any of the coefficients did reach significance, the general pattern suggested in Table 13.4 would be that having children would decrease a man's odds of self-employment. Clearly the effect of the number and age of children on a person's odds of self-employment is stronger for women than for men. This is consistent with the idea that it is women who are expected to make adjustments when home and work demands conflict, and that one of these adjustments may be becoming self-employed.

Again, these results are different from those found by Carr for the U.S. There is a relatively small, positive effect of having both a child who is aged 0–6 and one aged

6–17 on men's odds of self-employment for the United States, but no effect for having one child in either age category alone. From Table 13.4, it appears that men in Canada are even less likely to make work adjustments for balancing home and career than men in the United States.

In general, the patterns in the control variables for the men's results are the same as those for women. The notable exceptions are that married men and men whose spouses work part-time have greater odds of self-employment, unlike married women and women whose spouses work part-time. This reaffirms the point that the importance of marriage for self-employment is probably greater for men than for women.

Conclusion/Summary of Finding

Having children increased a woman's odds of being self-employed, and the more children a woman had, the greater were her odds of self-employment. These results are consistent with what Carr (1996) found for women in the United States.

Hypothesis 3, however, did not receive unqualified support. While women with very young children had higher odds of self-employment than women without children, women with preschoolers had the same odds of self-employment as women without kids. Women with school age kids again had greater odds of self-employment than women without children. Having preschoolers suppressed the positive effect of having very young children when children of both ages were present in the home, but it did not eliminate the increase in the odds when both preschoolers and school-age children were present. It was suggested that this situation is not well explained by existing theory, and an alternative argument about the duration and frequency of long-term work interruptions was proposed. While this proposition sheds light on this apparently anomalous result, further research on this issue is necessary before it can be accepted as an explanation of the patterns found in the data.

Finally, hypothesis 4 was also supported by the data. It is clear that women turn to self-employment as a way to near age the double day much more so than men. Having children has no effect on men's odds of self-employment. Additionally, the age of a man's children do not affect his odds of starting a business. This is more evidence in favor of the idea that it is women who are making the bulk of the adjustments to balance career and family.

In general, the results presented in this paper confirm previous findings on the ways in which men and women balance home and work responsibilities, as well as adding a new dimension to these debates. There are four main points which deserve consideration.

First, one of the clearest messages to emerge from Tables 13.3 and 13.4 is that it is women, and not men, who make adjustments in their work situation when the demands of home and work are in conflict. The relatively inflexible demands of having children, especially very young children, increases a woman's odds of self-employment versus women without children, but having children, of any age, has no effect on men's odds of self-employment. The results show that in addition to some of the other ways in which women adjust to the demands of the double day (Kalleberg and Rosenfeld 1992; Ginn and Sandall 1997), they also turn to self-employment to alleviate these pressures, at least in Canada, and in the United States (Carr 1996). This possibility is not something that has received sustained attention in Canada to date.

Second, Crompton and Harris point out that women in certain occupations are able to "satisfice" by achieving an acceptable level of performance in both the home and work. The same may be true of self-employment because it likely gives women all of the "planning" benefits that Crompton and Harris found for doctors. Self-employed women have control over the type of job they do, and likely have more control over their hours of work than employees, which might allow them to strike a satisfactory balance between home and work. The point is that it is not only certain occupations that offer the ability to satisfice. Self-employment can offer these benefits as well, and from the results above, some women are taking advantage of these benefits.

Third, Ginn and Sandall point out that women often end up taking lesser jobs when they are forced to make adjustments to balance home and work. If self-employment offers women the ability to satisfice between home and work, then it may be a preferable option to taking on lesser jobs. A woman's odds of self-employment increase if she works part-time, but part-time self-employment may be a more desirable form of work than part-time salaried or waged employment. On the other hand, since satisfying implies some sacrifices on the part of women, it may not be preferable to other methods of managing work and family conflicts. In all likelihood, self-employment will be a very good option for some women, but not for others, and the appeal of self-employment will depend on many individual, family and workplace factors.

Finally, the results reveal that the relationship between children's ages and the odds of a woman being self-employed is not straightforward. Ginn and Sandall (1997) and Carr (1996) suggest that the presence of younger children should elevate stress levels and demands because young children require more sustained attention than older children. Following this line of reasoning, the expectation was that the presence of younger children should raise a woman's odds of self-employment, but there should be less of an effect for older children. However, the results show that among younger children, this positive effect is only present for children under two, but not for three- to five-year-olds. In addition, older children increase a woman's odds of self-employment, which is not consistent with the ideas of Ginn and Sandall (1997) and Carr (1996).

Women turning to self-employment as a way to balance the pressures of the double day may be a peculiarly North American phenomenon, albeit with variations between Canada and the United States. Given that Kalleberg and Rosenfeld (1992) have shown that women in Canada and the United States face more difficulties in juggling home and work than women in Scandinavia, the likelihood that this pattern is unique is enhanced. With appropriate international data, it would be interesting to investigate this possibility.

References

This research was generously supported by an internal grant (partially funded by the SSHRC) from Wilfrid Laurier University and by a SSHRC standard research grant to the author. I would like to thank the anonymous reviewers for helpful comments on a previous version of this chapter.

Arai, A. B. 1995. "Self-Employment and the Nature of the Canadian Economy." Ph.D. diss., University of British Columbia.

———. 1997. "The Road Not Taken: The Transition from Unemployment to Self-Employment in Canada, 1961–1991." *Canadian Journal of Sociology* 22, no. 3: 365–382.

Beaujot, R. 1997. "Parental Preferences for Work and Childcare." *Canadian Public Policy* 23, no. 3: 275–288.

Bechhofer, F., and B. Elliott. 1978. "The Voice of Small Business and the Politics of Survival." *Sociological Review* 26, no. 1: 57–88.

Belcourt, M., R. J. Burke, and H. Lee-Gosselin. 1991. *The Glass Box: Women Business Owners in Canada.* Ottawa. Canadian Advisory Council on the Status of Women.

Bertaux, D., and I. Bertaux-Wiame. 1981. "Artisanal Bakery in France: How It Lives and Why It Survives." In *The Petite Bourgeoisie: Comparative Studies of an Uneasy Stratum,* ed. F. Bechhofer and B. Elliott, 154–181. New York: St. Martin's.

Blain, J. 1993. "'I Can't Come in Today, the Baby Has Chicken Pox!' Gender and Class Processes in How Parents in the Labor Force Deal with the Problem of Sick Children." *Canadian Journal of Sociology* 18, no. 4: 405–430.

Carr, D. 1996. "Two Paths to Self-Employment? Women's and Men's Self-Employment in the United States 1980." *Work and Occupations* 24, no. 1: 26–53.

Crompton, R., and F. Harris. 1998. "Gender Relations and Employment: The Impact of Occupation." *Work, Employment, and Society* 12, no. 2: 297–316.

Estes, S. B., and J. L. Glass. 1996. "Job Changes Following Childbirth: Are Women Trading Compensation for Family-Responsive Work Conditions." *Work and Occupations* 23, no. 4: 405–436.

Fast, J., and M. Da Pont. 1997. "Changes in Women's Work Continuity." *Canadian Social Trends* 46, no. 3: 2–7.

Giles, W., and V. Preston. 1996. "The Domestication of Women's Work: A Comparison of Chinese and Portuguese Immigrant Women Home-Workers." *Studies in Practical Economy* 51: 147–182.

Ginn, J., and J. Sandall. 1997. "Balancing Home and Employment." *Work, Employment, and Society* 11, no. 3: 414–431.

Granovetter, M. 1981. "Small Is Bountiful: Labor Markets and Establishment Size." *American Sociological Review* 49, no. 3: 323–334.

Hochschild, A., with A. Machung. 1989. *The Second Shift: Working Parents and the Revolution at Home.* New York: Viking.

Jackson, C. 1996. "Measuring and Valuing Households' Unpaid Work." *Canadian Social Trends* 42: 25–29.

Jurik, N. C. 1998. "Getting Away and Getting By: The Experience of Self-Employed Homeworkers." *Work and Occupations* 25, no. 1: 7–35.

Kalleberg, A. I., and R. A. Rosenfeld. 1992. "Work in the Family and in the Labor Market: A Cross-National, Reciprocal Analysis." *Journal of Marriage and the Family* 52: 331–346.

Light, I., and C. Rosenstein. 1995. *Race, Ethnicity, and Entrepreneurship in Urban America.* New York: Aldine de Gruyter.

Linder, M. 1992. *Farewell to the Self-Employed: Deconstructing a Socioeconomic and Legal Solipsism.* New York: Greenwood.

Luxtun, M. 1980. *More Than a Labor of Love.* Toronto: Women's Press.

Munch, A., M. J. McPherson, and L. Smith-Lovin. 1997. "Gender, Children, and Social Contact: The Effects of Child Rearing for Men and Women." *American Sociological Review* 62, no. 4: 509–520.

Nisbet, P. 1997. "Dualism, Flexibility, and Self-Employment in the UK Construction Industry." *Work, Employment, and Society* 11, no. 3: 459–480.

Portes, A. 1995. "Economic Sociology and the Sociology of Immigration: A Conceptual Overview." In *The Economic Sociology of Immigration,* ed. A. Portes, 1–41. New York: Sage.

Presser, H. B. 1994. "Employment Schedules, Gender, and Household Labor." *American Sociological Review* 59, no. 3: 348–364.

South, S., and G. Spitze. 1994. "Housework in Marital and Nonmarital Households." *American Sociological Review* 59, no. 3: 327–347.

Statistics Canada. 1997. *Labour Force Update: The Self-Employed.* Ottawa: Statistics Canada. Cat. no. 71-005XPB.

Steinmetz, G., and E. O. Wright. 1989. "The Fall and Rise of the Petty Bourgeoisie: Changing Patterns of Self-Employment in the Postwar United States." *American Journal of Sociology* 94, no. 5: 973–1018.

Waldfogel, J. 1997. "The Effect of Children on Women's Wages." *American Sociological Review* 62, no. 2: 209–217.

Waldinger, R., H. Aldrich, and R. Ward. 1990. "Opportunities, Group Characteristics, and Strategies." In *Ethnic Entrepreneurs: Immigrant Business in Industrial Societies,* ed. R. Waldinger, H. Aldrich, and R. Ward, 13–18. London: Sage.

Discussion Questions

1. Create a new work structure that you think both women and men workers would like.
2. What do you think would be the best nontraditional work structure if you were a working mother with young children? What if you were a working father with young children?
3. Assess what you believe are the three key advantages and the three key disadvantages to telecommuting. Note any anticipated gender differences in the preferences or disinclination of employees to consider this work option.
4. Do you believe the stigma that Epstein and her colleagues report afflicts part-time lawyers would probably affect part-time doctors as well? Why, or why not?
5. Drawing on some of the information in Rogers's article and speculating more broadly from a sociological perspective, why do you think temporary work has been a growing part of American employment?
6. Why have women traditionally not pursued self-employment? Why has self-employment been a more comfortable option for men?

Part V

GENDER MATTERS

M uch has been made about the wage gap between men and women. Though this gap has narrowed some since the 1970s, the difference in income persists between men and women, regardless of the setting and despite the advancement of women into typically masculine fields like law and medicine. The following readings review some of the explanations for these different outcomes, be they wage differences or experiential differences, for men and women. The structural and cultural explanations for how gender influences the work people do suggest a rather complex set of circumstances set off by different expectations for the achievements of men and women, and society's willingness to both appreciate and renumerate each sex differently.

In "The Wage Gap: Myths and Facts," from the National Committee on Pay Equity, we see the strong influence that education plays in earnings. It is also clear that, even in the jobs for which one need not be academically trained, men will out-earn women.

In "Peaks and Valleys: The Gendered Emotional Culture of Rescue Workers," Jennifer Lois provides a unique and fascinating look at the field of emergency rescue. She discovers that within these settings a rather gendered emotional culture develops to both sustain workers and further distinguish them from one another.

And finally, in "Career Commitments: Women and Men Law School Graduates," Kandace Pearson Schrimsher describes the different experiences for male and female graduates by measuring their continued employment and commitment to the profession of law. It turns out that support systems matter a great deal to those who pursue work in law and that these informal supports were harder to come by for women. In a similar vein, the ability to garner support during the college credentialing phase or later, when the person is engaged in the workplace, presents more challenges to women than it does for the men.

14

THE WAGE GAP
Myths and Facts

National Committee on Pay Equity

Wage Gap: 73%

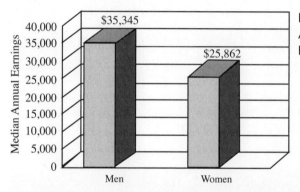

FIGURE 14.1   1998 Median Annual Earnings Year-Round, Full-Time Workers

FIGURE 14.2   1998 Median Annual Earnings by Race and Sex

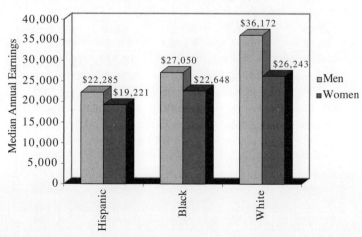

FIGURE 14.3   The Wage Gap by Race and Sex, 1998

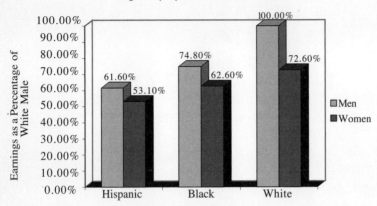

Notes

- The wage gap is a statistical indicator often used as an index of the status of women's earnings relative to men's. it is also used to compare the earnings of people of color to those of White men.
- The wage gap is expressed as a percentage (for example, in 1998, women earned 73 percent as much as men) and is calculated by dividing median annual earnings for women by median annual earnings for men.
- To calculate the wage gap for each race/sex group, median annual earnings are divided by those of White males, who are not subject to race- or sex-based wage discrimination.
- Individual earnings data for Asian/Pacific Islanders and Native Americans are available, yet they are from a very small sample and thus are not as reliable.
- Statistics are from the Census Bureau *Current Population Reports*, Series P-60, U.S. Commerce Department.

FIGURE 14.4   Changes in the Wage Gap, 1970–1998

Median annual earnings of black men and women, Hispanic men and women, and white women as a percentage of white men's median annual earnings.

Year	White Men	Black Men	Hispanic Men	White Women	Black Women	Hispanic Women
1970	100%	69.00%	N/A	58.70%	48.20%	N/A
1975	100%	74.30%	72.10%	57.50%	55.40%	49.30%
1980	100%	70.70%	70.80%	58.90%	55.70%	50.50%
1985	100%	69.70%	68.00%	63.00%	57.10%	52.10%
1990	100%	73.10%	66.30%	69.40%	62.50%	54.30%
1992	100%	72.60%	63.35%	70.00%	64.00%	55.40%
1994	100%	75.10%	64.30%	71.60%	63.00%	55.60%
1995	100%	75.90%	63.30%	71.20%	64.20%	53.40%
1996	100%	80.00%	63.90%	73.30%	65.10%	56.60%
1997	100%	75.10%	61.40%	71.90%	62.60%	53.90%
1998	100%	74.90%	61.60%	72.60%	62.60%	53.10%

FIGURE 14.5   The Wage Gap Since 1960; 38 Years Later, Still 27 Percent Behind

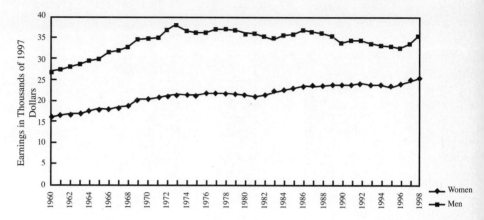

Over a 38-year period, the gap, in 1998 dollars, between women's and men's earnings has closed by more than $2,000. *Source:* Data from the Census Bureau, 1998.

FIGURE 14.6   The Wage Gap by Education, 1998

Following are wages reflecting the median earnings in 1998 for full-time, year-round workers, 25 years and older.

	H.S. Grad	B.A. Degree	Master's	Doctorate
All Men	$30,868	$49,982	$60,168	$69,188
White	$31,562	$50,614	$60,177	$71,715
Black	$25,203	$41,310	$42,323	—
Hispanic	$25,602	$38,078	$61,928	—

	H.S. Grad	B.A. Degree	Master's	Doctorate
All Women	$21,963	$35,408	$42,002	$52,167
White	$22,438	$35,408	$42,002	$51,662
Black	$19,381	$35,339	$40,766	—
Hispanic	$19,826	$32,289	$42,400	—

Source: U.S. Bureau of the Census.

Key Findings
• Female College graduates are behind male college graduates by $14,574.
• A black college-educated female earns $15,275 less annually than the college-educated white male.
• A Hispanic college-educated female makes $18,325 less annually than the college-educated white male.

FIGURE 14.7   The Wage Gap over Time: In Real Dollars, Women See Little Change

Year	Women's Earnings	Men's Earnings	Dollar Difference	Percent
1998	$25,862	$35,345	$9,483	73
1997	25,362	34,199	8,837	74
1996	24,632	33,394	8,762	74
1995	24,062	33,687	9,625	71
1994	24,423	33,935	9,512	72
1993	24,531	34,300	9,769	72
1992	24,833	35,083	10,250	71
1991	24,597	35,210	10,613	70
1990	24,721	34,518	9,797	72
1989	24,672	35,927	11,255	69
1988	24,258	36,728	12,470	66
1987	24,265	37,229	12,964	65
1986	24,141	37,561	13,420	64
1985	23,668	36,652	12,984	65
1984	23,187	36,425	13,238	64
1983	22,773	35,809	13,036	64
1982	22,189	35,937	13,748	62
1981	21,711	36,652	14,941	59
1980	22,176	36,862	14,686	60
1979	22,360	37,477	15,117	60
1978	22,579	37,985	15,406	59
1977	22,227	37,722	15,495	59
1976	22,225	36,922	14,697	60
1975	21,764	37,003	15,239	59
1974	21,890	37,258	15,368	59
1973	21,877	38,630	16,753	57
1972	21,671	37,453	15,782	58
1971	21,152	35,546	14,394	60
1970	21,008	35,386	14,378	59
1969	20,590	34,979	14,389	59
1968	19,270	33,136	13,866	58
1967	18,635	32,250	13,977	58
1966	18,273	31,748	13,475	58
1965	18,245	30,446	12,201	60
1964	17,746	30,003	12,257	59
1963	17,255	29,271	12,016	59
1962	16,956	28,595	11,639	59
1961	16,626	28,061	11,435	59
1960	16,487	27,173	10,686	61

Source: U.S. Bureau of the Census , March Current Population Survey.
Note: All figures in 1998 dollars.

Profile of the Wage Gap by Selected Occupations

FIGURE 14.8   Occupations with Estimated Earnings Under $20,000*

Occupation	Percent Women	Men's Wages	Women's Wages	Earnings Gap	Earnings Ratio (%)
Waiter/Waitress	72%	$343	$282	$61	82%
Cleaning & Building Service Occupations	29%	$358	$288	$70	80%
Bartender	55%	$379	$293	$86	77%
Dry Cleaning Machine Operators	55%	$301	$270	$31	90%

* Approximate annual earnings categories were estimated by multiplying median weekly wages for men by 52 weeks.

FIGURE 14.9   Occupations with Estimated Earnings Between $20,000 and $33,000

Occupation	Percent Women	Men's Wages	Women's Wages	Earnings Gap	Earnings Ratio (%)
Bus Driver	41%	$476	$352	$124	74%
Sales Worker; Retail & Personal	56%	$412	$272	$140	66%
Mechanics & Repairers	4%	$599	$519	$ 80	87%
Admin. Support, incl. clerical	76%	$518	$418	$100	81%
Construction Trades	2%	$545	$408	$137	75%

Data was analyzed using 1998 Household Data Annual Averages, Bureau of Labor Statistics.

FIGURE 14.10   Occupations with Estimated Earnings Above $33,000

Occupation	Percent Women	Men's Wages	Women's Wages	Earnings Gap	Earnings Ratio (%)
Accountants & Auditors	60%	$ 821	$618	$203	75%
Securities & Financial Service Sales	31%	$ 930	$598	$332	64%
Pharmacists	42%	$1,146	$985	$161	86%
Engineers	10%	$1,011	$831	$180	82%
Physicians	32%	$1,255	$966	$289	77%
Teachers, College & Univ.	37%	$ 998	$769	$229	77%
Lawyers	34%	$1,350	$951	$399	70%
Editors and Reporters	44%	$ 812	$616	$196	76%

FIGURE 14.11   Other Occupations in Which the Majority of Workers Are Women

Occupation	Percent Women	Men's Wages	Women's Wages	Earnings Gap	Earnings Ratio (%)
Registered Nurse	91%	$774	$734	$40	95%
Social Worker	65%	$609	$586	$41	93%
Elementary School Teacher	84%	$749	$677	$72	90%
Secretaries, Stenographers, & Typists	98%	$484	$436	$48	90%
Cashiers	75%	$302	$259	$43	86%

African American Women in the Workplace

FIGURE 14.13   Black Women by Occupation

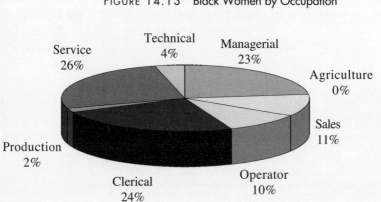

Job Description	Women's Median Weekly Earnings
Administrative Support	$419
Sales	$372
Service	$296
All Occupations	$456

Source: Bureau of Labor Statistics.

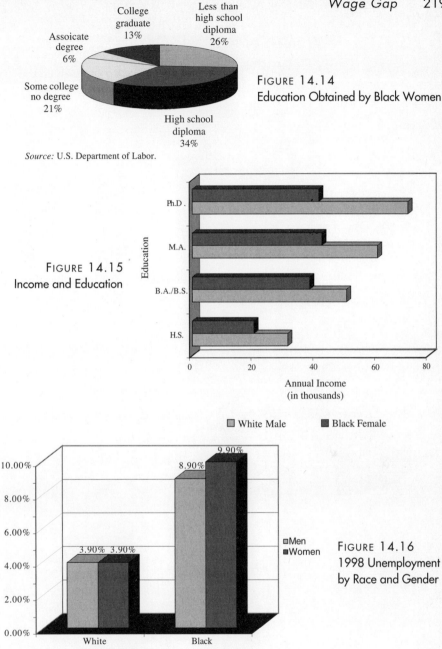

FIGURE 14.14
Education Obtained by Black Women

Source: U.S. Department of Labor.

FIGURE 14.15
Income and Education

FIGURE 14.16
1998 Unemployment
by Race and Gender

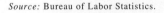

Source: Bureau of Labor Statistics.

Implications

This patter of substantially lower lifetime earnings affects the quality of life for African women and their families, limits their opportunity for promotion, and contributes to decreased savings, pensions, and Social Security payments for African American women in their senior years.

Women of Hispanic Origin
in the Workplace

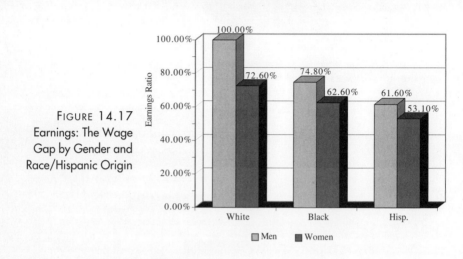

FIGURE 14.17
Earnings: The Wage
Gap by Gender and
Race/Hispanic Origin

FIGURE 14.18   Occupational Segregation:
Hispanic Women by Occupation

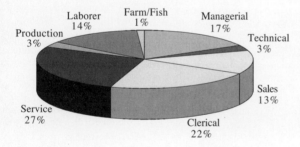

Source: Bureau of Labor Statistics.

FIGURE 14.19   Education of Hispanic Women, 1998

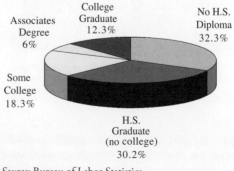

Source: Bureau of Labor Statistics.

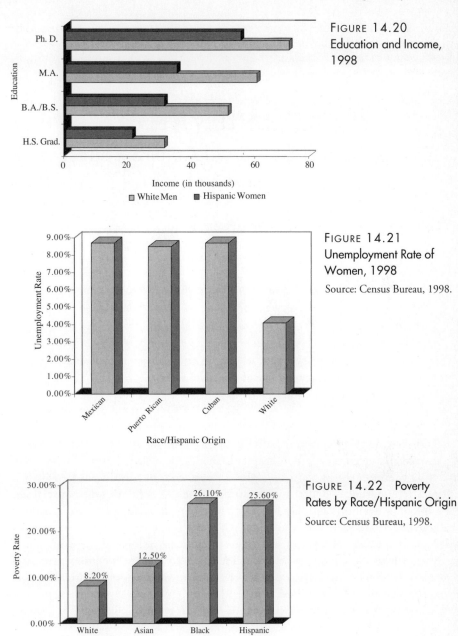

FIGURE 14.20
Education and Income,
1998

Income (in thousands)
☐ White Men   ■ Hispanic Women

FIGURE 14.21
Unemployment Rate of
Women, 1998
Source: Census Bureau, 1998.

Race/Hispanic Origin

FIGURE 14.22   Poverty
Rates by Race/Hispanic Origin
Source: Census Bureau, 1998.

Implications

This pattern of substantially lower lifetime earnings affects the quality of life for Hispanic women and their families, limits their access to education and health care, and contributes to decreased retirement security for Hispanic women in their senior years.

15

PEAKS AND VALLEYS
The Gendered Emotional Culture of Rescue Workers

Jennifer Lois

*There ain't nothin' glamorous about taking somebody's human remains,
stuffing 'em in a black bag, hauling 'em up a hill, and throwing 'em in
the back of the sheriff's van. There is nothin' glamorous about that. And
when I'm in those types of situations, there's a space I have to go to in my
head. And it's real no-nonsense; it's time to say, "Let's get the job done."*
—Jim, twenty-year member of Peak Volunteer Search and Rescue

Action in emergency situations calls for rational thinking in the face of potentially
overwhelming emotions. This chapter is about how male and female members of
"Peak," a volunteer search and rescue group, "managed" their emotions (Hochschild
1983) before, during, and after their most dangerous, stressful, or gruesome rescues.
At times their emotions and corresponding management techniques were consistent
with broader gender stereotypes; at other times they were not. In this article, I explore
these similarities and differences, showing how rescuers negotiated the (sometimes)
conflicting demands of both gender and emotion norms in high-risk crisis situations. I
also reveal how these negotiated courses of action resulted in power differences between the women and men in Peak.

These data are drawn from a five-and-one-half-year ethnographic study of a volunteer search and rescue group in a Rocky Mountain resort town.

• • •

There were four stages of edgework that members experienced in Peak's missions:
preparing for the edge, performing on the edge, going over the edge, and extending
the edge. These stages were distinctly marked not only by the flow of rescue events but
also by members' feelings in each stage. Yet, despite passing through the same stages of

edgework, women and men experienced edgework differently, interpreting and managing feelings in gender-specific ways before, during, and after the missions.

Preparing for the Edge: Anticipating the Unknown

Missions were variable events, and members were often required to use whatever resources they had to accomplish their task. Generally, the men in the group found it exciting not to know what to expect from a rescue, and they felt challenged by the prospect of relying on their cognitive and technical skills to quickly solve any puzzle that suddenly presented itself. Peak's female rescuers, however, tended to view the missions' unpredictability as stressful, and they worried in anticipation about performing under certain conditions.

Women commonly worried that they might be physically unable to perform a task either because they would not be strong enough or because they would not know what to do. Thirty-year-old Elena expressed uncertainty about knowing how to help an injured victim:

> I'm always wondering if I'm going to hurt somebody more than help them. I'm always wondering if I'm doing the right thing. "Do I move [the victim's] head, or could it break her back?" You know? I mean, I always second-guess myself in the field. I guess my problem is that I'm always unsure of myself. Like, I'd be afraid that I would do more damage than good, in a way. . . And that's where my hesitation always comes in. I mean, it's a big problem too because, like, I know what's right, and I don't speak up about it because I'm unsure of myself. You know?

Not only did Elena, a member of four years, worry about her preparedness to help victims, she also saw this apprehension as problematic; importantly, she felt that her lack of confidence in her ability was the source of the problem, not her ability level itself.

Women also tended to worry about their ability to maintain emotional control, realizing that they could encounter a particularly upsetting scene on a mission. For example, Maddie, a ten-year member, told me that one situation she dreaded was encountering a dead victim whom she knew. She expected that this situation would be one that most threatened her emotional control, the one in which she would be most likely to go over the edge:

> I think my biggest fear has always been that [the victim] is gonna be, eventually, somebody I know. And eventually it was. With Arnie [who was killed] in an avalanche. And yet, I was okay with that. I was more okay than I thought I might be. I always think I'm gonna lose it but, I guess you expect for the worst, and then you usually do better. Or, expect that "What would you do if you lost it?" or "How would you get it back?" And so I've planned ahead.

Worrying about what could arise on a future mission compelled many women to make a plan of action ahead of time, speculating about their potential reactions to stressful events. Preparing for edgework by imagining numerous different scenarios gave them some sense of control over the unpredictable future, and through such planning, they were able to manage their uncomfortable anticipatory feelings about the unknown, a dynamic found in other research on high-risk takers (Holyfield 1997; Lyng 1990).

Maddie's statement also typified another technique many female rescuers used in conjunction with planning and rehearsing future scenarios: They set low expectations for themselves. Part of their planning process was to prepare for the most demanding possible situations, the ones in which they were most likely to fail. This emotion management strategy served two functions. First, it made women acutely aware of their progress toward the edge on missions. Maddie said that on "gruesome" missions, she remained highly cognizant of her emotional state, always prepared to hand off her task to someone else. The second function of women's low expectations was that they would probably perform beyond them, which allowed them to remain within their limits while feeling good about surpassing their expectations.

Anticipating a poor performance was not very common among the men in the group, however. Most of the men in Peak used the opposite technique—sheer confidence—to prepare for emergency action. Brooke, a four-year member in her late twenties, told me that two seven-year members, twenty-eight-year-old Gary and thirty-two-year-old Nick, were able to perform at very high levels because of their high expectations for themselves:

I think that both of those guys see themselves as Superman. Which is not necessarily a good thing. They sort of see themselves as being invincible [and] I think that they might test their physical limits more than I would. They might go into a situation, would stand back and say, "I don't think that's safe." But they're convinced that nothing's going to happen to them. . . . But then again, I think that has a lot to do with mental aspect of it. You know, they see themselves as being more capable of doing something than I would. Therefore, as long as they see themselves being capable of it, they are capable of it. If that makes any sense.

According to Brooke, extreme confidence was effective for Gary and Nick, yet she did not think that it was a viable emotion management technique for her to employ.

When I asked Gary himself about his experience in extreme situations,: responded with incredible certainty in his ability, supporting Brooke's perception of him:

Gary: I like being thrown knee-deep [into challenging situations]. I like it when the shit hits the fan and having to get my way out of it.

Jen: Don't you get nervous that you might not be able to do that?

Gary: Nope.

Jen: Do you think you'll always be able to do that?

Gary: Yup. I am a cocky, young, think-I-can-do-it-all kid. I can get out of a situation. Probably because I have never not done it. I perform tremendously under pressure. That's when I shine at my absolute, top of my game. And I love being put in the hot seat. That's one of the reasons I do [search and rescue].

Gary highlighted an interdependent relationship between confidence and ability: Not only did confidence enhance performance but past performance also enhanced confidence.

Other men were extremely confident too, even when they were accused by others of overestimating their own ability. Roger, a twenty-seven-year-old member of six years, was highly experienced. He described his ability to assess avalanche danger, a highly unpredictable phenomenon, as better than most other members'. On one occasion when the team was practicing avalanche skills, Roger walked out to the edge of a cornice (a windblown pile of snow overhanging a steep hill or cliff, which can break off and cause an avalanche). Another highly experienced rescuer, Shorty, questioned Roger's judgment because if he broke the cornice and caused an avalanche, he could easily have been swept up in it, carried down the mountain, and buried under several feet of heavy snow. Roger was angered because he was very confident in his ability to assess how far out he could walk on any cornice without breaking it, reasoning that his past experience gave him this knowledge. He told me he had spent much recreational time in the back country, examining cornices and, through trial and error, learning where they typically break:

> I could probably tell a lot more [about avalanche potential than other members], and I can usually say, "Well this is where it's gonna break and this is where it's gonna slide." And sure as shit, when I get out there and I jump around, that's right where it breaks and that's right where it slides. If you're just a normal person walking out there, you're an idiot, but I don't think I am because I know what I'm doing. Shorty even questioned me, like, "Do you think it's really safe to be doing that?" And it's like, "Well, I wouldn't be doing it if it wasn't safe. It's not safe for you to be doing it, no, but it's safe for me because I know what I'm doing."

Roger's confidence helped him prepare for edgework in the event of a real mission. By stating where he thought cornices would break, he was quite literally reaffirming his ability to assess the edge—the boundary between safety and danger—which allowed him to feel in control of the situation. One way to view his activity was to consider it objectively dangerous: Roger had crossed the danger boundary, as evidenced by the many avalanches he had caused. Yet, he considered his actions safe: Even though he had caused many avalanches, each time he proved he was right, demonstrating his fine awareness and superior control of the edge, which signaled to himself and others that he could approach it and work there without going over it.

Many of Peak's men used these confidence displays to assert that they could outperform each other, which created a highly competitive environment. I witnessed many of these bravado sessions, mostly during social hours at the bars, where men discussed their own strengths as they anxiously awaited the opportunity to prove themselves on future missions. Several gender scholars have suggested that masculinity, but not femininity, must constantly be proven—that men are "only as masculine as [their] last demonstration of masculinity" (Beneke 1997, 43; see also Connell 1987; Kimmel 1996; Messner 1992). Thus, perhaps Peak's men were not only anticipating a chance to prove themselves as rescuers but also as men.

Wanting to prove ones' self and having confidence was much less tolerated for women in Peak, however. For example, when Robin, a six-year member in her early thirties, did display confidence about her abilities and experiences, other members doubted and criticized her. Although she held high rescue certifications and had a great deal of experience in many of the activities required for search and rescue, such as whitewater rafting and searching, other rescuers found her to be strange and weird, basing these judgments on her displays of confidence. Elena described what she thought bothered her (and others) about Robin:

> She brags a lot. About herself. And she shows off a lot. And I think that people perceive that as not necessarily a good thing. . . Sometimes I wonder if she doesn't feel like she just needs to always prove herself.

Clearly, Robin was being held to different standards than male rescuers, as she was negatively sanctioned for performing what I observed to be "masculine" behavior. Brooke, also commented on Robin's boasting: "That tells me something about this girl. That something's not right there. She's pumping herself up, you know?" Apparently, Brooke objected to Robin's displays of confidence because she saw them as gender inappropriate: They conveyed important information about "this girl." In preparing for missions, most female rescuers did not display confidence like their male counterparts; instead, they remained cautious and modest.

There are several explanations for this gendered difference in preparation strategies. First, in general, men were more experienced than women. Through their own recreation as well as through group-related activities, men's exposure to risk was both more frequent and more hazardous than women's. Yet, this gendered confidence pattern was not totally explained by differential risk exposure. For example, when I talked to equally experienced men and women, apprehension still dominated women's anticipatory feelings (except for Robin's), and confidence dominated men's. Furthermore, even when women performed well on missions, it did not seem to boost their confidence for future situations, while conversely, men's poor performance did not erode theirs.[1]

A second factor in explaining this pattern was that the masculine nature of rescue work made men feel more at ease in the setting, and thus they tended to display unwavering certainty that they could handle any situation that might arise. Women felt disadvantaged by this masculine environment and, taking this into account, set low expectations for themselves. In one way, their feelings were based in reality: They were aware that, on the whole, the men in the group were physically stronger and thus able to perform harder tasks than they. Brooke said that it was "obvious" and "completely understandable" that she would be second choice as a rope hauler because she was physically weaker than a man.[2]

In another way, though, women's insecurities were due to cultural and group stereotypes about men's superior rescue ability. For example, the belief that men are emotionally stronger than women made women question whether they would be able to perform edgework in potentially upsetting situations, while the same stereotype enabled men to have confidence that they would maintain control in those situations. Yet, my observations (discussed later in this article) yielded no gendered pattern of emotional control. Another stereotype that made women worry about their rescue ability was the belief that men were more technically inclined than they were. This stereotype came into play during trainings and missions when the group used any kind of mechanization, such as rope and pulley systems, helicopters, or snowmobiles. Cyndi, a three-year member in her late twenties, told me she felt "hugely" intimidated in her first year by the technical training, yet she later became quite adept in setting up and operating rope and pulley systems. Elena had a similar experience. She told me that during her first training, she looked around at "all the guys" and thought, "What am I doing here? I'm not even qualified for any of this." Cyndi's and Elena's feelings of inferiority acted as "place markers" where "the emotion conveys information about the state of the social ranking system" (Clark 1990, 308). In this case, they felt inferior because performing gender-appropriate behavior, or "doing femininity" (West and Zimmerman 1987), was inconsistent with "doing" edgework, which they perceived as a much more "masculine" endeavor.

Because women felt this gendered tension, they may have devised these distinct ways to moderate it. By remaining trepidacious and maintaining low expectations that they would often exceed, the women reaffirmed their place in the group as useful. Although they feared admitting when they would be unable to complete a task, because as Cyndi said, it meant "you're admitting to everyone else that you're not as good as them," many women in the group felt that bowing out early was preferable to competing and failing. Cyndi said others would think, "At least they didn't fuck the mission up. They stayed, and they helped, and they did something." Thus, trepidation and confidence emerged as gendered emotional strategies used in preparing for edgework.

Performing on the Edge: Suppressing Feelings

During Peak's urgent missions, clear thinking and rational action, core features of edgework, were seen as especially crucial. However, in such demanding situations, members' capacity for emotional and physical control was seen as more tenuous: Emotions threatened to push them over the edge, preventing them from physically performing at all. Rescuers who were easily scared, excited, or upset by a mission's events were considered undependable. Members employed several strategies to control these feelings during the missions, allowing them to perform under pressure.

Rescuers were particularly wary of the onset of adrenaline rushes because such potent physiological reactions threatened their composure; they felt that the emotions they experienced could "get in the way" of their performance. Yet, adrenaline was not totally undesirable; in fact, at lower levels, both male and female rescuers welcomed it because it helped them focus and heightened their awareness. Mostly, though, Peak's emotional culture cast adrenaline rushes—the involuntary physiological response that causes increased heart rate and breathing—as an important situational cue, one that rescuers should heed as a warning that they were at risk of losing control.

Although Peak's members talked about adrenaline as though it were an emotion, Schachter and Singer (1962) demonstrated that the physiological arousal associated with adrenaline does not signify a particular emotion in the absence of other situational information. After exploring what rescuers meant by the term adrenaline rush, I discovered they were actually referring to two distinct (and potentially problematic) emotional states associated with adrenaline: fear and urgency.

Excessive fear was dangerous because it could paralyze rescuers, rendering them ineffective and thus increasing risk for both their teammates and the victim. Cyndi expressed a typical perspective when she described the difference between helpful and harmful levels of fear. She described a time when she was trying to cross a river on a series of slippery rocks, each of which was just beyond her comfortable step, requiring her to jump from one to the next. Other rescuers were waiting for her to cross, and she knew that they would be able to reach her if she slipped and fell into the rushing water. Nonetheless, she could not do it:

> I mean, I knew that I was perfectly safe. And I was trembling like a leaf, and my heart was racing, and there wasn't a damn thing I could do about it! I could sit there all day long [saying to myself], "You're gonna be fine, you're gonna be fine, you're gonna be fine," and I just stood there shaking. I was just in one of these sort of states: huge adrenaline rush. . . . There's a point where some fear is a good thing—adrenaline—and it helps you focus, because you know that you need to be careful. If you're in a situation where there is some fear, maybe an avalanche or a river, you want to get whatever it is you're doing done quickly because the faster you get out of it, the safer you are. But then there's a point where it stops being an aid and it becomes a hindrance: Fear outweighs your ability to act. I think that's the worst thing in the world you could do for a mission, just freeze and panic, where you spend more time combating your fear than thinking about the situation you're in.

Interestingly, Cyndi equated adrenaline with fear. She used these terms interchangeably, noting the edge between useful and detrimental physiological reactions, both of which she experienced as fear. Her description highlighted both sides of the edge: the controllable side, where "some fear is a good thing" because rescuers could use their aroused feelings to create order and perform at higher levels. She also explained the chaotic side, where too much fear impeded rescuers' ability to act rationally and efficiently. They would become overwhelmed with emotion, a phenomenon that strips individuals of their ability to make self-indications and thus monitor and control their actions (Mills and Kleinman 1988).

Loss of control due to fear, however, was almost always associated with women's reactions to adrenaline, while becoming too "excitable" or feeling excessive urgency was only associated with men's reactions to adrenaline. Like too much fear, members considered excessive urgency to be a detrimental emotion during missions because it could cause rescuers to act irrationally and thus, unsafely. On one occasion, the mission coordinator selected two experienced members to enter a dangerous avalanche gully and evacuate a snowboarder who had a broken leg. While they were tending to the victim, two newer members, Patrick and Mitch, skied own into the gully without getting authorization from the mission coordinator, which endangered the two experienced members already in the gully by creating the possibility of triggering an avalanche above them. Furthermore, Patrick was unable to ski the difficult terrain, causing him to spend extraordinarily more time in the gully, thus exponentially increasing the risk to himself and others. Group members accused Patrick and Mitch of letting their adrenaline override rational, controlled action: They skied into the gully because it was exciting and risky, not because they were needed on the scene. Brooke said, "It was just poor judgment, they jumped the gun, they had the adrenaline running. I can't imagine what they were thinking." When I asked Patrick about this, he accounted for his actions by interpreting his adrenaline as urgency. He said, "The reason I went is because I wanted to get down to the victim. I wanted to help."

One reason men and women might have experienced adrenaline rushes differently was because they were simultaneously "doing gender" (West and Zimmerman 987). Men tended to be confident at the prospect of undertaking risk, which may have caused them to interpret their adrenaline during the mission as pleasurable and exciting. Since women, on the other hand, reported more cautious mind-sets in preparing for missions, worrying about their ability to exercise emotional and physical control in risky situations, perhaps they were more likely to define their adrenaline rushes as fear. It is important to note, however, that while too much adrenaline, Whether it be feminine fear or masculine urgency, was considered detrimental to the safety of the missions, urgency was less stigmatized than fear, perhaps because it was seen as easier to conquer or because it was a more pleasurable sensation. As a result, women had a harder time gaining status from their successful mission performances because they (and others) defined their adrenaline as fear.

Nevertheless, men and women managed their feelings of urgency and fear similarly: They suppressed them. For example, the most critical mission I experienced ad four casualties. A van had driven off the side of a dirt road and tumbled to the bottom of a 400-foot ravine. Search and rescue was called because the accident was accessible to the paramedics, who needed ropes to get down to the victims and a hauling system to get them out. Cyndi told me that while on that mission, she was in control of her emotions, successfully suppressing them, because she was working rope systems up on the road, unable to see beyond the drop-off down to the accident site. She felt differently, however, when one of the accident victims reached the hill in a panicked state. The victim, who had a broken arm, had managed to climb up the 400-foot embankment in an effort to catch up to the rescue team that was evacuating her critically injured mother. Cyndi was thrown off kilter by this height:

> Because I was up at the top, it wasn't real. You know, I could sort of disassociate, it's like, "Okay, let's just get the job done and not think about it." But then you're meeting this person [climbing out of the accident scene] who is just out of it. I mean, she was panicked and [she had] adrenaline [rushing], and I was just kind of like, "Okay, there really are real people down there, but I'm not gonna get panicked. I need to calm this person down, because she's not gonna help rushing up to the scene, and getting in the way of the paramedics [while] trying to get to her mother."

Cyndi's emotional control was threatened when the victim emerged from the trauma scene. The sight forced her to the edge, where her ordered, controlled action was threatened by her feeling of chaotic, uncontrolled panic. She quickly narrowed her focus further, successfully managing her own impending panic by monitoring the victim's behavior. In this way, she was able to keep her feelings at bay while she continued working. High-risk takers frequently report similar reactions: They narrow their focus so dramatically that they lose awareness of everything extraneous to the risk activity itself (Holyfield 1997; Lyng 1990).

Another way emotions interfered with performance was when members were disturbed by the graphic sight of the accidents they encountered. Recovering the body of a dead victim, for example, held great potential for upset feelings, especially if the death was violent or gruesome, leaving the body in pieces, excessively bloody, or positioned unnaturally (such as having the legs bent backward or a limb missing). Such situations could cause extreme reactions in rescuers, possibly preventing them from doing the job they were assigned. On the whole, men were assumed to be better suited for these graphic jobs because they were perceived to be emotionally stronger than women. For example, Brooke made a statement that reflected the idea that emotional strength and masculinity were intertwined when she said that under such extreme conditions, Peak's members had to "have the balls to go in and do what needs to be done. . . . I think you have to be [emotionally] strong to see what you see and to deal with what you deal with in this group."

Other members stated these gendered expectations more blatantly. Maddie told me she had noticed a common pattern in the ten years she had been in the group:

> I think there's an emotional consideration [to being in this group], because our society says men need to hold their emotions in check more so than women. It's expected. It's an expectation from our society. So in any kind of situation where emotions could come into play, you know, something that's really gruesome, [the mission coordinators] aren't gonna ask [the women], they'll ask the guys first.

Maddie's statement highlights how emotional stoicism was not only a critical feature of doing edgework but also of "doing masculinity." These two concepts, edgework and masculinity, were often so confounded that the gender order in Peak was implicitly justified, a point I return to later.

Jim, a mission coordinator, confirmed Maddie's observation when he told me that he tried to assign members to jobs according to their ability, regardless of gender, except in one situation:

> I do, however, hesitate to use women in body recovery-type situation. . . I want to protect 'em from exposure to that type of incident. I can't tell you why I wanna protect 'em, but that's what it is. 'Cause I think it's a horrible deal. My wife asks me all the time, "Why do you have to go do the body?" Been there. Done that. I can do that. Why subject somebody else to it?

Yet men were not immune to the potentially disturbing effects of gruesome rescues. In fact, Meg, a member for ten years, told me that despite stereotypes of masculine emotional strength, she had seen experienced men who had trouble dealing with dead bodies, even though they were willing to assist in the recovery task:

> I've seen people that are very, very macho and strong and opinionated become very sheepish in those situations. . . . [They] march right in and as soon as they get a visual on [the body], they're off doing something else. [They] walk away. Can't look, can't touch. . . . And for me, a body recovery is just like recovering a living person. You know, it's just a body of who was there, and the "who" part is gone. . . . So body recoveries are not so difficult for me, but for some people it's a real struggle.

Thus emotional upset even threatened some men who were expected to be emotionally tough.

In these gruesome situations, both male and female rescuers reported using one primary emotion management strategy to combat their upset feelings: depersonalizing the victims. Meg alluded to this by saying a body is not a person because the "who" part is gone. Such detachment is a common way people maintain instrumental control in emotionally threatening situations (DeCoster 1997; Jones 1997; Smith and Kleinman 1989). Tyler, an eight-year member in his early thirties, told me how some members detached when recovering dead bodies:

> Some people don't look at a dead person's face. And the reason is that a face is some one's identity. Someone's body—I mean, pretty much a body is the same on everyone. But a headless body lacks an identity. You know, you need to put a face with a person. You don't put feet with a person. And by not looking at someone's face, you really can take some of the identity out of it. And it almost can seem more surreal, and that what you're dealing with really isn't even a body. So it can be easier for some people. It really helps them control how they feel about it.

Members like Meg and Tyler had their own ways of depersonalizing their actions on missions—acts of bravery and heroism that would seem to be logically motivated by a deep concern for other human beings. Yet, in these intense incidents, rescuers emphasized the need to depersonalize the victims, to think of their bodies as inanimate objects that belonged to no one. Although group members believed that men would be able to accomplish this more easily, my data show no gendered pattern to this ability.

Fear, urgency, and emotional upset were some of the powerful feelings that threatened rescuers' control during missions in very gendered ways. Male and female rescuers, however, reported very similar ways of dealing with these threatening emotions to maintain "affective neutrality" (Parsons 1951) during missions: They suppressed their feelings by closely focusing on their task and depersonalizing the victims. This group norm of displaying affective neutrality signified a cool-headedness that was considered safe and effective, and the group considered those who could achieve it in the most critical of circumstances—those who could push the edge the farthest—their most valuable members. At times, these evaluations were based on individuals' past performances; at other times, they were based on gendered stereotypes of emotional capabilities.

Going over the Edge: Releasing Feelings

Immediately after missions, members' suppressed feelings began to surface. Both women and men viewed the sensations they got from successful mission outcomes, like reuniting victims with their family, as the ultimate reward, and I often witnessed them expressing these positive feelings upon hearing the news of a saved victim. They instantly discarded their objective demeanor and became jovial, slaphappy, and chatty. They released the pent-up stress that had been tightly managed throughout the missions by shouting, high-fiving each other, making jokes, and talking about what they had been thinking and feeling throughout the mission. Generally, they felt energized, which they regarded as a positive feeling of control and competence. For Lyng's (1990) skydivers, the whole point of edgework was to experience these feelings after a jump.

Not surprisingly, after missions with negative outcomes, both male and female rescuers reported highly unpleasant emotions, which usually hit them once they got home and were alone. At times, these feelings rushed forward uncontrollably, taking rescuers over the edge into emotional disorder and chaos. One source of upset feelings was recurring visual memories of emotionally disturbing scenes, which are common when people, such as medical students (Smith and Kleinman 1989), first see dead bodies. Not only did Peak's rescuers report being bothered by intrusive images of the graphic things they had seen but also by the things they experienced through their sense of hearing and of touch. One member told me that when he assisted in the body recovery of a fallen rock climber, he didn't sleep for three weeks because his mind kept replaying the crackling sound of the victim's legs as rescuers tried to fit him in the body bag. Another rescuer remembered feeling the weight of a dead body she helped carry out from the four-passenger van rollover: "I just remember how heavy it was. You know, they say 'dead weight'? That was one of the most memorable [missions]. That one lived with me for a while."

These upsetting flashbacks could be compounded when the rescue hit too close to home, and subsequently, members' confrontation with the stressful emotions was more intense. For example, Tyler told me that on one mission, he, Nick, and Shorty volunteered to travel to another county to extract the body of a kayaker from the middle of a rushing river. The kayaker was killed when the front of his kayak got sucked under the water and pinned between two rocks. The force of the water behind him pushed the back of his kayak up into the air and then folded it over on top of him, snapping both of his legs backward and trapping him in his kayak. The victim's friends were unable to reach him and he drowned. Nick found that particular mission more difficult to deal with than others, causing him several disturbing flashbacks. He told me that for days afterward he could not shake these strong, negative feelings:

Nick: It was really messing with my head. I mean, every time I looked at a river or just thought about rafting or kayaking or whatever, I would just focus on the way the body looked. . . . I didn't think it was gonna be that beat up. It was only in the river for a day before we got to it, but it was pretty beat up.

Jen: How do you feel when you see stuff like that?

Nick: A little nauseous. Nervous about getting hurt in that situation, you know, dying in that same situation that the person was in. Especially since the week before I checked into kayaking lessons! [laughs]
Jen: And did you follow up on that?
Nick: No.

Thus the negative effects of "failed" missions could make members feel vulnerable —like they could encounter the same fate—which diluted the emotional charge they got from edgework. As a result, both female and male rescuers tried to manage the uncontrolled flow of conflicting emotions in the immediate postmission period. In the most intense cases, they reported feeling overwhelmed with emotion, unable to control it and needing to release it in some way.

There were two ways in which members released these feelings, and these management techniques appeared to be highly related to gender. Women tended to cry. I talked to Elena, the four-year member who initially felt unqualified for search and rescue, shortly after her first (and only) dead-body recovery. She told me that she thought she was "okay" until she got home and was in the shower, where she started to cry. She felt that this initial release was enough to reduce the backlog of feelings that had piled up while she was suppressing them during the mission. It allowed her to regain her composure, reducing her stress and anxiety to manageable levels. In essence, she lost and regained her self-reflexivity, much like the battered wives Mills and Kleinman (1988) analyzed. Other women, too, reported that they sometimes "needed" to cry in the wake of a stressful mission, precisely to release "pent-up stress." Men, however, never reported crying as a means of dealing with the emotional turmoil of missions. Although it is possible that men and women did cry with equal frequency and masculinity norms prevented men from reporting it, it was more likely that women saw this as a more acceptable emotion management technique and coped in this way more often than men (see Gove, Geerken, and Hughes 1979; King et al. 1996; Mirowsky and Ross 1995; Roehling, Koelbel, and Rutgers 1996; Thoits 1995).

After the most traumatic missions, such as one occasion when members extricated the charred remains of several forest firefighters caught in a "fire storm" (an extremely hot, quick-moving, and dangerous type of forest fire), the group provided a professionally run "critical incident debriefing" session where they could talk about their feelings after the mission. While these sessions encouraged men (who were the ones most often involved in such intense missions) to express their feelings, there were only two of these sessions offered in my five-and-one-half years with Peak. As a general rule, Peak's culture did not encourage men to express their feelings after emotionally taxing rescues. For example, neither female nor male rescuers asked men how they felt after such events. Women, however, were accorded much more displayed concern after disturbing missions. I regularly witnessed both women and men asking women how they felt and touching them supportively, for example, by sympathetically rubbing their back or hugging them. These observations do not suggest that rescuers were not concerned about the men, however; in fact, they were often so concerned that they made sure to phone male rescuers a few days after a disturbing event and ask them "how things were going," an indirect way of checking up on them and reaching out to them emotionally.

That Peak's culture did not encourage men to display their emotions is not surprising, given that toughness and emotional stoicism are central features of many cultural conceptions of masculinity (Connell 1987; Kimmel 1996; Messner 1992). Instead, Peak's men coped with their anxiety and unpleasant feelings by drinking alcohol after negative-outcome missions, such as dead-body recoveries. After Tyler, Nick, and Shorty recovered the trapped kayaker's body in another county, Tyler told me that they bought a twelve-pack of beer for Nick and Shorty to drink while Tyler drove them home. In the three-hour drive, Shorty drank two of the beers and Nick drank the remaining ten. When I asked Nick about this, he told me that he drank beer after missions to try to

> calm down, to relax. . . . [I was tense] because I didn't think the body was gonna be that beat up. It's kinda like if you had a rough day at work, you drink a couple beers. . . . I think [it's] just part of releasing any tension, even if it's just adrenaline that you have stored up.

In this way, members used "bodily deep acting," manipulating their physiological state to change their emotional state (Hochschild 1990), by relaxing themselves with alcohol in an effort to dampen the chaos of their surfacing feelings.

Men coped in this way more than women. Although women went drinking with the men after intense and upsetting missions, they drank substantially less alcohol (averaging one to two drinks) than the men (who frequently drank five or more) and left the bar much earlier to go home. In her ten years with Peak, Maddie had concluded that men used alcohol to cope with emotional upset because of gender socialization:

> Maddie: I think the guys hide [their upset] a lot better [than the women]. And deal with it by going and drinking beers. I mean, that has always been the way they deal with it—for years. And I don't think that's good. Because [of] this posttraumatic stress [disorder], I mean, you can see it in a lot of our guys after a big, heavy-duty mission. You know, just going to the bar and drinking beers doesn't release it always. And then it starts to come out in their personal lives, and I don't think that's healthy at all. I think you need to do a little more than that.
>
> Jen: Like counseling?
>
> Maddie: Yeah, but then our guys think they're too cool to do that stuff.
>
> Jen: Have you ever seen any women dealing with their feelings by drinking alcohol?
>
> Maddie: No. Not at all.

Maddie explained men's higher alcohol consumption rate over women's with cultural expectations for them to hide their feelings and appear to remain emotionally unaffected, an observation supported by social research (Mirowsky and Ross 1995; Thoits 1995). In this way, male rescuers lived up to the emotionally stoic male stereotype by engaging in this phase of edgework in a distinctly "masculine" way. Maddie and other women, however, believed that this "masculine" coping strategy was a distinctly ineffective, and thus inferior, way of dealing with unpleasant feelings, an observation that has received inconclusive support in coping research (e.g., Patterson and McCubbin 1984; Robinson and Johnson 1997; Roehling, Koelbel, and Rutgers 1996; Sigmon, Stanton, and Snyder 1995).

Extending the Edge: Redefining Feelings

In the long term, positive-outcome missions allowed rescuers to extend the edge; members' success served as evidence that they could push their limits further next time. Negative outcomes, however, threatened to compress the edge, leaving rescuers wondering if they were capable and unsure of the risk they were willing to assume in the future. The fourth stage of edgework, then, was marked by members' ability to regain control of these negative feelings by cognitively processing and redefining their experiences, a process Kitsuse (1962) termed "retrospective interpretation." In this way, rescuers employed another type of "deep acting" where they "visualize[d] a substantial portion of reality in a different way" (Hochschild 1990, 121), which transformed their feelings about it. This helped them maximize their future edgework ability.

Women and men shared the same emotions and management techniques in this stage of edgework. For example, guilt was a stressful emotion for both male and female rescuers in the wake of unsuccessful missions because they could feel personally responsible for the outcome, for example, if they failed to save a victim. On one occasion, rescuers felt bothered by a mission where a kayaker died in a river race. Many of Peak's members were at the race, volunteering to act as safety agents on the river banks, throwing lines to any kayakers in trouble. One racer's kayak flipped upside down, and he was unable to right himself. Although many tried to reach him—fellow racers chased him down, people standing on the banks threw safety lines—no one could get to him until he floated through the finish line four minutes later. Many bystanders speculated that he must have been knocked unconscious while he was inverted and subsequently drowned. Jim told me that he went over and over the incident in his mind that night, trying to think of something he and the team could have done to reach the boater more quickly. He could find no flaws in the team's response yet found it difficult to accept that the boater was killed. Kevin, a ten-year member in his mid-forties, echoed Jim's feelings when he told me that he felt compelled to return to the scene in search of an answer:

> It bothered me that I wasn't able to do something. And I went back that night to stand by the river, to look at it, to reevaluate, and I came to the same conclusion: There was nothing I could've done, other than create a worse situation.

This incident was particularly troublesome for group members because they saw the accident and were so close by; standing there on the river bank they felt helpless while the kayaker drowned. Two days later, the local newspaper reported that the kayaker had died when, due to a genetic defect, his heart "exploded." Many members were relieved by this news because it confirmed the conclusions they had come to through their careful reanalysis: They could not have saved him.

One way in which members neutralized their guilt was by redefining their part in missions. One technique was "denying responsibility" (Sykes and Matza 1957) for the victim's fate, which could take the form of blaming the victims themselves. Cyndi told me how she reconciled her conflicting feelings about a dead victim she helped recover.

He had taken his brand-new pickup truck up a narrow, steep hiking trail to see how well the four-wheel drive worked and was killed when he rolled it off the trail into a ravine. Cyndi said she kept trying to remember that he did something "really stupid." Not only did members dodge guilt using these rationalizations, but they sidestepped vulnerability too. The victim's stupidity was the cause of death, and rescuers, who considered themselves much smarter, could avoid such a fate. Through these methods, both men and women were able to temper their feelings of guilt and vulnerability, which in turn helped them to maintain a positive self-image as well as to reassure themselves about their own ability to survive edgework.

Another technique both female and male rescuers used to counter the stress of emotionally taxing missions in the long term was to weight the successes more than the failures. Although they took great pains to separate themselves personally from failed missions, denying responsibility and downplaying meaning in those situations, members actively sought a personal connection with the successful missions, acknowledging their role in them and allowing their participation to be meaningful and important reflections of their self. This bias in self-perception is a common way people may "bolster their self-esteem, their affect, and. . . their public image" (Eisenberg 1986, 79). Personally accepting credit for successes protected rescuers by increasing their confidence and making them feel that they had control over risky conditions, a phenomenon found among other edgeworkers (Lyng 1990).

Several members reported that saving someone's life was the ultimate reward of search and rescue and was unlike any other feeling they had ever had. One search for a sixty-eight-year-old hiker lasted five days. The team had scoured the mountainside where she had last been seen, finding no clues, and becoming less optimistic that she would be found alive, if she were found at all. The mission coordinator sent Martin, a five-year member in his early fifties, and two other rescuers up in a search helicopter for one last sweep of the area before calling off the search. Martin told me that it was by "a miracle" that he spotted something red peeking out from underneath a boulder and directed the helicopter closer to investigate it. There they found the missing woman, severely dehydrated and weak, but alive. He told me how his part in the mission made him feel:

> The whole experience of finding her was the kind of feeling you want to get out of search and rescue. I mean, we saved somebody, there's no question in my mind, that really meant the difference between her being dead or alive. And it was so good a feeling. . . I feel good when we help people, but this was just so different because I honestly think we saved somebody's life. You know, we made a huge difference, and I made a big difference. I was the one that saw her. I was very involved in it. In my mind, "I found her." I can't deny it. I really felt good about myself. I felt that the time that I've put into the group, for all the good times we have and the bad times we have, it was worth it for that one thing. . . That was probably the biggest kick I ever got in my life! I can't tell you how good I felt about that!

Clearly Martin's experience was an emotionally rewarding one. He welcomed these feelings and openly expressed them. He noted that he did not want to deny his personal part in the mission—he couldn't deny it—he needed to identify personally with such a life-saving event. He allowed these feelings to significantly enhance how he felt about himself. When I asked him how long these feelings lasted, he said, "I was high for days! I still felt good, I was still floating on a high. Just from saving her." He had been able to draw on this experience repeatedly to help him counteract his negative feelings in previous and subsequent missions, steadfastly holding to the idea that all his rescue experiences were "worth it for that one thing." Many female and male rescuers used this technique: They defined their overall participation in search and rescue as valuable and thus were able to extend the edge—risk more emotionally and physically—because the rewards outweighed the costs. The gender similarities in these data suggest that in this stage of edgework, how rescuers accomplished gender did not conflict with how they redefined their feelings.

Conclusion

Peak's critical missions required members to pass through four stages of edgework. These stages were marked both by the flow of rescue events and the corresponding emotions they evoked. Rescuers risked both their physical and emotional well-being before, during, and after the missions, and maintaining a sense of order was a key concern in each stage. Because each of these four stages was characterized by different emotions that threatened their sense of order, members used several types of emotion management strategies as they prepared for, performed on, exceeded, and redefined the edge. Moreover, these feelings and management techniques varied by gender. The men in the group tended to feel confident and excited on missions and, although sometimes quite upset, tended to display emotional stoicism at negative outcomes. Conversely, the women tended to feel trepidacious and fearful on the critical missions and to express their upset feelings in their aftermath. Thus, the dynamics of edgework, emotions, and gender converged to create the distinct model of emotional culture presented here.

The emotions Peak's members experienced during certain stages of a mission, as well as the consequences of these emotions, prompted members to recognize their importance and to attach meaning to them. They developed beliefs about which emotions were useful or appropriate in each stage and constructed norms to help them achieve these desired emotional states. For example, they believed that emotions such as uncertainty, urgency, fear, upset, vulnerability, and guilt were undesirable because these powerful feelings were potentially disruptive. They could interfere with members' performance, causing them to sacrifice the efficiency of the mission as well as the safety of other rescuers and the victims. Working off this assumption—that during missions almost all emotions were dangerous obstacles to be overcome—Peak's members constructed an emotional culture that prioritized suppressing all emotions during missions and releasing them only after the crisis ended (see Irvine [1999] and Stearns [1994] for analyses of similar emotional patterns).

Peak's women and men shared this emotional culture, agreeing on the potentially disruptive nature of emotions as well as the corresponding need to suppress them and remain cool during crises. They also agreed on the need to release these pent-up feelings after crisis situations. But Peak's men and women differed in steps they took to bring themselves in line with these cultural beliefs. Thus, the abstract assumptions about emotions were shared, but the norms instituted to achieve them differed along gender lines.

These two ways of accomplishing edgework constitute two distinct "emotion lines," which Hochschild (1990, 123) has called a "series of emotional reactions [resulting from]. . . a series of instigating events." For example, women and men in Peak tended to interpret missions' "instigating events" differently, which set off a chain of feelings and management techniques unique to each gendered emotion line. The masculine emotion line was constructed around the interpretation of edgework as exciting. The men in the group tended to be confident in their abilities even before they knew what a mission might require of them and often held the belief that the more demanding the mission, the better. In general, they looked forward to being challenged by very difficult situations, and their vocabulary reflected this as they referred affectionately to these situations as on the verge of "going to shit" and to themselves as being "put in the hot seat." They thrived on excitement during the missions, interpreting their heightened arousal as urgency, and continued to expect that they would succeed. When missions ended unfavorably, they did not release the built-up tension all at once but let it leak out slowly, referring to it with telling metaphors such as "unwinding." Later, they neutralized their failure with emotional "justifying ideologies" (Cancian and Gordon 1988) that helped them maintain a positive self-image. Thus, it appears that the men tended to approach and engage in edgework with positive feelings (perhaps already suppressing negative feelings) and in the event of failure released these pent-up emotions slowly: They followed an "excitement/slow leak" emotion line of failed edgework.

The feminine emotion line was based on the idea of edgework as anxiety producing. Peak's women tended to be unsure of their ability to engage in edgework and were often anxious in anticipation of many physically and emotionally challenging situations. Many women openly questioned their potential for physical competence and emotional self-control. During critical missions, they generally remained anxious, often interpreting their heightened arousal as fear, and constantly worrying that they might fail. When missions ended unfavorably, they released their emotions abruptly by bursting into tears. They later used emotional justifying ideologies, like the men did, to reconceptualize their actions, which neutralized potentially damaging definitions of the self. Thus it appears that the women in the group tended to enact an "anxiety/outburst" emotion line of failed edgework.

To negotiate the often conflicting demands of edgework and gender, Peak's men and women devised these distinct but gender-appropriate emotion lines. These two emotion lines, however, were not equally respected ways of enacting edgework. In fact, it was the distinction between the two that stratified the group members, creating a hierarchy of emotional competence for edgework, with men at the top. When members evaluated the gendered ways of preparing for and enacting edgework, both men and women recognized the superiority of masculine "excitement" over feminine "anxiety." Although most women reported managing their anxiety in a relatively effective way (i.e., they performed edgework competently), they viewed themselves as "emotional deviants" (Thoits 1990) when it came to the first two stages: preparing for and acting in crisis. (Recall how they tended to consider their lack of confidence as problematic, to decline tasks they thought might overwhelm them emotionally, and to interpret their adrenaline as fear.)

Thoits (1990) has hypothesized that people who are marginalized in a subculture may recognize their own emotional deviance more frequently than nonmarginal members because their own emotions often conflict with those dominant in the subculture. By virtue of their fringe status, marginal subcultural members might, for example, feel pulled between two different emotional subcultures: the one in which they are marginal, and another with different norms and values, in which they better fit. Most women in Peak accepted their status as emotional deviants: They rarely challenged the low expectations others had for them and often held low expectations for themselves, generally believing that their feelings and management techniques were inferior to men's. They readily admitted that they might not be able to handle the emotional demands of a mission, often deferring to others, usually men, who displayed no reservations about entering potentially challenging, upsetting, or gruesome situations. Clark (1990, 314) has suggested that when it comes to emotions and status, "having no place, or feeling 'out of place,' can be more painful even than having an inferior place." Thus, Peak's women tended to validate their membership by volunteering to do less challenging tasks. In this way, they used inferior "place claims" (Clark 1990) to accept and reinforce their emotional place—subordinate though it was—in Peak's missions.

In the period after the missions, however, Peak's women generally did not feel that their norm of "outburst" was inferior to men's slow-leak method of ventilating emotions. In fact, they viewed their method as superior to men's and disparaged the slow-leak norm, because they believed that it caused negative emotions to become trapped and to fester. In this way, women made superior place claims in the group, insisting that the men were too constrained by strict gender roles to display their negative feelings through an emotional outburst. Yet, women's superior emotional place claims went unacknowledged. Most of Peak's men did not accept an inferior status when it came to their slow-leak method of releasing emotions. (Recall they were "too cool" to attend counseling.) They paid no attention to the women's denigration of their management technique and thus ignored the women's place claim to superiority in the emotional ventilation arena. Thus, the third phase of edgework, releasing emotions, was contested gender terrain; both women and men vied for the right to define normative ventilation methods.

It is possible that many women in the group perceived their position as inferior when it came to accomplishing edgework because they often felt as though it was a masculine domain, as much high-risk taking tends to be (Harrell 1986). After the danger had passed, however, when it came to dealing directly with emotions, women may have considered themselves the "emotional specialists." In her landmark study of a male-dominated corporation, Kanter (1977) identified this common stereotype of women, noting that both genders assumed women to be better equipped "naturally" to deal with emotional issues. More recently, other scholars have found evidence of this pervasive stereotype in more contemporary male-dominated settings as well (see Hochschild 1983; Pierce 1995), which suggests that specializing in emotional issues is still a core feature of "doing femininity" (West and Zimmerman 1987). Given this powerful belief, on one hand, it is easy to see why Peak's women felt justified in asserting the superiority of their "outburst" norm; by the same token, however, it is puzzling that women's place claims in the emotional realm were given little credibility by Peak's men.

One explanation for this phenomenon might be that norms of masculinity, including the norm of masculine emotional stoicism (Connell 1987; Kimmel 1996; Messner 1992), were so strongly entrenched and intricately connected to the edgework subculture that it gave men the "means of emotional culture production" (Cancian and Gordon 1988): They controlled the standards by which edgeworkers were judged. Furthermore, if emotions were the main avenue through which men distinguished themselves from women before, during, and after edgework, they may have felt that their appropriate gender performance—their very masculinity—would be threatened if they were to display emotions associated with a feminized edgework performance. This interpretation resonates with Connell's (1987) conception of "hegemonic masculinity," which is sustained because it dominates over other gendered forms, such as alternative masculinities held by gay men or nurturing fathers, and any kind of femininity.

These data show that there can be contested emotional terrain within one emotional culture. Although Cancian and Gordon's (1988) analysis of shifting love and anger norms in women's magazines demonstrated emotional culture contradictions, their work was only able to focus on the messages being sent to women about their emotions; it was unable to assess how individual women received these conflicting cultural messages. My research uncovers this aspect of an emotional culture. It shows how Peak's women evaluated themselves in terms of these discrepant cultural messages and how these self-interpretations guided their future action. In some cases, they acted to resist their subordinate position, drawing from the larger emotional culture to bolster their claims to a more respected place in the group. In other cases, they drew on gendered emotion norms to reinforce their subordinate status. Similarly, the men in the group accepted women's place claims in some cases yet denied them in others. By examining how women and men reacted to gendered cultural messages about emotions, these data reveal how gender may be constructed selectively by relying on culturally specific (and occasionally contradictory) emotion norms.

Notes

I would like to thank Patricia Adler, Peter Adler, Nan Boyd, Dan Cress, Alice Fothergill, David Franks, Joanna Higginson, Leslie Irvine, Joyce Nielsen, editor Christine Bose, and four anonymous reviewers for their helpful comments on earlier versions of this chapter.

1. There were very few exceptions to this pattern, and they were extreme cases. For example, when Patrick overestimated his skiing ability and created a dangerous situation (discussed later), he became more humble, but only after the board of directors formally disciplined him and group members overtly and harshly criticized him. His error was so egregious that members teased him for several years following the event. Perhaps Patrick was humbled by this situation because of the extraordinary pressure the group put on him; in almost all other cases, however, male rescuers maintained their confidence even after performing poorly.

2. There were some objective differences between women's and men's performance, which Peak's women realized. For the most part, this difference was physical. As Brooke noted, on the whole, the men in the group were stronger than the women, especially for the type of tasks required of rescue work, which can require a great deal of upper body strength. For example, the women were physically less able than the men to haul a rope, to carry the stretcher down a steep trail, or to ride a snow-

mobile (increased body mass greatly aids steering and control, as does upper body strength). Of course, there were women in Peak who were young and fit, and there were men who were old and out of shape. However, I never witnessed a situation where a woman outperformed a man when it came to upper body strength. Peak's women's physical strength lay in their endurance and in their legs. Thus, I observed many times when some women could outhike some men and even carry heavier packs. Overall, Peak's men physically outperformed the women.

References

Adler, Patricia A., and Peter Adler. 1987. *Membership Roles in Field Research*. Newbury Park, Calif.: Sage.

Beneke, Timothy. 1997. *Proving Manhood*. Berkeley: University of California Press.

Blumer, Herbert. 1969. *Symbolic Interactionism*. Englewood Cliffs, N.J.: Prentice Hall.

Cancian, Francesca M., and Steven L. Gordon. 1988. "Changing Emotion Norms in Marriage: Love and Anger in U.S. Women's Magazines Since 1900." *Gender and Society* 2: 308–342.

Clark, Candace. 1990. "Emotions and Micropolitics in Everyday Life: Some Patterns and Paradoxes of Place." In *Research Agendas in the Sociology of Emotions*, edited by Theodore D. Kemper. Albany: State University of New York Press.

Connell, R. W. 1987. *Gender and Power*. Stanford, Calif.: Stanford University Press.

DeCoster, Vaughn A. 1997. "Physician Treatment of Patient Emotions: An Application of the Sociology of Emotion." *In Social Perspectives on Emotion*, edited by Rebecca J. Erickson and Beverley Cuthbertson-Johnson. Vol. 4. Greenwich, Conn.: JAI.

Eisenberg, Nancy. 1986. *Altruistic Emotion, Cognition, and Behavior*. Hillsdale, N.J.: Erlbaum.

Fothergill, Alice. 1996. "Gender, Risk, and Disaster." *International Journal of Mass Emergencies and Disasters* 14: 33–56.

Geertz, Clifford. 1973. *The Interpretation of Cultures*. New York: Basic Books.

Glaser, Barney, and Anselm Strauss. 1967. *The Discovery of Grounded Theory*. Chicago: Aldine.

Gordon, Steven L. 1989. "Institutional and Impulsive Orientations in Selectively Appropriating Emotions to Self." In *The Sociology of Emotions: Original Essays and Research Papers*, edited by David D. Franks and E. Doyle McCarthy. Greenwich, Conn.: JAI.

Gove, Walter R., Michael Geerken, and Michael Hughes. 1979. "Drug Use and Mental Health Among a Representative National Sample of Young Adults." *Social Forces* 58: 572–590.

Harrell, W. Andrew. 1986. "Masculinity and Farming-Related Accidents." *Sex Roles* 15: 467–478.

Hochschild, Artie R. 1983. *The Managed Heart*. Berkeley: University of California Press.

_____. 1990. "Ideology and Emotion Management: A Perspective and Path for Future Research." In *Research Agendas in the Sociology of Emotions*, edited by Theodore D. Kemper. Albany: State University of New York Press.

Holyfield, Lori. 1997. "Generating Excitement: Experienced Emotion in Commercial Leisure." In *Social Perspectives on Emotion*, edited by Rebecca J. Erickson and Beverley Cuthbertson-Johnson. Vol. 4. Greenwich, Conn.: JAI.

_____. 1999. "Manufacturing Adventure: The Buying and Selling of Emotions." *Journal of Contemporary Ethnography* 28: 3–32.

Holyfield, Lori, and Gary Alan Fine. 1997. "Adventure As Character Work: The Collective Taming of Fear." *Symbolic Interaction* 20: 343–363.

Irvine, Leslie. 1999. *Codependent Forevermore*. Chicago: University of Chicago Press.

Jones, Lynn Cerys. 1997. "Both Friend and Stranger: How Crisis Volunteers Build and Manage Unpersonal Relationships with Clients." In *Social Perspectives on Emotion*, edited by Rebecca J. Erickson and Beverley Cuthbertson-Johnson. Vol. 4. Greenwich, Conn.: JAI.

Jorgensen, Danny L. 1989. *Participant Observation*. Newbury Park, Calif.: Sage.

Kanter, Rosabeth Moss. 1977. *Men and Women of the Corporation*. New York: Basic Books.

Kimmel, Michael. 1996. *Manhood in America: A Cultural History*. New York: Free Press.

King, Gary, Steven R. Delaronde, Raymond Dinoi, and Ann Forsberg. 1996. "Substance Use, Coping, and Safer Sex Practices Among Adolescents with Hemophilia and Human Immunodeficiency Virus." *Journal of Adolescent Health* 18: 435–441.

Kitsuse, John. 1962. "Societal Reactions to Deviant Behavior: Problems of Theory and Method." *Social Problems* 9: 247–256.

Konradi, Amanda. 1999. "I Don't Have to Be Afraid of You": Rape Survivors' Emotion Management in Court. *Symbolic Interaction* 22: 45–77.

Lyng, Stephen. 1990. "Edgework: A Social Psychological Analysis of Voluntary Risk Taking." *American Journal of Sociology* 95: 851–886.

Martin, Susan Ehrlich. 1980. *Breaking and Entering*. Berkeley: University of California Press.

Messner, Michael A. 1992. *Power at Play*. Boston: Beacon.

Metz, Donald L. 1981. *Running Hot*. Cambridge, Mass.: Abt.

Mills, Trudy, and Sherryl Kleinman. 1988. "Emotions, Reflexivity, and Action: An Interactionist Analysis." *Social Forces* 66: 1009–1027.

Mirowsky, John, and Catherine E. Ross. 1995. "Sex Differences in Distress: Real or Artifact?" *American Sociological Review* 60: 449–68.

Palmer, C. Eddie. 1982. "Trauma Junkies and Street Work: Occupational Behavior of Paramedics and Emergency Medical Technicians." *Urban Life* 12: 162–83.

Parsons, Talcott. 1951. *The social system*. New York: Free Press.

Patterson, Joan M., and Hamilton I. McCubbin. 1984. "Gender Roles and Coping." *Journal of Marriage and the Family* 46: 95–104.

Pierce, Jennifer L. 1995. *Gender trials*. Berkeley: University of California Press.

Robinson, Michael D., and Joel T. Johnson. 1997. "Is It Emotion or Is It Stress? Gender stereotypes and the Perception of Subjective Experience." *Sex Rolls* 36: 235–58.

Roehling, Patricia V., Nikole Koelbel, and Christina Rutgers. 1996. "Codependence and Conduct Disorder: Feminine Versus Masculine Coping Responses to Abusive Parenting Practices." *Sex Roles* 35: 603–18.

Schachter, Stanley, and Jerome E. Singer. 1962. "The Interactions of Cognitive and Physiological Determinants of Emotional State." *Psychological Review* 69: 379–99.

Sigmon, Sandra T., Annette L. Stanton, and C.R. Snyder. 1995. "Gender Differences in Coping: A Further Test of Socialization and Role Constraint Theories." *Sex Roles* 33: 565–87.

Smith, Allen C. III, and Sherryl Kleinman. 1989. "Managing Emotions in Medical School: Students' Contacts with the Living and Dead." *Social Psychology Quarterly* 52: 56–69.

Stearns, Peter N. 1994. *American Cool*. New York: New York University Press.

Sykes, Gresham, and David Matza. 1957. "Techniques of Neutralization: A Theory of Delinquency." *American Sociological Review* 22: 664–70.

Thoits, Peggy A. 1990. "Emotional Deviance: Research Agendas." In *Research Agendas in the Sociology of Emotions*, edited by Theodore D. Kemper. Albany: State University of New York Press.

———. 1995. "Identity-relevant Events and Psychological Symptoms: A Cautionary Tale." *Journal of Health and Social Behavior* 36: 72–82.

Thompson, Hunter S. 1971. *Fear and Loathing in Las Vegas*. New York: Warner.

West, Candace, and Don H. Zimmerman. 1987. "Observations on the Display and Management of Emotion in Naturally Occurring Activites: The Case of "Hysteria" in Calls to 9-1-1. *Social Psychology Quarterly* 61: 141–59.

16

CAREER COMMITMENTS
Women and Men Law
School Graduates

Kandace Pearson Schrimsher

This chapter is based on a larger study of the careers of women and men eleven years after they graduated from Case Western Reserve University School of Law. The study examined the similarities and differences of law school, employment, and family experiences. Specifically, this chapter focuses on the career commitment of the women and men graduates. Career commitment is measured by continued employment in the legal profession and the side bets (investments) trade in maintaining career commitment.

A qualitative and quantitative analysis of eight specific side bets found that (1) women and men had similar law school experiences, and class rank, not gender, influenced opportunities and experiences; (2) women were more committed than men to the legal profession, as measured by job mobility, which was increasing for both groups; (3) although the vast majority of graduates experienced stress in their work, the conflict experienced between work and family relationships was different among women and men; (4) the career satisfaction of prestige of position, prestige in community, and advancement opportunities differed between women and men; and (5) the women accepted restrictions on their careers if they came from their husbands. Most women were not getting the support they needed from their husbands or the workplace. What they did get was not as relevant to their careers as the type of spouse/partner career support received by their male counterparts.

The Legal Profession

The astonishing growth in the number of lawyers in the United States since World War II has been accompanied by an unprecedented increase in demand for legal services from both business clients and individuals. By 1990, the legal profession had become a $91 billion a year service industry, employing more than 940,000 people, and surpassing the medical profession in the number of licensed professionals (MacCrate 1992).

The rapid growth in the number of lawyers has affected the manner in which law is practiced and how law firms are structured and organized. It has allowed greater specialization in law practice and an increased division of labor among lawyers. New areas of law and regulation, for the most part designed by lawyers, have created whole new fields of legal services.

Along with the rapid growth of lawyers has been an increased demand for all kinds of legal services, particularly from the business community. For the past forty years, the economic base that supports legal services has expanded greatly, being matched by the steadily increasing number of clients willing and able to pay for legal services (MacCrate 1992).

In 1991, there were 805,872 lawyers in the United States, of which 80.2 percent were men and only 19.8 percent were women (Curran and Carson 1994). Practicing lawyers are employed in several types of settings, including private practice (solo and firm), private industry, and government employment (federal and state). Private practice is the most common organization of employment for lawyers. In fact, in 1991, 73 percent of lawyers were employed in private practice, of which 45 percent, worked solo and 55 percent in firms (Curran and Carson 1994).

Private practice may consist of firms ranging in size anywhere from one to over 100 lawyers. Generally, these firms may also include legal researchers and support staff. Lawyers employed in private practice are salaried professionals with an opportunity for profit sharing if and when they get promoted from associate to partner status.

Internal structures of law firms generally consist of administrations ordered by a series of committees and a system of ranks, each with distinctive obligations and privileges. The single most significant distinction in a law firm is that of rank. "Partners" own the firm and, therefore, divide its considerable profits at the end of the year. "Associates," on the other hand, do not share in the profits of the firm; they are its employees, working for a generous but nevertheless fixed salary (Spangler 1986, 35). The enormous differences between associate salaries and partnership salaries (sometimes more than 10 to 1) symbolize both the subordination of the former and the rewards that follow from accepting it gracefully (Abel 1989, 222).

Firms admit associates to partnership after seven to ten years of service to the firm. In all firms, the timetable for full partnership is similar: after a decade, attorneys expect to be full and permanent members of the partnership. Under the current system, then, salaried employment (associate status) is a temporary status designed to lead into either partnership (ownership) or exit from the firm. The possibility of a partnership secures the associates' loyalty, although the probability of being made partner is declining (Spangler 1986, 36).

Another position within a firm is that "of counsel." Traditionally, this position title applied to those individuals who were retired partners of their law limn. However, in the last decade or so, this position has been redefined. Currently, the status "of counsel" implies more of a lateral category; a nonequity salaried employer of the firm. Individuals who occupy this position are not considered associates because they are not on a partner track.

To a significant extent, firm size and practice setting have had a direct relationship to the types of clients served, the type of law practiced, and the financial rewards of practice. Community-oriented solo and small firm practitioners work predominantly for individuals, whereas lawyers in larger firms work predominately for business clients.

In general, the financial rewards for legal work for individuals (except for personal injury claims) have been less than the rewards for representing business. Various studies of the legal profession have indicated a strong relationship among the size of a firm arid the source of its income: as firm size increases, the percentage of fees from business clients also increases while the percentage of Ices from individuals decreases. Hence, the larger the firm, the greater the concentration of work front business clients and, thus, the larger the average income of the firms' lawyers.

Generally, working in the legal profession requires an involvement in cases, paperwork, and community. Moreover, in most first environments, carvings are to some extent dependent on initiative—ambition, drive, and motivation. Hence, the time demands of the work increase dramatically. A full day at the office is not enough for an aspiring lawyer. The norms of the legal profession equate success and excellence with hard work, measured in part by long hours. Putting in extra hours at night and working on weekends are not only common but generally expected. Furthermore, besides having the pressure to work hard, there is also the expectation of spending all extra time on legal affairs, such as taking classes (i.e., continuing legal education), bar association projects and meetings, and community services such as pro bono work.

The legal profession, as well as most professions in general, are what Coser (1974) describes as "greedy institutions." Not only do firms and corporations impose time demands on employees, but the employees themselves seek other options to get access to mime challenging and interesting work and/or seek to participate or increase participation in organizational problem .solving. 'Thus, in these types of settings, women and men have protects with goals (fiat require additional work and reflection beyond the time permitted at the office. Moreover, it is the organization's intention that time records and billing demands keep lawyers competitive and overproducing.

Concepts of
Career Commitment and Side Bets

In order to understand fully what is meant by career patterns, the concept of career must first be defined. In broad terms, Hughes (1958) defined the concept of career as "the more or less orderly and predictable course of one's work life" (1958, p. 12). According to Wilensky (1961), a career is "a succession of related jobs, arranged in a hierarchy of prestige, through which persons move in an ordered (more or less predictable) sequence (1961, 523).

Moreover, the work of one person is usually related to the work of another or a larger social unit. According to Lopata, Barnwaldt, and Miller (1986), this means that one's work is usually woven into social roles, defined as sets of interdependent social relations between a social person and a social circle involving duties and rights (Znaniecki 1965, as cited in Lopata et al. 1986; see also Lopata 1994). In other words, jobs are social roles containing work and other aspects of social relations with all members of a social circle, where the social circle consists of everyone with whom the person interacts in order to carry forth a role.

Throughout this discussion, Becker's (1960) concepts of commitment and side bets are used along with the side bets proposed in Lopata's (1992) article, "Career Commitments of American Women: The Issue of Side Bets." Although Lopata presented ten side bets, only those side bets that are relevant to the occupational/professional commitment of law school graduates are examined and discussed here. As Lopata did in her study, I broaden the concept of side bets to include relevant aspects of the total life space (professional and personal), which women and men graduates can bring into line because these can affect, with ease or with difficulty, the types of career choices made and the level of commitment desired and/or maintained.

When discussing the concept of commitment, Becker (1960) referred to two distinct types: (1) commitment to the organization, and (2) commitment to the occupation. I examined the investments and commitments the women and men graduates have to the legal profession, as opposed to their commitment to the organization of employment. Hence, for the purpose of this study, commitment to the profession will be measured by continued employment in the legal profession.

Side Bet Theory

Becker (1960) contended that commitment occurs through a process lie called "placing side bets," or types of investments. Becker asserted that the greater the number of side bets, the greater the degree of commitment of the individual to a course of action. It follows that these investments strengthen one's commitment to employment and career goals, both directly and indirectly, staking it beneficial to continue such commitments. In Becker's analysis, commitment to the organization and commitment to the occupation are the result of a series of conscious and unconscious side bets, or investments. A committed person has acted in such a way as to involve her or his other interests, originally unrelated to the action the person is engaging in, to he directly related to that action (Stebbins 1968, 527). For example, Stebbins (1970), in his study of job commitment, found that age, education, marriage, children, and salary were all associated with a strong degree of commitment as well as a strong development of professional identity. So it follows that these investments strengthen one's commitment to employment and career goals, both directly and indirectly, staking it beneficial to continue such commitments.

A consistent line of activity will often be based on more than one kind of side bet; several kinds of "things" valuable to the person may be staked into a particular line of activity. Ritzer and Trice (1969) asserted that there needs to he an analysis of values with which side bets can he made, by examining what kinds of things the individual desires and those types of losses feared. Hence, in order to understand commitment fully, one must discover the system of values upon which the side bets are made.

Lopata's (1992) study examined the side bets of American women in the form of education, occupational preparation, employer selection, full-time involvement, role conflict avoidance, incorporation of career into self-concept, and the building of a relatively congruent construction of reality. Following Becker (1960), Lopata contended that choosing an occupation or employing organization provides the individual with rewards that can be hard to give up; thus, leaving it may result either in penalties or in costs that the person can he increasingly unwilling to face. Thus, the side bets tie the person to that line of action in many ways that she or he may not be aware of until she or lie contemplates the decision to leave this occupation or organization. On the other hand, a person may consciously increase the ease of following the committed line of action by purposely building "side bets" into her or his life (Lopata 1992, 4). The focus of this analysis is on the latter, that most of the women and men graduates have purposely built side bets into their lives.

Several major studies of the changing commitments of women to family and work roles indicate possible forms of side bets. For example, a person who may perceive her or himself as committed to an occupation or a career line that demands high commitment is thus recognized as such by her or himself as well as by her or his closest "significant others," such as mentors, friends, and colleagues, and by the "generalized others," such as members of the profession.

Traditional research indicates that the greater the complexity of the occupation, as well as its status in the structure, the higher the commitment of the persons in it (Kohn and Schooler 1973, 1983; Lopata et al. 1985a, 1986, as cited in Lopata 1992). This paper utilizes eight of Lopata's hypothesized ten side bets. The eight side bets discussed here are:

1. Preparation for the profession through schooling;
2. Selection of an organization that can he expected to support commitment to professional goals;
3. Involvement in a job that enables one to work in that profession and/or pursue a career line and provide job complexity;
4. Positive feedback from above involvement;
5. Association with people of similar commitments, colleagues, and friends;
6. Support from spouse/ partner;
7. Support in the role of parent to make possible commitments; and
8. Developing a relatively congruent construction of reality at the socio-psychological and behavioral aspects of commitment.

These side bets are examined to identify similarities and differences in side bets among women and men and what effect, if any, these differences and/or similarities have on their measured commitment (continued employment) to the legal profession.

Lopata (1992) emphasized that these side bets have been expected for most men in modern America, due to the "vestige" of the two-sphere world in which a male's professional commitment to an occupation/employee role is taken for granted. This society was developed through a strong focus upon the economic institution, to be carried forth directly by men (Weher 1953, as cited in Lopata 1992). Until very recently, members of this half of the American population have needed no justification for organizing their lives around occupations. Socialization throughout the life course provided men with a solid base of a congruent construction of reality. The occupational system continues for the most part with "greedy" commitment demands, making it difficult for women who also must meet the demands of equally "greedy" families (Coser 1974; Coser and Coser 1974). Thus, career commitment by women and men in two-career families requires investment in many side bets, both internally, in terms of mutual support and self-concept, or identities; and externally, from the environment, especially from people in the various role circles in which they are involved (Lopata 1992, 11). However, studies indicate that women and men do not receive equal internal and external support in their careers.

Study Design and Methods

The findings of this study are based on the data of an alumni survey of the women and men 1981 graduates of Case Western Reserve University School of Law, Cleveland, Ohio, conducted during the summer of 1992. Approximately 45 percent of the graduates participated in the study—35 percent women and 65 percent men (which was also the actual gender composition of the class of 1981). The data were complied from a questionnaire that was twenty-two pages long and composed mostly of multiple choice questions that required participants to circle a number that best described their answers, as well as open-ended, and rank-ordered questions, The CWRU Alum Survey included the following sections: (1) personal background information, (2) law school experiences, (3) employment history, (4) current employment, (5) work projections, (6) additional background information, and (7) housework and child care responsibilities.

Other studies of law school graduates referred to throughout this chapter include the New Mexico Study (Teitelbaum et al. 1991), University of Michigan Study (Chambers 1990), the Minnesota Study (Mattessich and Heilman 1990), the Stanford Project (1988), the Harvard Project (Vogt 1986), and Liefland (1986).

Specifically, the New Mexico Study examined alumni of the University of New Mexico, classes of 1975–1986. The University of Michigan Study examined the class of 1985 (five years out of law school at the time of the survey). The Minnesota study was commissioned by the Minnesota Women Lawyers Task Force on the Status of Women in the Profession. That study examined the careers of law school graduates of 1975, 1978, 1982, and 1985 from three Minnesota law schools: University of Minnesota (35 percent), William Mitchell (44 percent), and Hamline University (21 percent). The Stanford Project was an empirical study that examined gender, legal education and the legal profession with law school graduates and current students. The Harvard Project examined the classes of 1959, 1969, 1974, and 1981 from seven northeastern law schools: Boston College, Boston University, Columbia University, University of Connecticut, Harvard, Northeastern, and Suffolk University. This study had a range of small, medium, and large schools, representing schools with regional or national prestige. Finally, Liefland's study examined the career patterns of male and female lawyers of the classes of 1976, 1977, and

1978 from four prominent law schools: University of California at Berkeley, Columbia University, University of Pennsylvania, and New York University.

Examination of Side Bets

The findings of this study suggest that eleven years after graduating from law school, most CWRU graduates have maintained a high level of commitment to the legal profession, as evidenced by the high number, 84 percent of the women and 81 percent of the men, who were practicing law. When eight of Lopata's (1992) proposed side bets were examined, many similarities and differences among the women and men graduates were revealed.

Side Bet 1: Preparation Through Schooling
Side Bet 1 examines commitment to professional goals by the graduates of the same law school by means of education. Clearly, all of the women and men made an investment in their career commitment through attaining a law degree. They invested their time, energy, and money in obtaining an undergraduate degree, prior to their three year commitment to earn a law degree.

Side Bet 2: Selection of an Organization of Employment
Side Bet 2 is the selection of an organization that can be expected to support commitment to professional goals. This investment was made by the majority of both women and men and is reflected in the high rate of job mobility among the graduates. During the first eleven years after graduating from law school, most graduates had held at least two different jobs. Moreover, 47 percent of the women and 50 percent of the men had held three or more jobs. Twenty-one percent of the women and 24 percent of the men had had yet another job after job three. This finding suggests that when professional goals are not being met or are perceived as being compromised in a job or an organization, most CWRU women and men will seek alternative employment perceived as more conducive to the achievement of professional goals and commitments. Therefore, the high rate of job mobility among the women and men indicates an unsatisfactory match between lawyer and organization at the beginning, and for some throughout their legal careers.

At the time of the survey, the majority of women and men practiced law in private firms (see Table 16.1). These findings were similar to several other studies, with the exception of first job after law school (no differences were found among CWRU women and men), where gender differences were found among organizations and positions of employment (Mattessich and Heilman 1990: Liefland 1986; Vogt 1986; Curran and Carson 1985; White 1965).

As indicated in Table 16.2, at the time of the CWRU survey, the then graduates had greater employment diversity among firm sizes, while the women were concentrated in the very small or the large firms. Moreover, many more men than women were employed outside of the legal profession. The majority of women employed in the legal profession practiced law; two were judges and two women were in other types of legal work. The majority of women who practiced law were employed in solo or

TABLE 16.1   Current Organization of Employment

	Female (%)	N	Male (%)	N
Private firm/solo	43	1	55	36
Federal government	3	1	5	3
State/local government	14	5	3	2
Quasi-government (World Bank)	0	0	2	1
Legal services/public defender	3	1	2	1
Public interest	0	0	2	1
Fortune 500 industry/service	14	5	8	5
Other industry/business	9	3	3	2
Banking/finance	6	2	5	3
Accounting firm	0	0	6	4
Other Service	9	3	9	7
		(N = 65)		(N = 35)

NOTES: F = .07; Sig. = .796

TABLE 16.2   Current Position of Employment

	Female (%)	N	Male (%)	N
Practice law	82	28	72	49
Trail/appellate judge	6	2	0	0
Other legal position	6	2	3	2
Non-law employment	6	2	25	16
		(N = 34)		(N = 67)

NOTES: F = .43; Sig. = .513

small firms of four or less and large firms of one hundred or more (see Table 16.3). Similar to the women, the majority of men practiced law, and two men did other legal work. However, the majority of men who practiced law were employed in firms of five to fifteen lawyers (36 percent), one-fourth were in large firms of one hundred or more, and 21 percent were in small firms of four or less.

The high concentration of women employed at solo and large firms may be because of the perceived advantages associated with each setting. Solo practice offers an environment with a sense of independence for setting one's own hours and the freedom to turn away and accept clients; also, solo practitioners need to answer to no one but themselves in pursuing cases that appeal to them) (Spangler 1985). Large firms, on the other hand, have made the greatest strides toward equality among men and women as they have elsewhere in the legal profession and in other professions. There is equality in recruitment; equality in pay in the initial years; access to specialization in all areas of the law; and institutionalization of policies such as maternity leave, unpaid leave, and availability of part-time work tracks (Epstein et al. 1995).

TABLE 16.3   Firm Size of Practicing Lawyers

	Female (%)	N	Male (%)	N
4 or less	47	7	21	9
5-15	7	1	36	15
16-29	0	0	2	1
30-49	0	0	5	2
50-100	7	1	12	5
More than 100	10	6	24	10
		(N = 15)		(N = 42)

NOTES: F = .03; Sig. = .852

TABLE 16.4   Current Law Firm Status

	Female (%)	N	Male (%)	N
Solo	40	6	13	5
Partner	33	5	69	27
Associate	13	2	8	3
Of counsel	7	1	3	1
Other	7	1	8	3
		(N = 15)		(N = 39)

NOTES: F = .26; Sig. = .610

These findings and differences must be explored further to determine the underlying factors prevalent in organizations of employment. For example, are these choices made by the women and men? Are they the result of unsuccessful employment in a different firm size and/or organization? Or are they the only alternative options available for personal responsibilities? Are women and men making their employment decision based on their own needs, or are they based on the needs of others?

At the time of the study, more than twice as many men than women had achieved partner status at their law firms. Among those women who were in firms with status-level positions, 33 percent were partners, 12 percent associates, 7 percent were of counsel, and 7 percent were employed in other firm positions (see Table 16.4). The majority of men were partners in their firms (69 percent); a further number were associates, 3 percent were of counsel, and 8 percent were employed in other firm positions. It should he noted that the differences among the firm positions of the women and men may he attributed to the fact that a high proportion of women were employed in solo practice, where generally there are no distinct associate and partner positions.

Another explanation of the differences of status level among the women and men may be that some of the women are taking or have taken nontraditional career paths. For example, in her study of women lawyers, Fritz (1990) found that many law firms provide maternity leave and offer flexible arrangements to those associates, virtually all of whom are women, who wish to work part-time or take extended leaves to care for their children. But those women who accept part-time arrangements (at a law firm, this can mean working thirty hours a week) generally forfeit the opportunity to become partners. In my study, 58 percent of the women and 16 percent of the men, at some point in their careers, had worked part-time and/or stopped employment; parental leaves had been taken by 42 percent of these women and only one man.

The Law Society's Working Party on Women's Careers found that with women's career advancements, "the principal difficulty that women have to face is the reconciliation of their social responsibilities for children with the needs of a career" ("Women in the Profession" 1988, 1l). The traditional male career model of success would suggest that a person occupy an associate status for five to seven years and then be promoted to partner status. However, the timing of associate status coincides with women's peak fertility, while men's fertility lasts much longer. The demands of the firm tend to be the highest at the associate status, a time when women may prefer to work less. The CWRU women who were at the associate level status may have "slowed" or stopped their career path for family/spouse obligations or commitments (Pearson 1990; Spencer and Podomore 1957; White 1984). Therefore, those women who took "nontraditional" career paths would be more likely to achieve partner status much later in their careers than those persons who followed the traditional male career model of the legal profession. Or, perhaps some women may have redefined their priorities and no longer aspire to partner status and the male career model of success.

Side Bet 3: Pursuit of Career Goals and Job Complexity

Side Bet 3 reveals that the majority of both women and men were involved in jobs which enabled them to work in the legal profession and/or pursue their career line and provide job complexity. Again, the investment of career commitment is reflected in the high rate of mobility within the legal profession among both women and men graduates.

The factors liked the most among both women and men about their current careers include intellectual stimulation, challenges, and problems solving—all characteristics of job complexity. Work-related stress was the aspect they liked the least. The majority of both women and men attribute their work-related stress to deadlines, which require immediate output, making quality work difficult. Also, many women attribute their work-related stress to their attempt to balance work and family demands, and problems with superiors. The men, on the other hand, attribute their stress primarily to client demands, problems with superiors and balancing work and family demands. Even though family was more frequently a source of stress for the women, among the men family demands were the fourth most common source of stress. Perhaps the differences in the acknowledgment and identification of stress due to family demands may be influenced by the fact that 66 percent of the men (as opposed to all of the women) have spouses who are also employed in the paid labor force. Hence, these men, as opposed to their male counterparts whose wives are not employed, may experience, to some extent, the potential career disadvantages that result from the time demands most women in the paid labor force experience in their attempt to juggle both work and family responsibilities and commitments.

At the time of the survey, most of the graduates had children who were quite young. However, in their study of women lawyers, Spencer and Podomore (1987) found that child care concerns and responsibilities are not just indicative to the early years. A senior barrister in their study pointed out that her teenage children made a lot of emotional demands "that you can't delegate" (Spencer and Podomore 1987, 55). Moreover, in her research on changing families in America, Stephanie Coontz (1997) reflects on her own family life and contends, "as a mother and a researcher, I've found that it's the parents of teenagers who need the most flexibility."

It could be argued that those women who aspire to achieve higher positions, or who occupy higher positions within their organization, have the potential to shoulder heavier "out of work" demands, particularly family responsibilities. Research suggests that women, despite their full-time employment status, continue to do the bulk of the family and household work (Hertz 1986; Hochschild 1989, 1997; Kanter 1989). Hence, like the women lawyers in Epstein's study (1981) and the women professionals in Hochschild's study (1997), the CWRU women graduates appear to have additional time demands, or what Hochschild (1997) terms "time binds," created by their multiple roles of professional, mother, and spouse.

Side Bet 4: Positive Feedback From Employment Involvement

Side Bet 4, a positive evaluation of both instrumental and secondary involvement, is evident in the graduates' evaluation of their career satisfaction. Regardless of the high level of stress experienced by the graduates, in the workplace and/or at home, the vast majority of both women and men had overall high levels of career satisfaction (see also Chambers 1990; Mattessich and Heilman 1990; Stanford Project 1988).

The majority of the women had the highest level of career satisfaction with solving problems, intellectual challenges, intellectual stimulation, and degree of independence. The majority of men had high levels of career satisfaction with: intellectual challenges, prestige of position, degree of independence, intellectual stimulation and solving problems.

Notes: The sample size of the women was 33, except for Prestige of Position, which was 34. The sample size of the men was 63, except for Advancement Opportunity, which was 61.

As indicated in Table 16.5, the significant statistical differences of sources of career satisfaction among the women and men was prestige of position, prestige in community, and advancement opportunities. The men had a much higher degree of career satisfaction from the prestige of their position than did the women. These dramatic differences among women and men may be indicative of the fact that more than twice as many men than women had achieved partner status in their law firm. High-status positions generally tend to be associated with high salaries and power and are occupied primarily by men. Therefore, it may he presumed that prestige in the community would be higher for those persons with high-level positions, salaries, and power, since generally these aspects tend to he admired in American society and are often directly correlated with each other, hence leading to higher job satisfaction.

TABLE 16.5   Gender Differences in Career Satisfaction

	Very Important		Somewhat Important			
	Female (%)	Male (%)	Female (%)	Male (%)	F	Sig.
Prestige of position	18	51	50	37	9.60	.00
Prestige in community	21	52	48	32	5.84	.01
Advancement in community	24	39	39	34	3.09	.08

NOTES: The sample size of the women was 33, except for Prestige of Position, which was 34. The sample size of the men was 63, except for Advancement Opportunity, which was 61.

The differences in sources of career satisfaction among women and men needs to be further investigated in order to discover whether the dissatisfaction is also related to job position, salary, organization of employment, or public perception of the significance of job positions.

Side Bet 5: Association with People of Similar Commitments

Side Bet 5, association with persons of similar commitments, also reveals differences among women and men. The American Bar Association (ABA) is the national professional organization of the legal profession. There are additional bar associations at the state, county, and city levels and also in different areas of specialty (special bars). Memberships in professional organizations allow persons to seek recognition from outside groups and professional groups. Therefore, membership affiliations are one indication of professional commitment and loyalty to the profession.

Gouldner (1957, 1958) studied the professional commitment and organizational loyalty of faculty members of a small liberal arts college. He distinguished between two types of members: "the cosmopolitan" and "the local." The cosmopolitan member has little loyalty to the local organization, a strong commitment to specialized skills, and a strong identification with reference groups representing professional specialty. The local member, on the other hand, displays a strong loyalty to the local organization and the profession, a weak commitment to specialized skills, and a strong identification with reference groups located within the organization.

When professional membership affiliations were examined using Gouldner's (1957, 1958) concepts of "local" and "cosmopolitan" professional role orientation, the findings of this study suggest that the women graduates took more of a "local" role orientation, while the men were more "cosmopolitan." The majority of the women were not members of the American Bar Association, while the majority of the men were.

Those women and men who did not participate in professional organizations identified time and/or financial constraints as the primary reasons for nonmembership. They did not have enough time to devote to being members, and/or the membership rate was too expensive, preventing them from joining if their firm did not pay for it, or causing them to pick and choose those organizations they believed to be the most beneficial to join. However, it should be noted that women were not allowed to join the American Bar Association until 1910, and currently there is a significant underrepresentation of women in the governance of the American Bar Association coupled with the commonly held perception that the American Bar Association caters to middle-sized and larger male firms. Moreover, the low rate of membership among the women may be attributed to the expenses and time commitments of bar involvement, which must be approved by firm partners, a position that, as revealed in this study and several others, is more often occupied by men than women.

Side Bet 6: Support from Spouse/Partner

Although it has been documented that the role of spouse/partner is regarded as being somewhat competitive to careers (especially for women), like most other studies, the majority of both women and men were married at the time of the CWRU survey (see also Chambers 1990; Mattessich and Heilman 1990). However, all of the women and only 66 percent of the men were involved in marriages where either both spouses had careers or one had a career and the other was employed full-time in the paid labor force (see Table 16.6).

Eighty-seven percent of the women had spouses/partners who were employed professionals (of whom 32 percent were lawyers). The remaining 13 percent of the husbands were also employed full-time. Among the men, however, only 46 percent had spouses/partners who were employed professionals (of whom 15 percent were lawyers). Thirty-one percent had wives who were homemakers, 21 percent had wives who were employed full-time, and 2 percent had wives who were college students. These findings were similar to the Michigan study (1990), where the women were typically linked with partners who earned about as much or more than they did. By contrast, the great majority of men with partners were linked to someone who earned much less than they did or did not have a job in the paid workforce.

This study hypothesized two possibilities of partner support: (1) the majority of women are married to professionals who are likely to be in "greedy" organizations and thus have their own competitive career goals, and (2) since fewer than half of the men are married to professionals or women who are employed full-time, and close to one-third are married to "homemakers," more of the men are likely to have spouses who support their own competitiveness, professional goals, and commitments.

It could be argued that those women and men who have spouses/partners with similar professional interests and goals may receive a greater degree of encouragement and understanding of their own work responsibilities and commitments. On the other hand, those persons involved in dual-career marriages or relationships, or one-career/two-income marriages or relationships, would tend to encounter different types of strains and tensions and different types of career support than a graduate who was the primary career person in the marriage, with a spouse who had little, if any, employment in the paid labor force.

The ways in which a spouse/partner gave career support declined drastically among women and men. The majority of women received "general career support," followed by consulting with work and career, and helping with child care and household responsibilities. On the other hand, the majority of men received spouse/partner career support in terms of tolerance of the time demands of their work, taking sole responsibility for child care and household responsibilities, and tolerance of their frequent and extensive travel.

TABLE 16.6   Spouse/Partner Employment

	Female (%)	N	Male (%)	N
Professional	55	17	31	17
Lawyer	32	10	15	8
Other employment	13	4	21	11
Student	0	0	2	1
Homemaker	0	0	31	17
		(N = 31)		(N = 54)

NOTES: F = 2.92; Sig. = 091

Among the men graduates, partner career support was defined more in terms of a tolerance of job responsibilities. For example, one man wrote, "[My wife] does most of the child care, manages my wardrobe, [and] consults on matters in her field." Another indicated, "[My wife] puts up with long hours [and] lots of travel. . . . She does a great job with our kids—reducing the stress on me." Still another man reported, "She stays home with the kids, which makes my work priorities easier to handle. She's also excellent with social matters." Another wrote, "[My wife] bore the burden of spending extra time with the children." Hence, most men, but few women, get full-time help from their spouse/partner.

The women tend to define spouse career support more in terms of general career support and help with child care and/or household responsibilities. The men, on the other hand, orient their spouse/partner support in terms of their own professional responsibilities—a characteristic related directly to career performance and commitment. This finding supports the "second shift" ideology (Hochschild 1989) that working women, in addition to their professional obligations and commitments, continue to be responsible for the lion's share of both child and household obligations and commitments. However, it should be noted that some of the men recognize the fact that their wives take sole responsibility for child care and household obligations, therefore giving them the opportunity to be more deeply involved with their professional obligations, commitments, and goals—something most of their female counterparts are not likely to ever experience.

Among the women, the husbands pose a major problem since the women's careers are not getting the support they need, and also the support provided by the husbands is not as relevant to their career commitment and goals as what the men graduates receive from their wives. In their study examining the position of women lawyers in eight New York City law firms, Epstein and her colleagues (1995) found that support from one's spouse was one of the greatest factors that their participants noted as an important influence in the career paths of women.

When spouse/partner career hindrances were examined, again differences among women and men were revealed. Many of the women claimed that simply choosing to have a family limited their choices, as did receiving little if any help with child care and household responsibilities. For most of the men, a spouse/partner hindered their career by complaining of the long hours they have to work, and in the tension they experience as the result of having a spouse who was also employed full-time.

Like Hochschild (1989), who found in her study that family responsibilities were a major theme in the problems of the women, this theme also prevailed in my study. For example, among the women of CWRU, responses such as these were all too common: "He does nothing to ease the responsibilities at home and with our child. By leaving those responsibilities to me, my career goals have had to be deferred." Another woman reported, "He does not do his share to run the household or child care responsibility." Yet another wrote, "Too many household chores fall on my shoulders."

Among the men, an intolerance of job responsibilities was the most frequently mentioned aspect of spousal career hindrance. For example, one man indicated, "[My wife] has, on occasion, been less than enthusiastic about. . . [my] long hours." Another wrote, "[My wife has] inflexible hours with her job." And yet another man indicated, "She has a full-time career also, so we have to juggle kids, household chores, etc." Changes in the attitudes of men begin to appear among those lawyers with children who have wives who are also employed full-time. Hence, these men, to some degree, experience the conflict and stress of juggling family and career obligations and commitments.

Side Bet 7: Support in the Role of Parent

Side Bet 7 examines support in the role of parent to make professional commitments possible. Although it has definitely been documented that the role of parent competes with careers of women (and as this study reveals, to some extent, men), the majority of both women and men graduates had two to three infant, preschool, or grade school-age children. Most graduates found that their work conflicted with their ability to devote enough attention to their children (see also Hochschild 1997). However, as indicated in Table 16.7, the women were twice as likely than the men to experience this conflict "often" or "very often."

For example, one woman wrote, "[The conflict is] time demands—sometimes when I travel, I won't see my kids for three days. I have missed parent/teacher conferences. Sometimes I feel I've not spent enough time with my children." Another woman reported, "[I'm] away from home for weeks at a time (including weekends). I've missed one full month of my baby's so far six-month life." And another woman wrote:

> I work all day, so the important times—lunch, right after school—for good communication, are missed. It's hard to he involved in school. And evenings are only three hours long, including dinner time. If I devote any time to my husband, to get emotionally prepared to go to work the next day, there is little time left for a child.

Therefore, if a woman professional decides to have children, she is faced with the dilemma of how much time should she devote to her children and her spouse/partner and how much to her career. This dilemma involves more than simply the allocation of time, as Coser and Rokoff (1971) pointed out. The issue of "family and career" implies conflict between deeply held social values, too: "Professional women are expected to be committed to their work 'just like a man.' At the same time they are normatively

TABLE 16.7   Conflict Experienced Between Work and Children

	Female (%)	N	Male (%)	N
Rarely	15	4	18	9
Sometimes	42	11	57	28
Often	23	6	16	8
Very often	19	5	8	4
		(N = 26)		(N = 49)

NOTES: F = 2.23; Sig. = .139

required to give priority to their family (Coser and Rokoff 1971, 535). Moreover, it has been documented in many studies that the conflict experienced by many women in the paid labor force, as indicated in the responses of the CWRU women, is often associated with guilt (see Pearson 1990; Hochschild 1997). Also, along with the guilt, some of the women appear to project a sense of sadness.

Among some of the men, lack of time to spend with their children also contributes to their stress. For example, one man wrote, "I am not able to spend as much time with [my children] as I would like, or attend doctor appointments, or games or programs. I am never home for dinner unless we eat out on a weekend." Another man reported, "I am not able to devote as much time to my daughter as I would like. Often I don't get home until after her bedtime." Still another man wrote, "It is extremely important for a parent to spend time (not just 'quality time,' but absolute quantitative time also) with children, and my work inhibits that occasionally."

Side Bet 8: Developing a Congruent Construction of Reality

Side Bet 8 examined the development of a relatively congruent construction of reality around career identity. Lopata (1992) hypothesized the higher the level of occupational/professional commitment, the more the person is likely to pull together a congruent image of the self, the job, and the environment. She contended that the very process of making conscious career commitments can push a person toward increased congruence. Therefore, projected career goals and the perceived possibility of their goal attainment could be reflective of the degree of occupational commitment and congruency.

It appears that the vast majority of the CWRU women and men graduates have pulled together a congruent image of the job. However, does this congruency of their professional goals and commitments come at a cost to their personal selves? According to the graduates, it most certainly does. When the extent that their work conflicts with their personal interests was examined, 45 percent of the women and 34 percent of the men experienced conflict "often" or "very often" and 33 percent of the women and 53 percent of the men "sometimes" experienced conflict. As discussed throughout this paper, "time demands" are the primary source of conflict.

One woman, in response to her work conflicting with personal interests wrote, "Are you kidding! I work, I raise two kids and I maintain our household—how much time can be left?" Another woman reported, "When there is simply not enough time, personal interests get sacrificed before family interests." And, one of the few women in this study who was not employed in the paid labor force wrote, "My 'work' is primarily raising the kids, with the exception of volunteer work on political campaigns or as director on a board. However, I've found that kids will eat up every available minute, often to the detriment of the parent's personal interests." Keeping this in mind, one can only imagine how those women with full-time careers and employment married to men with similar working commitments, experience time demands.

Time demands are also experienced by the men, as evident in this response, "There is just very little time to relax enough and do the personal things I like, and not take time from [my] wife and children." Another man indicated, "I can't read or play as much as I would like. I've had no time to learn golf and little time to travel."

In Hochschild's (1997) study of work and family "time binds" among the women and men employed at Americo, she asserted that the more women and men do what they do in exchange for money and the more their work in the public realm is valued and/or honored, the more, almost by definition, private life is devalued and its boundaries shrink (1997, 198–199).

Nevertheless, despite the conflict the graduates experience, whether it was with job changes, stress, or conflict with spouse or parental roles, most of the graduates had high levels of career satisfaction and continued to be employed in the legal profession. This holds true even when the vast majority of women and men experienced a high level of conflict with work and personal interests. Regardless, nearly half of the women and men were "very satisfied" with their family life today, and nearly one-third of both women and men were simply "satisfied" (see also Chambers 1987; Mattessich and Heilman 1990).

Perhaps the legal profession, and professions in general, which have incredible time demands and pressures—along with the socialization process at both the law school level and the professional level—drive and maintain the image of congruency. As a result, such congruency, as Lopata (1992) asserted, creates a strong commitment to the profession. This may be the only way to maintain the self, job, and the environment in order to maintain professional goals and commitments.

Hence, although the graduates cope daily with the stress and conflict of meshing their professional and personal lives, overall they are satisfied with the results and continue to be committed to their professional goals, evidenced by the fact that they generally do spend their time mainly on the job (see also Hochschild 1997).

Conclusion

Although the women and men graduates did equally well in law school, differences and similarities emerge in career and family experiences once outside of law school. An examination of the eight side bets revealed gender differences among the graduates that include: (1) men occupy different career positions, practice law in more diverse settings, and were more than twice as likely to have achieved partnership status in their firms; (2) dramatic differences emerged among three aspects of career satisfaction, with women being more dissatisfied with the prestige from their position, prestige in community and opportunities for advancement; (3) men were more involved in professional associations than women; and (4) men experienced spousal career support that is relevant to their career ambitions, goals, and advancements. The women, however, received more "tolerance," a positive attitude or supportive attitude toward their career commitments and goals. Moreover, when men did experience career hindrances from their wives, it was in the form of an "intolerance" of their long hours and frequent and extensive travel, a hindrance that is an attitude but not a direct barrier to career performance or advancement. The women, on the other hand, had hindrances that were the result of having the primary burden of child care and household responsibilities, hindrances that decrease the amount of time available for career commitments and obligations—a direct barrier to career performance and achievement.

The similarities among the women and men graduates appeared when men had children and wives who were employed full-time. These similarities include: (1) men who indicated having experienced work-related stress due to their attempt to balance work and family life; (2) men who reported their career hindrances were a direct result of having a wife who also had a career or was employed full-time; and (3) men who revealed that they experience stress because their professional obligations and commitments do not allow them to spend as much time with their families as they would have liked.

When examining career commitment of the women and men graduates, it may be concluded after looking at side bets that American society, the legal profession, and careers are not set up in such a way that women with spouse and child responsibilities can continue total professional commitment. So, although women can put all of their eggs in one basket for law school, afterward they have to withdraw some of them because of children and lack of cooperation and division of labor with a spouse. It appears, for the most part, that although the spouse is aware of and sympathetic to her needs, she is the one who adjusts her work schedule and shoulders the primary responsibility of the children.

This study indicates that women cannot maintain side bets as well and as easily as the men can. Many significant gender differences were rooted in child care/household responsibilities. This is an important issue, directly or indirectly, for most of the CWRU women and men graduates, especially since the vast majority have young children (infant, preschool, and early grade school age). Primary responsibility for family obligations and commitments has career consequences. As indicated in this study, most men tend to construct their lives around their jobs, while most women tend to construct their jobs around their personal lives.

The majority of the men do not experience the demands of child care/household responsibilities as being detrimental to their career opportunities and choices, but most women do. This could be because nearly one-third of the men have wives who are "homemakers," not currently employed in the paid labor force. As a result, the majority of the CWRU men are the sole career person and sole or primary source of income for their families. This puts less constraints on their time for professional responsibilities and obligations, which could put them at a professional advantage over most of their female counterparts in attaining positions of employment and salary. In turn, this places men at an advantage in maintaining the eight side bets.

Moreover, many women accepted restrictions on their careers if they came from their husbands. Not only are they not receiving support from their spouses, but they accept this. And for those women who receive career support, the vast majority are not getting the type of support they need, and what they get is not as relevant as the spousal career support received by their male counterparts. Therefore, this study suggests that career differences among women and men are not attributable to their law school experiences per se but to the lack of cooperation they receive from their spouses, and the workplace, for their family responsibilities and obligations.

While overall the graduates are relatively satisfied with their jobs, it is necessary to ask whether or not they will continue to he satisfied—as they appear to want to have *both* their family lives and their professional lives—if the profession continues to follow the traditional male career model of success, that is, for a woman with few, if any, responsibilities. This model appears to dissatisfy not only women but some men as well. Perhaps women and men may become increasingly dissatisfied if the legal profession fails to confront the idea that both women and men lawyers need to lead satisfying personal lives, and participate in their communities in addition to practicing law and remaining committed to their professional goals.

However, it should not be overlooked that CWRU women and men have similar high levels of career satisfaction. Perhaps women are, in their own ways, attempting to redefine the traditional male career model of success, making it mare conducive to fit their unique needs. Moreover, with the increase of men in solo firms, one can not help but wonder if they, too, are attempting to redefine the traditional male career model of success by defining success more on an individual level, as opposed to what is expected in the legal profession and in American society.

The overrepresentation of women in solo and large law firms reported by CWRU women and men deserves further attention. These differences suggest that while larger numbers of women have entered the practice of law and will continue to be employed in legal positions, the goal of fully assimilating women into the profession has not yet been met. The findings of this study suggest that a goal more conducive to full participation and maximum productivity of both women and men may be to integrate the unique needs identified in this study. After all, for many families, a mother in the paid labor force is not an option; it is necessary for economic survival. As revealed in this study, problems that have fallen solely on the shoulders of most women—the struggle of attempting to he accountable for both work and family responsibilities—are now being experienced by those men who also have a spouse employed in the paid labor force.

In conclusion, as Lopata (1992) contended, most men in modern America are expected to develop and maintain professional side bets. It has only been in recent years that men have needed to justify organizing their lives around their occupations. As evidenced in the literature, and as further indicated in the experiences of the CWRU women and men law school graduates, the occupational system continues to be a "greedy institution" with "greedy" commitments, demands, and expectations. Moreover, for many of the women, and for those men involved in dual-career or one career/two-paycheck marriages, the family is an equally "greedy institution" with equally "greedy" demands, commitments, and expectations of its own. Therefore, the degree of career commitment for most of the CWRU women and men is dependent upon the investment each makes in side bets in terms of self-concept and identities, and external contributions from the environment. Such investments help to maintain a continued involvement with their professional goals, which in turn dictate the strength of their professional commitment.

In other words, the differences in the careers of women and men are, to a great extent, a consequence of differences in whom they marry, child responsibility, and the type and degree of support women and men give each other in their career commitments and family/household responsibilities and obligations.

References

Abel, R. L. 1989. *American Lawyers*. New York. Oxford University Press.

American Bar Association Commission on Women in the profession. 1985. *Women in Law: Statistical Data*. Chicago: American Bar Foundation.

American Bar Association Commission on Women in the Profession. 1988. *Summary of Hearings ABA Mid-year Meetings*. Philadelphia, February 6–7.

_____. 1988. *Report to the House of Delegates*. Chicago, June.

Becker, H. S. 1960. "Notes on the Concept of Commitment." *American Journal of Sociology* 66: 32–40.

Becker, S., and J. Carper. 1956. "The Development of Identification with an Occupation." *American Journal of Sociology* 61: 289–298.

Chambers, D. 1987. "Tough Enough: The Work and Family Experiences of Recent Women Graduates of the University of Michigan Law School." Draft report, University of Michigan, Ann Arbor.

_____. 1990. "Accommodation and Satisfaction: Women and Men Lawyers and the Balance of Work and Family." *Law and Social Inquiry* 14: 251–287.

Coontz, S. 1997. *The Way We Really Are: Corning to Terms with America's Changing Families*. New York: Basic Books.

Coser, L., and R. L. Coser. 1974. "The Housewife and Her 'Greedy Family.'" In *Greedy Institutions*, edited by R. L. Coser, 89. New York: Free Press.

Coser, R. L., ed. 1974. *Greedy Institutions*. New York: Free Press.

Coser, R. L., and G. Rokoff. 1971. "Women in the Occupational World: Social Disruption and Conflict." *Social Problems*, Spring, 535–554.

Curran, B., and C. N. Carson. 1994. *The 1994 Lawyers Statistical Report*. Chicago: American Bar Foundation.

Epstein, C. F. 1971. "Law Partners and Marital Partners." *Human Relations*, December 24, 549–564.

Epstein, C. F. 1983. *Women in Love*. New York: Anchor.

Epstein, C. F., R. Stute, B. Oglensky, and M. Gower. 1995. "Glass Ceilings and Open Doors: Women's Advancement in the Legal Profession." *Fordham Law Review* 64, no. 2: 291–449.

Fritz, N. R. 1988. "In Focus: A Close-up Look at What's New in the HR Picture: Legal Equals?" *Personnel* 65: 45.

Gouldner, A. 1957. "Cosmopolitans and Locals: Toward an Analysis of Latent Social Roles—I." *Administrative Sciences Quarterly* 2: 281–306.

Gouldner, A. 1958. "Cosmopolitans and Locals: Toward an Analysis of Latent Social Roles—II." *Administrative Sciences Quarterly* 2: 444–480.

Hertz, R. 1986. *More Equal Than Others: Women and Men in Dual-Career Marriages*. Berkeley: University of California Press.

Hochschild, A. R. 1989. *The Second Shift.* New York: Viking.
_____. 1997. *The Time Bind.* New York: Metropolitan.
Hughes, E. C. 1963. "Professions." *Daedalus* 92: 665–668.
Kanter, R. M. 1978. "Reflections on Women and the Legal Profession: A Sociological Perspective." *Harvard Women's Law Journal* 1: 1–7.
Liefland, L. 1986. "Career Patterns of Male and Female Lawyers." *Buffalo Law Review* 35: 601–631.
Lopata, H. Z. 1992. "Career Commitments of American Women: The Issue of Side Bets." *The Sociological Quarterly* 34: 257–277.
_____. 1994. *Circles and Settings: Role Changes of American Women.* New York: State University of New York Press.
Lopata, H. Z., C. Miller, and D. Barnewolt. 1986. *City Women in America: Work, Jobs, Occupations, Careers.* New York: Preager.
MacCrate, R., ed. 1992. Legal *Education and Professional Development An Educational Continuum.* Student ed. New York: West.
Mattessich, P., and C. Heilman. 1990. "The Career Paths of Minnesota Law School Graduates: Does Gender Make a Difference?" *Law and Inequality* 9: 59–114.
Pearson, K. M. 1988. "Women and Men in the Legal Profession: Are the Scales of Justice Unbalanced?" Unpublished paper, University of Wisconsin–Milwaukee.
Pearson, K. M. 1990. "Illusions and Realities: An Examination of Women and Men Attorneys in Small Law Firms." Master's thesis, University of Wisconsin–Milwaukee.
Ritzer, G., and H. M. Trice. 1969. "An Empirical Study of Howard Becker's Side-Bet Theory." *Social Forces* 47: 459–479.
Schrimsher, K. P. 1996. "Professional Socialization, Career Patterns, and Commitments: A Gender Analysis of Law School Graduates." Ann Arbor, Mich.: UMI Dissertation Services.
Spangler, E. 1986. *Lawyers for Hire.* New Haven: Yale University Press.
Spencer, A., and D. Podorore. 1987. "Women Lawyers: Marginal Members in a Male-Dominated Profession." In *A Man's World: Essays ore Women in Male Dominated Professions,* edited by A. Spencer and D. Podomore. London: Tavistock.
Stanford Project. 1988. "Gender, Legal Education, and the Legal Profession: An Empirical Study of Stanford Law Students and Graduates." *Stanford Law Review* 40: 121–129.
Stebbins, R. 1970. "Career: The Subjective Approach." *Sociological Quarterly* 11: 32–49.
Stebbins, R. 1971. "The Subjective Career as a Basis for Redefining Role Conflict " *Pacific Sociological Review* 14: 383–402.
Teitelbaum, L., A. S. Lopez, and J. Gender. 1991. "Legal Education and Legal Careers." *Journal of Legal Education,* September-December, 443–481.
Vogt, L. 1986. "From Law School to Career: Where Do Graduates Go and What Do They Do?" Report prepared for Harvard Law School Program on the Legal Profession.
White, J. J. 1967. "Women in Law." *Michigan Law Review* 65: 1151–1122.
Wilinskey, H. 1964. "Careers, Lifestyles, and Social Interaction." *Social Sciences Journal* 12: 553–558.
"Women in the Profession: Accountants Should Share Lawyers' Fears." *Accountancy* 101: 11.

Discussion Questions

1. How does educational certification lead specifically to higher earnings?
2. Over time, what kinds of changes have women seen regarding the wage gap? What is meant by "real dollars" in the reading "The Wage Gap"?
3. According to Lois, how do rescuers manage their emotions differently, depending on their gender?

4. Do women and men consider the work of emergency rescue equally valuable to their sense of identity?
5. Why is looking at "side bets" important to how Schrimsher measures commitment to the profession of law?
6. Describe some examples of informal and formal support systems that would encourage men and women to stay committed to their chosen profession.

Part VI

PROBLEMS
ON THE JOB

"My boss propositioned me" is, unfortunately, not an infrequently heard comment. Sexual harassment is a troubling part of the working lives of men and women. Although perhaps always prevalent as more mixed-gendered work settings have become the norm in most fields, and as men and women in the contemporary spirit of open communication speak of these issues more willingly, sexual harassment at work has become a more frequently reported problem for men and women.

The first selection in this section, Linda Wirth's "Sexual Harassment," provides an excellent introduction and overview of the key definitions, issues, and data regarding sexual harassment. Wirth's discussion is placed in a global context, adding depth and breadth to the information.

This section also offers a real-life, somewhat sordid and brutal glimpse of sexual harassment in Betty Eisenberg's "Marking Gender Boundaries: Porn, Piss, and Power Tools." Women who work in the trades and in construction recount many open acts of assault, harassment, and sabotage.

The final chapter is a more optimistic look at the problem of sexual harassment. In "Resolving the Harassment Dilemma," Deborah Swiss suggests an array of concrete actions that can be used to fight and stop harassment, recommending that different resolutions and choices are appropriate for different individuals and situations.

The gender dynamics are complex in the case of sexual harassment. Although sexual harassment in this section focuses on women being harassed by male colleagues, other research and testimonials show that men are also victims of sexual harassment.

17

SEXUAL HARASSMENT

Linda Wirth

Sexual harassment is a new term to describe the age-old problem of unwelcome conduct of a sexual nature. It is a social phenomenon that can occur anywhere. The term "sexual harassment" was coined in the 1970s in the United States, which at that time began to recognize it as a specific type of conduct prohibited by the law. However, such behavior has also been given other names in the past in other parts of the world. More recently, in Japan the term *seku-hara* has been adopted. A Tanzanian report cites workers as saying: sometimes a supervisor will say or hint that he will be a bit lax on your reports if you are "good to him."[1] This chapter focuses on sexual harassment in the work situation.

While both women and men can be subjected to sexual harassment, more women suffer from it than men. In a number of countries, sexual harassment is regarded as a form of sex discrimination. This began in 1977 with a United States court case, which determined that sexual harassment constituted sex discrimination, reasoning that but for her womanhood (the complainant's) participation in sexual activity would never have been solicited. . . She became the target of her superior's sexual desires because she was a woman, and was asked to bow to his demands as the price for holding her job (reported in ILO 1992).

It is estimated in the United States that at least one out of every two women experiences sexual harassment at some point in her academic or working life (Fitzgerald and Ormerod 1991). It happens to women in their first job and to women who have been in the workforce for years. Women's groups in Malaysia point out that unwanted sexual attention is a form of sexual harassment often encountered by women in most public places. In such instances, one can ignore or walk away from it. But sexual harassment at the workplace is more disturbing—it becomes an irritant, a source of embarrassment and discomfort when encountered constantly. Under such circumstances, sexual harassment becomes a form of discrimination, as it can become a barrier to an individual's freedom of movement, full employment or opportunities at work.[2]

Over the past two decades, sexual harassment has been increasingly recognized as a common problem. It is considered a violation of human rights[3] and an affront to the dignity of the person. In particular, it is regarded as a manifestation of violence against women, an issue on which women's organizations in many countries are mobilizing.[4]

Sexual harassment at work has also been regarded as a contravention of obligations imposed by the law to be a good employer. According to the Commission of the European Union, as sexual harassment is a form of employee misconduct, employers have a responsibility to deal with it as they do with any other form of employee misconduct, as well as to refrain from harassing employees themselves. Since sexual harassment is a risk to health and safety, employers have a responsibility to take steps to minimize the risk as they do with other hazards (Commission of the European Union 1992).

There has been a steady growth in awareness of the serious consequences of sexual harassment for working women and for the achievement of equality. Awareness has also increased of the detrimental effects of sexual harassment on the efficiency of enterprises. Many countries have moved to legislate or are considering doing so.

The consequences of sexual harassment for the victim range from emotional stress resulting in feelings of humiliation, anxiety, fear, anger, anguish, powerlessness and depression, as well as physical reactions such as headaches, nausea, insomnia and high blood pressure (Fuentes et al. 1988). This in turn may cause increased absenteeism and lower productivity and can eventually lead to the person quitting the job (Danish Gallup Institute 1991). Refusal to grant sexual favors can mean failure to gain promotion. It can also be the reason behind the dismissal of many an employee whose work performance had formerly been satisfactory. For the enterprise, the cost of sick leave and employee turnover can be significant. Employers in those countries where court action may successfully result in awards for damages also run considerable financial risks if they do not put in place and enforce an explicit policy against sexual harassment.

The issue of sexual harassment is sensitive and difficult to address. When it occurs in the workplace, it is not so much a product of the working environment as a reflection of traditional social behavior between the sexes and of social attitudes towards women. It is extremely difficult for victims to complain about it without making their situation worse or for fear of losing their jobs. This is because sexual harassment in the workplace is not generally regarded as an employment issue, but rather as a "personal" problem between those involved. Without a policy explicitly indicating that sexual harassment will not be tolerated and that offenders will be sanctioned, would-be harassers may not even realize the harm they can cause not only to the victim, but also to the enterprise.

Sexual harassment is increasingly being recognized as a legitimate trade union concern, but the whole of the trade union movement is not yet fully at ease with the subject. This may be, as the Canadian Labor Congress acknowledges, because "there are situations in which one union member is harassed by another union member." Similarly, for employers sexual harassment is not an easy subject. A few years ago, employers tended to argue that sexual harassment is a question of individual behavior. Many employers are now recognizing it as a discipline problem, which can have detrimental effects on enterprise efficiency. With increasing awareness of the problem of sexual harassment, and of women's rights and the need to promote gender equality, it is also being increasingly recognized that much can be done by employers and trade unions at the workplace on this issue. Governments and nongovernmental organizations can also play an important role.

An attempt is made below to illustrate the importance of understanding what sexual harassment is and why it occurs. Secondly, it identifies practical ways of providing protection and of preventing the problem so that employees enjoy the right to a work environment free of sexual harassment. The chapter brings together data generated by a number of national reports on sexual harassment covering both the developed and the developing worlds.

What Is Sexual Harassment?

Sexual harassment has been defined in various ways. The definitions typically refer to unwanted conduct of a sexual nature, where either the rejection or imposition of such conduct can have negative employment consequences for the victim, as well as undesirable effects on the work environment. The Bureau of Women and Young Workers in the Philippines has, for example, identified two types of sexual harassment: sexual coercion and sexual annoyance. Sexual coercion has a direct consequence on the worker's employment status or the gain or loss of tangible job benefits. Sexual annoyance is sexually related conduct that is hostile, intimidating or offensive to the employee but has no direct links to any tangible job benefits or harm. This annoying conduct creates a bothersome work environment and the worker's terms and conditions of employment are dependent on the worker's willingness or capacity to endure that environment. This is especially experienced by women in nontraditional jobs.

In reviewing definitions of sexual harassment, the Bureau identified three forms: verbal, physical, and use of objects or pictures. Furthermore, the four basic components of sexual harassment were observed to be that: it is unwanted; it is repeated; it may be deliberate or done unconsciously; and it emphasizes a person's sexuality over her role as a worker.[5]

Some definitions clearly place the phenomenon of sexual harassment in the context of power relationships and/or sex discrimination. For example, the Organization of Tanzania Trade Unions (OTTU), in its sexual harassment policy and complaint procedure, defines sexual harassment as "one person(s) exercising power over another (others)." This includes: unwanted or unwelcome and unreciprocated behavior that is offensive to the recipient; unnecessary physical contact ranging from touching and patting through to rape; suggestive and unwelcome remarks or jokes, sexual propositions, unwanted comments on dress or appearance or verbal abuse of a sexual nature; leering and compromising invitations, display of pornographic pictures, suggestive movements and gestures, such as winking and touching; demands for sexual favors; physical assault and rape.[6]

The African Regional Federation of Commercial, Clerical, Professional and Technical Employees (AFRO-FIET), in a resolution on sexual harassment in November 1991, defined sexual harassment as any unwanted explicit or implicit, verbal or physical, sexual advances towards women workers in the workplace and in the trade union; sexual harassment is a hidden issue because it causes embarrassment and humiliation to women; and very few, if any, laws exist to protect women workers. Furthermore, "sexual harassment contributes to undermine the confidence of women, is a humiliating form of gender oppression of the worst kind and is a legitimate trade union issue" (AFRO-FIET 1991).

Definitions of sexual harassment at work can be classified into two types:

(i) a demand by a person in authority, such as a supervisor, for sexual favors in order to keep or obtain certain job benefits, be it a wage increase, a promotion, training opportunity, a transfer, or the job itself. In the United States this definition has been legally termed as quid pro quo sexual harassment (this for that), which involves a type of abuse of authority. Sometimes this type of sexual harassment is also referred to as "sexual blackmail."

(ii) unwelcome sexual advances, requests for sexual favors or other verbal, nonverbal or physical conduct of a sexual nature which interferes with an individual's work performance or creates an intimidating, hostile, abusive, offensive or poisoned work environment. In the United States this definition has been legally termed as "hostile working environment sexual harassment." (ILO 1992).

There is an increasing tendency to include both these dimensions in the formulation of legal definitions. However, sometimes only one form is used, as in the French legislation enacted in 1992, which included only the quid pro quo type. On the other hand, a Japanese court ruling in 1992 endorsed a definition of sexual harassment which refers only to the creation of a hostile work environment, and in 1993 the Labor Ministry in Japan recognized sexual harassment as "unpleasant speech or conduct with sexual references. that creates a difficult work environment" (*The Times* 1993).

The essential characteristic of sexual harassment as being conduct of a sexual nature that is unwanted by or unwelcome to the recipient distinguishes it from friendly behavior that is welcome and mutual. Determining whether such conduct is unwelcome or not has led courts in a number of countries to indicate that sexual harassment is conduct that the individual knew or ought to have known was unwelcome. More recently, courts in Canada, Switzerland, the United Kingdom, and the United States have opted for the "reasonable woman's" viewpoint as to whether the behavior was wanted or not, as it is women who mainly experience sexual harassment.

There are many kinds of verbal, nonverbal, and physical acts that may be considered sexual harassment. They vary according to cultural and social practices and the social contexts in which they occur. For instance, in some cultures physical touching upon greeting or communicating may be normal social behavior, while in other societies this would be interpreted as a sexual advance, whether wanted or not. Furthermore, in some traditions, a woman's explicit rejection of sexual advances may be regarded as a sign of her positive interest in the person making them. In some countries cultural difficulties still exist in understanding whether a woman finds a proposition of a sexual nature welcome or not. Thus, the Canadian Trade Union Congress supports the slogan No Means No, which is part of a national campaign to stem violence against women. In workplaces, the display of sexually suggestive posters would be tolerated by many workers and be considered by just as many others as offensive. A report on sexual harassment in Jamaica notes that "sexual by-play" makes sexual harassment a problematic issue in the Caribbean as it is an accepted part of communication styles between men and women.[7] Therefore it is not always easy to determine what is offensive and to whom. It is also often difficult for victims of sexual harassment to express their rejection of such behavior, because of fear or embarrassment.

Another issue in defining sexual harassment is whether the conduct has to be repeated to be considered as such. Usually, conduct of a sexual nature is regarded as harassment if it persists once it has been made clear that it is unwelcome. However, one incident may be regarded as sexual harassment if it is sufficiently serious, such as sexual assault or a demand for sexual favors in exchange for a job benefit.

The most common form of harassment reported by surveys is that involving unwelcome verbal comments, jokes, teasing, and propositions of a sexual nature. This is followed by unwanted physical touching and fondling. More serious forms of sexual harassment, while generally occurring to a lesser extent, can have particularly detrimental employment consequences for a significant number of victims. In the Philippines one survey reported that testimonies produced evidence of emotional stress, fear and voluntary job loss because of sexual harassment. The victims reported devastating economic effects, such as denied job promotions, poor job evaluation and job transfer. Seventy-five percent were harassed by supervisors or other individuals having direct influence on hiring, evaluation or promotion of the harassed women. Nineteen percent were harassed by coemployees, mostly in the form of verbal harassment.[8]

How Widespread Is the Problem?

In quite a number of countries, surveys have been conducted to determine the extent to which sexual harassment occurs, the groups that are typically affected, the profile of a harasser, the forms that harassment takes and its consequences. The validity of certain surveys, which up until now mainly emanate from the industrialized countries, can sometimes be questioned due to inadequacies of the samples, types of question posed, or the time frames used. Comparison between countries and cultures is also difficult owing to the widely varying survey samples and methodologies employed. The surveys nevertheless provide some insight into the nature and extent of the problem.

While estimated percentages vary considerably, a significant number of employees, the majority of whom are women, claim to have been sexually harassed. A study in 1988 commissioned by the Government of the Netherlands found that an overall 58 percent of women working in a small business, a large municipality, and an industrial company had experienced sexual harassment at work (ILO 1992). Similar results were obtained by a 1992 survey of 25 companies and international organizations in the city of Geneva in Switzerland (Bureau de l'egalite 1993). A government survey in Japan in 1993 showed that 26 percent of working women in Tokyo had suffered "at least one unpleasant sexual experience at work in the past two years" (*The Times* 1993). In the United States a survey of 23,000 federal employees in 1980 found that 42 percent of women reported some form of sexual harassment.[9] At the lower end of the scale, women reporting sexual harassment represented 11 percent of those surveyed in Denmark, 17 percent in Sweden, and 21 percent in France (ILO 1992).

A few surveys in developing countries also show that sexual harassment at work is a problem for many women workers. In Tanzania a survey of 10,319 women in 135 workplaces from 13 regions in 1988–1989 found that sexual harassment was a common problem affecting women workers. Sixty percent of the women indicated that sexual harassment occurred at their workplace and was so common that they did not report it.[10]

According to the Committee for Asian Women, in Thailand, women workers returning home from night shift in factories are at risk of being sexually abused, and some workers are sexually harassed by management and administrative staff. If the women refuse to give in, "they will be dismissed or harassed until they resign. Many employers deliberately select good-looking women when they recruit new workers" (Committee for Asian Women 1991).

In India, a study of indigenous women laborers in Bihar, India, describes the sexual exploitation of these women by their employers, contractors and coworkers as the greatest humiliation that these women are subjected to as a consequence of their extremely exploitative working conditions and lack of bargaining power. Rape and sexual abuse are common. Frequently the women are held in bondage and if they manage to escape it is not always possible to go back to their villages. Many end up in prostitution or just disappear altogether (Prasad 1988).

The results of some surveys would tend to suggest that the reported percentage of those experiencing sexual harassment is only the tip of the iceberg. There are more women who indicate that they know of others who have been sexually harassed than there are women who acknowledge having been sexually harassed themselves. In a Côte d'Ivoire radio program in early 1993, callers commonly indicated that while they had not been sexually harassed themselves, they all knew of women who had been victims. Similarly, in a survey in Japan in 1991 by the Tokyo Metropolitan Government, 51 percent of respondents reported having heard about sexual harassment cases.[11]

Given the reluctance and difficulties involved in making complaints, assessments made on the basis of the number of complaints filed in courts or made within enterprises or public administrations are only an indication of what is likely to be a more widespread phenomenon. The fact that sexual harassment is often viewed as a personal problem and not recognized as a legitimate labor issue, and the consequent lack of complaints' mechanisms make reporting the incidence of sexual harassment a heroic effort on the part of victims. Fear of losing one's job, of reprisals or making the workplace even more unbearable are very real obstacles for a victim of sexual harassment and, therefore, limit reporting.

Who Is Harassed and Who Harasses?

The link between the incidence of sexual harassment and women's relatively weak position in the labor market cannot be ignored. Sexual harassment of women workers is bound to persist while women occupy more precarious and lower-paid jobs than men. With economic restructuring in many countries and the subsequent rise in more precarious forms of employment, particularly for women, the problem of sexual harassment at work is likely to be exacerbated.

A number of surveys have identified the greater vulnerability of certain categories of women workers, such as those on precarious contracts, young women, single women, migrant workers and domestic workers. In addition, women working in sectors or occupations where women predominate or alternatively women working in traditional male jobs are also particularly at risk because of the imbalance between the sexes at the workplace. In some cases sexual harassment appears to occur least in situations where an equal number of men and women are employed in positions but more frequently when the traditional roles of men and women are challenged by women taking up employment in a traditionally male-dominated sector or when women are employed in higher-level positions.[12]

The Federal Human Rights and Equal Opportunities Commission in Australia has found that two-thirds of all cases heard by the Commission related to small businesses of under 100 employees. Over half of them involved sexual harassment. The complainants held mainly clerical and retail positions reflecting the occupations dominated by women. The Commission has also reported dealing with a number of complaints from male-dominated work areas, particularly by women promoted to a more senior level than many of the men.[13] In addition, 75 percent of the sexual harassment complaints that proceeded to a public hearing in Australia involved women under twenty years old. Young women are particularly vulnerable to sexual harassment in the workplace because of their age, inexperience, and limited knowledge of their rights and remedies (Elliot and Shanahan Research 1990). Over half had difficulties in finding employment prior to their harassment, and in most cases it was their first job.

The General Union of Workers in Spain found that women between 26 and 30 years old were more likely to be harassed than other age groups, given that this group of women combined what were regarded as important characteristics: youth and supposed sexual experience. Women who were separated, divorced, or widowed were not only more likely to be subject to sexual harassment, but they also experienced stronger forms of harassment (Fuentes et al. 1988). A survey of federal employees in the United States indicated that women have the greatest chance of being sexually harassed if they are single or divorced, between the ages of 20 and 44, have some university education, have a nontraditional job, or work in a predominantly male environment or for a male supervisor.[14]

Domestic workers are also among workers most exposed to sexual harassment. A Jamaican study in 1989 on domestic service reported sexual harassment as a problem, particularly for women from rural areas working in private homes in towns.[15] Studies in Indonesia and Sri Lanka have shown sexual harassment to be a serious problem for women from these countries working as domestic employees in the Middle East (ILO 1993). The Malaysian Trade Union Congress has reported a high incidence of sexual harassment of Filipina domestic workers in Malaysia.

In the Philippines, a report based on small surveys and reported incidents from labor unions concluded that sexual harassment exists in different work environments and can affect anyone—an ordinary worker, a professional, an executive, or an elected trade union official. However, there appeared to be a higher incidence of the problem in industries where physical appearance is important, such as in hotels, restaurants, banks, media, and entertainment; and in industries where women predominate, such as in garment and electronic manufacturing. A high incidence of sexual harassment has been observed in export processing zones, where male supervisors reportedly demand sexual favors from subordinates, mostly young and single women, in return for employment stability, promotion, or better working conditions.[16]

Sexual harassment may be perpetrated by a person in authority, such as a supervisor, or by a coworker or a client. Some surveys have not found significant differences between the representation of these groups. For example, in a French study the harasser was identified by 29 percent of the harassed women as the employer himself, by 26 percent as a superior, by 22 percent as a colleague, and by 27 percent as a client.[17]

A study of Zimbabwean women in industry noted that sexual harassment of women workers by male supervisors is becoming a problem. "Because women are in insecure and often casual positions, they are vulnerable to male supervisors who threaten them with dismissal if sexual favors are not granted." One woman organizer said that she had received numerous complaints from women, who, when seeking casual employment in industry, were bluntly told by male supervisors that jobs were only available to "those willing to provide favors" (Made and Lagerstrom 1985).

Consequences of Sexual Harassment

The effects of sexual harassment on the victim include emotional distress (stress, tension, feelings of humiliation and threat, depression, loss of self-esteem, absenteeism, and a decrease in productivity), and physical illness. Others include loss of employment benefits, dismissals, and resignations. In the Netherlands 25 percent of the harassed women claimed that there had been negative job effects, with a deterioration in the work environment and with some women actually leaving their job or transferring elsewhere.[18] A study in Germany found that 6 percent of the women interviewed had resigned from their job as a result of being sexually harassed. A Danish poll revealed that, in 17 percent of reported cases of sexual harassment, there was a change of workplace and, in 8 percent of cases, the women had been dismissed.[19]

In terms of financial loss to enterprises, a study of 160 companies in the United States in 1989 found that sexual harassment had cost the corporate employers an average of $6.7 million per year due to absenteeism, low productivity, and employee turnover (Husbands 1992).

An extremely serious consequence of sexual harassment that is beginning to be documented is the infection of victims with HIV and, therefore, AIDS and eventual death. This is particularly the case in those parts of the world where infection levels are high and where submission to sexual demands in the work context thus runs a high risk of HIV being transmitted.

Why Does Sexual Harassment Persist?

Sexual harassment has more to do with power relations than with sexual interest. For many it is a form of oppression, victimization, or intimidation based on relationships of power and authority. In some instances abuse of power is linked only to hierarchical rank, but in many countries women's groups, workers, and employers organizations and government agencies link abuse of power with the traditional status of women in society and observe that when harassed, a person's identity as a sexual being takes precedence over her identity as a worker.

On the other hand, fear of losing power or advantage can also be at the root of the harassing behavior. Fellow workers s may use harassment as an intimidation tactic to discourage women from applying for and working in traditionally male occupations. Sexual harassment can also be used to undermine the authority of women supervisors. A national trade union group (FNV) in the Netherlands points out that sexual harassment "is not a temporary phenomenon because men feel threatened in their status and authority by women's improved access to the labor market."[20]

The Fourteenth Conference of the Asian and Pacific Regional Organization of the International Confederation of Free Trade Unions, in August 1988, identified sexual harassment at the workplace as a "further discrimination suffered by women."[21] A study in the Philippines notes that "the existence of sexual harassment in the employment environment can be partly rooted in the society's concept of traditional sex roles. The notion which regards men as the economic providers and women as the inferior sex whose main role is tied to their reproductive capacities has produced inappropriate behavior among male workers in the workplace.[22]

In a survey by the Tokyo Metropolitan Government, 50 percent of respondents thought that sexual harassment occurred because women were not seen as equal partners; 21 percent put it down to lack of education on equality between men and women and 19 percent to women being seen as sex objects.[23] Sexual harassment also persists due to public opinion and lack of legal measures specifically sanctioning it as well as low levels of cases reported.

In 1983 a survey in the fish conservation industry in Peru found that "unsolicited sexual advances" generally involved men in a position of authority in the enterprise and that the silence around these incidents was due to the women's need to keep their jobs, the conviction of being unable to oppose, a superior and distrust and fear of the scorn of their colleagues.[24]

Combating Sexual Harassment

While sexual harassment has only fairly recently been recognized as a problem, there has been a remarkable response around the world in terms of awareness and adoption of legal and other measures within both public and private enterprises. Tackling sexual harassment, like many problems, involves changing social attitudes and perceptions, and is a long-term process covering the whole social and political spectrum and the adoption and enforcement of a range of measures.

Acknowledging the Problem

A first step is the recognition of sexual harassment in general as a problem, and in particular as a labor issue. National mass media and informal means of education have an important role to play in this respect. Recognition of the phenomenon of sexual harassment, in turn, contributes to its elimination. Initial court cases in countries often tend to attract media attention and start off a chain reaction.

A report from the Côte d'Ivoire, cited above, indicates that for legal protection from sexual harassment and effective enforcement, the laws need to be accompanied by an extensive awareness-raising campaign led by public authorities, employers, trade unions and human rights organizations to prevent and discourage the practice of sexual harassment. Such an effort should not be restricted to the modern economic sectors, but should extend also to rural areas and the informal sector where the majority of workers are to be found.

A number of government agencies, women's groups, and trade unions have conducted awareness-raising activities in their countries. They have produced leaflets and guidelines, and organized meetings and debates to make sexual harassment a subject for public discussion. Once the barrier of silence is broken, sexual harassment cases tend to be increasingly reported, as victims feel more encouraged to step forward.

Women's organizations have often initiated the launching of sexual harassment as a public issue in many countries. For example the European Association against all Forms of Violence against Women at work, based in Paris, aims to raise the awareness of enterprises and trade unions about the need for a policy to combat sexual harassment. It has also proposed texts for legislative reform in France and issues a periodical publication on sexual harassment and violence against women.

Similarly, in a number of developing countries this is occurring in the context of campaigns to combat violence against women. The Tanzanian Media Women's Association assisted in setting up a Crisis Centre on Sexual Harassment, Domestic Violence and Discrimination against Women and Children in Dar es Salaam. The Centre provides medical, legal, and counseling services to women and children: A Committee has also been established, with membership from different professional groups, that works for legal reform and focuses on stimulating people and groups to become aware of prejudice and discrimination. It identifies sexism as the root cause of violence against women and also promotes education about the problem using community radio, folk theatre, and popular educational materials.[25] Women's groups in the Philippines have published articles and conducted seminars and other activities to bring the issue to the attention of government, community organizations and the general public.[26] Trade unions have, in some cases, actually spearheaded national awareness-raising campaigns. For example, in 1988 the Malaysian Trade Union Congress launched a national campaign to combat sexual harassment, which received wide media coverage and to which the government has responded with a commitment to study possible legal measures. In Nicaragua, the Association of Agricultural Workers identified, in its 1993–1994 "plan of struggle," protection against sexual blackmail as an issue that should be included in the promulgation of a new labor code.[27]

In many countries, the mass media (television, radio, and newspapers) are already playing a crucial role in raising awareness of sexual harassment. It has even become a popular subject for filmmaking. In Sri Lanka sexual harassment has surfaced as an issue in video films and teledramas broadcast on the national networks.

Governments in several countries have initiated awareness-raising campaigns. In 1989–1990, the federal Human Rights and Equal Opportunities Commission in Australia launched a national media-based public awareness campaign targeted towards young women (SHOUT, Sexual Harassment is OUT). A campaign by the Belgian government involved the production of posters, stickers, pamphlets and information kits, which were sent to employers and workers in the public and private sectors, trade unions and women's organizations.[28]

Legal Protection

Major problems encountered in dealing with sexual harassment and sexual violence against women within the legal systems of many countries are the patriarchal concepts, unsympathetic judiciaries (the majority of whom may be men), the fact that the burden of proof rests on the complainant and the importance attached to the character of the victim. Moreover, in many countries discriminatory traditional customs are still in place, despite the fact that the statute books outlaw discrimination against women.

Quite a number of countries, however, have begun to adopt legislation which specifically addresses sexual harassment. This is particularly so in industrialized countries, although a few developing countries have recently begun to do likewise. In 1995, for example, both Costa Rica and the Philippines adopted laws specifically prohibiting sexual harassment. In the Caribbean, model legislation on violence against women has been prepared, with the assistance of the Commonwealth Secretariat, which includes the prohibition of sexual harassment.

Unless sexual harassment is explicitly recognized as a distinct legal wrong, labor laws that deal with sexual harassment indirectly through unjust dismissal cases are inadequate in addressing the problem. Similarly, criminal laws that treat sexual harassment as criminally indecent behavior are not particularly effective in addressing the problem owing to the strict requirements, for proving allegations. If sexual harassment remains a "hidden problem," the development of preventive measures will be hindered and victims will be discouraged from undertaking what can be lengthy and costly court procedures.

Depending on the national legal system, different types of law may be used explicitly to prohibit and actively prevent sexual harassment. These include equal opportunity, labor, tort, and criminal laws. Their implementation depends on the application of effective remedies and sanctions. Court cases can further interpret these laws or shape the law itself in countries with a common law legal system.

Equal opportunity laws which prohibit sex discrimination in employment have been used to provide protection against sexual harassment in a number of countries— Australia, Canada, Denmark, Ireland, Germany (Berlin), New Zealand, Sweden, the United Kingdom, and the United States. In a number of these countries sexual harassment is specifically mentioned in the statute, while in others courts have interpreted sexual harassment as a form of sex discrimination. In most of these countries, a victim of sexual harassment may find it easier to file a complaint because of the special procedures and institutional authorities that have been created under the equal opportunity laws. These may take the form of an equal opportunities or human rights commission, a board, an ombudsman or a commissioner (ILO 1992). In Puerto Rico a law adopted in 1988 specifically prohibits sexual harassment and recognizes it as a form of sex discrimination. The law makes the employer responsible for acts of sexual harassment in the workplace, whether committed by the employer or the employer's representatives or by supervisors and whether or not the particular acts were authorized or prohibited by the employer and independently of whether the employer knew or should have known of these acts. The law also provides for the award of financial compensation for damages and civil remedies whereby the employer could be ordered to promote or re-instate the employee and ensure that the sexual harassment ceases.[29]

Labor laws have been amended in a number of countries (Belgium, Canada, France, New Zealand and Spain) explicitly to prohibit sexual harassment. In Belgium the law directs the employer to protect workers against sexual harassment at work, including any actions of a verbal, nonverbal or physical nature which one knows or ought to know would offend the dignity of men and women employees. Canada's federal Labor Code states that all employees are "entitled to employment free of sexual harassment" (ILO 1992).

The 1992 Labor Code in the Dominican Republic provides that no employer may "commit any act against a worker which might be considered sexual harassment, or support or refrain from intervening in the event of his representative committing such an act."[30] In Namibia the 1992 Labor Act provides that a labor court may issue orders that unfair acts of harassment on the basis of the sex of an employee be discontinued or that the person harassing an employee perform or refrain from performing any acts specified in such orders.[31] The 1995 Anti-Sexual Harassment Act in the Philippines declares all forms of sexual harassment in employment, as well as in the education and training environment, unlawful.

Tort law can also afford protection against sexual harassment in most countries. A tort is a legal wrong, other than a breach of contract, such as a personal injury, for which a court can grant a remedy, most commonly in the form of damages and interest. Tort law encompasses both negligent acts resulting from carelessness or inattention, and intentional acts that can cause harm. Sexual harassment is by its nature an intentional act and would qualify as an intentional tort under most circumstances. Tort law has been found to prohibit sexual harassment in a number of countries (Japan, Switzerland, the United Kingdom and the United States). It can theoretically be applied to virtually all countries, except where a statutory scheme is the exclusive remedy, as in Canada (ILO 1992).

Criminal law, while also potentially applicable to sexual harassment, presents more difficulties in bringing a case to court, as the burden of proof is more substantial and in most countries the state prosecutor must decide whether the situation justifies bringing criminal action against the alleged harasser. This is the case in France, which has recently adopted a specific penal law on sexual harassment, designed to have general application to any abuse of authority involving requests for sexual favors (ILO 1992).

In a few countries the law requires positive action on the part of employers to prevent sexual harassment. In Sweden the equal opportunity law requires an affirmative action plan to be submitted annually by employers with more than ten employers; the plan should include an indication of what positive steps are to be taken to prevent sexual harassment in the workplace. The Canadian federal Labor Code requires employers, after consulting with the workers or their representatives, to issue a policy statement concerning sexual harassment. Belgian labor law also requires employers to adopt a policy against sexual harassment, and to institute certain procedures for complaints. French labor law has a provision that allows the works Safety, Health and

Working Conditions Committee to propose measures to prevent sexual harassment (ILO 1992).

To establish legal protection for victims of sexual harassment, it is logical that legal definitions be formulated so that legal action can be effectively pursued. Such definitions may be included in legal texts which specifically seek to prohibit, prevent or sanction sexual harassment, or may be defined in case law as a consequence of civil, labor, or penal court proceedings.

In a number of countries sexual harassment has been recognized and defined by a court decision (Australia, Canada, Ireland, Switzerland, the United Kingdom and the United States at federal and state levels). For example, the Supreme Court of Canada has broadly defined sexual harassment in the workplace as "unwelcome conduct of a sexual nature that detrimentally affects the work environment or leads to adverse job-related consequences for the victims of the harassment. . . When sexual harassment occurs in the workplace, it is an abuse of both economic and sexual power. . . Sexual harassment in the workplace attacks the dignity and self-respect of the victim both as an employee and as a human being."[32]

In most of the industrialized countries that have not enacted specific legislation on sexual harassment, it has been defined by implication as an activity which is in violation of a statute covering a subject other than sexual harassment, such as unfair dismissal, negligent or intentional acts causing harm, or criminal behavior (ILO 1992). This is also the case for some developing countries such as Brazil and Tanzania.

Enforcement problems can arise when laws against sexual harassment are passed without providing a legal definition. This is the case in Peru. The passage of proposed laws to address sexual harassment can also be delayed as a result of difficulties in defining sexual harassment or due to differing opinions as to which aspects should be legislated for. For example, in Argentina a number of draft laws addressing sexual harassment have been unsuccessfully tabled in Parliament during recent years.[33]

Legal definitions may be very specific and detailed as to the type of behavior constituting sexual harassment. One problem with listing the types of conduct prohibited is that this may be limiting, and other acts which could also amount to sexual harassment may go unrecognized as such.

On the other hand, legal definitions may employ broad terms to refer to the actual behavior and focus more on the employment consequences of unwanted conduct of a sexual nature. For example, the United States Equal Employment Opportunities Commission, the federal agency responsible for the enforcement of Title VII of the Civil Rights Act, which deals with employment discrimination, defines sexual harassment as a form of sex discrimination and indicates that unwelcome sexual advances, requests for sexual favors and other verbal or physical conduct of a sexual nature constitute sexual harassment when (1) submission to such conduct is made either explicitly or implicitly a term or condition of an individual's employment, (2) submission to or rejection of such conduct by an individual is used as the basis for employment decisions affecting such individual, or (3) such conduct has the purpose or effect of unreasonably interfering with an individual's work performance or creating an intimidating, hostile, or offensive working environment.[34]

Combating sexual harassment successfully through law depends also on how legal enforcement of such measures is undertaken. In this respect the issues of liability, complaint procedures, relief and damages for the victim and penalties need to be addressed. The issue of liability is important both from the point of view of potential damages which can be claimed and for its preventive effects. The Canadian Human Rights Act refers to the "liability of the person" which can include both the employer and the alleged harasser, while the Canadian Labor Code indicates that the employer has a responsibility to "make every reasonable effort to ensure that no employee is subjected to sexual harassment."

Procedures that allow the filing of sexual harassment complaints with the minimum of delay, cost and embarrassment are extremely important to facilitate the coming forward of victims. Such procedures also help more data to be collected on the nature and extent of the problem of sexual harassment and encourage its prevention.

Finally, the possibility for victims of sexual harassment to obtain monetary damages is important to compensate for any financial loss as a result of dismissal or missed promotion, as well as for injury to feelings and humiliation suffered. In the United States damages can amount to $100,000 or more, although smaller amounts are also common. In most other countries awards have been relatively small, of $10,000 or less, although theoretically they could be larger, particularly under unjust dismissal claims that often provide for six months' salary to be paid.

Courts may also order cessation of the harassment or action to repair harm caused, or both. Sanctioning of the harasser by transfer, demotion, temporary suspension or dismissal is usually the prerogative of the employer, although courts may determine whether to uphold this right or not in the case of dispute. Courts can also impose fines or prison sentences or both. The awarding of damages and/or the imposition of penalties are significant elements in combating sexual harassment at work as they can encourage victims to speak out and provide a stimulus for employers to take preventive action.

Conclusion

In many parts of the world sexual harassment has now been recognized and measures taken to combat it. However, progress is uneven and much effort is still required to mobilized governments, employers' and worker's organizations to address this "occupational hazard." While laws can do much to provide a framework for action, it is public opinion and changes in social attitudes towards women that will eventually have the greatest impact on eradicating sexual harassment. Recognizing the phenomenon of sexual harassment as harmful to victims, enterprises and society is the first and most important step, as well as probably the most difficult. A major shift in consciousness is needed to ensure that sexual harassment at work is not perceived as a trivial and personal matter and that it is treated as an act of sex discrimination and an unacceptable condition of work. Raising awareness in schools, universities and other educational institutions is of strategic importance for setting the stage later on in workplaces and social structures.

Acting on the problem of sexual harassment must include providing avenues for the victim of sexual harassment to complain without fear of retaliation or ending up as the accused through the stringent tests involved in proving allegations. Appropriate work-place complaint procedures are an ideal way to provide such guarantees. Legislation and government agencies can go a long way in assisting complainants where solutions cannot be found within the enterprise. Special attention will need to be given to devising ways of reaching women most vulnerable to sexual harassment.

Notes

1. Women and Youth Directorate, Organization of Tanzania Trade Unions, "Protection against sexual harassment at work in developing countries," Tanzanian country paper prepared for the ILO, September 1993.

2. Selangor Consumers Association, Women Graduates Association, Women's Aid Organization, Young Women's Christian Association, and the Malaysian Trade Union Congress Women's Section.

3. United Nations, Declaration on the Elimination of Violence Against Women, New York, A/RES/48/104, General Assembly, 20 December 1993.

4. Selangor Consumers Association, Women Graduates Association, Women's Aid Organization, Young Women's Christian Association, and the Malaysian Trade Union Congress Women's Section.

5. "Women: Where do you go from here?" *Philippine Labour Review* (Manila), January-June 1991.

6. Women and Youth Directorate, Organization of Tanzania Trade Unions, "Protection against sexual harassment at work in developing countries," Tanzanian country paper prepared for the ILO, September 1993.

7. "Measures to prevent sexual harassment in Jamaica," country paper prepared for the ILO, August 1993.

8. Country monograph on sexual harassment in the Philippines, prepared for the ILO, October 1993.

9. U.S. Merit Systems Protection Board, "Sexual harassment in the federal workplace: Is it a problem?" Washington: U.S. Government Printing Office, 1981.

10. Women and Youth Directorate, Organization of Tanzania Trade Unions, "Protection against sexual harassment at work in developing countries," Tanzanian country paper prepared for the ILO, September 1993.

11. Tokyo Metropolitan Government, Koyo biyodo o kangaeru 5: Sexual harassment he nanda ro? (Thinking about equal employment no. 5, What is sexual harassment?); Koyo biyodo o kangaeru 6: Romu kanritoshiteno sexual harassment (Thinking about equal employment No. 6: Sexual harassment. A labour relations issue), March 1992.

12. Study commissioned by the Dutch government and conducted by the University of Groningen. Information on sexual harassment in the Netherlands reported to the ILO by Alie Kuiper, May 1992.

13. Information reported to the ILO in 1992 by Quentin Bryce, Australian Federal Sex Discrimination Commissioner at the time.

14. United States Merit Systems Protection Board, 1981, "Sexual harassment in the federal workplace: Is it a problem?" Washington: U.S. Government Printing Office, 1981.

15. "Measures to prevent sexual harassment in Jamaica," country paper prepared for the ILO, August 1993.

16. Country monograph on sexual harassment in the Philippines, prepared for the ILO, October 1993.

17. Secretariat d'Etat aux droits des femmes et a la consommation, 1991, Le bareelement sesuel enquete aupres des frangais Perception, opinions et evaluation du phenomenon (Sexual harassment: Survey of the perceptions and opinions of the French and evaluation of the phenomenon), Paris.

18. Study commissioned by the Dutch government and conducted by the University of Groningen. Information on sexual harassment in the Netherlands reported to the ILO by Alie Kuiper, May 1992.

19. 1991 survey of approximately 1,350 women by the Danish Gallup Institute. Information reported to the ILO by Hanne Petersen and Gitte Mogensen, February 1992.

20. Women's Secretariat, FNV.

21. Resolution of the Fourteenth Conference of the Asian and Pacific Regional Organization of the International Confederation of Free Trade Unions, meeting in Bangkok, Thailand, August 4–6, 1988, on the Promotion of Equality in Employment and Development for Women, in Asian and Pacific Labour, July-August 1988.

22. Country monograph on sexual harassment in the Philippines, prepared for the ILO, October 1993.

23. Tokyo Metropolitan Government: Koyo biyodo o kangaeru 5: Sexual harassment he nanda ro? (Thinking about equal employment, no. 5, What is sexual harassment?); Koyo biyodo o kangaeru 6: Romu kanritoshiteno sexual harassment (Thinking about equal employment, no. 6: Sexual harassment A labour relations issue), March 1992.

24. M. Barrig, M. Chueca, and A. M. Yanez, 1984, *Anzuelo sin carnada. Obreras en la industria de conserva de pescado*, Lima.

25. The Committee against Sexual Harassment, "Domestic Violence and Discrimination against Women and Children," Dar es Salaam, Tanzania, October 1991–May 1992.

26. Country monograph on sexual harassment in the Philippines, prepared for the ILO, October 1993.

27. Resolution of the Association of Agricultural Workers, VIII Assembly of the Movement of Agricultural and Livestock Women Workers for Employment, Property and Equality. Not a Step Backwards, 6–7 March 1993, Managua.

28. Secretaire d'Etat a l'emancipation sociale, 1986, 'Sex collegue Ex-collegue: Un dossier sur le harcelement sexuel sur les lieux de travail', Brussels. 29. Act No. 17, 22 April 1988, Puerto Rico. 30. Dominican Republic, Section 47(9), Act Negating the Labour Code.

29. Act 17, 22 April 1988, Puerto Rico.

30. Dominican Republic, Section 47 (9), Act 16-29, 29 May 1992, promulgating the Labour Code.

31. Labour Act, 1992 (Act 6 of 1992), dated Gazette of the Republic of Namibia, 8 April 1992.

32. Janzen v. Platty Enterprises, 1989. op. cit.

33. Clarin, Buenos Aires, 17–23 August 1993.

34. 45 Federal Register 74,677 (10 November 1980) codified in 29 Code of Federal Regulations (CFR) Section 1604.11(a).

References

AFRO-FIET. 1991. Resolution on Sexual Harassment. Regional Women's Seminar for English-speaking Africa, Lusaka, Zambia, 11–14 November.

Bureau de l'égalité. 1993. *Harcèlement sexuel la réalité cachée des femmes au travail* (Sexual harassment: The hidden reality of women at work), Geneva.

Commission of the European Union. 1992. "Recommendation on the Protection of the Dignity of Women and Men at Work and Code of Practice on Measures to Combat Sexual Harassment." *Official Journal of the European Communities* 35, no. 49 (Brussels), February.

Committee for Asian Women. 1991. *Many Paths, One Goal: Organizing women workers in Aria, Hong Kong.*

Danish Gallup Institute. 1991. Survey of approximately 1,350 Women, Copenhagen.

Elliot and Shanahan Research. 1990. "Young Women in the Workplace: An Awareness and Attitude Survey, Sexual Harassment," in Pemberton Advertising, North Sydney.

Fitzgerald, L., and A. Ormerod. 1991. "Breaking silence: The sexual harassment of women in academia and the workplace." In F. Denmark and M. Paludi, eds., *Handbook of the Psychology of Women.* New York: Greenwood.

Fuentes, M. C., et al. 1988. *Discriminaciyn y acorn sexual a la mujer en el trabajo* (Discrimination and sexual harassment of women at work). Madrid, Fundacion Caballero.

Husbands, R. 1992. "Sexual Harassment Law in Employment: An International Perspective." *International Labor Review* 131, no. 6.

Made, P., and B. Lagerström. 1985. *Zimbabwean Women in Industry.* Harare: Zimbabwe Publishing House.

Prasad, S. Sahay. 1988. *Tribal Women Laborers: Aspects of Economic and Physical Exploitation.* New Delhi: Gian Publishing House.

The Times. 1993. 20 October, London.

WASH. 1990. *Sexual Harassment of Women in the Workplace: A Guide to Legal Action.* London: Women against Sexual Harassment.

18

MARKING GENDER BOUNDARIES
Porn, Piss, Power Tools

Betty Eisenberg

I don't worry about the ones who say things to me. That quiet person with that very controlled anger is the one I worry about. You can feel the anger, they don't have to voice it, you know it's there.
    And those are sometimes the ones who try to be the nicest to you. You have to watch them.

—Gay Wilkinson, Boston

Close to eleven on a Friday morning, the steward was walking around the forty-four-story job collecting $2 each from the roughly sixty electricians on the site to celebrate the general foreman's fiftieth birthday with a drinking party in the shack. The party would start at lunchtime and extend into the afternoon. A stripper would be performing.

I was, at that point, less than a year out of my time.

Several of the new journeywomen in my local, including myself, and several of our business agents had only recently gone through a training together on sexual harassment. Earlier that week a highly publicized rape in the Boston area—on a poolroom table at Big Dan's Tavern—had called public attention to sexual violence. And it was the same week as International Women's Day. Ignoring the situation didn't feel like an option.

The steward told me that I didn't have to contribute or come to the party. I countered that, if the steward was organizing a celebration of the GF's birthday, it should be done so that everyone could participate. And I explained why I didn't think there should be a drinking party with a stripper on a union jobsite. "Just because we have to take you in," the steward said, "doesn't mean anything has to change because you're here."

I knew I didn't want to go to the party or be working on the job that afternoon. I told my foreman I was going home. Before leaving, I called the union hall and told my business agent that I was walking off the job and why. He asked what the other two female electricians there thought. I said that since both were apprentices and more vulnerable, I hadn't talked with them. He explained that, given how late it was, there wasn't really anything he could do. I said I understood. And I went home. Expecting the party to go on.

Monday morning on the bus ride to work, I learned from a woman plumber who worked on the site that, after I'd left on Friday, my business agent had asked the steward to cancel the party and return everyone's money. My breath caught. I was surprised and impressed that the hall had acted, but I knew there would be retribution.

—Susan

On jobsites the behavior of those in authority—the foreman or general foreman representing the contractor (though they are also union members) and the steward representing the union—set a tone and an example for the crew to follow, and strongly affected a tradeswoman's sense of her welcome and safety. On her first job as an apprentice carpenter Lorraine Bertosa felt protected.

I remember my first foreman literally saying to the guys, "Watch how you talk." He said that in the first week I was on the jobsite. He was one of these guys that felt confident himself, wasn't out to prove anything. It was fine that women were there. A really unbelievable guy to get as a first foreman. If you were willing, then he was willing to meet you halfway He would say to the guys, "Don't talk like that. You can't talk like that around here" (cuss words, certain things they were saying). I think that pressure came directly from the office, from the contractor. We want to keep these women.

Where contractors and unions did not make such a clear commitment to "keep these women," new tradeswomen were less fortunate. Coworkers, foremen, or stewards who felt that women did not belong in the industry at times expressed that opinion through words, actions, or silence. Before affirmative action brought government support for a more diverse workforce, harassment, ranging from petty to criminal, had been a standard means to discourage those who strayed across the industry's gender and racial boundaries. It did not end when the government regulations began.

Tradeswomen were sharp observers, and most perceived themselves to be on their own in handling any hostility. They worried that requesting assistance could as likely bring retribution as help. Given the imbalance of power, many women put blinders on, kept their focus on the day's work, and waited for a bad situation to end by itself. Women, especially those unfamiliar with the safety practices of tools and equipment, were particularly vulnerable on their first jobs. Not only were they green, but they were not yet sworn into union membership. Probationary periods could range from a few months to two years, for those entering under special affirmative action guidelines. Kathy Walsh was sent driving on a wild goose chase looking for the foreman on her first day at work—hazing that might have happened to any new apprentice. But on her second day, when she knew where she was going, the ironworker who'd verbally expressed his resentment about having a woman on the job expressed those feelings again, this time physically.

> Everybody parked up on top of this embankment. It was about forty feet down to where we were working, very steep, and it was muddy and slippery. An ironworker pushed me from behind. And I slid most of the way down that embankment face first.
>
> Getting up from there—I can't remember whether I was crying or not, if I wasn't I was almost—and getting the mud off of my face and out of my tool pouch and going to work that day was one of the hardest things I'd ever done at that point. Mark, the guy that was nice to me, was like so nice to me that day. He gave the guy shit about it, and he came down as quick as he could and helped me get up. At the end of the day he said, "I don't know anybody that wouldn't have walked away at that point. You just keep it up, and fuck these guys." My first day I slammed my hand in the car door. My second day I went down face first down a muddy forty-foot embankment.
>
> The job lasted for about two weeks. They laid me off and I was like—uh. I think I made it back to my car before I started crying.
>
> —Kathy

Loyalty by trade is very strong in construction. Workers generally spend coffee breaks and lunch: carpenters with carpenters, ironworkers with ironworkers, painters with painters. For a journeyman of one trade to push down an apprentice of another trade is highly unusual, because normally, the full crew would rally to defend their apprentice. Attacks on women put men in the position of choosing between male bonding and union or trade solidarity. Only one of the carpenters came to Kathy's assistance. When she reported back to her apprenticeship coordinator after the layoff, she never mentioned the ironworker's action, or the tacit approval of most of her crew. "I was totally intimidated by the whole process, all of it. We didn't even join the union until we had at least 6,00 hours in."

The behavior of the union representatives a tradeswoman happened to encounter was critical to shaping her expectations of whether or not the union would assist her in handling harassment or discrimination. Although MaryAnn Cloherty would return to union construction years later and complete her apprenticeship with a different local, she quit the first time around. She was a second-year apprentice on a job where having a steward on the site only added to her problems.

> There was a lot of pornography on the job, and when I would complain about it they would take it down and they would put up more. Crotch shots, legs spread, blown up. I mean there was a crotch shot that was blown up that was at least three feet by five feet. I walked by it for three days, I didn't know what it was. I did not know what it was until I was on the other side of the picture and I saw a whole series of porno shots. I realized what the other shot must be. That was when I complained.

The offending stuff came down. And then the next day the whole jobsite was littered with it.

There was a union steward who was the worst offender. I really felt like there was nowhere to go. My steward when I first arrived on the job said, "Put your tools over here." After I put my tools down he said, "One thing you got to understand is, I used to throw gooks from helicopters in Vietnam." I didn't know what was that supposed to mean to me. I think he was trying to scare me or intimidate me or paint himself as a big ogre. I didn't really think I could relate to this guy.

A skilled construction worker must be able to climb scaffolding, use power tools, lift heavy objects, and perform countless other tasks that are inherently dangerous. But like driving a car on a freeway, they can be accomplished with relative safety given proper training, support, and equipment. Just as a student driver wouldn't feel comfortable in high-speed traffic accompanied by a driving instructor who was threatening, someone learning to splice live wires, walk an I-beam, or maneuver their way through the obstacle course of a construction site needed to trust their supervision in order to focus on the actual task at hand.

As a first-year apprentice plumber in Boston, Maura Russell was sent to a new building under construction, a good opportunity to see a project from the ground up. On the crew, though,

One guy was really a very sick fella. One day we were both carrying a length of 6- or 8-inch cast iron pipe. It was a stage of the underground, and he was on one end and I was on the other. We were carrying it from one place to a trench on another part of the job. We were walking by this one big pit that had all this rebar, reinforcing bar, sticking up in various patterns because they were going to be pouring a floor and also have some starts for some columns.

He gave me a shove with that pipe so that I went down into that pit with the pipe, which is heavy pipe. And it was really lucky—luck had a lot to do with it— that I landed on my feet, still holding the pipe. That I did not end up in a perforated sandwich, with the pipe on top of me, landing on a lot of that rebar which was vertical. I can still see him standing at the top of that pit with his little Carhartt jacket and reflector shades and Arctic CAT hat looking down. And with his little psycho voice saying, "Gotta watch out. You could get killed around here."

He was really creepy.

I'd be pouring lead in a pit, in a trench. It's a sunny day. This is totally outside. All of a sudden, cloud. And there'd be this Dick (which was his name, actually) totally bending over me, blocking the sun and whispering in my ear in his little creepy voice, "Watch out that you don't get any water in that lead. It could pop up and you'd get a face full of lead and, that wouldn't be too pretty, would it?"

Rather than bring the danger she felt from this journeyman to the attention of any authority, Maura just dodged him as best she could. She recognized the box he had her in—it was her word against his. And what's wrong with his warning her to be careful?

And who wouldn't believe that a green girl apprentice simply lost her balance carrying heavy pipe?

Women who had no reason to perceive the union as offering them protection, but were still committed to staying in the trade, often chose not to report even very serious harassment. Karen Pollak had applied to several Kansas City unions over the years before affirmative action regulations created an opening in the Carpenters. Having learned the trade from her grandfather, she passed the journeyman's test. She was allowed to enter as a first-year apprentice. Despite the opportunity to hire a skilled mechanic at apprentice rate, it was a year before a contractor would hire her. On her first day on the job as an apprentice carpenter, she could have reported her treatment to the union. Or to the police. Committed to keeping the job, she chose instead the silence she felt was required.

Since none of the carpenters wanted to work with her, Karen was partnered with a laborer who was "none too happy to be working with me. He was trying to do everything he could to drive me crazy. I lost him for several hours in the afternoon. I couldn't find him." Assigned to put in insulation at the edge of the building, Karen was given a safety belt that was too large for her. She eventually just left it "hooked up onto one of the lines, but it was laying over the edge of the floor." When the superintendent found her still working later that afternoon, he told her he'd assumed she'd fallen and died. While the super was admonishing her for not wearing the belt,

I look down and the laborer that I was paired up to was taking a sledgehammer and just demolishing my little red Volkswagen. It was like, "What did I do?" Well, he explained to me that we don't drive Communist cars onto union parking lots.

I couldn't leave my tools at work, because the gang boxes were full. I'm over in the middle of nowhere, with no way to get home and I can't leave my tools. So I just put my toolbox on my shoulder and we hitched a ride. This farmer picked me up alongside of the road about a half mile from the jobsite. I got home, though, several hours later than I should have. And the husband was real upset. He was like, "Where's your car?" That was the nicest car that we owned. "Well, we don't have it anymore." "What do you mean, we don't have it anymore?" And then I explained. And it was like, "Well, you have to press charges against this guy. You can't let him do this shit to you." "No, I can't do that. You don't understand. I will get pushed off the—building. You can't do those things."

I eventually got it towed home. We used parts off of it. I had nice seats and a nice shifter. But as far as the car—he had taken a cutting torch and cut the frame. I would assume it would have to be on work time, because I had the car at lunchtime. When I went back to work from lunch, it was fine.

After getting chewed out by this superintendent because I had left my safety belt and it was hanging over the edge of the floor and he thought that I had died, it was like, "Did you even go down to see if I was there?" "No, I just figured I'd worry about it when I got down there." Well, that told me where I stood. So that's why I was not going to press charges on my little Volkswagen. We just gritted our teeth and went on and bought a really old Volkswagen, and took and drove it to work. But from then on I parked it two or three blocks away from the jobsite.

These were real strong-valued people. It was not a union-made car and it represented to them, definitely I had to be a communist. I was driving a Volkswagen. I was a woman wanting to be a carpenter. So I had to be. That was my first day of work. Welcome to the real world.

Asking for help was not necessarily a more useful response, as Yvonne Valles learned. Attracted by the opportunity to work with her hands and the hope that she'd be able to buy a home once she made a journey level painter's salary, she was an eager first-year apprentice. She joined painters hanging vinyl wallpaper at a hotel in Los Angeles, and within the first two weeks faced harassment from her foreman.

I'm still kind of traumatized by the second job I got. The foreman on the job was a real jerk. Him and a couple of the other painters would always be talking real dirty about women all the time. They used to leave magazines of naked women in the bathroom that I'd use. They'd leave the book wide open and it would show. They'd think it was funny. They were harassing from day one.

There was a young kid apprentice that was about 18 years old. My foreman used to talk verbally abusive to him, call him a dickhead and all kinds of names. With me, I heard him making a crack one time, called me a dyke. Anyway, he was always bragging on breaks. He'd be talking to the guys, but I could overhear him because we'd eat in the same room. I mean, where was I going to go eat lunch? He used to pick up prostitutes. He'd be saying, I'm going to see so-and-so tonight.

One day, I was hanging up some wallpaper and he came to me. I was kneeling down. He goes, "Hey, you want to see some pictures of my girlfriend?" And I said, "No." He said, "Oh, come on, I'm training her to be an apprentice, too. Don't you want to see some pictures of how I train my apprentices?" I said, "No, why don't you just leave me alone?"

So anyway, I was kneeling down, spreading the wallpaper on the walls. All of a sudden he stuck a Polaroid picture in front of my face and he goes, "Look." And I looked. And he starts laughing.

It was a picture of a young woman laying down with her legs open and she had what they call in wallpapering a seam roller. It's got a little handle with the roller on it, you lay the seams down flat with that to get the air bubbles out. She had the handle inside her vagina. And he starts, "Yeah, that's how I train my apprentices."

Oh, man. I just said, "Get out of here, I don't want to see that!" I was really upset. I went home that day and I called the apprenticeship school and I told the head of the apprentice school, "I got a problem on the job. I'm being harassed and I just want you to know what's going on."

I told him about it, and I started crying 'cause I was really humiliated. He says, "Oh, gee, I'm sorry," and "That asshole," and he goes, "Yvonne, it's not always going to be like that." He says, "I'll talk to him."

But nothing ever happened. He had told me too, "You know, Yvonne, I can report this but it might not be good for you."

I said, "Well, there's only one thing I'm afraid of. I've heard that women that file lawsuits against their companies, they end up getting blackballed. I wouldn't want to have that mark against me." He said, "That's true, that could happen."

They don't care. They want to discourage you. It's like contractors have this attitude, from what I've heard, if a woman sues them—fine, they won't hire any more women at all.

I hated that guy. He was disgusting. He used to ask me if I'd want to snort some cocaine with him after work. I just kept my mouth shut because I needed the job. I needed to pay my rent, so I just tolerated it.

Any new worker wants to make the workplace more comfortable by developing congenial relationships with coworkers. Yet as Melinda Hernandez, a new electrical apprentice learned, friendliness could set off an invisible minefield.

On that job there was an apprentice—he wasn't a piece of shit, he was *the* piece of shit of life, the lowest of the low. But I didn't know this, see. He came off very nice. He happened to be Puerto Rican, too.

And he says, "Oh, it's nice to have a girl working side by side, why don't we hang out one day? We'll go out to dinner after work." So I didn't know. "It's just dinner. What's the big thing? What, are you afraid of me or something?" But he came off very nicely, so I said, all right. Maybe I can make a friend, you know, in the industry starting out.

So we went to dinner, and after dinner he wanted to go out dancing or whatever. And I said, "No, you know, I told you that I have someone, that I'm involved."

To make a long story short, that Monday we went to work, I think he told everybody what every man wants to hear—that we got intimate (and that's a very refined word coming from this character, okay). He did me, you know.

He became very nasty, openly, verbally cursing a lot, talking about who he screwed the night before to the men. And I'm sitting in the men's locker because the women weren't given their own locker. One day he actually brought in pornographic material, pictures that he had taken of a woman close up, with a flashlight. The reason I know this was because he was describing to them the pictures when I was in the room. And they were laughing. But none of them ever took a stand. I thought in their minds they figured, Well, it's not my daughter, or it's her own kind, it's a Puerto Rican just like her doing it to her. It's not us. Whatever it was, they justified it. Nobody ever said anything. And I remember there was a guy in the room that was sitting in the corner, he was a born-again Christian, reading a Bible.

I got up and I walked out, I just stepped out of the room. I realized that I was in for a long haul, because that was my first job. Wow, you know, what a drag. But I hoped. I had high hopes that things would get better.

Family support was key for Cheryl Camp when she faced hostility on her second job. The knowledge that her union rotated apprentices to a different shop every six months meant that even if treatment didn't improve, it would at least end. And the fact that men on her first job had been particularly supportive helped her ride through the hard times.

> There was an electrician on the job, a younger guy, too. And a minority, he was black. He went out of his way to harass me. It really irritated him to know that there was a female electrician on the job. And plus, I was an apprentice. He had gone through the trainee program and, you know, there was a stigma always attached to the people that came through the trainee program. I can't repeat the things that he said. He had the filthiest mouth, I mean really filthy the things that he would say. And then he would describe his outings the night before with ladies of the night and go off into really intricate details of his endeavors and make sure that I could hear every single word. If I was walking someplace, he would start, walking behind me and making rude comments about how women are.
>
> What I really hated was, all the guys on the job knew that he was doing this to me, that he was harassing me. And no one intervened and talked to him to tell him, Why don't you back off and leave her alone. They knew that I was new, that I was an apprentice, and as an apprentice you're supposed to be seen, and not heard, you're lower than whale crap. You really aren't supposed to have anything to say to a journeyman as an apprentice, other than asking questions, if they allow you to ask questions. I really don't think that they even considered my feelings in the matter. When I told them that I was taking him up on charges for harassment, they told me, Well, this is just the way he is, and Don't let it bother you. But that's impossible for it not to bother you.
>
> There was another female on this job. She was a plumber, but we didn't work in the same area. He was harassing her too, but her husband is also a plumber, so he straightened him out so he didn't say anything else to her. But I had no one to intervene for me. And he was the type of individual that you could not just approach personally, and say, "Why don't you just back off and leave me alone." It was the foreman that came through and ended up having him apologize to me. He ignored me after that.
>
> I was under so much stress with him, from what he was saying and the way that he made me feel every day, I was ready to quit the trade at that time. My mother talked to me and was saying, "Well, Cheryl, you don't remember what your ultimate goals are. You wanted to finish this and see it through. You know the first shop that you worked for was so great and the guys were different there, so it's not going to always be this way. Just bear with it and try to see it through and it could get better." My mom was a real source of comfort.

The effect of a harasser's action was compounded when others on the job knew about it but did not intervene—as though he were acting on their behalf. Contractors and unions tended to underestimate the gravity of harassment and in some instances even condoned the behavior, tacitly or explicitly. Institutional procedures for prevention or punishment were rare.

Acts of passive aggression could cause serious injury without anyone seeming to be responsible. Although with an inexperienced worker it might be difficult to distinguish between a true accident and an intended one, it was the responsibility of the supervising journeyman to look out for an apprentice's safety, and the responsibility of the training program to properly prepare apprentices. Karen Pollak saw the failure to train apprentices in the proper use of power tools not as some malevolent attack on women, but merely as the result of assuming that apprentices knew how to use them, which had traditionally been true. Karen had been trained to use a skill saw safely when she was five or six years old (by her grandfather, who showed the grandchildren his missing finger). But other female apprentices received. . .

Lots and lots of injuries. Eye injury. Feet. Hands. We had a woman that lost three fingers. Because no one told her how to use the table saw. Another one was cutting stakes out on the jobsite, cut off her whole hand. All because no one took the time to really, really explain that these things can hurt you. I knew how to use the tools. I had an unfair advantage to a lot of the women. Basically what they taught you was how to put the saw blade into the saw and make sure that the guard worked, if there was a guard. That was about it.

They would say to the woman that it happened to, See? I told you, you should have stayed home. A broom wouldn't do that to you. And then they would make it a point that you knew that someone had gotten hurt.

They told me when the lady cut her hand off. She was using a big radial arm saw, a 16-incher, out on the jobsite. She had put her hand down to hold the material. The material started to move. The saw got bound. And somehow or another her hand got back behind the saw, so it pulled itself right back across her. They were able to save it, but she didn't have full function of her hand. It's not the same. And never will be. That's something that could have been easily prevented.

Even if it began as an unintentional oversight, once women started to experience so many injuries, an adjustment should have been quickly made to incorporate power tool safety into the training. Instead, the pattern of accidents became not only proof that women didn't belong, but an amulet to frighten women into leaving.

Some job situations had the feel of trench warfare. Men who wanted to drive women out; women who were determined to stay. Knowledge of tools and experience at the trade did not prevent an "accident" that broke Karen Pollak's nose, when a journeyman did not want her—not only a woman, but a Cherokee Indian—working with him.

I had a sledgehammer dropped on me. This was a job that they had to have a woman. And they needed a minority. It was like, Give me a black woman or somebody who I can mark as a double and then I only have to have one of them. It was just a little tiny library for the University of Kansas Medical Center.

We were down in the hole and I was stripping forms. The guy above me was on the next set of scaffolding working on the next layer. I kept noticing that hairpins, which are a form-type hardware, would fall down and hit the hardhat. Every

Marking Gender Boundaries   295

once in a while it'd hit the bill and knock the hat off, You'd bend over and pick the hat up, look up and go, "Can't you be careful?" "Yep, I just dropped it, sorry."

The superintendent had yelled at him about something. I was standing below and he was going, "Well, make her do it. She doesn't do anything."

"She's stripping. That's all she's here to do.

I was going, "Well, I'm willing to learn. I can handle doing more things than just pulling nails."

"Nah. Not with me you're not." At lunchtime, the foreman said that I was going to go help him after lunch.

He got up on top of the wall before I did. He was standing up on the scaffolding he had just built. I was just starting to climb up the form. BAM! The sledgehammer hit me, it rang my bell.

It was like, Okay, that *could* have been an accident. He throws the rope down. I hook up the sledgehammer and he pulls it back up. I make sure I'm away from the rope. If he happens to slip again, no problem.

For some odd reason, he didn't nail down his scaffolding like you're supposed to do. He told me he did. I stepped on the far end of the board and the scaffolding went smack with the board right in the face. Straight down, back into the hole.

The hole had mud in it. And water. I had hip waders on earlier that day stripping it out. It was an ugly sight. I had broke my nose. The superintendent comes over and says, "Well, this isn't going to work. He doesn't really want you up there."

"Oh, I just thought it was an accident that the sledgehammer fell."

"Probably was on his part, Karen."

"And that's why he didn't nail down the boards, huh?"

"Well, maybe he was getting ready to move them over to the next set of scaffolding."

"Right. He knew I was climbing up there."

I stayed on the bottom and stripped. He would drop things if I was underneath him. I soon got the idea, Stay away from him.

The wisdom of Karen's response—to outwit her journeyman's efforts to injure her while keeping up production—is made clear by the actions of the superintendent who both represents the contractor on the job and belongs to the union. The journeyman responsible for her safety not only drops a sledgehammer and other objects on her, but lies to her about the scaffolding being nailed down, resulting in her fall and broken nose. Rather than laying off the journeyman or bringing him up on charges in the union, the super accommodates his wishes. All three understand the unspoken ground rules: not only is it acceptable to refuse to work with a woman, it is acceptable to communicate that refusal through actions which, out on the street, could result in prosecution for assault and battery.

Harassment could result not only in a stressful work environment or physical but also in economic costs, both short- and long-term. It was not unusual for a tradeswoman to be transferred or laid off after attention was called to harassment. Barbara Trees found that her skill training was also affected.

It was a second-year apprentice working for this contractor doing ceilings—this concealed kind, the hard kind of ceiling—and I was really trying to learn them. The bar isn't revealed, you don't see it, so they're kind of complicated. I wasn't finding it easy to begin with. I was up on the Baker [staging] by myself and the electricians opened up the computer floor around me. They opened up enough tiles so I couldn't move my Baker. I said to them, "You know, I need to move this Baker. Will you put back those tiles?" They just wouldn't do it.

I'd be working on a Baker and they'd be having their coffee break and I would hear my name fairly continuously. "Barbara…Barbara…Barbara…" I got sick of it, so I called over to them and I said, "Is there something you want to say to me?" And, "Oh, no, no, there's nothing we want to say to you."

That was really all it took.

I went home that night and I came back into work the next morning and these guys obviously had written on my Baker in letters a foot high, "PROPERTY OF THE CUNT." I didn't know what to do about it. I didn't really think there was anything I *could* do about it. But what happened is that my sub-foreman came over and he saw it. I didn't really want him to see it or anything. I was embarrassed, actually. So he says, "What's this?" I said, "Well, I think those electrician guys wrote this on here, you know, because we had word yesterday." He says, "Well, we can't have this. I'll speak to the foreman." I was really surprised by his reaction. I felt he was trying to help me.

So the foreman came over to me and asked me what happened. And he said, "We can't have other trades harassing our carpenters. We're going to have a meeting of all the trades later in the day. I'll let them know that they can't do this." I thought, you know, this sounded good, this sounded like what he was supposed to say to me.

I guess they had the meeting and what happened is that I was transferred out of there. They just decided that I was too much trouble. I remember as I walked down the street I passed one of those electrician guys and he almost tried to hide in the building. He saw me and he kind of put his eyes down. I think he must have realized what he had done.

This was my introduction to how they help you out. This guy was so sincere— Oh, we can't have them harassing our carpenters, we're not going to put up with this. I remember thanking him, thinking, This is really great.

Whenever I see ceilings now, I sort of panic. I actually kind of get a cold sweat going. I started to realize what it's from is that the two opportunities I had to learn ceilings both ended where I was laid off or taken off the job. I still feel bad about this. That was my chance to learn.

So this is what happens. Your training suffers. You feel guilty. You don't know what you did wrong. You're feeling like kind of an awful person. And you don't learn your ceilings.

A tradeswoman who changed contractors or crews—particularly if she bounced between situations where coworkers were friendly and fair and situations where she faced hostility and humiliation—could find it hard to build self-confidence and gain her bearings as a developing mechanic. Like many tradeswomen, Helen Vozenilek, an apprentice electrician in Albuquerque, struggled to understand the cause of harassment, looking for how she might prevent or avoid it.

I made the shithouse walls. It was something like, FUCKING LESBIAN ELEC-TRICIAN BITCH. I somehow knew that had to be me. You know, process of elimination.

On that job, the steward was terrible. I don't think he liked women. It was just a bad collection of people. You know how men can get—when they're alone, they're fine, they're actually brothers! And then they get in a group and they're just beasts! I think that was the situation there. They sort of got beastly.

I did feel really harassed there and I didn't quite get it. I remember going home a couple of nights and just crying myself to sleep. I think the steward had talked to me that day, said they were going to run me off or something and it was like, I didn't get it. The hardest thing is the capriciousness, not knowing what you did or what you were being held responsible for, or irresponsible for.

Some of the men who saw tradeswomen as invaders of their domain marked territory with graffiti, pornography, or bodily fluids. Although Irene Soloway, a New York City carpenter, "really didn't experience a great deal of sexual harassment."

I had one incident that upset me for quite a while, which was a job that I was determined to do well on and keep. After six months of coming in every day, I took a day off. When I came back, the shanty had porno pictures all over it, real disgusting ones. The foreman and I didn't get along. It turned out his brother had spent the entire day plastering the shanty on company time. I really was truly shocked, because I had been on the job for six months and pornography was not an issue. So I felt it was terribly personal. It's like, you don't even know where to look! The men were all sitting on their benches and I knew that they weren't comfortable with it, either. I mean, you have a shanty that's clean and decent, you have your little nail and your little hook and your little lunch, and then one day you come in and it's—you know, open cunts all over the wall. It made a lot of people uncomfortable, but I knew that nobody would say a word. I had a screaming fight with the foreman outside the shanty. I was a second-year apprentice.

The reason why I had a problem with the foreman in the first place was because I told him, in front of a group of men, "I'm an apprentice, I'm not an animal, and if you want to call me, I have a name." He used to call black people Nigger, you know. I guess he must have called me Girl. He was furious with me and he told me so in no uncertain terms. And then this happened. I ended up being sent off the job, and I never felt that I had any retribution for that.

They sent me to another job and then two days later I got laid off. So they sort of diffused it that way. I always felt I had to find some like really, really remarkable way to turn the situation around. You think you have to deal with this on your own and you have to be able to stay in the industry, you know. That was my philosophy. I always thought of how would I turn this around and have him be shocked and upset and angry. Which is stupid. I mean, he's the boss. I'm not. So you can't turn it around in that way, in a personal way. But that was the way I used to think.

As an apprentice plumber, Maura Russell never had the opportunity to work with another woman in her trade. On one job with several hundred workers, though, she was able to work with two other tradeswomen, an electrician and a taper, building apartments for the elderly.

We hung around together, which was really nice. But they have a hard time with women getting together on jobs.

There was one time when the three of us were having lunch in K —'s car. This one guy who was there just for two days, an asphalt contractor putting in the parking lot, came over to where we were eating our lunch and pissed on the side of the car. Quite unbelievable. Looking at him coming over, at first I thought his truck must be parked next to us. And then K — is like, "Wait a minute! Is he doing what I think he's doing?" Really.

He'd left by this point. We convinced K — that what she should do is talk to the super. The guy's in his truck and he denies it. K — say's, "Oh, bullshit, you did this." At which point, the super went insane that she swore. And just said, "If you talk like that, you don't deserve to be treated, like a lady."

He was just going to walk away and not deal with it. And that was the point at which K — took out her little Swiss Army knife and told the guy that she would slash his tires if he didn't apologize. He'd been laughing at the incident, which is what really enraged her. He finally did say, "Oh, I'm sorry I'm sorry I'm sorry."

She said, "No. You got out of the car to piss on my car, and now you have to get out to apologize."

So he did. He was angry at that point that he was compelled to do that. And the super was jumping up and down livid, like she was a maniac. He didn't want her on his job anymore. He went running to the trailer to call her company to get her fired (which he was unsuccessful in doing).

But that incident later, we joked, would become that she had a ten-inch knife or something to this guy's throat—and it has pretty much gone around the circuit like that. But that was definitely, Talk like a lady if you expect to be treated like one.

Laborer boss said that to me later in the day, "My wife, she just would have turned her head."

Really.

Although, for women, responding in kind to harassment could bring on more trouble, Maura was sure that if there had been three men in that car,

They would absolutely have pummeled him. And what would the super have done about that? He would have turned his little head. He would have expected that. Oh, they would have gone insane if something like that had happened to a man.

That was really quite an interesting statement of, You're not welcome. Gross, really: gross.

Hostility could be triggered by small acts of self-empowerment. Like three women sitting together in a car. Or a woman becoming more assertive. Doubly vulnerable, as an African American woman, Gloria Flowers found that her worst harassment came when she decided to speak up for herself, after she reached "a point where I wanted to have some respect, I wanted to be talked to like I had some sense."

Towards the end of my apprenticeship I was really catching the blues. That last year, I said to myself, I'm not taking this crap anymore. I'm going to start telling some of these guys off. Well, that was the worst thing I could have done. It's almost like, when you get revenge, it's not as sweet as you think it's going to be.

That last year was my worst year by far. I remember this super telling me, maybe I shouldn't have gotten in the trade. "Why don't you just give up and give out?"

I fell out with a lot of the guys. Some of the guys I had liked previously, we ended up just rubbing each other the wrong way. They started rotating me, working me every other week. At the time I didn't know it was because they wanted to lay me off and couldn't figure out a way to really do it.

This one job I was on, the Ohio Bell Building, downtown Cleveland, there was this black guy on the job, he hated my guts for some reason. He had problems with women, he was like in his third or fourth marriage. That was the worst, the darkest period, I have to say, because he got physically abusive.

He pushed me, physically pushed me down stairs when nobody was watching, in a subbasement. I remember being so mad and so hurt, I wanted to kill that guy. But he was a body builder, he was really built.

A lot of times they had raffles for different things on the jobs. It just so happened that on this job—I don't know why this happened to me, God was trying to show me something—they were raffling a .357 magnum. I don't know what made this guy ask me if I was interested that particular day. Generally I had my little blinders on. I was kind of kept in the dark on a lot of things.

But that particular time—and feeling the way I was feeling—I wanted in on that raffle. I remember coming home. I talked to a girlfriend about it, and she said, Pray about it, and don't do nothing stupid. You can't take on no man, blah, blah, blah.

She really brought me back down to the ground. I prayed about it and it ended up working out. He got laid off, and I got laid off shortly thereafter.

That guy wanted to hurt me. He did. I never told any of the guys about it because, you know, they didn't care. That job had gone sour for me. None of the guys wanted to have anything to do with me on that particular job because I just wasn't taking any stuff.

Accidents set up against women or people of color were particularly insidious. When "successful" they accomplished two things: eliminating or frightening the target, and framing them to look incompetent, not only as individuals but, by extension, as a representative of their gender or race. As an apprentice electrician, Nancy Mason learned to be extra cautious, in case work was sabotaged.

> I was deliberately set up, actually, on two occasions. Once I had circuits turned on when I was trimming out receptacles in a high-rise office space. I don't know who turned the circuits on. And another time I'd been hooking up fire alarm exit signs and I went back to check some. I was up at a light exit sign, and someone had actually tied the ground wire into the hot wire on the other end of the Scotchlok and as I was taking it out, someone turned it on and it blew up in front of me.
>
> I did not get hurt, but obviously someone was hoping I probably would have, or gotten scared or whatever. Those incidents both happened, I think, when I was a fourth-year apprentice. I was getting pretty tuned in to always checking stuff with my own meter. But the turning on the circuit while I was at that exit sign was probably the most dangerous thing, because of the higher voltage. It was a 277 situation.

Bernadette Gross, who went through her carpentry apprenticeship in Seattle, was on many jobs where "the object was to buck me off, and I rode them like that. It was like, I'm not going anywhere." But harassment, even when handled, carried an additional personal cost—to one's sense of trust in other people. On a job early in her apprenticeship, Bernadette fell from a ladder that was not properly secured.

> I was up on a second story framing a window, and the ladder wasn't tied off and it slid from under me.
>
> I had a sheet of plywood dropped on my hardhat. I mean, it hit my hardhat really hard. I was bent over and it could have broke my back, really—and there was just never anything done.
>
> At that time I didn't have sense enough to think that someone had set out to hurt me. Just later on, it was like putting it all together. I was still pretty new, right? And then, I never had that many accidents after that. In my second year, I knew better. If somebody told me to go up a ladder, I'd check it, you know. But in life, it took me a long time to believe that people had malice in their heart. I always believed that they were sort of going their way and you got in the way and they knocked you over. It wasn't anything that they set out to say, I'm going to knock her over, you know.
>
> But I found out that there were people who did, you know, sit down and plot that. It's kind of a hard blow for me.

Such experiences happened to women who graduated from apprenticeship programs. They cast an ironic light on the common explanation for those who did not, the new women apprentices who quit after only a day, a month, or a year, were the ones who supposedly "found it wasn't for them."

19

RESOLVING THE
HARASSMENT DILEMMA

Deborah J. Swiss

At 19, I was shocked and silent when I encountered harassment. When I was 28, I was disgusted by it. At 37, I take it for granted and tell the man that his wife and daughter wouldn't appreciate his behavior.
—Government officer in upper middle management

According to the 1990 Equal Employment Opportunity Commission (EEOC) guidelines, sexual harassment is defined as follows:

Unwelcome sexual advances, requests for sexual favors, and other verbal and physical conduct of a sexual nature will constitute harassment when: 1. Submission to such conduct is made either explicitly or implicitly a term or condition of a person's employment; 2. Submission to or rejection of such conduct by an individual is used as a basis for academic or employment decisions affecting that individual; or 3. Such conduct has the purpose or effect of unreasonably interfering with an individual's academic or work performance or creating an intimidating, hostile or offensive academic or work environment.

No one really knows how many women are harassed at work each day. Fear of reprisal and even concern about losing their jobs hold many women back from reporting sexual harassment. Anita Hill's testimony appeared to give many other women the courage to speak out about their own experiences: Between 1991 and 1993, harassment complaints filed with the EEOC nearly doubled—from 6,892 in 1991 to 12,537 in 1993. But evidence is strong that most harassment goes unreported.

Fifty percent of the women in my sample of 325 have experienced harassment according to the EEOC definition. Many indicated that they have been harassed more than once. Eighty-five percent of the time, they handled the incident privately with the offending individual, largely due to the stigma attached to those who file complaints. Thirty percent of the time, they reported the incident. Offenders were most likely to be superiors, followed by clients, and then peers.

Since language, from a legal standpoint, constitutes one of the "gray" areas in the definition of harassment, I asked the women in my survey a separate question about whether they had experienced language demeaning to women in their current position. Sixty-nine percent responded that they had, some on a daily basis and others less frequently. My findings are similar to those of a 1992 Korn/Ferry survey of 439 women executives in which 59 percent reported that they had experienced sexual harassment at work, but only 14 percent reported it. Many women suffer in silence.

Some of those senior enough to have less concern about job security confront their harassers privately and directly. Some extricate themselves from difficult situations by changing jobs while claiming other reasons for their move.

Mary Rowe, ombudsperson at the Massachusetts Institute of Technology (MIT) and a pioneer in strategies to remedy all forms of harassment, estimates that of the 6,000 concerns about harassment she heard over a sixteen-year period at MIT—from inside and outside the institution—at least 75 percent of those affected worried about negative consequences for bringing forward charges: job reprisal, social rejection, peer and family disapproval, loss of goodwill, and, in some cases, violence.

In any work setting, the unwritten rules place an extraordinarily high value on "goodwill"—getting along with the team, avoiding behavior that appears disloyal, keeping the peace between coworkers. Being labeled a troublemaker can mean quiet death for a career. The fallout for bringing forward an allegation of sexual harassment can be destructive to a woman's career from several angles: when the woman's name is not considered for committee leadership, when the invitations stop for the important client dinners, when she is silently excluded from informal office exchanges. She, rather than the harasser, becomes the outcast in her organization. What can a woman do to counteract the indignity of being forced, for fear of reprisal, to suffer in silence?

Even when the harassment line is definitively crossed, women fear career reprisal for going public with an allegation. Yet they also worry about personal integrity for taking no action at all. As a woman who manages a large, male-dominated staff explains, "Passively accepting harassment would diminish my authority."

To remedy a situation that involved wolf whistles and sexual innuendo every time she walked past a colleague, she spoke to the offender directly. When it became apparent that the meaning of her words had not sunk in, she called a meeting with both the harasser and his boss. She made it clear that she would not report the harasser if, and only if, the offensive behavior stopped immediately. "I didn't want him to lose his job; I just wanted the harassment to stop." And it did. She may, in fact, have saved the person's job since soon after the harassment stopped, the president of her organization issued a firm directive on zero tolerance for sexual harassment.

Does a woman sacrifice her integrity when she chooses this approach? No, say many of the women I met, not if your intention is to stop the harassment and keep your career moving.

A new, perhaps more political and realistic attitude prevails among courageous women who are helping to set new standards for what is acceptable and what is not for workplace behavior. They are, one by one, putting a stop to behavior that makes the workplace a battle zone for women—without having to go to court.

Formal complaints and litigation are not the answer for the vast majority of women who have suffered harassment. It's expensive. It's time consuming. And even if a woman wins her harassment case, her career is the likely loser. The threat of litigation has done little to change corporate behavior. It has only pushed it underground a bit.

Must Boys Be Boys?

Law partner Catherine Lee describes a common form of harassment experienced by many of the women in my survey. As Catherine explains, "I've put up with being called 'honey' and 'sweetie' for years. I bit my tongue when a major client prospect commented on my legs. But the day a European client called me 'pussycat' (after weeks and weeks of 'sweetheart') I drew the line. That was more than I was prepared to take from anyone." Catherine immediately told the client, "I do not want to be called pussycat. In fact," she added in a lighter tone, "in this country, people can go to jail when they make persistent and unwanted comments like that." Her client, at first, laughed, but then, says Catherine, "He woke up and got the point for the rest of the time I represented him."

Catherine feels a responsibility to stop harassment in a way that will, if possible, educate the offender. She has changed her strategy as she has moved up the ranks and explains, "The challenge is to try to say something that will be understood, that will be heard—as opposed to earlier in my career when I was less confident and less secure in my position and I felt more angry." As is the case for many women, the anger and frustration that come with being harassed have a great deal to do with not having the power to stop it.

An episode of the television show *Grace Under Fire* portrayed a too easy, yet commonly accepted, rationale for "boys will be boys" behavior: the majority rules, defend-the-pack excuse. When challenged about his tolerance for demeaning and sexist comments, one oil refinery manager counters, "What am I supposed to do—tell nineteen productive workers to change or tell one worker to get with the team? Grace, that's not harassment," he argues, "that's math."

The price for becoming one of the boys can exact a terrible toll on a woman's business credibility in the long term. Susan Cohen's story points to the danger in accepting, tolerating, and even imitating the machismo of male colleagues. To conduct business with a young, primarily male Wall Street crowd, Susan thought she could gain acceptance as "one of the guys" by following their lead in heavy drinking and using crude language. When she decided she needed to work under higher standards, none of her colleagues took her seriously. Susan now offers a stern warning to her younger, female colleagues. "Once you accept their behavior, once you go along to a 'girlie' show because you think you have no other choice, you live with these standards forever."

Despite the possibility of misunderstanding certain kinds of comments or actions, most harassment is painfully clear in its intent. Taken individually, comments like "Let's invite her to the meeting; she's easy on the eyes," or "What's the matter? Got PMS today?" seem unworthy of response or attention. Experienced cumulatively—at the coffee machine, after a client presentation, on the way into an important meeting—they demean a woman's business talent and undermine a fair chance at professional respect. The long-term impact is wearing and demeaning.

Finding Resolution Right for You

For Caryn Moir, harassment began with irritating comments from the man in the next office: "Would you like to go to Tahiti with me?" "Would you marry a man who'd been married three times?"

Caryn, known for her confident, no-nonsense style, would answer with characteristic humor, "I wouldn't even date a man who had been married three times." When the harassment turned perverted, Caryn's humor and patience with her offensive colleague began to wane. Pregnant with her first child, she began to receive pornographic videotapes in the mail—on her birthday, on holidays.

Physically sick from a difficult pregnancy, Caryn understandably could not find the energy to file a formal grievance, but she wanted her harasser to know that she was "on to him." Caryn recalls how she felt when she finally confronted him. "I was eight months pregnant and big as a house. I felt like a tank—being 60 pounds heavier. And we had lost our cat the night before; he'd gotten hit by a car." And this was the morning the harasser chose to make nasty comments about Caryn's membership in the company's women's organization. Thinking more about the videotapes than his insults that morning, Caryn says, "Finally, I told him, 'Back off!'" His verbal harassment stopped, but the tapes began to arrive with greater frequency.

"I didn't want everyone to think I was a crybaby," explains Caryn. "All my life I've heard that if you want to be successful in business, 'Don't go whining about stuff you can handle yourself.'" But after nearly a year of regular deliveries of X-rated films, Caryn worried that she might need some sort of protection in case the harassment got even worse. She quickly learned that even when a company's official policy denounces harassment, the burden to prove and document the case falls on the woman herself. "In those early days when I was handling the harasser myself, I needed to document every conversation. Well, we all know how busy our lives are—and I have to write down every snaky comment he makes to me?! I don't think so." As Caryn points out, even in a company that offers full support in resolving harassment, much of the burden of proof falls on the victim.

A woman may begin to feel that the harasser is controlling her life in a different way when she begins the often frustrating process of documenting his actions. As Caryn suggests, "It's difficult to think about going through some kind of legal action while I'm working in an environment where I'm supposed to be a team player. Also, I may have to implicate people who may not want to get involved. There's a lot of 'Whatever you do, don't involve me!' And I have to continue to work in this environment."

Caryn admits, "Confronting harassment becomes extremely personal. For me, it was frightening for awhile, thinking that this guy might come after me. It was something that almost struck fear in me." Fear, becoming "prey" to a harasser, becomes another form of a harasser's potentially destructive power.

Despite conflicting emotions about what course she should follow, Caryn says, "I finally made it really loud and clear in the office that I had been receiving these tapes. I made it obvious that I was going to prosecute and made comments about getting fingerprints." Soon after this, the harasser left the company.

What is instructional about Caryn's case is not so much the disgusting nature of the harassment she experienced but the fact that her first concern was about being perceived as an oversensitive, whining female if she pursued a formal investigation. "Everybody agreed that I was being so cooperative," she says. "They thought I was being mature and 'a big girl.' The kind of feeling I got was 'Boy, you're being such a good sport about all this.'" Women like Caryn recognize that they are often scrutinized closely for how they handle these extremely delicate situations even in the context of an open and supportive work culture. And, Caryn adds, "I love working for Pacific Bell. I would not stay here if this were not a healthy environment."

If a woman like Caryn, who works in a company committed to resolving sexual harassment, was reluctant to speak out about this egregious version, it comes as no surprise that most women choose not to go public about the more common, if less extreme, forms of harassment. Caryn's story also explains why women need to choose a course of action that is absolutely comfortable for them.

What do the experts on resolving the harassment dilemma advise? Even they do not always agree on what is the best course of action. Lynne Slater, equal opportunity manager for the Goddard Space Flight Center, suggests that choosing an effective remedy depends on the individual situation as well as the style and temperament of the person being harassed. "Some women are strong enough to just go to the guy and say, 'Look, buzz off.' A lot of women are not. But if they are, I think that's the best way to go." The ability to take such a direct approach is highly dependent on the strength, or perceived strength, of a woman's professional position. A woman with a long track record and a supportive boss is in a much better position to speak up than a woman who has not been part of a company long enough to build political alliances and a solid professional reputation.

Because every employee at the Goddard Space Flight Center has received training on sexual harassment, Lynne Slater can, in good conscience, recommend warning a harasser directly or asking a boss to intervene "so there's a common language," she says. "The managers and staff know what the game plan is." Although Lynne admits that not every manager is entirely comfortable with her approach, everyone in the organization has been given the opportunity to understand what is acceptable behavior and what is not. And Lynne knows that top management supports her position.

Even in an organization like the Goddard Space Flight Center, where employees are well-educated and there are clear procedures for anyone who is harassed, women still fear reprisal for speaking out about harassment. Women have relayed to Lynne again and again observations that point to the insignificance with which many managers regard the issue. For example, she often hears comments like "I mentioned the harassment to my boss and he handled it, but he thought I was stupid for not just ignoring it." And the perception that a woman is "stupid" or oversensitive will influence whether or not her boss considers her for assignments and growth opportunities.

And what if the harasser is someone who can hold your job security or the completion of an important project over your head? The "Now look creep, this can't go on" strategy may not be a wise course if the offender is your boss or someone who can have an impact on your paycheck or career movement. When the offender is someone's immediate supervisor, Lynne brings the case to the supervisor's boss. When it is an outside contractor who is doing the harassing, Lynne asks the internal contracting officer to call the harasser directly and put pressure on him to "clean up his behavior." Their consistent message is, "These are the rules you will work under. If you cannot, we will terminate the contract." The message is simple and straightforward. And the word gets out to other contractors. As Lynne adds, "That's one thing that I don't mind leaking out."

A Whistle-Blower's Courage

In 1991, Frances Conley, M.D., decided that expecting women to handle the humiliating experiences she encountered every step of the way from graduate school to the top of her profession was too steep a price to pay for someone whose profession is life-saving surgery. By virtue of her unusually high organizational value as one of a tiny number of female neurosurgeons nationwide, Dr. Conley took the calculated and courageous risk of resigning from her job to protest the promotion of a known harasser.

At the time she resigned, Frances was chair of the medical faculty senate at Stanford and had just been elected to a prestigious University committee. She was also running an internationally known research program. So, she says, "It was obvious to everybody that I was not crazy." Just why did she resign? Because a man widely known for his consistently demeaning language to women, including Frances, was appointed department chair. She could no longer tolerate his behavior in the hallway, in meetings, and in other public settings, where he would yell comments such as "You're being difficult today. You must have PMS," or "You're not being a team player. You must be 'on the rag.'" Frances knew that other women had filed sexual harassment charges against this surgeon, but they had basically been ignored.

Frances made her point. A committee investigated the allegations against the surgeon, and, after demoting him, they asked Frances to return to her professorship in neurosurgery. She did. Frances was able to take courageous action because, as she explains, "I was dealing from a hand of tremendous strength. I have tenure. I'm a full professor." But even for a woman with her professional clout, courage has come at a price. "I am persona non grata at Stanford and will not go any further in deanships or medical administration."

Overall, however, Frances knows she did what she needed to do and has received more than a thousand letters of support confirming that opinion.

Frances advises other women to "take a good look at the pluses and minuses before you act. And if the minuses outweigh the pluses in terms of the career you would like to have, then you had better swallow hard. Try to diffuse the harassment in any way you can, but start documenting what's happening right at the start until you have a critical mass of facts. Then you have the evidence if you decide to make your move."

The Gray Area

Should we feel any sympathy for the man who says, "All this talk about what I can and cannot do is making me paranoid. I'm afraid to even talk to the women in my office"? Is it harassment when a man compliments a woman on her new suit? Certainly not, if his behavior is consistently professional in all respects. But yes, it could constitute harassment if the comment follows a series of her refusals to the question, "Won't you come to my beach house this weekend?"

Most reasonable people have good instincts about what constitutes demeaning, offensive, and harassing behavior. Many women decide that they will take a higher road than that chosen by their harasser. As MIT's Mary Rowe notes, "I do feel a social obligation to allow anyone who isn't a truly awful person to save face." A natural and understandable reflex to a demeaning incident is an angry retort or a stern lecture. When the purpose is both to stop the behavior and to avoid career reprisal, some women decide to allow the offender to save face: "If this a social invitation, I'm very honored, but I won't be able to come." No emotion, no explanation needed.

Even the best definition of what constitutes a hostile work environment is highly situation dependent. As Mary Rowe suggests, "Harassment is an unusual 'wrong': It exists in part in the eye of the person wronged rather than having a wholly objective life of its own. For example, sexual harassment is legally defined in part as being unwanted sexual attention."

Mary describes the difficulty in clarifying where poor judgment ends and harassment begins. "There isn't a clear line except as defined by each person. Imagine, for instance, somebody who has been abused in childhood. She may need a workplace that has no images in it that recall gender to her. And conversely, somebody brought up as the only sister among eleven brothers—who was the best football player among them—may have no problems at all with raunchy chitchat."

Difficulty in definition does not excuse the need for resolution of a troubling, if often secret, workplace dilemma. How can managers set standards that are equitable and fair while covering a broad spectrum for individual levels of tolerance? How does a woman define for herself where her own lines of tolerance will be drawn?

Caryn Moir hesitated at first to take action against an extreme form of harassment largely because she was concerned that confronting the offender would do more harm to her career and her state of mind than the harassment itself. And if the stakes seem this high for the outrageous behavior that Caryn faced, dealing with the "gray" areas of harassment are all the more difficult. Women who "cry wolf" do all women a disservice. Caryn knows a woman "who knee jerks to every comment and is threatened by everything. Nobody pays attention to her after awhile, and she makes it harder for other women to speak out."

The best way to handle a hostile situation depends on how a woman evaluates the intent of the offender: Is his behavior simply poor judgment? A generational gap? Or does he know better? Is he just busting my chops? Karen Hoyt, an executive in a manufacturing firm, suggests, "There are things I will say to some people that I wouldn't dare say to somebody else. You have to take the pulse of the situation, and you certainly don't want to do anything that will publicly embarrass the other person, regardless of what he's done to you, because then you're on his list forever."

Trying to classify language as either offensive or hostile or showing poor judgment often means walking a delicate line. At a company conference, Karen was approached by a vice president who greeted her with a "Hi, sweetheart, how are you doing?" She replied with a, "Well, hi, poopsie, I'm fine. How are you?" After a brief look of amazement, Karen says, "He just gave me a big smile and walked away. I had done this jokingly so he knew I wasn't being malicious, but I was making a point about respectful language."

Karen bristles when she thinks of other situations—like business social gatherings and professional conferences—where women are expected to tolerate a different standard for physical contact. Frequently at such events, she extends her hand, intending to shake hands with a male colleague who instead puts his arm around her and plants a kiss on her cheek. "That just blows my mind," she says, "because I don't even know these people well. I don't like people touching me and I certainly don't want them kissing me unless they're a really close friend. And even for a friend, I wouldn't expect them to kiss me in a business setting." These are the situations where women find extrication difficult and embarrassing. As Karen concludes, "In these cases, I just get out quick and don't go near the person again. You can't make this an issue when you're in the middle of a group of people. Not if you want to survive."

Sexual Harassment's Long-Term Memory

As women described their experience with sexual harassment, many talked of never having told anyone—not even a friend or family member—about the incident. They have learned to hide the human toll of the embarrassment and shame they feel—for something over which they had no control. One woman, now in a corner executive office, recalls an early point in her career when harassment was not widely recognized. "We were at an offsite conference. I was walking to my car and I noticed an older man whose car was far away, so I said, 'Do you want a ride?' And he said, 'Sure.' He got in my car and immediately grabbed me and kissed me. And I was just horrified. It was the last thing in the world I expected. I was very upset about it. I didn't know what to do so I told no one."

The real import of harassment is not in how it is defined but in what it does to the person who experiences it. Regardless of the specific circumstances, harassment is disturbing, demeaning, embarrassing, annoying, and frustrating. Women who've been sexually harassed carry the heavy burden of wondering whether they should have said something to the harasser, whether they did anything to cause the, incident, why they were unable to take action that might prevent the next woman from being harassed.

Karen Hoyt still carries the vivid memory of the explicitly drawn nude woman that greeted her the first day she entered the executive dining room. "In my wildest imagination, this was not something I expected." As the only woman among forty male managers, Karen nervously sat down at one of the two tables reserved for executives. "All of a sudden, the lazy Susan stops in front of me, and there's a white sheet of paper on which someone has drawn a naked woman, spread eagle. Nothing is left to the imagination. And I'm thinking, 'Gee, do I make an issue out of this? Do I react? What are they waiting for?'" Karen decided not to say a word. After a few more spins around the table, an older male noticed the drawing and said, "This is terrible," as he removed it from the table.

Sitting at this lunch, Karen recalled the advice she had heard from Carole St. Mark, then a vice president at Pitney Bowes, who spoke at a Simmons College management course. "Choose your battles very carefully. You can't win them all." Karen had made the political decision not to give in to the emotional reaction the group at her table expected from her. "I decided this was really petty and childish, and that I didn't want to get involved in it. They were looking for me to get upset, so they could say, 'See, we told you she wouldn't be able to handle this job.'" And, she adds, her decision was probably a wise one. "One of those guys ended up being my boss a couple of years later."

Even if simmering hostility toward managerial women does not turn destructive, it can cause these women to question their personal integrity and can undermine their professional confidence. Although Karen has never before spoken about this incident, she now reflects, "I've never forgotten that. It left such an indelible mark in my brain. I will remember it forever. And it really does something to you because every time I see one of those guys, I wonder, 'What did they think of me as a person that would make them do something like that? Just what were they trying to tell me?'"

Over the years, Karen has maintained her cool in a variety of other hostile encounters with her male peers and colleagues. When asked whether this less-than-welcoming experience fortified her for other challenges, Karen replied, "I now know that I can rise above that kind of behavior. I don't need to deal on their level. It wouldn't serve any purpose."

The Clout That Seniority Brings

When the young men on Wall Street bellow across the floor, "Hey babe, great job on the latest sell!" senior vice president Marianne Bye excuses the language as pure foolishness, unworthy of her time or attention. "They're not going to change, so why fight it?" she asks. She has learned to ignore some of the macho posturing that compels certain colleagues to make up stories about their sexual conquests. Marianne even dismissed the behavior of a pathetic colleague who unknowingly bragged to Marianne's boyfriend that he had been intimate with her on their business trip, which was completely false.

When I asked Marianne, "Weren't you enraged by this? Didn't you find his outrageous lie demeaning?" she replied, "I only take action when it becomes an issue of power or control, when the occasional client has the nerve to approach me as a sex object rather than a competent analyst. Like the time," she continues, "when a business contact tried to physically assault me on a company boat in the middle of the day."

Marianne is senior enough to practice what she considers the ideal strategy for sending a powerful message to the man who tried to assault her. She simply told all of her business colleagues about the incident, putting the word out on the street "that the guy is a creep," and she refuses ever to do business with him again. Taking this kind of stand against a harasser exerts economic penalties on both the offender and on his company.

The Generic Solution

Few women are in a senior or secure enough position to take the kind of action that Marianne did. But many have found creative solutions that stop the harassment without having to worry that their careers will suffer.

At one East Coast company, all the senior executives work along a mahogany row, each with a secretary. One morning, ten of the secretaries came in early, at 6:00 A.M., to cover the mahogany panels with copies of the company's sexual harassment policy. The notices couldn't be missed, and the CEO asked, "What brought this on?" After some discussion it became clear that the configuration of all-male managers and all-female support staff had set up a situation where harassment went unchallenged. The CEO insisted upon mandatory training, which put the offending managers on notice. The women who had been harassed avoided the stigma attached to whistle-blowers and protected themselves from the power and potential wrath of senior-level harassers. No one lost her privacy or put her career at risk.

A generic solution is most valuable when someone who has been harassed and wants the behavior to stop also wants to remain anonymous. This approach is particularly appealing when the offender is a boss, a superior, or a client. It relies on a third party acting as a go-between with a manager in the department where the harassment occurred. At MIT, examples of generic actions include holding a discussion about harassment at a general department meeting, posting copies of MIT's harassment policy in prominent locations, holding training sessions and showing films on what constitutes harassment, or talking informally with managers about how to resolve problems.

Pacific Bell's women's employee organization acts as a neutral party whenever an allegation of sexual harassment is brought to its attention. As Caryn Moir explains, "Instead of hoping that someone will sweep the problem under the carpet, we essentially go in and shine a light on the area." In one case, a woman who worked with the mostly male telephone installation crew found herself at a loss for how to remedy a hostile work environment.

After attempting to resolve the issue through formal channels, the female installer approached the women's committee. The committee, in turn, got the process moving by approaching the company officer responsible for the installer's business unit. Without taking sides in the harassment allegation, they simply asked the officer, "Are you aware that this is going on?" Within weeks, the harassed woman, who had been preparing for a promotion, was upgraded and transferred to a different department. And all of the installers participated in mandatory training on workplace harassment.

Requesting harassment training through an intermediary such as an advocacy committee, a trusted senior executive, or a personnel officer is one alternative to direct confrontation with a harasser. Although a generic solution is not the answer to every case of harassment, it can resolve many without resorting to a formal grievance process. In most organizations, it is virtually impossible to guarantee confidentiality once a formal charge is filed, but a woman can maintain her privacy if she relies on the generic approach.

A woman may fear that she does not have enough evidence to definitively prove her case and may abandon hope for any remedy. "There is quite understandably a strong 1990s concern about the rights of defendants," Mary Rowe points out. "Employers are less comfortable about making career-affecting decisions on the basis of 'he said/she said' evidence." But, she stresses, getting harassment to stop does not always involve having to prove the case in a formal setting. Mediation, shuttle diplomacy, interruption by a concerned bystander, dealing with the harasser directly, or adopting the generic education approach do not require absolute evidence of guilt.

The Good, the Bad, and the Courageous: What Bystanders Can Do

The humiliation of sexual harassment has traditionally been defined in terms of an assertion of power, and sympathetic bystanders can diffuse the power of the offender and the powerlessness of the harassed. The value of a bystander's intervention is that no one need feel adversarial and worry about retaliation. The harasser is, by default, given a chance to clean up his behavior, and the woman can maintain her privacy and avoid career reprisal. Peer pressure matters in every age group: when they witness harassment, bystanders can serve the role of either censor or educator.

Janet Blake was too embarrassed to tell her husband what a male vice president on her quality work team said at the reception celebrating the completion of their work, "Well, now that we're on the same team, do you think we could start showering together?" Janet's shock and embarrassment might have been mitigated if only the other executive standing next to her had said something like, "You know, statements like that offend us all. I think you owe Janet an apology."

In other situations, a statement or question directed toward the offending behavior rather than the offending individual can effectively challenge the rules that perpetuate a hostile work environment: "We don't need that kind of talk here."; "Do you really want to put up that *Playboy* poster?"; "It's really not a good idea to tell those jokes at the holiday party." Bystanders can perform an invaluable role with very few words. A single statement from a very senior male manager or a board member can be enough to clean things up immediately. It's not always that simple, but it can be.

The Collective Solution

Even when a hostile work situation offends an entire department or perhaps the whole company, women may hesitate to come forward as a group for fear that they will automatically be labeled as troublemakers and find themselves isolated from their male colleagues and from business opportunities in the company.

Helen Wallace had just joined the management team at a new firm when she was invited to a company party following a local professional conference. The events planned at an off-site conference included a celebration of another woman's birthday. The company birthday "gift" turned out to be a male stripper. After briefly pondering, "What century are we in? Is this really happening?" Helen snapped into her strategic planning mode and called all the women together for a quick caucus in her hotel room.

"Our first inclination," Helen explains, "was to come out with guns blazing and confront the company president then and there, but we decided we wouldn't make a big deal of the incident that night." Each woman decided to go back to her own manager and to explain factually—without emotion—what was wrong with the company picture that night. Helen, as the company's most senior woman, volunteered to speak to the president. When she met with him, she came prepared with a draft letter in which he apologized for allowing the offensive incident to take place and defined the legalities of harassment.

Had there been an enlightened bystander at the party, he might have made a statement—more powerful than the president's—about company standards that very night. A humane man with a good sense of humor could have said to the stripper, "I'm glad you have the skills to dance, but we won't be needing you tonight. I wish you well. Now, could I invite you outside so that you can get paid?"

From a political perspective, a message like this is more likely to be heard and remembered when the messenger is a man. Female bystanders, concerned about using up too much credibility, may be reluctant to speak up when they are focusing on bigger gender battles. And the birthday woman, though deeply offended, does not want to appear ungracious. Ideally, a senior executive, in a quiet and pleasant way, could have quickly dismissed the stripper and proposed a decent alternative: "Let's get some cake and sing 'Happy Birthday'" or "Where can we send out for ice cream?"

The Organization's Imperative

The highest cost in reporting harassment is not embarrassment or loss of pride—it is fear of career reprisal. Just the potential loss of good working relationships may make a woman feel that she does not want to come forward when she has been harassed. And when word of harassment allegations leaks out through an organization's informal communication channels, a woman may be ostracized for maligning a member of "the team" or jeopardizing the company's reputation.

How can an organization create a culture that minimizes the possibility of career reprisal and loss of business relationships? What is the best strategy for protecting employee privacy while encouraging the reporting of harassment without penalty?

Training sessions on sexual harassment that say "here's the line—don't cross it" may put a stop to the most egregious versions of harassment. With a strong message from the top, training and role play can also be effective in defining the gray areas for harassment. But it takes more than a stern warning and an explanation of what can land an offender in court to educate people in a way that changes their daily behavior. Diffusing a hostile work environment is rarely accomplished by a single one-time effort.

Provide a menu of options that places discretionary control in the hands of the person who has been harassed—at least for most cases. Recognize that most women who have been harassed are not looking to do battle. They simply want the harassment to stop. The following strategies can set the tone for a workplace in which harassment is clearly defined as unacceptable conduct:

- Do everything possible to guarantee confidentiality and freedom from reprisal for the woman who's been harassed. Once harassment has been reported, watch for any retaliation in the form of unfavorable job references or other negative actions against the person who reported it. Promote educational rather than adversarial solutions.

- Offer generic and problem-solving options: corporate- or department-wide sexual harassment training, office meetings in which a leader regularly reminds everyone about the types of behavior that the organization will not tolerate regular written communication to all staff members about the possible legal consequences for those who create a hostile work environment.
- Demonstrate genuine commitment from senior management to provide people with the courage to do what they know is right. Such commitment can serve as a guidepost to the bystander, who can mediate a potentially explosive incident; to the manager, who can require training; and to the woman, who can be assured of her right to be treated with respect after strong action has been taken in response to a harassment incident.
- Give managers and supervisors the support, training, and information they need to prevent or diffuse a hostile work environment. Define their obligation to take action if they observe or hear about harassment: to offer a woman a range of options to stop the harassment, to prevent reprisal, and to get things back to normal after the harassment has been resolved.
- Consider a confidential hot line for information and advice so that women can consult an expert in harassment to determine their best course of action. An ombudsperson's office or a women's committee can also serve this purpose.
- Compose your organization's harassment policy in gender-neutral language. Include remedies for all potential forms of harassment.

What a Woman Can Do

When a woman who has been harassed sees Linda Wilcox, an ombudsperson for the Harvard Medical Area schools, Linda begins by helping her build a decision tree about all possible courses of action, weighing the risks and benefits of each. What is the likely organizational response if you did this? What's the worst that could happen if you followed this course of action? For the woman who tells Linda she feels so humiliated by the experience that "I cannot look myself in the mirror," Linda tells her, "You probably need to do something." Linda's general advice is to choose a plan that stops the harassment with the lowest risk of retribution. As she explains, "The fewer people involved in your problem the better. Ideally, you stop the harassment at the lowest possible level, which is with the offender. If this doesn't work, speak with someone in your organization who you are certain will maintain confidentiality."

With career survival in mind, any woman can conduct her own risk/reward analysis before deciding how to stop the harassment and whether to file a formal complaint. Every woman I interviewed who has experienced sexual harassment advises others: trust your instincts. If you think you've been harassed, then you probably have. When formulating your response to sexual harassment in the workplace, consider the following advice:

- Do whatever it takes to stop the harassment. Choose an option that feels right for you.
- You may not need to go public to get harassment to stop. You may be able to handle the incident privately and directly with the offending individual. This can take the form of a letter or a conversation. Write a letter to the harasser, even if you never send it. You can use the letter to organize your thoughts for a face-to-face conversation. Role-play first with a colleague or friend to work out how you will handle putting the harasser on notice.
- Seek assistance via an intermediary—a boss, a mentor, a trusted senior executive—if you are uncomfortable confronting your harasser directly. You can also send a clear, yet anonymous, "generic" message. Mail the harasser a highlighted version of your company's sexual harassment statement. Post copies of the policy on every bulletin board in your department.
- Put in writing the dates and details of the harassment—if only for your private files at home. Pay particular attention to incidents that can be substantiated by others. Six months after the incident, you may want to read the file to find assurance that you did nothing to bring on the harassment. This strategy may be helpful in putting aside embarrassment or self-blame. And if the harassment should continue, you will have the historical documentation to take action.
- Consider a political approach and a long-term view. When in doubt, consider allowing a harasser to save face. Allowing the offender to save face, once the harassment has stopped, can reduce the likelihood of career fallout. In certain situations, it may, however, be absolutely repugnant to allow a harasser to save face. When harassment involves physical contact or an explicit threat if a sexual favor is not granted, a formal complaint may be the only answer.
- Formulate a backup plan. For example, "If telling my harasser directly doesn't work, I will speak to my boss next week," or, "If the training that I requested through my personnel officer doesn't work, I will investigate other options."
- Tell a trusted friend or family member what happened. Women who keep harassment incidents to themselves find it can slowly eat away at them.
- Don't blame yourself. This doesn't require you to excuse the injustice you have suffered. If the actions of the harasser destroy your self-confidence, then the wrong person has won.

Discussion Questions

1. As defined in Wirth's article, list five specific examples of verbal sexual harassment.
2. How do you think the women should have reacted differently to two of the incidents of sexual harassment in Eisenberg's article? Why do you feel your proposed reaction is better? Note any risks your recommended action would entail.
3. If you were being inappropriately touched by your supervisor in public (or in private, or in both circumstances), what action would you take from the options in the Swiss article? What if you were a young widow or widower with two small

children and you did very specialized work in a bad job market with no likely prospect of finding other employment?

4. Why do you think people engage in sexual harassment? Provide at least three different explanations.

5. What is different about sexual harassment if the victim is male?

6. Have you, or anyone you know, encountered sexual harassment? If you are comfortable with doing so, describe the situation you or someone you know experienced, or create a detailed fictionalized case study of sexual harassment.

Part VII

WORK/HOME CONFLICT: TIME AND DOMESTIC LABOR

A constant concern for anyone who works is how to manage the demands of work and home life. What makes this particularly more challenging to women is the strong cultural expectation that women ought to worry about managing the home and children first, and more so than men. Regardless of how many hours women work or even the kind of paid work they do, they will spend more of their time managing these many obligations to all "others," like employers, children, spouses, and extended family members. The next three readings offer insight into how some men and women respond to the often overwhelming demands of home and work, and how society itself may hinder the men who want to be more involved in home than we might ordinarily expect them to be.

Arlie Hochschild's work in *Time Bind* is both compelling and real. She takes the reader through the daily experiences of working parents from different levels inside the walls of a large employer. Despite the intentions of even this family-friendly corporation, women and men still tread most delicately when balancing their home and professional commitments.

In *Family Man,* Scott Coltrane explores uncharted terrain by asking men to delve into and discuss their own views of their responsibilities when it comes to home and family. Interestingly, we see that men offer some solutions to the binds of competing obligations—solutions that are indeed gendered.

Household labor is often an important way to measure commitment to a home life. Beth Anne Shelton and Daphne John, in "White, Black, and Hispanic Men's Household Labor Time," describe the differences across race and class as well as gender. The notion of egalitarianism is one both sought after and misunderstood. As these authors attest, how to run a home while engaged in employment is often a very individual, if not inventive, process that can be vastly improved when there are more structural forces outside the purview of the family home.

20

TIME BIND

Arlie Hochschild

Almost from the beginning of my stay in Spotted Deer, I could tell that the family-friendly reforms introduced with so much fanfare in 1985 were finding a curious reception. Three things seemed true. First, Amerco's workers declared on survey after survey that they were strained to the limit. Second, the company offered them policies that would allow them to cut back. Third, almost no one cut back programs that allowed parents to work undistracted by family concerns were endlessly in demand, while policies offering shorter hours that allowed workers more free or family time languished.

To try to make sense of this paradox I began, first of all, to scrutinize the text of the policy and the results of employee surveys. Amerco defines a part-time job as one that requires thirty-five hours or less, with full or prorated benefits.[1] A job share is a full-time position shared by two people with benefits and salary prorated. As with all attempts to change work schedules, I learned, the worker has to get the permission of a supervisor, a division head, or both. In addition, workers under union contract—a full half of Amerco's workforce including factory hands and maintenance crews—were not eligible for policies offering shorter or more flexible hours.

But I discovered that among eligible employees with children thirteen and under, only 3 percent worked part time. In fact, in 1990, only 53 out of Amerco's 21,070 employees in the United States, less than one-quarter of 1 percent of its workforce, were part-timers, and less than 1 percent of Amerco's employees shared a job.

Amerco also offered its employees a program called "flexplace," which allowed workers to do their work from home or some other place. One percent of employees used it. Likewise, under certain circumstances, an employee could take a temporary leave from full-time work. The standard paid parental leave for a new mother was six weeks (to be divided with the father as the couple wished). If permission was granted, a parent could then return to work part time with full benefits, to be arranged at his or her supervisor's discretion. Most new mothers took the paid weeks off, and sometimes several months more of unpaid leave, but then returned to their full-time schedules. Almost no Amerco fathers took advantage of parental leave, and no Amerco father has ever responded to the arrival of a new baby in the family by taking up a part-time work schedule.

By contrast, "flextime," a policy allowing workers to come and go early or late, or to be in other ways flexible about when they do their work, was quite popular. By 1993, a quarter of all workers—and a third of working parents—used it. In other words, of Amerco's family-friendly policies only flextime, which rearranged but did not cut back on hours of work, had any significant impact on the workplace. According to one survey, 99 percent of Amerco employees worked full time, and full-time employees averaged forty-seven hours a week. As I looked more closely at the figures I discovered some surprising things. Workers with young children actually put in more hours at work as those without children. Although a third of all parents had flexible schedules, 56 percent of employees with children regularly worked on weekends. Seventy-two percent of parents regularly worked overtime; unionized hourly workers were paid for this time (though much of their overtime was required), while salaried workers weren't. In fact, during the years I was studying Amerco, parents and nonparents alike began to work longer hours. By 1993, virtually everyone I spoke with told me they were working longer hours than they had only a few years earlier, and most agreed that Amerco was "a pretty workaholic place."

Amerco is not alone. A 1990 study of 188 Fortune 500 manufacturing firms found that while 88 percent of them informally offered part-time work, only 3–5 percent of their employees made use of it. Six percent of the companies surveyed formally offered job sharing, but only 1 percent or less of their employees took advantage of that. Forty-five percent of these companies officially offered flextime, but only 10 percent of their employees used it. Three percent of the companies offered flexplace—work at home—and less than 3 percent of their employees took advantage of it.[2] (The 1993 Family and Medical Leave Act requires all companies employing fifty or more workers to offer three months of unpaid time off for medical or family emergencies. Although it is not yet clear what effect this law will have, research suggests few workers are likely to take advantage of it. Studies of earlier state family and medical leave laws show that less than 5 percent of employees actually use the leave.)

As Amerco's experience would suggest, American working parents seem to be putting in longer and longer hours. Of workers with children aged twelve and under, only 4 percent of men, and 13 percent of women, worked less than forty hours a week.[3] According to a study by Arthur Emlen of Portland State University, whether or not a worker has a child makes remarkably little difference to his or her attendance record at work. Excluding vacation and holidays, the average employee misses nine days of work a year. The average parent of a child who is left home alone on weekdays misses fourteen and a half days a year: only five and a half days more. Fathers with young children only miss half a day more a year than fathers without children.[4]

The idea of more time for family life seems to have died, gone to heaven, and become an angel of an idea. But why? Why don't working parents and others too, take the opportunity available to them to reduce their hours at work?

The most widely accepted explanation is that working parents simply can't afford to work shorter hours. With the median income of U.S. households in 1996 at $32,264, it is true that many workers could not pay their rent and food bills on three-quarters or half of their salaries. But notwithstanding the financial and time pressures most parents face, why do the majority not even take all of the paid vacation days due to them? Even more puzzling, why are the best-paid employees—upper-level managers and professionals—among the least interested in part-time work or job sharing? In one Amerco survey, only one-third of top-level female employees (who belong to what is called the "A-payroll") thought part time was of "great value." The percentage of women favoring part time rose as pay levels went down: 45 percent of B-payroll (lower-level managers and professionals) and administrative women (who provide clerical support) thought part time was of "great value." Thus, those who earned more money were less interested in part-time work than those who earned less. Few men at any level expressed interest in part-time work.

Again, if income alone determined how often or how long mothers stayed home after the birth of their babies, we would expect poorer mothers to go back to work more quickly, and richer mothers to spend more time at home. But that's not what we find. Nationwide, well-to-do new mothers are not significantly more likely to stay home with a new baby than low-income new mothers. A quarter of poor new mothers in one study returned to work after three months, but so did a third of well-to-do new mothers. Twenty-three percent of new mothers with household incomes of $15,000 or under took long leaves (fifty-three weeks or more), and so did 22 percent of new mothers with household incomes of $50,000 or more.[5]

In a 1995 national study, 48 percent of American working women and 61 percent of men claimed they would still want to work even if they had enough money to live as "comfortably as you would like."[6] When asked what was "very important" to their decision to take their current job, only 35 percent of respondents in one national study said "salary/wage," whereas 55 percent mentioned "gaining new skills" as very important, and 60 percent mentioned "effect on personal/family life."[7] Money matters, of course, but other things do too.

According to a second commonly believed explanation, workers extend their hours, not because they need the money, but because they are afraid of being laid off. They're working scared. By fostering a climate of fear, the argument goes, many companies take away with one hand the helpful policies they lightly offer with the other.

Downsizing is a serious problem in American companies in the 1990s but there's scant evidence that employees at Amerco were working scared. During the late 1980s and early 1990s, there was very little talk of layoffs. When I asked employees whether they worked long hours because they were afraid of getting on a layoff list, virtually everyone said no. (Although there were, in fact, small-scale layoffs in certain divisions of the company, the process was handled delicately through "internal rehiring" and "encouraged" early retirement.) And when I compared hours of work in the few downsized Amerco divisions with those in nondownsized divisions, they were basically the same. Supervisors in the two kinds of divisions received just about the same number of requests for shorter hours.

Hourly workers were more anxious about layoffs than salaried workers, but fear of losing their jobs was not the main reason they give for working long hours of overtime. For one thing, Amerco is a union shop, where layoffs are allocated by seniority, regardless of hours. In fact, even among a particularly vulnerable group—factory workers who had been laid off in the economic downturn of the early 1980s and were later rehired—most did not cite fear for their jobs as the only, or main, reason they sought over nine hours.

One possible explanation is that workers interested in and eligible for flexible or shorter hours don't know they can get them. After all, even at a place like Amerco, such policies are fairly new. Yet on closer inspection, this proved not to be the case. According to a 1990 survey, most Amerco workers were aware of company policies on flextime and leaves. Women were better informed than men, and higher-level workers more so than lower-level workers. The vast majority of people I talked with knew that the company offered "good" policies and were proud to be working for such a generous company. Employees who weren't clear about the details knew they could always ask someone who was. As one secretary remarked, "I don't know exactly how long the parental leave is, but I know how to find out." So why didn't they?

Perhaps the roadblock to getting shorter hours was not on the worker's side, but on the company's. Were family-friendly policies just for show? Perhaps companies like Amerco wanted to look good but not to do good. Perhaps they wanted to attract the best new workers and shine brightly before the corporate world by offering family-friendly policies but not to suffer the nuisance of implementing them. As this line of reasoning has it, the CEO winks at his middle managers and whispers, "We don't really mean this." He says this because he believes it's not in the company's basic interest to reduce employee time on the job.[8]

This may be true in many companies, but I concluded that it was probably not the case at Amerco. First of all, Amerco workers themselves generally believed that their CEO was sincere. When asked, 60 percent thought "senior management supported the family or personal needs of its workers." This reflects a high degree of confidence in top management's goodwill on this issue. Moreover, there is considerable evidence that flexible schedules benefit companies, not simply workers, and that many companies like Amerco know it.

Amerco saw strong business reasons to institute family-friendly programs. For one thing, "hiring the best" now often means hiring a woman. Women now make up half of the graduates of departments of business administration and receive a third of all bachelor degrees in computer and information sciences.[9] One way to gain an edge in what looked like an increasingly competitive hiring environment, the company figured, was to outshine its competitors in its work-family policies. A study of women engineers at the chemical company Du Pont found that it was the best performers, not the worst, who were leaving in search of jobs with better work-family balance. Skilled workers who leave voluntarily cost companies dearly. On average, for each skilled employee who quits, it costs a company $40,000 to hire and train a replacement. A study of Merck and Company found that losing an exempt employee costs the company one and a half times that employee's annual salary, and losing a nonexempt employee costs the company 0.75 times the worker's salary.[10] Also it takes a new worker at least one year to perform as well as the worker he or she replaces.

In a national study of fifty-eight employers, thirty-one claimed that family-friendly policies help attract desirable employees. Three-quarters claimed such policies lower absenteeism. Two-thirds felt they improve worker attitudes.[11] Companies may also enjoy reduced medical insurance costs as a result of lowered stress levels at work.

Beyond this, studies well known to Amerco management have demonstrated the costs of not instituting such policies—in increased absenteeism and tardiness, and lowered productivity. A 1987 study conducted by the National Council for Jewish Women found that women working for family-friendly companies were sick less often, worked more on their own time, worked later into their pregnancies, and were more likely to return to work after a birth.[12] Moreover, the study found that workers who took advantage of family-friendly policies were among the best performers, and the least likely to have disciplinary problems. All in all, there is no proof that flexible hours are not in a company's long-term interest, and substantial evidence that they are. It seems that Amerco would stand to benefit by having at least some workers use its family-friendly policies.

It might be argued, then, that such policies are in the interest of the company but not of the hapless middle manager who has to implement them. Amy Truett, the most forceful proponent of family-friendly reforms at Amerco, believed the real bottleneck was in the impermeable "clay layer" of middle management—and that there was no getting around it. The company brochure describing work-family policies notes in small print that any arrangement needs the approval of one's "immediate supervisor or division manager." This, of course, leaves power in the hands of a manager who may see such policies as a matter of privilege, not rights.

We might call this the Balashev theory. In an episode in Leo Tolstoy's *War and Peace*, the Russian Tsar Alexander dispatches his trusted envoy Balashev to deliver an important warning to Napoleon, emperor of France, to withdraw his forces from Russia. Alexander gives Balashev exact instructions on what to say—that Russia will consider itself at war with France so long as French soldiers are on Russian soil. Balashev sets off. But along the way, he is detained by one person, then another, each with an urgent concern, each affecting Balashev's frame of mind. At last, he is brought, awestruck, before Napoleon. Swayed by more immediate influences, at the last moment Balashev softens the tsar's message. Napoleon need not withdraw his troops from Russian soil at all, only to the other side of a nearby river. Inadvertently, Balashev alters world history and war breaks out.

Perhaps expedient company managers in the outlying provinces of Amerco "do a Balashev." Although most employees felt that senior management supported family-friendly policies, they were convinced that fewer middle managers did; and indeed some middle managers did tell me that flexible schedules were "one more headache to manage." As the head of a large engineering division told me in a pleasant, matter-of-fact way, "My policy on flextime is that there is no flextime."

But if manager resistance were the main reason for the low usage of part time, job sharing, and leaves of various sorts, then friendly progressive managers should receive more requests for flexible or shorter hours than recalcitrant managers. In fact, offices with progressive managers had only slightly more part-timers, job sharers, and flextimers than offices with resistant managers. Progressive managers received roughly the same number of requests as did resistant managers. For the most part, it was not that workers were applying and being turned away. It was that workers weren't applying.

For some women in male-dominated fields, one reason to work long hours, or at least to avoid shorter ones, may be the need to ward off "the evil eye" of male resentment. As an anonymous male respondent to a company survey declared, "Let's hope we're not starting another minority and women crisis [by introducing family-friendly policies]. White males can't stand another one like in the 1970s." A woman engineer (and mother) commented from the other side: "Two of my coworkers, older men, won't say it to my face, but I know they think I got their promotion. Truth is I got my promotion. I earned it. But at work I feel I have to prove it. I don't know if that's behind my sixty-hour week or not."

In the formal company culture, white men are not supposed to resent white women and minorities, but some do. Many men have become good at disguising their disgruntlement, but women have become equally adept at detecting hidden expressions of it. The female newcomers I talked with "knew" just how resentful each man in each job classification was, or how recently he had "changed his tune." Still, the theory of the evil eye doesn't explain why women outside of "envy environments" do not try to claim more time at home; nor does it explain why these envious men themselves shy away from parental leave or shorter hours.

All of the explanations listed above have real merit. In certain circumstances, some of the obstacles were overwhelming. But by themselves, these road blocks are not formidable enough to account for such widespread acquiescence to long hours. In those cases where workers can afford to earn less money, are not afraid of being fired, have informed themselves of the new policies, lack envious coworkers, and work for a company that values balance and that has trained its "Balashevs" to do the same, the clues point to another underlying explanation for why workers are not trying to get more time for themselves.

A 1985 Bureau of Labor Statistics survey asked workers whether they preferred a shorter work week, a longer one, or their present schedule. Sixty-five percent preferred their schedule to remain the way it is. Of the remainder, three-quarters wanted longer hours. Less than 10 percent said they wanted a cut in hours. In every age group, more women wanted a longer work week than wanted a shorter one.[13] In a 1993 study by the Families and Work Institute in New York, researchers Ellen Galinsky, James T. Bond, and Dana Friedman asked a large random sample of workers how much time and energy they actually give to work, to family and friends, and to themselves. Then they asked how much time each respondent would like to devote to each of these. People responded that they actually give 43 percent of their time and energy to family and friends, 37 percent to the job, and 20 percent to themselves.[14] But when asked what they would like, the answers were nearly the same: Forty-seven percent to family and friends, 30 percent to the job, and 23 percent to themselves. Such studies imply that working families aren't using family-friendly policies in large part because they aren't asking to use them,[15] and they aren't asking for them because they haven't formulated in their minds a need urgent enough. Certainly, some parents have tried to shorten their hours. Twenty-one percent of the nation's women voluntarily work part time, as do 7 percent of men.[16] A number of others make informal arrangements that don't show up in survey results. Still, while hurried working parents report needing more time, the main story of their lives does not center on their struggle to get it.

Why aren't working parents forging a "culture of resistance" parallel to the social movement that professionals like Amy Truett are quietly creating on their behalf? Where is *their* mission statement, their vision? Even if parents don't dare knock on their managers' doors to ask for 85 percent work schedules, for instance, why aren't they privately questioning their own use of time? Parent's lives are too crowded, their time with their children too limited. They, claim they want extra time at home. But do they want something else even more?

Notes

1. These part-time jobs are not to be confused with jobs without benefits or job security, jobs in the so-called contingency labor force. The growth of "bad" part-time jobs may, indeed, be chilling the quest for "good" ones. See Vicki Smith, "Flexibility in Work and Employment: Impact on Women," *Research in the Sociology of Organizations* 11 (1993): 195–216.

2. See Galinsky et al., *The Corporate Reference Guide* (1991), 85–87. Nationwide, a far higher proportion of firms claim to offer flexible schedules than report workers using them.

3. Galinsky et al., *The Corporate Reference Guide* (1991), 123.

4. Arthur Emlen, "Employee profiles: 1987 Dependent Care Survey, Selected Companies" (Portland: Oregon Regional Research Institute for Human Services, Portland State University, 1987), reported in Friedman, *Linking Work–Family Issues to the Bottom Line* (1991), 13.

5. Hofferth et al., *National Child Care Survey* 1990 (1991), 374. See also Bond and Galinsky, Beyond the Parental Leave Debate (1991), 74.

6. Families and Work Institute, *Women: The New Providers*, Whirlpool Foundations Study, Part 1, survey conducted by Louis Harris and Associates, Inc., May 1995, 12.

7. See Galinksy et al., *The Changing Workforce* (1993), 17.

8. For one thing, family-friendly part-time jobs come with full-time benefit packages, requiring the company to pay more money for less work. These benefits could be prorated, of course, but when companies have to give up something, they generally prefer to raise wages rather than lower hours. See Schor, *the Overworked American* (1991).

9. "The Workforce 2000," an influential 1987 Hudson Institute Report, predicted a shortage of skilled labor by the year 2000 due to the low U.S. birthrate in the 1970s. The report also noted that fewer white males and more of everyone else would be applying for jobs. To be sure, the layoffs of the 1980s put more skilled white men back on the market, but this has not significantly changed the long-term trend toward a more diversified workplace.

10. Friedman, *Linking Work–Family Issues to the Bottom Line* (1991), 12.

11. Barbara Presley Noble, "Making a Case for Family Programs," *New York Times*, 2 May 1993: 25.

12. Studies of Johnson & Johnson, the pharmaceutical giant, and of Fel Pro, a maker of automotive sealing products, found that family-friendly policies made workers more content and more likely to stay with their companies. See Friedman, *Linking Work–Family Issues to the Bottom Line* (1991), 47–50.

13. Janet Norwood, "American Workers Want More: More Work, That Is," *Across the Board*, November 1987 (New York: The Conference Board). Based on a 1985 Bureau of labor Statistics survey, Norwood notes that 28 percent of workers said they wanted a longer work week. Less that 10 percent wanted a cut in hours with reduced pay (60).

14. Galinksy et al., *The Changing Workforce* (1993), 98.

15. According to Dana Friedman, "Perhaps the greatest obstacle to company activity is the absence of employee demand" (Dana Friedman, "Work vs. Family: War of the Worlds," *Personnel Administrator*, August 1987, 37.

16. Callaghan and Hartmann, *Contingent Work* (1991), Table 6: 38. Also see Deborah Swiss and Judith Walker, women and the Work/Family Dilemma: How Today's Professional Women Are Finding Solutions (New York: Wiley, 1993), a study of 1,644 female Harvard alumnae and their travails taking parental leave.

21

FAMILY MAN

Scott Coltrane

We contacted dual-earner couples through word-of-mouth referrals and inter-viewed mothers and fathers separately. To correct for omissions in previous studies of dual-career or minority families, we recruited middle-class two-job Chicano couples with at least one school-aged child. Since the majority of Latino two-job families in the United States comprise husbands and wives with service sector jobs, we began by interviewing white-collar workers (e.g., secretaries, clerks, social workers). In addition, we interviewed some people who held jobs that were working class (e.g., mechanic, laborer, painter) or professional (e.g., attorney, teacher, administrator). We screened potential couples on the basis of husband and wife both holding jobs, rather than on any statements they made about sharing domestic tasks.

The Chicano husbands and wives tended to be in their mid-thirties with children of preschool and school age. Most lived in suburban neighborhoods, though a quarter lived in smaller rural towns. Few were first-generation immigrants and most had lived in southern California for their entire lives. Virtually all considered themselves middle class, but almost all had parents who were working class.

Elsa Valdez and I asked husbands and wives who initiated various tasks, who set standards for their performance, and whether they felt that their division of family work was fair. It was evident from the initial card sorting that wives were responsible for most housework and many child care tasks, and that husbands did mostly out-side work and shared some child care. These findings are not surprising. The Chicano couples shared somewhat less than the couples in the first study, in part because they had younger children and in part because they were not selected based on egalitarian self-identification. Many more tasks were shared than in the hypo-thetical "average" family. Many domestic tasks were allocated according to conven-tional gender expectations.

Table 21.1 shows wives' and husbands' perceptions of who did which family tasks. The two spouses' ratings are listed separately to illustrate how they saw things differently. For housecleaning, wives rated themselves as doing most of the vacuuming, mopping, sweeping, dusting, cleaning sinks, cleaning toilets, cleaning tubs, making beds, picking up toys, tidying the living room, hanging up clothes, and spring cleaning. Wives listed only cleaning the porch and washing windows as shared, and indicated that husbands

TABLE 21.1 Wives' and Husbands' Perceptions of Domestic Task Performance

	Wife's Perception			Husband's Perception		
	Wife More	Both Equally	Husband More	Wife More	Both Equally	Husband More
House Cleaning						
	Vacuum	Clean porch	Take out trash	Mop	Clean porch	Take out trash
	Mop	Wash windows		Sweep	Wash windows	
	Sweep			Dust	Vacuum	
	Dust			Clean toilets	Clean sinks	
	Clean sinks			Make beds	Clean tub	
	Clean toilets			Hang up clothes	Pick up Toys	
	Clean tubs				Tidy living room	
	Make beds				Spring cleaning	
	Pick up toys					
	Tidy living room					
	Hang up clothes					
	Spring cleaning					
Meal Preparation and Clean-Up						
	Plan menus	Put food away		Plan menus	Put food away	
	Prepare breakfast			Prepare breakfast	Prepare lunch	
	Prepare lunch			Cook dinner	Make snacks	
	Cook dinner			Bake	Put dishes away	
	Make snacks			Wash dishes	Wipe kitchen counters	
	Bake			Grocery shop		
	Wash dishes					
	Put dishes away					
	Wipe kitchen counters					
	Grocery shop					

(continued)

TABLE 21.1 Wives' and Husbands' Perceptions of Domestic Task Performance (continued)

	Wife's Perception			Husband's Perception		
	Wife More	Both Equally	Husband More	Wife More	Both Equally	Husband More
Clothes Care						
	Laundry	Iron		Laundry	Iron	
	Hand laundry			Hand laundry	Shoe care	
	Shoe care			Sew		
	Sew			Buy clothes		
	Buy clothes					
Home Maintenance and Repairs						
	Redecorate	General yardwork	House repairs		Redecorate	House repairs
		Water lawn	Car maintenance		Clean rain gutters	Car maintenance
		Mow lawn	Car repairs			Car repairs
		Garden	Wash car			Wash car
		Interior painting				General yardwork
		Exterior painting				Water lawn
		Clean rain gutters				Mow lawn
						Garden
						Interior painting
						Exterior painting
Finances and Home Management						
	Run errands	Prepare taxes		Pay bills	Run errands	
	Pay bills	Make investments		Contact relatives/friends	Prepare taxes	
		Handle insurance			Make investments	
		Decide major purchases			Handle insurance	
		Plan couple dates			Decide major purchases	
		Contact relatives/freinds			Plan couple dates	

(continued)

TABLE 21.1 Wives' and Husbands' Perceptions of Domestic Task Performance *(continued)*

	Wife's Perception			Husband's Perception	
Wife More	Both Equally	Husband More	Wife More	Both Equally	Husband More
Child Care					
Put children to bed	Supervise children		Awaken children	Put children to bed	
Awaken children	Discipline children		Help children dress	Drive children	
Help children dress	Play with children		Help children bathe	Supervise children	
Help children bathe	Plan outings with children		Take child to doctor	Discipline children	
Drive children			Care for sick child	Play with children	
Take child to doctor			Arrange babysitting	Plan outings with children	
Care for sick child					
Arrange babysitting					

most often took out the trash. Husbands also listed trash as their chore, but rated more tasks as equally shared than as being done by their wives.

A similar pattern was evident for meal preparation and cleanup. Wives listed all tasks in this area as being performed by themselves, with the exception of putting food away, which was listed as shared. Husbands again placed almost half the tasks in the shared pile, with many of the less time-consuming tasks being rated as being performed by husbands and wives about equally. Such tasks included putting food away, preparing lunch, making snacks, putting dishes away, and wiping kitchen counters. Both husbands and wives indicated that wives were primarily responsible for planning menus, preparing breakfast, cooking dinner, baking, washing dishes, and shopping for groceries.

The discrepancies between husbands' and wives' accounts were much smaller in the area of clothes care, primarily because both agreed that wives did almost all of it. Wives were rated as performing the laundry, the hand laundry, the sewing, and purchasing clothes. In an unexpected finding, both husbands and wives listed ironing as a shared activity. This was the only stereotypically "feminine" housework task that was consistently ranked as shared. Few of the Anglo men in the first study shared ironing with their wives, but among the Chicano couples, even the women considered this a shared activity. Wanting the entire family to appear well-dressed in public, especially on Sundays, motivated some men to iron their own clothes and sometimes also their children's and their wives' clothes. Ironing is also a task that some men reported they could do while watching sports on television.

The same general trend observed for housework was also evident for child care. Here, both spouses listed more tasks as shared, but husbands listed as many tasks in the equal column as in the wife's column. In contrast, wives listed only supervising, disciplining, playing with, and planning outings with the children as shared activities. Husbands said that putting children to bed and driving them places were also shared activities. Bodily care aspects of child rearing, including getting children up in the morning, monitoring bathing, helping them dress, taking them to the doctor, tending them when sick, and arranging for babysitters, were all listed by both spouses as the province of the wife.

Similar discrepancies were evident between spousal reports for tasks traditionally considered "manly" activities. Wives listed 7 of 12 home maintenance and repair tasks as performed equally by both spouses, and one—redecorating—as performed principally by themselves. Husbands, in contrast, listed only two tasks as shared, with all others listed as being performed principally by themselves.

In the area of finances and household management, both spouses listed six of eight tasks as shared, and two in the wife's domain. Both spouses listed paying bills as being primarily the wife's task. Wives saw themselves as running errands more often, whereas husbands considered errands to be an equally shared activity. Wives indicated that spouses shared phoning and writing relatives and friends, but husbands saw wives as being primarily responsible for these social and "kin-keeping" activities. This was the only task that men listed as performed by wives more often than the wives themselves did. Perhaps because keeping contact with kin has been stereotyped as the wife's obligation in both Chicano and Anglo families, men overestimated their wife's efforts and underestimated their own.

To summarize, wives thought they had sole or primary responsibility for many more housework and child care tasks than their husbands gave them credit for and husbands thought they had more responsibility for outside work than their wives gave them credit for. Disagreement was especially likely for frequently performed tasks of short duration that were stereotyped as being women's work or men's work.

Living in Separate Worlds

Looking at the patterns of disagreement described above, we could say that husbands and wives were living in different worlds. In fact, this view might shed some light on what happens with family work in most families. The sociologist Jesse Bernard suggests that every marital union actually contains two distinct marriages—"his" and "hers."[1] Because the activities, rights, duties, and obligations of husbands and wives are so different, spouses often experience married life as two separate realities.

His marriage and her marriage are different because of historical conventions and power inequities, but seeing family work differently also comes from some routine biases in perception. Social psychologists have documented how vivid and rare events are more likely to be recalled than common, everyday events.[2] What could be more mundane than wiping the kitchen counter or putting away the dishes? Routine housework activities are therefore not likely to be precisely attended to, stored in memory, or quickly retrieved. If, however, one rarely performs such activities, the tasks can become more salient. Thus, some men remember every housecleaning or child-related task they perform because these events are more vivid to them. Similarly, women might remember changing the oil or mowing the lawn precisely because these are relatively rare events for them. Whether one performs the tasks or not, however, both inside and outside household chores are relatively unremarkable, which makes them more difficult to recall precisely. This increases the chances that a second type of perceptual distortion might come into play.

Another cognitive tendency is for memory distortions or miscalculations to be ego enhancing. That is, we are likely to remember those things that make us look good, and forget those that make us look bad.[3] For women, family work is routine, but they typically know what needs to be done and feel good about themselves when the work fulfills the needs of other family members. Depending on whether they feel better about being the only one who does the work, or having a husband who helps, they are subject to different bias in their estimates of who does what. For example, consider a hypothetical household in which the husband and wife spend equal time on cooking, but her efforts are concentrated on serving hot "sit-down" meals and his efforts are focused on shopping, washing and chopping vegetables, stocking the refrigerator with lunch and snack foods, and packaging leftovers for later consumption. If the woman's self-image is based on the caring and feeding that she performs during family meals, she is likely to "see" her cooking contribution as greater than her husband's. If, on the other hand, her self-evaluation is more dependent on being a woman who shares the kitchen work, she will "see" his contribution as equal to her own.

For men, doing family work is typically less routine than it is for women, so when they do it, it is likely to be relatively vivid or salient. If they are involved in smoldering chore wars and agree they should do more of it, they are even more likely to overestimate their domestic contributions, for it enhances their self-image as an involved and caring husband. Some of the wives we talked to complained that their husbands remembered every time they made a small contribution to kitchen cleanup, but hardly noticed the countless times the women shopped, chopped, cooked, cleaned, washed, and tidied the kitchen. In reporting who does what, men and women thus tend to focus more on their own activities, because these things are ego enhancing and cognitively more available.

Men are likely to give extra weight to the rare housework tasks they perform, but what about those that they don't notice? Because men usually don't have responsibility for initiating housework and because their identity is not usually tied to doing it, they often don't pay much attention to it in the first place. The most common complaint heard from both Anglo and Chicano wives was that husbands "just didn't see" when things needed doing or take responsibility for initiating the important details of housekeeping. Most wives thus remained in control of setting schedules and generating lists for domestic chores. Unfamiliar with the details of running the household, men were likely to underestimate their wives' contributions and to escape the full range of tensions and strains that come with the second shift of family work. By "not seeing" what needed to be done, and missing the full extent of their wife's contributions, the men enjoyed a privileged position in many of the families we interviewed (even though most of them "saw" more than the average husband).

Although the Chicano couples did not agree on which tasks were shared, they independently reported that their current arrangements fell short of being fair. Because previous studies have found that even unbalanced divisions of labor are labeled "fair" by husbands and wives, I was surprised that these couples said things were unfair. After sorting the task cards, some of the men noticed that their wife's pile dwarfed their own, with one commenting, "Gee, I guess I don't do as much as I thought." Seeing many more cards in her pile did not fit with their ideal that things should be shared, so some men may have been encouraged to acknowledge that things were unequal. When asked directly, most wives did not think of their divisions of labor as fair, yet few expected much change in the future. Housework, in particular, was viewed as a mundane burden that they had to shoulder alone or seek help with, simply because they were women.

Ranking the Amount of Sharing

Though husbands and wives saw things differently and work was divided in relatively conventional ways, some noticeable shifts in work and family responsibilities were underway in these families. I averaged the husband–wife scores for each task so that I could compare across families and figure out why some couples shared more than others. I combined the various tasks associated with housecleaning, meal preparation, meal cleanup, and clothes care into a single housework measure and used the twelve child-related tasks to form an overall measure of child care. Fathers uniformly spent more time in direct interaction with their children than their own fathers had with them, but fewer than half of the individual child care tasks were ranked as shared when husbands' and wives' ratings were averaged. In the more traditional families, the wives still exercised control over all child care and reported that they were responsible for facilitating father–child interaction. In other families, however, the fathers themselves initiated and sustained regular contact with their children. In some cases, fathers' commitments to spend more time with their children created work/family conflicts that we typically associate only with mothers. At least some child care tasks were shared in every family and a few families even divided responsibility for the children about in half.

Looking at housework, as well as child care, I focused the analysis on why some men were sharing more of the planning and performance of tasks conventionally assumed by women. One of the important issues that emerged was the extent to which wives were defined as sharing the economic provider role with their husbands. After presenting some theoretical ideas about how paid work and family work fit together, I turn to the interviews with the Chicano couples.

The families we interviewed did not think of themselves as having chosen to become two-job families. Like the couples in previous studies, they were simply responding to financial necessity. Few couples talked about the joys of sharing either market or household labor, and few mentioned that they were motivated to share family work because they wanted to change gender roles in the larger society. Most husbands talked as though they were coerced into their present arrangements with comments like "we were pretty much forced into it" and "we didn't really have any choice."

According to most social science explanations, paid work and family work should influence each other, yet we do not understand exactly how and why this is so. "New" home economics theories assume that family members allocate responsibility for various tasks based on "tastes" for certain types of work and the underlying desire to maximize benefits for the entire family unit. Efficiency is supposed to be the driving force behind why women do most of the housework, though there is some question why it is efficient to pay women lower wages for similar work in the wage-labor market.[4] Feminist and structural conflict theories assume that all family members' needs are not equally served by conventional task allocation, and that responsibility for housework can be seen as a measure of women's oppression.[5] Finally, most social role theories suggest that the boundaries between work and family are "asymmetrically permeable," with men's paid work excusing them from family obligations, but women's family commitments allowed to intrude on their work roles.[6] All three of these theoretical approaches assume that changes in paid work will promote shifts in family work, but most empirical studies have not been able to isolate how and why.

To understand the interplay of work, family, and gender, the sociologist Jane Hood suggests that we must accurately measure the economic provider role. Her assumption is that divisions of paid and unpaid labor are shaped by gender-linked notions of who is responsible for providing financially for the family and who is responsible for direct care to family members.[7] According to Hood, only when wives are accepted as economic providers will husbands assume more of the parent/homemaker role.[8] We looked at this issue by asking husbands and wives how they felt about performing paid work and family work.

Although all the Chicano husbands and three-fourths of the Chicana wives we interviewed were employed full time, the couples varied in the extent to which they accepted the wife as a co-provider. By considering the employment and earnings of each spouse, along with each spouse's attitudes toward the provider role, I divided the twenty families into two general groups: main providers and co-providers.[9] As Hood predicts, this distinction, with minor variations, makes a big difference in who does what around the house.

Main Provider Families

In almost half the families, husbands made substantially more money than wives and assumed that men should be primary breadwinners and women should be responsible for home and children. Families were categorized as main providers because they generally considered the wife's job secondary and treated her income as "extra" money to be earmarked for special purposes.[10] One main provider husband said, "I would prefer that my wife did not have to work, and could stay at home with my daughter, but finances just don't permit that." Another commented that his wife made just about enough to cover the costs of child care, suggesting that the children were still her primary responsibility, and that any wages she earned should first be allocated to cover "her" tasks.

The main provider couples included all five wives who were employed part time, and three wives who worked in lower status full-time jobs. Wives in these families made substantially less money than their husbands, contributing an average of 20 percent to the total family income. In main provider households, wives took pride in the homemaker role and readily accepted responsibility for managing the household. One part-time bookkeeper married to a law clerk studying for the bar described their division of labor by saying, "It's a given that I take care of children and housework, but when I am real tired, he steps in willingly." Husbands typically remained in a helper role: in this case, the law clerk told his wife, "Just tell me what to do and I'll do it." He said that if he came home and she was gone, he might clean house, but that if she was home, he would "let her do it." Neither spouse questioned the underlying obligation of the wife to be in charge of making sure that daily family needs were taken care of. She was the household manager and he was a helper.

The lawyer-to-be was very conscious of the difference in occupational status between he and his wife, even though he had not yet reached his full potential earnings. He talked about early marital negotiations that seemed to set the tone for some smoldering arguments and resentments about housework that both he and his wife hinted were always present.

> When we were first married, I would do something and she wouldn't like the way that I did it. So I would say, "Okay, then, you do it, and I won't do it again." That was like in our first few years of marriage when we were first getting used to each other, but now she doesn't discourage me so much. She knows that if she does, she's going to wind up doing it herself.

His resistance and her reluctance to press for change reflected an economy of gratitude that was as unbalanced as their household division of labor. When he occasionally contributed to housework or child care, she was indebted to him. She complimented him for being willing to step in when she asked for help, but privately lamented that she had to negotiate for each small contribution. Firmly entrenched in the main provider role and somewhat oblivious to the daily rituals of housework and child care, he felt justified in needing encouragement. When she did ask him for help, she was careful to thank him for dressing the children or for giving her a ten-minute break from them. While these patterns of family work and inequities in the exchange of gratitude were long-standing, tension lurked just below the surface. He commented, "My wife gets uptight with me for agreeing to help out my mom, [because] she feels she can't even ask me to go to the store for her."

Another main provider couple reflected a similar pattern of labor allocation, and claimed that the arrangement was fair to them both. The woman, a part-time teacher's aide, acknowledged that she loved being a wife and mother and "naturally" took charge of managing the household. She commented, "I have the say-so on the running of the house, and I also decide on the children's activities." Although she had a college degree, she described her current part-time job as ideal for her. She was able to work 20 hours per week at a neighborhood school and was home by the time her children returned home from their school. While she earned only $6,000 per year, she justified the low salary because the job fit so well with "the family's" schedule. Her husband's administrative job allowed them to live comfortably since he earned $48,000 annually.

This secondary provider wife sorted the household task cards in a conventional manner: Her piles contained all the cleaning, cooking, clothes care, and child care tasks, while his piles included yard work, home repairs, finances, and home management. Her major complaints were that her husband didn't notice things and that he created more work for her. "The worst part about housework and child care is the amount of nagging I have to do to get him to help. Also, for example, say I just cleaned the house; he will leave the newspaper scattered all over the place or he will leave wet towels on the bathroom floor." When asked whether there had been any negotiation over who would do which chores, the husband responded, "I don't think a set decision was made, it was a necessity." His wife's response was similar, "It just evolved that way, we never really talked about it."

His provider role was taken for granted, but occasionally she voiced some muted resentment. For example, she commented that she gets discouraged and upset when he tells her that she should not be working because their youngest child is just five years old. Additionally, she mentioned in passing that she was sometimes bothered by the fact that she had not been able to further her career, or work overtime, since that would interfere with "the family's" schedule.

Wives of main providers not only performed virtually all the housework and child care, but both spouses accepted this as "natural" or "normal." The wife's commitment to outside employment was generally limited, and her income was considered supplemental. The husbands' few domestic contributions were seen as aiding the wife and he took more credit for his housework contributions than his wife was willing to grant him. Another main provider husband admitted, "She tells me to do lotsa things, but whatever she tells me to do, then I do half." The husbands in main provider couples consistently failed to see most of the details of running the household, and since they were not "supposed" to be responsible for such tasks, they were rarely challenged by wives to redefine housework as their responsibility.

Main provider husbands assumed that financial support was their duty. When one man was asked how it felt to make more money than his wife, he responded by saying: "It's my job, I wouldn't feel right if I didn't make more money. . . . Any way that I look at it, I have to keep up my salary, or I'm not doing my job. If it costs $40,000 to live nowadays and I'm not in a $40,000 a year job, then I'm not gonna be happy." This same husband, a small-town auto mechanic and shop manager, worked between 50 and 60 hours every week. His comments revealed how main provider husbands sometimes felt threatened when women began asserting themselves in previously all-male occupations.

As long as women mind their own business, no problem with me, you know. If you get a secretary that's nosy and wants to run the company, hey, well, we tell her where to stick it. . . . There's nothing wrong with them being in the job, but when you can't do my job, don't tell me how to do it.

The mechanic's wife, also a part-time teacher's aide, subtly resisted by "spending as little time on housework as I can get away with." Nevertheless, she still considered it her sole duty to cook, and only when her husband was away at military reserve training sessions did she feel she could "slack off" by not placing "regular meals" on the table each night.

The Impact of Failed Aspirations.   Main provider couples allocated most of the family work to the wife, but a few of these couples—those with husbands who had unfulfilled career goals—tended to share more than the others. Using the combined measures for housework and child care, these couples were rated as sharing significantly more family labor. What appeared to tip the economy of gratitude away from simple male privilege was the wife's sense that the husband had not fulfilled his career potential. For example, one main provider husband graduated from a four-year college and completed two years of postgraduate study without finishing his master's thesis. At the time of the interview, he was making about $30,000 per year as a self-employed house painter and his wife was making $13,000 a year as a full-time secretary. His comments show how her evaluation of his failed or postponed career aspirations led to more bargaining over his participation in routine housework.

> She reminds me that I'm not doing what we both think I should be doing, and sometimes that's a discouragement, because I might have worked a lot of hours, and I'll come home tired, for example, and she'll say, "You've gotta clean the house," and I'll say, "Damn I'm tired, I'd like to get a little rest in." But she says, "You're only doing this because it's your choice." She tends to not have sympathy for me in my work because it was more my choice than hers.

He acknowledged that he should be doing something more "worthwhile" and hoped that he would not be painting houses for more than another year. Still, as long as he stayed in his current job, she would not allow him to use fatigue from employment as a way to get out of doing housework.

> I worked about sixty hours a week the last couple of weeks. I worked yesterday [Saturday], and today. If it had been my choice, I would have drank beer and watched TV. But since she had a baby shower to go to, I babysitted my nephews. And since we had you coming, she kind of laid out the program: "You've gotta clean the floors, and wash the dishes and do the carpets. So get to it buddy!" (Laughs)

Although this main provider husband capitulated to his wife's demands, she was the one to set tasks for him and reminded him to perform them. In responding to her "program," he used the strategy of claimed incompetence that other main provider husbands also used. While he admitted that he was proficient at the "janitorial stuff," he was careful to point out that he was incapable of dusting or doing the laundry.

> It's amazing what you can do when you have little time and you just get in and do it. And I'm good at that. I'm good at the big cleaning, I'm good at the janitorial stuff. I can do the carpet, do the floors, do all that stuff. But I'm no good on the details. She wants all the details just right, so she handles dusting, the laundry, and the things that I couldn't do, like I would turn everything one color.

By recategorizing some of the housework as "big cleaning" and "janitorial stuff," this husband rendered it accountable as men's work. Thus, he continued to "do gender" as he did housework. While he drew the line at laundry and dusting, it is significant that there was at least some redefinition of tasks like vacuuming and mopping. He was complying, albeit reluctantly, to many of his wife's requests because they agreed that he had not fulfilled "his" job as sole provider. He still yearned to be the "real" breadwinner and shared his hope that getting a better paying job would mean that he could ignore the housework.

> Sharing the house stuff is usually just a necessity. If, as we would hope in the future, if she didn't have to work outside of the home, then I think I would be comfortable doing less of it. Then she would be the primary house care person and I would be the primary financial resource person. I think roles would change then, and I would be comfortable with her doing more of the dishes and more of the cleaning, and I think she would too. In that sense, I think traditional relationships, if traditional means the guy working and the woman staying home, is good. I wouldn't mind getting a taste of it myself!

A similar failed aspirations pattern was found in another main provider household, even though the husband had a good job as an elementary school teacher. While his wife earned less than a sixth of what he did, she was working on an advanced degree and coordinated a nonprofit community program. In this family, unlike most others, the husband performed more housework than he did child care, though both he and his wife agreed that she did more of both. Nevertheless, he performed these household chores reluctantly, and only in response to prodding from his wife. "Housework is mostly her responsibility. I like to come home and kick back. Sometimes she has to complain before I do anything around the house. You know when she hits the wall, then I start doing things. So I get out of the house on weekends."

This main provider husband talked about how his real love was art, and how he had failed to pursue his dream of being a graphic artist. The blocked occupational achievement in his case was not that he didn't make good money in a respected professional job, but that he was not fulfilling his "true" potential. His failed career goals increased her willingness to make demands on him, influenced their division of household labor, and helped shape feelings of entitlement between them. "I have talents that she doesn't have. I guess that's one of my strongest strengths, is that I'm an artist. But I have not done it. She's very disappointed in me in the sense that I have not done enough of it, and that I do not spend enough time helping my daughter be creative."

Another main provider household followed a similar failed aspirations pattern. He was a telephone lineman making $34,000 a year and she had recently quit an "outside" job, and was now running a family day care center in their home that earned about $10,000 per year. She regretted that he didn't do something "more important" for a living. He said, "She's always telling me, 'You're pretty smart, you're too smart for what you are doing.'" Like the other two failed aspirations husbands, he did more family work than other main providers, but resentment came through when he described what he didn't like about "the wife" working outside the home.

What I didn't like about it was that I used to get home before the wife, because she had to commute, and I'd have to pop something to eat. Most of the time it was just whatever I happened to find in the fridge. Then I'd have to go pick up the kids immediately from the babysitter, and sometimes I had evening things to do, so what I didn't like was that I had to figure out a way to schedule baby watch or baby sitting when I had evening things.

Thus, even when main provider husbands began to assume some of the domestic chores in response to "necessity" or "nagging," they seemed to cling to the idea that it wasn't fully their responsibility. According to their accounts, this seemed to justify their resentment at having to do "her" chores. Not incidentally, most of the secondary provider wives reported that they received very little help unless they "constantly" reminded him. Wives didn't like their husband's reluctance to assume responsibility for family work, but the women also continued to accept the homemaker role. In addition, the wives appreciated their husband's substantial financial contributions. When performance of the provider role was deemed to be lacking in some way (as in failed aspirations or low occupational prestige), wives' resentment appeared closer to the surface and couples reported that the wives were more persistent in demanding help.

Co-Provider Couples

The remaining families were classified as co-providers, based on an evaluation of their employment, earnings, and ideology. Compared to main provider couples, co-providers tended to have more equal earnings and to value the wife's employment more highly. Among the twelve co-provider couples, wives averaged 44 percent of the family income compared to 20 percent for main provider couples. There was considerable variation among co-provider husbands, however, in terms of their willingness to accept their wives as equal providers, or to assume the role of equal homemaker or parent. Accordingly, I categorized these families into ambivalent co-providers (5 couples) and full co-providers (7 couples). The ambivalent co-provider husbands accepted their wives' jobs as important and permanent, but often used their own job commitments as justifications for why they did so little at home. I discuss both types of co-providers, considering variation between them in terms of earnings, job status, ideology, role attachments, and divisions of family work.

Ambivalent Co-Providers

Compared to their wives, ambivalent co-provider husbands usually held jobs that were roughly equivalent in terms of occupational prestige and worked about the same number of hours per week. All these husbands earned more than their wives, however, with average annual husbands' earnings of $39,000, compared to $30,000 for the wives. While both husbands and wives thus had careers that provided "comfortable" incomes, the husbands, and sometimes the wives, were ambivalent about treating her career as equally important to his. For example, few ambivalent co-provider husbands let their family work intrude on their paid work, whereas wives' family work often interfered with their paid work. Such asymmetrically permeable work/family boundaries are common in single earner and main provider families, but must be supported with subtle ideologies and elaborate justifications when husbands and wives hold similar occupational positions.

Ambivalent co-provider husbands remained in a helper role at home, perceiving their wives to be more involved parents and assuming that housework was also their wives' responsibility. Husbands used their breadwinner responsibilities to justify their absence, but most lamented not being able to spend more time with their families. For instance, one husband who worked full time as a city planner was married to a woman who worked an equal number of hours as an office manager. In talking about the time he put in at his job, he commented, "I wish I had more time to spend with my children, and to spend with my wife too, of course, but it's a fact of life that I have to work." His wife, in contrast, indicated that her paid job, which she had held for fourteen years, did not prohibit her from adequately caring for her three children, or taking care of "her" household chores. Ambivalent co-provider husbands did not perform significantly more housework and child care than main provider husbands, and generally did fewer household chores than main provider husbands with failed career aspirations.

Not surprisingly, ambivalent co-provider husbands tended to be satisfied with their current divisions of labor, even though they usually admitted that things were "not quite fair." One junior high school teacher married to a bilingual education program coordinator described his reactions to their division of family labor.

To be honest, I'm totally satisfied. When I had a first-period conference, I was a little more flexible, I'd help her more with changing' em, you know getting them ready for school since I didn't have to be at school right away. Then I had to switch because they had some situation out at fifth-period conference, so that, you know, now she does it a little bit more than I do, and I don't help out with the kids as much in the morning because I have to be there an hour earlier.

This ambivalent co-provider clearly saw himself as "helping" his wife with the children, yet made light of her contributions by saying she does "a little bit more than I do." He went on to reveal how his wife did not enjoy similar special privileges due to her employment, since she had to pick up the children from day care every day, as well as take them to school in the mornings.

She gets out a little later than I do, because she's an administrator, but I have other things outside. I also work out, I run, and that sort of gives me a time away, to do that before they all come here. I have community meetings in the evenings sometimes too. So, I mean, it might not be totally fair—maybe 60/40—but I'm thoroughly happy with the way things are.

While he was "thoroughly happy" with the current arrangements, his wife thought that their division of labor was decidedly unfair. She said, "I don't like the fact that it's taken for granted that I'm available. When he goes out he just assumes I'm available, but when I go out I have to consult with him to make sure he is available." For her, child care was a given. For him, it was optional, as evidenced by his comment, "If I don't have something else to do then I'll take the kids."

Ambivalent co-provider husbands also tended to lament the way they saw their family involvement limiting their careers or personal activities. For instance, the school teacher discussed above regretted that he could not do what he used to before he had children.

> Having children keeps me away from thinking a lot about my work. You know, it used to be, before we had kids, I could have my mind geared to work—you know how ideas just pop in, you really get into it. But with kids it doesn't get as—you know, you can't switch. It gets more difficult, it makes it hard to get into it. I don't have that freedom of mind, you know, and it takes away from aspects of my work, like doing a little bit more reading or research that I would like to do. Or my own activities, I mean, I still run, but not as much as I used to. I used to play basketball, I used to coach, this and that.

Other ambivalent co-provider husbands talked about the impact of children on their careers and personal lives with less lament and more appreciation for establishing bonds with their children. Encouraged by their wives to alter their priorities, some reinterpreted the relative importance of career and family commitments. For example, another teacher and coach talked about how having a family changed his feelings about his job.

> I like the way things are going, let's put it this way. I mean, it's just that once you become a parent, it's a never-ending thing. I coach my kid, for example, this past week we had four games and I'm getting ready to go out there, you know and I'm getting ready to change a door knob here. I just think that by having a family that your life becomes so involved after awhile with your own kids, that it's very difficult. I coached at the varsity level for one year and I was taking so much time away from it that I had to give that up. In other words, I had to give up something that I like to do, for my own kids' sake. I would leave in the morning when they were asleep, and I would get out of coaches' meetings at ten or eleven at night. My wife said to me, "Think about your priorities, man, you leave when the kids are asleep, come back when they are asleep," so I decided to change that act. So I gave it up for a year, and I was home all the time. And now I am going to coach again, but it's at lower levels, and I'll be home every day. I have to make adjustments for my family. So your attitude changes, it's not me that counts anymore.

Whereas family labor was not shared equally in this ambivalent co-provider couple, the husband, at his wife's urging, was beginning to accept and appreciate that his children were more important than his job. Like many other husbands, he was evaluating his attachment to his children on his wife's terms, but he was beginning to take on more responsibility for them. Unlike the main providers, ambivalent co-provider husbands were more conflicted about giving up job time to perform family work. Like the main providers, however, they did not relinquish the assumption that the home was basically the wife's domain.

Hiring Outside Help

Two of the ambivalent co-provider couples attempted to alleviate stress on the wife by hiring outside help. For instance, we asked a self-employed male attorney making $40,000 per year if he thought their division of household tasks was fair: "Do you mean fair like equal? It's probably not equal, so probably it wouldn't be fair. That's why we have a housekeeper." His wife, a social worker earning $36,000 per year, talked about how the household was still her responsibility, but that she now had fewer tasks to do. "When I did not have help, I tended to do everything, but with a housekeeper, I don't have to do so much." She went on to talk about how she wished he would do more with their five- and eight-year-old children, but speculated that he would as they grew older.

Another couple paid a live-in babysitter and housekeeper to watch their three children during the day while he worked full time in construction and she worked full time as a psychiatric social worker. Although she labeled the outside help as "essential," she noted that her husband contributed more to the mess than he did to its cleanup. He saw himself as an involved father because he played with his children and she acknowledged this, but she also complained that he competed with them in games as if he were a child himself. His participation in routine household labor was considered optional, as evidenced by his comment, "I like to cook once in a while."

Only one other family, a full co-provider couple who shared most of the housework, talked about paying for household help. In their case, they hired a gardener to do some of "his" chores, freeing him to do more of the child care and housework. This strategy reflected an assumption that the husband "should" share in family work, an assumption that most main provider and ambivalent co-provider husbands did not willingly make.

Full Co-Provider Couples

Over a third of the Chicano couples were classified as full co-providers. Husbands and wives in these families took the wife's employment for granted and considered her career to be just as important as his. Like the more ambivalent couples discussed above, full co-provider husbands and wives worked about the same number of hours as each other, but, on the whole, the co-provider couples spent a total of about ten more hours each week on the job than their more ambivalent counterparts. Despite working more hours, co-providers tended to have significantly lower incomes.

The sharing of family work was substantially greater for full co-providers than for any other groups. (No co-provider couple had a mean husband–wife housework/child care score over 3.0—the true midpoint of the combined scale—but five of the seven families had mean husband–wife scores of 2.5 or higher, indicating substantial sharing of these tasks.) Since husbands tended to take more credit than their wives granted them, I also looked specifically at the wives' ratings in the co-provider couples. Six of seven co-provider wives rated child care as shared, and two of these wives also rated housework as shared. The co-provider families thus represent the most egalitarian families in this sample of dual-earner Chicano couples and show the direct link between accepting the wife as co-provider and the husband as a co-caregiver. On the following pages I explore some factors that the couples indicated led to sharing these roles.

Like the more ambivalent co-providers, husbands in full co-provider families discussed conflicts between work and family and sometimes alluded to the ways that their occupational advancement was limited by their commitments to their children. One husband and wife spent the same number of hours on the job, earned approximately the same amount of money, and were employed as engineering technicians for the same employer. When asked how his family involvement had affected his job performance, he responded by saying, "It should, because I really need to spend a lot more time learning my work and I haven't really put in the time I need to advance in the profession. . . . I would spend more time if I didn't have kids. I'd like to be able to play with the computer or read books more often." Nevertheless, the husband repeatedly talked about how such adjustments were not really sacrifices because he valued time with his children so highly. He did not use his job as an excuse to get out of family work like the ambivalent co-providers, and he seemed to value his wife's career at least as much as his own.

> I think her job is probably more important than mine because she's been at that kind of work a lot longer than I have. And at the level she is—its awkward the way it is, because I get paid just a little bit more than she does, I have a higher position. But she definitely knows the work a lot more, she's been doing the same type of work for about nine years already, and I've only been doing this type of engineering work for about two and a half years, so she knows a lot more. We both have to work, that's for sure.

Because they recognized that they were equal providers, this couple shared more of the family work. In the interview and the card sorts, the husband indicated that he did more child care and housework than she did. In contrast, she gave her husband credit for doing a substantial amount of the child care, though less than she. She described his relationship with their seven-year-old son as "very caring," and noted that he helps the boy with homework more often than she does. She also said that he did most of the heavy cleaning and scrubbing, but, contrary to his classification, rated herself as doing many more of the total housework tasks. She also commented that he doesn't clean toilets and doesn't always notice when things are dirty.

The husband also raised issues about standards and styles for housework. Similar to some of the men in the first interviews, he suggested that he does more of the routine maintenance and general cleaning jobs but leaves the "little things" and major redecorating to her.

> Some of the things she does, I just will not do. I will not dust all the little things in the house. That's one of my least favorite things, is dusting. I'm more than likely to do the mopping and vacuuming and trying to make things fit. And she's more than likely to want to move something around that's going to require a new piece of furniture to make it work.

His comments reveal how arguments shift to differences over housework standards once both spouses accept that they should share responsibility for the housework. "She has high standards for cleanliness that you would have to be home to maintain. Mine tend to acknowledge that hey, you don't always get to this stuff because you have other things to do. I think I have a better acceptance that one priority hurts something else in the background."

Although this couple generally agreed about how to raise their son, standards for child care were also subject to debate. He saw himself as doing more with his son than she did, as reflected in comments such as "I tend to think of myself as the more involved parent, and I think other people have noticed that too." While she had only positive things to say about his parenting, he offered both praise and criticism.

> She can be very playful. She makes up fun games. She doesn't always put enough into the educational part of it, though, like exploring or reading. . . . She cherishes tune-up time [job-related study or preparation], and sometimes I feel she should be using that time to spend with him. Like at the beach, I'll play with him, but she'll be more likely to be under the umbrella reading.

Like many other husbands, he went on to say that he thought their division of labor was unfair. Unlike the others, however, he indicated that he thought their current arrangements favored her needs, not his. "I think I do more housework [and] it's probably not fair because I do more of the dirtier tasks. . . . Also, at this point, our solution tends to favor her free time more than my free time."

In this family, comparable occupational status and earnings, coupled with a relatively egalitarian ideology, led to substantial sharing of family work. The husband took more credit for his involvement than his wife gave him, but we can see a difference between their talk and that of some of the more conventional families discussed above. While other husbands sometimes complained about their wife's high standards, they treated housework, and even parenting, as primarily her duty. They often resented being nagged to do more around the house, but rarely moved out of a helper role to consider it their duty to anticipate, schedule, and take care of family and household needs. In this co-provider household, that unbalanced allocation of responsibility was not so taken for granted. Because of this, negotiations over housework and parenting were more frequent than in the other families. Since they both held expectations that each would fulfill both provider and caretaker roles, resentments came from both spouses—not just from the wife.

Sharing provider and homemaker roles seems to be easier, when, like the family above, the wife's earnings and occupational prestige equal or exceed those of her husband. For instance, in one of the couples reporting the most sharing of child care and housework, the wife earned $36,000 annually as executive director of a nonprofit group and as a private consultant, whereas he earned $30,000 as a self-employed general contractor. This couple shared most of the housework according to both, and although she rated him as doing fully half of the child care, he rated her as performing more than he did.

This couple started off their marriage with fairly traditional gender expectations and a conventional division of labor. While the husband's ideology had slowly changed, he still talked like most of the main provider husbands.

As far the household is concerned, I divide a house into two categories: one is the interior and the other is the exterior. For the interior, my wife pushes me to deal with that. The exterior, I'm left to it myself. So, what I'm basically saying is that generally speaking, a woman does not deal with the exterior. The woman's main concern is with the interior, although there is a lot of deviation.

In this family, an egalitarian belief system did not precede the sharing of household labor. The wife was still responsible for setting the "interior" household agenda and had to remind her husband to help with housework and child care. When asked whether he and his wife had arguments about housework, this husband laughed and said, "All the time, doesn't everybody?"

This couple was different from most others because she made more money than he did, and had no qualms about demanding help from him. While he had not yet accepted the idea that interior chores were equally his, he reluctantly performed them. In the card sorts, she ranked his contributions to child care equal to hers, and rated his contributions to housework only slightly below her own. While not eagerly rushing to do the cooking, cleaning, or laundry, he complied with occasional reminders, and according to her, was "a better cleaner."

His sharing stemmed, in part, from her higher earnings and their mutual willingness to reduce his "outside chores" by hiring help. Instead of complaining about their division of labor, he talked about how he has come to appreciate his situation.

Ever since I've known my wife, she's made more money than I have. Initially—as a man—I resented it. I went through a lot of head trips about it. But as time developed, I appreciated it. Now I respect it. The way I figure it is I'd rather have her sharing the money with me than sharing it with someone else. She has her full-time job and then she has her part-time job as a consultant. The gardener I'm paying $75 per week, and I'm paying someone else $25 per week to make my lunch, so I'm enjoying it! It's self-interest.

The power dynamic in this family, coupled with their willingness to pay for outside help to reduce his chores, and the flexibility of his self-employed work schedule, led to substantial sharing of cooking, cleaning, and child care. Because she was making more money and working more hours than he was, he could not emulate other husbands in claiming priority for his provider activities.

A similar dynamic was evident in other co-provider couples with comparable earnings and career commitments. One male IRS officer married to a school teacher now made more money than his wife, but talked about his feelings when she was the more successful provider.

It doesn't bother me when she makes more money than me. I don't think it has anything to do with being a man. I don't have any hang-ups about it, I mean, I don't equate those things with manhood. It takes a pretty simple mind to think that way. First of all, she doesn't feel superior when she has made more money. I guess if the woman felt that she could expect more because she was making more money, that's when the guy might feel intimidated.

This husband's statement implied that his wife did not use her equal or superior earnings as a basis for making demands on him. Contrary to his portrayal, however, she commented that he was "better" at housework than she was, and that she "nagged him" to get him to do it. Although only two wives in this sample of families earned more than their husbands, the reversal of symbolic provider status seemed to raise expectations for increased family work from husbands. Both of the husbands we interviewed who made less than their wives performed more of the housework and child care than other husbands.

Even when wives' earnings did not exceed husbands', some co-providers shared the homemaker role. A male college admissions recruiter and his executive secretary wife shared substantial housework according to mutual ratings and most child care according to her rating. He made $29,000 per year working an average of fifty hours per week, while she made $22,000 working a forty-hour week. Like the contractor/executive secretary couple above, she was willing to give him more credit than he was willing to claim for child care. In both cases this appeared to reflect the wife's sincere appreciation for her husband's parenting efforts and a desire to praise him for doing so much more than other fathers. For their part, the husbands placed a high value on their wives' unique parenting skills and seemed to downplay the possibility that they might be considered equal parents.

Like most men, the college recruiter husband was reluctant to perform many housecleaning chores. Like other co-provider husbands, however, he managed to redefine these routine household chores as a shared responsibility. For instance, when we asked him what he liked least about housework, he laughingly replied: "Probably those damn toilets, man, and the showers, the bathrooms, gotta scrub 'em, argghh! I wish I didn't have to do any of that, you know the vacuuming and all that. But it's just a fact of life." Even though he did more than most men, he still acknowledged that he did less than his wife. He also admitted that he had used his job to get out of doing more family work. "I think there might be room for a more equal distribution than in the past. But then, I also have always used my job as a justification, you know, for doing less. I'm on the road and stuff, that makes it kinda hard." Whereas other wives often allowed husbands to use their jobs as excuses for doing less family work, or assumed that their husbands were incapable of performing certain chores like cooking or laundry, the pattern in this family resembled that in the failed aspirations families. In other words, the wife did not assume that housework was "her" job, did not accept her husband's job demands as justification for his doing less housework, and sometimes challenged his interpretation of how much his job required of him. He commented, "Sometimes she's not always understanding of my work. I mean, it's like 'Why are you doing this, it's not even your job.' Because the typical thing is always like, you know, 'Well, this is my job, this is what I do for a living and you just have to accept it.'"

When he described who did what around their house, this husband provided some insight into how his wife was able to get him to do more.

Sometimes she just refuses to do something. . . . An example would be the ironing, you know, I never used to do the ironing, hated it. Now it's just something that happens. You need something ironed, you better iron it or you're not gonna have it in the morning. So, I think, you know, that kinda just evolved, I mean, she just gradually quit doing it so everybody just had to do their own. My son irons his own clothes, I iron my own clothes, my daughter irons her own clothes, the only one that doesn't iron is the baby, and next year she'll probably start.

Hood describes this strategy as "going on strike," and suggests that it is most effective when husbands feel the specific task must be done.[11] Since appearing neat and well-dressed was a priority for this husband, when she stopped ironing his clothes, he started doing it himself. Because he felt it was important for his children to be "presentable" in public, he also began to remind them to iron their own clothes before going visiting or attending mass.

Many co-provider couples said that sharing housework was contingent on continual bargaining and negotiation. Others focused on how the sharing of family work "evolved naturally." One co-provider husband, director of a housing agency, reported that he and his wife didn't negotiate; "we pretty much do what needs to be done." His wife, an executive secretary, confirmed his description, and echoed the ad hoc arrangements of many of the role-sharing couples in the first study. "We have not had to negotiate. We both have our specialties. He is great with dishes, I like to clean bathrooms. He does most of the laundry. It has worked out that we each do what we like best."

When both spouses assume that household tasks are a shared responsibility, negotiation can be less necessary or contentious. For example, a co-provider Chicano husband who worked as a mail carrier commented, "I get home early and start dinner, make sure the kids do their homework, feed the dogs, stuff like that." He and his wife, also an executive secretary, agreed that they rarely talked about housework. She said, "When I went back to work we agreed that we both needed to share, and so we just do it." While she still reminded him to perform chores according to her standards or on her schedule, she summed up her appreciation by commenting, "at least he does it without complaining." Lack of complaint was a common feature of co-provider families. Whereas many main provider husbands complained of having to do "her" chores, the co-providers did not talk about harboring resentments about contributing to housework or child care. Time was short and the work was often tedious, but they rarely assumed that they were being forced into it by their wives. Neither did co-provider husbands complain about not having the services of a stay-at-home wife like the main provider husbands sometimes did.

Getting Involved as Fathers

Some Chicano fathers spoke of making explicit choices to become actively involved in their children's lives. One co-provider husband talked about the uniqueness of a mother's love, but focused on his decision to "invest" in his kids.

Fathers are always going to be at a disadvantage in the whole nurturing thing simply because it can't be the same [as it is with mothers]. But I think that fathers can make it their choice to become as nurturing as they want to. I think that if they consider the relationship that they will have with them for the rest of their life they can see that it is the most important investment they can make.

Involved fathers characterized what they were doing as a decision to put their children's needs first. Main provider husbands, in contrast, tended to use their jobs as excuses for spending little time with their children. Ambivalent co-providers similarly lamented how children sometimes detracted from their careers. Co-provider husbands, on the other hand, even though they were employed as many hours as the others, talked about making a definite choice to spend time with and care for their children. None voiced regret over such a choice.

When asked whether fathers could provide the same type of nurturance that mothers did, the majority of co-providers said no, even while affirming that it was very important for fathers to be involved with their children. Most of the main provider husbands, in contrast, answered that men could nurture like women, but only if they were somehow compelled to do so by some unusual circumstance. For instance, one main provider said, "If it was necessary, yes I think a father could. . . you know, you can adapt to anything, so if their mother couldn't do it, their dad could." Ambivalent co-providers generally did not claim credit for men being able to parent like women, yet their answers resembled those of the main providers. One said, "Maybe men could provide the same nurturance if they were the only parent, but mother nurturance is more important." Another ambivalent co-provider answered, "Probably, I don't know about permanently, but they probably could if they had to, if they were left in a situation where they had to." Whereas main providers and ambivalent co-providers focused on how men could parent when they were forced to do it, co-providers stressed the fact that one had to choose it voluntarily.

Sharing and Reluctance

For these dual-earner Chicano couples, we found considerable sharing in several areas. First, as in previous studies of ethnic minority families, wives were employed a substantial number of hours and made significant contributions to the household income. Second, like some researchers, we found that couples described their decisionmaking to be relatively fair and equal. Third, fathers in these families were more involved in child rearing than their own fathers had been, and seven of 20 husbands were rated as sharing most child care tasks. Finally, although no husband performed fully half of the housework, a few made substantial contributions in this area as well.

One of the power dynamics that appeared to undergird the household division of labor in these families was the relative earning power of each spouse, though this was modified by occupational prestige, provider role status, and personal preferences. When the wife earned less than a third of the family income, the husband performed little of the routine housework or child care. In two families, wives earned more than their husbands. These two households reported sharing more domestic labor than any of the others. Among the other couples who shared family work, we found a preponderance of relatively balanced incomes. In the two families with large financial contributions from wives, but little household help from husbands, couples had hired housekeepers to reduce the household workload.

Relative income thus makes a difference, but there was no simple or straightforward exchange of market resources for domestic services in these families. Other factors like failed career aspirations or occupational status influenced power differentials and helped to explain why some wives were willing to push a little harder for change in the division of household labor. In almost every case, husbands reluctantly responded to requests for help from wives. Only when wives explicitly took the initiative to shift some of the housework burden to husbands did the men begin to assume significant responsibility for the day-to-day operation of the household. Even when they began to share the family work, men tended to do some of the less onerous tasks like playing with the children or washing the dinner dishes. When we compare these men to their own fathers, or those of their mothers, however, we can see that they are sharing more domestic chores than the generation of parents that preceded them.

Acceptance of wives as co-providers and wives' delegation of a portion of the home-maker role to husbands were especially important to creating more equal divisions of household labor. If wives made lists for their husbands or offered them frequent reminders, they were more successful than if they waited for husbands to take the initiative. But remaining responsible for managing the home and children was cause for resentment on the part of many wives. Sometimes wives were effective in getting husbands to perform certain chores, like ironing, by stopping doing it altogether. For other wives, sharing evolved more "naturally," as both spouses agreed to share tasks or performed the chores they most preferred.

Economies of gratitude continually shifted in these couples as ideology, career attachments, and feelings of obligation and entitlement changed. For some main provider families, this meant that wives were grateful for husbands' "permission" to hold a job, or that wives worked harder at home because they felt guilty for making their husbands do any of the housework. Main provider husbands usually let their job commitments limit their family work, whereas their wives took time off from work to take children to the dentist, care for a sick child, or attend a parent–teacher conference.

Even in families where co-provider wives had advanced degrees and earned relatively high wages, women's work/family boundaries were more permeable than their husbands'. For example, one professional woman complained that her teacher husband was a "perpetual" graduate student and attended "endless" community meetings. She was employed more hours then he, and made about the same amount of money, but she had to "schedule him" to watch the children if she wanted to leave the house alone. His stature as a "community leader" provided him with subterranean leverage in the unspoken struggle over taking responsibility for the house and children. His "gender ideology," if we had measured it with conventional survey questions, would undoubtedly have been characterized as "egalitarian." He spoke in broad platitudes about women's equality and was washing the dishes when we arrived for the interviews. He insisted on finishing the dishes as he answered my questions, but in the other room his wife confided to Elsa in incredulous tones, "He never does that!"

In other ambivalent co-provider families, husbands gained unspoken advantage because they had more prestigious jobs than their wives, and earned more money. While these highly educated attorneys and administrators talked about how they respected their wives' careers, and expressed interest in spending more time with their children, their actions showed that they did not fully assume responsibility for sharing the family work. To solve the dilemma of too little time and too many chores, two of these families hired housekeepers. Wives were grateful for this strategy, though it did not alter inequities in the distribution of housework and child care, or in the allocation of worry.

In other families, the economy of gratitude departed dramatically from conventional notions of husband as economic provider and wife as nurturing homemaker. When wives' earnings approached or exceeded their husbands', economies of gratitude shifted toward more equal expectations, with husbands beginning to assume that they must do more around the house. Even in these families, husbands rarely began doing more chores without prodding from wives, but they usually did them "without complaining." Similarly, when wives with economic leverage began expecting more from their husbands, they were usually successful in getting them to do more.

Another type of leverage that was important, even in main provider households, was the existence of failed aspirations. If wives expected husbands to "make more" of themselves, pursue "more important" careers, or follow "dream" occupational goals, then wives were able to get husbands to do more around the house. This perception of failed aspirations, if held by both spouses, served as a reminder that husbands had no excuse for not helping out at home. In these families, wives were not at all reluctant to demand assistance with domestic chores, and husbands were rarely able to use their jobs as excuses for getting out of housework.[12]

The leisure gap, common among Anglo couples, is also clearly present in dual-earner Chicano families. Nevertheless, in couples where the economy of gratitude is more balanced, the leisure gap begins to shrink. It becomes much less significant, though it doesn't disappear entirely, when both spouses consider the woman's job as important as the man's. In subsequent chapters we will see that this tends to happen when wives' earnings approach those of husbands'.

The economies of gratitude in these families were not equally balanced, but many exhibited divisions of household labor that contradicted cultural stereotypes of male-dominated Chicano families. Particularly salient in these families was the lack of fit between their own class position and that of their parents. Most parents were immigrants with little education and low occupational mobility. The couples we interviewed, in contrast, were well educated and relatively secure in middle-class occupations. The couples could have compared themselves to their parents, evaluating themselves as egalitarian and financially successful. While some did just that, most compared themselves to their Anglo and Chicano friends and co-workers, many of whom shared as much or more than they did. The couples had no absolute or fixed standard against which to make judgments about themselves. Implicitly comparing their earnings, occupational commitments, and perceived aptitudes, these individuals negotiated new patterns of work and family commitments and developed new justifications for their emerging arrangements.[13] These were not created anew, but emerged out of the popular culture in which they found themselves. Our findings confirm that families are an important site of new struggles over the meaning of gender and the rights and obligations of men and women to each other and over each other's labor.

One of our most interesting findings has to do with the class position of Chicano husbands and wives who shared the most household labor: white-collar working-class families shared more than upper-middle-class professionals. Contrary to findings from some nationwide surveys, the most highly educated of our well-educated sample of Chicano couples shared only moderate amounts of child care and little housework.[14] Contrary to other predictions, neither was it the working-class women in this study who achieved the most balanced divisions of labor.[15] It was the middle occupational group—the executive secretaries, clerks, technicians, teachers, and midlevel administrators—who extracted the most help from husbands. The men in these families were similarly in the middle in terms of occupational status for this sample—administrative assistants, a builder, a mail carrier, a technician—and in the middle in terms of income. What this means is that the highest status wives—the program coordinators, nurses, social workers, and office managers—were not able to, or chose not to, transform their salaries or occupational status into more participation from husbands. This was probably because their husbands had even higher incomes and more prestigious occupations. The lawyers, program directors, ranking bureaucrats, and "community leaders" parlayed their status into extra leisure at home, either by paying for housekeepers or ignoring the housework. Finally, Chicano wives at the lowest end fared least well. The teacher's aides, entry-level secretaries, day care providers, and part-time employees did the bulk of the work at home whether they were married to mechanics or lawyers. When wives made less than a third of what their husbands did, they were only able to get husbands to do a little more if they were working at jobs considered "below" them—a telephone lineman, a painter, an elementary school teacher.

These interviews with Chicano couples corroborate results from previous in-depth interview studies of Anglo couples and suggest that the major processes shaping divisions of labor in middle-class Chicano couples are about the same as those shaping such divisions in other couples.[14] That is not to say that ethnicity did not make a difference to the people we talked with. They grew up in recently immigrating working-class families, watched their parents work long hours for minimal wages, and understood firsthand the toll that various forms of racial and ethnic discrimination can take. Probably because of some of these experiences, and their own more recent ones, our informants looked at job security, fertility decisions, and the division of family work somewhat differently than their Anglo counterparts. In some cases, this may give Chicano husbands in working-class or professional jobs license to ignore more of the housework, and might temper the anger of some working-class or professional Chicanos who are still called on to do most of the domestic chores. If our findings are generalizable, however, it is those in between the blue-collar working class and the upper-middle-class professionals who might be most likely to share family work.

Assessing whether my findings apply to other two-job Latino or other minority couples will require the use of larger, more representative samples. If the limited sharing we observed represents a trend—however slow or reluctant—it could have far-reaching consequences. More and more mothers are remaining full-time members of the paid labor force. With the "postindustrial" expansion of the service and information sectors of the economy, Chicanos and other minorities, will be increasingly likely to enter white-collar working-class occupations. As more minority families fit the occupational profile of those we studied, we may see more assumption of housework and child care by the men within them.

Regardless of the specific changes that the economy will undergo, we can expect ethnic minority men and women, like their white counterparts, to continue to negotiate for change in their work and family roles. Economic and institutional factors will undoubtedly play a major part in the shaping of these roles, but social and personal factors will also be important. Reluctant husbands will be unlikely to accept even partial responsibility for the homemaker role unless wives are accepted as co-providers.

Notes

1. Jesse Bernard. *The Future of Marriage.* New York: World, 1972.

2. R. Nisbett and L. Ross. *Human Inference Strategies and Shortcomings of Social Judgment.* Englewood Cliffs, NJ: Prentice Hall, 1980.

3. S. C. Thompson and H. H. Kelley. "Judgment of Responsibility for Activities in Close Relationships." *Journal of Personality and Social Psychology* 41(1981): 469–477.

4. Gary Becker. *A Treatise on the Family,* (Cambridge, Mass.: Harvard University Press, 1981)

5. Heidi Hermann. "The Family as the Locus of Gender, Class, and Political Struggle," *Signs* 6 (1981): 366–394.

6. Joseph Pleck. "The Work-Family Role System." *Social Problems* 24 (1977): 417–427.

7. Jane Hood. "The Provider Role in Meaning and Measurement." *Journal of Marriage and the Family* 48 (1986): 349–359.

8. See Jane Hood, *Becoming a Two-Job Family* (New York: Praeger, 1983); John Scanzoni, *Sex Roles, Women's Work and Marital Conflict* (Washington, D.C.: Lexington, 1978).

9. See Hood, (*The Provider Role,* 1978).

10. Ibid.

11. See Hood, (*Two-Job Family,* 131).

12. For a discussion on the ways that economies of gratitude are shaped by past events, see Karen Pyke and Scott Coltrane, "Entitlement Obligation and Gratitude in Remarriage" (paper presented at the Annual Meeting of the Pacific Sociological Association, San Francisco, California, April 1995), and Karen Pyke, *Gender and Society* (1992).

13. Judith Stacey. *Brave New Families: Stories of Domestic Upheaval in Late Twentieth Century America* (New York: Basic Books, 1991), 17.

14. Donna H. Berardo, Constance Shehan, and Gerald R. Leslie, "A Residue of Tradition: Jobs, Careers, and Spouses, and Housework," *Journal of Marriage and the Family.* 49(1987): 381–390; Catherine E. Ross, "The Division of Labor at Home," *Social Forces* 65 (1987): 816–833.

15. Patricai Zavella. *Women's Work and Chicano Families: Cannery Workers of the Santa Clara Valley* (Ithaca, New York: Cornell University Press, 1987).

16. See for example, Hochschild, *Second Shift;* Hood, *Two-Job Family.*

22

WHITE, BLACK, AND HISPANIC MEN'S HOUSEHOLD LABOR TIME

Anne Shelton and Daphne John

Most of the recent research on household labor concerns the impact of women's labor force participation on the allocation of tasks or responsibilities. Researchers routinely recognize that women's household labor time is associated with their employment status, as well as with a variety of other sociodemographic characteristics, including age and education. A great deal has been written about the ways in which time commitments and sex role attitudes affect the division of household labor (Coverman 1985; Huber and Spitze 1983; Perrucci, Potter, and Rhoads 1978; Pleck 1985; Ross 1987). Men are by definition included in the analyses that focus on the division of household labor, but these studies typically ignore the relationship between men's work and family roles.

Some researchers have examined the relationship between men's work and family roles (Coverman 1985; Pleck 1977, 1985), but the relative scarcity of these studies means that although some questions about men's household roles have been examined, a number of issues remain unexamined. In particular, there has been little research on the impact of men's paid labor time on their household labor time and there has been only limited research on racial and ethnic variations in men's household labor time.

In this analysis we begin to examine some of the neglected issues in the study of men's household labor time by focusing on how married men's paid labor time affects their family roles as defined by their household labor time and specific household tasks. Although there is less variation in men's paid labor time than in women's, there is some variation, and just as paid labor time affects women's household labor time, it may also affect men's. Moreover, the amount of time men have available to them may affect the specific household tasks they perform, with men with more time performing more nondiscretionary tasks than men who have less time available to them.

Recently, increased awareness of the need to examine links between gender and race have led many to argue that race and gender cannot, in fact, be discussed separately (Collins 1990; Reid and Comas-Diaz 1990; Zinn 1991). Moreover, "gender studies" should not be limited only to women. Therefore, we assess the impact of selected sociodemographic characteristics on men's household labor time with a special emphasis on race and ethnicity.

Literature Review

The changes in women's labor force participation have resulted in a large number of dual-earner couples. Kimmel (1987) notes that this shift has created not only new role demands for women, but also new demands for men. Just as women have expanded their roles in the paid labor force, men also have expanded their roles in the family. The transition in men's and women's roles may, however, vary by race and ethnicity because of the historically different patterns of black, white, and Hispanic women's labor force participation (Beckett and Smith 1981; McAdoo 1990).

Although researchers routinely examine the impact of women's paid labor time on the household division of labor, the impact of men's paid labor time on the household division of labor is generally ignored. The lack of attention to the impact of men's paid work time on their household labor time may reflect the fact that there is less variability in men's paid labor time than in women's. Those studies that have examined the impact of men's paid work time on their household labor time have yielded conflicting results (Barnett and Baruch 1987; Coverman and Sheley 1986; Pleck 1985; Thompson and Walker 1989). Some find that men's time spent in paid labor is negatively associated with their household labor time (Rexroat and Shehan 1987; Atkinson and Huston 1984), whereas others find no association (Kingston and Nock 1985). Because this research rarely focuses on racial/ethnic variation, we have little information about the ways that paid labor and household labor demands may be related differently for white, black, and Hispanic men.

Research on black and Hispanic households indicates that the images of the egalitarian black household and the gender-stratified Hispanic household may be inaccurate depictions of reality derived from superficial examinations. In the case of black households, egalitarianism is commonly attributed to black women's high rates of labor force participation (McAdoo 1990). If, however, black women's labor force participation reflects economic pressures rather than egalitarian sex role attitudes (Broman 1988, 1991), women's employment may be unrelated to the division of labor.

Research on the division of labor in black households does not consistently indicate how black and white households differ. Some research on the division of household labor finds that black families have a more egalitarian division of labor than white families (Beckett 1976; Beckett and Smith 1981; Broman 1988, 1991). Other studies by J. A. Ericksen, Yancey, and E. P. Ericksen (1979) and Farkas (1976) also suggest that black men do more household labor than their white counterparts (see also Miller and Garrison 1982). However, Broman (1991, 1988) argues that although some egalitarian patterns do exist in black households, there is not gender equity. For example, in married couple households the proportions of men who state they do most of the household chores is much smaller than the proportion of women responding that they do all the household chores. Although unemployed men respond that they do more of the household chores more frequently than employed men, they do not make this claim nearly as often as women, regardless of women's employment status. Broman (1988) also notes that women are likely to report being primarily responsible for traditionally female tasks.

Other researchers argue that the image of the egalitarian black family is inaccurate (Cronkite 1977; Staples 1978; Wilson, Tolson, Hinton, and Kiernan 1990). For example, Wilson et al. (1990) point out that black women are likely to be responsible for child care and household labor. Cronkite (1977) says that black men prefer more internal differentiation in the household than do white men. That is, she argues that they prefer a more traditional division of household labor, with women responsible for housework and child care. Others claim that black families are similar to white families in egalitarianism and that the differences that do exist often are based on social class rather than on race per se (McAdoo 1990; Staples 1978). Staples (1978) also claims that class differences are consistent across race. McAdoo (1990) argues, in much the same vein, that black and white fathers are similarly nurturant to their children and that black and white middle- and upper-income fathers have similar parenting styles. In contrast to the view that black men are less traditional than white men, Ransford and Miller (1983) find that middle-class black men have more traditional sex role attitudes than white middle-class men.

The literature regarding the division of household labor within Hispanic households is more limited, and much of what is available deals only with Chicanos, excluding other Hispanics. The research on Hispanic households yields conflicting results. Golding (1990) finds that Mexican American men do less household labor than Anglo men, whereas Mexican American women do more household labor than Anglo women. Differences between Hispanic and Anglo men's housework and child care time, like the differences between black and white men, may be due to other differences between them (Golding 1990; McAdoo 1990; Staples 1978). Golding (1990) finds that education is correlated with ethnicity and household labor time such that after removing the effects of education, the impact of ethnicity on the division of labor in the household is not significant. Thus, although she finds a more traditional division of labor within Mexican American households than in Anglo households, this division of labor reflects educational differences rather than solely ethnicity effects. Similarly, Ybarra (1982) finds that although acculturation does not significantly affect who performs the household labor, wives' employment does. She finds that the division of labor in dual-worker households is more equal than in male provider households.

In other research, Mirande (1979) discusses the patterns of shared responsibility for domestic work in Mexican American households. Although men's participation in household labor may give the appearance of egalitarianism, it does not necessarily indicate equality. For example, men may participate but spend less time than women. Vega and colleagues (1986) argue that Mexican American families are similar to Anglo families but that in terms of their adaptability to change in family roles they appear to be more flexible than Anglo families. Thus the male provider role may be less firmly entrenched in Mexican American than in Anglo households, resulting in a less rigid division of household labor. Similarly, Zinn (1980) asserts that Mexican American women's changing work roles may change their role identification.

There also is research indicating that decision making is not shared in Hispanic households (Williams 1990). Williams (1990) finds that Mexican American men continue to have more authority than wives, but that the patterns of decision making are not as traditional as in the past.

Some research suggests that the differences among white, black, and Hispanic men's family roles may reflect differences in the way that they internalize the provider role. Wilkie (1991) argues that black men's ability to fulfill the provider role may be associated with their rates of marriage (see also Tucker and Taylor 1989). Similarly, Stack (1974) found that when black men are unable to provide financially for their family, they also are less likely to participate in the household (e.g., housework and child care) (Cazenave 1979; Wilkie 1991). Although the findings of Wilkie (1991) and Tucker and Taylor (1989) do not directly indicate a relationship between the provider role and men's participation in the household, we can speculate that this association may exist. Thus, to the extent that there are differences among black, white, and Hispanic men's internalization of the provider role, we might also expect to find that the relationship between work and family roles varies by race/ethnicity.

We focus on the definition of egalitarianism based on the division of labor within the household. Hood (1983) notes that there are a number of ways in which an egalitarian marriage is defined. For our purposes, egalitarianism is defined in terms of household labor time. Some studies discuss decision making and role sharing, which are logically associated with the division of household labor, but which are not unproblematically related to it (Blumstein and Schwartz 1983).

A problem with much of the research on men's household labor time is the failure to incorporate wives' characteristics into the analyses. Just as men's paid labor time may act as a constraint on their household labor time, wives' paid labor time may create a demand for them to spend more time on household labor. The use of couples as the units of analysis in this chapter helps us understand the interaction between spouses' characteristics.

We further examine white, black, and Hispanic men's household labor time to determine the nature of the association between men's paid labor time and household labor time. In addition, we examine racial/ethnic differences in men's household labor time and assess the extent to which any observed differences may reflect differences in paid labor time, education, or other sociodemographic characteristics. We also incorporate wives' paid labor time and attitudes about family roles into our analysis to determine the ways in which husbands' and wives' characteristics interact to affect men's household labor time.

Data and Methods

The data for this study are from the 1987 National Survey of Families and Households (NSFH) (Sweet, Bumpass, and Call 1988), a national probability sample of 9,643 persons with an oversampling of 3,374 minority respondents, single parents, cohabiting persons, recently married persons, and respondents with stepchildren. One adult per household was selected randomly to be the primary respondent and his or her spouse/partner (if applicable) was also given a questionnaire designed for secondary respondents. Portions of the main interview with the primary respondent were self-administered, as was the entire spouse/partner questionnaire. In this analysis, we include only married respondents with a completed spouse questionnaire.

In the analyses to follow we begin by describing black, white, and Hispanic men's and women's household labor time. In addition to comparing household labor time across racial/ethnic groups, we also compare this time by work status.

In the second stage of the analysis, we examine the relationship between ethnicity and men's household labor time after controlling for a variety of other factors, including age, education, sex role attitudes, and both husbands' and wives' paid work. We use multiple regression analysis to determine if there are race/ethnic differences in household labor time or in the impact of paid labor time on household labor time that are independent of sociodemographic differences between white, black, and Hispanic men.[1]

In addition to determining whether or not a race/ethnicity effect on household labor time exists once other characteristics have been taken into account, we look at the relationship between husbands' and wives' paid labor and household labor time. We expect to find that men who spend more time in paid work will spend less time on household labor once other characteristics have been held constant. Moreover, to the extent that wives' market work time may act as a demand on men, we expect to find that the more time wives spend in paid labor the more time husbands will spend on household labor, once other variables have been held constant.

Our analyses include separate estimates of white, black, and Hispanic men's and women's household labor time. Hispanics include Mexican Americans as well as other Hispanic respondents. Paid labor time is measured in hours usually spent per week at work for both respondents and spouses. Education and age are measured in years.

Respondents' and spouses' sex role attitudes are measured by their responses to two attitude items. Each item was scored from 1 to 5. Respondents were asked if they agreed with the following statements:

1. If a husband and a wife both work full-time, they should share household tasks equally.
2. Preschool children are likely to suffer if their mother is employed.

Responses to the two items were summed and divided by two so that the range of the summated measure is 1 to 5. A high score indicates more liberal sex role attitudes and a low score indicates more traditional sex role attitudes.

Presence of children was included as an independent variable in some of the analyses. A score of 0 indicates that the respondent has no children under the age of 18 in the household, whereas a score of 1 indicates that there are children under the age of 18 in the household.

Findings

Findings in Table 22.1 reveal that black and Hispanic men spend significantly more time on household labor than do white men. Women's household labor time also varies by race/ethnicity, but in a different pattern. Hispanic women spend significantly more time on household labor than white women. They also spend more time on household labor than black women, but a t-test of the difference is not significant. Nevertheless, the gap is of substantive interest because the lack of statistical significance is largely a function of inflated standard deviations due to the small number of black and Hispanic respondents. As the results in Table 22.1 indicate, the divergent patterns of variation in household labor time by race and gender combine in such a way that men's proportionate share of household labor also varies by ethnicity.

Black men spend an average of 25 hours per week on household labor compared to 19.6 hours for white men and 23.2 hours for Hispanic men. The absolute size of the gap between black and Hispanic men's household labor time is small, with both groups of men spending significantly more time on household labor than white men. Nevertheless, black men spend more time on household labor than Hispanic men, although the gap is not statistically significant. This pattern both partially confirms and contradicts earlier research. Black men's relatively high household labor time is consistent with the view that black households may have a more equal division of labor than other households. The data in Table 22.1 do not, however, allow us to determine the source of black men's household labor time investments. It is possible, for example, that on average, black men spend less time in paid labor and therefore more time on household labor. The pattern also could reflect a number of other possible differences in the sociodemographic characteristics of black and white men that we examine in a later section.

Hispanic men's relatively high time investment in household labor is consistent with previous research finding that Hispanic men participate at least as much as Anglo men in household labor, and contradicts those who argue that Hispanic men participate in household labor less than Anglo men. Of course, much of the research on Hispanic men's family roles examines decision making or the distribution of power, rather than household labor time. Most of the research on household labor assumes that it is onerous duty and that only someone without the power to avoid it (or without any decisionmaking authority) will do it (Ferree 1987). Thus, researchers whose focus is on decision making often assume that egalitarian patterns of decision making are associated with an egalitarian division of household labor.

Women's household labor time also varies by race/ethnicity, with Hispanic women spending significantly more time on household labor than either black or white women. Hispanic women spend an average of 41.8 hours per week on household labor compared to 37.3 hours for white women and 38 hours per week for black women. Thus, Hispanic men and women spend significantly more time on household labor than white men and women, whereas black women's household labor time is not significantly different from white women's household labor time. Women's and men's different investments in household labor time affect men's proportionate share of household labor time. The data on black men and women indicate that black men do 40 percent of the household labor (done by men and women only) whereas Hispanic and Anglo men do 36 percent and 34 percent of the household labor, respectively. Thus, Table 22.1 confirms earlier research reporting that black households have a

TABLE 22.1   Household Labor Time by Gender and Race/Ethnicity

	White	Black	Hispanic	T-Test Blk/Wht	T-Test Hsp/Wht	T-Test Blk/Hsp
Men	19.6	25.0	23.2	2.3**	2.2*	.6
	(19.3)	(28.7)	(19.2)			
Women	37.3	38.0	41.8	.3	1.9*	1.2
	(21.6)	(26.3)	(24.5)			
Men's % of Household Labor Time	34%	40%	36%			

Notes: *p ≤ .05; **p ≤ .01. Standard deviation in parenthesis.

more equal division of household labor than white households and also confirms research indicating that Anglo and Hispanic households may have few differences in division of labor. In addition, the findings for Hispanic households suggest that there may be even more changes in the traditional patterns of Hispanic households than Williams's (1990) research on decisionmaking indicates.

We begin to examine the source of some of the gap in Table 22.2, where we present white, black, and Hispanic men's household labor time by employment status using multiple classification analysis. We do this in order to determine if black men's relatively high levels of household labor time reflect their lower paid labor time.

With respect to employment status, there are some interesting patterns. For both white and Hispanic men, those who are employed spend less time on household labor than those who are not employed, although the pattern is statistically significant only for white men. For blacks, however, the pattern is quite different. Black men who are not employed spend less time on household labor than black men who are employed, although the difference is not statistically significant. These findings indicate that the relationship between paid labor time and household labor time varies by race/ethnicity and that differences in black, white, and Hispanic men's household labor time are not simply a function of differences in their employment status.

The relationship between black men's employment status and their household labor time may indicate that black men who are not employed are different from nonemployed white and Hispanic men. To the extent that black men are not employed involuntarily, the results in Table 22.2 may reflect the age structure of those who are not employed. It also may indicate the presence of a distinct group of black men characterized by both low time investments in paid labor and low investments in household labor. The argument that the apparent egalitarianism of the black family may be a function of black men's reduced hours in paid labor is not supported by these findings. If anything, these findings indicate that, among blacks, the division of household labor is likely to be more equal in households where the man is employed than in households where he is not. Although this is in some sense counterintuitive, it may in-

TABLE 22.2   Men's Household Labor Time by Race/Ethnicity and
Employment Status

	White	Black	Hispanic
Employment Status			
Not employed	23.5	19.5	23.0
Employed PT (1-39 hrs.)	19.1	26.6	22.7
Employed FT	18.2	27.0	22.3
Eta	.12***	.13	.03
N	2798	183	164

Notes: We use 39 hours as our break between part-time and full-time in order to ensure an adequate *n* for the part-time category. Eta is a measure of association.
*** p ≤ .001.

dicate that the "breadwinner" role is internalized in such a way that even black men who are not employed may opt out of the family per se, rather than compensating for their reduced paid work with more household labor (Komarovsky 1940; Stack 1974). Among the men in this sample, the expression of their "opting out" may be to avoid household labor. (See Cazenave 1984; Hood 1986, for more discussion of the importance of subjective perceptions of work and family roles.)

Up to this point we have examined men's household labor time without taking into consideration a variety of sociodemographic characteristics, sex role attitudes, or wives' work status. Thus, some of the observed race/ethnic differences may reflect other differences among white, black, and Hispanic households. In Table 22.3 we examine the impact of race/ethnicity on men's household labor time by estimating the direct effect of race/ethnicity on household labor time as well as by estimating the ways that paid labor time may affect white, black, and Hispanic men's household labor time differently, after taking other factors into account. Thus, in Table 22.3 we can determine if the previously observed association between race/ethnicity and household labor time or the race/ethnic differences in the impact of paid labor time on household labor time are artifacts of other differences among white, black, and Hispanic men.

The results in Table 22.3 show that after controlling for respondents' education, age, children, sex role attitudes, wives' sex role attitudes and paid labor time, race/ethnicity is not significantly associated with men's household labor time. Thus, the differences among white, black, and Hispanic men's household labor time that we observed earlier appear to reflect other differences among them. For example, they may reflect differences in social class or education as McAdoo (1990) and Golding (1990) have argued. They may also, however, reflect differences in the presence of children or in wives' paid labor time.

Although we find no direct effects of race/ethnicity on men's household labor time in our multivariate analysis, the differential effect of paid labor time on men's household labor time remains.[2] For white and Hispanic men, each additional hour spent in paid

TABLE 22.3   Regression of Men's Household Labor Time on Paid Labor Time, Race/Ethnicity, Presence of Children, Education, Age, Sex Role Attitudes, Wives' Paid Labor Time, and Wives' Sex Role Attitudes

	b	$s.e.$
Paid labor	-.10***	.02
Black	-3.4	2.4
Hispanic	-.67	3.2
Black/paid	.27***	.07
Hispanic/paid	.08	.08
Children	3.7***	.81
Education	-.15	.12
Age	.02	.03
Men's sex role attributes	1.5***	.52
Wives' paid labour time	.07***	.02
Wives' sex role attitudes	.76	.51
Constant	13.4	3.4
R^2		.033
N		2782

Notes: **$p \leq .01$; ***$p \leq .001$.

labor is associated with their spending slightly more than six fewer minutes per day on household labor. For black men, however, each additional hour in paid labor is associated with them spending more time on household labor, even after controlling for sociodemographic and household characteristics. Thus, the pattern we observed in the bivariate analyses is repeated in the multivariate analyses. The more time black men spend in paid labor the more time they spend on household labor, whereas the association between paid labor time and household labor time is negative for Anglo and Hispanic men.

There are a variety of possible explanations for the different association between paid labor time and household labor time for black men than for white or Hispanic men. Black men may define the breadwinner role more narrowly than white or Hispanic men, such that when they are not employed and unable to contribute to their family's financial well-being they may retreat from the family in other ways (Stack 1974). The race/ethnic variation in the association between men's paid labor time and household labor time may reflect differences in housing patterns. If households with nonemployed black men are more likely to live in apartments, and those with employed black men are more likely to live in single-family houses, the pattern we see may reflect the amount of household labor that must be done. The different association for white and Hispanic men may be the result of different housing patterns. That is, households with nonemployed white or Hispanic men may not be as concentrated in apartments as is the case with black households. Thus there may be variation in the amount of household labor that must be done associated with men's employment status.

The pattern of the effects of some of the control variables is also interesting. For example, men with children spend more time on household labor than men without children, and men with more egalitarian sex role attitudes spend more time on household labor than men with more traditional attitudes. Wives' sex role attitudes are not associated with men's household labor time, but the more time wives spend in paid labor, the more time husbands spend on household labor. Interestingly, after controlling for other variables, men's age is not significantly associated with their household labor time.

In Table 22.4 we further examine the relationship between men's employment status and their household labor time by examining white, black, and Hispanic men's time spent on specific household tasks, after controlling for sociodemographic and household characteristics. Among those men employed full-time, black men spend more time than white and Hispanic men cleaning house, shopping, and repairing automobiles. Cleaning house and shopping are typically "female-typed" tasks indicating that employed black men's household labor time represents less gender stratification rather than simply more time spent on tasks typically done by men. Nevertheless, there are some "female-typed" tasks on which white men spend more time. White men employed full-time spend more time on laundry than black or Hispanic men. Not all of the differences in housework time result from variation in time spent on "female-typed" tasks. White and black men employed full-time spend more time than Hispanic men on outdoor tasks, and black and Hispanic men employed full-time spend more time paying bills than white men.

Among those who are employed part-time or not at all, Hispanic men are most likely to spend more time on specific household tasks than either white or black men, although in a number of cases black and Hispanic men's household task time is similar. Hispanic men employed part-time spend the most time cleaning house, but black men also spend more time cleaning house than white men. Similarly, black men spend significantly more time washing dishes than other men, although Hispanic men spend almost as much time as black men. Among those who are not employed, Hispanic men spend more time than black or white men preparing meals, washing dishes, and cleaning house; thus more time among "female-typed" tasks than other men.

The patterns observed in Table 22.4 indicate that there is more variation by race/ethnicity among men who are employed full-time than among those who are employed part-time or not at all. Although we should use care when comparing across employment statuses in Table 22.4 (because there may be sociodemographic differences among the groups), we can see that black men's greater household labor time, with respect to white and Hispanic men, appears to be among those who are employed full-time, whereas there are fewer and less definite patterns among those employed fewer hours or not at all.

With respect to specific household tasks, Table 22.4 shows that black men who are employed full-time spend more time on a variety of household tasks, rather than on only a few or male-typed tasks. The pattern of greater involvement in traditionally female tasks among black men employed full-time indicates that among black households there are more egalitarian patterns of family work when the husband is employed than when he is not.

TABLE 22.4   Men's Time Spent on Specific Household Tasks by Employment Status and Race/Ethnicity

	Not Employed	Employed Part-Time	Employed Full-Time
Preparing Meals			
White	3.3	2.9	2.3
Black	4.2	4.9	3.3
Hispanic	5.8	3.2	2.2
beta	.09+	.09	.02
Washing Dishes			
White	2.7	2.2	1.9
Black	1.6	4.5	2.7
Hispanic	4.0	4.1	2.1
beta	.06*	.22**	.05
Cleaning House			
White	2.3	1.8	1.7
Black	2.3	3.2	3.0
Hispanic	4.3	3.9	2.2
beta	.08+	.20**	.11***
Outdoor Tasks			
White	7.5	5.0	5.6
Black	5.8	4.8	5.4
Hispanic	5.2	3.7	3.9
beta	.06	.06	.06*
Shopping			
White	2.9	2.4	2.3
Black	2.7	2.6	4.0
Hispanic	2.5	3.5	3.1
beta	.02	.08	.14***

(continued)

Conclusion

Our findings point to several important patterns. Just as women's paid labor time is associated with their household labor time, we find that men's paid labor time is associated with their household labor time. Thus, although there is less variation in men's paid labor time than in women's, there is enough that it warrants some research atten-

TABLE 22.4   *(continued)*

	Not Employed	Employed Part-Time	Employed Full-Time
Laundry			
White	.7	.8	1.2
Black	.9	1.5	.6
Hispanic	1.3	.4	.6
beta	.06	.11	.08***
Paying Bills			
White	1.6	1.4	1.5
Black	2.5	2.2	2.4
Hispanic	2.1	4.1	2.5
beta	.07	.26***	.09***
Auto Maintenance			
White	1.4	1.6	2.0
Black	1.4	2.5	3.4
Hispanic	2.1	3.2	2.9
beta	.04	.21***	.08***
Driving			
White	1.2	1.3	1.5
Black	1.1	1.7	2.7
Hispanic	1.9	1.4	1.5
beta	.04	.04	.08

Notes: Controlling for respondents' sex role attitudes, education, age, spouses' paid work time, spouses' sex role attitudes, and number of children. Beta is a partial measure of association.
$+p \leq .10$; $*p \leq .05$; $**p \leq .01$; $***p \leq .001$.

tion. Interestingly, the pattern of association between paid labor time and household labor time varies by race/ethnicity. Employed black men do more household labor than those who are not employed, whereas employed white and Hispanic men do less household labor than those who are not employed. These different patterns illustrate the dangers of analyses that fail to examine not only the direct effect of race/ethnicity on household labor time but also the way that race/ethnicity may affect the relationship among other variables. The relationship between men's work and family roles is not such that we can talk about a relationship: the relationship varies by race/ethnicity. This difference in the relationship between work and family suggests that we need to conduct more research on the nature of work and family trade-offs and how they vary by race and ethnicity.

Our analyses also indicate some differences in the family roles (as measured by household labor time) of white, black, and Hispanic men. Our findings from bivariate analyses show that Hispanic and black men spend more time on household labor than white men. Even with Hispanic women's relatively high levels of household labor time, Hispanic men's proportionate share of household labor time is higher than white men's. Black men's relatively high proportionate share of household labor time confirms earlier research indicating that black households may be more egalitarian than white households. Unlike some speculation, however, we find that this pattern is not the result of differences in black men's paid labor time, but that employed black men are the ones who are spending more time on household labor. This somewhat surprising finding indicates the need to examine the relationship between black men's work and family roles in more detail. Given previous findings about black men's attachment to family and work roles (Cazenave 1979), black men's attachments to the provider role as well as their perceptions of family obligations may be the most fruitful place to begin future studies. In addition, the different patterns observed indicate the complex nature of the work–family linkage for men more generally. Further analyses might also focus on the characteristics of nonemployed black men as compared to nonemployed white and Hispanic men to determine what may account for the different patterns of work and family role trade-offs.

Finally, we find that higher household labor time among black men employed full-time reflects their greater time investments in traditionally female tasks, rather than differences in time investments in "male-typed" tasks. In addition, the pattern of Hispanic men's time spent on specific household tasks indicates that they often spend more time on female-typed tasks than Anglo men. Thus, even though Anglo and Hispanic men's total household labor time is not significantly different once sociodemographic characteristics have been taken into account, Hispanic men may spend more time on typically "female-typed" tasks like meal preparation, washing dishes, and cleaning house than do Anglo men (see also Mirandd 1985; Zinn 1980). In addition, our findings indicate that there may be more changes in the Hispanic household than some who have found changing patterns suggest (Mirandd 1985; Williams 1990).

In future research we must give more attention to racial/ethnic variation in men's family patterns as well as to the different trade-offs that men may make between work and family. We simply cannot assume that the trade-offs are the same for men as for women, just as we have often argued that we cannot assume that women's labor force experiences can be modeled in the same way that we model men's. At the same time, our findings argue for the systematic inclusion of ethnicity and race in studies of the work–family trade-off for both men and women. We need to examine differences among black, white, and Hispanic men's perceptions of their family responsibilities if we are to understand how they balance work and family responsibilities.

Notes

We appreciate the very helpful comments of Jane Hood, Norma Williams, Maxine Baca Zinn, and Marta Tienda.

1. The lack of statistical significance is a result of the relatively small number of black and Hispanic respondents in the survey.

2. To determine the differential effects of paid labor time for white, black, and Hispanic respondents we included interaction terms for race/ethnicity and paid labor time in our analysis. The nonsignificant effect for the interaction term between Hispanic and paid labor time indicates that the impact of paid labor time on Hispanic men's household labor time is not significantly different from the impact of paid labor time on white men's household labor time. The significant interaction term for black men indicates that there is a significant difference in the impact of paid labor time on black and white men's household labor time. By adding the coefficient for paid labor time to the coefficient for the black/paid labor time interaction term, we can see that even after controlling for sociodemographic and household characteristics, paid labor time is positively associated with black men's household labor time. Thus, the more time black men spend in paid labor the more time they spend in household labor, whereas the association between paid labor time and household labor time is negative for Anglo and Hispanic men.

References

Atkinson, J., and Huston, T. L. 1984. "Sex Role Orientation and Division of Labor Early in Marriage." *Journal of Personality and Social Psychology* 46, no. 2: 330–345.

Barnett, R. C., and Baruch, G. K. 1987. "Determinants of Fathers' Participation in Family Work." *Journal of Marriage and the Family* 49: 29–40.

Beckett, J. O. 1976. "Working Wives: A Racial Comparison." *Social Work,* November, 463–471.

Beckett, J. O., and Smith, A. D. 1981. "Work and Family Roles: Egalitarian Marriage in Black and White Families." *Social Service Review* 55, no. 2: 314–326.

Blumstein, P., and Schwartz, P. 1983. *American Couples.* New York: Pocket Books.

Broman, C. 1988. "Household Work and Family Life Satisfaction of Blacks." *Journal of Marriage and the Family* 50: 743–748.

———. 1991. "Gender, Work-Family Roles, and Psychological Well-Being of Blacks." *Journal of Marriage and the Family* 53: 509–520.

Cazenave, N. 1979. "Middle-Income Black Fathers: An Analysis of the Provider Role." *Family Coordinator* 28: 583–593.

———. 1984. "Race, Socioeconomic Status, and Age: The Social Context of Masculinity." *Sex Roles* 11, no. 7–8: 639–656.

Collins, P. H. 1990. *Black Feminist Thought: Knowledge, Consciousness and the Politics of Empowerment.* Cambridge, Mass.: Unwin Hyman.

Coverman, S. 1985. "Explaining Husbands' Participation in Domestic Labor." *Sociological Quarterly* 26, no. 1: 81–98.

Coverman, S., and Sheley, J. F. 1986. "Change in Men's Housework and Child-Care Time, 1965–1975." *Journal of Marriage and the Family* 48: 413–422.

Cronkite, R. C. 1977. "The Determinants of Spouses' Normative Preferences for Family Roles." *Journal of Marriage and the Family* 39: 575–585.

Ericksen, J. A., Yancey, W. L., and Ericksen, E. P. 1979. "The Division of Family Roles." *Journal of Marriage and the Family* 41: 301–313.

Farkas, G. 1976. "Education, Wage Rates, and the Division of Labor Between Husband and Wife." *Journal of Marriage and the Family* 38: 473–483.

Ferree, M. M. 1987. "Family and Job for Working-Class Women: Gender and Class Systems Seen from Below." In N. Gerstel and H. E. Gross, eds., *Families and Work,* 289–301. Philadelphia: Temple University Press.

Golding, J. M. 1990. "Division of Household Labor, Strain and Depressive Symptoms Among Mexican Americans and Non-Hispanic Whites." *Psychology of Women Quarterly* 14: 103–117.

Hood, J. C. 1983. *Becoming a Two-Job Family.* New York: Praeger.

_____. 1986. "The Provider Role: Its Meaning and Measurement." *Journal of Marriage and the Family* 48: 349–359.

Huber, J., and G. Spitze. 1983. *Sex Stratification: Children, Housework and Jobs.* New York: Academic Press.

Kimmel, M. S. 1987. "Rethinking 'Masculinity': New Directions in Research." In M. S. Kimmel, ed., *Changing Men: New Directions of Research on Men and Masculinity,* 9–24. Newbury Park, Calif.: Sage.

Kingston, P. W., and Nock, S. L. 1985. "Consequences of the Family Work Day." *Journal of Marriage and the Family* 47, no. 3: 619–630.

Komarovsky, M. 1940. *The Unemployed Man and His Family.* New York: Dryden.

McAdoo, H. P. 1990. "A Portrait of African American Families in the United States." In S. E. Rix, ed., *The American Woman 1990–1991: A Status Report,* 71–93. New York: Norton.

Miller, J., and Garrison, H. H. 1982. "Sex Roles: The Division of Labor at Home and in the Workplace." *Annual Review of Sociology* 8: 237–262.

Mirandé, A. 1979. "A Reinterpretation of Male Dominance in the Chicano Family." *Family Coordinator* 28, no. 4: 473–480.

_____. 1985. *The Chicano Experience: An Alternative Perspective.* Notre Dame, Ind.: University of Notre Dame Press.

Perrucci, C. C., Potter, H. R., and Rhoads, D. L. 1978. "Determinants of Male Family-Role Performance." *Psychology of Women Quarterly* 3, no. 1: 53–66.

Pleck, J. H. 1977. "The Work-Family Role System." *Social Problems* 24: 417–427.

_____. 1985. *Working Wives/Working Husbands.* Beverly Hills: Sage.

Ransford, E., and Miller, J. 1983. "Race, Sex, and Feminist Outlooks." *American Sociological Review* 48: 46–59.

Reid, P. T., and Comas-Diaz, L. 1990. "Gender and Ethnicity: Perspectives on Dual Status." *Sex Roles* 22, no. 7–8: 397–408.

Rexroat, C., and Shehan, C. 1987. "The Family Life Cycle and Spouses' Time in Housework." *Journal of Marriage and the Family* 49, no. 4: 737–750.

Ross, C. E. 1987. "The Division of Labor at Home." *Social Forces* 65, no. 3: 816–834.

Stack, C. B. 1974. *All Our Kin.* New York: Harper Colophon.

Staples, R. 1978. "Masculinity and Race: The Dual Dilemma of Black Men." *Journal of Social Issues* 34, no. 1: 169–183.

Sweet, J., Bumpass, L., and Call, V. 1988. *The Design and Content of the National Survey of Families and Households.* Working Paper NSFH-1. Madison: University of Wisconsin-Madison, Center for Demography and Ecology.

Thompson, L., and Walker, A. J. 1989. "Gender in Families: Women and Men in Marriage, Work and Parenthood." *Journal of Marriage and the Family* 51: 845–871.

Tucker, M. B., and Taylor, R. J. 1989. "Demographic Correlates of Relationship Status Among Black Americans." *Journal of Marriage and the Family* 51: 655–665.

Vega, W. A., Patterson, T., Sallis, J., Nader, P., Atkins, C., and Abramson, I. 1986. "Cohesion and Adaptability in Mexican American and Anglo Families." *Journal of Marriage and the Family* 48: 857–867.

Wilkie, J. R. 1991. "The Decline in Men's Labor Force Participation and Income and the Changing Structure of Family Economic Support." *Journal of Marriage and the Family* 53, no. l: 111–122.

Williams, N. 1990. *The Mexican American Family: Tradition and Change.* Dix Hills, N.Y.: General Hall.

Wilson, M. N., Tolson, T. F. J., Hinton, I. D., and Kiernan, M. 1990. "Flexibility and Sharing of Childcare Duties in Black Families." *Sex Roles* 22, no. 7–8: 409–425.

Ybarra, L. 1982. "When Wives Work: The Impact on the Chicano Family." *Journal of Marriage and the Family* 44: 169–178.

Zinn, M. B. 1980. "Gender and Ethnic Identity Among Chicanos." *Frontiers* 2: 8–24.
_____. 1991. "Family, Feminism, and Race in America." In J. Lorber and S. A. Farrell, eds., *The Social Construction of Gender,* 110–134. Newbury Park, Calif.: Sage.

Discussion Questions

1. What kinds of offerings does Amerco make to its employees with family commitments?
2. According to Hochschild, are working parents doing enough on their own to make their busy lives more manageable?
3. Are men and women really living in separate worlds when it comes to the demands of family and home?
4. How open to change are the men and women Coltrane writes about? Specifically, where there are conflicts over responsibilities, how do men and women resolve them differently?
5. How are African American households different from white households in terms of role expectations for men and women?
6. Do Shelton and John believe that one race or ethnic group can learn from another in terms of managing home and work obligations?

Part VIII

THE PARENT TRAP

Can parents juggle it all? Combining home and work is often an overwhelming challenge for most mothers and fathers. The readings in this section provide a sociological snapshot of the lives of working parents. Although some women with young children have always worked, particularly women of color and lower social class, there has been a steady increase in the number of mothers who work and in the number of hours they work. There has also been a significant shift, although not numerically large, in the number of "Mr. Moms," or fathers who stay at home to care for children.

In the first article, "Mothers at Work: Effects on Children's Well-Being," Lois W. Hoffman and Lise M. Youngblade discuss the impact of working mothers on their children. Hoffman and Youngblade say the effects of having a working mother are mostly positive, particularly as measured by achievement test scores and social skills. Nonetheless, the relationship between working mothers and children's academic and social skills is complex and can vary with the gender of the child, the marital status of the mother, and the social class of the family.

Kathleen Gerson, in "Dilemmas of Involved Fatherhood," provides an interesting perspective on men who want to become more involved with their own fatherhood but are discouraged by social disapproval and employer intransigence in accommodating their roles as fathers. Nonetheless, Gerson highlights many men who transcend these barriers and who find tremendous intrinsic rewards in making family their priority and their work secondary.

"Men Don't Do This Sort of Thing: Househusbands," by Calvin D. Smith, contains narratives from househusbands and features the difficulties most of these men encountered adjusting to their nontraditional roles as the main child-care provider and "nurturer" of the family. More specifically, Smith delves into the question of how these men have struggled and resolved self-identity questions about their masculinity.

In the final selection, we learn from Kathryn Edin and Laura Lein, in "Why Don't Welfare-Reliant Mothers Go to Work?" just how complicated the issue of welfare reliance is for poor mothers. Despite popular misconceptions, many mothers who collect welfare do so only after numerous experiences working at low-wage and unskilled labor.

Juggling is difficult. Choosing what kind of balance each parent, male and female, wants to achieve in combining caring for children and work, and choosing to work or not to work, is one of life's most difficult choices.

23

MOTHERS AT WORK
Effects on Children's Well-Being

Lois W. Hoffman and Lisa M. Youngblade

Overall, children with employed mothers score higher on academic achievement tests in reading, mathematics, and language. In general, this finding held true across ethnic groups, for children with married mothers, for children with single mothers, and for the subgroup of children living in poverty. Moreover, among children with married mothers, teachers rated children with employed mothers as having fewer learning problems than children with nonemployed mothers, a finding that seems to support the pattern of results on the standardized achievement tests. In general this pattern of higher achievement test scores for children with employed mothers fits with findings in past research of higher academic achievement for daughters of employed mothers and of higher cognitive scores for children in poverty. However, reports of lower school performance for middle-class sons of employed mothers were not supported in the current study, and in fact, the results were in the opposite direction.

With respect to behavior patterns, on the other hand, middle-class boys with full-time employed, married mothers seem to exhibit more acting-out behaviors. This pattern did not hold for middle-class boys whose mothers were employed part-time. Further, the pattern for middle-class boys may need to be considered in the context of the low level of acting out and aggressive behavior in the middle class generally. In the working-class married group, it is the children whose mothers are full-time homemakers who received the highest peer ratings of hitting and teacher ratings of acting out.

In other aspects, and particularly for girls, children with employed mothers seemed to be functioning in a more socially and emotionally skilled manner than children with nonemployed mothers. Teachers rated children with employed mothers as higher in peer social skills than children with nonemployed mothers. Daughters of married, employed mothers had more frustration tolerance than daughters of married, nonemployed mothers. And, for the subgroup of white, working-class girls with married mothers, daughters of employed mothers were better liked by peers than daughters of full-time homemakers.

In addition, the findings of the current study suggest that girls with nonemployed mothers present a pattern characterized by a more external locus of control (for girls with married mothers, and for African American girls with single mothers) and more shyness and less assertiveness (for girls with single employed mothers). In contrast, daughters of employed mothers appear more assertive, and have more of a sense of internal control.

Previous research has found that children of employed mothers have less traditional attitudes toward sex roles than do children of full-time homemakers. In this research, we differentiated stereotypes about "female" activities from stereotypes about "male" activities. The stereotype measure about "female" activities tapped whether one thinks men, like woman, can cook, clean the house, and take care of children. Thus, it is not surprising that it is only in the married-mother families that we find the children of employed mothers are less stereotyped on this measure, for it is only in the married families that the children see their fathers taking on these roles. In this study, as in previous research, fathers in dual-wage families participate more in child care tasks traditionally assigned to women.

The stereotype measure about "male" activities, however, showed a different pattern. For boys, there was no evidence that those with employed mothers were less stereotyped about traditionally male activities. In fact, in single-mother families, boys were more stereotyped about male activities when their mothers were employed than when they were not. The reason for this is not clear. It may be that these boys are called on by their employed mothers to help in the house to fill in for the absent father. That single, employed mothers, faced with dual role of employee and sole parent, may enlist their sons' help by appealing to the idea that they have to take on the man's role.

For girls, on the other hand, less stereotyped views about masculine activities were found in single-mother families, as well as in married-mother families, when mothers were employed. In employed-mother families, children see women filling the role of breadwinner, which has traditionally been considered the man's role. Girls may identify with their mothers and see them as role models; in consequence, girls may become less stereotyped about masculine activities when their mothers work, while boys do not.

In summary, for the group of children with married mothers, these results, based on examining the effects of maternal employment during the child's first year, revealed that children whose mothers were employed in the child's first year appear more aggressive than children whose mothers were not employed during the child's first year. Teachers and peers corroborated these differences in aggressiveness between the employed and nonemployed groups.

These findings are consistent with previous research, which has indicated that children with early day care experience are more aggressive and noncompliant (Belsky 1990; Clarke-Stewart, 1989). However, it should be noted as well that these findings are in contrast to data reported by the NICHD Early Child Care Research network (1998), which showed little evidence that early, extensive, and continuous care is related to problematic behavior at twenty-four and thirty-six months. In the NICHD study, both quality of care and greater experience in groups with other children predicted socially competent behavior at twenty-four months. On the whole, however, family variables were much stronger predictors of child behavior than any of the child care variables.

Why might children whose mothers had worked during these preschool years be more aggressive, in the third and fourth grades, than children whose mothers had been full-time homemakers? One possible answer is the different child care experiences of these two groups. Compared to the children whose mothers are full-time homemakers, children with employed mothers are more likely to experience longer hours of nonmatenal care, in multiple settings, during their preschool years. This could account, in part for the aggressive behavior of these children.

These are other reasons, however, why we might expect these two groups to differ. For example, mothers who choose to work in the child's first year may be different from mothers who do not choose to work in the child's first year, in personality, parenting philosophies, or other characteristics. It might be, then, that these differing parental qualities actually account for different child outcomes, rather than the fact that the mother worked or did not work in the child's preschool years. The data reported by the NICHD group (1998) showing that family variables lends weight to this notion.

24

DILEMMAS OF INVOLVED FATHERHOOD

Kathleen Gerson

Work's a necessity, but the things that really matter are spending time with my family. If I didn't have a family, I don't know what I would have turned to. That's why I say you're rich in lots of ways other than money. I look at my daughter and think, "My family is everything."

—Carl, a thirty-four year-old utilities worker

Social disapproval and economic inequality put full-time domesticity out of reach for almost all men. Yet most also found that economic necessity and employer intransigence made anything less than full-time work an equally distant possibility. Few employers offered the option of part-time work, especially in male-dominated fields. Arthur, a married sanitation worker planning for fatherhood, complained:

> If it was feasible, I would love to spend more time with my child. That would be more important to me than working. I'd love to be able to work twenty-five hours a week or four days a week and have three days off to spend with the family, but most jobs aren't going to accommodate you that way.

Yet, even if part-time work were available, involved fathers still needed the earnings that only full-time and overtime work could offer. Lou, the sewage worker who worked the night shift in order to spend days with his young daughter, could not accept lower wages or fewer benefits:

> If I knew that financially everything would be set, I'd stay home. I'd like to stay more with my daughter. It's a lot of fun to be with a very nice three-year-old girl. But if I work less, I would equate it to less money and then I wouldn't be taking care of my family. If it meant less work and the same or more money, I'd say, "Sure!" I'd be dumb if I didn't.

Dean, the driver for a city department of parks, agreed that his economic obligations could not take a backseat to his nurturing ones:

> It always comes down to the same thing: I would like to have more time to spend with my children, but if I didn't have money, what's the sense of having time off? If I could work part-time and make enough money, that would be fine and dandy.

Since involved fathers tried to nurture as well as support their children, they made an especially hard choice between money and time. Like many mothers, they had to add caretaking onto full-time workplace responsibilities, but employers are generally reluctant to recognize male (or female) parental responsibility as a legitimate right or need.[1] Worse yet, paternal leaves are rarely considered a legitimate option for men even if they formally exist. Involved fathers wished to take time off for parenting, but like most men they were reluctant to do so for fear of imperiling their careers.[2] And even though most employers allow health-related leaves with impunity, they have not been so flexible when it comes to the job of parenting. Workers receive the message that illness is unavoidable, but parenting is voluntary—an indication of a lack of commitment. Our current corporate culture thus makes parenting hazardous to anyone's career, and choosing a "daddy track" can be just as dangerous as the much-publicized "mommy track." Juan, a financial analyst, knew he could not pull back from his job for more than a few days or a week without jeopardizing his job security. To parental leave,

> I'd say yes, but realistically no. It would be a problem because it's very difficult for me to tell my boss that I have to leave at such a time. I have deadlines to meet. If I leave the office for two or three months, my job is in jeopardy.

Because employers did not offer flexible options for structuring work on a daily basis or over the course of a career, some involved fathers looked to self-employment or home-based work for more flexibility and control. Craig, the ex-dancer currently working in an office, hoped he would be able to integrate work and parenting by working at home:

> I would like to find myself in the situation where I'm not locked into a nine-to-five schedule. Ultimately, I hope I'm doing consulting on my own at home, which means time close to the family. So that in the middle of my own workday, at the house, I'm available. I can just put my work aside and play Daddy.

Most could not even entertain this option. They had to fit parenting in around the edges of their work lives.[3]

Domestic arrangements also impede full equality. Child rearing remains an undervalued, isolating, and largely invisible accomplishment for all parents. This has fueled women's flight from domesticity and also dampened men's motivation to choose it. Russell, the legal aid attorney and father of two, recognized that child rearing was less valued than employment:

I think I would feel somewhat meaningless to not be engaged in any form of productive work, although certainly raising children is productive work. But I couldn't be responsible for that on a full-time basis. While I love my guys, I don't think I could be around them all the time.

Child rearing can be invisible as well as undervalued. Unlike the size of a paycheck or the title one holds at work, there are few socially recognized rewards for the time a parent devotes to raising a child or the results it produces. This made only the most dedicated, like Hank, willing to consider full-time parenting:

> Nobody will know the time and the effort I put in the family. They will look down on it. I would devote time, hours, and nobody will be happy with it except me because I'll know what I was trying for.

The forces pulling women out of the home are stronger than the forces pulling men into it. Since the social value of public pursuits outstrips the power and prestige of private ones, men are likely to resist full-time domesticity even as women move toward full-time employment. This process is similar to the one pulling women into male-dominated occupations while leaving men less inclined to enter female-dominated ones. In addition, just as women in male-dominated occupations face prejudice and discrimination, fathers who become equal or primary parents are stigmatized—treated as "tokens" in a female-dominated world.[4] Roger shied away from the pervasive questioning about his life as a custodial parent:

> I think I've become somewhat more introverted than I used to be because I get tired of explaining my situation at home. . . The thing that blows all the kids' minds—they're all living with Mommy and my kids are living with Daddy.

In the face of such disincentives, most involved fathers rejected staying home for the same reasons many women do and more. Female breadwinning and male home-making did not seem acceptable even when they made economic sense. Robin, a stockbroker, rejected domesticity precisely because his poor work prospects left him in no state to bear the additional stigma of becoming a househusband. Although he was making a lot less money than his wife was, he felt too "demoralized" to consider staying home. "I'm not secure enough, I guess, to stay home and be a househusband."

Of course, involved fathers actively resisted the discrimination they encountered. They asserted their nurturing competence and insisted on being taken as seriously as female parents are. The prevailing skepticism about men's parental abilities, however, made this an uphill battle. Ernie complained:

> I believe I have as much right in raising the child as she does, but I found a lot of reverse discrimination—people assuming that the mother takes care of the child. It's a lot of stereotyping, a lot that's taken for granted. Like pediatricians: they speak to my wife; they won't speak to me. I say, "Hey, I take care of her, too." They look past me like I'm

invisible. The same thing with the nursery school. I went out on all the interviews. They looked at me like, "What're you doing here?"

Economic, social, and ideological arrangements thus made involved fatherhood difficult. The lack of workplace and domestic supports diluted and suppressed the potential for involvement even among the most motivated men. In the absence of these hurdles, fathers who wished to be involved might have participated far more than they actually did. They might, in fact, have made choices that now remain open to a rapidly diminishing number of women. Ernie wished he had options that only full-time mothers enjoy:

> I'm not the type that has career aspirations and is very goal-oriented. If I didn't have to work, I wouldn't. But I would volunteer. I would work in a nursery school. I would do a lot more volunteer work with my daughter's school. I would love to go on trips like the mothers who don't work, be more active in the P.T.A. I would love that. But I can't.

As the supports for homemaking mothers erode, supports for equal and primary fathers have not emerged to offset the growing imbalance between children's needs and families' resources. Fathers have had to depend on paid help, relatives, and already overburdened wives even when they did not wish to do so.

These obstacles not only left mothers giving up more. They also made involved fathers appear heroic about whatever they did. Comparisons with other men could be used to ward off complaints and resist further change.

Ernie maintained:

> Sometimes she didn't think I did enough. I couldn't stand that because I thought I was doing too much. I really felt I was doing more than I should, whatever that means. I told her to go talk to some of her friends and see what their husbands are doing.

Nurturing fathers faced deeply rooted barriers to full equality in parenting. Social arrangements at work and in the home dampened even willing men's ability to share equally. The truncated range of choices open to most of these men limited the options of their wives, ex-wives, and partners as well. We can only guess how many mothers' helpers would become equal parents if these obstacles did not exist or, better yet, were replaced by positive supports for involved fatherhood.

Benefiting from the Loss of Privilege: Incentives for Change

If full equality remained beyond the reach of most involved fathers, they nevertheless moved a notable distance toward it. They were not simply forced to make concessions; nor were they just being altruistic. They also perceived offsetting, if unheralded, benefits. After all, parenting can be its own reward—offering intrinsic pleasures and a powerful sense of accomplishment. Rick explained:

I have an extremely close relationship with my kids, and that makes me feel good. The fact that they're both doing very well in school—I know that at least a little bit of that comes from having been with them when they were young. So there's all those interactions in seeing them on their way to being healthy and vibrant kids.

These feelings took on added significance when other avenues for building self-esteem were blocked. Todd, the aspiring actor who became a construction worker, hoped his talents could be channeled toward his daughter instead of his job:

If there's any Creator at all up there, She or It or They're going to ask for some sort of accounting at the end. They're going to be pleased if they gave you a certain amount of gifts and you were able to do something with them. I'd still like to be a part of something more meaningful than putting in a new fire hydrant—I guess through my influence on this little one's life.

If children offered a source of pride for those whose workplace aspirations had not been met, this was not just a concern for passing on genes or the family name. Contributions of time and emotions counted more. Carl, who chose utility repair work so that he could care for his daughter after school, saw his "investment" reflected in her talents and achievements:

I've had a lot of compliments on her, and I take them as a compliment also. It's something that became part of you—teaching them different things, helping them grow up. They'll do something, and it's like seeing a reflection of you.

As work opportunities stall in an age of stagnant economic growth, parenting offers men another avenue for developing self-esteem. But economically successful fathers also reaped benefits from involvement because it balanced lives that would otherwise have been more narrowly focused on paid work. For Charles, the attorney with a young son, caretaking provided a legitimate reason for limiting the demands of work: "I'm working a little less hard, taking on fewer responsibilities. . . But I think it's great. I don't need all the other shit."

Children also provided the hope of permanence in an age of divorce. Even happily married fathers came to see their children as the bedrock of stability in a shaky world, the one bond that could not be severed or assailed. Having been reared by a single mother, Juan viewed his children rather than his wife as the best chance for enduring emotional ties: "What if one day my wife and I get sick of each other after so many years? So I would like to have children."

Involved fatherhood also provided emotional supports by creating a bond between husbands and wives. Married men were less likely to feel rejected by their wives and excluded from the new relationships that form with the birth of a child. Timothy, the worker at a city dump, could not understand why less involved fathers complained of being rejected when a new baby arrived:

They have these books about how fathers are supposed to go through the blues because the wife is giving her attention to the child. Is this some kind of maniac that wrote this? I take care of him just as much as she does.

Sharing the load of caring for a newborn also seemed to decrease the chances that a mother would feel overwhelmed and alone during a critical and trying turning point in a marriage.[5] Carlos hoped that sharing the caretaking would help him avoid the hostility that he felt unequal arrangements would generate:

I think it's a great burden to have one parent do all the caretaking. It would burn out that person, and they're not going to be able to respond to you. Then I would start feeling resentment towards her and possibly the child. So the only way I could see avoiding that is by sharing the responsibility.

Since involved fathers believed that a satisfying relationship depended on both partners being able to meet their needs, thwarting a partner's dreams by refusing to participate seemed to be a Pyrrhic victory. The costs of not sharing appeared greater than the costs of sharing. Carl was pleased to escape his parents' pattern:

My parents are the old school. He never really touched a dish. I like what I'm doing better. The older way, I feel the woman will think, "I never really had an opportunity to do things." She will become resentful later on. Where my wife can't say nothing because she's had her freedom, she's worked, she's not stayed in the kitchen barefoot and pregnant, and I did what I had to do. I feel in the long run it pays off. The other way, maybe she would have left.

Involved fatherhood thus offered two ways of coping with the risks of marriage in an era of divorce. It provided another source of emotional sustenance in the event that the marital bond did not survive. And it offered a way to build less rancorous relationships by reducing wives' resentment. Indeed, there is growing evidence that egalitarian relationships do provide benefits to husbands and wives. In one report, wives whose husbands participate in domestic duties showed lower rates of depression than those with husbands who don't, while another found that the more housework a husband does, the lower are the chances that his wife has considered divorce.[6] Emotional gratification and marital peace were not the only payoffs. In agreeing to share the domestic load, men can also share the economic load. Their wives' income lessens the pressure to work long hours and take on second jobs. Wesley was pleased to exchange extra hours at work for domestic sharing:

If Cindy wants to be home, she can stay home. But that would probably mean I would have to either get myself another job or work overtime on the job I have. I would do it. She knows that. But she doesn't want me to. We spend more time with each other this way.

Involved fathers also believed their children would benefit in both the short and long runs—perceptions that research on both married and divorced fathers supports.[7] Larry observed:

Having spent a lot of time with both of us, she's not really dependent on either one of us. Mommy's like daddy; daddy's like mommy. At times I am her mother. It's good to switch roles. She don't run to mommy or run to daddy. She runs to both of us.

They hoped their example would help their daughters and sons develop a flexible approach to building their own lives. Ernie decided his involvement created a better domestic environment for his daughter:

The sharing—it's a good role model for her. She sees me cook. I'm trying to teach her baking, and I think it's nice my daughter is learning baking from her father. So I'm hoping she sees that it's split and not that just the wife does this and the man does that.

He also hoped his participation would give his daughter a sense of self-reliance, agreeing with a growing group of psychologists who argue that girls no less than boys need their fathers. Both sexes identify in varying degrees with both parents, and girls look to fathers as well as mothers to provide models for living:

Raising my child, that is my priority—seeing that she's raised well in the sense of preparing her to face the world, trying to get her exposed as much as possible, so she may find out what she likes to pursue. I hope she has a career. I hope she finds something she really likes and works for it.[8]

These men concluded that their domestic arrangements would also benefit their sons, echoing recent research showing that sons of involved fathers are likely to show a more developed capacity for empathy.[9] Wesley thus concluded that his two sons "feel close to the two of us. Maybe when they get married, they'll share in the house."

Just as these fathers created families that differed from the households in which they were reared, so their children will take the lessons of their childhood into unknown futures. Involved fathers' belief in the advantages of domestic sharing cannot guarantee a similar response in their children, but it can and did strengthen their own resolve to create a more egalitarian household. As more fathers become involved, their growing numbers should prompt wider social acceptance of egalitarian households, bolstering the option to make such choices.

Ultimately, however, men's movement toward domestic equality will depend on their ability to overcome the obstacles to change and their desire to resist the social pressures to conform. Equal fathers were willing and able to defy social expectations, to overcome social constraints, and to reject the pathways of the past. There is good reason to believe that their outlooks and choices reflect a simmering mood among many American men, who long for more work flexibility and fewer work demands. There is even reason to believe many would be willing to relinquish some earnings in exchange for spending more time with their families. A *Time* survey found that 56 percent of a random sample of men said they would forfeit up to one-fourth of their salaries "to have more family and personal time," and 45 percent "said they would probably refuse a promotion that involved sacrificing hours with their families.[10] Carl reflects this mood:

> It's amazing how many people don't understand the way I feel. I would prefer to be home than work overtime, where they would kill to get it. They say, "What are you, rich?" No, but you only need a certain amount of money to live. God forbid you walk down the street and get struck by a car, or whatever, and it's over. I don't want to say, "Why didn't I spend more time with my family?" It's not going to happen to me. You can control it.

By focusing on the advantages and discounting the drawbacks of their choices, men are able to overcome some of the social and ideological barriers to equal parenting. In adding up the sacrifices and the gains, Larry spoke for the group: "I've given some things up, sure, but the changes in my lifestyle are eighty or ninety percent in the positive."

Though few in number, equal fathers demonstrate that men can discover or acquire nurturing skills and find pleasure in using them. Those men who did find support for being an equal father made contingent choices just like those who did not. In both instances, different circumstances could easily have produced different outcomes. It is not surprising that Rick found his rare and unexpected path to be a matter of chance:

> I have very conservative attitudes in many respects. The fact that we got married and had children was very conservative. The fact that within those parameters, we shared, co-shared, work and family—that was not conservative. We've never discussed it, but I feel that the outcome is built much more on chance. I may not have always felt that way, but my own experiences confirmed it.

Chance, however, is just another way of saying that his choice was based on unusual and unexpected opportunities. Given how rare are the supports for involved fathering and how pervasive the obstacles, its rise is even more significant than its limited nature. For the potential of the many men who wish to be more involved to be realized, however, the unusual circumstances that now prompt only a small fraction of men to become equal parents must become real for a much larger group.

Notes

From No Man's Land: Men's Changing Commitments to Family and Work by Kathleen Gerson, 247–255. Copyright © 1993 Basic Books, a division of HarperCollins Publishers, Inc. Reprinted by permission of Basic Books, a member of Perseus Books, LLC.

1. See Carol Lawson, "Baby Beckons: Why Is Daddy at Work?" *New York Times,* May 16, 1991; C1. The Family Leave Act that finally became law in 1993 is an important first step, but much more will be needed for men to feel able to choose equal parenting.

2. Joseph H. Pleck. "Husbands' Paid Work and Family Roles: Current Research Trends," *Research in the Interweave of Social Roles: Jobs and Families* 3 (1983): 251–333.

3. Barbara J. Risman and Maxine P. Atkinson, "Gender in Intimate Relationships: Toward a Dialectical Structural Theory" (paper presented at the National Council on Family Relations Theory, Construction, and Research Methodology Workshop (November), Seattle, Washington, 1990. According to Risman and Atkinson, "No matter how involved 'new feminist' fathers become in child-care, they. . . are expected to work harder and are constrained from leaving less than optimal jobs because of their economic responsibilities. When they do care for their children after work, they are praised highly by friends, family members, and wives as wonderful, modem, 'involved' fathers" (pp. 15–16).

4. Hal Strauss. "Freaks of Nature," *American Health,* January–February 1989, 70–71; Rosabeth M. Kanter, *Men and Women of the Corporation* (New York: Basic Books, 1977); Bryan E. Robinson, "Men Caring for the Young: A Profile," in Robert A. Lewis and Marvin B. Sussman, eds., *Men's Changing Roles in the Family* (New York: Haworth, 1986), 151–161. Men who become primary parents face barriers similar to those faced by the first female managers, who had to cope with being "tokens." Strauss discusses the stigmatization and social isolation of househusbands Kanter analyzes how the first female managers were tokens in the corporation. Robinson (1986), reports that male caregivers who work in nursery schools and day care programs also face discrimination and stigma from employers, co-workers, and even parents.

5. See Alice A. Rossi, "Transition to Parenthood," *Journal of Marriage and the Family* 30 (1960): 26–39.

6. Joan Huber and Glenna Spitze. *Sex Stratification: Children, Housework, and Jobs* (New York: Academic, 1983); Catherine E. Ross, John Mirowskv, and Joan Huber, "Dividing Work, Sharing Work, and In-Between: Marriage Patterns and Depression," *American Sociological Review,* December 1983, 809–823; See also Michael E. Lamb, Joseph H. Pleck, and James A. Levine, "Effects of Increased Paternal Involvement on Fathers and Mothers," in Charlie Lewis and Margaret O'Brien, eds., *Reassessing Fatherhood: New Observations on Fathers and the Modern Family* (Newberry Park, Calif.: Sage, 1987), 103–125; Arlie R. Hochschild with Anne Machung, *The Second Shift: Working Parents and the Revolution at Home* (New York: Viking, 1989).

7. See Frank F. Furstenberg Jr., S. Phillip Morgan, and Paul D. Allison, "Paternal Participation and Children's Well-Being After Marital Dissolution," *American Sociological Review* 52, no. 5 (1987): 695–701; Shirley M. H. Hanson. 1986. "Father/Child Relationships: Beyond Kramer vs. Kramer," in Robert A. Lewis and Marvin B. Sussman, eds., *Men's Changing Roles in the Family* (New York: Haworth), 135–150; Michael E. Lamb, ed., *The Role of the Father in Child Development* (New York: Wiley, 1976); J. W. Santrock and R. A. Warshak, "Father Custody and Social Development in Boys and Girls," *Journal of Social Issues* 32 (1979): 112–125; J. W. Santrock, R. A. Warshak, and G. L. Elliot, "Social Development and Parent-Child Interaction in Father-Custody and Stepmother Families," in Michael E. Lamb, ed., *Nontraditional Families: Parenting and Child Development* (Hillside, N.J.: Erlbaum, 1982), 289–314.

8. Victoria Secunda. *Women and Their Fathers: The Sexual and Romantic Impact of the First Man in Your Life* (New York: Delacorte, 1992).

9. Daniel Goleman, "Surprising Findings About the Development of Empathy in Children," *New York Times,* July 10, 1990, C1.

10. Reported in Judith Stacey. "Backwards toward the Post-Modern Family," in Alan Wolfe, ed., *America at Century's End,* 17–34 (Berkeley: University of California Press). See also Phyllis Moen and Donna I. Dempster-McClain, "Employed Parents: Role Strain, Work Time, and Preferences for Working Less," *Journal of Marriage and the Family* 49, no. 3 (1987): 579–590; Eli Chinoy, *Automobile Workers and the American Dream* (New York: Random House, 1955). If Chinoy found that automobile workers in the 1950s dreamed about retiring, inheriting wealth, or opening their own businesses as an alternative to dead-end factory jobs, then the decline of well-paying, secure manufacturing jobs over the last decade has given this dream of independence through self-employment new life.

25

"MEN DON'T DO THIS SORT OF THING"

Househusbands

Calvin D. Smith

Prior research has found that househusbands suffer alienation and ostracism from a variety of sources. Based on in-depth interviews with eleven househusbands, this article builds on such research by outlining and analyzing some of the mechanisms of this alienation and some of the adaptations these men made to deal with these experiences. Of particular interest are the problems the men report having with being seen by others as legitimately involved in child care and (to a lesser extent) housework. These data strongly support the idea that the men's sex category overrides other positionings that may be relevant, such as "competent housekeeper" or "full-time househusband and child carer." Put differently, hegemonic conceptions of who ought to be minding the children and the house subvert or thwart these men's attempts to validate themselves and these practices. The consequences are a feeling of illegitimacy on one hand and social isolation on the other.

The Study

In 1992, I interviewed eleven men about their experiences as househusbands. Such men ostensibly are in breach of the norms for their gender. They had given up full-time careers to stay at home and care for children. They lived with and were supported by women who had given up full-time child care and housework and taken up full-time paid work. They are engaged in what is commonly understood as *role reversal.*[1] Their story is one of men who not only experience negative reactions to their form of life (from both men and women) but who are relatively powerless to transform the views of others. They instead adopt a variety of strategies for coping with these negative reactions.

In this article, I recount some of these experiences, focusing in the first part on the dual issues of the men's feelings of illegitimacy as househusbands and their isolation from various groups of mothers, their potential peers. In the second part of the article, I describe the men's responses to their sense of illegitimacy and the social isolation that results from this transgressive form of life. I will be using the men's own words to carry the analysis, and I will describe the experiences leading to the sense these men had of being socially isolated as househusbands. I conceive of the problem as one of the validation of transgressive gender practices. Put in the simple and commonsense terms of the gender ideologies underpinning the gender order, men are not meant to mother.

"So, What's It Like Being a Househusband?"

In this section, I outline the social factors contributing to these men's sense of illegitimacy and their social isolation. The experiences these men recount of being househusbands easily can be grouped into three domains of phenomena, as follows:

1. *Personal processes* of self-identification and appeals to internalized beliefs (or the internalization of new beliefs) that these men used to justify to themselves the value of their new identity and social location
2. *Interpersonal interactions* through which people express intentionally or otherwise their assumptions and prejudices
3. *Material manifestations* of the gender order that arise in the architectural and sociophysical features of the urban landscape and in which are embedded the physical consequences of the taken-for-grantedness and stability of assumptions about or ideologies of gender

The drama of these men's struggle with their unusual vocation is played out in these three domains, as we shall see in more detail in the following sections.

Personal Processes

Rejecting Hegemonic Masculinity, Identifying with "Mothering."   In this study, the success of the passage from extradomestic to domestic work emerged as the phenomenon of greatest importance for these men. Most had achieved a degree of awareness of gender as a range of beliefs that could, indeed must, be challenged if a man is to feel right about being a househusband. This is because of the strong ideological link between women and child care (and other household) work. Therefore, one way to legitimate being a househusband is to reject gender discourses that are inherently delegitimizing. Hegemonic masculinity (Connell 1987, 184–187) is such a gender discourse. Thus, several of the men drew a distinction between themselves and "macho men." Macho and nonmacho were variously defined as having some or all of the attributes listed in Table 25.1, which details the kinds of characteristics the men used to conceive of the difference between themselves and macho men.[2]

The men in this sample may be denying their (macho) "maleness" to be seen more plausibly as potentially successful nurturers. Their central problem is how to fashion a

TABLE 25.1: Personal Identification Work: "Macho" and "Nonmacho"

Characteristics identified as macho

Beer swilling

Being in adolescent mode

Selfishness

Having smokes all the time

Preferring the company of men to women

Thinking that a woman's place is in the home and a man's is in the workplace, earning the money

Not accepting responsibilities when children come along

Taking an interest in cars or football

Being interested in politics

Desire to dominate friends, family, or spouse

Hesitancy to show emotions

Unwillingness to introspect

Setting and realizing personal job-related goals

Ambition

Incapacity to accept human failings in themselves and others

Putting on more of a front than they would like to let on

Characteristics identified as nonmacho

Getting on with women better than with men

Taking responsibility

Liking to cook

Not liking to talk football or motor cars

Being skilled at cooking

Overtly showing love to child(ren)

Following a child's lead, not trying to organize the child's play

Ability to accept human failings in themselves and others

Developing patience and being patient

NOTE: The information on which this table is based is very rich and interesting and deserves an independent treatment. Such a treatment is beyond the focus of this article, however.

legitimate place for themselves as full-time nurturers and house workers. As Connell (1987) points out, discourses of gender are intimately tied both to social organization (e.g., the division of labor) and to personal identity. Successful adaptation to being a househusband seemed to be achieved in part by respondents personally identifying with a nonmacho masculinity. All respondents showed some signs of this, although the degree to which this was true varied from man to man. Note that although the macho list seems longer, if we delete from it those items that have an opposite term in the nonmacho list, the numbers even out (ten to nine, respectively).[3] Also note the strongly practical themes that link the nomnacho with the work of nurturing. Cooking, being responsible, showing love to children, and developing patience are practical achievements of parenting. Compare these with May and Strikwerda's (1991) specifications of nurturant fatherhood:

On reflection, though, it seems quite clear that what we are doing as fathers is quite similar to what, when done by mothers, is called nurturance. To be a nurturer is (1) to display caring behavior for an extended period of time, (2) to have an intellectual commitment to that caring, and (3) to identify oneself as a nurturing person. (p. 30)

Whereas these men may seem to be oriented to the first two of May and Strikwerda's constituents of nurturing behavior, this analysis is about the trials of being at once a male and a nurturer. As we will soon see, it is their identification as nurturers, or more generally as househusbands, that these men find problematic.

Notwithstanding such personal identifications with nonmacho masculinities, the men in this sample lament their failure to become integrated and accepted into the world of mothers and house workers in a variety of contexts. In fact, there is a striking disparity between their endorsements of the work and their disaffection toward its social implications: they are at once, on the whole, both enthusiastic advocates of the reversal and disaffected emigrés to a social position that yields little to their implicit challenge to gender ideology.

Self-Imposed Illegitimacy.   Most of the disaffection exhibited by these men is not of their own making, and I will be discussing its sources at length below. However, it is important to acknowledge the internal cause of this problem: personal gender ideologies.

Greg, for example, thinks that his gender is a barrier to future communication with his daughter, particularly as she enters puberty, so he is thinking of "standing aside" to let more of a bond develop between the daughter and her mother. This intention to stand aside is associated with a general belief that women are natural mothers, the evidence of which is his wife's "intuition" about their children's moods (an intuition he thinks he lacks), and therefore can be interpreted as a pragmatic solution to a problem created by ideological beliefs and interpreted through ideological lenses, as it were.

For Greg, his gender is a factor that he sees as limiting his potential suitability, in the eyes of his daughter, as a confidant. When asked why he would consider reverting to a more traditional division of labor in the home, he replied,

> The motivating factor is I think that the girls are getting to a stage where they need a mother—they need someone basically their own gender who knows the situations that could arise and they would want someone to talk to. I think—this is only my personal thoughts and K is of the same opinion, I think—that as N gets a little bit older and she's going through these changes, I don't think she's going to want to talk to me about them—because I'm a man—not because I'm her dad—I'm a man.

Thus, Greg sees himself as incapacitated by his maleness but not just because of the anticipated delicacies of puberty. Later, Greg said that he thought he found the work harder than a woman would:

> **A:** I find it is a lot harder for me than it is for them [other mothers]. . . to do it.
> **Q:** Than a woman?

A: Yeah, cos I think their instincts are there. . . . I've found at times that my wife can pick up certain attitudes from the girls that I don't and it's just something that's intuitive.

Q: Do you think that it's an instinctual thing that she has?

A: Yeah I think it is. . . . I think it's in-built.

Q: Not because they're girls and she's a woman?

A: No.

Q: If you had boys she'd still pick up stuff—?

A: Yeah, I think it'd still be there.

This reaction is less definite in the other men, but it is still lurking subtly. For instance, Jan merely emphasises that he would not have been as happy about the reversal had his children not treated him as their primary carer (i.e., the way a child treats and is bonded to and dependent on his or her mother). I suggest that these attitudes about the prospects of the men's success reveal that they lack confidence in their capacities as mothers, based on beliefs about both what successful mothering looks like and which sex is most likely to achieve it.

This is similar to Scott Coltrane's (1989, 484–485) findings that showed that different genetic resources of men and women were invoked to justify the division of labor in "manager-helper," dual-income families.

Interpersonal Interactions

Negotiating the Reversal. The home environment constitutes a primary site for the negotiation of the legitimacy of a reversal. One way of legitimizing these reversals is to justify them in terms of a legitimizing discourse. This is most easily done in the home. More than any other, the home is a site in which the individual has relatively influential input into the discursive references that can justify his at home status. Those who have engaged in the swap by choice rather than by happenstance have no legitimate excuse, in contexts outside the home, for leaving the world of paid work that defines most men (Pleck and Sawyer 1974, 94; see also Pleck 1976, 1983, 1987; Tolsen 1977). However, "choosers" have a higher degree of legitimacy in the home context because the choice to engage in the reversal is a negotiated outcome involving both partners and a variety of shared assumptions. The following is an example of one man who has a very high degree of support for the reversal from his spouse:

> I said to her a while back "I think I'll look for a full-time job" and she said "no, no, I want you to stay at home"—she's never had it so good—she comes home and says—and I cook really lovely meals y'know—she's just so happy that she comes home and doesn't have to do any housework. (Keith)

But the home is not always a site of unambiguous legitimacy for the reversal. Whereas Keith is a chooser, Jan is not:

TABLE 25.2: Main Reason(s) Given for Commencing Reversal

Parental ideals with economic factors	4
Personal illness	3
Spouse's committment to/investment in career	2
Illness of spouse	1
Egalitarian ideals	1
Total	11

The major issue I've found—I've been doing this three years in October, and the main—the major difficulty for me was um, family and friends' expectations, and even my wife's expectations. Of what I should do. Because I've often said to H [spouse] that *when she was home with the kids and I was working there was never never never any expectation that she should go to work* or that she should ever work. It was just that y'know "you're at home with the children, if you want to do that one day that's fine;' but there was never expectation, *yet with me being at home, even with her there's always expectation like, you'll work one day—always*—like we had to process that, and work through it so that it's not there now, like it was (uh huh) but I used to always feel that pressure. (Jan, emphasis added)

This finding validates Coltrane's (1989) assertion that "the essential nature of men is taken to be that of provider" (p. 488). Even between spouses engaged in a reversal, it is the "default" construction of men, and it requires active interpersonal negotiation to effect a change.

By far the most common source of legitimacy at home are those negotiations that are based on shared values and assumptions. As can be seen from Table 25.1, a range of contingencies is given to account for the advent of the reversals.[15] Of these, two (illness of self and illness of spouse) represent circumstances of little choice compared with the others.

It is in the home that the initial decision to engage in reversal is given its normative force and legitimacy, through negotiations that are based on a variety of discourses, the legitimating force of which is shared between negotiators (e.g., parental values, economic rationality, egalitarian ideals).[16]

The point being made here is simply that, in the first instance, a reversal must be negotiated between the spouses. That these reversals have taken place generally means that some basis justifies the reversal. It should not be inferred, however, that those partners therefore are equally happy about it or that neither agrees to the reversal begrudgingly. I merely wish to articulate that there is a process that makes the domestic context more likely than the "outside world" to be a context of legitimacy. In the current political climate, legitimating discourses in the home context are necessary but not sufficient to make these men feel legitimately involved in their respective reversals. This is why the "choice" and "happenstance" distinction (with reference to the advent of the reversals) is important. In all of the former cases, the men enjoyed the greatest at-home legitimacy. But in some of the latter, they or their spouses only begrudgingly accepted the reversal as a "solution" to the prevailing antecedents that necessitated it.

This leads to the first theoretically interesting observation from these data: social identity is evidently a contextual matter to the extent that how invisible its negotiation is to ourselves and others, and how happy we are with our own, is a function of its contextual legitimacy. The problem for these men is that their other-attributed identity as men keeps overriding their self-attributed identity as househusbands. The degree to which this fractures their own views of themselves and forms a basis for the sense of illegitimacy is a function of the discursive constitution of various contexts in which they operate. This is why the domestic context provides a basis for the greatest isomorphism between their own views of themselves and those of others (spouse, children) in that context. The fact that the "extradomestic" context provides the greatest number of challenges to the legitimacy of their identities as househusbands is the main focus of this article.

Explicit Challenges.   Some challenges to their legitimacy as househusbands that these men experienced were issued explicitly by others using a reference discourse (e.g., hegemonic masculinity) that invalidates the reversal by implication. The degree to which these reversals are seen as illegitimate has no doubt changed over time. For example, Eddie (in reversal eleven years) can recall a time (a decade ago) when househusbands were topical, freakish, and, according to one of his peers, "obviously" homosexual. He contrasts this with the present, a time when nurturing behavior by men toward their children, along with less rigidly defined "sex roles" in nuclear families, are more acceptable, even though still relatively rare. Eddie recounts an incident that occurred in the early 1980s, with a woman who had seen a television program about househusbands:

> I was a househusband[10] and she knew I was a househusband and ahh I said "yes" and she said, "they're all poofs y'know," I said, "really?" and she said "oh yes, you can tell," I said, "how do you work that out?" "well it's obvious isn't it?" y'know (laughter) I said "Well it's not obvious to me, explain it," and she couldn't she said "no, you can see that: they must be." (Eddie)

Continuing the conversation with the same woman, Eddie asked her whether she also would classify him as a poof, since he too was a househusband:
> I said, "but I'm a househusband, does that put me in the same category?" and she said, "oh no, no, cos you coach a football team, and you have a drink with my husband; that's different," I said, "well its not really y'know—I'm sure these fellows drink too," she said, "no they can't possibly—you could tell." Her mind was fixed and nothing was gonna change it—even though she had the evidence before her. . . that was the perception they had of househusbands about ten or twelve years ago. (Eddie)

The woman here decides that certain "facts" about Eddie (viz., that he coaches football and drinks with her husband) carry definitional priority over other "facts" about him (viz., that he is a househusband). This example demonstrates how contextual, or indexical, legitimacy is: in the context that she knows him as a coach and drinking friend of her husband's, the claim that he is a househusband is not consistent with the claim that he is a poof, but outside that context the inference that a househusband must he a poof is the default. Last but not least in offering direct challenges to their legitimacy is the family:

> Oh I s'pose I felt as though family—and I got this from other members of the family too— I felt like I was a bludger, y'know, I felt as though "men don't do this sort of thing." My stepfather told me I was living off the earnings of my wife and um, and it's a really suck thing to do y'know cos my mother's never worked y'know, she's just always—stays at home y'know and just cooks and stuff. . . . it's been that way for at least two years I'd say. (Jan)

Being Ignored By Potential Peers

Another experience of illegitimacy is Greg's recollection that many of the women at the créche he attends are unfriendly toward him:

> I find it very difficult to interact with other women at kindergartens or playgroups or whatever. . . . I went to a playgroup once and I sat here [hits table with hand] and the women sat here [hits table elsewhere]. I moved here [hits table place representing where women were sitting], they still talked around me—that's one of the difficulties I've found—they didn't want to [talk to me]. . . There are a lot of women out there that think males shouldn't be at home. And I found a problem that way. . . y'know I'm dropping off at kindy and picking her up and a lot of women will walk around me—y'-know I'm talking to someone else and they want to [talk to that person]—they might come over and start talking to that other person and totally shut me out.

The behavior of these women is consistent with Ehrensaft's (1980) suggestion that women may resist the occupation by men if realms in which they have power and over which they have control. However her argument that "[w]omen under advanced capitalism spend too much time feeling powerless to relish a situation where, under the auspices of liberation, they find themselves with less power" (p. 51) implicitly ignores women's active role in the reproduction of gendered expectations about what men and women ought rightly to be and to do, and by playing down their active role in the constitution of gender and gendered patterns of behavior, it also excuses women, exempting them from analysis and protecting them from criticism. That men may have an interest in maintaining their power has not excused, exempted, or protected men in that regard.

Being Tested.   There seems to be an attitude of suspicion on the part of other mothers, indeed women generally, that these men are not really doing the job in its entirety, doing all of the implied tasks tout ensemble. Several of the men complained of this attitude. They felt that before being accepted they had to prove themselves in some way and that some women engaged in a kind of "testing" game. For instance, Greg recounts that women who had been less than supportive of his presence at the kindergarten his daughter was attending were not so unfriendly after he had done one of the "mothers' rosters" there. Other mothers also cast a skeptical eye over the proceedings when a man takes on this kind of work. When explaining why he feels some pride in or self-satisfaction over his success in the role of nurturer and house worker, that "being a male [he] could do it as well—cook meals and bake cakes all those things," Bob described the skeptical attitude of his peers toward him: "the women around—the other mothers and so forth around—they tend to sort of ahh keep an eye on you to see if 'what's he doing?' y'know. 'Can he really do that or what?' y'know." (Bob)

Faux Pas. The social interactions I have called faux pas are those in which the man's status as a full-time home worker and child care is overlooked, deliberately or accidentally, by an interlocutor, and the basis for the identification of the man (by the other) reverts to "man-as-not-fully-responsible-for-the-children." I call them faux pas because, from the men's perspectives, they are interactional "false steps," based on faulty inferences their interlocutors make from that-they-are-men to that-they-are-not-mothers, when the interlocutors could be expected to know better (because, for instance, they already had been told the person in question was a househusband).

Thus, a complaint repeatedly made by these men is that many people, particularly women, assume that they must be nonnurturers, full-time breadwinners, and if they are obviously looking after children at any time, then they are doing it only temporarily. Even when they explicitly state that their involvement in nurturing, care, and housework is full-time and that it is their spouses who are the breadwinners, this information is often not taken seriously or it is forgotten even during the same conversation in which it is conveyed.

Allan tells the story of a woman who knew quite well (or, at least, who ought to have known quite well) but simply forgot that he was a full-time househusband. They had met at a swimming class both their children were attending. A few minutes earlier in a conversation, he had told her that he had an interest in yachting and, in the same conversation, she simply forgot that he had full-time child care commitments just like her own and assumed he would be able to join her husband on a yachting trip each Wednesday:

> [The] lady [I was talking to] down at the swimming pool said to me: "look um he goes sailing every Wednesday"—this is the husband—and I said "Jesus, there's no way in the world I can be there: I've got to pick N [son] up at two o'clock, I've got to race from L [suburb] to pick up K [daughter] at kindy, I've got to get dinner ready" and she looked at me almost as if she'd forgotten that I was really a proper househusband—not one of these persons who is just looking after the kids for the day. . . but she knows that I've been looking after K and I had N there in the pram (yeah) right, and she's in the swimming lessons. . . she assumed I'd be dashing off with her husband sailing all day Wednesday. And I said "No, no, no, no. Wait on. . . " "I'm a proper househusband" I say to them, because I think a lot of them get to think that again you're just looking after them while your wife's on holidays.

Of course, from their interlocutors' perspectives it is a perfectly ordinary and appropriate inference from the attribution "male" to a range of attributes including "not the primary caregiver of children." That is the whole point. Because being a man excludes the attributions "motherlike, full-time nurturer," and so on, these men repeatedly found themselves being cast as men-as-instrumental-carers or men-as-breadwinners, over and above the possibility of their being seen as men-as-mothers. So, although in May and Strikwerda's (1991) view men may be able to nurture, there is a big step from that philosophical "revelation" to social integration. It was merely salt into their wounds that such mistakes occurred when someone who already knew of their circumstances "forgot."

Other men, too, were guilty of assuming away the degree of involvement anticipated by these men," when for the first time they had to tell work colleagues that they were leaving their jobs and why.

Q: What sort of reactions did you get from the people you told?
A: Questioning from males. . . one guy. . . could not understand how you would fill in your day, his main worry was "what are you going to do?" I did a supply day back there and he said "have you been playing golf[11]—he sort of thought I'd be playing golf three times a week—there was this conception of all this spare time, which if you take on the tasks of what females do, you don't have a lot of time—it's repetitive, day after day, but there's not these masses of spare time—if you're going to replicate the cooking the ironing and so on—so his was "what are you going to do?" (David)

The faux pas reveals the inferences made by people when confronted with men who claim to be engaged in full-time child care and housework. Those inferences are based on assumptions about men qua men, which sometimes override the fact that they are househusbands.

Sexual Suspects.   Another common theme was a feeling of not being fully accepted because of sexual stereotyping:

> I felt I was under suspicion because I was a male. This has happened on several occasions as if I'd say to them—one of them couldn't do nappies she asked if I knew a way to do nappies so they wouldn't leak blah blah (mm hmm) I said "Look y'know come round for a cup of coffee, bring the kids—or the baby—and I'll show you how to do it," and she came, but other girls I'd say "oh why don't you come over for coffee and scones and have a chat," and um they always seem to be very hesitant and (mm hmm) I often sort of got the feeling that because I was I male, and perhaps they thought I was trying to lure them round to my place for a coffee. And that's happened a few times so you feel a little bit alienated in that situation although my good friends, obviously they just come over. (Allan)

The uniform result of this suspicious attitude is attenuation of the men's social contacts with other mothers. Coffee mornings are an important example. Coffee mornings are get-togethers of two, three, four, or more at-home mothers. Many of the men believe their exclusion from this site of integration on the part of their potential peers contributes to their sense of isolation and segregation. A simple visit to the home of another woman seems to be something of a taboo in the men's eyes, and it rarely happens. To some of these men, it is a major symbol of their lack of integration with their potential peers (other mothers at home) that they are never invited to coffee mornings. Most believe that they occur on a regular basis, and most theorize similar reasons for the fact that they are not invited to visit other women. The following is a typical account of the problem:

> **A:** My wife goes to the clinic, and they always have the mothers' meetings things— um I didn't actually get told I couldn't come—the nurses there were very helpful they said "oh yeah, come round any time, I'll look forward to it," but some of the other mothers were a bit strange about it y'know like as if like I've entered a domain you should not enter, y'know like "this is women's work, go away."
> **Q:** How do they express that to you?
> **A:** Well, I've never been invited anywhere basically. Y'know like you're just gone—like there's morning teas and coffee mornings going on all round Brisbane but men don't go to them, ahh cause women just don't invite them, which I think is partly sexual—um y'know like they don't want to invite strange men into their houses—but ah you miss out because a lot of the support group you get just doesn't exist. (Colin)

We can begin to see how the gendering of these men leaves them unconnected from the informal social support networks that may be more readily accessible to female at-home carers (see Wearing 1984). In the next section, this theme is developed beyond interpersonal interactions as more general manifestations of the gender order become relevant.

Material Manifestations of the Gender Order

In the following section, I detail experiences whose delegitimizing force derives from the fact that they occur in and around physical structures that have been designed with the gendered division of labor in mind or simply signify it in some way or other. For example, shopping centers have baby change rooms in them, but until recent times, these have often been a built-in part of women's toilets; or again, signs indicating change rooms often carry a female symbol for the parent or the phrase "mothers' room"; and, of course, suburban neighborhoods themselves are mostly peopled during the day by women.

Social Isolation in the Neighborhood.

> The worst thing about being at home and as a caregiver—in that situation is the immense isolation, social isolation—there ain't no boys out there that you can sit down and talk to about your football with or whatever. (Mark)

The physical context of the suburb, in which much of this legitimization drama is played out, is a social space in which women are concentrated, at least during business hours. These men are not incorporated into that wider, daytime suburban community. As one man put it,

> The aspect that interests me the most is the problem of the suburbs for men right—the suburbs aren't instituted between " in the morning and five at night for men—in as

much as the people are resident in the suburb—there's more women working and there's a transition happening—they exist for women um—ahh—from the tennis club and various networks that do exist. (Mark)

This problem is most salient when understood and experienced in terms of the consequences it has for access to the informal networks of mothers that are a source of information and skill sharing. Wearing (1984) has detailed the importance of rich, informal networks that suburban mothers establish as a source of social interaction, help, and support (p. 176). Colin recalls an occasion when his daughter was distressed with colic, and he had to phone a friend in another town because he did not have a neighborhood network to fall back on for information and support:

It [not having someone to call on if something is going wrong] scares you. But if I was a woman on my own I think I would've got a lot more help to some extent because um— women would come over—(You mean. . . just in the normal course of the day?) In the normal way, yeah, yeah so we tend to have missed out on that little y'know.

Mark points out the essential contrast between his circumstances and those of Swedish men, namely, the visible presence of carers who are men, in substantial numbers, in the public arena during the day.

Of course its different in Sweden—I know the situation in Sweden—not only women but men can get maternity leave so its an overall situation that they stay at home so you walk around in Stockholm and there's all these men pushing prams around in the middle of the day.

Legitimacy for this man would be higher were there more men doing child care; then it would be more "normal."

Just being recognized as a man alone with a baby can sometimes elicit unusual responses from people, such as being stopped in the street and asked if you are okay (the assumption presumably being that something must be wrong if there is a man with children and no woman to be seen).

I'm just looking in shop windows y'know going out for a walk in the morning and y'-know there's these people stopped me—three or four people stopped me—cause I'm just standing there with the baby and the pram looking in shop windows enjoying myself and three—there was an old lady, a young couple stopped me, and a couple of girls about eighteen: "are you okay," "yeah fine," "no worries just wandering around"—because they saw the baby and everyone stopped and said, "ooh ahh, lovely baby," and there's a woman there who was pregnant, had a baby in a stroller and shopping bags, and nobody took a blind bit of notice. (Colin)

Again, Coltrane (1989) has found similar examples of the "noticeability" of men when they are doing their day-to-day activities with their children:

[Fathers] described their sense of parenting responsibility as taken-for-granted and did not consider it to be out of the ordinary or something worthy of special praise [or attention).. . . Thus fathers discounted and normalized extreme reactions to their divisions of labor and interpreted them in a way that supported the "natural" character of what they were doing. (p. 486)

By contrast, my data suggest that what is "natural" is the issue, and it was the house-husbands' failure to achieve being seen as engaging in nurturing "just naturally" that these men lamented.

Shopping Centers, Toilets, and Baby Change Rooms.   Shopping centers during the day, like neighborhoods, are predominantly peopled by women. Taking a child to the toilets in a shopping center poses certain problems for househusbands. Some of the men recount that they have been given "strange looks" by people when they have taken their young daughters into the men's toilet. But the converse (i.e., a mother taking her son into the women's toilet) is culturally benign (as many men will tell you).

There's always that difficulty—well, not difficulty—like I was talking to some other friends recently—like going to the toilets like when you're out shopping y'know I still get weird looks off these old dears when I take her to the men's toilet y'know—people don't think anything of it taking the boys into the girls toilets, but taking her in, they sort of look at me.

But much more salient issues for the men in my sample are the problems of the sexist nature of the design of change rooms." Change rooms are often situated within women's toilets. They sometimes have a dual function as sites where women can comfortably breast-feed their children as well as change nappies. Sometimes the change room is an antechamber to the toilet area; sometimes they are contiguous. The men experience this as explicit evidence that what they are doing is not culturally sanctioned.

This problem is common, and the men often "solve" it by avoiding the change rooms altogether. One wryly attested to having "changed the baby in some pretty strange places." The following quote is typical:

A: I've found it pretty awkward really because trying to change the baby when you go out can be fun too because half the mothers' rooms are in women's toilets and you get some very strange looks when you start to go in.

Q: Are they antechambers to the toilets or right inside the toilets?

A: Sometimes yeah. But you're very reluctant to find out. I mean when was the last time you walked into a ladies toilet: when you were about two? So some of them. . . have got completely separate areas for changing babies which is help-ful. . . . But some you go in it's always in the ladies toilets and that means you end up doing it on the concrete. (Jan)

Even when the change room is an antechamber or a separate room altogether, there is still a further complication—that breast-feeding mothers seem to be alarmed by the very presence of a man in the same room as themselves.

> A few times when I've gone into change rooms and there have been y'know mothers in there who have been perhaps nursing their children you sort of get a shocked reaction, but normally its only just that initial shock of seeing a male walk into the room. (David)

Tennis Club, Golf Club, and Other Leisure Activities.   Some of the men in this sample also noted that some organizations (e.g., golf clubs) provide child care services on certain days but that these are called "mothers' days" or "ladies' days," and they find that this linguistic usage is alienating, implying as it does that the only likely consumers of such services will be women. This use effectively excludes male "mothers," even though such men's needs for relief care are the same as those of any woman in similar circumstances who wants to participate in leisure or sport activities.

Women and "Women's Stuff."   For the most part, these men just felt out of place and ill at ease in the contexts where women were dominant, if only in terms of their physical presence. Some could say exactly what it was about the behavior of women in groups such as play groups that alienated them, but others simply felt out of sorts. Just approaching a group of mothers together, especially for the first time, represented a frightening prospect for some of these men. Henry recounted his "first day" fears when he took his son to kindergarten:

> The car almost didn't stop—it almost turned around. It was something I had to over-come—it is a real feeling: you see twenty-five women up there and you think "far out" y'know—it was a little bit imposing knowing that you're going to be the only male there.

The basis of isolation for these men, after the initial approach to a group of women in, for instance, the play group, is the conversation. Several of the men mentioned that the conversations often were oriented around topics that only a woman could legitimately comment on, in particular, gynecological problems and the childbirth experience:

> Even at play group I've found that it was sort of quite awkward um y'know the women that'd be there—y'know I was the only male there—and that didn't bother me as much, but at the same time, socially you just sort of felt slightly on the outer y'know they were quite happy to talk about—y'know: whatever they wanted to talk about—and of course, y'know a lot of conversation—particularly in the early stages—was all related to birthing [sic] and everything else, and they certainly felt very awkward about it—y'know it didn't worry me—ahh. (But you couldn't share that with them?) No, I couldn't share the deeper experience of it despite the fact that I was there for the birth [of my own children]. (David)

To summarize, the men in this study encountered the gender order in all its force at the level of experience: in microsocial encounters, in architecture, in the demographics of suburbia; the structural, cultural, and symbolic realities of the gender order affected them in a way that challenged the legitimacy of their transgressive form of life.

Notes

I am grateful to Maree Boyle and Jim McKay, who commented on earlier drafts of this article. I would also like to thank the anonymous reviewers for their helpful comments. Final responsibility for the article, however, rests with me. An earlier version of this article was presented at the annual conference of the Australian Sociological Association, Macquarie University, December 1993.

1. When I use the term "role," I do not refer to the concept of role as it is understood by role theorists. For example, what I mean by the phrase "identification with role" is something more like "identification with the discourses that define the commonsense concepts of the role in question." Connell (1979) has pointed out the theoretical problems with the use of the concept of role; however, in the present analysis the concept and the imperatives of its social logic are native.

2. Although all statements about either "macho" and "nonmacho" imply their own negations for the opposite category (what is true of macho men is false of nonmacho men, by definition), I have not constructed table 25.1 by filling out the list of characteristics in one column by their implications from the characteristics in the other column (readers can do this for themselves). Rather, each of the items was mentioned by at least one (though sometimes by more than one) of the men in this sample.

3. This kind of denial of hegemonic masculine gender characteristics is reminiscent of the process of "defeminization" found by Hochschild (1974) in a study of professional women (scientists). The women Hochschild studied seemed to deny or diminish their identification with their gender status–appropriate characteristics to strengthen their claims to be identified with gender status–inappropriate characteristics (professionalism, skills, and success as scientists) (Chase 1988, 280–281).

4. The revised macho list would include beer swilling, being in adolescent mode, selfishness, having smokes all the time, thinking that a woman's place is in the home, being interested in politics, desire to dominate, unwillingness to introspect, setting and realizing personal job-related goals, putting on more of a front than they would like to let on.

5. The interested reader should compare these data with Grbich (1992), who found that reasons given for the onset of a reversal were mostly related to the male's work, the major reason cited being the male partner's low commitment to his career. In Smith (n.d.), I suggested that this belied a voluntaristic bias or an insufficiently thorough approach to the matter. Coltrane (1989, 477) found that the sharing of housework and child care in his dual-earner families was underpinned by two ideological themes: child-centeredness and equity ideals. Whereas Coltrane's "child-centeredness" is a focus on the children's welfare and time spent with them when the couple was not working, my "parental ideals" relate more to the idea that there ought to be at least one parent who stays at home to raise the child in the first few years.

6. It should be remembered that when asked for their reasons for engaging in the reversal, most men gave more than one reason. In such circumstances, I would then ask them to tell me what the main reason was, and it is to this response that my categories refer. Singling out "main reasons" produces a misleading sense that these reason categories are mutually exclusive, and each is sufficient alone as a motivation. In contrast, when giving reasons for the advent of their reversals, the men in my sample did not give a single reason each but a cluster of related reasons. Note especially the response "parental ideals and economic rationality," the dual elements of which I could not separate to emphasize one over the other because they were always presented in tandem.

References

Abrahams, B., S. Feldman, and S. C. Nash. 1978. "Sex Role Self-Concept and Sex Role Attitudes: Enduring Personality Characteristics or Adaptations to Changing Life Situations?" *Developmental Psychology* 14, no. 4: 393–400.

Astrachan, A. 1986. *How Men Feel: Their Response to Women's Demands for Equality and Power.* New York: Doubleday.

Badinter, E. 1981. *The Myth of Motherhood.* Translated by R. DeGaris. London: Souvenir.

Bell, R. A. 1991. "Gender, Friendship Network Density, and Loneliness." *Journal of Social Behavior and Personality* 6, no. 1: 45–56.

Berger, P., and T. Luckmann. 1967. *The Social Construction of Reality: A Treatise in the Sociology of Knowledge.* Harmondsworth, U.K.: Penguin.

Chase, S. E. 1988. "Making Sense of 'The Woman Who Becomes a Man.'" In *Gender and Discourse: The power of talk,* edited by A. D. Todd and S. Fisher, 275–295. Norwood, N.J.: Ablex.

Coltrane, S. 1989. "Household Labor and the Routine Production of Gender." *Social Problems* 36, no. 5: 473–490.

Connell, R. W. 1979. "The Concept of Role and What to Do with It." *Australian and New England Journal of Sociology* 15 no. 3: 1987 7–17.

_____. 1987. *Gender and Power: Society, the Person, and Sexual Politics.* Sydney, Australia: Allen & Unwin.

Ehrensaft, D. 1980. "When Women and Men Mother." *Socialist Review* 10, no. 49: 37–73.

Fairclough, N. 1989. *Language and Power.* London: Longman.

Farrell, W. 1977. *The Liberated Man: Beyond Masculinity: Freeing Men and Their Relationships with Women.* New York: Random House.

Fausto-Sterling, A. 1985. *Myths of Gender: Biological Theories About Women and Men.* New York: Basic.

Garfinkel, H. 1967. *Studies in Ethnomethodology.* Englewood Cliffs, N.J.: Prentice-Hall.

Goffman, E. 1979. *Gender Advertisements.* London: Macmillan.

Grbich, C. 1992. "Societal Response to Familial Role Change in Australia: Marginalisation or Social Change?" *Journal of Comparative Family Studies* 23, no. 1: 79–94.

Haas, L. 1990. "Gender Equality and Social Policy: Implications of a Study of Parental Leave in Sweden." *Journal of Family Issues* 11, no. 4: 401–423.

Harper, J. 1980. *Fathers at Home.* Harmondsworth, U.K.: Penguin.

Hearn, J. 1987. *The Gender of Oppression: Masculinity and the Critique of Marxism.* Sussex, U.K.: Wheatsheaf.

Herek, G. M. 1987. "On Heterosexual Masculinity: Some Psychical Consequences of the Social Construction of Gender and Sexuality." In Changing Men: New Directions in Research on Men and Masculinity, edited by M. S. Kimmel. London: Sage.

Hochschild, A. 1974. "Making It: Marginality and Obstacles to Minority Consciousness." In *Women and Success: The Anatomy of Achievement,* edited by R. Kundsin. New York: William Morrow.

Kessler, S. J. 1990. "The Medical Construction of Gender: Case Management of Intersexed Infants." *Signs* 16, no. 1: 3–26.

Kessler, S. J., and W. Mckenna. 1978. *Gender: An Ethnomethodological Approach.* New York: John Wiley.

Kimmel, M. S., ed. 1987. *Changing Men: New Directions in Research on Men and Masculinity.* London: Sage.

LaRossa, R. 1988. "Fatherhood and Social Change." *Family Relations* 37: 451–457.

Lewis, C., and M. O'Brien. 1987. "Constraints on Fathers: Research, Theory and Clinical Practice." In *Reassessing Fatherhood: New Observations on Fathers and the Modern Family,* edited by C. Lewis and M. O'Brien. London: Sage.

Lorber, J., and S. A. Fanell. 1991. "Principles of Gender Construction." In *The Social Construction of Gender,* edited by J. Lorber and S. A. Farrell, 7–11. Newbery Park, Calif.: Sage.

May, L., and R. Strikwerda. 1991. "Fatherhood and Nurturance." *Journal of Social Philosophy* 22, no. 2: 28–39.

Minichiello, V., R. Aroni, E. Timewell, and L. Alexander. 1990. *In-Depth Interviewing: Re Searching People.* Melbourne, Australia: Longman Cheshire.

Money, J. 1986. *Venuses Penises: Sexology, Sexosophy and Exigency Theory.* Buffalo, N.Y.: Prometheus.

Pleck, J. 1976. "The Male Sex Role: Definitions, Problems, and Sources of Change." *Journal of Social Issues* 32, no. 3: 155–164.

_____. 1983. "Husbands Paid Work and Family Roles." In *Research in the Interweave of Social Riles,* edited by H. Lopata and J. Pleck, 251–333. Greenwich, Conn.: JAI.

26

WHY DON'T WELFARE-RELIANT MOTHERS GO TO WORK?

Kathryn Edin and Laura Lein

In 1990, Brianna Kerry had graduated from high school and was earning $4.55 an hour as a clerk in a large discount chain store. Because she could not get full-time hours (only twenty-six to thirty-four hours a week), she grossed about $600 a month. She had looked for better jobs, but the San Antonio economy was depressed, and she could find none. When Kerry learned she was pregnant, she called several day care centers for information and learned that the fee for full-time infant care equaled her paycheck. Because she did not see her economic situation improving any time soon and since she had planned to have children eventually, Kerry decided to have the baby. Shortly before her daughter's birth in 1991, she quit her job and applied for AFDC, food stamps, and Medicaid.

When we spoke with Kerry in 1992, she had been on the welfare rolls for almost two years and had tried to make good use of her time on welfare. She had completed one training program (a year-long business course offered by a proprietary school) but felt that the program had been a waste: that "ripoff school," as she called it, had put her $1,300 in debt and had not led to a job. Now, she told us, she was nearly finished with a second training program. This time the Job Opportunities and Basic Skills (JOBS) training program had paid for the course.

Kerry was enthusiastic about leaving welfare for work. When she finished her training as a home health aide, she was told she could earn $6 an hour, a much higher wage than she had earned previously. In the first year of work, she thought she could make ends meet because her living expenses were low (she shared the rent with her father and another couple) and because she would have a day care subsidy and Medicaid. Under the welfare rules at the time, both were continued for the first year after a mother left welfare for work. She was worried, though, about what would happen in the second year when she would have to pay for day care and doctor visits on her own. In her optimistic moments, she thought her child's father might get a steady, well-paying job and marry her, solving her economic problems. When she felt less optimistic, she feared he would never make more than "chump change." In these moments, she predicted that when the day care subsidy ran out, economic exigencies would force her back on welfare and into yet another training program.

The Decision to Stay on Welfare

Social scientists often analyze individual decision making processes in terms of incentives and disincentives, or what social scientists call "rational choice" models (Bane and Ellwood 1994). These models assume that women like Brianna Kerry choose between welfare and work by calculating the costs and benefits of each option, and then determining which has the biggest payoff. When economists apply these models, they typically focus on the economic costs and benefits associated with welfare as opposed to work and assume that individuals consider the long run as well as the short-run economic consequences of their choices. Sociologists usually concentrate on the short run and take into account a somewhat broader array of costs and benefits.

In his influential book *Losing Ground* (1984), Charles Murray put forward what was essentially a rational choice argument to explain the growth of welfare between 1960 and 1980. In the 1950s, he argued, relatively few women used the welfare system because it paid very low benefits, married women were not eligible, and the "man in the house" rule meant that single mothers could not live with a man to whom they were not married and retain their benefits. During the 1960s and 1970s, all this changed. Welfare benefits became more generous, food stamps and Medicaid were added, more families became eligible, and the Supreme Court struck down the "man in the house" rule.

Murray argued that these changes fundamentally altered the rules by which poor people lived, and that these rules were the reverse of those mainstream Americans lived by. First, because welfare benefits now came closer to what mothers could earn by working, there was little economic incentive to leave the welfare rolls for a job, according to Murray. Second, since unmarried mothers who cohabited with men could now get benefits, they had far less incentive to marry. Murray explicated the latter change rather dramatically with the story of a mythical couple, Harold and Phyllis, who chose to live together but not get married because Phyllis could then claim full benefits and combine them with Harold's wages. In short, the new rules rewarded nonwork, nonmarriage, and out-of-wedlock childbearing. Murray claimed these behaviors, in turn, increased the likelihood that poor families would remain poor. The only way to mend this system, he concluded, was to abolish AFDC.

Along with conservatives like Murray, political moderates and liberals have also applied the language of incentives and disincentives to welfare policy. Until 1968, mothers who earned a dollar from work lost a dollar in AFDC benefits. In 1968, a Democratic Congress passed a law allowing welfare recipients who worked part time to keep more of their benefits. Under the law, caseworkers were required to disregard both the first $30 of earned income and one-third of a welfare recipient's additional earnings when calculating the reduction in her AFDC benefits. This was called the "$30 and one-third" rule. Liberal lawmakers assumed that decreasing the penalty (or "tax rate") on wage income would encourage work. Ironically, Ronald Reagan persuaded Congress to eliminate the rule in 1981, because he claimed it discouraged mothers from working full time. More recently, the Clinton administration employed the language of incentives to justify expanding the earned income tax credit, which the administration believes will increase single mothers' incentive to work.

Social scientists have little direct evidence of how single mothers themselves view the incentives and disincentives associated with welfare or work. Do mothers make their decisions using a cost-benefit approach? How do government policies influence these decisions? Could government policies do more to encourage work? In our 1992 interviews, we spoke to welfare-reliant mothers at length about their economic circumstances and how they chose to deal with them. This chapter records what mothers actually said about the incentives and disincentives of welfare and work in the early 1990s. These firsthand accounts of the factors that influenced their welfare/work decisions provide important insights to those who seek to formulate welfare policies that are effective in moving mothers from welfare to work for good.

Our data lend a good deal of support to the idea that mothers choose between welfare and work by weighing the costs and benefits of each. Most of the welfare-reliant mothers we interviewed had an accurate view of the benefits they would lose by going to work—although they did not always know the exact dollar amount—and they made reasonable assessments of how much they would need to earn to offset the added costs of work. Mothers' views of the incentives and disincentives of each, however, were quite different from those assumed by many social scientists, including Murray. For poor single mothers, the welfare/work choice was not merely a problem of maximizing income or consumption. Rather, each woman's choice was set against a backdrop of survival and serious potential material hardship. The mothers with whom we spoke were less interested in maximizing consumption than in minimizing the risk of economic disaster. We return to this point later in the chapter.

We interviewed 214 welfare-reliant women, most of whom said that their decision regarding whether to leave welfare was predicated on their past labor market experiences. These experiences shaped their estimates of their current job prospects. Contrary to popular rhetoric, mothers did not choose welfare because of a lack of work experience or because they were ignorant of their job options. Most of the welfare-reliant mothers we interviewed had held a job in the formal sector of the labor market in the past: 83 percent had some work experience and 65 percent had worked within the last five years. National data, though not directly comparable, suggest an even higher rate of labor market participation; 60 percent of all welfare recipients surveyed by the Panel Study of Income Dynamics (PSID) had worked during the previous two years (U.S. House of Representatives 1993, 718). On average, our welfare recipients had accumulated 5.6 years of work experience before their current spell on welfare.

Elsewhere, we have demonstrated that their experience in the low-wage labor market taught these mothers several lessons about their likely job prospects (Edin and Lein 1997). First, returning to the kinds of jobs they had held in the past would not make them better off—either financially or emotionally—than they were on welfare. Indeed, this was precisely why most mothers were receiving welfare rather than working. Second, most mothers believed that taking a low-wage job might well make them worse off, because the job might vanish and they might be without any income for a time, since it took months for the welfare department to redetermine welfare eligibility and cut the first check. Consequently, working might put them and their children at risk of serious hardship. Third, no matter how long they stayed at a job and no matter how diligently they worked, jobs in what some called "the five-dollar-an-hour ghetto" seldom led to better jobs over time. Fourth, since job clubs and other components of the federal JOBS program were designed to place mothers in the types of jobs they held in the past, they saw little reason to participate in these programs: JOBS training programs added little to mothers' earning power. Finally, mothers took noneconomic as well as economic factors into account when deciding between welfare and work. Although most mothers felt that accepting welfare carried a social stigma, they also feared that work—and the time they would have to spend away from home—could jeopardize the safety and well-being of their children.

Given these realities, it was surprising to us that most mothers still had plans to leave welfare for work. Some planned to delay leaving welfare until their children were older and the cost of working was lower. Others like Brianna Kerry planned to use their time on welfare to improve their skills so they could get a better job when they reentered the labor force. In the long run, the goal of most mothers was to earn enough to eliminate the need for any government welfare program and to minimize their dependence on family, friends, boyfriends, side jobs, and agencies.

Half the mothers in the welfare-reliant group were engaged in some form of work (formal or informal) to make ends meet. Most had also worked at a job in the formal sector at some time in the past, and the vast majority planned to do so in the future, indeed, they all knew that they would have to work in due course, since their children would eventually reach adulthood, making the family ineligible for welfare. Only a tiny portion had no concrete plans to work in the formal sector.

When welfare-reliant mothers thought about welfare and work, the vast majority calculated not only how their prospective wages would compare with their cash welfare and food stamp benefits but how much they would lose in housing subsidies and other means-tested benefits. They also calculated how much more they would have to spend on child care, medical care, transportation, and suitable work clothing if they were to take a job. This mother's comment was typical:

> One day, I sat down and figured out the balance of everything that I got on welfare [including fuel assistance and Medicaid] and everything that I [earn] and have to spend working. And you know what? You're definitely better off on welfare! I mean absolutely every woman wants to work. I always want to work, but it's hard.

Because the costs and benefits associated with leaving welfare for work were constantly on their minds, many of the women we interviewed could do these calculations off the top of their heads, and some were able to show us the backs of envelopes and scraps of notebook paper on which they had scribbled such calculations in the last few weeks. Although respondents' estimates were seldom exact, most mothers were able to describe their prospective loss in benefits and potential increase in expenses. They were also able to calculate how holding a regular job would affect their ability to supplement their income in various ways. In addition, mothers considered a variety of noneconomic "costs" of working: whether full-time work would leave them enough time to be competent parents and whether they could manage to keep their children safe from the potentially lethal effects of their neighborhoods. Mothers' concerns about their children's welfare were often as important as purely economic gains or losses in their decisions.

"A Total Trap"

One Boston woman had only recently gone on welfare after seven years of working as a police dispatcher. Her top wage at this job was $7 an hour—a relatively high wage compared with the other women in our sample. She made ends meet on this wage only because she had a housing subsidy and a live-in boyfriend who paid a lot of the expenses. Despite the fact that she worked full time, she could not afford to move out of the projects. After her boyfriend left her and stopped contributing to her budget, she could not pay her bills. Thus, after seven years, she returned to welfare and went back to school:

> There's nothing in a low salary job because. . . your rent be so high. . . You know, people don't believe that people who work and live in the projects be paying $400–$500 for rent. But that's true because you can't really afford—for three bedroom, you can't really afford to go out and be paying $1,000 for a private apartment. You go out and get a job and then they take your rent subsidy away from you. You pay that much rent and it's hard just trying to maintain the low standard of living you had on welfare. You're in the same position, so it don't matter if you're working or not.

For women living in subsidized housing, working meant a double tax on earnings because housing subsidies are determined on the basis of cash income. For welfare-reliant mothers, only the cash welfare payment (and not food stamp benefits or the value of Medicaid) is used in determining rent. This means that even if a mother took a job that paid the equivalent of her combined cash welfare, food stamp, and Medicaid benefits, she would have had to pay more rent.

Another mother spoke of the combined effect of losing medical coverage, food stamps, and part of her housing subsidy when she took her last job as a housekeeper for a cleaning service:

> They say that they want mothers to get off the aid and work, okay. There's a lot of mothers who want to work, okay, like me. I want to work. And then you work, they don't give you a medical card. And sometimes, it depends on how much you make, they cut off your medical card, and when you go out and get those jobs you don't make enough to pay rent, then medical coverage and bills. It's really not worth it to go out working when you think about it, you know. It's not worth it 'cause you have kids and then they gonna be sick and you gonna have to go to the doctor and you gonna have to

pay hundreds of dollars and that's why—that's mainly why lots of mothers don't go out and get jobs, because they don't think it's worth it. . . . You're losing double.

Mothers also had to calculate the effect that work would have on their abilities to garner the additional income that allowed them to survive on welfare. Those mothers who relied exclusively on their social networks for extra help each month felt they could more easily afford the time spent working at a job in the formal sector; mothers who relied on side jobs or agency handouts were far less sanguine about their ability to keep up these strategies while working a full-time job. One mother captured this sentiment particularly well:

> I'm going to have to lose a lot in terms of what I earn from under-the-table housecleaning to gain anything from a job. I'm a workaholic. I'm so unhappy with welfare. But I can't leave welfare for work. I'm ready to move back home with my mother, tell welfare to screw—excuse my French—and try to get child support so I could live off of work. Even if I get a part-time job, though, they take so much from you. I'm very creative, I'm very smart, and I know that I could get my way out of this. But, now, I just feel like I'm all boxed in.

Apart from believing that working was a financial wash, women also felt they would gain little self-respect from the minimum-wage jobs they could get with their current skills. Nearly all of our welfare-reliant respondents said they would feel better about themselves if they could make it without welfare, but this boost to their self-esteem seemed to depend on a working life that offered somewhat higher wages and better prospects for advancement than most of the jobs they thought they could get with their current skills and job experience.

Risking the Future

The cost-benefit calculations that mothers made about leaving welfare for work were colored by the economic and social contexts of these women's lives. As we mentioned earlier, the mothers we interviewed had to weigh the utility of work against the real possibility that a subsequent layoff or reduction in hours could lead to serious material hardship. The jobs these mothers could get were among the least reliable in the U.S. economy. Typically, they demanded work at irregular hours, did not guarantee how many hours a worker would be able to work in a given week, and were subject to frequent layoffs. Nowhere was this more true than in the fast food industry. When we asked "What's the problem with working at a place like a fast food restaurant?" one welfare-reliant Chicago mother with eight years of experience in fast food restaurants told us,

> They work you really hard and you can't even get full-time hours. Those jobs are for the kids. I wouldn't go back because there would be no money. There is not even enough money for the teenagers, let alone for an adult supporting a family. It's for teenagers I feel, and I'm beyond that.

Fast food chains typically impose unpredictable schedules on workers, sending them home when business is slow. As a result, women could not predict how many hours they would be able to work. One mother recounted,

> Like I was supposed to work until 11:00 today. They turned around and sent me home at 9:30 in the morning. I get so mad. They make you slave and [then] they don't give you regular hours.

Even worse, if the job failed, it usually took several months to get their benefits going again, leaving these mothers with no source of legal income in the interim. A Chicago respondent expressed the frustration with the lag in benefits this way:

> [Because of the way the system is set up] it's just really hard to get off of [welfare]. When you go get a job, you lose everything, just about. For every nickel you make, they take a dime from you. [I have been] on and off welfare. Like when I [tried] working at a nursing home, I was making $4.50 an hour [and] they felt like I ma[de] too much money. Then they cut me off. And I just couldn't make ends meet with $4.50 an hour, because I was paying for day care too. So I [had] to quit my job to get back on it. It took me forever to get back on, and meanwhile I had to starve and beg from friends.

Another woman commented,

> One thing they should change is not to wait three months for things to catch up with you. They're like three months behind so like, say if I worked in April [I wouldn't get any benefits] in June, [even though I had no work] income in June. That's where a lot of people can't make it. That's what threw me off. Because like in April I made so much money with my job, and I was expecting my check to go down, but by the time it caught up with me I no longer had a job.

Even women who had not yet risked leaving welfare themselves learned to be cautious based on the experiences of their friends, relatives, and neighbors:

> The friend I have. . . I could see being on aid was really bothering her, and I could understand where she was coming from because for a couple of months she tried to leave welfare for a job. She found out she couldn't make it working after a couple of months. And then she had to quit her job and wait three months . . . to get back on. It was hard. She had to come over here and borrow money from me! And I gave her food. She couldn't even pay her rent or anything. Her mother was paying her rent for her. So I was thinking about this. I want to work but this scares me.

To aggravate matters, a large proportion of those respondents who stayed at one job in order to work their way up were eventually laid off. Gottschalk and Danziger (1989) found that women working in low-wage jobs were three times more prone to job layoffs than other workers (see also Blank 1995). One might expect that unemployment insurance would provide a safety net for such workers, but this is seldom the case. The percentage of job losers who collected unemployment declined throughout the 1980s. At the end of the decade, less than one in three jobless workers reported receiving unemployment benefits (about 34 percent were eligible), and those in the low-wage sector were the least likely to have coverage (Burtless 1994, 69; U.S. House of Representatives 1987, 330). This is presumably because an increasing proportion of Americans are working at jobs that are not covered by these benefits. Roberta Spalter-Roth, Heidi Hartmann, and Beverly Burr (1994) found that only 11 percent of welfare recipients with substantial work hours were eligible for unemployment insurance.

Dead-End Jobs

The vast majority of those who had worked also found that hard work rarely led to anything better. Their past jobs had seldom produced the type of "human capital" (training, experience, or education) that they could parley into better jobs. Nor did they produce the "social capital" (professional contacts and links with other jobs or employers) that might improve their career prospects, since they worked with other women in equally low level jobs. In short, these women were unable to build careers; if they chose to work, they were much more likely to move from one dead-end job to another. Thus, women learned that the kinds of jobs available to them were not avenues to success or even to bare-bones self-sufficiency; they were dead ends.

One respondent from the low-wage worker group, an African American woman in her late thirties with a high school diploma, had spent twenty years working for a large regional grocery chain. She worked the first fifteen years as a cashier, earning the minimum wage. In 1986, management promoted her to the service counter and raised her hourly wage from $3.35 to $4.00 an hour. In 1991, after five years in her new position, she had worked her way up to $5 an hour, the highest wage she had ever received. She had virtually never been late or taken a sick day, and her boss told her she was one of his most competent employees, yet her hourly salary over the past twenty years had risen by a total of $1.65.

Nonetheless, this mother was able to make ends meet for three reasons. First, her children were all in their teens and needed no day care; their truancy rate, however, was so high that she felt they would not finish high school. Second, she had a Section 8 housing subsidy, which allowed her to live in a private apartment within walking distance of her job. Third, she had lived with a succession of steadily employed boyfriends (three men over the past twenty years) who paid a lot of her bills. Her twenty-year-old daughter was raising her two-year-old twins on welfare and was a part of our welfare-reliant sample. Although her daughter also lived in a Section 8 apartment close to the central business district, she had two children who would have required day care if she went to work, and she did not have a boyfriend who could pay her bills. Because of this, she turned down a job where her mother worked.

Most of the welfare-reliant mothers we interviewed felt they could get a job if they were willing to do minimum-wage work. Even in Boston and San Antonio, where the labor market was slack, most mothers thought they could get work. At a minimum, however, they wanted a job that would leave them slightly better off than they had been on welfare. The mothers' most common dream was to earn enough to move out of project housing and into a better neighborhood. Other mothers wanted to buy better clothing for their children so their peers would not ridicule them. Yet, few mothers had had work experiences that led them to expect such rewards from work; they knew firsthand that a minimum-wage job would get them nowhere.

Most mothers told us they had originally entered the labor market with high hopes. They believed that if they could manage to stay at one job long enough or, alternatively, use each job as a stepping stone to a better one, they could make ends meet through work. After a few years in the low-wage job sector, they saw that instead of achieving their goals they were getting further and further behind in their bills. Not surprisingly, mothers concluded that the future they were building through low-wage work was a house of cards.

Iris, a Chicago welfare-reliant mother with twelve years of low-wage work experience, had spent her last seven working years as head housekeeper at a large hotel. Although this job gave her benefits and a two-week paid vacation, after seven years she had gone from $4.90 to only $5.15 an hour. Two years prior to our interviews, she had left this job for welfare with the hope that she could use the time off to search full-time for a better job. After months of persistent searching, she concluded that better jobs were simply not available for someone with her skills and experience.

One displaced housewife, Bonnie Jones, applied for AFDC when her husband deserted her and her savings ran dry. Because she had substantial secretarial experience, she found a job quickly. Her persistently low earnings, however, meant that she was back on welfare after two years.

I went on Public Aid when my ex left [1987]. He just up and poof, that was it. My daughter was four. And I was like "Oh God." I hadn't worked in five years. I lived on my savings until it ran out and then I went on welfare. After a few months on AFDC I went on an interview and I was hired at a computer supply store. . . for $5.50. I took it because I was living free with my mother and I figured it was a foot in the door. I already had office experience, but I had a five-year gap in my work history because of my child. I figured I would get in as a switchboard operator and push my way up as high as I could. [But] there's no ladder. It's unbelievable. I just quit there in September. They drilled me to the ground. My top wage was $6.90 in two years when I quit.

National data echo these mothers' experiences. First, a large body of research has shown that low-wage work does not pay a living or family wage. Charles Michalopoulos and Irwin Garfinkel (1989) estimate that workers with demographic profiles resembling those of typical welfare-reliant mothers could expect to earn only $5.15 an hour (in 1991 dollars) if they left welfare for work. Diana Pearce's (1991) analysis of PSID data also shows that for 70 percent of welfare-reliant mothers in the 1980s, spells of low-wage employment left them no better off than they had been before. The kinds of jobs that are available to these women more often end up being chutes, not ladders.

Second, there is growing evidence that low-wage jobs provide little or no access to better future jobs. In their book *Working but Poor*, Sar Levitan and Isaac Shapiro (1987) write,

Evidence of mobility among the working poor should not obscure the serious and enduring labor market problems that this group faces. Their prospects may be better than those of the non-working poor, but many of the working poor have long-term earnings problems. More than any other indicator, including demographic characteristics such as education or race, the best predictor of future status in a low-wage job is whether or not a worker is currently in a low-wage job. A core group of the working poor remains impoverished for many years. . . . [Furthermore], the deteriorating conditions of the 1980s stay have exacerbated the labor market difficulties of the working poor and extended the duration of their poverty spells. (p. 25)

Unless the typical unskilled or semiskilled single mother finds an unusually well-paying job or has medical benefits, a child care subsidy, and very low housing and transportation costs, she cannot work her way from dependency to self-sufficiency. Despite this reality, many single mothers remained committed to the work ethic and tried to leave welfare again and again. Many had such varied job histories that their employment records sounded like the newspaper's "help wanted" advertisements. Most mothers had moved from one job to another, always looking for some slight advantage—more hours, a better shift, a lower co-payment on a health plan, more convenient transportation, less strenuous manual labor, or less monotonous work—without substantially improving their earnings over the long term.

Nonetheless, some researchers have criticized women workers in the low-wage sector both for not moving enough and for moving too much. Lawrence Mead (1992), for example, argues that,

The notion of the dead-end job misrepresents the nature of mobility in the economy. Most jobs are dead-end in the sense that any given employer usually offers employees only limited chances for promotion. Most workers move up, not by rising within the organization, but by leaving it and getting a better job elsewhere. Mobility comes not in a given job but from a work history that convinces each employer that the job seeker will be a reliable employee. Advancement is something workers must largely seek out for themselves, not something given to them by employers. (p. 96)

At the same time, Mead (1992) remonstrates that "These workers exhibit what Hall termed 'pathological instability' in holding jobs" (p. 96).

What Must a Single Mother Earn to Leave Welfare?

We asked each welfare-reliant mother what she felt she would need to earn in order to leave welfare for work. Roughly 70 percent of mothers cited what economists call a "reservation wage" between $8 to $10 an hour. Mothers with only one child gave slightly lower estimates—averaging roughly $7.50 an hour—while mothers with more than three children and mothers whose children would need full-time child care tended to give slightly higher estimates.

The loss of health benefits so often associated with leaving welfare for work pushed reservation wages toward the upper end of this $8 to $10 range. We asked one work-ready Boston-area mother, "What is a decent wage? What could you support your family with?" She told us, "at least $8 an hour and with benefits." We then asked, "What would you do if you were offered a job for $8 an hour with no benefits and without possibility for advancement?" She answered, "I wouldn't take it. I would go into training or back to school, but I wouldn't take it."

This respondent's children had experienced serious health problems in the past, making it necessary for her to retain her medical benefits. Mothers whose families had no history of medical problems were more willing to risk their health benefits, but even these mothers believed that a job without benefits would have to pay more. Mothers' estimates of how much more varied, depending mostly on a family's health history and current health status.

How much did these mothers need to earn to maintain the same standard of living that welfare afforded? The average welfare-reliant mother in 1991 needed $876 a month to pay her expenses; those who paid market rent needed over $1,000 a month. It seems reasonable to argue that if welfare-reliant mothers needed to spend an average of $876 a month to meet their expenses, working mothers would need to spend even more, because working adds extra costs to the monthly budget. Working mothers usually spend substantially more on medical care because they lose Medicaid, because few low-wage employers offer health care benefits, and because those employers who do usually require copayments and have deductibles. Most working mothers also pay more for transportation because of commuting costs and travel to and from their day care provider. In addition, working mothers probably need to spend more for child care than welfare-reliant mothers. Finally, some working mothers need to purchase more and better clothing than they had on welfare.

In previous work, Edin and Jencks (1992) used the 1984–1985 Consumer Expenditure Survey to provide rough estimates of how much more working single mothers spent on these items than their welfare-reliant counterparts. They found that single mothers who worked spent $2,800 more each year on these four items—medical care, transportation, child care, and clothing—than their welfare-reliant counterparts. If we inflate these numbers to 1991 levels, the figure is roughly $3,500. We also looked at a group of 165 working mothers who earned about what our welfare-reliant mothers reported having earned in the past. These mothers spent about $37 a month more for health care, $67 a month more for transportation, $58 a month more for child care, and $27 a month more for clothing than welfare-reliant mothers did. Taken together, these additional expenses total $189 a month, or $2,268 a year.

By adding the extra costs of working to the average amount privately housed welfare recipients spent each month ($1,077 + $189), we calculate what the average mother would need to take home each month from a job if she were to maintain the standard of living she had on welfare—roughly $1,300 in take-home pay. On an annual basis, she would have to gross roughly $16,000, or between $8 and $9 an hour depending on how many hours she could be expected to work. Yet, Michalopoulos and Garfinkel

(1989) have shown that a full-time, year-round worker with characteristics similar to the average welfare-reliant single mother in the 1980s could expect to earn only $5.15 an hour. Kathleen Mullan Harris (1996) has made comparable estimates using PSID data for all women who left welfare for work during the 1980s. On average, during this ten-year period, she found that women who left welfare for work were paid $6.11 an hour in 1991 dollars. The difference between Michalopoulos and Garfinkel's predictions and Harris's results reflects the fact that women who actually leave welfare for work have greater earning power than those who remain on welfare (or leave the rolls for other reasons).

If a single mother worked forty hours a week for fifty weeks of the year at $5.15 an hour, she would earn $858 a month, or about $10,000 a year after subtracting taxes and adding the EITC. If she worked thirty-five hours a week for fifty weeks—the average number of hours our low-wage sample reported working—she would earn only $751 a month, or about $9,000 after taxes and the EITC. These figures mean that the average mother who left welfare for full-time work would experience, at minimum, a 33-percent gap between what she could expect to earn and what she would need to maintain her standard of living.

The break-even point—using our own data and national-level expenditure data—thus ranges from $8 to $9 an hour. Recall that our mothers' reservation wages ranged from about $8 to $10 an hour. Because most mothers in our sample knew they could not expect to earn this much given their current skills, it seems reasonable that they chose to delay work until their potential work-related costs decreased or until they had enhanced their education and training to a point where they could earn more.

The "Welfare Trap"

The Omnibus Budget Reconciliation Act of 1981, the Family Support Act of 1988, and the welfare reform law of 1996 all tried to push the welfare poor into low-wage employment. All evolved from two related assumptions:

1. Most welfare-reliant mothers have little or no work experience;
2. Employment at a low-wage job will provide access to better jobs in the future.

In other words, the welfare problem has been defined as an issue of labor force participation—once a mother gets a job, any job, policymakers assume she can move up. For this reason, welfare reform has focused on pushing unskilled and semiskilled mothers "out of the nest" as soon as possible. The astoundingly high rates of welfare recidivism show, however, that while such tactics may marginally reduce costs, fledgling working mothers more often crash than fly. Using longitudinal data from the PSID, Harris (1993, table 4) estimates that nearly one-quarter of all mothers who exit welfare for work return within one year, 35 percent within two years, and 54 percent within six years. Subsequent exits from welfare are also rapid: within twelve months of their return, half leave welfare again. Some of them then return to welfare yet again (Harris 1993, table 2).

The Institute for Women's Policy Research (IWPR) has studied the work behavior of welfare-reliant mothers using data from the Survey of Income and Program Participation (SIPP). IWPR found that seven of ten mothers reported some participation in the formal sector of the U.S. labor market during the two-year period of its study. However, their jobs were unstable (averaging only forty-six weeks), seldom provided health coverage (workers were covered in only one-third of the months they worked), paid poorly (an average of $4.29 an hour in 1990 dollars), and were concentrated in the lowest rungs of the occupational ladder (39 percent worked as maids, cashiers, nurse's aides, child care workers, or waitresses) (Spalter-Roth et al. 1995).

This chapter, too, has shown that many single mothers spend much of their adult lives cycling between welfare and work. The essence of this "welfare trap" is not that public aid warps women's personalities or makes them pathologically dependent, although that may occasionally happen. Rather, it is that low-wage jobs usually make single mothers even worse off than they were on welfare.

Because our data represent a snapshot rather than a longitudinal portrait of how welfare-reliant mothers were living in the early 1990s, we cannot fully describe how single mothers moved between the federal welfare system and work over time. Our data do allow us, however, to present monthly budgets (ones that balance) for poor persons—something that no national survey of low-income families has managed to accomplish. These budgets provide a clear picture of the cost that welfare-reliant mothers must take into account when making the decision between welfare and work. Our open-ended interviews with mothers also offered insights into how many women viewed the trade-off between welfare and work, and how they thought these tradeoffs might affect their children.

What is interesting, then, is the continuing attraction of work for these women. Like mothers everywhere, these women dreamed of moving to a better neighborhood, making it a month without running out of food, regularly giving their children and loved ones birthday and Christmas gifts, taking their children down South to meet their kinfolk, buying their children good enough clothing that they would not be ridiculed at school, and maybe having a little nest egg for emergencies. Faced with the reality that welfare would never get them any of these things, and with the deadening knowledge that welfare receipt was daily eating away at their own and their children's self-respect, mothers planned ways in which they could make work more profitable for themselves and less of a threat to their children's well-being.

References

Blank, Rebecca. 1995. "Outlook for the U.S. Labor Market and Prospects for Low-Wage Entry Jobs." *In The Work Alternative*, edited by Demetra Smith Nightengale and Robert H. Haveman. Washington, D.C.: The Urban Institute Press. Cambridge Mass.: Harvard University Press.

Burtless, Gary. 1994. "Public Spending on the Poor: Historical Trends and Economic Limits." In *Confronting Poverty*, edited by Sheldon H. Danzinger. Gary D. Sandefur and Daniel H. Weinberg. Cambridge, Mass: Harvard University Press: New York: Russell Sage Foundation.

Edin, Kathryn, and Christopher Jencks. 1992. "Welfare" In *Rethinking Social Policy*, edited by Christopher Jencks. Cambridge, Mass.: Harvard University Press.

Edin, Kathryn, and Laura Lein. 1997. "Work, Welfare and Single Mothers Economic Survival Strategies." *American Sociological Review*. 62: 253–266.

Gottschalk, Peter, and Sheldon Danzinger. 1986. "Unemployment Insurance and the Safety Net for the Unemployed." Working Paper.

Harris, Kathleen Mullan. 1991. "Teenage Mothers and Welfare Dependency: Working Off Welfare." *American Journal of Sociology*, 912: 492–518.

———1996. "Life after Welfare: Women, Work and Repeat Dependency." *American Sociological Review*. 61: 207-246.

Levitan, Sar A. and Isaac Shapiro. 1987. *Working but Poor: America's Contradiction*. Baltimore: Johns Hopkins University Press.

Mead, Lawrence M. 1992. *The New Politics of Poverty: The Nonworking Poor in America*. New York: Basic Books.

Michalopoulos, Charles, and Irwin Garfinkel. 1989. "Reducing Welfare Dependence and Poverty of Single Mothers by Means of Earnings and Child Support: Wishful Thinking and Realistic Possibilities," Discussion Paper 882–89. Madison: Institute for Research on Poverty, University of Wisconsin.

Pearce, Diana. 1991. "Chutes and Ladders," Paper Presented at the American Sociological Association Annual Meeting, Cincinnati, Ohio (August).

Spalter-Roth, Roberta, Heidi Hartmann, and Beverly Burr. 1996. *Income Insecurity: The Failure of Unemployment Insurance to Reach Working AFDC Mothers*. Washington, D.C.: Institute for Women's Policy Research.

U.S. Bureau of Census. 1991. *Who's Supporting the Kids?* SB/91-18. U.S. Department of Commerce, Economics and Statistics Administration. Washington: U.S. Government Printing Office.

U.S. House of Representatives. Contingence on Ways and Means. 1987. Overview of Entitlement Programs (Green Book). Washington: U.S. Government Printing Office.

———1993. Overview of Entitlement Programs (Green Book). Washington: U.S. Government Printing Office.

Discussion Questions

1. Extend the discussion in the Hoffman and Youngblade excerpt, and identify what you believe are the potential key negative effects of working mothers on their children. What do you think are the potential key benefits?

2. How involved was your father in your childhood? Thinking about the issues raised in the Gerson reading, how do you wish your father's involvement was different? In what ways could your father have been more involved?

3. Projecting fifty years into the future, what percentage of fathers do you believe will be househusbands? Justify your projected percentage. Will the issues of identity and masculinity be as strong for househusbands in fifty years, compared with how strong Smith reports these issues are now?

4. Do you think welfare mothers should work? How do you respond to Lein's discussion of the choices welfare mothers make between staying at home to care for their children and going to work?

5. How have employers responded to the working parents on their staff? Is it the employer's responsibility to consider the status of working parents at all? If so, to what degree?

6. Assume you are married or have a partner and that you have school-age children, and that both you and your spouse or partner plan to work full-time. How could you effectively juggle work and family issues?

Part IX

WORK OVER THE LIFE COURSE

How does the work we do really change who we are? Over time, our labor says as much about our choices in life as it does our limits or expectations therein. For women and men, the ability to work is often affected by their personal obligations and choices at home or at least away from work. And when we leave work, either temporarily or for good, we fully realize the impact and import of that work identity and status in our lives. The following articles, which conclude the book, all attest to how work can speak volumes about an individual's demands and social status at various stages over the life course.

In "The Quest for Children," from *Creating a Life*, Sylvia Ann Hewlett describes the impact of work for the highly educated, highly motivated woman. She argues that as women prepare for a valuable career, their reproductive capacity will diminish. In the end, women will often have to make difficult choices regarding their professional and personal intentions in life.

In "Jobs for Mothers: Married Women's Labor Force Reentry," Wei-hsin Yu suggests that for middle-aged women, structural explanations, not personal ones, account for the "channeling" of women into the transient work and keep them from full-time, more coveted positions in Japan.

And finally, Toni Calasanti's "Retirement: Golden Years for Whom?" contends that at the end of people's work lives, the concept of retirement is elusive for many women, while this is not so for most white men. The notion that workers will spend time in leisure after they end their time in paid labor is both imagined and much less real to the many who cannot afford to stop working. Moreover, with the normal, continuous duties of maintaining a household, women will rarely stop working, for pay or otherwise. The notion of a work identity for some men, then, creates the sense that there is more entitlement for them in how they choose their work and when they choose to end it. For a woman, on the other hand, the work identity is second and more conditional to her identity as mother, partner, and more. This subordinate ranking of work means that women's choices will be highly influenced by the choices of others over the life course.

27

THE QUEST FOR CHILDREN

Sylvia Ann Hewlett

In January 2001, in partnership with Harris Interactive and the National Parenting Association, I fielded a nationwide survey designed to explore the professional and private lives of highly educated/high-earning women. In this survey, called High-Achieving Women 2001, we targeted the top 10 percent of women—measured in terms of earning power—and focused on two age-groups: the breakthrough generation, ages 41–55, and their younger peers, 28–40. We distinguished between high-achievers (those earning over $55,000 or $65,000 depending on age) and ultra-achievers (those earning over $100,000), and included a sample of "high-potential" women—highly qualified women who have left their careers, mainly for family reasons. In addition, we added in a small sample of men.

The findings of this survey are startling—and sobering. Here are some of the highlights.

Childlessness Haunts the Executive Suite

Thirty-three percent of high-achieving women are childless at age 40, and this figure rises to 42 percent in corporate America. Among ultra-achieving women in corporate America (those earning more than $100,000 a year) the childlessness figure rises to 49 percent. In contrast, only 25 percent of high-achieving men are childless at age 40, and this figure falls to 19 percent among ultra-achieving men (those earning more than $200,000 a year).

For High-Achieving Women, Childlessness Is Not a Choice

The vast majority of these women did not choose to be childless. Looking back to their early twenties, when they graduated college, only 14 percent said they definitely had not wanted children. Indeed, among those women who had children, a significant proportion (24 percent) wanted more than they were able to have.

More than a quarter of all high-achieving women in the 41–55-year-old age bracket said they would still like to have children, and this figure rises to 31 percent among ultra-achievers. Given the odds against these midlife women bearing children, these responses point to a mother lode of pain and yearning.

High-Achieving Women Are Extremely Unlikely to Have a Child After Age 39

Among high-achieving women aged 41–55, only 1 percent had a first child after age 39. And among ultra-achievers, no one had a first child after age 36. Most of the women in each group who were mothers had their first child in their early or mid-twenties.

High-Achieving Women Are Extremely Unlikely to Get Married After Age 35

When high-achieving women marry, they tend to marry young. In the older group, only 8 percent got married for the first time after age 30, and only 3 percent after age 35.

For Women, It's Lonely at the Top

Only 60 percent of high-achieving women in the older age-group are currently married, and this figure falls to 57 percent in corporate America. By way of contrast, 76 percent of older men are currently married and this figure rises to 83 percent among ultra-achievers.

African American Women Face an Even More Difficult Reality

Only 33 percent of high-achieving African American women are currently married and 43 percent have children. In the older age-group, (41–55) 48 percent are childless. Indeed, among older African American women, no one had a child after age 37 and no one was married after age 28. Balancing career and family seems to be a particularly difficult challenge for women of color.

The "Second Shift" Is Alive and Well

High-earning women continue to take prime responsibility for home and children. Indeed, 40 percent of high-achieving wives feel that their husbands create more work for them around the house than they contribute.

This is even true for ultra-achieving wives (half of whom are married to men earning less than they do). In these marriages only 8 percent of husbands take prime responsibility for helping children with homework, and a mere 5 percent take prime responsibility for cleaning the house.

Hype Trumps Reality on the Fertility Front

Despite the fact that 21 percent of women in the younger age group have experienced fertility problems, 89 percent of young, high-achieving women believe that they will be able to get pregnant into their forties.

In High-Altitude Careers, Hours at Work Are Long and Getting Longer

The more successful the woman, the longer her workweek. Twenty-nine percent of high-achievers and 34 percent of ultra-achievers work more than 50 hours a week (medicine, law, and academia are particularly time-intensive). Among ultra-achievers, a significant minority (14 percent) work more than 60 hours a week. A third of these women work longer hours than they did five years ago.

Women Entrepreneurs Do a Much Better Job Balancing Their Lives Than Women in Corporate America

Self-employed, high-achieving women are much less likely to be childless than women who work in corporate America (22 percent versus 42 percent in the older age-group). This gap widens even further among ultra-achievers (22 percent versus 49 percent). Self-employed women are also more likely to be married than women in corporate America (67 percent versus 57 percent).

Younger Women Face Even Harder Choices

The tough trade-offs faced by breakthrough-generation women dog the footsteps of younger women. Indeed, if you compare women in the younger age-group with women in the older age-group by calculating what proportion had a child by age 35, younger women seem to be in worse shape. Only 45 percent of younger women have had a child by age 35, while 62 percent of older women had had a child by this point in time. In other words, young women are having a harder time balancing work and family than their older sisters.

High-Potential Women Who Left Their Careers Want to Get Back on Track

A large proportion of high-potential women who left their careers when a child was born feel that this decision was forced on them by long workweeks, unsympathetic employers and inflexible workplaces. The majority (66 percent) would like to be back at work.

Workplace Policies Make a Difference

High-achieving mothers who stay in their careers work for companies that offer a rich array of work/life options-flextime, paid leave, reduced hour jobs, and so on. In sharp contrast, many high-potential mothers currently not in careers left companies that had much less in the way of work/life policies.

Childfree Employees Often Resent Parent "Perks"

Fifty-four percent of high-achieving women without children say that in their workplaces people without children are unfairly expected to pick up the slack for those who have children. This rift between working parents and the "childfree" has the potential of becoming ugly.

High-Achieving Women Are Skeptical About "Having It All"

Only a small proportion of high-achieving women (16 percent) feel that it is very likely that a woman can "have it all" in terms of career and family. Women tend to think men fare better on this front: 39 percent of high-achieving women feel that men can "have it all."

28

JOBS FOR MOTHERS

Married Women's Labor Force Reentry

Wei-hsin Yu

Sociological research has paid increasing attention to so-called nonstandard atypical, or contingent jobs (Appelbaum 1987; Kalleberg 2000; Parker 1998; Tilly 1996). Within the category of nonstandard work arrangements, part-time employment has been the dominant form, and it has increased most rapidly of all types of nonstandard, employment, particularly in advanced industrial countries (Blossfeld and Hakim 1997; Houseman and Osawa 1995; Smith et al. 1998). The continuous expansion of the share of part-time workers in the labor force in advanced economies makes part-time employment an important topic to study (e.g., Rosenfeld and Birkelund 1995; Tilly 1996).

The growth of part-time employment across advanced economies corresponds to a great extent to the increase in female labor force participation in nonagricultural sectors (Blossfeld 1997; Hakim 1997; Rosenfeld and Birkelund 1995). The matching of women, in particular married women, to part-time employment attracts much attention from both economists and sociologists (e.g., Ermisch and Wright 1993; Folk and Beller 1993; Miller 1993; Nagase 1997; Rosenfeld and Birkelund 1995). In view of evidence that part-timers are likely to obtain lower wage returns to individual qualifications than full-timers (Kalleberg 2000), the feminization of part-time jobs generally indicates increasing gender inequality. Thus, explaining women's concentration in part-time work enhances our understandings of gender stratification.

This study, using the case of Japan, searches for a further understanding of married women's apparent restriction to part-time employment. It has been well-documented that Japan, among developed countries, has a relatively high proportion of women in nonstandard work arrangements, in particular part-time employment (Brinton 1993; Rosenfeld and Birkelund 1995). What makes the Japanese case particularly puzzling is that older married women, rather than mothers with young children, constitute the majority of part-timers in the society. As the following section will show, the Japanese case presents empirical challenges to several existing theories on married women's concentration in part-time work. This study aims to solve this empirical puzzle by factoring the characteristics of standard employment into the equation. I argue that structural barriers embedded in the standard employment system play a critical role in pushing new types of participants in the labor market—married women who reenter the labor force in the case of Japan—into nonstandard employment. By solving this empirical puzzle, this study develops a general explanation of women's employment options over the life cycle.

Although most studies addressed and discussed in this paper, and in particular the studies on Western countries, consider only part-time employment, I combine part-time and all kinds of temporary jobs into one category for the Japanese case. I do so because (1) these types of employment indeed share certain features of nonstandard employment status; (2) the survey data and various government-generated statistical reports used in this study coded part-time and some types of temporary employment together; and most importantly, (3) the definitions of nonstandard employment in Japan are so fluid that the classification based on the designated status would not be very meaningful. There are several ways of designating part-time and temporary workers in Japan, including *pato* or *arubaito, rinjikoyo, haken, keiyaku, shokutaku,* and so forth. Although each category listed above has slightly different implications for forms of work, lines drawn between the categories are somewhat obscure, and uses of the terms vary from employer to employer (Houseman and Osawa 1995, 1998; JIL 1991). Moreover, part-time employment in Japan often refers to the status of a job rather than the amount of time spent working, so using "hours on the job" would not necessarily help distinguish part-time from temporary employment. There is great variation among part-time workers with respect to hours spent at work (JIL 1991), and a good proportion of those classified as part-timers by their employers work as much as their regular, full-time counterparts (Houseman and Osawa 1995; Gottfried and Hayashi-Kato 1998).

Combining part-time and temporary workers as a research category does not mean that there are no differences between the two groups. Rather, this research intends to acknowledge shared features of part-time and temporary employment such as instability and low return on individual qualifications despite the heterogeneity among the incumbents (Gottfried and Hayashi-Kato 1998). Nevertheless, it is important to note that among married female workers in Japan the number of temporary workers (i.e., *rinjikoyo, haken, keiyaku* and *shokutaku* workers) is far smaller than the number of part-timers (i.e., *pato* or *arubaito* workers) (Gottfried and Hayashi-Kato 1998; JIL 1991). In view of this proportion, I argue that it is not inappropriate to compare this study with previous ones on women and part-time employment. A later section defining variables for the statistical analysis present more discussion on the similarities and differences between part-time and temporary workers in Japan.

Theoretical Background and Empirical Challenges

Prior research has adopted several approaches to explain married women's concentration in part-time nonstandard employment. The family cycle arguments focus on women's need to resolve family-work conflicts and demonstrate that women's life cycles and domestic responsibilities greatly effect their movement into part-time employment (Drobnic et al. 1999; Folk and Beller 1993; Miller 1993; Mincer 1985; Moen 1985; Perry 1988 1990; Walsh 1999). Requiring fewer work hours and providing more flexibility than full-time employment, part-time employment is argued to be attractive to those managing child rearing and employment at the same time. Also emphasizing labor supply conditions, Hakim (1995, 1996) argues that a good number of married women work part-time because they prioritize non-market activities. This group of arguments implies that part-time employment is a transitional form of work and women will move back to full-time employment once the demand for child care or their orientation toward nonmarket activities changes. This type of explanation to some extent assumes that women can move between part-time and full-time employment at no cost.

The Japanese case renders empirical challenges to this group of theories. The family cycle argument does not explain Japanese women's movement between full-time and part-time employment as well as it does in Western countries. Japanese women rarely move back to full-time employment after life cycle stage changes. To illustrate this, I show the percentage of women in regular, full-time employee status in contrast to the percentage of all female workers by age-group in 1995 (Figure 28.1). A large proportion of older working women in Japan were not regular, full-time employees. The results are striking when we compare women in their thirties with women in their forties, two groups that were likely to be in different phases in the family cycle and have different family responsibilities. There was only a small increase in the percentage of women in standard, full-time employment between these two age-groups despite a much greater proportion of women in the labor force in their forties.

In fact, older women constitute the majority of part-timers in Japan. According to Houseman and Osawa (1995), 70.4 percent of women in *pato* employment (the dominant type of part-time employment status) in 1992 were over forty years. Nagase's research reports an even more peculiar finding (1997). Her multinomial logit results indicate that among working women with preschool children, full-time employment is more common than part-time employment. These empirical results indicate that women's labor supply over different stages of the family life cycle alone is insufficient to explain Japanese women's employment patterns.

One may argue that married women in Japan remain in part-time employment after the early stage of child rearing because they prioritize nonmarket activities. This is accurate perhaps for some Japanese women. Nonetheless, work hours of part-time employment are not necessarily short or flexible in Japan (Houseman and Osawa 1998). In addition, reported statistics of the Employment Security Bureau suggest that there are many involuntary part-timers. For example, the total number of new applicants for part-time jobs throughout the year of 1995 was 13,300, while 114,120 part-time job placements were arranged by all public job-matching services during the same year. The number of part-time jobs available largely outnumber applicants. The numbers suggest that many part-time job placements were made without applicants wanting a part-time job in the first place.

Furthermore, according to the Ministry of Labour of Japan (1995) more than 70% of full-time jobs for women are managerial, professional and clerical, while almost two-thirds of part-time and temporary jobs are in manufacturing, sales, and service occupations; these require more manual labor and have low occupational status. The low status of part-time and temporary jobs in Japan makes it unlikely

FIGURE 28.1   Percentages of female workers, nonagricultural female workers, and nonagricultural regular employees in the female population by age-group, 1995. *Source:* Statistics Bureau Management and Coordination Agency, Japan, *Annual Report on the Labour Force Survey, 1995.*

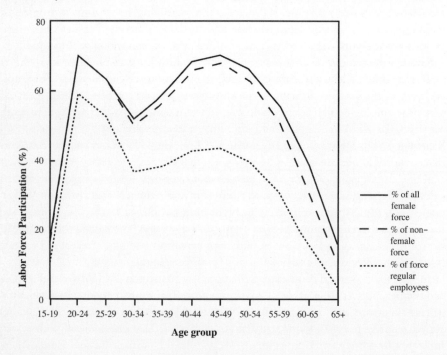

that older women, who are not tightly restrained by domestic responsibility, would actually prefer part-time or temporary work to full-time, regular employment.

The apparent existence of involuntary part-timers makes labor demand explanations more plausible. This type of explanation emphasizes employers' interests in using part-time or temporary labor to increase staff flexibility as well as reduce labor costs (Houseman and Abraham, J. 1993; Houseman and Osawa 1995 1998; Kalleberg 2000; Rosenfeld and Kalleberg 1990; Tilly 1996). It suggests that the growth of women in part-time employment in developed countries results from the fact that employers have intentionally chosen more part-time labor at the expense of full-time employment.

Despite a drastic increase in Japan in the demand for part-time or temporary work over the last two decades (Gottfried and Hayashi-Kato 1998; Houseman and Osawa 1998; Lincoln and Nakata 1997; Yu 1999), this type of explanation still does not explain why older married women are the ones filling the increasing part-time positions. The increasing demand for part-time workers has not affected all demographic groups equally. According to *Hataraku josei no jijo* (The Situation of Working Women), prepared by the Ministry of Labour in 1995, about 95 percent of *pato* (part-time) workers are women. Male nonregular employees are mostly *arubaito* workers, who by definition have a main job elsewhere or are still students. Furthermore, among male *pato* workers, the dominant group comprises workers over sixty years (Houseman and Osawa 1995 1998). The statistics indicate that men work part-time only before they leave school and start their "real jobs," or after they are forced to retire from regular, full-time employment, while part-time jobs are still predominately "women's jobs." Therefore, the increasing demand for part-time and temporary workers is not met even in part by the more expensive labor force of male workers. The level of demand in nonstandard employment alone is not sufficient to explain this fact.

Several other studies explain women's concentration in part-time employment by examining state policies and their effects on married women's employment. For example, comparative studies show that countries with beneficial family policies penalize part-time employment less and therefore encourage more married women to work part-time (Blossfeld and Hakim 1997; Rosenfeld and Birkelund 1995; Rosenfeld and Kalleberg 1990). However, Rosenfeld and Birkelund, acknowledged that the considerable proportion of part-timers among female workers in Japan cannot be explained by beneficial family policies or a sizable public sector (1995).

Other related studies show that patriarchal states that perpetuate the male-breadwinner model drive married women into nonstandard types of employment as a way to secure the traditional "gender contract" while facilitating women's labor force participation (Gottfried and Hayashi-Kato 1998; Gottfried and O'Reilly 2000; Pyle 1990). This type of argument suggests that the Japanese state plays an essential role in women's employment options by, instead of alleviating the penalty of part-time work, discouraging married women's career opportunities in the standard employment system through social policies (Gottfried and Hayashi-Kato 1998; Gottfried and O'Reilly 2000). While previous studies have discussed many structural constraints that are important in understanding the Japanese case, they provide little analysis of how women react to the identified institutional constraint and what triggers their movement into nonstandard employment. In particular, because older married women are the ones crowding into part-time employment, prior research does not explain why the impact of institutional barriers on women's employment seems to differ for women in different life cycle stages.

Explanatory Framework and the Context

The case of Japan calls for an alternative explanation of why married women fill part-time and temporary employment. While neither denying employers' interest in a flexible and cheap labor force nor neglecting factors that affect married women's labor supply, I argue that a proper explanation must take into account the context in which the alternative of the standard full-time employment is quite inaccessible for new demographic groups in the labor market.

I develop my theoretical framework by following the perspective frequently used to assess formal and informal economic activities. Studies on the "informal economy" (Beneria and Roldan 1987; Portes 1994; Portes and Sassen-Koob 1987) often include contingent, non-regular jobs. It has been argued that the persistence of informal employment is a response to overly rigid formal employment. Much employment activity is formal because employers are constrained by legal institutions and common practices. The

FIGURE 28.2   Changes in female labor force participation by age-group. Source: Ministry of Labour, Japan, *Yearbook of Labour Statistics,* 1960 and 1995.

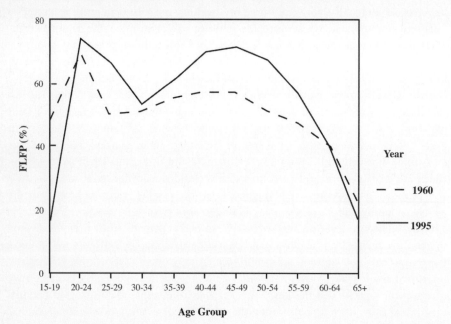

cost of formality becomes high when there are numerous rules and regulations to follow. In a highly regulated economy, the cost of entering formal employment is particularly high for new groups of participants such as married women and immigrants because the established practices in the formal economy are not designed to accommodate their needs or appreciate their qualifications. As a result, new participants have to adopt less formal but more flexible forms of work, that is, nonstandard or contingent work (DeSoto 1989; Piore and Sabel 1984; Portes and Benton 1984).

I expect to show that explanations focusing on the rigidity of formal economies can be extended to explain married women's concentration in part-time and temporary employment in Japan. I argue that part-time and temporary employment tends to absorb newcomers in the labor market primarily when the standard, full-time employment system creates barriers and constraints against new demographic groups in the labor force. The macrolevel statistics in Japan support the assertion that middle-aged married women who return to the labor force after the early stage of child rearing have constituted the majority of new demographic groups in the labor force.

The proportion of middle-aged women in the labor force has increased drastically from 1960 to 1995 (fig. 28.2), a result of the drastically declining fertility rate, increasing educational attainment, and prolonged life expectancy of women (Brewster and Rindfuss 2000; Kelly 1993; Yu 1999). While the labor force participation among women younger than age thirty has increased as well, to a large extent this change reflects the fact that Japanese women nowadays marry later and are more likely to withdraw from the labor force upon childbearing instead of marriage (Yamaguchi 1997).

Thus, this increase signifies an extension of labor force participation of an existing group, rather than a new source of labor supply. As Japan has been reluctant to accept immigrants (Douglass and Roberts 2000), middle-aged married women have become the dominant group of new participants in the labor force over the past several decades.

Following the theoretical approach emphasizing the rigidity of formal economies, the increasing supply of middle-aged women and the growing demand for part-time workers mesh only when the formal, full-time employment system sets high barriers that block new participants from entering the labor force. The rigidity of the standard employment system in Japan results from the fact that many employment practices are strictly designed for the "usual" labor force—that is, men before the mandatory retirement age and young, single women—and by definition are incompatible with the needs of others. For example, the "permanent employment" system and its associated practices (Cheng and Kalleberg 1997; Kaneko et al. 1996; Lincoln and Nakata 1997; Van Wolferen 1988; Vogel 1979), as I will discuss below, are tailored for continuous service without work interruption and become barriers that block the less usual work force such as labor force reenterers.

Two conventional recruitment practices make standard, full-time employment in Japan not as accessible for middle-aged married women as in other industrial societies. First, strong ties between schools and firms exist (Rosenbaum and Kariya 1989), which send students directly to firms after graduation. Most firms prefer fresh graduates, rather than experienced workers (Ishida 1993). Large firms in particular recruit regular, full-time employees only once a year, at the time of graduation. This recruitment practice is based on the belief that new graduates are the most suitable for on-the-job, firm-specific training; the latter is essential to the standard Japanese employment system featuring long-term employment and a seniority-based promotion and wage system (Cole 1971; Crawcour 1978; Koike 1987).

Second, even though recruitment practices are looser among small- to medium-sized firms, it is common for small employers to set upper age limits for recruitment. According to a survey (*Gyokyo to Koyo ni Knttsuru Anketo Chosa,* Business Situation and Employment Survey) done in 1996 on small- to medium-size employers by a job advertisement company in Tokyo, more than half of the employers surveyed set upper age limits when they recruited regular, full-time employees. Most Japanese firms set upper age limits because the seniority-based wage system often is essentially an age-based system; full-time, regular employees are assumed to be men and single women whose seniority is highly correlated with age. According to the Ministry of Labour (1995), age rather than work experience qualifications, education, ability, or previous job positions, was the second most important determinant for the wage of a mid-career person—that is, a person who has prior work experience elsewhere before entering the job—across all sizes of firms, and was less important only than a "balance with the wages of those who have been serving." Employers cannot maintain this age-based reward system without jeopardizing the balance between age and existing employees' wages if the labor force reenters with relatively long work interruptions. Therefore, upper age limits for new employees hired avoid confusing the system. As a result, upper age limits automatically exclude many women who intend to go back into the labor force after child rearing.

Furthermore, assuming the labor force to be constituted by men and single women, Japanese firms adopt a familism ideology and demand high devotion from their "family members," that is, regular, full-time employees. Such high devotion in practice becomes long work hours despite legal restrictions (Roberts 1996; Yu 2001). Although female full-time employees in general spend less time on overtime work and after-hours *tsukiai* (informal social functions, which are customary among coworkers as a way of reinforcing social ties) than their male counterparts (Brinton 1993; Ogasawara 1998), a moderate demand of after-hours time is sufficient to make full-time employment incompatible with married women's responsibilities since most of them have an overworked husband who rarely contributes to housework or child rearing. Thus, the normalization of overtime work in the standard employment system forms another barrier to full-time employment of married women.

Finally, while common employment practices in the economy actively deter married women from entering standard employment, state policies make nonstandard employment more appealing (Gottfried and HayashiKato 1998; Gottfried and O'Reilly 2000). The income tax system provides a good example. The Japanese tax system is actually in favor of two-earner families, given that the individual, rather than the household, is the unit to file tax (Feldstein and Feenberg 1996; Ishii 1993). However, the tax system also provides a relatively high tax threshold, which makes part-time jobs seem tax-free and hence appealing (Ishii 1993; Shoven 1989; Wakisaka and Bae 1998). One individual in 1995 would be free from income tax if he or she earns 1,030,000 yen or less. Based on the average hourly pay for women reported by the Ministry of Labour in the same year, this amount would mean 22–30 hours of work a week, depending on the geographical area, industry, and enterprise scale. With the addition of "special allowances for spouses" in 1987, husbands with wives who earn less than 700,000 yen a year receive twice the spousal deduction, while husbands of wives who earn up to 1,410,000 annually can still receive tax deductions of various amounts. This addition of tax regulations further encourages part-time wives to extend their hours at part-time jobs, even though long hours of work do not change their overall status to full-time.

Another common practice among Japanese firms further enhances the impact of the existing income tax system. Firms are obligated to pay for the health and pension (*nenkin*) insurance of an employee as well as his or her dependents. A part-time working wife is entitled to the same dependent benefits as long as her income is under the tax threshold (earning under 1,030,000 yen in 1995) because her husband's firm considers her, and wives who are full-time homemakers, both financially dependent. In addition, *many* firms, in particular large ones, provide family subsidies (*kazoku teate*) male employees with financially dependent wives. Therefore, when a married woman's earnings are over the tax threshold, she has to bear the opportune cost of losing the family subsidy and health as well as the pension insurance premium from her husband's employer. This company policy significantly increases the cost of taking a full-time job for married women.

The discussion above suggests that the standard employment system in Japan could play a critical role in matching new sources of labor supply to nonstandard employment. Conventional recruitment practices and time demands in the standard employment system have been intentionally designed to support the existing labor force, men and single women, rendering standard employment too rigid to accommodate middle-aged married women reentering the labor force. Meanwhile, tax regulations and family subsidy programs provide inducements to consider part-time employment as an appealing alternative. These inducements further enhance the relative cost for married women reentering full-time employment.

In summary, this study focuses on the rigidity of the formal economy explaining the concentration of newcomers in the "informal economy," and suggests that nonstandard employment is likely to absorb an emerging group of labor force participants primarily when the standard type of employment is extremely inaccessible to newcomers. This perspective explains why only a small proportion of married women are able to reenter full-time, regular employment after the domestic responsibilities decline.

Discussion

The statistical analysis supports the argument that part-time or temporary employment in Japan is not the means for women to remain in the labor force during child rearing, nor does it serve as a bridge to full-time employment later. Rather, part-time and temporary employment is a common destination for older married women who reenter the labor force. Results from the multinomial logit models show that the probability of being recruited as full-time employees is much smaller than as part-time or temporary employees for married women of all ages. Nonetheless, part-time and temporary work eventually becomes older women's work because married women who reenter the labor force are likely to do so after their children reach school ages. The analysis also supports the proposition that the difficulty of reentering standard employment requires most married women to remain in part-time or temporary employment in later stages of their family cycles. Therefore, the concentration of middle-aged married women in non-standard employment in Japan is best explained as a mismatch between over-supplied older women and overly rigid full-time employment.

During my personal interviews, this mechanism of matching married women to part-time and temporary employment is supported by individual stories. For example, I asked all women working part-time whether they considered finding a full-time job. Many of them, in particular the older ones, had the same reaction. They laughed and said: 'This is not about what I want to do—I simply can't. There are upper age limits (*nenrei seigen*)!" In addition, labor force reentering experiences of many married women whom I interviewed provide good illustrations of my argument. The following is one of them, from a 35-year-old married woman who worked part-time in a family-owned dental clinic

> When I first went back to work (after giving birth), I tried to find a full-time job. I had obtained my license for denture making then, so I tried to find a job in those medium-sized firms that made dental materials. I told every employer during my job interview that I could only work until seven o'clock in the evening, because I needed to be home by then to cook dinner and take care of my kids. I told them that I didn't mind getting

less pay but I couldn't do overtime work. The firm I went to said yes to me. So I started to work there. Then right after I went to work, I found it impossible for me to stay away from overtime work. I wanted to leave by seven, but they always kept me late. There was so much work to do. I went to tell the employer that I couldn't stay that late, and he was really upset and said it was my responsibility. He expected me to finish my job as a worker; no matter how late it took me. I was angry and told him that he lied to me about the work condition. I only worked there for a month and I quit. Then I thought: that's it. Full-time jobs don't work. I would have to do overtime work any-way—they always lie about it. So I didn't try to look for full-time jobs any more.

This had an additional part-time job, from midnight to 6 o'clock in the morning, to make *bento* (box lunches) for convenience stores nearby. The two part-time jobs added up to 11 hours of her everyday life. She explained that she had to take two part-time jobs because part-time jobs did not pay well enough to support her family, since her husband was self-employed and had suffered greatly from the economic recession. It was obvious to me she would prefer to take one full-time job rather than two part-time jobs if a full-time job allowed for less overtime work at night.

The experience of another interviewee's labor force reentry also supports the hypothesis that the barriers to regular full-time employment are high for married women. She was 45 years old and had a university degree and relatively continuous work experience. She told me what happened when she looked for a full-time job shortly after having left the premarital job.

I had anybody to help me if my kids got sick, etc. He went on and on. Finally, the top-level manager, a foreign man, who was also interviewing me, stopped the Japanese man and said: "Well, since she is here to apply for the job, she must have solved all these family issues." I almost laughed. That was really funny.

In contrast, becoming a part-timer is relatively easy for married women. Ethnographic studies have shown the differential treatment of part-time and full-time female workers (Roberson 1998; Roberts 1994). I found similar results in the field research. Part-time employment is frequently offered with the words *"shufu* (housewives) are welcome" in its advertisements. Some employers even put extra efforts to attract mothers to part-time work. When I visited an enterprise union for a large textile firm, which regularly hires part-time workers in many of its factories, a male official in the union proudly spoke to me about what the firm had done for female workers.

In our factories in Chiba, we have child care centers for part-timers. So those mothers can bring their children to work and put them in the day care. I think it is rare in Japan. . . No, we don't provide any day care service for regular employees. Full-time employees don't need it.

The above comment is interesting particularly in the way that this union official denies the need for child care for full-time workers while acknowledging it for part-timers.

This attitude is consistent with my argument that standard employment in Japan has been designed for men and single women, who do not have the need for child care. It further supports the proposition that we need to take into account the exclusionary characteristics of full-time employment in order to explain the matching of middle-aged married women to nonstandard employment.

One may challenge this explanation by arguing that married women are prone to part-time or temporary employment upon labor force reentry because they receive financial support from their husbands and they have a greater desire for time flexibility. However, the analysis in the previous section showed that, regardless of gender attitudes, once a woman left the job she obtained before marriage, her destination for labor force reentry is very likely to be part-time, temporary employment, rather than full-time employment. Hence, I argue that even though gender attitudes indeed influence women's employment decisions, they do not explain why the destination of married women's labor force reentry is disproportionately part-time or temporary employment. The following statement from a fifty-year-old woman who worked part time in a post office illustrates that a woman's orientation to work may not be the only concern

> I wish I could work longer hours. My husband was sent to a branch in another area and my son moved to school. Now I live by myself and have a lot of time to work. But, see, my husband gets 1,500,000 yen annually as the family subsidy. If my income is under 900,000 yen a year—I think it is 900,000 yen now—I don't need to pay tax.

Without understanding the structural constraints that drive married women in Japan away from standard, full-time employment, we cannot explain their concentration in nonstandard employment. An increasing number of studies pay attention to and examine nonstandard employment as a separate category. Surprisingly, the characteristics of full-time employment are hardly discussed in this group of studies. Studies on women's part-time employment tend to emphasize the importance of relative wage offer (e.g., Ermisch and Wright 1993), relative work hours and flexibility (e.g., Addabbo 1997; Burchell et al. 1997), and family or life cycle effects (e.g., Coutrot et al. 1997; Dex 1987; Perry 1988). All these factors create an impression that women are pulled into part-time employment, rather than pushed to part-time employment by a rigidly defined formal employment system. This chapter, however, calls attention to the importance of standard employment characteristics while studying nonstandard forms of employment.

Conclusion

This chapter illustrates the relationship between married women and nonstandard employment in Japan; neither labor supply nor labor demand alone explains this relationship sufficiently. Alternatively, this study demonstrates that requirements for full-time, regular employees can become barriers for new groups in the job market when they are designed specifically for exclusive participating groups, namely, men and single women in the case of Japan. As discussed, certain standard employment practices in Japan, such as upper age limits for recruitment and time demands for full-time jobs, were not established for the purpose of discriminating against a given group, but they de facto discourage new demographic groups to enter full-time employment. As a result, non-standard types of work have absorbed an increasing number of middle-aged women who are looking for opportunities to reenter the labor force. This study has shown that the high proportion of married women, in particular older married women, in part-time and temporary employment, results from the fact the formal employment system is reluctant to adjust to a group who rarely appeared in the paid labor force until recently. Thus, using the example of Japan, this study reveals the shortcomings of neglecting the role of the formal employment structure in explaining married women and nonstandard employment.

This study has two implications for issues on gender inequality. First, the interaction of structural barriers and gender differences in work trajectories through the life cycle increases the gap in earnings and occupational prestige between men and women as they age. As the number of nonstandard jobs continues to grow in developed countries, gender segregation by occupation is no longer the only type of segregation that contributes to gender inequality in the workplace. Men and women become increasingly segregated by type of employment in many societies. This study demonstrates that gender segregation by type of employment becomes more severe in societies where the cost of reentering standard employment is much higher than nonstandard employment; this is so because women on average experience more work interruptions than their male counterparts do.

The second implication concerns legal changes that are made to enhance gender equality. This study has revealed a critical flaw of the Equal Employment Opportunity Act (EEOA) in Japan that has not been discussed in prior research. The EEOA was passed in 1985 and revised in 1997. Several studies show that the EEOA did not provide enforcement measures and led to little change to enhance gender equality in the workplace (Gottfried and Hayashi-Kato 1998; Lam 1993; Shire and Ota 1997). Nonetheless, even if the EEOA were fully effective, it would not change the increase in married women in nonstandard employment. Overall, married women's employment is caused by retention in the labor force through marriage and childbearing or labor force reentry at a later date. This study shows that the reentering group tends to find standard employment extremely inaccessible in Japan. The EEOA never took into account the institutional barriers reentering women encounter, and therefore would only have covered the interests of the uninterrupted group at best. While requiring employers to treat men and women equally upon recruitment, the EEOA does not acknowledge that single and married women could also be treated differently. As a result, there is no restriction against collecting information on marital status or setting upper age limits. This is probably why statistics show that the percentage of part-time employment among female workers continues to increase since the passage of the EEOA (Hanami 2000). Legal reform concerning equal employment opportunities of men and women has to understand the heterogeneity of female workers and pay extra attention to institutional barriers upon married women's labor force reentry.

The final note of this study concerns the recent economic recession in Japan. Will the rise of middle-aged married women in nonstandard employment continue in view of the common belief that the Japanese employment system will change because of the bursting of the bubble economy and worsening financial problems? Some changes in the standard employment practices may occur, but it is unlikely that the economic recession will reduce the barriers to standard employment discussed in the paper, given the shrinking labor demand for standard, regular employment. Rather, the decrease of labor demand may further exclude less essential groups, such as older men and single women, from the regular labor force. In fact, part-time employment has been one of the solutions to the economic difficulty that has perpetuated the existing system for the formal labor force (Lincoln and Nakata, 1977). As the data in this study are all from the mid '90s, we can conclude that married women's concentration in irregular, nonstandard jobs has not yet been affected by the economic recession. Furthermore, because the changes in women's life cycles remain, and a decrease in men's income is foreseeable because of the economic stagnation, married women are likely to become even more eager to reenter the labor force. As a result, we can expect, unfortunately, an ever-increasing number of married women in irregular jobs in Japan, regardless of experience, qualification, or need.

References

An earlier version of this chapter was presented at the 1998 annual meeting of the Association for Asian studies, Washington, D.C.

Addabbo, Tinadara. 1997. "Part-time work in Italy." In Hans-Peter Blossfeld and Catherine Hakim (eds.), *Between Equalization and Marginalization*: 113–132. New York: Oxford University press.

Applebaum, Eileen. 1987. "Reconstructing work: Temporary, part-time, and at-home employment." In Heidi Hartmann, Robert Kraut, and Louise Tilly (eds.), *Computer Chips and Paper Clips: Technology and Women's Employment* Vol. 2: 269–310. Washington, D.C.: National Academy of Sciences.

Becker, Gary. 1964. *Human Capital*. New York: National Bureau of Economic Research, Columbia University Press.

Benaria, Lourdes, and Martha Roldan. 1987. *The Crossroads of Class and Gender: Industrial Housework, Subcontracting and Household Dynamics in Mexico City*. Chicago: University of Chicago Press.

Bielby, Denise D. 1992. "Commitment to Work and Family." *Annual Review of Sociology* 18: 281–302.

Blossfeld, Hans-Peter. 1997. "Women's Part-Time employment and the Family Cycle: A Cross-National Comparison." In Hans-Peter Blossfeld and Catherine Hakim (eds.), *Between Equalization and Marginalizaion*: 315–324. New York: Oxford University Press.

Blossfeld, Hans-Peter, and Catherine Hakim. 1997. "Introduction: A Comparative Perspective on Part-Time Work." In Hans Peter Blossfeld and Catherine Hakim (eds.), *Between Equalization and Marginalization*: 1–21. New York: Oxford University Press.

Brewster, Karen L., and Ronald Rindfuss. 2000. "Fertility and Women's Employment in Industrialized Nations." *Annual Review of Sociology* 26: 271–296.

Brinton, Mary C. 1995. *Women and the Economic Miracle: Gender and Work in Postwar Japan*. Berkeley: University of California Press.

Brinton, Mary C., Yean-Ju Lee, and William L. Parish. 1995. "Married Women's Employment in Rapidly Industrializing Societies: Examples from East Asia." *American Journal of Sociology* 100: 1099–1130.

Burchell, Brendan J., Angela Dale, and Heather Joshi. 1997. "Part-Time Work Among British Women." In Hans-Peter Blossfeld and Catherine Hakim, eds., *Between Equalization and Marginalization*, 210–246. New York: Oxford University Press.

Cheng, Mariah Mantsun, and Arne L. Kalleberg. 1997. "How permanent was permanent employment: Patterns of organizational mobility in Japan 1916-1975." *Work and Occupations* 24: 12–32.

Cole, Robert E. 1971. "The Theory of Institutionalization: Permanent Employment and Tradition in Japan." *Economic Development and Cultural Change* 20: 47–70.

Coutrot, Laurence, Irene Fournier, Annick Kieffer, and Eva Leievre. 1997. "The Family Cycle and the Growth of Part-Time Female Employment in France: Boon or Doom?" In Hans-Peter Blossfeld and Catherine Hakim, eds., *Between Equalization and Marginalization,* 133–163. New York: Oxford University Press.

Crawcour, Sydney. 1978. "The Japanese Employment System." *Journal of Japanese Studies* 4: 225–245.

DeSoto, Hernando. 1989. *The Other Path: The Invisible Revolution in the Third World.* New York: Harper & Row.

Dex, Shirley. 1987. *Women's Occupational Mobility: A Lifetime Perspective.* London: Macmillan.

Dore, Ronald. 1976. *The Diploma Disease: Education, Qualification, and Development.* Berkeley: University of California Press.

Douglass, Mike, and Glenda S. Roberts. 2000. "Japan in a Global Age of Migration." In Mike Douglass and Glenda S. Roberts, eds., *Japan and Global Migration: Foreign Workers and the Advent of a Multicultural Society,* 3-37. London: Routledge.

Drobnic, Sonja, Hans-Peter Blossfeld, and Gotz Rohwer. 1998. "Dynamics of Women's Employment Patterns Over the Family Life Course: A Comparison of the United States and Germany." *Journal of Marriage and Family* 61: 133–146.

Ermisch, John F., and Robert E. Wright. 1993. "Wage Offers and Full-Time Employment by British Women." *Journal of Human Resources* 28: 111-133.

Feldstein, Martin, and Daniel R. Feenberg. 1995. "The Taxation of Two-Earner Families." In Martin Feldstein and James M. Poterba, eds., *Empirical Foundations of Household Taxation,* 3976. Chicago: University of Chicago Press.

Folk, Karen Fox, and Andrea H. Beller. 1993. "Part-Time Work and Child Care Choices for Mothers of Preschool Children." *Journal of Marriage and Family* 55: 146-157.

Gottfried, Heidi, and Nagisa Hayashi-Kato. 1999. "Gendering Work: Deconstructing the Narrative of the Japanese Economic Miracle." *Work, Employment, and Society* 12: 25-46.

Gottfried, Heidi, and Jacqueline O'Reilly. 2000. *The Weakness of a Strong Breadwinner Model: Part-Time Work and Female Labour Force Participation in Germany and Japan.* Occasional Paper Series. Wayne State University.

Hakim, Catherine. 1996. "A Sociological Perspective on Part-Time Work." In Hans-Peter Blossfeld and Catherine Hakim, eds., *Between Equalization and Marginalization,* 2270. New York: Oxford University Press.

Hanami, Tadashi. 2000. "Equal employment revisited." Japan Labor Bulletin 39(1): 5–10.

Houseman, Susan, and Katherine G. Abraham. 1993. "Female Workers as a Buffer in the Japanese Economy." The American Economic Review 83: 45–51.

Houseman, Susan, and Miachiko Osawa. 1998. "What Is the Nature of Part-time Work in the United States and Japan?" In Jacqueline O'Reilly and Colette Fagan (eds.), *Part-time Prospects: An International Comparison of part-time Work in Europe, North America, and the Pacific Rim*: 232–251. London: Routledge.

——. 1995. "Part-time and temporary employment in Japan." Monthly Labor Review, October: 10–18.

Ishida, Hiroshi. *Social Mobility in Contemporary Japan.* Stanford, CA: Stanford University Press.

Ishii, Hiromitsu. 1993. *The Japanese Tax System,* 2nd ed. Oxford: Clarendon Press.

JIL (The Japan Institute of Labour). 1991. "Patotaimu Rodo Jitai Chosa Kenkyu Hokokusho" (Report for survey on part-time labor force participation). JIL Survey Reports, No. 11. Tokyo: JIL

Kalleberg, Arne L. 2000. "Nonstandard employment relations: Part-time, temporary and contract work." Annual Review of Sociology 26: 341–365.

Kaneko, Kazuo, *Hiroki Sato, and Hiroshi Uchida. 1996. Labor and Management Dealing with Employment Protection.* Tokyo: Tokyo Metropolitan University Labor Research Institute.

Kelly, William W. 1993. "Finding a Place in Metropolitan Japan: Ideologies, Institutions, and Everyday Life." In Andrew Gordon (ed.), *Postwar Japan As History*: 189–238. Berkeley: University of California Press.

Koike, Krazuo. 1987. "Human Resource Development and Labor-Management Relations." In Kozo Yamamura and Usukichi Yasuba (eds.), *The Political Economy of Japan* Vol. 1: 289–330. Stanford: Stanford University Press.

Lam, Alice C.L. 1993. "Equal Employment Opportunities for Japanese Women: Changing Company Practice." In Janet Hunter (ed.), *Japanese Women Working*: 197–221. New York: Routledge.

Lincoln, James, and Yoshifumi Hakata. 1997. "The Transformation of the Japanese Employment System: Nature, Depth, and Origins." *Work and Occupations* 24: 33–55.

Miller, Carole F. 1993. "Part-Time Participation over the Life Cycle Among Married Women Who Work in the Market." *Applied Economics* 25: 91–99.

Mincer, Jacob. 1985. "Intercountry Comparisons of Labor Force Trends and of Related Developments: An Overview." *Labor Economics* 3: 1–32.

Ministry of Finance, Japan. 1996. *An Outline of Japanese Taxes*.

Ministry of Labour, Japan. 1995. *Year Book of Labour Statistics*.

Moen, Phillis. 1985. "Continuities and Discontinuities in Women's Labor Force Activity." In G. H. Elder (ed.), *Life Course Dynamics: Trajectories and Transitions, 1968–1980*. New York: Cornell University Press.

Nagase, Nobuko. 1997. "Wage Differentials and Labour Supply of Married Women in Japan: Part-time and Informal Sector Work Opportunities." *The Japanese Economic Review* 48:29–42.

Ogasawara, Yuko. 1998. *Office Ladies and Salaried Men: Men Power, Gender, and Work in Japanese Companies*. Berkeley: University of California Press.

Parker, Robert E. 1998. "Temporary Clerical Workers." In Amy Wharton (ed.), *Working in America: Continuity, Conflict, and Change*: 447–469. Mountain View, CA: Mayfield. Parker, Robert E. 1998. "Temporary Clerical Workers." In Amy Wharton, ed., *America: Continuity, Conflict, and Change,* 447–469. Mountain View, Calif.: Mayfield.

Perry, Stephen. 1990. "Part-Time Work and Returning to Work After the Birth of the First Child." *Applied Economics* 22: 1137–1148.

———— 1988. "The Supply of Female Part-Time Labour Over the Life Cycle." *Applied Economics* 20: 1579–1587.

Piore, Michael J., and Charles F Sabel. 1984. *The Second Industrial Divide: Possibilities for Prosperity*. New York: Basic.

Portes, Alejandro. 1994. "The Informal Economy and Its Paradoxes." In Neil J. Smelser and Richard Swedberg, eds., *The Handbook of Economic Sociology,* 427–449. Princeton: Princeton University Press.

Portes, Alejandro, and Lauren Benton. 1984. "Industrial Development and Labor Absorption: A Reinterpretation." *Populations and Development Review* 10: 589–611.

Portes, Alejandro, and Saskia Sassen-Koob. 1987. "Making It Underground: Comparative Material on the Informal Sector in Western Market Economies." *American Journal of Sociology* 93: 3061.

Pyle, Jean Larson. 1990. *The State and Women in the Economy: Lessons from Sex Discrimination in the Republic of Ireland*. Albany: State University of New York Press.

Roberson, James E. 1997. *Japanese Working Class Lives: An Ethnographic Study of Factory Workers*. London: Routledge.

Roberts, Glenda S. 1994. *Staying on the Line: Blue-Collar Women in Contemporary Japan*. Honolulu: University of Hawaii Press.

————. 1996 "Careers and Commitment: Azumi's Blue-Collar Women." In Anne E. Imamura, ed., *Reimaging Japanese Women,* 221–243. Berkeley: University of California Press.

Rosenbaum, James, and Takehiko Kariya. 1988. "From High School to Work: Market and Institutional Mechanisms in Japan." *American Journal of Sociology* 94: 1334–1365.

Rosenfeld, Rachel A., and Gunn Elisabeth Birkelund. 1995. "Women's Part-Time Work: A Cross-national Comparison." *European Sociological Review* 11: 111–134.

Rosenfeld, Rachel A., and Arne Kalleberg. 1989. "A Cross-National Comparison of the Gender Gap in Income." *American Journal of Sociology* 96: 69–106.

Shire, Karen, and Madoka Ota. 1996. "The First Decade of Equal Employment Opportunities in Japan: A Review of Research." *Journal of Social Science* 36: 51–62.

Shoven, John B. 1990. "The Japanese Tax Reform and the Effective Rate of Tax on Japanese Corporate Investments." *Tax Policy and the Economy* 3: 97–115.

Smith, Mark, Colette Fagan, and Jill Rubery. 1997. "Where and Why Is Part-Time Work Growing in Europe?" In Jacqueline O'Reilly and Colette Fagan, eds., *Part-Time Prospects: An International Comparison of Part-time Work in Europe, North America, and the Pacific Rim,* 35–56. New York: Routledge.

Tilly, Chris. 1996. *Half a Job: Good and Bad Part-Time Jobs in a Changing Labor Market.* Philadelphia: Temple University Press.

Van Wolferen, Karel 1988. *The Enigma of Japanese Power.* New York: Random House.

Vogel, Ezra. 1979. *Japan No. 1: Lessons for America.* New York: Harper & Row.

Wakisaka, Akira, and Haesun Bae. 1997. "Why Is Part-Time Rate Higher in Japan Than in South Korea?" In Jacqueline O'Reilly and Colette Fagan, eds., *Part-Time Prospects: An International Comparison of Part-time Work in Europe, North America, and the Pacific Rim,* 252–264. New York: Routledge.

Walsh, Janet. 1999. "Myths and Counter-Myths: An Analysis of Part-Time Female Employees and Their Orientations to Work and Working Hours." *Work, Employment, and Society* 13: 179–203.

Yu, Wei-hsin. 1999. "Unequal Employment, Diverse Career Paths: Gender Stratification in Japan and Taiwan." Unpublished Doctoral Dissertation. The University of Chicago.

———. 2000. "Family Demands, Gender Attitudes, and Married Women's Labor Force Participation: Comparing Japan and Taiwan." In Mary C. Brinton (ed.), *Women's Working Lives in East Asia*: 70–95. Stanford: Stanford University Press.

29

RETIREMENT
Golden Years for Whom?

Toni Calasanti

The golden years. Retirement is a time of freedom, of relaxation, of leisure. Retirees can enjoy themselves, live without schedules or the daily grind; they can travel, spend time on hobbies, and simply enjoy their later years. This is the American dream, the reward for a lifetime of hard work. Yet, as is true of so many aspects of the American dream, the golden years are a myth except for the most privileged: white, middle-class men and, perhaps, their spouses.

This brief overview of the lives of retirees will use a life-course perspective to demonstrate the ways in which socioeconomic stratification influences the ability of retirees (those over age 65) to experience a life of leisure or freedom. Through the primary focus on women, the chapter reveals, first, that work involves more than paid labor and, second, the ways in which the life course influences the interdependence between employment and family labor into the retirement years. Race and class hierarchies intersect with gender relations over the life course to determine who will retire and what their lives will be like.

Putting women's lives at the center of analysis reveals the wide range of productive activities that men and women perform that have value, including paid labor, unpaid labor, and services provided to others (Calasanti and Bonanno 1992; Herzog et al. 1989). First, it is clear that women perform more productive activities than men do at all times throughout the life course (Herzog et al. 1989). Second, "retirement" does not free women from labor. Gender relations structure the productive activities in which men and women engage: which ones they do and the rewards for these activities. When one considers race and class as well, one finds that the "golden years" of retirement pertain only to a select group of predominant) white, middle-class men. Privileged men have choices: they can choose to engage in paid work, and they can choose to be involved in domestic labor. The voluntary nature of these activities underscores power differences based on gender as well as on race and class.

A life-course approach demonstrates the cumulative impact of gender relations in three interacting arenas: the state, the family, and the workplace. Sensitivity to gender relations in these spheres reveals, for instance, that women continue to work in old age because of their low income in retirement. Such work is not freely chosen when it is predicated on financial need; nor is their income situation simply a result of poor decisions or planning over their lifetimes. Instead, these economic needs are structured into workplace and state policies, as well as normal behavior within families—the expectation (and mandate) that women will have primary responsibility for domestic labor.

There is a second aspect to the notion that "a woman's work is never done." Women retirees also continue domestic labor, typically regardless of class or race, including different kinds of caregiving. By contrast, men's ability to partake of the golden years free of work is based on their gender, which continues to free them from obligatory domestic labor. At the same time, many men do live this dream. White, middle-class men's advantage in the labor market, including their ability to secure stable "career" jobs, is related to the disadvantages experienced by women and by people of color.

To debunk the myth of retirement as a time of leisure, this chapter will draw upon previous studies and data on income and Social Security. In addition, it will illustrate some points using qualitative data gathered from in-depth interviews of fifty-seven retired white men and women in 1987. Respondents were urban and rural residents of a Southeastern state. The men represented managerial and working classes, while the women were primarily working class.

Gender, the State, and Retirement Income: Social Security

Social Security, the public pension program in the United States, is an important source of income in retirement. Enacted in 1935, Social Security legislation included initial assumptions about gender that continue to influence retirement benefits: that women always depend upon men in heterosexual (marital) relationships, and that women will be homemakers and men will be breadwinners. Just as the "family wage" assumed a patriarchal family head who would provide for other members (May 1987), Social Security legislation assumed the same in retirement. Thus men's presumed labor-force history—a long-term, stable career with ever increasing rewards—formed the basis of benefit eligibility and calculations. Never mind that minority and working-class men were virtually excluded by this formulation as they were shut out of family wages and careers. Indeed, the original act assigned benefits to the breadwinner exclusively; only in 1939 did it add wives and widows as beneficiaries (Harrington Meyer 1996). Social Security reinforced women's subordination by distinguishing between deserving and undeserving women. That is, while widows could collect Social Security based on their spouse's work histories, divorced women could not, even if they divorced for spousal abuse (Rodeheaver 1987). Only since 1972 has gender-neutral language even allowed men to collect benefits as a dependent spouse (Quadagno 1999).

At the same time that household labor was seen to be a woman's job and her basis for economic support, it was not valued as highly as men's paid labor; a spouse "dependent" was (and is) entitled to only half of the main benefit amount. Despite some changes in Social Security since the original legislation, such as the ability of divorced women to collect benefits if they were married for at least ten years, the devaluation of women's reproductive work relative to the main breadwinner's evident in the reduced spousal benefit remains today.

Social Security ignored the reality of female breadwinners—despite the fact, for instance, that 40 percent of black women held jobs compared to 15 percent of white women (Amott and Matthaie 1996). Indeed, by assuming only one breadwinner and tying benefit levels to earnings (discussed below), Social Security gives a dual-earner couple with an annual income of $60,000 lower benefits than it pays to a traditional couple in which the man earns that same amount alone (Quadagno 1999). Thus women's lower wages did not appear to be a concern, nor was the way in which their family obligations might interfere with continuous labor force participation. Indeed, so devalued is women's reproductive labor that women cannot count years engaged in reproductive labor in their own benefit levels.

To understand the cumulative impact of gender relations within the family on retirement requires some knowledge of how Social Security benefits are calculated. First, benefit levels are tied to earnings; the more one earns, the greater the likelihood that one will receive the maximum benefit, which was $1,373.10 per month in 1999 (Social Security Administration 1999). Women tend to be clustered in a relatively small array of low-paid jobs, which deflate Social Security benefits. In addition, benefits are also based on the earnings of the best thirty-five years of work. It is important that men's ability to have, on average, only one zero year out of thirty-five, compared to women's average of twelve zero years (Harrington Mever 1996), is firmly rooted in the gender division of family labor. Women who leave the labor market due to family obligations are likely to have their departure reflected not only in the pay they receive upon their return but also later in their Social Security checks.

Thus, gender relations in family and work influence the retirement experiences of both men and women through the formation of pensions themselves. These programs are fashioned on the basis of men's experiences of work and production, as well as traditional, heterosexist notions about the domestic sphere; household labor is ignored (Quadagno and Harrington Meyer 1990; Scott 1991). As a result, men's work is seen to be more valuable and is more highly rewarded than women's in retirement, despite the fact that their ability to engage in more highly paid forms of labor likely relied upon a woman's household labor. Married women, then, are exploited: they are unpaid for domestic labor and then underpaid by Social Security while all the time they are improving the wages and benefits of their husbands. Finally, women's dependence on men for financial security in old age is reinforced by the assumption that individuals remain permanent members of traditional, heterosexual nuclear families (Harrington Mever 1990; Rodeheaver 1987).

As a result, one finds that even among presently married retirees, having been divorced or widowed earlier in their lives has an important influence on women's, but not on men's, retirement incomes. Women who had been continuously married to the same person had a monthly average retirement income that of $83.52 less than similar men, By contrast, presently married women whose marital history was interrupted received an average of $356.35 less than men with interrupted marital histories.

An additional racial bias is also embedded in the original Social Security legislation, which excluded occupations typically held by people of color, particularly agricultural labor and domestic labor. Figures from the 1940s, important years in the earnings history of present retirees, reveal that retired women of color were often employed as domestic laborers. Over one-fifth of American Indian women, over one-quarter of Puerto Rican and Japanese American women, one-third of Chicano and Filipina American women, and over one-half of African American women were employed as domestic laborers, compared to only 12 percent of European American women (Amott and Matthaei 1996; King 1992). Although legislative changes have now enabled almost all workers to be covered, only 83 percent of blacks aged 65 or more (men, 81 percent and women, 84 percent) and 74 percent of nonwhite Hispanics (men, 77 percent and women, 72 percent) received Social Security in 1996, compared to over 90 percent of white men and women (Social Security Administration 1998a, Table 1.9).

Finally, class privilege in Social Security benefits is also evident. Working-class citizens, who enjoy less job stability than middle-class workers, receive lower benefits because of the rules concerning number of years of continuous work needed to calculate benefit levels. Further, tying benefit levels to earnings is an advantage to higher earners. While the replacement rate—the percentage of pre-retirement income that Social Security replaces—is greater for low earners, the actual dollar amount high earners receive is substantially greater.

Taken all together, the bases for Social Security benefits put women at a disadvantage, especially minority or working-class women, who might otherwise rely on their own work histories for benefits.

Gender Relations Within the Family: The Division of Domestic Labor

Despite their increased participation in the labor force, women bear primary responsibility for household tasks (Coverman andd Sheley 1986; Press and Townslev 1998). First, this domestic division of labor influences retirement through its impact on the types of jobs women and men obtain and on their upward mobility. Among present-day retirees, women often entered the labor force later than men and had to work particular shifts, turn down promotions (where they existed), or enter particular types of jobs so as to maintain their domestic-labor roles. Second, time spent on domestic labor has an impact on other labor market outcomes such as earnings (Coverman 1983). This situation does not imply that women expend less energy at work; in fact, evidence indicates that they work harder than men (Bielbv and Bielby 1988). Finally, among older employed women, acting as unpaid care-givers for frail elderly can impede labor-force activity (Harrington Meyer 1990; Stoller 1993).

Gender Relations in the Workplace

Compared to men's jobs, women's jobs—predominantly in the service sector—pay substantially less and have less mobility and fewer benefits, including pensions. They earn less and so receive lower Social Security benefits. Recent data reveal that women still make only 73 cents to the male dollar (U.S. Bureau of the Census 1998). As is shown below, this labor-force discrimination has a cumulative effect as it translates into less ability to save for the future while one is employed and less retirement income later.

Pensions

Coverage.   Receipt of private pensions, a potentially important source of retirement income, depends upon the job: whether or not it includes pension coverage. At this time, about 56 percent of full-time workers are covered by pensions. These workers are disproportionately white and well educated and work for large firms (Johnson, Sambamoorthi, and Crystal 1999, 320). The kinds of jobs women and many minorities and lower-status workers tend to hold, such as service jobs, are among those with the lowest rates of pension coverage (Stoller and Gibson 2000). Even in jobs with coverage, private pensions tend to put women at a disadvantage in the same way that Social Security does as they also assume continuity of work and so penalize women with intermittent work histories (Quadagno 1988).

Receipt.   Coverage rates, low as they are, do not tell how many actually receive pensions. In 1996, less than half (45 percent) of those 65 and over received a pension and only one-quarter of women did (Chen 1994; Estes and Michel 1999). One-third of whites but only one in six blacks or Hispanics receive pensions (Chen and Leavitt 1997). The intersection of race and gender is apparent when one looks at marital status. In 1996, among those who were not married, 44 percent of men but only 33 percent of women had pension benefits. Of the latter, only 23 percent of black women and 13 percent of Hispanic women received pensions. By contrast, one-third of both black and Hispanic couples and 59 percent of white couples received pensions (Estes and Michel 1999, 5). Finally, pension receipt is closely related to class, with those in the upper three quintiles of income receiving the bulk of pensions (Woods 1996).

Amounts.   As should be apparent, pensions serve to expand inequities in old age. Less than one-fourth of all elderly households receive almost 70 percent of all pension and annuity income (Woods 1996, 22). In fact, almost one-third of this income goes to those with the top 10 percent of income (Woods 1996, Table 11, 24). Women's mean pension benefit is only about one-half that of men's (Johnson, Sambamoorthi, and Crystal 1999), $3,679 and $6,442, respectively (Social Security Administration 1998, cited in Estes and Michel 1999). So, men are twice as likely to receive a private pension, and their benefits are twice that of women's. This gender gap will continue, as a substantial gender gap in pension wealth remains in current jobs, where men's median pension wealth is 76 percent greater than women's (Johnson, Sambamoorthi, and Crystal 1999).

"Careers" versus Jobs

These inequities result not from individual choice, but from the structure of employment. A better understanding of the intersections of gender, race, and class helps elaborate this point. For example, the likelihood of people having "careers" is not merely gendered. Working-class, black, retired men, for instance, face marketplace barriers that prevent them from experiencing the dichotomy of work and retirement. Racial discrimination and the placement of blacks in secondary labor-market jobs means that these African Americans move into and out of the marketplace throughout the life course (Gibson 1987). As a result, they generally do not experience the clear demarcation of retirement that is more typical of middle-class white men's withdrawal from the labor force. Further, a lifetime of low-paid, unstable employment with few if any benefits translates into a need to continue working, whether in the formal or informal labor market (Calasanti and Bonanno 1992).

Similarly, and in contrast to the work histories of white women, black women's laborforce participation has been relatively continuous throughout the twentieth century (Amott and Matthaei 1996). As a result, among present-day women retirees, African American women report more years of employment and fewer interruptions (Belgrave 1988). Despite their more stable work histories, however, black women receive relatively low wages; consequently, among present retirees, they have among the lowest incomes. The accumulation of disadvantage over their life courses leaves racial and ethnic minority women, particularly black women, with the highest poverty levels in old age (Social Security Administration 1998b).

Income in Retirement

The recent portrayal of the old as very well-to-do is based on a partial picture of a small minority. Over the course of a lifetime the privileges associated with gender, race, and class build upon one another in a way that is more multiplicative than additive. As a result, the greatest inequities are exhibited among the old (Pampel 1998).

To be sure, there are fewer old people below the poverty line —10.5 percent—than in the past (Social Security Administration 1999, Table 3E.4, 151). Much of the poverty, among the old was alleviated when Social Security benefits were tied to the cost of living in the 1970s. By the same token, a large proportion of old people are "near poor"—just above the poverty line. For example, the 1998 poverty threshold for old individuals was $7,818, while the median income for this same group was $12,719 (Social Security Administration 1999, Tables 3.E1, 150 and Table 3.E3, 152). This means that half of old individuals have incomes just over 150 percent of the poverty line (163 percent = $12,743).

Financial status in old age is important for understanding which groups have the greatest need to be employed in "retirement." Social Security is the largest source of income for those over age 65, providing about 40 percent of income for this group. but its importance varies by income group (Grad 1994, 109). For instance, in 1998, Social Security constituted only 18 percent of the income among those in the top fifth; pensions provide more income for this group. By contrast, among the poorest fifth, Social Security constituted 82 percent of their income and pensions only 3 percent (Social Security Administration 1999, 22).

Given this situation, a gender discrepancy in Social Security benefits comes as no surprise. At the end of 1998, retired men's average monthly benefit was $877; women received $675.50 (Social Security Administration 1999, 18). Examining financial status more closely by race and gender reveals a more complex situation. Whites of either gender have much lower poverty rates than other race and gender groups. Compare the 1997 poverty figures for whites aged 65 and over (men, 6 percent and women, 11.7 percent) to those for balck men (22.2 percent) and women (28.9 percent) or Hispanic men (23.6 percent) and women (28.1 percent) (Social Security Administration 1998b, 13).

The policy bias toward traditional families is apparent when one examines subgroups of elderly poor. Old women make up three-fourths of the elderly poor, and these rates are highest among unmarried women (Glasse, Estes, and Smeeding 1999). Divorced women, whose poverty rate is 22.2 percent, fare even worse than widowed women, 18 percent of whom are poor (respective numbers for men are 15 percent and 11.4 percent) (Estes and Michel 1999, 3). Again, it is critical to note that minority women are especially at a disadvantage in this regard. Finally, a woman's likelihood of experiencing financial difficulties in old age increases over time. For many long-term unmarried women retirees, only their own continued earning keeps them out of poverty (Shaw, Zuckerman, and Hartmann 1998).

Work in Retirement

The popular image of a forty-year career followed by permanent withdrawal from the labor force is increasingly rare. Although this image most closely approximates men's work lives, between one-third and one-half of men report that they do not permanently leave the labor force when they leave their full-time jobs. Instead, they may reduce their hours, take temporary jobs, or leave and re-enter numerous times (Pampel 1998; Quinn, Burkhauser, and Myers 1990).

Thus, continued labor force participation in retirement is not uncommon. At the same time, retirees' reasons for continuing and ability to continue and the types of labor-force activity differ by gender, race, and class. Some research suggests that higher-status, more-educated workers will reenter (Han and Moen 1999). Given their greater likelihood to receive a pension, such workers might retire from one job in order to receive their pension and then enter another to gain supplemental income (Pampel 1998). The well-educated stand in stark contrast to retirees who reenter the labor force because they need the money (Han and Moen 1999). Because intermittent work histories predict greater likelihood of postretirement employment (Han and Moen 1999), women are more likely than men to need and seek reentry, even women whose poor health spurred retirement (Han and Moen 1999). Apparently, men's work histories allow them greater financial stability and security than women's do.

Formal Labor

Gender also influences the forms reentry will take. Types of postretirement labor in the formal market tend to be bimodal. Those with greater education appear to have more opportunities to find work (Han and Moen 1999). Professionals, for example, may continue to work as consultants. These "working retirees" are often very well paid but are still a bargain to employers, who no longer need to pay benefits. By contrast are the female, working-class, and racial-ethnic retirees who are more likely to get the low-paid, service-sector jobs. In fact, global competition has driven some employers to look specifically for older people to work in minimum-wage or low-wage jobs to supplement their Social Security benefits (Calasanti and Bonanno 1992).

Older workers, whether men or women, face problems in the labor market such as job segregation and low pay. Gender plays an additional role, however, as women are considered "old" and unattractive at younger ages than men are. Consequently, in many workplaces women face the problems of age discrimination sooner than men do (Rodeheaver 1990). Thus, one finds that women seeking to reenter the labor market have greater difficulty finding employment than do men (Hardy 1991). Given the narrowness of social standards of attractiveness, racial and ethnic women are even more at a disadvantage, both earlier in life and later, as they are often seen to be "old" even more quickly (Blea 1992; Rodeheaver 1990). Class has an additional impact. While they are motivated by greater financial need, working-class retirees have fewer opportunities to gain employment (Pampel 1998).

Informal Labor

Those unable or unwilling to secure employment in the formal economy may opt instead to engage in the informal economy, that is, jobs not regulated by laws or obtained through formal channels. Examples include jobs paid under the table or off the books, and work for barter. Whether activities are paid or not, informal labor among all age-groups tends to be differentiated on the basis of gender-typed tasks and even spatial locations. Men do more outside work that takes them away from the home, for example, while women engage in crafts, gardening, baby-sitting, sewing, and other activities that can be accomplished in the home and often alongside their own domestic labor (Nelson 1999). Similarly, women retirees' cottage industries tend to be based more on home skills, such as altering clothing or making craft objects to sell.

Marie is a good example of this kind of work situation among the working-class women in my study. Her health problems, exacerbated by her employer's unwillingness to allow her to take the short, frequent breaks she needed, forced her to retire in her fifties. She had worked most of her life, from her early teen years on, in a long series of often unstable jobs. Eventually, she was employed at the same multinational firm for her last twenty years. Still, her pay and subsequent Social Security benefits were low and her pension provided only $100 a month. To supplement her income, Marie made quilts until, as she says, her fingers hurt from being pricked. Then she turned to making yarn poodles, painted eggs, and other crafts to sell. While these do not bring in much money, not nearly enough to compensate for the time she puts into them, she says she is grateful for the income when, at the end of the month, she cannot otherwise afford her medications (Calasanti 1987).

Working for pay or barter, formally or informally, is only one way in which women, among others, may continue working in retirement.

Retirement for Women:
Is Woman's Work Ever Done?

The cliché that "a woman's work is never done" is usually meant to reflect the life of a wife and mother raising a family. Much like the 1960s television images of the ideal family, the earnings brought home by the male breadwinner implicitly justified her work at home. Many couples believe that they divide household work according to their schedules and time availability so that, upon retirement, women and men will share tasks more equitably (Szinovacz and Harpster 1994). Women, however, continue to bear primary responsibility for domestic labor as patterns established earlier in a marriage continue, despite the fact that a more equitable division of labor increases the happiness, and marital satisfaction of wives (Pina and Bengtson 1995).

Indeed, perhaps the most critical way in which retirement differs for women and men revolves around women's continued responsibility for domestic labor, a reality I slowly came to realize in my study. In my interviews both men and women described retirement in terms of "freedom." But for men the term meant freedom from punching a time clock, from being supervised, in short from the sorts of activities relevant to paid work. Women, by contrast, often spoke of their relief at having the "freedom" to "do laundry any day I like" instead of having to fit such domestic chores into a paid-work schedule. In effect, for them, retirement was a reduction, but not a cessation, of work: they went from two (or more) jobs to one. In a nutshell, women's retirement experiences reveal power differentials embedded in gender hierarchies. The work is not forsaken, but women are "free" to "reshape" it, as Loin observations demonstrate: "When I worked I had to do a lot of work at night, housework laundry, ironing, everything, and now I don't even have a certain day to do my laundry. I do it when I want to and I just don't feel like I'm on a tight schedule."

These different retirement experiences rested squarely on women's disadvantageous (and men's advantageous) positions within the home and workplace. To be sure, the ability of some middle-class white men to feel free in retirement—to engage in domestic labor, for example, because they choose to do so, or to have the financial resources to enjoy these years—rests upon women's responsibility for housework. Such gendered power relations are obvious in research on the ways that spouses' employment status—retired or still employed—influences their participation in gender-typed household tasks. Only wives take on more household tasks when they retire and their husbands are still employed; retired men do not increase their time in domestic labor when their wives are still working (Szinovacz and Harpster 1994).

The same gender expectations pervade care giving, in its broadest sense. Caring for others extends not only to spouses or parents (their own or their spouses') but also to their children, grandchildren, great grandchildren, and communities. For many African American women retirees, both paid and unpaid work beginning in childhood continues throughout their lives. In their retirement years, their work expands to include increased service to others and their communities (Allen and Chin-Sang 1990). In my study of white women, men were involved in greater family care. For example, both Ethel and Jenny had divorced or unemployed children who moved back into their homes. Indeed, in addition to still sewing clothes for all six of her children, Jenny had offspring she directly cared for a the time that I spoke with her. Her daughter and two children were living with her until the daughter's divorce was finalized. Her divorced son also lived with her, requiring her to get up early in the morning to make him breakfast before work and to care for her visiting grandchild. Sally, like Jenny and several others, watches her grandchildren while her daughter works. Husbands did take on some duties at times, but only when the women were themselves physically incapable, a situation similar to that found in other studies (Szinovacz and Harpster 1994). This in addition to possible continued participation in the formal or informal economy, for the most part it is women who continue to engage in a wide range of domestic labor in retirement.

Conclusion

Gender, race, and class relations make the golden years of retirement a myth for the vast majority. For the most part, women will continue to Work at household tasks and caring for others—elderly parents, their own children who have moved back home, or their grandchildren. In addition, many women, people of color, and members of the working class will continue to participate in the formal or informal economy, even while receiving Social Security benefits. At the same time, it would be a mistake to assume that these gender differences in retirement experiences are necessarily negative. In addition to the extra income garnered, work of all kinds—paid and unpaid—can provide intrinsic satisfaction. Women's domestic labor may also provide them advantages in old age relative to men. For example, the time that women spend maintaining family and friendship ties gives them more confidants and a larger support network so that they are not reliant only on spouses—isolation being a problem many men face if their spouses die before them. Similarly, despite their greater likelihood of poverty upon death of a spouse, widows fare better than do widowers on some criteria because of their domestic labor experience. For example, widowers are at greater risk of institutionalization in the months following death of their spouse than are widows, in part due to the men's lack of daily household skills (Blieszner 1993).

What of the future, as the population ages and women increasingly work for wages? There is little reason to expect major changes in the conditions leading to women's work in retirement. In terms of domestic labor, between 1951 and 1997, married women's labor force participation nearly tripled, to 62 percent (U.S. Bureau of the Census 1998). This fact has not led, however, to significant change in the division of, or responsibility for, household labor. As a result, it is unlikely that women's responsibility for domestic labor in retirement will show much change. In terms of retirement income, again the key problems are low wages and lack of pension coverage, and these have not altered substantially either. In fact, the increased presence of defined-contribution plans and various Social Security "reform" proposals may even exacerbate retired women's poor financial situation. For example, increasing the years of eligibility needed to obtain Social Security benefits to thirty-eight would create even more zero years of earnings for women. Despite women's increased labor force participation, in

2030 only 40 percent of women will have the full thirty-five years of contributions presently required (Quadagno 1999, 350). And finally, increased aging of the population also means increased care giving—primarily performed by women. Without changes in the ways gender inequities are embedded in social institutions, demographic trends or increased labor-market participation will not alter gendered retirement experiences in fundamental ways.

References

The author thanks Neal King for his helpful comments and editorial help on this manuscript, and Maureen Clark and Laura Montgomery for their assistance in final preparation.

Allen, Katherine, and V. Chin Sang. 1990. "Lifetime of Work: The Context and Meanings of Leisure for Aging Black Women." *Gerontologist* 30, no. 6: 734–740.

Amott, Teresa, and Julie Matthaei. 1996. *Race, Gender, and Work: A Multi-Cultural Economic History of Women in the United States.* Rev. ed. Boston: South End.

Belgrave, Linda L. 1988. "The Effects of Race Differences in Work History, Work Attitude Economic Resources, and Health on Women's Retirement." *Research on Aging* 10, no. 3: 383–398.

Bielby, Denise D., and William T. Bielby. 1981. "She Works Hard for the Money: Household Responsibilities and the Allocation of Work Effort." *American Journal of Sociology* March 93: 1031–1059.

Blea, Irene I. 1992. *La Chicana and the Intersection of Race, Class, and Gender.* New York: Praeger.

Blieszner, Rosemary. 1993. "A Socialist–Feminist Perspective on Widowhood." *Journal of Aging Studies* 7, no. 2: 171–182.

Calasanti, Toni M. 1987. "Work, Gender, and Retirement Satisfaction." Ph.D. diss., University of Kentucky.

Calasanti, Toni M., and Alessandro Bonanno. 1992. "Working 'Overtime': Economic Restructuring and Retirement of a Class." *Sociological Quarterly* 33, no. 1: 135–152.

Chen, Yung-Ping. 1994. "Improving the Economic Security of Minority Persons As They Enter Old Age." In J. S. Jackson, ed., *Minority Elders: Five Goals Toward Building a Public Policy Base,* 22–31. Washington, D.C.: Gerontological Society of America.

Chen, Yung-Ping, and Thomas D. Leavitt. 1997. "The Widening Gap Between White and Minority Pension Coverage." *Public Policy and Aging Report* 8, no. 1: 10–11.

Coverman, Shelley. 1983. "Gender, Domestic Labor Time, and Wage Inequality." *American Sociological Review* 48, no. 6: 623–637.

Coverman, Shelley, and Joseph Sheley. 1986. "Change in Men's Housework and Child-Care Time, 1965–1975." *Journal of Marriage and the Family* 48: 413–422.

Estes, Carroll L., and Martha Michel. 1999. *Fact Sheet on Women and Social Security.* Washington, D.C.: Gerontological Society of America.

Freidland, Robert, and Laura Summer. 1999. "Is Demography Destiny?" *Public Policy and Aging Report* 9, no. 4: 1–14.

Gibson, Rose C. 1987. "Reconceptualizing retirement for black Americans." *Gerontologist* 27, no. 6: 691–698.

Glasse, Lou, Carroll L. Estes, and Timothy Smeeding. 1999. "Older Women and Social Security." *GSA Task Force on Women.* Washington, D.C.: Gerontological Society of America.

Grad, Susan. 1994. *Income of the Population 55 or Older 1992.* Publication 13-11871. Washington, D.C.: Social Security Administration, Office of Research and Statistics.

Han, Shin-Kap, and Phyllis Moen. 1999. "Clocking out: Temporal patterning of retirement." *American Journal of Sociology* 105, no. 1: 191–236.

Hardy, Melissa A. 1991. "Employment after Retirement: Who Gets Back in?" *Research on Aging* 13, no. 3: 267–288.

454   Gender and Work in Today's World: A Reader

Harrington Meyer, Madonna. 1990. "Family Status and Poverty Among Older Women: The Gendered Distribution of Retirement Income in the United States." *Social Problems* 37, no. 4: 551–563.
_____. 1996. "Making Claims As Workers or Wives: The Distribution of Social Security Benefits." *American Sociological Review* 61:449–465.
Herzog, A. Regula, Robert L. Kahn, James N. Morgan, James S. Jackson, and Toni C. Antonucci. 1989. "Age differences in Productive Activities." *Journal of Gerontology* 44, no. 4: S129–S138.
Johnson, Richard W., Usha Sambamoorthi, and Stephan Crystal. 1999. "Gender Differences in Pension Wealth: Estimate Using Provider Data." *Gerontologist* 39, no. 3:320–333.
King, Mary C. 1992. "Occupational Segregation by Race and Sex, 1940–1988." *Monthly Labor Review* 115, no. 4: 30–36.
May, Martha. 1987. "The Historical Problem of the Family Wage: The Ford Motor Company and the Five Dollar Day." In N. Gerstel and H. E. Gross, eds., *Families and Work,* 111–131. Philadelphia: Temple University Press.
Nelson, Margaret K. 1999. "Between Paid and Unpaid Work: Gender Patterns in Supplemental Economic Activities Among White, Rural Families." *Gender and Society* 13, no. 4: 518–539.
Pampel, Fred C. 1998. *Aging, Social Inequality, and Public Policy.* Thousand Oaks, Calif.: Pine Forge.
Pina, Darlene L., and Vern L. Bengtson. 1995. "Division of Household Labor and the Well-Being of Retirement-Aged Wives." *Gerontologist* 35, no. 3: 308–317.
Press, Julie E., and Eleanor Townslev. 1998. "Wives' and Husbands' Housework Reporting: Gender, Class, and Social Desirability." *Gender and Society* 12, no. 2: 188–218.
Quadagno, Jill S. 1988. "Women's Access to Pensions and the Structure of Eligibility Rules: Systems of Production and Reproduction." *Sociological Quarterly* 29, no. 4: 541–558.
_____. 1999. *Aging and the Life Course.* Boston: McGraw-Hill.
Quadagno, Jill S., and Madonna Harrington Meyer. 1990. "Gender and Public Policy." *Generations* 14, no. 2:64–66.
Quinn, Joseph F., Richard V. Burkhauser, and Daniel A. Mvers. 1990. *Passing the Torch: The Influence of Economic Incentive on work and Retirement.* Kalamazoo, Mich.: W. E. Upjohn Institute for Employment Search.
Rodeheaver, Dean. 1987. "When Old Age Became a Social Problem, Women Were Left Behind." *Gerontologist* 27, no. 6: 741–746.
_____. 1990. "Labor Market Progeria." *Generations* 14, no. 2: 53–58.
Scott, C. G. 1991. "Aged SSI Recipients: Income, Work History, and Social Security Benefits." *Social Security Bulletin* 54, no. 8: 2–11.
Shaw, Lois, Diane Zuckerman, and Heidi Hartmann. 1998. *The Impact of Social Security on Women.* Washington, D.C.: Institute for Women's Policy Research.
Social Security Administration. 1998a. *Income of the Population 55 or Older, 1996.* Office of Research, Evaluation, and Statistics. Washington, D.C.: U.S. Government Printing Office. www.ssa.gov/statistics/incpop55toc.html.
_____. 1998b. Women and Retirement Security. Office on Policy. www.ssa.gov/policy/sswomen.pdf.
_____. 1999. *Social Security Bulletin: Annual Statistical Supplement.* Washington, D.C.: U.S. Government Printing Office.
Stoller, Eleanor P. 1993. "Gender and the Organization of Lay Health Care: A Socialist–Feminist Perspective." *Journal of Aging Studies* 7, no. 2: 151–170.
Stoller, Eleanor P., and Rose C. Gibson. 2000. *Worlds of Difference.* 2d ed. Thousand Oaks, Calif.: Pine Forge.
Szinovacz, Maximilliane. 1989. "Retirement, Couples, and Household Work." In M. Szinovacz, D. J. Ekerdt, and B. Vinick, eds., *Families and Retirement,* 33–58. Newbury Park, Calif.: Sage.
Szinovacz, Maximilliane, and Paula Harpster. 1994. "Couples' Employment/Retirement Status and the Division of Household Tasks." *Journal of Gerontology: Social Sciences* 49, no. 3: S125–S136.

U.S. Bureau of the Census. 1998. "Married Women Joining Work Force Spur 150 Percent Family Income Increase, Census Bureau Finds in 50-Year Review." www.census.gov/Press-Release/cb98-181.html.

_____. 1999. "Household Income At Record High; Poverty Declines in 1998, Census Bureau Reports." *Money Income in the United States, 1998.* Current Population Reports, P60–206. Washington, D.C.: U.S. Government Printing Office. www.census.gov/Press-Release/www/1999/cb99-188.html.

Villa, Valentine M., Steven P. Wallace, and Kyriakos Markides. 1997. "Economic Diversity and an Aging Population: The Impact of Public Policy and Economic Trends." *Generations* 21, no. 2: 13–18.

Woods, James. 1996. "Pension Benefits Among the Aged: Conflicting Measures, Unequal Distributions." *Social Security Bulletin* 59, no. 3: 330.

Discussion Questions

1. According to Hewlett, is childlessness a choice for executive women?
2. How can an employer make it easier for high-achieving women to have a family while they maintain their high-level work status?
3. Why is it that Japanese women, according to Yu, rarely return to full-time work after their life cycles change?
4. How does the Japanese tax system affect women's decisions to reenter the world of paid labor ?
5. How does retirement become a gendered concept, according to Colasanti?
6. In the social security system, workers who retire are paid lifetime federal benefits based on their paid labor contributions over their life course. How can it be argued that women, who earn less in their lifetimes, are then not fairly remunerated during retirement years?

Bibliography

Arai, A. Bruce. 2000. "Self-Employment as a Response to the Double Day for Women and Men in Canada." *Canadian Review of Sociology and Anthropology* 37: 125–142.

Calasanti, Toni. 2001. "Retirement: Golden Years for Whom?" *Gender Mosaics* 300–310. Los Angeles: Roxbury Publishing Company.

Cherry, Robert. 2001. *Who Gets the Good Jobs: Combating Race and Gender Disparities?* New Brunswick, NJ: Rutgers University Press.

Coltrane, Scott. 1996. *Family Man: Fatherhood, Housework, and Gender Equity*. Oxford: Oxford University Press.

Edin, Kathryn, and Laura Lein. 1997. "Why Don't Welfare-Reliant Mothers Go to Work?" In *Making Ends Meet* 60–87. New York: Russell Sage Publications.

Ehrenreich, Barbara. 2001. *Nickel and Dimed: On Not Getting by in America*. New York: Metropolitan Books.

Eisenberg, Betty. 1998. "Marking Gender Boundaries: Porn, Piss, Power Tools." In *We'll Call You if We Need You: Experiences of Women Working Construction*. Ithaca, NY: ILR Press.

Epstein, Cynthia Fuchs, Carroll Seron, Bonnie Oglensky, and Roger Saute. 1999. "Part-time Work as Deviance: Stigmatization and its Consequences." *The Part-time Paradox: Time Norms, Professional Lives, Family and Gender* 29–37. New York: Routledge Press.

Gerson, Kathleen. 1993. "Dilemmas of Involved Fatherhood." *No Man's Land: Changing Commitments to Family and Work* 247–255. New York: Basic Books.

Hewlett, Sylvia Ann. 2002. *Creating a Life: Professional Women and the Quest for Children*. New York: Talk Miramax Books.

Hochschild, Arlie Russell. 1997. *The Time Bind: When Work Becomes Home and Home Becomes Work*. New York: Henry Holt Publishers.

Hoffman and Youngblade. 1999. *Mothers at Work: Effects on Children's Well-being*. Cambridge: Cambridge University Press.

Hondagneu-Sotelo, Pierette. 2001. *Doméstica: Immigrant Workers Cleaning and Caring in the Shadows of Influence*. Berkeley, California: University of California Press.

Lawson, Helene M. 2000. *Ladies on the Lot: Women, Car Sales, and the Pursuit of the American Dream*. New York: Rowman and Littlefield.

Lee, Wendy. 1991. "Prostitution and Tourism in South-East Asia." In N. Redclift and M.T. Sinclair (eds.), *Working Women: International Perspectives on Labour and Gender Ideology*, 79–103. London: Routledge Press.

Lois, Jennifer. 2001. "Peaks and Valleys: The Gendered Emotional Culture of Edgework." *Gender and Society*, vol. 15, no. 3 (June): 381–406. Thousand Oaks, California: Sage Press.

Martin, Susan E. 1994. "Outsider Within the Station House: the Impact of Race and Gender on Black Women Police." *Social Problems*, vol. 41, no. 3 (August). California: University of California Press

National Committee on Pay Equity. 2001. "The Wage Gap: Myths and Facts." In P.S. Rothenberg (ed.), *Race, Class, and Gender in the United States: An Integrated Study* 292–304.Worth Publishers.

Ogasawara, Yuko. 1998. *Office Ladies and Salaried Men: Power, Gender, and Work in Japanese Companies*. Berkeley, California: University of California Press.

Pierce, Jennifer. 1993. "Rambo Litigators: Emotional Labor in a Male-Dominated Occupation." In C.Cheng (ed.), *Masculinities in Organizations* 1–27. Thousand Oaks, California: Sage Publishers

Rogers, Jackie Krasas. 2000. *Temps: The Many Faces of the Changing Workplace.* Ithaca, New York: Cornell University Press

Schrimsher, Kandace Peason. 1998. "Career Commitments: Women and Men Law School Graduates." *Current Research on Occupations and Professions* 10: 193–215. Jai Press Inc.

Shelton, Beth Anne and John, Daphne. 1993. "Ethnicity, Race and Difference: a Comparison of White, Black, and Hispanic Men's Household Labor Time." In Jane C. Hood (ed.), *Men, Work, and Family.* Newbury Park: Sage Publishers.

Smith, Calvin D. 1998. "Men Don't Do this Sort of Thing: A Case Study of the Social Isolation of House Husbands." *Men and Masculinities*, vol. 1, no. 2 (October). California: Sage Publishers.

Swiss, Deborah J. 1996. "Resolving the Harassment Dilemma." *Women Breaking Through: Overcoming the Final 10 Obstacles at Work* 90–112. Princeton, New Jersey: Peterson/Pacesetter Books.

Williams, Christine. 1992. "The Glass Escalator: Hidden Advantages for Men in the Female Professions." *Social Problems* 39: 253–267. California: The University of California Press.

Wirth, Linda. 1997. "Sexual Harassment at Work." In E. Date-Bah (ed.), *Promoting Gender Equality at Work: Turning Vision into Reality for the Twenty-first Century.* London: Zed Books.

Woods, James D. 1993. "Coming Out, Moving On." *The Corporate Closet* 171–222. New York: Free Press.

Yu, Wei-Hsin. 2003. "Jobs for Mothers: Married Women's Labor Force Reentry and Part-time, Temporary Employment in Japan." *Sociological Forum*, vol. 17, no. 3. New York: Plenum Press.

Index